DYNAMIC PHYSICAL EDUCATION FOR SECONDARY SCHOOL STUDENTS

CURRICULUM AND INSTRUCTION

SECOND EDITION

Robert P. Pangrazi
Arizona State University

Paul W. Darst
Arizona State University

MACMILLAN PUBLISHING COMPANY
New York
COLLIER MACMILLAN CANADA
Toronto

Editor: *Robert Miller*
Production Supervisor: *Katherine Evancie*
Production Manager: *Nick Sklitsis*
Text and Cover Designer: *Pat Smythe*
Cover photograph: *Robert P. Pangrazi*

This book was set in ITC Garamond by V&M Graphics, Inc. and printed and bound by Halliday Lithograph. The cover was printed by Phoenix Color Corp.

Macmillan Publishing Company
866 Third Avenue, New York, New York 10022

Collier Macmillan Canada, Inc.
1200 Eglinton Avenue East
Suite 200
Don Mills, Ontario M3C 3N1

Library of Congress Cataloging-in-Publication Data

Pangrazi, Robert P.
    Dynamic physical education for secondary school students:
curriculum and instruction / Robert P. Pangrazi, Paul W. Darst.
        p. cm.
    ISBN 0-02-390674-X
    1. Physical education and training—United States—Curricula.
2. Physical education and training—Study and teaching (Secondary)—
United States. 3. Physical education and training—Canada—
Curricula. 4. Physical education and training—Study and teaching
(Secondary)—Canada. I. Darst, Paul W. II. Title.
GV365.P36 1991
613.7'0973—dc20   90-5410
                    CIP

Printing: 1 2 3 4 5 6 7   Year: 1 2 3 4 5 6 7

BRIEF CONTENTS

DETAILED CONTENTS

PREFACE

The second edition of *Dynamic Physical Education for Secondary School Students* is a major revision. The changes reflect an increasing understanding of the rudiments of curriculum and instruction. New chapters on planning, management strategies, and maintaining an effective learning environment are included. Increased emphasis is placed on integrating disabled students into instructional settings. A strong attempt has been made to separate junior and senior high school programs. More often than not, junior high school programs have been replications of high school programs. In this edition, a separate chapter is devoted to helping teachers understand the needs of junior high students and how these characteristics impact on the development of a meaningful curriculum.

Second Edition Modifications and Additions

In many states, secondary school physical education is disappearing as the back-to-basics approach takes its toll. The authors maintain that physical education is basic and have added a new chapter that reviews the research supporting the need for a physical education program as part of the total school curriculum. Sections on the impact of activity on growth, the increased incidence of hypokinetic diseases among students, and the long-term effects of exercise during the school years are included. Research has revealed a number of guidelines for exercising secondary school students safely, and they are clearly discussed.

Physical Fitness

An issue that continues to receive public attention is the lack of physical fitness among youngsters of all ages. Certainly, no issue reflects more negatively on the effectiveness of secondary school physical education programs. Many adults have felt that fitness might be the only reason physical education

should be required in junior and senior high schools. Chapter 18 gives increased coverage of this issue, with special emphasis on health-related fitness development. Directions and guidelines for implementing the Fitnessgram and Physical Best fitness batteries are included. New fitness routines and activities have been developed in order to offer the widest range of fitness activities possible for students. In addition, Chapter 16 offers activities for maintaining wellness and developing an understanding of the basic components of lifetime fitness. It is important that the secondary school teacher offer fitness activities coupled to a better understanding of wellness.

Curriculum Planning

The majority of teachers, at one time or another, have the opportunity to develop the curriculum they will teach. Unfortunately, too often the curriculums have been developed by teachers based on their personal likes or dislikes and their perceived level of competency in presenting an activity. This often leads to a curriculum with a narrow focus and one that does not meet the needs of all students. With this in mind, the authors increased the coverage of curriculum planning. Chapter 3 describes the steps to follow to assure the development of a comprehensive curriculum. Coverage is given to a variety of curriculum models currently utilized in various school districts, showing the strengths and weaknesses of the various models. An understanding of this chapter will help teachers realize the importance of a philosophical framework to undergird the curriculum.

Chapter 4 discusses the critical years of adolescence in the physical education setting and how students' growth and development characteristics impact on the design of the curriculum. A review of junior high school curriculum and a suggested curriculum are offered for 7th and 8th graders. A separate section is devoted to the 9th grade curriculum because it is critical if teachers expect students to continue participating in physical education in high school.

Chapter 5 reviews the growth and development of high school students. A lengthy discussion helps teachers understand the difficult decisions that must be made to assure the curriculum is relevant. High school curriculums must be interesting for students to participate, and Chapter 5 encourages this kind of thinking.

Instructional Effectiveness

Planning has always played an important role in effective teaching. Chapter 7 places strong emphasis on planning for success through lesson, unit, and yearly planning. Practical strategies are offered to help both the beginning and the experienced teacher organize meaningful and sequential learning experiences. An extensive section has been added that applies Hunter's essential elements of instruction concepts to physical education. Also included are a number of practical methods to ensure that students learn effectively.

Chapter 8 presents organizational material for an effective instructional environment. Advice for effective communication with students is presented step by step. Important facets of teaching are presented such as the development of instructional cues and the demonstration, observation, and maintenance of class performance. A large section of this chapter is devoted to helping teachers adapt instructional tasks to individual needs while effectively utilizing instructional feedback. Finally, an in-depth section helps teachers better understand how to design and implement meaningful policies and procedures to assure student cooperation.

Chapter 9 is filled with many new activities and techniques for managing and disciplining students in a positive and caring manner. Typically, this area has been a principal concern of teachers and parents yet has not been covered in detail in physical education textbooks. Teachers are shown how to reinforce desired behavior and develop a positive, yet assertive, discipline style. Punishment, although discouraged, is discussed, and guidelines for its acceptable use are presented.

This edition reflects a determination on the part of the authors to ensure that teachers perform their duties in a manner that is technically correct and in line with current research. The chapters on pedagogy reflect a body of knowledge related to effective teaching and indicate that it is no longer acceptable to "teach as we were taught."

Chapter 10 focuses on teaching styles and the effective implementation of such styles. The depth of coverage given to teaching styles is increased in an effort to help teachers understand when different styles are best used. A number of practical examples have been added to the chapter to help students visualize how the use of a different teaching style can enhance and increase the quality of student learning.

Liability and Students with Disabilities

The important aspects of liability and teaching students with disabilities are seldom covered in secondary school physical education textbooks. Legal liability continues to be a major concern of teachers. Chapter 13 describes situations teachers should avoid, focuses on safety, and offers a checklist for analyzing possible situations that might result in a lawsuit. Teaching students with disabilities is discussed in detail in Chapter 6. This important chapter offers a step-by-step approach to the development of an individualized education program (IEP) and presents guidelines for screening and assessment. Criteria are offered for the placement of students in the least restrictive environment, with emphasis on a positive and constructive approach. An expanded section of practical ideas for modifying activities to assure maximal student success is included. Finally, specific disabilities with accompanying requisite instructional procedures are described in detail.

Systematic Observation of Instruction

Chapter 11 is a new addition; it focuses on helping teachers develop a systematic approach for improving their instructional effectiveness. Setting realistic goals and finding meaningful methods for gauging successful accomplishment are covered. Methods of systematic observation of instruction are discussed and presented in a manner that is straightforward and easy to implement. In addition, a number of combination systems for observing teacher and student effectiveness are included.

Potpourri

New activities have been added, particularly adventure activities. The focus of the units of activity is to help teachers understand the different approaches and teaching devices that can be used in activity presentations. Included with each unit are practical ideas for skill work, lead-up activities, and specific learning contracts. The instructional units have been separated into four chapters: team sports, individual sports, dual sports, and outdoor adventure activities. This division should help students view the need for including units of instruction from all areas in their total curriculum. Finally, a number of suggested readings for each activity are offered so students can secure in-depth information written by experts.

Kudos

This book is the result of the help of many people. We are most appreciative of the professional staff at Macmillan Publishing Company. Special thanks go to our editor, Robert Miller, for his guidance and support. In addition, Steve Fedorchek, Ken Coyle, and Donald Hicks of the Tempe School District, Tempe, Arizona, helped field-test and evaluate the instructional units. Uncompromising thank yous go to our wives, Debbie and Charlene, for their constant support and patience.

Special thanks go to reviewers who helped guide our efforts including Jim Batesky of the University of Wisconsin at La Cross, Pat Flaugher of Eastern Illinois University, and Thomas W. Steele of the State University of New York at Cortland.

R.P.P.
P.W.D.

1

THE ROLE OF PHYSICAL EDUCATION IN THE SECONDARY SCHOOL

Physical education in the secondary school is often misunderstood by students, faculty, administrators, and the community. One misconception is that the physical education program is synonymous with the school's athletic program. Too many people believe that a school with a good football team must inherently have an effective physical education program because the latter helps to develop and prepare athletes for the sports program. An example is the school principal who advocates the expansion of weight training classes in the physical education curriculum in order to improve the athletic program. Unfortunately, administrators and some members of the general public seldom understand that the goals of physical education are directed toward meaningful educational experiences for all students and at all ability levels. When teachers (who also coach) try to maintain excellence in teaching and coaching, it may be difficult to achieve the single goal of the athletic program and the multiple goals of physical education.

People have varied images of the physical education environment. Some envision a rigid class in which students dress in the required uniform and exercise in straight lines under the watchful eye of a regimental instructor. A negative atmosphere exists when running laps and exercise are used as punishment for dress-code infractions or lack of self-discipline. Others view physical education as a subject to be avoided because of crowded classes, smelly locker rooms, and a lack of time for changing clothes. Often, activities only include a core of traditional team sports a teacher selected from a repertoire of activities developed years earlier. Current and popular physical fitness activities and sports are missing from the program.

Some people remember physical education as a time for playing some type of game on a daily basis. Little or no organized teaching or learning occurred in the process. Teachers simply rolled out the ball and let students play a game or tournament for several weeks. George Leonard (1977), noted author

and philosopher, describes a traditional secondary school physical education class in the following manner:

> Students scramble into their gym clothes and then stand at attention for dress inspection. Next, a period of group calisthenics including push-ups, jumping jacks, and sit-ups is followed by a lap around the track. Students then choose up sides and move on to the traditional game of the day, i.e., flag football, basketball, softball, and volleyball. The final activity of the day is the shower and in many schools, a shower inspection to make sure that all students have participated. Coed activities and individualized instruction are unheard of in these situations. (p. 2)

This situation creates a number of problems, and it is a pity that these scenarios have existed in schools for years. Physically active forms of sport and play, can have a positive impact on today's adolescent students. Many adults still have these negative situations etched in their minds. Even more unfortunate, however, is that these same scenarios still exist in schools across the country. Physical miseducation is a dragon that rears its ugly head for various reasons, and it is extremely tough to slay.

On the other side of the coin, the scene is quite different in some schools. Physical education is a positive, exciting experience that has been set up by a group of dedicated teachers. Secondary students are getting an opportunity to choose between activities such as cycling, golf (Figure 1.1), rock climbing, disc sports, and wilderness survival. A high school in California offers 45 elective choices, including sailing, scuba diving, martial arts, Frisbee, and yoga. Short 2-week minicourses as well as semester-long, in-depth units are offered. An Arizona high school offers several adventure and wilderness courses that include caving, rock climbing, stream fishing, and backpacking as part of the physical education program. Junior high schools are offering a wide variety of short units including juggling, new games, initiative challenges, ropes course activities, bicycling, and orienteering.

FIGURE 1.1 Golf instruction

Many schools are changing to a relaxed, humane atmosphere. Strict dress codes are being relaxed and students are being given a voice about clothes they want to wear for activity. Instructional procedures include learning stations in which students work on different tasks at different levels. Teachers move about the gymnasium, giving information to, correcting, encouraging, and praising students.

Physical fitness activities may include many choices such as aerobic dancing, rope jumping, circuit training, obstacle courses, partner resistance activities, stationary bicycles, rowing machines, or running an orienteering course. These activities are arranged in a systematic progression that enables all students to find personal satisfaction and success. Highly skilled students are provided with challenging activities that force them to expand their physical limits (Figure 1.2).

Clearly, the two aforementioned programs have

FIGURE 1.2 Exercising using an obstacle course

many differences. One can easily see why many people have misunderstood physical education. Programs vary significantly from place to place and situation to situation. Knowledge, attitudes, and behaviors toward activity are strongly influenced by the type of physical education program students experience. Consequently, in developing an effective physical education program, we must start with a clear understanding of what physical education is and what it should be doing in school settings.

WHAT IS PHYSICAL EDUCATION?

Physical education is a learning process that focuses on increasing knowledge and affecting attitudes and behaviors relative to physical activities, including exercise, sports, games, dance, aquatic activities, and outdoor adventure activities. It can occur inside or outside the schools. It can be formal or informal. It might include a father teaching his son how to play golf or a boy receiving information from the coach of a youth soccer team. It could include a girl taking private gymnastics lessons or a mother explaining to her son about pacing during a 10-km run. It can be a young boy explaining the rules of football to his grandfather or a wife teaching her husband how to play racquetball. It is a group of 7th graders learning to play badminton in a junior high school or high school students learning the concepts of health related fitness in a classroom setting. Physical education is the passing of information, attitudes, and skills from one person to another (Figure 1.3).

The process of physical education is an important function of our schools. Physical education instructors have a tremendous responsibility to develop and teach from a systematically organized curriculum for kindergarten through grade 12 that favorably influences all students and enhances their physical activity habits. Young people deserve a well-conceived and well-developed program of physical education because it can improve their quality of life and have an impact on their life-styles. This transmission of knowledge, skills, and attitudes is certainly a legitimate educational concern.

WHAT SHOULD A PHYSICAL EDUCATION PROGRAM ACCOMPLISH?

Physical educators have long purported to accomplish a wide variety of goals in the schools. Claims have been made in the areas of physical fitness,

FIGURE 1.3 Aerobics is a popular fitness activity

motor abilities, intellectual skills, character development, and personal social-emotional adjustment, among others. These claims have varied from time to time and place to place, depending on the trends in education and society.

Recently, it seems as if the schools, including the physical education programs, have been asked to accomplish more while resources to support programs dwindle. Educational critics continually cite the ineffectiveness of school programs in meeting instructional goals. Perhaps expectations of the physical education program are unrealistic. The focus of programs should be narrowed somewhat to emphasize fewer major goals.

The following sections offer insight about what physical education programs should be offering to students. It is critical to know what physical education should accomplish for its participants in order to assure that activities and strategies are directed toward these ends.

Incorporate Physical Activity into Life-Style Patterns

An important goal of a secondary school physical education program should be to help students incorporate physical activity into their life-styles. This requires curriculum, instruction, and teachers to have a positive impact on student's knowledge, attitudes, and skill behaviors relative to physical activities. It does not mean that the secondary program should avoid other goals in different areas. It does mean that this is the most important goal and should be strongly emphasized.

A successful physical education program is not measured by the current level of knowledge or the physical skills of students, nor by the number of participants on the varsity athletic teams. Certainly

it is not the number of victories that the football or basketball teams accumulate. The ultimate measure of success is the number of students who participate in physical activities such as exercise, sport, dance, and outdoor adventure activities throughout their lives. As Siedentop (1980b) states

> We teach because we hope to influence not only the present abilities of students but also their future behavior and predispositions to continue to engage in our subject matter. We are interested in the growth of the student now, but education just for now makes little sense. Most of what we hope to provide for the student is really directed toward the future of the student. We naturally want the student to learn and perform well now, to have fun now, and to enjoy the learning experience now. But, the nature of education has always been that it attempts to do things now that will have long-term effects, that is, that will affect the future behavior of the student. We are interested, in the final analysis, in what happens to students after they finish our course; indeed, after they finish all formal education. (p. 267)

Physical educators should be interested in passing on knowledge and developing the physical skills of students; however, a strong, organized emphasis must be placed on the affective dimension of learning. For example, students may learn the physical skills of basketball, including dribbling, passing, and rebounding. They also may learn information about traveling, offensive fouls, and strategies for attacking a zone defense. If they do not learn to enjoy or find success in playing basketball, however, the probability of their incorporating basketball into their life-style is reduced.

For the physical educator, impact on the affective dimension of learning is not an easy task compared with the relative ease of showing gains in students' knowledge and physical skills areas. Because of this difficulty, many physical educators have not planned carefully for the affective area. Dodds (1976, p. 109) explains: "I submit that physical educators have expended much effort on cognitive and psychomotor teaching tasks, but have only paid lip service to the affective domain."

Without proper planning and systematic arrangement of the learning environment, the probability of developing positive student attitudes and physically active life-styles is greatly reduced. Secondary curriculum plans and instructional strategies should be concerned with developing learning environments that help students enjoy physical activities for a lifetime.

Improve Physical Skills

Another important program goal is to help students improve their physical skills. People tend to repeat activities they do well or find rewarding. Success is a great motivator. If students improve their volleyball bumps, Frisbee sidearm throws, or tennis serves, the chance is better that they will repeat the activity and incorporate it into their life-styles. Skill development does not occur overnight or in a three-week unit. Students should be counseled about procedures and opportunities for developing physical skills outside the school program.

Teachers need to provide a support system for students as their skills improve and the positive benefits of physical activity begin to appear. Students start to change their attitudes toward physical activity when personal skill levels improve. They need to be aware that physical skill development is not easy and demands long, continuous effort. Too many students expect instant success. Teachers should help students find individual levels of success, for success can be different for different people.

Develop Physical Fitness

Physical educators must provide students with successful encounters in exercise and physical activities that lead to improved health-related physical fitness. This includes cardiovascular efficiency, flexibility, body fat reduction, and muscular strength and endurance. Students need to experience the types of activities that result in the benefits of physical fitness on a first-hand basis. They should understand how to develop and arrange suitable fitness routines that will positively impact their health. Physical educators must do much more than lecture students on the benefits of physical activity and tell them to run a lap around the track. Improving health-related physical fitness means putting students through organized activities that improve fitness systematically throughout the year so that students learn that there are several pathways to fitness.

Physical fitness development is similar to physical skill development in that it requires time, energy, and self-discipline. Students need to be aware of the factors that influence fitness development. Eating habits, types of activities, heredity, and frequency of activity are just a few of the factors that students must understand. Physical education programs play an important role in helping students develop activity habits that will benefit their physical health.

Enhance Social-Emotional Functioning

Physical activity environments provide a number of unique opportunities for students to experience and develop social-emotional skills. Getting along with other people, being part of a team, accepting an official's judgment, losing the final game of a tournament, dealing with peers who have varying levels of ability, or changing clothes in a crowded locker room are just a few of the many experiences that may occur in a physical education class. These are important experiences for students. Physical educators have a responsibility to help guide and direct students in understanding these various social-emotional behaviors.

Develop Requisite Knowledge for Lifetime Activity

A physical education program should provide students with a wide range of knowledge about all of the aforementioned goals. A knowledge component is intertwined with these objectives. Indeed, accomplishing any objective is impossible if students do not have a certain amount of knowledge. For example, getting students to enjoy tennis without understanding the rules, strategies, and etiquette is difficult, and most people cannot incorporate an aerobic activity into their life-style without understanding the possible health-related benefits.

As students increase their knowledge of physical activities, they should also increase their enjoyment and rate of participation. This is unfortunately not always the case. Many people understand the rules, regulations, and benefits of physical activity and yet have not incorporated any activity into their life-styles. This is why physical education programs must do more than just provide students with knowledge about physical activity. Students must experience success while participating in these activities.

DEVELOPING EFFECTIVE PHYSICAL EDUCATION PROGRAMS

Certainly the accomplishment of all of these goals is a difficult challenge for physical educators. Given the circumstances in many schools, goals will not be fulfilled quickly or easily. However, the best way to reach these goals is to simply develop a sound program and teach it effectively. Curricula and teaching methods have been field-tested and studied with these goals in mind, and procedures are available to help maximize the effectiveness of physical education programs. The following are suggestions for developing programs that help students incorporate physical activity into their life-styles. Specific curricula and instruction examples will be presented in Chapters 4 and 5.

Create a Positive Learning Environment

The instructor is the most important factor in the learning environment. Regardless of the teaching method or curriculum design, a perceptive, analytical teacher is paramount to student learning. A good teacher creates a teaching-learning atmosphere that is both positive and caring. Instructional procedures should be planned carefully so students can experience immediate success. The instructor's reactions to student failure should be kept minimal and momentary. Teachers must focus their feedback and reactions on positive student behaviors rather than always using a "correction complex" that responds only to students' mistakes. Contract approaches and individualized instruction have been used successfully to shape skill behaviors. Teachers are realizing that they must take an active role in the teaching-learning process by demonstrating, participating, encouraging, giving feedback, and hustling. Students are influenced significantly by someone who has incorporated physical activities into his or her life-style.

Many teachers are now using positive methods to discipline, teach, and motivate. Students are taught to enjoy physical education instead of learning to avoid the environment. Running and exercise are not used as a form of punishment. Students are rewarded for competitive efforts even if their team happens to lose on a given day. Teachers use students' first names and interact with all students on a daily basis. Students are given a degree of choice and freedom in the learning process, and they are consequently better motivated.

To some educators, these positive approaches sound like ideals that cannot be carried out in the "real world," yet all of the procedures discussed are occurring now in schools across the country. New ideas and programs are not developed and implemented easily, but when a better program is developed and when the teaching-learning process is improved, teachers feel more optimistic and more involved in their profession.

Research on teaching continues to provide information about ways to improve the teaching-learning process. Teacher modeling behavior can be an effective strategy for influencing specific types of student behavior (Westcott, 1978). Guidelines concerning the ways modeling can be used are available (Landers, 1978; McKenzie, 1982). Students need to see models of persons who have incorporated physical activity in their life-styles. Teachers can discuss their exercise habits with students and allow students to see them participating in and enjoying physical activity. Teachers should be aware of the powerful effect their behavior has on students, and should use this to help students develop healthy activity habits.

Teacher enthusiasm is another behavior that can be quite useful in a physical education environment (Locke and Woods, 1982). Evidence shows that this difficult-to-define behavior is a teaching skill that is associated with student learning (Roberts and Becker, 1976). Teachers need to display their love of and excitement for physical activity and their joy in teaching.

Teacher expectations are another critical factor in developing a positive atmosphere for teaching (Brophy and Good, 1974). If students are expected to be unmotivated and troublesome, then the possibility is strong that these behaviors will occur. If students are expected to learn and work hard, then the chance is better that they will. Abundant evidence shows that teachers' expectations for students will come to fruition. This is called the Pygmalion effect, or self-fulfilling prophecy (Rosenthal and Jacobson, 1968).

Many physical educators across the country have taken a hard look at the overall atmosphere of the physical education program. Students sometimes do all they can to avoid the subject. Activity offerings are often out-of-date. Classes are almost always overcrowded. Inflexible dress requirements cause students to rebel. Showers are required after every activity, and time allotted for showers frequently makes it impossible to get to the next class on time. Teachers may do little or no actual teaching and sometimes act like military drill instructors. Grades are often based on a negative approach, and exercise is sometimes used as punishment. With this picture in mind, we can easily see why many physical educators are advocating a change in the overall atmosphere.

Many schools have relaxed or liberalized the dress codes and grading procedures. Students at San Rafael High School in California (Kaplan, 1976) stated that what they liked best about the physical education program was not the 45 electives and numerous exotic activities, but a relaxed dress code that enabled them to wear clothes of their choice. In some schools, the grading procedures have been switched to a pass-fail basis. In other situations, students are able to choose the type of grading option they prefer.

Physical educators need to look carefully at the effects of the policies and procedures that they are using in programs. If these procedures are discouraging students from a lifetime of physical activity, they should be reevaluated. If dress codes and grading procedures are chasing students away and developing avoidance behaviors, acceptable alternatives must be developed. The overall atmosphere of the physical education environment does have a tremendous impact on students and on their attitude toward physical activity. Teachers should look carefully at all policies, procedures, dress codes, evaluation practices, and other aspects of the environment that affect students. When students leave the physical education environment, they should have a good feeling about physical activity and a desire to return for more.

Offer Elective or Selective Curricula

The elective or selective approach to physical education curricula has had an impact on schools across the nation. The terms (elective and selective) have, however, been used differently in various situations. Usually they refer to students' choosing to take an optional or elective year of physical education, or the students' choosing between several options during each activity interval of 3 to 6 weeks. Students can select either tennis, weight training, or soccer during the first 3-week unit, and either racquetball, archery, or flag football during the second 3 weeks. The choice can occur not only during the elective year but also during the required year or years. The choice process starts in some schools as early as the 7th or 8th grade, while in others it does not begin until the 10th grade. This type of program gives students an opportunity to choose activities of genuine interest to them, and to avoid activities in which they have little interest. At Greenway High School in Arizona (Wilson and Altieri, 1978), school officials found that some students would not elect an extra year of physical education because they wanted to avoid one or two specific activities such as swimming, gymnastics, or wrestling. Students would sacrifice an entire year of physical education to avoid certain activities. Because of this situation, curriculum planners need to implement an elective program in which students can choose from four or five activities during each unit of the elective year.

Another advantage of the elective approach is that students will be more motivated when they have influenced the selection of learning activities. Fewer problems should occur in the areas of participation and discipline. More students involved in the program can also mean more teachers, equipment, and facilities. Teachers in this type of program should be able to specialize in several activities and teach repeated units in their areas of expertise. This in turn improves the instructional process because of the reduced number of teacher preparations.

Flexibility in class size is yet another advantage. Certain activities can easily accommodate more students, depending on the equipment and facilities. For example, golf and tennis might have smaller classes than soccer and flag football.

Finally, considering the above advantages, teachers should be more motivated and enthusiastic about teaching in this type of program. The elective program can thus improve the motivational level of both students and teachers. Any educational practice that can affect the teaching-learning environment should be considered when developing programs in secondary school physical education. Problems do have to be worked out concerning grades, registration procedures, teaching attitudes, and class roll procedures. There are, however, several solutions available to a teaching staff that believes in the advantages of the approach.

Elective programs can be an influence in a positive direction. A number of secondary school physical education programs that have converted to elective programs have experienced an increase in students (Wilson and Altieri, 1978). Documentation shows that an elective program offers advantages such as increased student participation, enthusiasm, and motivation, as well as increased enthusiasm and motivation of teachers (Klappholz, 1978). Students in the 10th grade and above should have choice in all of their physical activities and should not be forced into activities that they are not interested in learning and that might cause them repeated failure. Students in grades 7–9 should be required to take several categories of activities such as team sports, lifetime sports, fitness activities, dance, aquatics, and adventure activities. This ensures a measure of breadth in activity experiences. If possible, they should be permitted to choose from a number of activities in each category. In the fitness area, for example, they might choose aerobic dance, weight training, or jogging. In the lifetime sport area, the choices might be tennis, golf, or bowling.

Offer Students a Choice of Activities

Evidence indicates that 7th-grade students begin to narrow their activity interests and specialize in specific activities (Anderson, 1958). This narrowing of interests continues as students progress through high school into adulthood. The implication is that junior high school students are ready to begin making some choices about the kinds of physical activity they want to include in their life-styles. This does not imply that programs should be based totally on the activity interests of 7th and 8th graders. Students at this age need direction and counseling in many categories of activities. As they move from 7th through 12th grade, they should be given increasing responsibility for choosing a personal activity program.

Offer a Variety of Activities

The curricula of physical education have expanded greatly in recent years. New and exciting activities such as Frisbee, aerobics, yoga, and rock climbing are included in programs across the country. A broad-based program increases the possibility that all students will find an enjoyable physical activity.

FIGURE 1.4   Adventure activity   (photograph courtesy of Old Town Canoe Company, Old Town, ME)

FIGURE 1.5   Playing handball, a lifetime sport

Physical educators should try to offer as many activities as possible. A balance among team sports, individual sports, dance, aquatics, outdoor activities (Figure 1.4), and physical conditioning activities should be a major program goal. The following categories illustrate the wide range of activities that can be incorporated into an exemplary program.

Lifetime Sports

In the past 25 years, the most significant change in secondary school physical education offerings has been the inclusion of the "lifetime" or "carryover" sports. These sports are primarily individual or dual activities that can be used for a lifetime as opposed to team sports that are difficult to continue after the school years. A major factor in the development of the lifetime sports concept was the Lifetime Sports Education Project (LSEP) sponsored by the American Alliance for Health, Physical Education, Recreation, and Dance (AAHPERD).* The LSEP originally focused on bowling, archery, badminton, tennis, and golf. Instructional materials and teaching clinics were developed by the LSEP to encourage physical educators to expand their curriculum (Figure 1.5).

Lifetime sports have become tremendously popular and have been expanded to include a host of new activities such as Frisbee, racquetball, and squash. The AAHPERD estimates that 75% of the nation's secondary schools emphasize lifetime sports in their physical education programs. This expanded offering has provided many participation opportunities for students and adults who are not interested in traditional team sports. Secondary school physical education programs are better able to serve all students when a wide variety of lifetime sports is offered, since different students are successful with different activities. Every student should be able to find success in some kind of physical activity (e.g., some students enjoy Frisbee much more than football and basketball).

Outdoor Adventure Activities

Another category of activity gaining popularity in the past fifteen years is the outdoor adventure or wilderness sports. Backpacking, rock climbing, orienteering, and bicycling are just a few of the activities in this category (Darst and Armstrong, 1980). These activities are similar to the lifetime sports and are primarily individual or dual activities that can be enjoyed over a lifetime. The emphasis is on risk and excitement in using the earth's natural environments such as snow, water, mountains, ice, rivers, and wilderness areas. Exploration, travel, and adventure are important elements in these activities. To train students in outdoor adventure skills, many schools are developing on-campus facilities such as climbing walls, rope courses, and orienteering sites (Figure 1.6), as well as using nearby community environments such as ski slopes, parks, rivers, and mountains. These activities emphasize competition with oneself and the environment in contrast to competition with other people. This is an attractive feature for many students. Outdoor adventure activities can also be enjoyed with family and friends during expanded leisure hours. They give people an opportunity to get away from the city and experience the natural environment in a time of vanishing wilderness areas.

*This organization formerly was called the American Alliance for Health, Physical Education, and Recreation (AAHPER). In 1980, the name was changed to reflect a growing involvement in dance. The abbreviation AAHPERD will be used for all organization references in this text, regardless of the actual name at the time.

FIGURE 1.6 Orienteering (reprinted from *Outdoor Adventure Activities for School and Recreation Programs* by P. W. Darst and G. P. Armstrong, 1980. New York: Macmillan Publishing Co., p. 152)

Health-Related Physical Fitness Activities

A combination of the running craze, the wellness movement, and the fitness renaissance that has emerged across the nation is rekindling interest in physical fitness types of activities. Aerobic rhythmic exercise, Jazzersize, jogging, weight training (Figure 1.7), and weight control classes are extremely popular with secondary students and adults. Schools are offering numerous classes called Superstars compet-

FIGURE 1.7 Weight lifting class

ition, shipshape class, systematic conditioning, and aerobics, which emphasize such areas as nutrition, obesity, coronary heart disease, flexibility, and strength. The AAHPERD has developed a new health-related fitness test called Physical Best (1988) that focuses on cardiovascular efficiency, abdominal strength and endurance, flexibility, upper body strength, and body composition. Various awards and motivational materials are available to aid students, teachers, and parents with information on the health-related parameters of physical fitness. Now is an opportune time for physical educators to develop learning experiences for students in this area.

Eastern-Influenced Activities

Eastern philosophy has had some influence on secondary school programs. Various forms of the martial arts, including judo, karate, aikido, kendo, and tae kwan do, are popular at the college and university level and are slowly filtering into the secondary school curricula. Yoga, transcendental meditation, relaxation techniques, and self-defense classes are common in many high school and junior high school programs.

New Team Sports

Finally, the development of new or modified team sports is continuing in many schools. Activities such as team handball, global ball, speed-a-way, broomball, flickerball, angleball, modified lacrosse (Figure 1.8), and pillow polo are a few of the newer team sports that are popular in various areas of the country. Some of these are new activities, whereas others are modifications of existing sports. They add another positive dimension to programs because of the increased variety and opportunities for success with certain types of students.

New team sport activities provide many interesting and exciting challenges for both students and instructors. In teaching almost any activity, there may be problems with safety, liability, competent instruction, equipment, and teacher's comfort zones, but the advantages of offering new team sports are well worth the encountered problems. A wide variety of activities should enhance the objective of developing in all students a positive attitude toward a lifetime of physical activity.

Assure Depth of Instruction

A new development in some of the larger high schools has been the offering of different levels of instruction such as beginning and intermediate classes. Some schools have even used the classifications of beginning, team, and recreational. Three-week

FIGURE 1.8 Playing modified lacrosse

units are being offered for beginning basketball, team basketball, and recreational basketball. The beginning class might cover dribbling, passing, pivoting, rebounding, and so forth, while the team class would cover such areas as offensive strategy, zone defenses, and techniques on beating a half court trap. The final recreational class would focus primarily on team play and tournaments. Students could take three units in a progressive, systematic procedure. An advantage of this approach is that teachers can do a better job of instruction because classes are more homogeneous in motivation. Students usually feel more comfortable in a group in which similar attitudes and abilities prevail.

In grades 10–12, instructors should make every possible attempt to create programs that offer intermediate and advanced levels of instruction. Students at these developmental levels are ready to choose one or two activities in which they want to excel. Advanced instruction is different from a free-play recreational situation that is commonly found in many programs. Depth refers to organized instruction rather than simply increasing the amount of participation time. Physical educators must move away from the notion that physical education programs should focus only on beginning levels. Many students do not participate in intramurals, sport clubs, athletics, or outside-school programs, and therefore the physical education program should provide in-depth instruction for students. A high level of skill development usually increases a person's tendency to repeat and enjoy activity.

The length of activity units has shortened over the past decade, especially at the junior high level. In quality programs, 6- to 9-week units are becoming obsolete. In many junior high programs, 2- to 3-week units are the norm. These shorter units have enabled physical educators to expand the breadth of their programs and to give students an introduction to a wider variety of activities. Some people are critical of this trend because of the reduction in depth of instruction, but students will choose to develop depth in an activity after they have had a successful encounter early in their school career. The short units also reduce boredom and frustration, which are common among junior high age students. With more program breadth, educators have a better opportunity to provide all students with some type of physical activity that they can currently enjoy and continue to use.

Depth in an activity is available in many high school curricula in which students can choose a semester-long unit. This specialized approach is part of an elective or optional program instead of a required program. This type of class gives students a chance to gain in-depth skill in an activity of their choice after they complete the required program. Many schools are offering semester- or year-long units focusing on popular activities such as dance, gymnastics, tennis, and physical conditioning. The approach is productive if the school can afford to make the offerings without reducing the quality of the basic required program. The junior high program should provide breadth, and the high school program should add depth and a wide variety of elective activities.

Diagnose and Counsel Students

Students in grades 7–9 should receive early formal guidance and counseling, which directs them toward activities that match their interests and physical abilities. The physical educator can help students understand their physical shortcomings and the possibilities for alleviating problems. This means data collection and the development of procedures for interpreting the data for students and parents. Obese students, for example, should be channeled into activities in which they can find success. However, they must understand the need for participation in aerobic activities that help to burn calories and aid in weight control. Students with strong upper bodies should be encouraged to try activities that require this physical feature. Students with poor cardiovascular efficiency should be introduced to aerobic activities. An assigned activity counselor can help each student make wise decisions about physical activity.

Students in grades 10–12 should be reminded of the benefits of physical activity and the types of activities available. They also need counseling in several other areas such as behavioral self-modification techniques to aid them in the change and maintenance of fitness habits (Hall, 1978). Students should understand environmental factors and obstacles that work against their attempts to participate in physical activities. Employment parameters, marriage, children, and climate are factors that affect activity life-styles. Learning to keep records, set goals, and establish reinforcement procedures can help students with their activity habits.

Another important area of activity counseling deals with changing interests and activities of people as they grow older. Many adults have been conditioned to think that physical activity is only for the young (Gordon et al., 1976; Ostrow, 1982). This attitude needs to be changed in light of the revelation that numerous benefits are derived from being active at all age levels. Fitness and play activities are important regardless of age.

Some secondary schools have designed a series of compulsory units that require students to assess their physical abilities and make decisions about physical activities in which they can find success and remediate weaknesses. An organized counseling program helps channel students into physical education activities that can enhance their strengths and alleviate weaknesses. For example, a 3-week unit for high school freshmen students might focus on testing a wide variety of health and motor parameters. The Fitnessgram System (1987) test could be administered (Figure 1.9) and a physical fitness report card could be sent home with students at regular grading intervals. Students could use the results to help them make decisions about their activity preferences now and in the future.

The testing and counseling procedures should be set up in a systematic, organized fashion. A physical education advisor should be assigned to each student to guide her or him through the process in an attempt to give students information on which they can base sound decisions about their future. This type of testing and counseling program combined

with the previously described elective-selective program is an effective way to fuse students' interests with their physical ability requirements. This model provides a blend of information about physical activity and gives students experiences in improving physical skills and physical fitness. Students should leave the program with approach tendencies for physical activity instead of avoidance behaviors.

Offer After- and Outside-School Activity Programs

After-school activity programs such as sport clubs, intramurals, and interscholastic athletics can be effective environments for students to improve their skills and become more proficient. These programs also provide opportunities for young people to meet others with similar interests. A variety of important qualities can be experienced through these programs (e.g., teamwork, dedication, perseverance, deferred rewards, and loyalty). These qualities should be nurtured in today's youth.

Outside-school activity programs include youth sport, YMCA, parks and recreation, and private sport-oriented programs. When possible, physical educators should become involved in the leadership aspects of both the after- and outside-school programs. This should help to ensure the quality of these programs and guard against the many possible abuses. Unqualified leaders with inappropriate goals for a program can be a disastrous experience for a group of young, immature students. These programs must be developed with the idea of fostering a love of physical activity in students (rather than promoting escape or avoidance behaviors). Physical educators should be able to help parents, other teachers, and adults to organize these programs with the proper goals in mind (Figure 1.10).

Curriculum planners and physical education teachers need to consider and deal effectively with these suggestions. Such ideas can be incorporated into a program, at least to some degree, without much strain on the budget. Each situation has a number of practical factors (e.g., students, facilities, teachers) that will influence the degree to which such suggestions can be developed. A program of curriculum and instruction that focuses on these areas will have an excellent chance of helping students incorporate physical activity into their life-styles.

Siedentop (1980a) has argued that the physical education curriculum functions in a cultural transmission mode rather than promoting social reconstruction. Physical education programs have incorporated activities that follow the activity choices of society, rather than provide a leadership role in shaping activity preferences. For example,

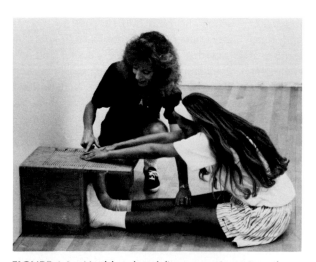

FIGURE 1.9 Health-related fitness testing (sit and reach test for flexibility; calf skinfold)

FIGURE 1.10   A soccer club in action

society's recent interest in wellness, wilderness sports, and the martial arts are having an effect on physical education curricula. This theory suggests that many adult activity interests and habits are formed outside school physical education programs in settings such as the private sports instruction industry. Perhaps it is time to focus physical education programs on social reconstruction. We need to develop programs that do influence students' activity habits and preferences, and these preferences should include types of activities that offer health-related benefits and a form of play.

Clearly, if physical educators want to affect lifetime physical activity habits positively, they must consider the ideas and steps presented. Programs that continue to use a negative atmosphere and focus primarily on the highly skilled athlete involved in team sports will not be successful. Teachers should be enthusiastic role models interested in all students and in a variety of lifetime activities. Curricula need to be organized so that students will be committed to activities that can be enjoyed for a lifetime.

FACTORS IMPACTING SECONDARY SCHOOL PHYSICAL EDUCATION PROGRAMS

A number of trends and related issues have impacted the development of secondary school physical education programs. Some of the factors which need to be considered when developing a program are discussed in the following section.

Conceptual Physical Fitness Programs

A development that started at the college level and has slowly filtered down to the secondary school level is called the conceptual approach. An example of the conceptual approach is the *Fitness for Life* text by Corbin and Lindsey (1990). This approach

has been called a lecture-laboratory method. Students spend time receiving information in a lecture situation and then try out or test the information on themselves or on peers in a laboratory setting. Emphasis is placed on information, appraisal procedures, and program planning. Students are expected to understand the "how, what, and why" of physical activity and exercise. They learn to use diagnostic tests in areas such as cardiovascular endurance, muscular strength and endurance, flexibility, body composition, and motor ability.

A variety of conceptual programs have been field-tested in various situations. In some schools, concepts make up the entire physical education program, while in others, the concepts may be only a portion of the requirement, such as a semester class or 6-week unit. Several books are available with lesson sequences and other instructional materials such as slide-tape lectures, scripts, review questions, tests, dittos, overhead transparencies, and laboratory experiments.

AAHPERD has sponsored the development of the Basic Stuff Series (1987), which is a compilation of current knowledge from the subdisciplines of physical education (e.g., exercise physiology, kinesiology, motor development, and motor learning). This series consists of nine booklets of information aimed at helping the physical educator incorporate knowledge concepts into the curriculum grades K–12. This series is an example of the trend toward inserting knowledge concepts into the physical education curriculum. This series will be discussed in Chapter 3 as part of a curriculum model emphasizing knowledge concepts.

The conceptual approach seems to be popular for several reasons. First, many believe that an academic approach focused on knowledge and cognitive growth instead of on physical skill is a more respectable educational endeavor. Others believe that when student knowledge is increased, attitudes and behaviors will also change, causing physical activity to be incorporated into the student's life-style. This is not a proven phenomenon. Increasing a person's knowledge does not ensure a change in behavior, and students must also experience and attempt physical activity and fitness as well as understand conceptually. Concepts should be an important part of a physical education program, but there must be a balance of both knowledge and physical skill development in the physical education curriculum.

Interdisciplinary Courses

In a few secondary schools, physical education is being combined with other disciplines such as health, biology, geology, and geography. In these programs, students have opportunities to learn about subjects such as drugs, alcohol, diseases, safety, first aid, hunting and fishing, taxidermy, rock formations, and environmental concerns. Emphasis is placed on combining physical skill development with knowledge. For example, students can learn about the flora and fauna of an area while concurrently learning camping and backpacking skills. This is the basic thesis of many outdoor education programs in which several disciplines are integrated to teach students about the outdoors.

This approach also balances the acquisition of knowledge and physical skill development, and offers some interesting challenges for students and teachers. Teachers can take advantage of geographical locations, different learning environments, and the interests of students living in these areas. The physical education teacher can team teach with teachers from other subject areas such as biology, zoology, or geography. In this way many interesting learning experiences can be developed. A major problem with this approach is that the time available for physical skill development is usually reduced in favor of more knowledge time.

Independent Study Options

Independent study programs give students an opportunity to earn physical education credit for advanced study or off-campus courses that are not available in the basic curricula. Students at a high school in California can earn credit for off-campus study involving surfing, ice skating, horseback riding, bowling, golf, and other disciplines. These programs are usually available to students only after they have completed the basic requirements. Some type of monitoring and weekly check-in procedure is arranged with the student, parent, and teacher agreeing to a contract. Many of these programs also contain a fitness component, and students must show some evidence of maintenance or improvement in the fitness area (e.g., body composition or cardiovascular endurance).

Students keep a log of their various activities with an anecdotal record of skill work, games, scores, opponents, and evaluation procedures. Written work is usually required on rules, etiquette, current personalities, research areas, or officiating. If problems occur with students not completing their work, they are returned to the regular program or are dropped from the independent study program. Some schools have special independent study areas in the library or in a room close to the gymnasium where students can check out materials or view video tapes and loop films.

Some problems may occur with students abusing the program and with monitoring procedures, equip-

ment check-out, legal liability, financial arrangements, and evaluation procedures. The program does, however, offer some possibilities for advanced and new activity study and can add an exciting dimension to the curricula. The independent study approach may help students develop self-management skills and become self-motivated because they have selected activities that appeal to them, and they are largely responsible for what they learn from the experience.

Use of Off-Campus Community Facilities

Another interesting trend that can be positive for school programs is the use of off-campus community facilities. This approach allows schools to use community bowling alleys, golf courses, ski slopes, and skating rinks to enhance the physical education program. Many schools are bussing students to a nearby bowling alley or golf course each Friday during a 3-week unit. A school in Pennsylvania takes students to a ski slope for downhill skiing lessons. Sometimes the schools provide the transportation and participation funds; in other cases, students pay the expenses. Funding can also be provided through car washes, candy sales, and raffles. Programs and procedures are limited only by a teacher's ingenuity and creative direction.

The nearby facilities in the community can add a valuable dimension to secondary programs. Physical educators need to broaden their areas of competency and to use the resources at their disposal. A noted physical educator once asked a physical education teacher who taught at a school situated near a beautiful lake, "Do you teach swimming, boating and sailing here?" "No," replied the teacher, "we don't have the facilities." Finding a way to use community resources for the betterment of students is surely possible. Qualified personnel from the community can also add instructional expertise in new activities.

State and Local Education Requirements

Each state department of education sets requirements for physical education. Policies differ from state to state. Some require a number of minutes per week for each grade level, whereas others specify a number of days per week. Several states have no physical education requirement. Each school district usually sets requirements within the framework provided by the state department of education. This is not a new policy, but it is important for physical educators to understand that requirements are developed within this framework. Consequently, district policies can be changed significantly and still be within the state guidelines. As an example, in

Arizona there is no requirement at the state level for physical education, yet most Arizona high schools have at least a 1-year physical education requirement. Other Arizona schools have a 2- or 3-year requirement, and some offer only an elective physical education program. The state requirement will significantly affect the curriculum, the students, and the teachers.

Teachers and curriculum planners must be informed about state and local requirements. Currently, the general trend has been for states to reduce physical education time in favor of more time for mathematics, science, and English. Many people still consider physical education to be a "frills" area, and it appears that physical educators will have to continue to justify their existence in the schools.

A newer approach to requirements at the local level in the selective-elective type of curriculum involves specifying requirements by activity category, such as team sports, lifetime sports, gymnastics, aquatics, recreational activities, and dance. An example would be requiring a student to complete 12 activities in one year. The requirement might be that three of the activities must be team sports, three must be lifetime sports, and one each must be selected from the areas of dance, aquatics, and gymnastics. The remaining activity choices would be left to the student. This procedure gives students a **choice within a requirement** and ensures that students will receive a variety of activities as well as the opportunity to choose according to their interests. Students have choice but not total freedom, so a more balanced curricular approach is thus assured.

Federal Mandates: Title IX and Coeducational Classes

Title IX of the Educational Amendments Act of 1972 has had a significant impact on most secondary school physical education programs. The law is based on the principle that school activities and programs are of equal value for both sexes. Students should not be denied access to participation in school activities on the basis of sex. This law has stirred up much debate and controversy. Interpretations and details are still being worked out by school districts, state departments of education, and the judicial system.

Legal ramifications have forced schools to provide equal access to physical education activities for both boys and girls (Figure 1.11). Coeducational classes have become the rule instead of the exception. Separate classes for males and females have been eliminated. This does not imply that both sexes must wrestle together, share locker facilities, or have the

FIGURE 1.11 Coeducational class

same activity interests. It does mean that males can participate in a dance class or females can elect a weight training class if they have interest in these respective areas. In principle, the law also means that instruction is provided by the most qualified person regardless of sex.

The law does allow schools to group students by ability, even if the result is groups consisting of primarily one sex. The law also allows teachers to segregate sexes during the game or competitive aspect of contact sports such as wrestling, basketball, football, ice hockey, and others. Teachers must also be sure that grading standards or procedures are not having an adverse effect on one sex, because this is a specified regulation of Title IX. Standards must be equally fair to both sexes.

Title IX has created some problems for physical educators. Teachers have been forced to expand their comfort zones in dealing with students of the opposite sex. Grading procedures, safety, locker room policies, and sexuality issues are a few of the areas that teachers have had to rethink with coeducational classes. For some, these changes have been interesting, exciting, and challenging, but for others the law has brought about negative feelings. For the latter, Title IX has been the cause of all that is wrong with today's physical education programs.

Amidst all of the controversy, it is important to examine the objectives of the physical education program and to focus on developing a situation that will meet the requirements of Title IX. There are new problems, but this is a small price to pay for inequalities that have existed in terms of opportunities for learning and participating in sport and physical education. Law or no law, physical education is just as important for females as it is for males. There are also clear advantages to coeducational programs in the areas of social development, activity offerings, and instructional quality. Teachers should be responsible for all students in their classes, regardless of ability, sex, or race. Many of the complaints that arise are often nothing more than a smoke screen for laziness, ineptness, or bias.

The Handicapped Student and Public Law 94–142

Public Law 94–142, the Education of All Handicapped Children Act, was signed in 1975 by President Ford. This law ensures that all youngsters with handicaps receive an appropriate public education that serves their unique needs. Physical education has been specified as an important part of the handicapped student's curricula or individualized education program (IEP). The IEP is prepared jointly by the teacher, the parent, and the student, if appropriate. It contains extensive information covering the student's present status, program objectives, learning activities, and evaluation procedures.

The law has compelled physical educators to develop specialized classes and programs for many students with handicaps. Other students have been mainstreamed into the regular physical education program as part of the least restrictive environment advocated by P. L. 94–142. School districts have been required to hire qualified instructors for these programs, as well as to encourage current teachers to develop skills for providing meaningful experiences for mainstreamed children with handicaps.

A federally validated program for students with handicaps that is being implemented throughout the country is the Physical Education Opportunities Program for Exceptional Learners (PEOPEL) (Long et al., 1980). The program involves a one-to-one peer teaching model in which student volunteers who are nonhandicapped are paired with students who are handicapped. The volunteers are put through an extensive training program and receive physical education credit for their efforts. The program has been field-tested and offers many advantages for students, such as a high rate of feedback, individual attention, and more instruction.

The law clearly creates some problems for physical educators in planning, organizing, managing, and evaluating daily and yearly programs for the handicapped. In most situations, the teacher must establish learning environments concurrently for students with and without handicaps. It is important to remember that physical education is as important to disabled students as it is to the other students. The handicapped deserve quality physical education experiences, and program offerings must continue to improve in this area, regardless of difficulties.

ISSUES IMPACTING PHYSICAL EDUCATION TEACHERS

A number of issues arise in all professions which determine the working conditions of practicing members. Currently, the following issues are hotly debated among physical education professionals.

Teaching and Coaching

Many people have a difficult time separating the physical education program from the athletic program. The athletic program is concerned with recruiting, coaching, and administering teams that will compete against other school teams. These goals are significantly different from the goals of the secondary school physical education program, yet athletics and physical education are often linked because the programs must share facilities, equipment, fields, and teachers. In addition, a great deal of pressure often comes from the local community to produce winning teams. The pressure to develop outstanding physical education programs is not nearly as great, and the visibility of the two programs is markedly different. This creates a difficult situation for the teacher-coach. The coach may support the concept of an outstanding curriculum, but may not find enough time and energy to do both. The physical education program often takes a back seat in many situations.

This problem has no simple solution. Many teachers want to work in both programs. The pressure to produce winners is apparent, and the individual instructor will determine the quality of the physical education program that is implemented. Many people do excellent work in both areas, but it is not an easy task.

Instruction, Management, and Free Play

For many years, physical educators were viewed favorably by administrators and peers for having identically dressed students in neat, straight lines. Many people still adhere to this practice, and students may be completely "under control" even though little instruction and learning are taking place. In fact, students may be learning to dislike or avoid physical activity and exercise because of their instructor's control procedures. Teachers sometimes become so concerned with management and discipline that they lose sight of the primary goals of physical education. If students are learning to dislike physical education because of the control techniques used, teachers need to look carefully at their procedures. A degree of management and discipline is necessary for an effective learning environment, but not a degree of control that destroys students' love of activity.

In contrast, there are many situations in which students have come to believe that secondary school physical education class is a time to play a game without any instruction or a time to work on the physical skills needed for successful game participation. Some students think they should always have free time for game participation. This attitude is a result of the policy of "rolling out the ball" espoused by many teachers. It becomes difficult for other teachers to organize a structured learning environment when students are accustomed to the free play approach.

Equipment, Facilities, and Class Size

A continuing problem that physical educators at all levels face is the problem of inadequate equipment and facilities. For some reason, many administrators believe that physical education classes can be larger and can manage with less equipment than an academic class. They fail to realize that it is impossible to learn to dribble a basketball without having access to a basketball on a regular basis. Students are also frustrated by standing in line and waiting for a turn to dribble the ball. Teachers have a difficult situation with 40 students on 6 tennis courts. Economic conditions make these problems difficult, and physical educators must strive to get a fair share of the budget. Students are not asked to learn to read and write without books, paper, and pencils. Physical education is as important as other discipline areas and should receive an equal share of the budget dollar.

Legal Liability

Many lawsuits appearing in various aspects of society are of concern to physical educators. Teachers are not immune to liability lawsuits as evidenced by an increasing number of cases of parents and students suing teachers, administrators, and school boards. This situation is unnerving when teachers attempt new activities or use new teaching techniques that involve any type of risk. Many teachers and administrators have become extremely cautious and conservative about activities that have a reputation of any danger, yet often many of these activities are actually safer than those traditionally included in the curriculum. A teacher can refuse to offer new activities for fear of a lawsuit. Ultimately, students become the victims in this process because teachers refuse to offer any units that have some degree of risk.

Teachers certainly need to acquire adequate knowledge about safety and instructional procedures before implementing a new activity. They should not be scared off solely on the basis of ignorance. Legal ramifications must be understood when developing a broad and balanced curriculum. With proper information and careful planning, the instructional risks of various activities can be minimized. If sound policies and procedures are followed on a daily basis, teachers should not worry about legal liability. An in-depth discussion of legal liability can be found in Chapter 13.

Private Sports Instruction

Opportunities for sports and fitness instruction in the private sector continue to expand rapidly. These programs are quite effective in meeting the demands of consumers. Gymnastics clubs, soccer leagues, Pop Warner football, motocross bicycle racing, little league baseball, and racquet clubs are a few examples of programs that are available to students. Students receive in-depth instruction, practice with adequate equipment, have many competitive opportunities, and receive trophies, T-shirts, and similar rewards. Many of these programs are excellent and provide students with valuable experiences. They do, however, create two major problems for school-based physical education programs.

The first problem is that private instruction creates a wide range of backgrounds, experiences, and abilities among students who are participating in school physical education. Students from middle- and upper-class families may have a wealth of experience in sports such as tennis, golf, soccer, and gymnastics, whereas students from lower income families will probably have little experience. It is difficult with limited equipment to develop a beginning gymnastics unit that is meaningful to 8th grade students who have had 5 years of intensive training at a private sports academy. This same point can be illustrated by comparing students involved in a soccer league for several years with students who have never played the game. Teachers face a difficult challenge in motivating students with such diverse backgrounds.

The second problem can be more significant in terms of impact on the school program. As opportunities in the private sector increase, public support for the school physical education curricula may lessen. Some people currently believe that secondary school physical education programs can be eliminated because of the many opportunities in the private sector. "Let students learn physical activities outside the school setting so there is more time and money for academic subjects" is the viewpoint often voiced. An opposing viewpoint argues that private instruction opportunities are available only to the upper middle class and that lower socioeconomic groups will have limited opportunities. The trend toward private instruction is continuing to grow and the possibility is strong that the private sports industry may become a serious competitor of school programs. Physical educators face the challenge of developing quality programs that provide meaningful learning experiences for all students regardless of background.

REFERENCES AND SUGGESTED READINGS

AAHPERD. 1988. *Physical Best.* Reston, VA: AAHPERD.

AAHPERD. 1987. *Basic Stuff Series.* Reston, VA: AAHPERD.

Anderson, J. Growth and development today: Implications for physical education. Paper presented at the National Conference on Social Changes and Implications for Physical Education and Sports Recreation, Estes Park, Colorado, June 1958.

Brophy, J. and Good, T. 1974. *Teacher-Student Relationships.* New York: Holt, Rinehart & Winston.

Corbin, C., and Lindsey, R. 1990. *Fitness for Life.* 3rd ed. Glenview, IL: Scott, Foresman & Co.

Darst, P., and Armstrong, G. 1980. *Outdoor Adventure Activities for School and Recreation Programs.* Minneapolis, MN: Burgess Publishing Co.

Dodds, P. 1976. Love and joy in the gymnasium. *Quest* (Summer): 109–116.

Gordon, C., Gaitz, C. M., and Scott, J. 1976. Leisure and Lives: Personal expressivity across the life span. In R. H. Binstock and E. Shanas (eds.) *Handbook of Aging and the Social Sciences.* New York: Van Nostrand Reinhold Co.

Hall, D. 1978. Changing attitudes by changing behavior. *JOPERD* 49(4): 20–21.

Huizinga, J. 1962. *Homo Ludens: A Study of the Play Element in Culture.* Boston: Beacon Press.

Klappholz, L. 1978. The case for selectives in physical education. *Physical Education Newsletter,* February issue.

Landers, D. 1978. How, when, and where to use demonstrations: Suggestions for the practitioner. *JOPERD* 49(1): 65–67.

Leonard, G. 1977. Why Johnny can't run and other gym class scandals. *Arizona JOHPERD* 21(1): 2–7.

Long, E., Irmer, L., Burkett, L., Glasenapp, G., and Odenkirk, B. 1980. PEOPEL. *JOPERD* 51(7): 28–30.

Locke, L., and Woods, S. 1982. Teacher enthusiasm. *Journal of Teaching in Physical Education* 1(3): 3–14.

McKenzie, T. 1982. Research on modeling: Implications for teacher training programs. *Journal of Teaching in Physical Education* 1(3): 23–30.

Ostrow, A. 1982. Age grading implications for physical activity participation among older adults. *Quest* 33: 112–123.

Roberts, C. and Becker, S. 1976. Communication and teaching effectiveness. *American Educational Research Journal* 13: 181–197.

Rosenthal, R. and Jacobson, L. 1968. *Pygmalion in the Classroom.* New York: Holt, Rinehart & Winston.

Siedentop, D. 1980(a). Physical education curriculum: An analysis of the past. *JOPERD* 51(7): 40–41.

Siedentop, D. 1980(b). *Physical Education — Introductory Analysis.* 3rd ed. Dubuque, IA: Wm. C. Brown Group.

Westcott, W. 1977. Effects of teacher modeling on the subsequent behavior of students. Doctoral dissertation, The Ohio State University. In *Dissertation Abstracts International, 1978,* 38: 6605A–6606B.

Wilson, B., and Altieri, P. 1978. Complying with Title IX — Increasing participation through the elective program. *Arizona JOHPERD* 21(2): 6–7.

2 PHYSICAL ACTIVITY: WHAT RESEARCH TELLS THE TEACHER

Adolescence is a time of rapid growth and development. During the elementary school years, students are able to learn motor learning patterns in a period of rather steady growth and development. However, the junior high school years and puberty give rise to a rapid growth spurt. Adolescence is defined here as occurring somewhere between the ages of 8 and 19 for females and 10 to 22 years for males (Malina, 1986). There is much variation in the actual onset of adolescence and entry into adulthood. However, it is that period of time when the body matures physically and sexually.

THE GROWING ADOLESCENT

Growth patterns are generally controlled by genetic makeup at birth. Although unhealthy parents or poor dietary practices can have a negative impact on proper growth and development, the focus in this section is on normal maturation common to the majority of youngsters. All students follow a general growth pattern; however, each person's timing is unique. Some students will be advanced physically for their chronological age whereas others will be identified as slow maturers. Only when the aberration from the norm is excessive should teachers and parents become concerned.

Growth Patterns

Teachers and parents are interested in how fast youngsters are growing. When heights and weights are plotted on a graph from year to year, a distance curve can be developed. These curves (Figure 2.1) give an indication of how tall and heavy young people are in a specific year of life. Another method of examining growth patterns is to look at a velocity curve. The velocity curve is quite useful because it reveals how much a youngster grows on a year-to-year basis (Figure 2.2). Children go through a rapid period of growth from birth to age 5. From age 6

to the onset of adolescence, growth slows to a steady but increasing pattern. During adolescence, rapid growth occurs again until adulthood is reached. During the elementary school years, males are generally taller and heavier. Females reach the adolescent growth spurt first, and grow taller and heavier during the 6th- and 7th-grade years. Males quickly catch up, however, and grow larger and stronger. Growth charts based on a larger and more recent sample of children have been developed by the National Center for Health Statistics (Figures 2.3 and 2.4). These tables can be consulted to identify both height and weight percentiles for youngsters aged 2–18. The tables offer excellent opportunity to visualize any marked differences among teenagers from a so-called "normal" population.

Body Physique

A student's physique can affect the quality of motor performance. Sheldon et al. (1954) developed the original scheme for identifying physiques based on

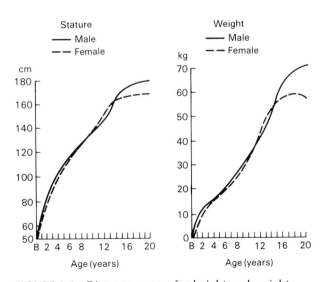

FIGURE 2.1 Distance curves for height and weight (from Malina, R. 1975. *Growth and Development: The First Twenty Years in Man*, p. 19. Minneapolis, MN: Burgess)

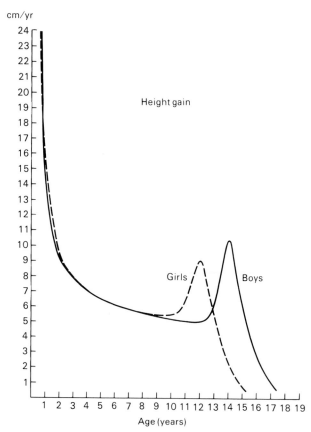

cm/yr

Height gain

Girls

Boys

Age (years)

FIGURE 2.2   Growth velocity curve for height   (from Tanner, J. M., Whitehouse, R. H., and Takaishi, M. 1966. *Archives of Diseases in Childhood*. 41:467)

the contribution of different components to the body as a whole. The components are termed *endomorphy, mesomorphy,* and *ectomorphy.* Each component is assessed individually from standardized photographs. Rating is done on a 7-point scale with 1 being the least expression and 7 the most expression of the specific component. The ratings of each component give a total score that results in identification of an individual's somatotype.

In general, youngsters who possess a mesomorphic body type perform best in activities requiring strength, speed, and agility. The mesomorph is characterized by a predominance of muscle and bone and is often labeled "muscled." These students usually perform well in most team sports because these activities require strength, speed, and agility. On the other hand, the ectomorph is identified as being extremely thin, with a minimum of muscle development, and is characterized as "skinny." These students may perform poorly in activities requiring strength and power, but do well in aerobic endurance activities such as jogging, cross-country running, and track and field. The third classification is the endomorph, who is soft and round, with an excessively protruding abdomen. These youngsters are

usually regarded as fat and often perform poorly in many areas, including aerobic and anaerobic skill-oriented activities. The obese student is generally at a disadvantage in all phases of the physical education program.

Physique Changes Caused By Growth

During adolescence, growth in weight and height accelerates rapidly. Males grow faster than females and for a longer period of time. Most females reach peak growth velocity around the age of 11 where as males do not peak until 13 years of age. It is common to see females grow larger than males in early adolescence, however, the males will quickly catch up and surpass them. In addition, males will broaden at the shoulders relative to their hips, whereas females broaden at the hips relative to the shoulders. The key difference in growth patterns between the maturing sexes lies in the area of body somatotype. There are more endomorphic body types among females than males. Among males, the mesomorphic body type becomes much more common. Males become stronger and increase the amount of muscle tissue whereas females increase the percentage of body fat. Obviously, this change in body physique impacts the athletic performances of both sexes. The purpose here is not full comprehension of the system of somatotyping, but to understand that a student's physique can directly affect motor performance. It also obviates, once again, that youngsters are dramatically different, necessitating that instruction accommodate individual differences.

Physical Maturity

The concept of maturity is used often by teachers in physical education. Usually, students are identified as being early, late, or average maturers, with teachers examining the social maturity rather than the physical maturity of the youngster. Physical maturity, however, has a strong impact on a student's performance in physical education. The most commonly used method to identify maturity rate is to compare chronological age with skeletal age. Ossification (hardening) of the bones occurs in the center of the bone shaft and at the ends of the long bones (growth plates). The rate of ossification gives an accurate indication of a youngster's rate of maturation. This rate of maturation or skeletal age (which can be identified by X-raying the wrist bones and comparing the development of the subject's bones with a set of standardized X rays) gives a truer sense of the student's physical maturity (Gruelich and Pyle, 1959). If the chronological age is greater than skeletal age, the youngster is said to be a late (or

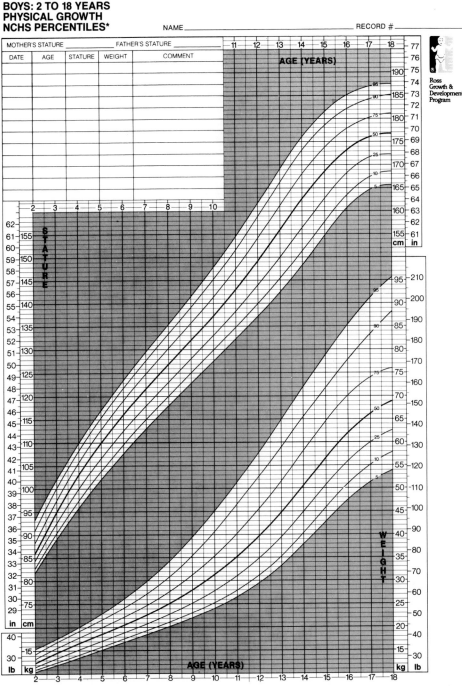

BOYS: 2 TO 18 YEARS
PHYSICAL GROWTH
NCHS PERCENTILES*

FIGURE 2.3 Physical growth percentiles for boys 2 to 18 years   (adapted from Hamill, P. V. V., Drizd, T. A., Johnson, C. L., Reed, R. B., Roche, A. F., and Moore, W. M. 1979. Physical growth: National Center for Health Statistics percentiles. *American Journal of Clinical Nutrition* 32: 607–629. Data from the Fels Research Institute, Wright State University School of Medicine, Yellow Springs, OH. Used with permission of Ross Laboratories, Columbus, OH)

slow) maturer. On the other hand, if the skeletal age is ahead of chronological age, the student is labeled an early (or fast) maturer.

Early-maturing students of both sexes are generally heavier and taller for their age than are average- or late-maturing students. In fact, obese youngsters (endomorphs) are often more mature for their age than are normal-weight youngsters. Early-maturing youngsters also have larger amounts of muscle and bone tissue, due to their larger body size. However, the early maturer also carries a greater percentage of body weight as fat tissue (Malina, 1980). Late-maturing youngsters will usually catch up to early maturers in height, but not in weight. In addition,

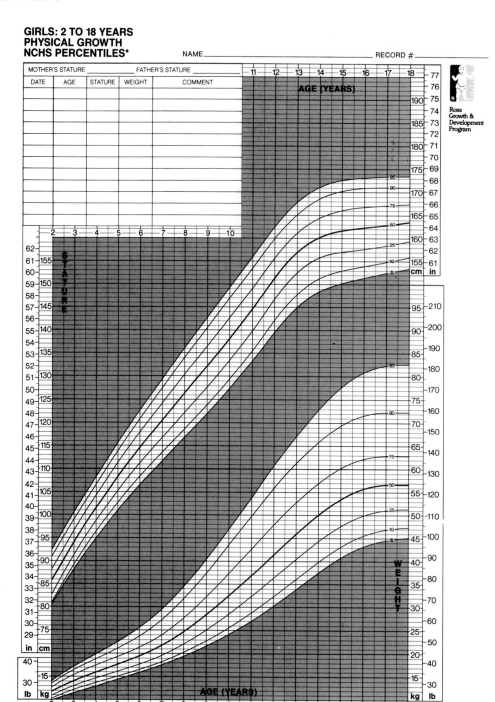

FIGURE 2.4   Physical growth percentiles for girls 2 to 18 years   (adapted from Hamill, P. V. V., Drizd, T. A., Johnson, C. L., Reed, R. B., Roche, A. F., and Moore, W. M. 1979. Physical growth: National Center for Health Statistics percentiles. *American Journal of Clinical Nutrition* 32: 607–629. Data from the Fels Research Institute, Wright State University School of Medicine, Yellow Springs, OH. Ross Laboratories, Columbus, OH)

an early-maturing student in elementary school will also be an early maturer in secondary school. Generally, early-maturing males will have mesomorphic physiques, and early-maturing females will be characterized by endomorphy. These differences in body size and composition probably account for the superiority of males in activities that require strength and power. The differences help explain the superiority of females in activities requiring flexibility and balance.

The motor performance of males is related to skeletal maturity in that the more mature youngster usually performs better on motor tasks (Clarke, 1971). For females, however, motor performance appears not to be related to physiological maturity. In fact, a study by Malina (1978) found that late maturation is commonly associated with exceptional motor performance. Because many sports require size and strength, it is quite likely that early maturers have a strong advantage in athletic endeavors. This points out the need to design a physical education curriculum that will meet the needs of both early and late maturers. It demands that units of instruction be offered that emphasize activities that rely less on strength and size and more on aerobic capacity, agility, balance, and coordination. In addition, programs often place importance on learning at the same rate or participating in activities with other students regardless of skill level, even though this practice may be detrimental to the development of students who are developing at a faster or slower rate. Teachers sometimes expect all youngsters to be capable of performing the same activity at the same time, regardless of maturation. Unfortunately, students do not mature at the same rate and are therefore not at similar levels of readiness to learn. If physical education is for all students, emphasis must be placed on assuring that part of the curriculum offers successful experiences for the less mature youngsters.

PHYSICAL ACTIVITY AND GROWTH

Teachers often want to justify physical education based on the impact of physical activity on growth. Unfortunately, it appears that activity has no impact on the stature of maturing students (Malina, 1986). However, regular training does not have a negative effect on growth and development. Some people have theorized that strenuous physical activity would disrupt normal developmental patterns; there is no evidence to support such concern.

Active youngsters are more lean than those who don't participate in regular activity. Involvement in activity obviously impacts the body composition of participants. The long-term effect of such activity is not known, however, and it is quite possible that once students quit participating they may return to a body type similar to nonexercisers. A number of studies with teenagers show that short-term training has a strong impact on muscular development. Muscular hypertrophy occurs due to training teenagers in a manner similar to adults. However, if the activity is not continued, lean body mass will decrease and fat levels will slowly increase.

Activity affects skeletal growth. Vigorous activity can improve internal bone structure so that bones are much more resistant to pressure, tension, and ultimately, to breakage. The bones also increase in diameter and density in response to activity. Inactivity for prolonged periods causes demineralization and makes the bones more prone to fracture. This increased bone density developed during adolescence can help guard against osteoporosis in adult life (Haymes, 1986).

Vigorous activity appears to cause the bones to grow to a shape that is mechanically advantageous for muscle attachments (Rarick, 1973). The skeletal system is not totally rigid and responds to stress by changing its posture. This mechanical advantage may allow the student to perform physical challenges at a higher level in later years when sport activities are more meaningful. This phenomenon helps to explain why a small person can throw a baseball as fast as a larger person with longer levers. An increased mechanical advantage allows the smaller person (with shorter levers) to generate an increased force.

Even though activity does enhance skeletal density, it does not appear to effect the rate of skeletal maturity. Those youngsters who are most mature at an early age are still most mature when evaluated later in adolescence. It is safe to say that exercise assures optimum growth of bones in maturing youngsters. The only cause for concern in this area is to assure that injury to the growth plates of the bones does not occur due to excessive pressure. As is usually the case, exercise should be administered in a progressive and reasonable manner.

Aerobic Capacity

Maximal aerobic power is an individual's maximum ability to use oxygen in the body for metabolic purposes. The oxygen uptake of an individual, all other factors being equal, determines the quality of endurance-oriented performance. Adults interested in increasing endurance-based athletic performance therefore train extensively to increase aerobic power.

Aerobic power increases with chronological age during the elementary school years in males and females at a similar rate, even though males exhibit higher levels as early as the age of 5 (Bar-Or, 1983). However, at the age of 12 the oxygen uptake continues to increase in males and stops improving in females after the age of 14. Since maximal aerobic power is closely related to lean body mass, this tapering off in aerobic power among older females is probably explained by the increase in necessary reproductive body fat. However, if aerobic power is related to the muscle mass that performs the activity, the differences are virtually nonexistent.

Another method of viewing aerobic power in youngsters is to adjust their maximum oxygen uptake on a per kilogram of body weight basis. When adjusted in this manner, it shows little change for males (no increase) and a continual decrease for females (Bar-Or, 1983). Again, this decrease in females may be due to an increase in body fat and a decrease in lean body mass. This lack of increase raises the question as to whether training youngsters will increase their aerobic performance. The research results differ. Some researchers have found an increase in aerobic power through training, whereas others report that training has no impact on the aerobic system. There is little doubt that aerobic power increases in adolescents with training. However, the key point in assuring that junior and senior high school youngsters participate in aerobic activity is to enhance health and well-being rather than show an increase in aerobic capacity. Lifetime fitness entails being involved in aerobic activities on a regular basis. The physical education program should cultivate a positive attitude toward activity and be based on regular exercise. This contrasts with the common practice of training and testing youngsters to see if they can reach their maximum capacity and physical limits. Few adults will ever exercise at a level that is overly demanding and physically exhausting.

The Impact of Obesity on Aerobic Capacity

Obese students seldom perform physical activities on a par with leaner youngsters (Bar-Or, 1983). In part, this is because of the greater metabolic cost of the obese student's exercise. Obese youngsters require a higher oxygen uptake capacity to perform a given task. Unfortunately, their capacity is usually lower than that of normal-weight youngsters, which means that they must operate at a higher percentage of their maximum capacity. This forces obese students to operate at a higher percentage of their aerobic capacity, so they have less reserve. The lack of reserve probably explains why these youngsters perceive aerobic tasks as demanding and unenjoyable. Teachers should bear this in mind when they ask obese youngsters to try to run as far and as fast as normal-weight youngsters. The task is absolutely more demanding for the obese student.

Obesity takes a great toll on a student's aerobic power because of the greater metabolic cost of exercise. Obese youngsters must perform at a higher percentage of their maximal oxygen uptake. Their maximal uptake values are unfortunately often lower than those of lean youngsters. This gives them less reserve and makes them perceive higher exertion when performing a task. These reactions contribute to the well-known perception among teachers that "obese youngsters don't like to run." This reaction is irrelevant because it doesn't solve the problem. To deal with this paradox, teachers must accept that the obese student is working harder and that work loads must be adjusted accordingly. Because the obese student is working harder than the normal weight youngster, it is necessary to understand that aerobic demands will not be similar. There is no acceptable premise, physiological or psychological, for asking all youngsters to run the same distance regardless of ability.

Work loads should be based on time rather than distance. Undoubtably, the most efficient runner will move farther than the obese youngster during a stipulated time period. However, this is expected when teachers follow the principle of individual differences. All students *do not and should not* have to do the same amount of exercise. Just as one would not expect elementary school youngsters to perform the same work load as that of high school seniors, it is unreasonable to expect obese students to be capable of work loads similar to those of lean, ectomorphic youngsters.

Weight Control

Body composition refers to the varying amounts of muscle, bone, and fat within the body. Over half of the fat stored in the body is stored in a layer just below the skin. This is the reason that skin folds are used to estimate the amount of fat carried within the body. Depending on the criteria used to evaluate the ratio of fat, from 25% to 35% of youngsters have been identified as being overfat or obese.

Obesity not only decreases a youngster's aerobic capacity, but it also has a negative impact on motor performance. The study of obesity in adolescents has produced some disturbing findings. Many obese people appear to have a decreased tendency for muscular activity. As weight increases, the impulse for physical exertion decreases further. As youngsters become more obese, they find themselves in a cycle that appears to be out of control. In most cases, physical activity appears to be the crucial factor in dealing with weight control. In comparisons of the diets of obese and normal youngsters, no substantial difference in caloric consumption was usually found. In fact, in some cases, obese youngsters actually consumed less food than did normal-weight youngsters (Corbin and Fletcher, 1968).

The lack of physical activity is common among obese youngsters. In a study of 9th-grade females (Johnson et al., 1956), females who were obese ate less but also exercised two-thirds less (in total time) than did normal-weight females. Movies taken of normal-weight and overweight teenagers (Corbin and Fletcher, 1968) demonstrated a great difference in the activity level of the two groups, even though diets were quite similar. A number of researchers have identified the effectiveness of increased activity in reducing obesity (Eisenman, 1986). However, just increasing activity may only be a short-term solution. It is necessary to change the attitudes of the youngster and to assure that they develop a positive feeling about the role of exercise in maintaining an optimum weight level. Many educators feel it is best to deal with obese youngsters in a positive fashion rather than by trying to solve their problem by requesting that they exercise more. If the treatment is not successful, students may feel as though they are failures and there is less chance the situation will be rectified.

Adults often make the statement: "Don't worry about excessive weight; it will come off when the student reaches adolescence." The opposite is usually true, however. Eighty percent of obese youngsters grow into obese adults; however, 96% of obese teenagers become obese adults (Johnson et al., 1956). Youngsters clearly do not grow out of obesity; they grow into it. Student obesity needs to be challenged at an early age, and this challenge must come from increased movement and activity. In addition, teachers must understand that many obese students are victims of their home environment. For example, Griffiths and Payne (1976) selected 4- and 5-year-old youngsters for study based on their parents' level of obesity. At the time of the study, the youngsters were of similar body composition. Youngsters of obese parents were, however, less active and also ate less than did the offspring of leaner parents. If the behavior continued, these youngsters of obese parents would probably become obese due to lack of activity. Obviously, students are not in total control of their destiny and solving problems of obesity are difficult at best. There are no easy answers, and to solve such complex problems as obesity, parents, nutritionists, counselors, nurses, and physicians need to be involved in the process.

The advantage of using physical activity to treat obesity is that it increases energy expenditure and may suppress appetite. In contrast to rigid diets, exercise will minimize the loss of lean body mass and will stimulate fat loss. Physical activity is inexpensive, easy to do in a variety of situations, and can be a social experience.

Strength Development

In the elementary school years, muscular strength increases linearly with chronological age (Malina, 1980) until adolescence, at which time a rapid increase in strength occurs. Strength is related to body size and lean body mass. When differences in strength between the sexes are adjusted for height, there is no difference in lower body strength from age 7 through 17. When the same adjustment between the sexes is made for upper body strength, however, males have more upper extremity and trunk strength (Malina, 1980). Males and females are thus competing on somewhat even terms in activities demanding leg strength, particularly if their size and mass are similar. On the other hand, in activities demanding arm or trunk strength, males have a definite advantage, even if they are similar to females in height and mass. These considerations are important when pairing students for competition. Many problems occur when a student is paired with someone who is considerably taller and heavier and therefore stronger.

MUSCLE FIBER TYPE AND PERFORMANCE

The number of muscle fibers that an individual possesses is genetically determined. An increase in muscle size is accomplished by an increase in the size of each muscle fiber. The size of the muscles is determined first by the number of fibers and second by the size of the fibers. An individual is therefore somewhat muscularly limited by genetic restrictions.

Skeletal muscle tissue contains fibers that are fast contracting (fast twitch [FT]) and others that are slow contracting (slow twitch [ST]) (Saltin, 1973). The percentage of fast- versus slow-contracting fibers varies from muscle to muscle and among individuals. The percentage of each type of muscle fiber is determined during the first weeks of postnatal life (Dubowitz, 1970). Most individuals are believed to possess a 50:50 split; that is, half of the muscle fibers are FT and half are ST. A small percentage of people have a ratio of 60:40 (in either direction), and researchers have verified that some people possess an even more extreme ratio.

What is the significance of variation in the ratio of muscle fiber type? The ST fibers have a rich supply of blood and related energy mechanisms. This results in a slowly contracting, fatigue-resistant muscle fiber that is well suited to endurance-type (aerobic) activities. In contrast, the FT fibers are capable of bursts of intense activity, but are subject to rapid fatigue. These fibers are well suited to activities demanding short-term speed and power (e.g., pull-ups, standing long jump, and shuttle run). The ST fibers would facilitate performance in the mile run or other endurance-oriented activity. On the other hand, the same student may do poorly in a physical education program dominated by team sports that place a premium on quickness and strength. Designing a program that offers activities demanding a wide range of physical attributes (i.e., endurance, balance, flexibility) is thus essential.

STRENGTH AND MOTOR PERFORMANCE

Strength is an important factor in performing motor skills. A study by Rarick and Dobbins (1975) identified and ranked the factors that contribute to the motor performance of students. The factor identified as most important was strength or power (or both) in relation to body size. Youngsters who demonstrated high levels of strength in relation to their body size were more capable of performing motor skills than were those with lower strength levels.

Deadweight (fat) was the fourth-ranked factor in the motor performance study and was weighted in a negative direction. The more obese a student was, the less proficient he or she was in performing motor skills. Deadweight acts as a negative factor in motor development because it reduces the student's strength in relation to body size. Obese students may be stronger than normal-weight youngsters in absolute terms, but they are less strong when strength is adjusted for body weight. This lack of strength causes obese students to perceive a strength-related task (e.g., push-up or sit-up) as much more difficult than the same task might seem to normal-weight peers. The need for varied work loads accompanied by teacher understanding and empathy is important to assure all youngsters the opportunity for success in strength-related activities. Strength must be developed in all youngsters so that they have the tools to find success in motor development activities.

HYPOKINETIC DISEASES

An area of national concern is the lack of physical fitness among youngsters. The President's Council on Physical Fitness and Sports issued a report recently showing that American youngsters showed no improvement, and in some cases a decline, in physical fitness since 1976. The school environment is not providing enough time and organized activity to develop an adequate level of fitness among its youth. Schools may be shortchanging youth in the area of health and wellness by refusing to offer physical education programs that offer emphasis and organization for health-related fitness development.

During the past decade, the interest in physical fitness and increased awareness of the benefits derived from an active life-style have spawned a wide assortment of health clubs, a vast array of books and magazines concerning exercise and fitness, a weekly smorgasbord of distance runs and triathalons. Exercise equipment has been streamlined, and apparel is available for virtually any type of physical activity. Unfortunately, most of this interest and life-style change has occurred among middle- and upper-class Americans. The truth of the matter is that very little change in fitness activity has occurred in lower middle- and lower-class families.

Sadly, the nation's enthusiasm for fitness and physical activity has not trickled down to school-age students. A recent statement issued by the American Academy of Pediatrics reported that youngsters from the ages of 2 to 12 watch about 25 hours of television per week, more time than they spend in school (Hastad, 1986). Only about a third of our youngsters and youth participate daily (Ross et al., 1987) in school physical education programs nationwide, and that amount is both declining and insufficient. This compares unfavorably to the Surgeon General's 1990 goal of a 60% rate for physical education (U.S. Department of Health and Human Services, 1980).

The current status of youngsters' physical fitness levels offers reason for concern. A report from the U.S. Department of Health and Human Services concluded that about half of American youngsters were not developing the exercise and fitness skills to develop healthy hearts and lungs (Ross and Gilbert, 1985). In addition, concern was expressed that youngsters were not developing a sound fitness base that would serve them throughout adulthood.

Heart Disease

Coronary heart disease affects over 5 million people and accounts for 1.5 million heart attacks each year (McGlynn, 1990). The yearly medical costs associated with heart disease in America amounts to over $26 billion (Freedson, 1986). Surely, there can be no greater rationale for increasing the amount of exercise for junior and senior high school students. It has long been thought that heart disease is of geriatric origin and manifests itself only in older adults. In a study by Glass (1973), 5,000 youngsters in the Iowa public schools were examined over a 2-year period. Of these students, 70% had symptoms of coronary heart disease, including 7% who had extremely high cholesterol levels, a large percentage with high blood pressure, and at least 12% who were obese.

In examining the developmental history of heart disease in humans, Dr. Kenneth Rose (1968) identified the first signs as appearing around the age of 2. The good news is that he also determined that the disease process is reversible until the age of 19. Unfortunately, if youngsters' exercise habits are not altered, they may be burdened with high blood pressure and/or obesity as they mature into adults.

There are no longitudinal studies to document that early control of coronary heart disease risk will reduce the onset of premature death in adult life (Gilliam et al., 1982). However, it appears that youngsters with high blood pressure, lipids, and obesity tend to retain those high levels into adulthood.

Students are not naturally active during a typical school day. A study by Gilliam et al. (1977) documented the fact that youngsters do not voluntarily engage in high-intensity activity. By the authors' definition, high-intensity activity occurred when the heart rate was elevated to at least 60% of its maximum. The heart rate of youngsters was monitored to see how much time during a 12-hour period was spent in high-intensity activity. Less than 2% of the time was spent by youngsters in high-intensity activity, and 80% of the time was spent in low-intensity activity. Researchers also found that females were even less active than males.

In addition, the study revealed that the school environment decreased the physical activity of youngsters. Compared to summer activity, youngsters' activity patterns decreased during the school year. Another interesting finding showed that if females were given the opportunity, they would increase their activity to those levels comparable to or above those of most moderately active males. The authors concluded that daily activity patterns can be changed and coronary heart disease decreased through increased cardiovascular activity.

Obesity and Diabetes Mellitus

There are other diseases associated with a lack of physical activity. One of the areas of grave concern is the high incidence of obesity among youngsters. Depending on the source of statistics and the criterion used to define obesity, anywhere from 30 to 60% of American youngsters have been identified as obese. Closely related to the obesity problem is that of diabetes mellitus. About 1.5 per 1,000 young-

sters (ages 0 to 15 years) are afflicted with this serious ailment. Properly administered exercise programs can be an effective approach for positively influencing this chronic disorder among children. Diabetic children who are physically active show lower levels of blood glucose and a more stable metabolism than sedentary youngsters (Larrson, 1984). The fitness of diabetic teenagers, caused by lack of exercise, is lower than that of nondiabetic students. This probably occurs because nurses and teachers fear exercise-induced hypoglycemia (Larrson, 1984). Proper management of diet and insulin is the key factor, which usually means assuring that the energy intake is increased while the insulin dose is maintained. Unfortunately, teenagers usually decrease the amount of their voluntary activity on entering junior and senior high school.

Lack of Flexibility and Upper Body Strength

A lack of flexibility and upper body strength has been a recurring problem regardless of the source of testing and research. This lack often leads to poor posture and lower back pain in adulthood. The need is clear: develop healthy youngsters today who are capable of maintaining a healthy life-style during adulthood.

The evidence shows that many youngsters are not healthy. Even though few youngsters die of heart disease and related health problems such as obesity and diabetes mellitus, there is a need for concern. For too long, parents and teachers have assumed that because teenagers seldom complain about their health status, they are healthy. Physical educators owe youngsters a legacy of personal fitness. A physical education program without a strong fitness component is taking away the only opportunity that youngsters will have to learn to maintain their health.

EFFECTS OF PHYSICAL EDUCATION ON STUDENTS

One of the more difficult questions to answer about physical education programming is the long-term effects such a program has on participants. Many physical educators speak loudly about the many benefits of their program with little evidence in hand. This has led many administrators and parents to doubt some of the wilder claims. An excellent chapter on different studies dealing with a number of benefits can be found in the text *Physical Activity and Well-Being* (Vogel, 1986). The unfortunate fact revealed by this study is that most studies conducted have not provided for maturity of students and thus provide little or no evidence. The need for longitudinal studies of youngsters in physical education programs is obvious. Related to this problem is the dearth of studies related to junior and senior high school programs. The majority of the research deals with elementary school students.

Within the limitations of the studies reviewed by Vogel (1986), the following lists the impact of physical education on the development of various parameters. It must be understood that many of the studies had a number of weaknesses and would have to be replicated in a similar manner in order to assure similar effects. Also, due to the limitations of the studies, it is quite possible that the effects could not be generalized to other populations. If the reader is interested in finding supporting data for a physical education program, it is recommended that they review the chapter mentioned previously before making sweeping statements that are unsupported.

Convincing Evidence to Support Improvement in the Following Areas

1. Student physical activity levels
2. Aerobic fitness
3. Knowledge related to healthy life-styles
4. Motor performance
5. Muscular endurance
6. Muscular power
7. Muscular strength
8. Physical fitness

Some Evidence to Support Improvement in the Following Areas

1. Flexibility of the hip and spine
2. Selected measures of perceptual motor performance (however there is no evidence to support the effect of perceptual-motor performance on academic achievement)
3. Movement speed
4. Cardiovascular health factors including cholesterol, risk factor reduction, and diastolic blood pressure

No Evidence to Support Improvement in the Following Areas

1. Agility-coordination
2. Alterations in height, weight, or girth
3. Alteration of nutritional practices
4. Acceleration or retardation of the maturation process
5. Self-concept or personality
6. Anaerobic fitness

SKILL LEVEL AND PHYSICAL EDUCATION

Students who feel incompetent in the physical skill area eventually drop out of physical education, and when they leave school, have a negative opinion of an active life-style. Dropping out of physical education commonly occurs at the junior high school level, although the process often begins in the elementary school years.

Dropping out of activity due to lack of skill competency during elementary school is most unfortunate. Predicting who will be an outstanding athlete in junior or senior high school by observing elementary school performance is, in fact, quite difficult. In a study by Clarke (1968), coaches rated males who were outstanding athletes. Of the males who were rated as outstanding between the ages of 9 and 15 years, only 25% received this rating at the elementary and junior high school age. Of the males, 45% were rated as outstanding at the elementary school level, but not at the junior high school level; and 35% of the group were rated as outstanding in junior high school, but not in elementary school. Thus, only 25% of the predictions were correct. Most people would not take a risk if the odds were against them 75% of the time. Teachers, however, often label youngsters at an early age, even though their predictions may be incorrect three out of four times.

This lack of predictive ability among teachers emphasizes the need for the physical education program to keep youngsters enthusiastic until they are capable of performing successfully. The purpose of a physical education program is not to develop athletes, and the program should not be presented so that it allows the athletically gifted to excel and prosper at the expense of less-talented youngsters. Physical education is for **all** youngsters. Gifted youngsters have a myriad of opportunities to enhance their skills. However, students who are less-skilled have only the physical education program to help them develop and improve. To reiterate, trying to identify youngsters as athletes in a physical education setting is not only inaccurate, but may be detrimental to their future development.

INTELLECTUAL DEVELOPMENT AND PHYSICAL EDUCATION

For years, physical educators have attempted to demonstrate a relationship between physical education and improvement in a student's intellectual development. Indeed, if intellectual development or academic achievement could be linked to physical education, it would rank higher as an educational priority. However, according to Shephard (1984a), "Strong proof is lacking." Shephard identifies the many limitations of such investigations, which include

1. Studies of special populations such as the mentally handicapped or athletes;
2. "Halo" effects, because teachers reward star performers with higher marks;
3. Self-image gains by athletes due to teacher and peer praise;
4. Short duration of training programs;
5. Possible side effects from curtailment of academic instruction;
6. Use of retrospective data relating observed academic performance to measures of activity or physical ability.

Thomas and Thomas (1986) offer a clear and concise summary statement: "However, attempts to improve or remediate cognitive function through the use of movement are not theoretically sound, nor does this approach have any empirical support in the research literature." In any case, physical educators must justify inclusion of physical education in the total school curriculum on the basis of its unique contributions: motor skill development and the understanding and maintenance of physical fitness. Since these contributions are unique to physical education and contribute to the physical well-being of youngsters, convincing administrators and parents further that intellectual development is enhanced by physical education should not be necessary. The public will support a physical education program if it aids, nurtures, and shows concern for the physical development of all students.

A study that has created much interest is the Trois Rivieres regional experiment (Shephard, 1984b). The study provides a well-conceived design for increased physical education programming. Even though students received more time for physical education (and less for academics), their academic performance was not decreased. These results appear to counter the objection that more physical education will result in poorer academic performance due to less time spent in the classroom. Administrators need to consider this study, particularly today, when many schools have a back-to-basics emphasis. This emphasis usually means "back to the classroom," without physical activity or the arts. One wonders if this lack of concern for the body, our "home of the brain," is not detrimental to the children's total development. The ability to read becomes unimportant if one's health has degenerated. No priority in life is higher than physical well-being.

LONG-TERM EFFECT OF EXERCISE

Many experts believe that the physical activity undertaken during the school years has a lifetime impact. Saltin and Grimby (1968) conducted a research project to learn whether the benefits of childhood activity carried over to adult life. They compared the ability to adjust to effort of three groups of subjects aged 50 to 59. One group comprised former athletes who had not participated in activity for over 20 years and who worked in sedentary jobs. A second group consisted of former athletes who kept up a regular training and exercise program during their adult years. The third group consisted of individuals who were not athletes in youth and who were inactive as adults. Results showed that the nonathlete group was capable of the least effort (measured by maximal oxygen uptake). The group that was active during youth but took part in little activity during adulthood scored significantly higher than did the nonathlete group. The athlete group that had maintained training scored a great deal higher than the other two groups. The essence of the study is that functional capacity as an adult appears to be partly a result of activity during the growing years.

GUIDELINES FOR EXERCISING YOUNGSTERS SAFELY

Few, if any, healthy students are permanently injured by exercise. However, when exercise is not conducted properly or is pushed to excess, serious problems can occur. The following sections offer guidelines for exercise related to areas teachers most often question.

Moderation in Exercise

As is usually the case, moderation is the best way to ensure that youngsters grow up enjoying different types of physical activity. Moderate exercise, coupled with opportunities to participate in recreational activity, help to develop a lasting desire to move.

Educators are sometimes concerned that a student may be harmed physiologically by too much or too vigorous activity. To date, there is no evidence that a healthy student can be harmed through vigorous exercise. This does not mean that a student is capable of the same unadjusted physical work load as an adult. Evidence does indicate, however, that youngsters can withstand a gradual increase in work load and are capable of work loads comparable to those of adults when the load is adjusted for height and size.

There was concern at one time that the large blood vessels do not grow in proportion to other body parts. This, it was theorized, placed the heart and the circulatory system under stress during strenuous exercise. Research has now established that fatigue causes healthy youngsters to stop exercising long before any danger to health occurs (Shephard, 1984a). In addition, the student's circulatory system is similar in proportion to that of an adult and is not at a disadvantage during exercise.

Exercising in Warm Climates

Teachers must be cautious when exercising youngsters in hot climates. The arrival of warm weather does not mean that exercise must stop, but certain measures should be used to avoid heat-related illness. Youngsters are not just little adults, and they do not adapt to extremes of temperature as effectively as adults do for the following physiological reasons (Bar-Or, 1983):

1. Youngsters have a higher surface area/mass ratio than those of adults. This allows a greater amount of heat to transfer between the environment and the body.
2. When walking or running, youngsters produce more metabolic heat per unit mass than adults produce. Youngsters are not as efficient in executing movement patterns, so they generate more metabolic heat than do adults performing a similar task.
3. Sweating capacity is not as great in some teenagers as in adults, resulting in a lowered ability to cool the body.
4. Ability to convey heat by blood from the body core to the skin is reduced in youngsters because of a lower cardiac output at a given oxygen uptake.

These physiological differences show clearly that youngsters are at a distinct disadvantage compared to adults when exercising in an environment where the ambient air temperature is higher than the skin temperature. In addition, the physical maturity of teenagers varies a great deal, so it is quite possible that some youngsters are similar to adults whereas others are still childlike in terms of their maturation level.

Individuals do acclimatize to warmer temperatures. However, youngsters appear to adjust to heat more slowly than adults (Bar-Or, 1983). Often, teenagers do not instinctively drink enough liquids to replenish fluids lost during exercise. The American Academy of Pediatrics Committee on Sports Medicine (1982b) offers the following guidelines for exercising youngsters in hot climates.

1. The intensity of activities that last 30 minutes or more should be reduced whenever relative humidity and air temperature are above critical levels (zone 3 in Figure 2.5). Information concerning relative humidity can be obtained from a nearby U.S. National Weather Service office or by use of a sling psychrometer (School Health Supplies, Box 409, 300 Lombard Road., Addison, IL 60101; approximate cost, $30.00) to compare dry-bulb and wet-bulb temperature levels.
2. At the beginning of a strenuous exercise program or after traveling to a warmer climate, the intensity and duration of exercise should be restrained initially and then increased gradually over a period of 10 to 14 days to accomplish acclimatization to the effects of heat.
3. Before prolonged physical activity, youngsters should be fully hydrated. During the activity, periodic drinking (e.g., 5 oz of cold tap water every 30 minutes for a student weighing 88 lb) should be enforced.
4. Clothing should be lightweight and limited to one layer of absorbent material to facilitate evaporation of sweat and to expose as much skin as possible. Sweat-saturated garments should be replaced by dry ones. Rubberized sweat suits should never be used to produce weight loss.

The committee identifies youngsters with the following conditions as being at a potentially high risk for heat stress: obesity, febrile (feverish) state, cystic fibrosis, gastrointestinal infection, diabetes insipidus, diabetes mellitus, chronic heart failure, caloric malnutrition, anorexia nervosa, sweating insufficiency syndrome, and mental deficiency.

Distance Running and Youngsters

The question often arises as to how much and how far youngsters should be allowed to run, particularly in a competitive or training-for-competition setting. The answer is complex, since parents, teachers, and coaches seldom see the long-term effects. The American Academy of Pediatrics Executive Committee (1982a) identifies some of the concerns: Lifetime involvement in a sport often depends on the type of early participation and gratification gained. Psychological problems can result from unrealistic goals for distance running by youngsters. A student who participates in distance running primarily for parental gratification may tire of this after a time and quit, or the student may continue, chafing under the parental pressure. In either case, psychological damage

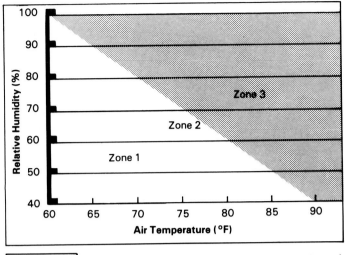

Safe

Caution

Danger

FIGURE 2.5 Weather guide for prevention of heat illness during prolonged strenuous exercise   (adapted from E. L. Fox, R. W. Bowers, and M. L. Foss, *The Physiological Basis of Physical Education and Athletics*, 4th ed. Copyright © 1988 W. B. Saunders Company. Reprinted by permission of Wm. C. Brown Publishers, Dubuque, IA. All rights reserved.)

may be done, and the student may be discouraged, either immediately or in the long run, from participating in sports. A student should be allowed to participate for the enjoyment of running without fear of parental or peer rejection or pressure. A student's sense of accomplishment, satisfaction, and appreciation by peers, parents, and coaches will foster involvement in running and other sports during school years and in later life.

A strong position taken by the International Athletics Association Federation (IAAF) Medical Committee (1983) in part states: "The danger certainly exists that with over-intensive training, separation of the growth plates may occur in the pelvic region, the knee, or the ankle. While this could heal with rest, nevertheless definitive information is lacking whether in years to come harmful effects may result."

In view of the preceeding, it is the opinion of the IAAF Medical Committee that training and competition for long-distance track and road-running events should not be encouraged. Up to the age of 12, it is suggested that not more than 800 meters (½ mile) should be run in competition. An increase in this distance should be introduced gradually, with, for example, a maximum of 3,000 meters (nearly 2 miles) in competition for 14 year olds.

Weight Training

Weight training for preadolescent youngsters has generated a great deal of concern among educators.

Many worry about safety and stress-related injuries, and others question whether such training can produce significant strength gains. Accepted thinking for some time has been that prepubescents are incapable of making significant strength gains because they lack adequate levels of circulating androgens. Research evidence is continuing to build that contradicts this point of view. A study by Cahill (1986) demonstrated significant increases in strength among 18 prepubescent males. A study by Servedio et al. (1985) showed significant strength gains in shoulder flexion. It appears that strength can be increased through weight training in prepubescent youngsters.

Note that the term *weight training* is used here to denote the use of barbells, dumbbells, or machines as resistance. It is in sharp contrast to *weight lifting* and/or *power lifting*, which is a competitive sport for the purpose of determining maximum lifting ability. There is strong agreement among experts that weight training is acceptable for youngsters, but weight lifting is highly undesirable and may be harmful. In a statement of strength training recommendations, the American Orthopaedic Society for Sports Medicine (AOSSM) (Duda, 1986) states: "(1) competition is prohibited, and (2) no maximum lift should ever be attempted." In addition, AOSSM recommends a physical exam, proper supervision by knowledgeable coaches, and emotional maturity on the part of the participating youngster. Obviously, safety and prevention of injury is a serious consideration for those interested in weight training for youngsters. Educators must consider seriously whether weight training is an appropriate activity for a typical class of youngsters in a physical education class. When injuries were reported, most occurred because of inadequate supervision, lack of proper technique, or competitive lifting. If knowledge and expertise in weight training is limited, these programs for youngsters should be avoided. It takes a knowledgeable instructor to provide an effective and safe program.

There are no studies that examine the long-term effects of strength training in youngsters. In addition, many experts worry about highly organized training programs that place great emphasis on relative gains in strength. A weight training program should be only one component of a comprehensive fitness program for youngsters. The National Strength and Conditioning Association (1985) recommends that 50–80% of the prepubescent athlete's training must include a variety of different exercises such as agility exercises (e.g., basketball, volleyball, tennis, tumbling) and endurance training (e.g., distance running, bicycling, swimming).

If a decision is made to develop a weight training program for youngsters, it should be done in a thoughtful and studied manner. Proper supervision and technique are key ingredients in a successful program. Program prescription recommended by AOSSM and NSCS are

1. Training is recommended two or three times a week for 20- to 30-minute periods.
2. No resistance should be applied until proper form is demonstrated. Six to fifteen repetitions equal one set; one to three sets per exercise should be done.
3. Weight or resistance is increased in 1- to 3-lb increments after the prepubescent does 15 repetitions in good form.

REFERENCES AND SUGGESTED READINGS

American Academy of Pediatrics. 1982a. Risks in long-distance running for children. *The Physician and Sportsmedicine* 10(8): 82–86.

American Academy of Pediatrics. 1982b. Climatic heat stress and the exercising child. *The Physician and Sportsmedicine* 11(8): 155–159.

Bar-Or, O. 1983. *Pediatric Sports Medicine for the Practitioner.* New York: Springer-Verlag.

Cahill, R. R. 1986. Prepubescent strength training gains support. *The Physician and Sportsmedicine* 14(2): 157–161.

Clarke, H. H. 1968. Characteristics of the young athlete: A longitudinal look. *Kinesiology Review* 3: 33–42.

Clarke, H. H. 1971. *Physical Motor Tests in the Medford Boy's Growth Study.* Englewood Cliffs, N.J.: Prentice-Hall.

Corbin, C. B., and Fletcher, P. 1968. Diet and activity patterns of obese and non-obese elementary school children. *Research Quarterly* 39(4): 922.

Dubowitz, V. 1970. Differentiation of fiber types in skeletal muscle. In E. J. Briskey, R. G. Cassens, and B. B. Marsh (eds.) *Physiology and Biochemistry of Muscle as a Food*, Vol 2. Madison, WI.: University of Wisconsin Press.

Duda, M. 1986. Prepubescent strength training gains support. *The Physician and Sportsmedicine* 14(2): 157–161.

Eisenman, P. 1986. Physical activity and body composition. In V. Seefeldt (ed.) *Physical Activity and Well Being.* Reston, VA: AAHPERD.

Freedson, P. S. 1986. *Cardiorespiratory Diseases.* In V. Seefeldt (ed.) *Physical Activity and Well Being.* Reston, VA: AAHPERD.

Gilliam, T. B., Katch, V. L., Thorland, W. G., and Weltman, A. W. 1977. Prevalence of coronary heart disease risk factors in active children, 7 to 12 years of age. *Medicine and Science in Sports and Exercise* 9(1): 21–25.

Gilliam, T. B., MacConnie, S. E., Greenen, D. L., Pels, A. E., and Freedson, P. S. 1982. Exercise program for children: A way to prevent heart disease? *The Physician and Sportsmedicine*, 10(9): 96–101, 105–106, 108.

Glass, W. 1973. Coronary heart disease sessions prove vitally interesting. *California AHPER Journal* (May/June): 7.

Griffiths, M., and Payne, P. R. 1976. Energy expenditure in small children of obese and non-obese parents. *Nature* 260: 698–700.

Gruelich, W., and Pyle, S. 1959. *Radiographic Atlas of Skeletal Development of the Hand and Wrist*, 2nd ed. Stanford, CA.: Stanford University Press.

Hastad, D. N. 1986. Physical fitness for elementary school children. *Educational Theory* 1: 12–14.

Haymes, E. M. 1986. Nutrition and ergogenic aids. In V. Seefeldt (ed.) *Physical Activity and Well Being.* Reston, VA: AAHPERD.

International Athletics Association Federation (IAAF). 1983. Not kid's stuff. *Sportsmedicine Bulletin* 18(1): 11.

Johnson, M. L., Burke, B. S., and Mayer, J. 1956. The prevalence and incidence of obesity in a cross section of elementary and secondary school children. *American Journal of Clinical Nutrition* 4(3): 231.

Larrson, Y. 1984. Physical performance and the young diabetic. In R. A. Boileau (ed.) *Advances in Pediatric Sport Sciences.* Champaign, IL: Human Kinetics Publishers.

Malina, R. M. 1978. Physical growth and maturity characteristics of young athletes. In R. A. Magill, M. H. Ash, and F. L. Smoll (eds.) *Children and Youth in Sport; A Contemporary Anthology.* Champaign, IL.: Human Kinetics Publishers.

Malina, R. M. 1980. Growth, strength, and physical performance. In G. A. Stull and T. K. Cureton (eds.) *Encyclopedia of Physical Education, Fitness, and Sports.* Salt Lake City, UT: Brighton Publishing.

Malina, R. M. 1986. Physical growth and development. In V. Seefeldt (ed.) *Physical Activity and Well-Being.* Reston, VA: AAHPERD.

McGlynn, G. 1990. *Dynamics of Fitness*. Dubuque: Wm. C. Brown Publishers.

National Strength and Conditioning Association. 1985. Position paper on prepubescent strength training. *National Strength and Conditioning Association Journal* 74: 27–31.

Rarick, L. G. (ed.) 1973. *Physical Activity, Human Growth and Activity*. New York: Academic Press.

Rarick, L. G., and Dobbins, D. A. 1975. Basic components in the motor performances of children six to nine years of age. *Medicine and Science in Sports* 72: 2.

Rose, K. 1968. To keep people in health. *Journal of the American College Health Association* 22: 80.

Ross, J. G., and Gilbert, G. G. 1985. The national children and youth fitness study: A summary of findings. *Journal of Physical Education, Recreation, and Dance* 56(*1*): 45–50.

Ross, J. G., Pate, R. R., Corbin, C. C., Delpy, L. A., and Gold, R. S. 1987. What is going on in the elementary physical education program? *Journal of Physical Education, Recreation, and Dance* 58(9): 78–84.

Saltin, B. 1973. Metabolic fundamentals of exercise. *Medicine and Science of Sports* 5: 137–146.

Saltin, B., and Grimby, G. 1968. Physiological analysis of middle-aged and old former athletes, comparison with still active athletes of the same ages. *Circulation* 38(6): 1104.

Servedio, F. J., Bartels, R. L., Hamlin, R. L., et al. 1985. The effects of weight training, using Olympic style lifts, on various physiological variables in prepubescent boys. Abstracted. *Medicine and Science in Sports and Exercise* 17: 288.

Sheldon, W. H., Dupertuis, C. W., and McDermott, E. 1954. *Atlas of Men: A Guide for Somatotyping the Adult Male at All Ages*. New York: Harper & Row.

Shephard, R. J. 1984a. Physical activity and child health. *Sports Medicine* 1: 205–233.

Shephard, R. J. 1984b. Physical activity and "wellness" of the child. In R. A. Boileau (ed.) *Advances in Pediatric Sport Sciences*. Champaign, IL.: Human Kinetics Publishers.

Thomas, J. R., and Tennant, L. K. 1978. Effects of rewards on changes in children's motivation for an athletic task. In F. L. Smoll and R. E. Smith (eds). *Psychological Perspectives in Youth Sports*. New York: Hemisphere Publishing.

Thomas, J. R., and Thomas, K. T. 1986. The relation of movement and cognitive function. In V. Seefeldt (ed.) *Physical Activity and Well-Being*. Reston, VA: AAHPERD

U.S. Department of Health and Human Services. 1980. *Promoting Health/Preventing Disease: Objectives for the Nation*. Washington, D.C.: U.S. Government Printing Office.

Vogel, P. 1986. Effects of physical education programs on children. In V. Seefeldt (ed.), *Physical Activity and Well-Being*. Reston, VA: AAHPERD.

Wilmore, J. H., and McNamara, J. J. 1974. Prevalence of coronary disease risk factors in boys, 8 to 12 years of age. *Journal of Pediatrics* 84: 527–533.

3

DEVELOPING A SECONDARY SCHOOL PHYSICAL EDUCATION CURRICULUM

Physical education teachers are usually involved in curriculum design and modification. This process for a secondary school can be quite complex and involves many factors and people. One of the first steps is to understand the confusing vocabulary of educators. Part of the confusion over curriculum vocabulary arises from the various meanings attributed to the same term. Because the cooperation of many people is necessary to develop a quality curriculum in a secondary school, it is especially important to speak the same language as your colleagues. The first section of this chapter focuses on curriculum definitions, concepts, and perspectives. This section is followed by a discussion of the most popular curriculum models currently used in secondary schools. Finally, a presentation and analysis of the steps necessary for developing a new curriculum plan are offered. Future curriculum planners in physical education should carefully consider all areas as they begin to prepare a specific curriculum for a specific situation.

CURRICULUM DEFINITIONS, CONCEPTS, AND PERSPECTIVES

The traditional manner for discussing or viewing curriculum is that of a separate, formal course of study. The focus of this perspective is on the planned in-class program. Examples of this include the history, mathematics, music, or physical education curriculum. Each academic area has a sequence of courses and specific topics or activities within each course. These courses of study are carefully planned and arranged so the stated objectives are accomplished. Curriculum emphasis, study, and research have focused primarily on this perspective. Teachers in physical education and in other subject areas channel the majority of their professional efforts into this curriculum aspect.

A newer view of the curriculum that focuses on a more broad, comprehensive approach is sometimes referred to as the physical education program (Siedentop et al., 1986). This approach includes all experiences and activities where students engage and learn about physical activity and sports. In addition to the in-class instruction program, this approach includes athletics, intramurals, sport clubs, noon-hour aerobics, and any other after-school activity that could impact students. For many years, activities outside the formal program were called extracurricular because they were viewed to be "extra" to the main, formal curriculum. In recent years, these extracurricular activities have been referred to as cocurricular in order to give them a more equal and important status. It is important to understand that students and parents certainly do not view these activities as "extra" to the main function of the school. In fact, many would argue that these activities are the most important. We think that the term cocurricular gives more status to these activities and helps people understand that these activities are important contributors to a school's overall goals.

The third perspective for viewing curriculum is called the "functional" curriculum (Berliner, 1979). The term refers to the actual amount of instructional lesson time a student spends on the specific subject matter. This time is called academic learning time (ALT) and is being studied extensively in physical education environments (Darst, Beauchamp, and Thompson, 1989). Time spent dribbling, passing, or shooting a basketball with a low error rate is high ALT, while time spent waiting in line, changing clothes, or rotating stations is not included in ALT. Studies show that many physical education environments are characterized by low rates of ALT. In some classes, no more than 15% of class time was spent engaged in ALT (Metzler, 1979).

The functional curriculum and the concept of ALT are representative of a scientific approach, which uses empirically derived data to make decisions about curriculum and instruction. This approach is a sound strategy for improving the quality of physical education programs for students at all levels. It provides hope for improvement in areas that have historically been tied to untested assumptions and hypotheses.

A fourth curriculum perspective that focuses on unplanned learning that occurs in all areas of the school and cuts across all of the above curriculum perspectives is called the "hidden" curriculum (Bain, 1975). The hidden curriculum is all of the unplanned and unrecognized values that are imparted through the educational process. Often, teachers and administrators have not looked carefully at their behavior toward students, the policies and procedures used, and the decisions that were made on funds, activities, schedules, or personnel. Because they do not personally review these areas, discrepancies or inconsistencies exist between what teachers say and what they actually do. Their implicit values are not consistent with their explicit philosophy. Areas of hidden values include: the development of student approach tendencies; the roles of females in sport and exercise activities; teachers' attitudes toward winning and losing; teachers' treatment of various social groups, races, and genders; and administrators' allocation of funds within the physical education program.

A good example of this situation is a teacher purporting to develop positive attitudes in students toward physical activity but then forcing students to run laps or do push-ups for lack of effort or for failure to "dress out" properly. Other teachers develop a negative atmosphere with grading or overly critical instructional procedures that cause students to do everything possible to escape or avoid the environment. The hidden curriculum of the school can contribute to the development of approach or avoidance tendencies (Mager, 1968). Students are learning continually to like or dislike school and the process of learning. Efforts must be made to study and develop the hidden curriculum so that it can have a positive effect on what students learn.

Physical educators usually evaluate the contributions of the specific activities in the formal course of study. However, they may neglect to consider carefully such aspects of the hidden curriculum as dress codes, showering policies, grading techniques, discipline procedures, instructional strategies, or teaching behaviors. Clearly, curriculum planners need to have information about and skills in all four of the curriculum perspectives. Ignoring any of these areas will have a significant negative impact on students.

For example, a teacher who does not look carefully at the effect of an imposed dress code may have some major problems with student participation. Grading procedures will have a powerful impact on students' attitudes toward physical educa-

tion. A well-developed formal curriculum plan will be ineffective if low rates of academic learning time (ALT) are prevalent in classes. The absence of coeducational activities, lifetime sports, or dance activities deprives students of a well-balanced curriculum. A teacher's emphasis on winning certainly affects students when the losing team always runs an extra lap or performs some extra duty. Physical educators must consider carefully the four perspectives when policies, procedures, yearly plans, daily plans, and other aspects of dealing with students are formulated. Specific suggestions will be made throughout this text with respect to each of these four areas.

FORMAL COURSE OF STUDY

The formal curriculum is an overall plan for all in-class instructional activities. It contains the scope, sequence, and arrangement of learning activities for each school year. The scope of the curriculum delineates the content for each year, and assures that the content of the program will be covered in a systematic and accountable fashion. The scope should offer as many activities as possible that will help accomplish the established objectives of the curriculum. The sequence of activities is arranged progressively throughout the year and from year to year. Each succeeding year in the curriculum should build on the program activities offered in previous years. Figure 3.1 is an example of a page from a scope and sequence chart. The formal curriculum is intended to guide teachers in developing and conducting learning experiences that give an opportunity to acquire knowledge, attitudes, and behaviors identified as goals or objectives. It is the "what" and "why" of education as opposed to the "how." The "how" is referred to as instruction.

Planning for curriculum and instruction should not be separated because they are interdependent. For example, the accomplishment of curriculum objectives are significantly affected by the instructional emphasis. A direct or task style of instruction has a different impact on students than a problem-solving or process-oriented approach. The length, content, and organizing arrangement of a unit also influences the type of instruction that will be most effective. Teachers need to be aware of how curriculum and instruction affect each other, and consequently, the two areas should be studied together.

The formal curriculum can be arranged around several major themes, called organizing centers. Learning experiences or activities are arranged around the organizing centers to accomplish the goals of the program. The most common organizing centers for physical education curricula have been

	PRESCHOOL	ELEM.	MIDDLE	SENIOR	K	1	2	3	4	5	6	7	8	9	10	11	12
C. Archery																	
1. History															I	I	R
2. Safety — Rules — Strategy															I	I	R
3. Equipment															I	I	R
4. Shooting															I	I	R
D. Badminton																	
1. History															I	I	R
2. Safety — Rules — Strategy	I	P							I	R					I	I	R
3. Equipment	I	P							I	R					R	R	R
4. Skills	I	P							I	R					R	R	R
a. Grip	I	P							I	R					R	R	R
b. Serve	I	P							I	R					R	R	R
c. Strokes	I	P							I	R					R	R	R
E. Bowling																	
1. History												I	R		I	I	R
2. Safety — Rules — Strategy	I	R										I	R		I	I	R
3. Equipment	I	R										I	R		I	I	R
4. Skills	I	R										I	R		I	I	R
a. Grip	I	R										I	R		I	I	R
b. Approach	I	R										I	R		I	I	R
c. Delivery	I	R										I	R		I	I	R
F. Cross-Country Skiing																	
1. History															I	I	R
2. Safety — Rules — Strategy	I	R													I	I	R
3. Equipment	I	R													I	I	R
4. Skills	I	R													I	I	R
a. Kick glide	I	R													I	I	R
b. Stop	I	R													I	I	R
c. Turns	I	R													I	I	R
d. Poling	I	R													I	I	R
e. Climb	I	R													I	I	R
G. Curling																	
1. History															I	I	R
2. Safety — Rules — Strategy															I	I	R
3. Equipment															I	I	R
4. Skills															I	I	R
a. Delivery															I	I	R
b. Sweeping															I	I	R
H. Golf																	
1. History															I	I	R
2. Safety — Rules — Strategy															I	I	R
3. Equipment															I	I	R
4. Skills															I	I	R
a. Grip															I	I	R
b. Full swings															I	I	R
c. Approach shots															I	I	R
d. Putting															I	I	R

FIGURE 3.1   An example of a page from a scope and sequence chart   (courtesy of LaCrosse, WI, Public Schools).
I—Introduce: initial instruction of psychomotor, cognitive, and affective skills that are explained, demonstrated and practiced.
R—Review and reinforce continued instruction of skill level improvement and increased knowledge of techniques.
P—Proficiency: the attainment of an individual's maximum skills level through instruction and practice.

movement forms, sport, and physical activity. Commonly included are units on basketball, softball, square dancing, and jogging. Additional organizing centers used in physical education include

1. Physical fitness components such as cardiovascular efficiency, strength, and control of body fat;
2. Wellness knowledge and activities involving stress management, nutrition, weight control, substance abuse, personal safety, physical fitness, environmental awareness, and behavioral self-control;
3. Movement themes such as propelling, catching, striking, and balancing;
4. Analysis of movement elements such as force, time, space, and flow;
5. Student motives such as appearance, health, and achievement;
6. Disciplinary knowledge from such areas as biomechanics, motor learning, exercise physiology, and sport philosophy;
7. Social themes such as competition, cooperation, and sportsmanship.

Most programs follow an eclectic philosophy that focuses on several themes from several of these areas.

The yearly and year-to-year curriculum plans should serve as tools for teachers. Curricula are organized in two planes, horizontal and vertical. The horizontal organization is the yearly plan and is concerned with arranging activities for the school year. The vertical curriculum is concerned with scope and sequence for all of the school years, from kindergarten through grade 12. Both should reflect the overall philosophy of the program and be organized to accomplish desired outcomes. The curricula offer direction to both teachers and students, and should be posted in the teaching area. Several specific horizontal (yearly) curriculum plans will be presented in Chapters 4 and 5.

A yearly plan avoids the pitfall of running out of time or activities. It gives departments of physical education a singular purpose and eases the burden when equipment and facilities are shared. Instructors can agree on the units that should be taught and on the amount of time that should be consigned to each unit. Each instructor then has a curriculum with similar content, differing only in the order of presentation of units. This allows effective use of equipment and facilities that have to be shared in most secondary school settings.

Another important reason for yearly planning concerns curriculum evaluation. If department members desire to evaluate their program of study, evaluation would be difficult if each teacher taught a unique curriculum. Similarly, if there is no yearly plan, determining the strengths and weaknesses of the curriculum becomes impossible. Why were physical fitness scores low? Why do students choose not to participate in the program? What activities should be added or deleted? Which activities are of high interest or low interest? These and other questions can be answered when the curriculum framework is known. In turn, parts of the curriculum can be modified and evaluated later. There is no substitute for a stable and well-planned curriculum.

CURRICULUM MODELS

Curriculum models provide an overall philosophy that underlies the physical education curriculum or program. The curriculum model includes a set of beliefs and goals that evolve from a value base. These models also provide a physical education curriculum planner with a basis for the selection and organization of objectives and content, the structure and sequence of activities, and the evaluation of the yearly curriculum plan. The scope and sequence of activities for the formal, in-class instructional program evolves from the curriculum model. It may also predict interrelationships between content and the instructional process. The curriculum may be implemented in a variety of ways, making it important for curriculum planners to understand the popular physical education curriculum models that are currently used in secondary schools. In building a quality physical education curriculum, a school system can take one of the following approaches:

1. Adopt a model that is functioning in another school.
2. Adapt an existing model to meet the local interests, preferences, and school priorities.
3. Build or create a new model.

Multi-Activity Model

By far the most common curriculum model in use today at the secondary level is the multi-activity approach focused on various forms of human movement. This is a traditional approach using units of physical activity or movement forms as the basic organizing center. There is no specific theme or focus. These activities not only provide the content of the model; they also provide the structure or format. The units vary in length from one week to one year depending on the school. The specific activities are culturally important forms of physical activity. There is a constant adding and subtracting of activities. The forms are usually classified in the following categories:

1. Team sports: basketball, softball, or soccer;
2. Individual or lifetime sports: gymnastics, tennis, or Frisbee;
3. Dance: folk, square, modern, or country swing;
4. Physical conditioning activities: jogging, weight training, or aerobics;
5. Recreational games: horseshoes, shuffleboard, or table tennis;
6. Outdoor adventure activities: bicycling, skiing, or orienteering;
7. Aquatics: swimming, skin diving, or water sports.

The multi-activity curriculum is usually arranged with a balance of activities from these categories. Activities are included on the basis of a number of practical factors such as student interest, teacher interest and expertise, community interest, class size, facilities, equipment, and climate. New activities or modified forms of old activities are occasionally added to the curriculum by an enterprising teacher who has picked up ideas from a professional journal or convention. Activities in the curriculum generally follow the activity preferences of society, usually with a significant time lag. The arrival of the "new" activities in physical education curricula—such as activities reflecting the fitness renaissance, the wellness movement, the interest in outdoor adventure activities, and the Eastern influence in the martial arts and yoga—are thus indicative of the desires of the people whom the program serves.

Instruction in these activities proceeds from introductory lessons to advanced and specialized courses. Students are grouped by grade level rather than by ability or developmental level. In most situations, students proceed through a sequence of required physical activities in a year. An effective trend is the elective (or selective) format that allows students to choose activities in which they would like to participate. Sometimes, students have to make choices from the various categories of activities in the curriculum such as taking a certain number of team sports, lifetime sports, or physical conditioning units. This choice format enhances the interest, enthusiasm, and motivational level of both students and teachers.

The use of activities or movement forms in this model is based on the idea that they contribute to the goals of general education (i.e., developing the total person socially, emotionally, intellectually, and physically). The popular "education through the physical" philosophy emphasizes the use of physical activities for personal development in the areas of physical fitness, motor abilities, mental abilities, and social abilities. Another current philosophy places emphasis on the intrinsic value of physical activities as a form of play (Siedentop, 1980b). This theory advocates movement forms for the intrinsic meaning and satisfaction they provide people. Activities do not have to be justified on the basis of external values such as fitness or social development.

It is easy to understand the popularity of the multi-activity model because of its diversity and flexibility for meeting the changing interests and desires of today's students. This model can provide novelty and excitement as the students explore, experiment with, and experience a wide variety of physical activities. There are many curricular opportunities for students to compete with other students, with the environment, or with themselves in different units. Teachers need to continually expand their teaching competencies in order to accommodate student interests in new activities. Teaching is still important even if there are many units with short periods for instruction. Classes should not be organized recreation periods with little or no instruction.

Knowledge Concepts Model

A curriculum model that has gained popularity in many universities, colleges, high schools, and junior high schools that focuses on imparting physical fitness concepts to students is called *Fitness for Life* (Corbin and Lindsey, 1990). This approach to physical education and fitness development places an instructional emphasis on lecture, laboratory experiments, and developing exercise programs for a lifetime of activity. This particular program is organized around the following questions:

1. Why is physical activity important to every person?
2. How should physical activity take place?
3. What forms of physical activity are available?

Information and activities are provided on the following topics: cardiovascular fitness, strength, endurance, flexibility, fat control, skill-related fitness, correct ways to exercise, and how to plan an exercise program. Students learn to diagnose and solve various physical fitness problems. They also have opportunities to develop exercise programs to remediate the various problems.

Several options are available for incorporating fitness for life into a school curriculum. Students may take a 6-wk unit or an entire semester using the fitness for life model, depending on the priorities of the school district. A wide variety of curriculum and instructional materials is available to teachers, such as books for students, lesson plans for teachers, slides, dittos, overhead transparencies, review questions, laboratory experiments, and test materials.

Another similar knowledge concepts approach to secondary curriculum focuses on the components of human wellness (see Chapter 16). Wellness is viewed by many as an important state of health that is an ongoing process throughout life. It is a preventive approach to health and expands on the fitness concepts model. Students need information and skills that pertain to human wellness. Advocates of this theory point to the numerous health problems that abound in our society. A healthy life-style for all students is the major objective of this model.

The wellness model is more comprehensive than the fitness concepts theory. Units of instruction in the wellness theory include stress management, alcohol and drug abuse, nutrition, weight control, physical fitness, coping skills, personal safety, environmental awareness, behavioral self-control, and problem-solving skills related to these specific topics.

Both approaches focus primarily on knowledge and understanding of physical fitness and wellness. People who advocate these models find the emphasis on knowledge to be an advantage since it adds credibility to the program. It is important to understand that an increase in time spent on lecture and analysis means a reduction in time spent performing physical skills. Students need information, but they also need successful encounters with physical activity, and that means time allotted for practicing and performing physical skills. Determining exactly how much time should be spent on knowledge acquisition and how much on physical skill development is difficult. The bottom line is getting students to incorporate physical activity into their life-styles.

Most schools using a knowledge concepts approach offer a balance of physical activity and knowledge concepts. An effective approach is to offer several units on wellness activities (including fitness) to supplement or complement the secondary school physical education curriculum (see Chapters 4 and 5). The secondary school curriculum should not focus exclusively on fitness, wellness, or movement, but should have objectives in all three areas.

Movement Analysis Concept Model

Curriculum models using an application of movement analysis concepts have primarily affected elementary physical education, although some junior and senior high school programs have been influenced by Rudolf Laban's (1963) movement concepts of time, space, force, and flow. Curriculum content focuses on teaching movement elements which serve as the basic organizing center. The units focus on such elements as force, balance, striking, motion, stability, and leverage. These movement elements or concepts can be applied to many sport skills (Seidel et al., 1980).

This curriculum model also emphasizes terminology, knowledge, and analytical abilities. Instructional emphasis includes indirect methods called problem solving or guided discovery. For example, students spend time analyzing various levels of movement for dribbling a basketball or playing defense in basketball. In racquetball, court position and relationships with opponents might be studied in a discovery approach. Again, as with the fitness concepts model, when more time is spent on knowledge and analysis, less time may be available for developing physical skills. This is an important consideration for a curriculum planner.

Student Motives or Purposes Model

Jewett and Mullan (1977) have developed a purpose-process curriculum framework for physical education based on students' motives or purposes for participating in physical activity. The model focuses on three major purposes that all people share: individual development, environmental coping, and social interaction. These three major purpose concepts are made up of 22 purpose elements, including circulo-respiratory efficiency, catharsis, challenge, awareness, teamwork, competition, and leadership. The content of the curriculum model provides experiences related to all of the purpose elements. This framework is designed to help teachers make curricular decisions based on a theoretical model.

The Basic Stuff Series (1987) sponsored by the AAHPERD is a compilation of knowledge gleaned from the subdisciplines of physical education into a format useful for physical education teachers. A booklet is available for each of the following areas: exercise physiology, humanities in physical education, kinesiology, motor development, motor learning, and psychosocial aspects of physical education. The intent of the series is to promote the inclusion of disciplinary knowledge in physical education curricula, grades K–12. It provides a resource for physical education teachers as they develop new curricula materials. Series I of the material focuses on the knowledge concepts, and Series II provides learning experiences that teachers can use for teaching the concepts.

The Basic Stuff Series is discussed here because the knowledge sections in the series are arranged around student motives or purposes for participating in physical activity. Common student motives that are identified and discussed include: achievement (doing better), health (feeling good), appearance (looking good), social interaction (getting along), and coping with the environment (surviving). These motives or purposes can serve as an organizing center for a curriculum. A curriculum based on this model could offer a balance of activities from these areas, and students could select activities that best fit their perceived motives. Some secondary schools are using the disciplinary knowledge in conjunction with student motives. The Basic Stuff Series fits nicely into this model because it offers content from the various subdisciplines for each motive (Series I) and instructional activities for three age levels around each motive (Series II).

A curriculum that is based on student motives devotes time to discussing values, motives, and knowledge concepts. Again, these discussions may divert time from physical skill development. Weighing these areas of emphasis carefully is important because time available is finite. If one area is emphasized, then another area may have to be reduced or eliminated. Knowledge concepts are important, but if the increased emphasis reduces the time available for physical skill development, then an important program objective may be slighted. Knowing about physical activities is not the same as experiencing them. If students are to incorporate activities into their life-styles, they need opportunities to experience success and to develop competency with various physical activities.

Outdoor Pursuits and Adventure Activities Model

A growing number of secondary schools have added outdoor, adventure-type activities to the physical education curriculum during the past 15–20 years. Some of the popular activites included in this category are cycling, orienteering, backpacking, skin/scuba diving, canoeing, cross-country skiing, downhill skiing, caving, rock climbing/rappelling, group initiatives, and ropes course activities. Some schools have included a limited number of short units (either elective or required) as part of the multi-activity program, while others have required an entire semester sequence of adventure activities. Many high schools are offering a year-long elective course made up of a variety of outdoor, adventure pursuits. For example, a middle school in Iowa offers a 2-wk unit on bicycling and a 2-wk unit on canoeing during the regular curricular sequence. A high school in Arizona offers two levels of a year-long elective wilderness adventure class in the physical education program that includes instruction and field trips for rock climbing, rappelling, caving, beginning and advanced backpacking, and day hikes.

This approach creates a significant change for teachers, students, administrators, and parents. Many of the activities must be done off-campus in the community at various outdoor locations. For example, rock climbing areas, wooded or desert locations,

caves, rivers, and lakes must be utilized. This means travel arrangements and flexible time schedules for classes. After-school, weekend, and vacation period times must be used for these classes. This means new arrangements for teaching loads and student credit arrangements.

The safety and liability problems related to these activities require special safety and insurance arrangements and administrative support. Many administrators and parents think little about the injuries related to after-school athletic programs such as football, wrestling, and gymnastics, but will think carefully about adventure activities with a certain amount of risk. Most of the activities also require specialized equipment, such as compasses, climbing ropes, and camping gear, along with the financing to purchase this equipment. Teachers need specialized instructional skills and must be highly qualified because there is a large difference between teaching volleyball poorly and teaching rock climbing poorly.

With the problems to be faced in this curricular model, why are physical educators willing to take the time and do the extra work? The reason is that many secondary students are interested and enthusiastic about the activities. There are many reasons for this increased motivation. Some students focus on the novelty of the activities, others like the risk and excitement, the challenge of the environment, or the opportunity to make decisons, while still others like the social opportunities without the competition between people. These activities satisfy the goals of the physical education curriculum and are well worth the extra effort involved to get them started. To a certain group of students, this will be the most popular and important area of physical education activities.

Parker and Steen (1988) have pointed out that physical educators need to dispel four myths that often block the introduction of outdoor pursuits into the physical education curriculum. The myths are:

1. The school must be located near major outdoor areas or state parks.
2. The teacher must have advanced skill levels in outdoor activities.
3. There are insurmountable obstacles regarding safety, legal liability, and insurance.
4. The cost of outdoor pursuits is too expensive for schools.

Schools and physical educators are overcoming these problems in a number of ways. By starting small and being creative and innovative, much can be accomplished. Many activities are quite simple and can be started on campus with a limited budget. With proper training and supervision, students can experience a safe and rewarding experience with outdoor activities.

Sports Education Model

The sports education curriculum model developed by Siedentop, Mand, and Taggart (1986) allows all students, regardless of ability level, to experience the positive values of sports similiar to the positive side of being involved in the interscholastic sports program. Hopefully students will experience such qualities as working to reach deferred goals, teamwork, loyalty, commitment, perserverance, dedication, and concern for other people. The model emphasizes the importance of teams, leagues, seasons, championships, coaches, practice, player involvement, formal records, statistics, and competitive balance. These characteristics are usually emphasized in sport programs but not in the physical education program. This model gives all students a chance to experience a quality competitive sports program that is organized and supervised by an unbiased physical educator who will protect the important values of sport. Students learn to compete and to be good competitors.

Siedentop, Mand, and Taggart (1986) point out at least six characteristics that make the sports education model different from the more traditional approaches to physical education. They are:

1. Sports education involves seasons rather than units;
2. Students quickly become members of teams;
3. There is a formal schedule of competition;
4. There is usually a major culminating event;
5. Records are kept and publicized;
6. Teachers assume the role of coaches.

Each season starts with time for instruction and the development of team strategies according to teams' strengths and weaknesses. The teacher helps organize the class into teams, elect a student captain, and provide feedback to the team members about skill development. The students on the teams must take initative to organize practice, decide on players' positions, and decide on strategies for playing other teams. Students can take on more responsibility as the program evolves and they begin to understand its goals.

The program can be implemented in several ways, depending on the situation and the comfort zone of the teacher. It could take place in a single class where only one teacher and one class is involved. It could involve several classes that meet during the same period of the day. Practice during the regular class period followed by competition outside the class time or some combination of competition in

and out of class could be offered. Depending upon student interests and available facilities, different activities can be selected for the program. Traditional team sports such as basketball, volleyball, and softball could be selected or modified into activities such as three-person volleyball or basketball, or novel activities such as ultimate frisbee, team handball, or modified lacrosse.

Social Development Model

Don Hellison (1978, 1985) orignated a curriculum model for secondary school physical education that focuses primarily on the development of social competence, self-control, responsible behavior, and concern for others. Emphasis on fitness and the development of sport skills and knowledge is reduced in order to accomplish the primary goal of social competence. Hellison and many other teachers, administrators, and parents feel that social problems in society and our homes have created a situation that requires schools to offer this type of focus. Society is complex, giving adolescents many choices with little control over their lives; making it necessary to change the focus of physical education programs. In addition, professionals subscribing to this model believe that students are more disruptive and difficult to manage, making it the school's responsibility to provide better social development training. This model has been developed to address these goals. It has been field-tested successfully with troubled or alienated youth as well as with the general student body.

In this model, students proceed through six developmental levels of social competence. Different students enter at different levels and then proceed upward through the steps. The following are the levels of social development:

Level 0: Irresponsibility. Students do not participate and are totally unmotivated and undisciplined. They interrupt and intimidate other students and teachers. They make excuses and blame others for their behavior. Teachers find it difficult to manage or accomplish much with these students.

Level 1: Self-control. Students at the self-control level can control themselves without the direct supervision of the teacher and do not infringe on the rights of other students or the teacher. They can begin to participate in class activities and enhance their learning.

Level 2: Involvement. Level two involves student self-control and desired involvement with the subject matter of fitness, skills, and games. Students are enthusiastically involved in the program without constant prompting supervision of the teacher.

Level 3: Self-responsibllity. Students at level three begin to identify their interests and start to make choices within the parameters of the program. Motivation and responsibility are characteristics of these students. They start to take more responsibility and explore options for their lives outside the program. This stage represents a start of their own identity.

Level 4: Caring. The caring stage has students moving outside themselves and showing concern for other students and the teacher. Students are cooperative, helpful and show a genuine interest in the lives of others. There is a real concern about the world around them.

Level 5: Going Beyond. The highest level is characterized by student leadership and additional responsibility for program decisions. Students get involved with the teacher on decisions that will affect all students in the program. Students become coworkers with teachers.

This model can be implemented in different ways depending on the specifics of the school situation and the type of students. Hellison (1985) suggests an option that uses a daily program with each week arranged so that two days are spent on sport skills and game activities, two days on individual physical fitness routines, and one day on cooperative and sharing activities focusing on social development. Each day, teachers begin or end a class with a "self-control" activity or strategy that reminds students of the important social goals of the class (self-control, involvement, self-responsibility, and caring). Examples of strategies available to the teacher are teacher talk, modeling, reinforcement, reflection time, student sharing, the talking bench (where two students go to work out a problem), student checklists, student achievement records, and behavior contracts between the student and the teacher. Many strategies are available to the teacher for each of the social development levels (0–4).

The day spent entirely on cooperative activities each week should be designed to help students interact with peers and the teacher. Initiative activities, new games, and cooperative activities are excellent possibilities (see Chapter 23). The model requires that students gradually take on more responsibility throughout the year and provide more input on the daily and weekly activities.

CONSTRUCTING A CURRICULUM GUIDE

The formal curriculum guide should be written in an organized, systematic manner. It is recommended that these steps be followed for establishing a quality, meaningful, and well-planned curriculum guide.

Step 1: Develop a Program Philosophy

The curriculum guide should start with a definition of physical education and a discussion of the values of the physical education department. As discussed in Chapter 1, physical education is a process that focuses on increasing students' knowledge and affecting their attitudes and behaviors in a positive manner relative to physical activities, including sports, exercise, games, dance, aquatic activities, and outdoor, adventure activities. It is an instructional program with developmental goals and achieveable outcomes. Physical education focuses primarily on psychomotor goals, but also makes a valuable contribution to the affective and cognitive learning domains. It is an important part of each student's overall educational experience because of the unique contributions to the following areas:

1. The development of physical skills that can be used for a lifetime of enjoyment and recreation;
2. The development and maintenance of a personalized level of health-related physical fitness;
3. The acquisition of knowledge that is necessary to be successful and to enjoy the various physical activities and fitness routines;
4. The development of a positive attitude toward regular physical activity and physical fitness participation.

Step 2: Examine the Desires of Society

Years ago, people banded together and decided to set aside land and build schools, because they wanted their children to acquire certain information, attitudes, and skills in a systematic manner from a trained specialist. These people had certain ambitions for their youth. Even though society has changed dramatically since that time and much new information has been discovered, people still have a number of desires that they want passed on to the next generation. Many of these desires have direct implications for curriculum construction in physical education. Curriculum planners need to analyze the desires of society.

Desire to Be Physically Fit, Healthy, and Attractive

Being fit, healthy, and attractive is especially important to physical educators because of the contribution that physical activity makes in these areas. Proof that activity aids in achieving weight control, cardiovascular efficiency, flexibility, and strength is well documented. The public is aware of the humiliation and problems that individuals face throughout life if they are obese, weak, or unattractive. Physically fit people feel positive and successful, and portray a positive image to others. These successes add up to a positive self-concept. In contrast, obese people often have difficulty with simple daily activities like dressing, sitting, and walking. They may have a negative self-image, and often cannot participate in or enjoy many activities.

Desire to Play

Play has been frequently discussed as an important behavior that permeates all cultures in a variety of forms. Sports, dance, and various types of physical activity are serious forms of play. Many other forms of play, including music, drama, and art, are also important in society. Indeed, play is as important to most people as work, and an enjoyable play life is as valuable as a productive work life. In fact, to many, play is the most important aspect of their life. It is what they would call "paradise" or "the good life." They look forward to a round of golf, a jog along a canal, or a backpacking trip in the mountains. Physical education can make a significant contribution to this universal desire to play.

Desire for Knowledge

The human race continues to search for knowledge in all areas. People are curious about the world around them. Physical education has an extensive body of knowledge that contains various subfields. These are exercise physiology, kinesiology, motor learning, history of sport, philosophy of sport, sport psychology, and sport sociology. Many opportunities and areas of physical education are available to satisfy this desire for information.

Desire for Success, Approval, and Satisfaction

People tend to repeat activities that provide them with success. They also tend to avoid activities in which they are not successful. Various types of success usually lead to recognition, approval, or self-satisfaction. People participate in activities in which they are successful because feelings of success lead to satisfaction and happiness. Physical activities are in this category and thus make a significant contribution to one's life.

Desire for Social and Emotional Competence

Most people are concerned about how other people feel about them. People want to be accepted, respected, and liked. Adults want their children to develop acceptable social and emotional skills so that they can enjoy life. Schools are the major social agency in our culture. Information is imparted in the school setting regarding dating, mental health,

sex education, nutrition, driver education, and many other important areas. Physical education offers unique opportunities in this social-emotional area because of the nature and arrangement of its subject matter. Competitive situations (involving winning, losing, and accepting referee decisions) and codeucational activities (with emphasis on movement skills) provide a rich source of social and emotional experiences for youth. Physical education teachers can have a tremendous impact on students in these areas.

Desire to Compete

Most societies are competitive. Indeed, competition is present in almost all aspects of our culture. People learn to compete at an early age, and many employers believe that the best competitors are the most successful workers in the business world. Adults want their children to be competitors and winners. In many youth sport leagues, children are forced at an early age to compete for league championships, trophies, and adult approval. In bicycle motocross racing, 5-year-old children in beginning, novice, and expert classes race around a track in pursuit of victories, trophies, and points that may bring them a funding sponsor so they can travel across the country to more races. Some people believe that this early competitive experience is beneficial for youngsters, but others seriously question these practices. Regardless of the stand taken, the fact is that most societies are competitive. The competitive nature of sports and physical activity requires physical educators to have a stand on competition. Physical education programs can have a strong influence on youth and their ability to compete.

Desire for Risk, Adventure, and Excitement

Perhaps because of increased urbanization, mechanization, and impersonal, fast-paced life-styles, many people are turning to high-risk adventurous activities for fun. Physical activities such as rock climbing, skiing, white water canoeing, and backpacking are increasing in popularity and give people an opportunity to do something new, risky, and exciting. The physical education curriculum can provide many experiences to satisfy this desire.

Desire for Rhythmic Expression

Most people enjoy listening to and moving to rhythmic sounds. Many forms of rhythmic activity have been popular in a wide variety of cultures throughout history. They can include many forms of dance, such as folk, square, and aerobic, as well as sport movements, such as jumping rope, running hurdles, or excercising to music. Rhythms can be both enjoyable and motivational. A variety of rhythmic activities is an important part of a physical education curriculum.

Desire for Creative Expression

People are looking for ways to express their autonomy and individuality. Clothes and hair styles have been especially popular ways to reveal oneself to the world. Play and leisure time is another opportunity for self-expression. The work world usually puts so many limits on individuality that people channel their creative and individual desires into play or leisure pursuits. Physical activities provide numerous possibilities for creative outlets structured by the rules that govern the activities. In basketball, students enjoy developing Isaih Thomas-type shots or Magic Johnson-type passes and assists. In gymnastics, the opportunity to develop a creative routine to music or to perfect new moves may be challenging. New plays and defenses are always being created in football. The challenges are unlimited, and the opportunities for creative expression appeal to students. Physical education curricula should be planned carefully to help satisfy this desire.

Step 3: Study the Characteristics and Interests of Students

The next step in curriculum construction is to take a close look at the developmental level, the characteristics, and the interests of students for whom the curriculum is being designed.

A cynical teacher once said, "Teaching would be a good job if it weren't for all those students." Without students, there would be no need for teachers, teaching strategies, or curriculum. Students are the most important factor to consider when developing a physical education curriculum. They are our basic resource, and teachers must remember this at all times. Potential teachers should spend time with students to learn about their interests, characteristics, and abilities. This can be accomplished by reading information, by talking with students and parents, and by formally collecting data.

Student characteristics are those typical or distinctive features that represent a given developmental or age level. As students grow and develop, certain characteristics appear and disappear. Within a specific age range, most of the students will exhibit similar characteristics. There will always be extreme ends of the normal curve regarding developmental levels. Students will vary in height, weight, social abilities, and in many other areas at each chronological age.

Developmental characteristics are usually examined by chronological age level. The problem

with this approach is that four or five different developmental age levels may exist within a given chronological age range (i.e., the 7th grade may have students with developmental ages from 10 to 14 years). Most schools, however, group students by chronological age rather than developmental level because of administrative ease. Physical education teachers must be aware of the wide range of developmental levels that can exist at a given grade level. These developmental differences will affect physical abilities and performance in physical activities.

Student characteristics can be categorized as physical, social, emotional, and intellectual. Curriculum planners need to consider carefully all of these areas, because physical education programs can contribute to all four. Some physical educators believe mistakenly that their program contributes only to the physical area, but physical activities do not occur in a learning vacuum: students are also involved mentally, socially, and emotionally.

The developmental characteristics of students are a key factor in the design of a curriculum. Social, emotional, physical, and intellectual characteristics are important variables in determining the types of activities, the length of units, the amount of student choice, and the content to be emphasized.

The characteristics of junior high school students are different from those of senior high students, and their developmental levels need to be considered as separate entities. It is difficult to sort out characteristics by each of the four categories. In the following sections on junior high and senior high school students, two areas will be discussed: the physical area, and a combination of the social, emotional, and intellectual areas.

Physical Area—Junior High Students, Ages 11–14

The following physical characteristics should be considered carefully when planning curriculum for the junior high level:

1. Students undergo a rapid and uneven growth spurt.
2. Girls experience this spurt about 1.5 years earlier than do boys.
3. Girls are usually taller and more physically mature early in this period. Once boys experience the growth spurt, they pass girls in height and weight.
4. Awkwardness, poor coordination, low strength, and low endurance are common during rapid growth spurts.
5. Students usually need more sleep during a growth spurt.
6. An increase in appetite occurs.

7. Posture is often poor due to social pressure.
8. Ossification of the bones is usually incomplete.
9. A wide range of physical maturity exists.
10. Students go through puberty and develop secondary sexual characteristics. Boys experience facial hair, pubic hair, a voice change, and genital and shoulder development. Girls develop breasts, pubic hair, a widening of the hips, and an accumulation of body fat.
11. Motor abilities develop slowly because of the increase in growth velocity.
12. The range of motor ability broadens, and the skill level differences of students become increasingly apparent.
13. Boys are stronger and may have more endurance than girls.
14. Many girls have an advantage over boys in the areas of balance and flexibility.

Social, Emotional, and Intellectual Areas — Junior High Students

Because physical education also involves other areas besides the physical, curriculum planners for the junior high level should keep in mind these characteristics of youngsters ages 11–14:

1. Students have a strong desire for independence. They believe that adults (authority figures) are old-fashioned. Most desire to make decisions for themselves.
2. Students are torn between adult and peer values.
3. Moods change quickly, for this is an emotional and unpredictable period. Students may be unstable, angry, fearful, and easily upset.
4. Fighting with parents and peers is common at this age, as is competitiveness.
5. Peer groups provide the standards for behavior. The peer group represents independence because of the absence of adults. Leaders, followers, and loyalty start to evolve from group dynamics.
6. Students are interested in improving themselves, especially in the physical area. Weight training, body building, and figure control or development are of special interest.
7. Strong concerns about size and abilities are common. Grooming, clothes, and appearance become important. Students are self-conscious about their bodies.
8. Romantic interests begin in this age range. Many students try to impress the opposite sex in various ways. Girls are usually ahead of boys socially and may begin to date older boys.
9. Social activities become important, and dances, movies, parties, and athletic events become social meeting places.

10. Intellectual development continues throughout this period. Students can concentrate longer, are able to understand more complex concepts, and are better able to follow directions. An interest in the "why" of physical activity occurs. Daydreaming and fantasizing lessen for many students.
11. The variety of student activities decreases continually throughout this period and into adulthood. Students are beginning to make decisions about areas in which they want to specialize. This has strong implications for future sport and physical activity participation.
12. Students have often lived in several places and have traveled to many areas.
13. A strong interest in risk, excitement, and adventure is common.

In summary, this is a challenging and difficult period for students. They are confused by their changing physical appearance and the transition process from childhood to adulthood. Many important decisions are being made about their careers and goals for life. For physical education teachers, the situation is extremely challenging, and can be quite frustrating and demanding as well as rewarding. Physical education can play a significant role in these students' lives.

Physical Area — Senior High School Students, Ages 15–18

The following are physical characteristics of senior high school students that need to be considered if the curriculum is to enhance the students' physical development:

1. Increases occur in motor abilities, coordination, strength, endurance, and speed. Boys surpass girls in these areas.
2. Boys surpass girls in height and weight. Sexual characteristics reach maturity in both boys and girls.
3. Boys continue to develop muscularly. Bone growth and the ossification process are usually complete.
4. By the end of this period, most students are physically mature. It is a good time to develop motor abilities.
5. Students continue to have large appetites.

Social, Emotional, and Intellectual Areas — Senior High School, Ages 15–18

High school students continue to change and develop in these areas. The following are characteristics common to this age group:

1. The peer group and its activities are a dominant factor in students' lives.
2. Social activities continue to be important and expand outside the home and school.
3. Dating, going steady, marriage, and careers dominate the activities and interests during this period.
4. Students are still critical of adults, teachers, and other authority figures. The conflict continues between peer and adult values.
5. Competition increases with grades, athletics, and dating.
6. Students are still very emotional, even though many have made adjustments to their new bodies and to the nature of school. Senior high students are usually better adjusted and happier than the junior high school youngsters.
7. Students continue to be concerned about their appearance and abilities. They are interested in ways to improve themselves and impress the opposite sex.
8. Students are approaching their full intellectual potential. Their memory, ability to reason, ability to concentrate, and imagination are improving and developing. They have more experience and knowledge on which to base decisions.
9. Strong concerns about security, attention, and affection exist for most students. Divorce, single-parent families, multiple moves, and changing American values have had an impact on young people by the time they reach this period.
10. This group is looking for risk, excitement, and adventure. Many students will be interested in physical activities that include these components.
11. The continued narrowing of interests and the development of specializations are important factors in physical education curriculum development. Students need an opportunity to express their independence by choosing specialized, in-depth activity classes. They should not be forced into activities in which they are not interested.

The senior high school years are important in transforming adolescents into adults. Students must face the realities of the world and make decisions about education, careers, marriage, religion, politics, and life-styles. Teachers have a valuable responsibility for imparting information, attitudes, and skills.

Physical Activity Interests of Students

Historically, the physical activity interests of the public have strongly influenced physical education curriculum. As people's interests change, programs have evolved from an early fitness-oriented model to a team sports approach, and finally, to an emphasis on individual lifetime activities. Currently popular activities, such as aerobic dance, outdoor adventure activities, distance running, and the martial arts, are slowly filtering into school physical education curricula because these activities are popular and they fulfill program goals.

The general activity interests of society and the specific interests of students in a secondary school are important factors in curriculum construction. A curriculum formulated without concern for the interests of students will probably not accomplish its objectives or help a teacher to develop positive student attitudes. In addition to popular new activities, various communities will generate a special interest in areas such as golf, tennis, or sailing, while others may focus more on basketball, baseball, or football. The geographic location, the economic situation, and the background of the community members will all have an impact on the activity interests of students, and these activity interests are important in helping an educator decide which units to offer in the curriculum.

Program planners should continually examine student interests and the types of activities that are being offered. Too often, programs are based on the activity interests of teachers, administrators, and parents, rather than students. In particular, many teachers will not teach activities in which they are not skilled. The activity comfort zone of teachers is often too narrow to accomplish program goals. This is why many students develop escape or avoidance behaviors in physical education. They actually like physical activity, but do not like the activities presented or the way that they are being taught. Teachers need to expand their teaching repertoire of activities and methods to include students' interests.

In a selective-elective curriculum, schools have mistakenly offered activity units that educators presumed would be popular with students. In reality, the students were not interested and did not enroll. Problems arise with scheduling, facilities, and teaching assignments. For example, an inner-city school tried offering 3-wk units on golf, bowling, and archery in an elective curriculum. In each section, only 1–5 students registered for the units. Clearly, students were not interested in these activities. The classes were cancelled and different activities were offered.

In another example at a high school (Wilson and Altieri, 1978), a survey of seniors helped to determine that students were not returning to physical education after the required freshman year because the curriculum did not provide any choice of specific units. All the units were required for all students if they chose to take an optional year of physical education. Many students were avoiding the entire year because they did not wish to take one or two of the 3-wk units. In other words, students would avoid an entire year because of one or two compulsory activities. Not all students reacted to the same activity; some were not interested in wrestling, while others disliked swimming or gymnastics. Eventually, school officials developed a program in which students had four or five activity choices. As a result of the new curriculum approach, student enrollment showed a large increase. Grades 10–12 are not the time to force students into activities in which they have little or no interest.

The Utah State Office of Education conducted a survey of high school students' interests in physical activity (Lindeman et al., 1981). The sample included 1,834 students from 15 high schools in the Salt Lake City area. Most of the students were in the 11th and 12th grades, with an equal distribution of boys and girls. One of the survey questions asked, "Which physical activities would you be most interested in taking as a physical education class?" The top ten selected activities are as follows:*

1. Outdoor survival—68.9%
2. Body conditioning, figure control—67.6%
3. Jogging, running—62.9%
4. Martial arts—57.3%
5. Weight training—53.8%
6. Lifesaving, water safety—47.8%
7. Racquetball—47%
8. Recreational games—46.7%
9. Tennis—46.4%
10. Cycling—45.3%

A traditional team sport did not appear until number 15 on the list. The results of the Utah survey seem to reflect society's general interests in the wellness movement, outdoor adventure activities, and the martial arts. Many physical educators, however, believe that students are interested primarily in team sports like football, basketball, and baseball. These educators may be expressing their personal interests and misrepresenting the interests of students.

Determining Student Interests

Many schools are beginning to use surveys or checklists to gather data about specific student activity interests. Surveys should be completed in the spring to help determine the curricular offerings for the following fall and spring semesters. In some cases, the survey will be given to students who will be feeding into the school the following year. For example, 6th graders should be surveyed before they enter junior high school, and next year's beginning senior high school students should be surveyed while still in junior high.

The survey should be administered every other year to all demographic groups within the schools (i.e., boys, girls, athletes, nonathletes, various racial groups, and various grade levels). As many students as possible should be surveyed to ensure valid information. Ideally, the survey can be administered in a class or homeroom period (math, science, or English) that is required for all students.

Most schools have access to data processing and computers, and a specialist is usually available to help set up programs for data analysis. A program can be designed to analyze the student population in many ways that are useful in constructing curriculum. For example, interests can be analyzed by age, sex, or racial group.

The interest survey should include all possible physical activities that could accomplish the objectives of physical education. It is important to avoid restrictive thinking when describing activity offerings in a survey. For example, the lack of a pool, racquetball courts, ski slopes, or various types of equipment for specific activities should not prohibit an educator from including these activities on the survey. Travel to off-campus facilities in the nearby community may be possible in the future. Most communities have nearby golf driving ranges, racquet clubs, bowling alleys, pools, ski slopes, or wooded areas that could be used for the school program. Data collected from surveys can be a basis for expanding physical facilities, or adding a pool, racquetball courts, tennis courts, or a weight lifting room. If student interest can be shown, administrators may be convinced that facilities and equipment, course offerings, or new teachers should be added to the physical education program.

An example of an interest survey is shown in Figure 3.2. The survey should be revised every other year, and new activity trends should be included. Professional and popular literature will help provide information about the new activity patterns and habits. Interests in the community can be determined by looking at various recreation programs offered through the YMCA, the parks and recreation department, private clubs, community leagues, and corporations. The number of facilities such as bowling alleys, golf courses, ski slopes, and swimming pools will provide additional information about interests in the community. The interests of community adults will have an impact on students. This is important information for the curriculum planner.

---

* The percentage is that portion of students who indicated that they would be interested in the activity.

PHYSICAL ACTIVITY INTEREST SURVEY

Name _____

Grade _____ Age _____ Sex _____

Athletic team _____

Instructions: Which of the following physical activities or sports would you be most interested in taking as a course in the physical education program? Please list your top 5 choices on the line provided. Place a number 1 in front of your highest choice, a number 2 in front of your next choice, and so on until you reach choice number 5. Remember to make only 5 choices.

Aquatic Activities
_____ Lifesaving, water safety
_____ Skin and scuba diving
_____ Surfing
_____ Swimming, diving
_____ Water sports (polo, volleyball, basketball)

Individual Activities
_____ Archery
_____ Badminton
_____ Fencing
_____ Frisbee
_____ Golf
_____ Gymnastics
_____ Handball
_____ Racquetball
_____ Recreational games (bowling, horseshoes, shuffleboard, etc.)
_____ Roller-skating
_____ Skateboarding
_____ Squash
_____ Tennis
_____ Track and field

Physical Conditioning Activities
_____ Aerobic dance
_____ Body conditioning, weight control
_____ Martial arts (judo, karate, kendo, etc.)
_____ Weight training
_____ Yoga

Outdoor Adventure Activities
_____ Backpacking
_____ Canoeing, kayaking

_____ Cycling (bicycling)
_____ Fishing
_____ Horseback riding
_____ Hunting
_____ Ice skating
_____ Outdoor survival
_____ Orienteering
_____ Rock climbing
_____ Sailing
_____ Skiing (cross country)
_____ Skiing (downhill)
_____ Snow shoeing

Rhythmic Activities
_____ Ballet
_____ Country swing dance
_____ Disco
_____ Folk and square dance
_____ Jazz dance
_____ Modern dance
_____ Social dance

Team Activities
_____ Baseball
_____ Basketball
_____ Field hockey
_____ Flag football
_____ Ice hockey
_____ Lacrosse
_____ Soccer
_____ Softball
_____ Speedball-speed-a-way
_____ Team handball
_____ Volleyball
_____ Wrestling

Directions for the teacher: Remind students to select only 5 choices, using the numbers 1–5 on the lines beside the activities. When analyzing the data, it is helpful to transpose numbers 1 and 5 and numbers 2 and 4. In other words, a 1 becomes a 5 and a 5 becomes a 1. A 2 is worth 4 and a 4 worth 2. The numbers are added for each activity. The activities with the most points are the most popular and those with the least points are the least popular.

FIGURE 3.2   Physical activity interest survey

Step 4: Determine Program Objectives

Formulating objectives is the fourth step in writing the curriculum guide. The objectives for an educational program should evolve from the desires of the people whom the program serves. Objectives should be formulated with the desires of both the public (parents and students) and physical education professionals in mind. In other words, a program based only on the desires of the public sector may not be educationally sound. The knowledge and understanding of trained professionals must be considered.

Objectives are behavioral goals to be reached by the students in a program. They provide focus and direction for the program. There are two types of objectives that are necessary for the curriculum. They are called institutional and student-centered objectives. Institutional objectives are general in nature and determine the direction of the program as desired by the school district. They specify the long-term goals of the program. These objectives should be written for the three learning domains: psychomotor, cognitive, and affective. The following are examples of general institutional objectives that could be used as overall curriculum objectives:

Affective Domain

1. The students will incorporate physical activity into their life-styles on a regular basis;
2. The students will display a positive attitude toward physical activity;
3. The students will develop social and emotional skills that will enable them to be responsible sports participants;
4. The students will feel good about their physical selves;

Psychomotor Domain

5. The students will develop an appropriate level of health-related physical fitness;
6. The students will develop specialized sport skills so that they can enjoy lifetime sports;

Cognitive Domain

7. The students will acquire knowledge about sports, games, dance, exercise, and fitness;
8. The students will develop a basic understanding of the underlying principles of movement.

After general institutional objectives have been determined, it is necessary to write the student-centered objectives. These objectives should be written in specific behavioral or performance terms. They should specify in terms of student behavior what physical skills, knowledge, and attitudes students will possess when they finish various units and daily lessons. Examples of specific behavioral or performance objective might be:

Psychomotor Domain

1. The student will run 1.5 mi in 12 min;
2. The student will do 35 push-ups in 1 min;
3. The student will bump the volleyball 12 consecutive times against the wall above a 10 ft line;

Cognitive Domain

4. The student will identify five exercises that develop low back flexibility;
5. The student will determine a training heart rate for a 15-year-old female;
6. The student will identify three exercises that develop the abdominal muscles;

Affective Domain

7. The student will demonstrate a positive attitude toward Frisbee activities by practicing during free time;
8. The student will demonstrate an understanding of cooperation by working with teammates in soccer games;
9. The student will show a positive attitude toward lifetime activity by joining the school's jogging club.

Overall institutional objectives for the curriculum should be written in general terms, but unit plans and daily lesson plans should use specific student-centered objectives with precise behavioral definitions. The sum of the specific daily lesson objectives should equal all of the objectives for one unit. The sum of the unit objectives should equal the total curricular objectives. The sum of the curricular objectives from each academic area should equal the objectives of the total school curriculum.

Specific behavioral or performance objectives that are useful for lesson and unit plans will be discussed in the planning and teaching styles chapters (Chapters 7, 8, and 10). For review of the general objectives of physical education that can be used for institutional objectives, refer to Chapter 1.

Step 5: Review the Practical (Restrictive) Factors

Step five focuses on the analysis of the many practical factors that must be considered while organizing the curriculum. These factors can influence the program in a positive or negative manner. The specifics of each situation, the people, the programs, and the facilities, will determine whether the factor is positive or negative. It is important for curriculum planners to think in positive terms, because negative or restrictive thinking will only hinder the development of a quality program. Negative factors can usually be changed and turned into positive factors as the curriculum develops, but people who think in restrictive terms will find this difficult.

Philosophical Position of Teachers

Since a secondary school physical education program usually involves several people, it is important that all members of the department have an understanding of the philosophy of physical education. Careful consideration should be given to the following questions:

1. What is physical education?
2. What are the objectives of physical education?
3. What activities should be used to accomplish these objectives?
4. How should these activities be arranged and packaged?
5. What policies and procedures should be used as guidelines?

All physical educators should think carefully about these questions and should verbalize the answers to students, faculty, administrators, school board members, and community members. An existing curriculum cannot be changed or a new one developed without an organized philosophy of physical education. Often, physical educators have not organized their opinions about the curriculum. An undeveloped philosophy can restrict curriculum construction.

A philosophy can be restrictive if a teacher is afraid of change and will not expand his or her "comfort zone." Physical education curricula continue to evolve and change. New activities are slowly filtering into programs. Someone who clings to a philosophy that was developed years earlier may be teaching a curriculum that is developing escape or avoidance tendencies in students. Physical educators should continually reevaluate their philosophy of physical education, and efforts should be made to bring the curriculum in line with that philosophy. A well-conceived philosophy based on sound educational principles is certainly a positive factor in curriculum construction.

All staff members should be involved in interpreting a sound philosophy to other interested and appropriate people. Staff members do not have to follow the same philosophy, however, but they must show respect for the ideas of peers, especially in front of other people. A positive situation exists when staff members have developed and shared philosophies with their colleagues. Compromises must be worked out privately when differences of opinion exist. Extremely different philosophies on a staff can create a restrictive situation.

Physical activity interests and abilities of the staff are important factors in curriculum development. A well-balanced curriculum demands a wide range of activity interests and abilities on the staff (i.e., dance, aquatics, wilderness activities, team sports, physical conditioning activities, and lifetime sports). In an elective-type curriculum, staff members can specialize in several activities. A specialist can greatly improve the quality of instruction in an activity.

An important factor in hiring staff members should be their teaching competence and how these abilities blend with the existing staff's competencies. A positive situation exists when a staff has a wide variety of activity interests and abilities. It is also a plus if staff members are willing to expand their teaching abilities through in-service training and additional course work.

The number of staff members is another important consideration in curriculum construction. If a choice needs to be made between staff and equipment, an increase in staff size is desirable. An additional teacher means reduced class sizes, more activity offerings, and an increase in student-teacher contact. If physical educators believe their subject matter is as important as any other curriculum area, they should defend the concept of a teacher-student ratio in physical education equal to the ratio in math, science, or English classes.

The School Administration

The support of various school administrators has a significant impact on the physical education curriculum. It is important for physical education teachers to communicate the goals of the program to administrators. Many administrators, have misconceptions about physical education. Communication between the staff and the administration is therefore an important positive factor. In most cases, administrators will agree with and support the philosophy of the physical education staff if they perceive it to be built on sound educational principles.

The administration can help the physical education curriculum in the following areas:

1. Determining the number of staff members and class size;
2. Hiring staff to fill specific departmental needs;
3. Constructing or developing facilities and teaching areas (e.g., racquetball courts, weight room, parcourse, or swimming pool);
4. Purchasing equipment and teaching aids (e.g., golf clubs, bowling sets, loop films, or jump ropes);

5. Supporting innovative ideas or new activities (e.g., pilot unit on orienteering, an off-campus cross country skiing lesson, or a team-teaching presentation of a golf unit);
6. Maintaining existing teaching stations (e.g., watering the fields, cleaning the gymnasium, or repairing weight machines);
7. Supporting staff development with in-service workshops, professional conferences, and current literature;
8. Providing useful and meaningful feedback to teachers on their teaching performance (e.g., collecting data on management time, productive time, active learning time, or behavior patterns).

Physical educators need to make an active effort to gain the support of the school administrators. This support can yield many positive dividends over time, because administrators have the power to influence situations and implement strategies.

Community Influences

The school's surrounding community is an important factor for consideration. Physical educators should become familiar with people in the community. Occupations, religions, educational levels, cultural values, and physical activity habits are factors that can affect curriculum development. Parents have a strong influence on the activity interests and habits of their children. By secondary school age, students have acquired specific habits that the physical education department must be aware of as they develop a program. Students in a suburban, upper-class community will be quite different from those in an urban, inner-city community because of their parents and various learning experiences. Both situations have pros and cons, and physical educators need to be aware.

The geographic location and the climate of the area are important factors. The terrain of the mountains, deserts, or plains combined with weather conditions of each area have an effect on people's activity interests. Extremely hot or cold climates strongly influence what activities can be arranged in the curriculum and at what time of the year they should be scheduled. Cross country skiing, bicycling, and outdoor swimming are examples of such activities. In addition, the climate influences how an activity is taught. For example, outdoor jogging during midday in September in central Arizona is next to impossible because of the extreme heat. Plans and alternatives for rainy and cold climates must also be developed by curriculum planners.

Public interests and the climate of the community can be used as factors in curriculum development.

The initial core of activity offerings can be built around currently popular activities. Students will probably have an interest in these activities and will be motivated to participate and learn. Teachers should use these high-probability activities or events to create a positive, successful atmosphere so that students develop a backlog of success. This is helpful when the teacher then attempts low-probability events or activities that may not be initially interesting or motivating (e.g., exercising or jogging). The climate and weather can be used positively by offering interesting units that require the snow, ice, desert, or wooded areas.

Physical educators should think positively about the community and the climate. Little can be done to change the climate, but influencing and changing the people of the community may be possible. Many citizens have misconceptions about physical education and physical activity in general. There are many ways to help educate the public and gain citizens' support. Chapter 15 discusses procedures for enhancing public relations.

Facilities and Equipment

The available teaching facilities will dictate, in part, the activities that can be offered in the curriculum. Facilities include on-campus and off-campus areas in the neighboring community. On-campus facilities are areas such as the gymnasium, wrestling room, weight room, tennis courts, field space, and hallways. Off-campus facilities might be a golf driving range, a horseback riding stable, a sailing pond, a stream for canoeing, a community swimming pool, or a hiking trail in a nearby park. Equipment includes materials such as bats, balls, tennis racquets, badminton birds, jump ropes, and records. Equipment is usually defined as the materials used on or with a teaching facility.

Teachers should continually strive for ways to improve and expand existing facilities and equipment. On-campus facilities can be increased by using a foyer area for aerobic dance, adapting an old storage area for golf, or expanding a locker room into a weight room. A creative look at existing facilities may provide new teaching areas.

Off-campus facilities can open a new world of teaching environnments. Many areas may be close by, within walking distance, whereas others may require transportation. The school may be able to provide a bus or special funds may be raised for transportation. Many schools are now bussing students to nearby bowling alleys, ski slopes, and hiking areas. When off-school facilities are used, school officials should be asked to look into the legal liability aspects of each situation.

Equipment can be added with departmental funds or with special funds raised by students for physical education. Some types of equipment can be made by school maintenance departments or by students as industrial arts projects. Safety factors should be checked carefully in all cases. In some units, students can bring equipment from home, such as tennis racquets, racquetballs, or bicycles. Curriculum planners need to be creative and to consider every possibility for expanding the facilities and increasing equipment.

Laws and Requirements

The laws, regulations, and requirements at the national, state, and local levels are another factor demanding consideration. Physical educators must understand various regulations in order to develop programs that comply with the laws. However, these laws and regulations were developed by people and are subject to change. People can modify laws if the legislation is not helping programs achieve their objectives. Appropriate procedures are available to change laws and government regulations, and educators must become actively involved in the process when change is necessary.

At the national level, Title IX of the Educational Amendments Act of 1972 and Public Law 94–142 have had a significant impact on physical education curriculum. Specifics of these laws, as discussed in Chapter 1, are still being debated and interpreted differently by school districts, state departments of education, and the judicial system. Physical educators need to evaluate these laws carefully and develop curricula that are in compliance. Each state department of education has regulations and guidelines governing the physical education requirements for that particular state. The local school district then develops guidelines within the framework of the state requirements.

School Schedule

The schedule or organizational pattern of the school will have an impact on implementation of the curriculum. There are two basic types of schedules: the block or traditional schedule and the flexible schedule.

The block or traditional plan (Figure 3.3) divides the school day into five or six equal time blocks or periods. Each class, such as math, science, or physical education, meets for the same length of time on each day of the school week. The advantage of the traditional schedule is that it is easier to set up, more economical, and easier to administer. Students are in the same class at the same time each day. This provides students and administrators with a stable routine.

Flexible schedules (Figure 3.4) provide a varying length of time for classes depending on the nature of the subject matter and the type of instruction given. A biology lecture might meet three days a week for 45 min, while a laboratory for biology would meet for 1.5 hr. A flexible schedule might allow physical education students to travel to a local ski slope and meet for a 3-hr block of time one day a week.

Period	Time	Monday	Tuesday	Wednesday	Thursday	Friday
Homeroom	8:00–8:15					→
1	8:15–9:10	General math				→
2	9:15–10:10	English				→
3	10:15–11:10	Biology				→
Lunch	11:15–11:45					→
Study hall	11:45–12:15					→
4	12:15–1:10	Physical education				→
5	1:15–2:10	History				→
6	2:15–3:10	Home economics				→

FIGURE 3.3 Block or traditional schedule

Module	Time	Monday	Tuesday	Wednesday	Thursday	Friday
1	8:00–8:15	English	Industrial arts lab	English	Biology lab	English
2	8:15–8:30	English	Industrial arts lab	English	Biology lab	English
3	8:30–8:45	English	Industrial arts lab	English	Biology lab	English
4	8:45–9:00	General math	Industrial arts lab	General math	Biology lab	General math
5	9:00–9:15	General math	Industrial arts lab	General math	Biology lab	General math
6	9:15–9:30	General math	Industrial arts lab	General math	Biology lab	General math
7	9:30–9:45	Biology lecture	Industrial arts	Biology lecture	Industrial arts	Open
8	9:45–10:00	Biology lecture	Industrial arts	Biology lecture	Industrial arts	Open
9	10:00–10:15	Biology lecture	Industrial arts	Biology lecture	Industrial arts	Open
10	10:15–10:30	History	Typing	History	Typing	History
11	10:30–10:45	History	Typing	History	Typing	History
12	10:45–11:00	History	Typing	History	Typing	History
13	11:00–11:15	Open	Typing	Open	Typing	Open
14	11:15–11:30	Lunch	Lunch	Lunch	Lunch	Lunch
15	11:30–11:45	Lunch	Lunch	Lunch	Lunch	Lunch
16	11:45–12:00	Physical education	Open	Physical education	English lab	Physical education
17	12:00–12:15	Physical education	Open	Physical education	English lab	Physical education
18	12:15–12:30	Physical education	Open	Physical education	English lab	Physical education
19	12:30–12:45	Physical education	Open	Physical education	English lab	Physical education
20	12:45–1:00	Physical education	Open	Physical education	English lab	Physical education
21	1:00–1:15	Physical education	Open	Physical education	English lab	Physical education
22	1:15–1:30	Typing lab	Open	Open	Open	Open
23	1:30–1:45	Typing lab	Open	Open	Open	Open
24	1:45–2:00	Typing lab	General math lab	Open	History lab	Open
25	2:00–2:15	Typing lab	General math lab	Open	History lab	Open
26	2:15–2:30	Typing lab	General math lab	Open	History lab	Physical education
27	2:30–2:45	Typing lab	General math lab	Open	History lab	Physical education
28	2:45–3:00	Open	General math lab	Open	History lab	Physical education
29	3:00–3:15	Open	General math lab	Open	History lab	Physical education

FIGURE 3.4   Flexible schedule

Schools use different types of flexible schedules designed to meet the needs of the people involved. In physical education, a flexible schedule can provide time for travel off campus, the option of grouping students for different types of instruction (large or small groups), or the use of limited and specific types of equipment. Some administrators and teachers complain about "dead spots" of time in a flexible schedule. Students may have 15 min of free time between classes, which causes concern because they need a place to go and may abuse the use of the free time. Many schools have provided a "commons" area where students can gather during these intervals.

The advantages of the flexible schedule would seem to enhance the physical education curriculum. The problems created can be managed by careful planning and the joint efforts of teachers and administrators. Physical education can add off-campus activities and improve the quality of instruction with an organized flexible schedule. A traditional block schedule limits physical education to a 45–60 min daily period, including time required for changing clothes. This obviously hinders many possibilities for activities and instructional methods.

Budget and Funding

Budget and funding procedures differ among school districts. Usually, the physical education department head is involved with developing and submitting the budget. It is therefore important for him or her to understand the funding procedures and to carefully plan an aggressive strategy for obtaining a fair share of the school's budget. Often administrators have misconceptions about class size and amounts of equipment that physical educators need to develop an effective program. Physical educators should seek parity with other school departments in terms of class size and equipment. Students cannot learn to read and write without materials and supplies, and they cannot learn physical skills without the necessary equipment.

The department's budget is usually focused on equipment and supplies. Funds for personnel and facilities come from a larger, total school budget. Physical educators need to understand the overall school budget and funding procedures, because personnel, facilities, and equipment are important factors in curriculum construction. The priority should always be additional personnel before new facilities or equipment.

In addition to the basic departmental budget, funds may be available through outside sources. Sometimes the athletic department will share equipment with the physical education department.

Boundary cones, jump ropes, and basketballs, for example, can be used by both departments. With tight budgets, this is an effective way to cut costs. Various community and parent groups like the Lions or Rotary Club may help with short-term funding for special facility or equipment needs such as a weight room, racquetball courts, or tennis racquets. Some schools allow departments to have special fund-raising campaigns involving the students and faculty. Car washes, candy sales, or admission to special sports demonstrations are useful projects for generating funds.

The best programs are not necessarily the ones with the most funding, but a certain amount of funding helps in producing a high-quality curriculum. All possible options for funding should be considered, and educators must be aggressive in their search for adequate funding.

Athletics, Intramurals, and Sports Clubs

These programs should be an adjunct to the basic physical education curriculum. The programs can serve a valuable function by offering additional opportunities for students to participate in physical activities and develop positive activity habits. All students should be able to find success in one or several of these programs. The programs give students a variety of experiences, depending on the specific situation (i.e., winning, losing, teamwork, friendships, deferred goals, perserverence, and dedication). The experience depends in part on how each program is developed and emphasized.

Physical educators should be aware that the availability, leadership, and emphasis of these three programs can have a significant positive or negative impact on the physical education curriculum. Many schools use the physical education curriculum as training for the athletic program. In many situations, athletes lift weights year round and receive physical education credit for athletic program participation. These students become highly specialized and do not have an opportunity to learn any lifetime sport skills. The educator must remember that the goals of the athletic program should be different than the goals of the physical education program. Community pressure can be extremely powerful in influencing the athletic program. Physical educators need to take leadership roles in all three programs and make sure that proper goals are stressed and protected.

Athletic, intramural, and sport club programs can be used to develop interest and enthusiasm for the physical education curriculum. Efforts should be made to coordinate offerings in the curriculum with offerings from athletics, intramurals, and sport clubs. A student taking a basic junior high basketball class may decide to play intramural basketball or to try out for the freshman team. A student in the school ski club may elect to take skiing in the physical education curriculum. A student playing intramural tennis may improve enough to make the varsity tennis team. Equipment and facilities can be bought, developed, and shared by all four groups. These programs can complement each other in a number of ways if a cooperative effort is made by program leaders. Physical educators should use their experience and knowledge of these programs to help develop other leaders from the school and community. With help and training, a math or science teacher can direct the intramural program or organize a sailing club for students, or a parent from the community might work with a teacher in organizing a backpacking or fishing club.

The Elementary School Physical Education Program

A sound secondary school physical education program should be built on the foundation of the elementary school physical education curriculum. Many school districts do not have adequate communication between elementary and secondary program organizers. Each section may act autonomously, without regard for other grades. Secondary curriculum planners should consider the elementary school program goals, activities, and teaching procedures. The transition from elementary to secondary programs will be smoother if learning activities and teaching procedures progress with continuity.

The daily format of the junior high program can be similar to the elementary school format with an introductory activity, a fitness activity, and a lesson focus. Students can learn about continuity drills, management procedures, and sideline soccer in the elementary school and then follow through with similar, but advanced, activities in the junior high program. Drills and skill work for basketball at the senior high level can be based on the junior high drills and skill work. Physical fitness activities such as circuit drills, exercises to music, and squad leader exercises can be used at all three levels (elementary through secondary) with modification. Similar teaching styles, methods, and behaviors are used advantageously at various times for all levels (e.g., station work, contracts, or teacher-leader activities).

A well-organized and educationally sound elementary curriculum that is linked with a similar secondary school physical education curriculum is certainly a positive situation for students and teachers. Many advantages are possible in terms of time management, learning progressions, staff motivation, student motivation, equipment purchasing, and idea sharing. An articulated physical education curriculum, K–12, can offer a number of interesting advantages.

Step 6: Determine Areas of Program Emphasis

Curriculum planners need to determine if specific areas within the model are going to be emphasized. Is the model going to focus on one or two areas such as outdoor adventure activities, knowledge concepts, or physical fitness routines and units? Is the model going to be focused on a multi-activity arrangement with a balance of a wide variety of short units to ensure breadth of exposure to all students? A percentage of time could be alloted to the various categories of activities such as team sports, lifetime sports, water sports, recreational games, and dance activities. Are longer units available for depth of exposure? Will students have a choice of activities or will the yearly sequence of units be required?

Some physical educators feel that a curriculum should focus on accomplishing only one or two objectives (Siedentop, Mand, and Taggart, 1986). The type of program and the amount of emphasis within each program is going to be determined by the public, the facilities, and the support available in each situation. A new curriculum at the secondary level cannot be all things to all people. It takes time and patience to get started and to gain the type of support necessary. It is best to think big but start small and progress slowly toward the goals.

Step 7: Select Appropriate Activities

Appropriate activities must be selected to accomplish program goals. These activities should blend the desires of society with the objectives of the program and the interests of the students. A program planner should realize that the interests of students cannot be the sole basis for a curriculum. Students cannot make all decisions on the courses and activities in the curriculum because they are not trained in educational programming. This does not mean, however, that activities selected by the educator cannot be interesting or enjoyable.

For example, 8th graders going through the adolescent growth spurt should be required to take short units covering a wide variety of physical activities to provide them with success in basic skills like running, dribbling, and throwing. Long, indepth units featuring specialized skills could be boring and frustrating for less-skilled students at this developmental level. Conversely, an 11th grader should have an opportunity to choose a semester unit in modern dance, tennis, racquetball, or another area that is highly specialized and in line with her or his interest. Senior high school is not the time to require students to take a unit they have little or no desire to pursue. A 7th grade girl should be required to try a variety of health-related fitness activities, but should also be able to choose an aerobics unit from available options. A 10th grade boy interested in body building should have the option to choose from several levels and types of resistance training.

Activity selection should not be based solely on the interests or teaching competencies of teachers directing the programs. Often, teacher interests were determined 10–15 years earlier, and are not activities that are popular in our society today. This emphasizes the need for teachers to continually expand their activity knowledge and expertise.

The curriculum planner should try to provide a balance of activities from different categories. Common categories emphasized are team sports, lifetime sports, physical conditioning, dance activities, aquatic activities, adventure activities, and self-testing activities. Activities in various categories can overlap, depending on the definition of the category. An important point is to assure that all students have experience with several activities selected from as many categories as possible in each school setting. Too often, the curriculum is heavily tipped toward team sports because of class size, facilities, equipment, or the instructor's lack of interest or ability.

An unbalanced curriculum is not appropriate for students who are interested in activity categories not offered. For example, many students enjoy Frisbee, orienteering, modern dance, or skin diving. They may not enjoy football, basketball, wrestling, or volleyball. If the curriculum is unbalanced, then these students will not have access to potentially fulfilling activities. Teachers must make every effort to offer a balanced program.

Activities should be selected and directed with the objectives of the program in mind. The skillful curriculum planner chooses activities that influence the habits of people in both the health-related and play areas. Activities cannot be justified unless they are fulfilling program goals. Initially, many students may not be interested in health-related fitness and have to be positively directed toward those activities. They need a gentle push to engage in the activities until the reinforcing aspects of physical exercise have developed a "positively addicted" person. All students should be able to find activities for play and health-related fitness in the physical education curriculum. Physical education programs must take a leadership role in trying to shape activity preferences, and teachers should select activities with this goal in mind.

Step 8: Arrange Units into a Year-Long and a Year-to-Year Sequence

After selecting the activities, the next step is to sequence them over the length of the school year, and from the first year to the second year, and so on until the students have graduated. A number of theoretical and practical factors should be considered in the arrangement of activities.

Horizontal versus Vertical

There are two major concerns in activity arrangement sequence. The first is horizontal articulation and deals with activities that are to be taught during the school year for a specific grade level. Horizontal organization of the curriculum is most often developed by physical educators. It describes to the instructors what activities are to be taught, when they are to be taught, and how long they will be taught. Without this organizational scheme, teachers would have little direction and knowledge about how to help students achieve desired goals.

Vertical articulation is less often tended to by curriculum planners. It delineates what activities will be taught at different grade levels. When done correctly, the vertical curriculum demands that teachers at the elementary, junior high, and senior high schools be keenly aware of what is being taught at each respective level. In physical education, the common practice has been to teach the same activities, in much the same manner, year after year. Important concepts such as sequence, progression, and continuity have been ignored as teachers at different grade levels work autonomously. Effective vertical articulation assures that related knowledge, skills, and attitudes are distributed over the 10- to 12-year school career of students. School districts with well-developed curricula have coordinated the efforts of physical educators at all levels.

Depth versus Breadth

The length of an activity unit varies from 1 week to 1 semester. Developmental level and interests of students affect the length of a unit, as does the school schedule and the number of days per week that a class meets. Finally, departmental philosophy on the concepts of depth and breadth in an activity will influence the length of units and the arrangement of varying levels of units.

Breadth in a curriculum refers to the offering of many short units throughout the year. A curriculum that offers 18 two-week-long units illustrates breadth of curriculum. Depth in a curriculum refers to the offering of fewer but longer units. A curriculum that offers 4 units, each of which is 9 weeks long, has depth in these activities. Depth can be added to a curriculum by offering intermediate- and advanced-level units in addition to beginning units (see Chapter 5). Generally, a junior high school program should provide activity breadth, while the senior high school program focuses on depth.

Progression and Continuity

Activities should be arranged from simple to complex. Students need to experience success quickly and then find challenges in the activities after experiencing success. The arrangement should also move from safe activities to activities with a controlled element of risk and danger. Proper steps, intervals, or sequences should be provided between activities so that students will be successful and develop positive attitudes. Curriculum planners build on students' previous skills and knowledge. This can be done both within the year (horizontally) and between the years (vertically). For example, team handball uses skills from soccer, basketball, and volleyball, and can be included after these three units have been taught. Intermediate basketball should build on beginning basketball activities, and soccer in the 8th grade should build on soccer experiences learned in the 7th grade.

A curriculum coordinator or department head within each school should supervise the arrangement of activities for that school. A coordinator at a higher level should supervise communication and progression of activities between the elementary and junior high, and between the junior high and senior high schools.

After-School Programs

Athletics, intramurals, sport clubs, YMCA and YWCA leagues, and parks and recreation programs offer students many activity programs after school. Specific activities are usually offered at the same time each year. Interest and motivation in specific activities usually increase during the time of the year when the activities are offered. Physical educators can capitalize on this heightened interest period by coordinating the physical education sequence of activities with after-school programs. For example, a track and field unit could be scheduled to end when the city track meet sponsored by the parks and recreation department occurs. Soccer could be offered in the fall in conjunction with the popular YMCA soccer leagues. Basketball could be coordinated with the school intramural program, and wrestling offered before an AAU wrestling tournament. Coordinating activities with all after-school programs can be dif-

ficult. The effort will be worthwhile, however, in terms of student motivation and increasing the number of students in after-school programs.

Weather and Facilities

The sequence of activities must be coordinated with weather conditions and the availability of equipment and facilities. Skiing, sailing, ice skating, and other outdoor activities require specific weather conditions that occur only at certain times of year. Some schools have outdoor pools available during the early fall and late spring periods. Off-campus areas may be available only during certain times of the year due to climate or public interest in the activity (e.g., golf ranges, bowling alleys, or surfing beaches). All factors should be checked carefully before making the final arrangement of activities.

Step 9: Evaluate and Modify the Curriculum

The final and on-going step in maintaining an effective curriculum is evaluation. Program evaluation that focuses on the general objectives of the program is called summative evaluation. Summative evaluation provides information about how well the curriculum as a whole affects students. Differentiating between curriculum and instruction is difficult. These areas intertwine and a program will not improve without constant evaluation in both areas.

Evaluating curriculum involves looking at three aspects: the curriculum itself, the performance of the students, and the effectiveness of the instructor. To evaluate curriculum, summative evaluation can be completed using a variety of checklists, rating scales, and self-appraisal instruments. Student responses can be analyzed and their performance evaluated with knowledge tests, fitness tests, performance objectives for physical skills, attitude and self-concept inventories, and free-time activity questionnaires (see Chapter 12). Instruction and teaching procedures can be evaluated using several coding instruments and devices (see Chapter 11).

Curriculum evaluation should serve to remind the instructor of the program goals and objectives, and should offer insight into program direction and progress. Figure 3.5 is an example of an evaluation instrument. Figure 3.6 is a formal instrument that can be used to evaluate programs on a point basis. The list of items presented can be a self-evaluation tool for analyzing the program. Each item should be rated according to the scale explained at the top of the form.

CURRICULUM EVALUATION QUESTIONS

1. Are students incorporating physical activity into their life-styles?
2. Are students returning to optional programs after they have completed the mandatory years?
3. Are students acquiring competency in physical skills?
4. Do students understand the concepts of developing and maintaining personal fitness for a lifetime?
5. Are students reaching a desirable level of physical fitness through participation in the program?
6. Do students possess the requisite knowledge required to participate in a wide variety of sports, games, and exercises?
7. Have students acquired social and emotional skills necessary for productive participation in school and society?
8. Does the curriculum leave students with a broad understanding of the wealth of physical activities available to them (balance)?
9. Does the curriculum allow students to leave school with a high level of competency in a few activities (depth)?
10. Does the curriculum follow a progressive sequence within the school year as well as between school years (horizontal and vertical curriculum)?

FIGURE 3.5   Curriculum evaluation questions

PROGRAM EVALUATION

0 points: Unacceptable. There is no compliance with the stated criteria.

1 point: Inadequate coverage. There is doubt about any compliance and little attention is paid to the stated criteria.

2 points: Adequate coverage. It is apparent that attention has been given to the criteria; however, there is room for improvement.

3 points: Excellent coverage. The program is exemplary in meeting the stated criteria.

Read each criterion, determine the extent to which there is compliance, then write in the appropriate scale score. If there is doubt about meeting certain criteria, list the lower of the two scores.

PHILOSOPHY AND PROGRAM IMPLEMENTATION

_____ 1. A written statement is available that describes the philosophy and principles on which the program is based.

_____ 2. Physical education is seen as an integral part of the total school curriculum and receives support similar to any other area of the school curriculum.

_____ 3. The program is constructed based on the desires of its constituency.

_____ 4. A written and updated version of a K–12 curriculum guide is available for the conduct and implementation of the program.

_____ 5. The physical education curriculum delineates horizontal and vertical structure. Teachers know what is to be taught during the school year as well as what is taught at different grade levels.

_____ 6. Activities are listed in units of instruction in proper progression and sequence.

_____ 7. Daily lesson plans are developed from the units of instruction and provide direction for instruction.

FIGURE 3.6   Formal program evaluation instrument

_____ 8. Physical education is regarded as an instructional program with emphasis on educating the child in contrast to providing time for tournaments or free play.

_____ 9. Students are taught the "how and why" of physical activity. Emphasis is placed on cognitive learning as well as on psychomotor learning.

_____ 10. All students take part in a regular program of physical education. Substitution of music, driver education, and athletics for physical education does not occur.

_____ 11. Programs at the junior high school level emphasize variety and exposure to a large number of activities.

_____ 12. The high school program allows students to elect the activities in which they choose to participate.

_____ 13. Students with handicaps can participate fully in the program and are offered a wide range of opportunities.

_____ 14. Students with medical problems are identified and monitored for follow-up examinations regularly.

_____ 15. A physician's written statement is the only way students are permanently excused from physical education.

_____ 16. The school has a nurse trained to treat accidents.

_____ 17. Provisions are made for dealing with students desiring to be excused from physical education classes. The plan is consistent and educationally sound.

_____ 18. The grading system used in physical education is consistent with that used in other curriculum areas.

_____ 19. There are provisions for public relations and sharing the program with parents. Demonstrations and information are shared regularly with the public.

_____ 20. The physical education faculty has a plan for professional growth that includes in-service training, professional meetings, university course-work, conferences, and independent study.

_____ 21. Instruction is regarded as a dynamic process and is analyzed through self-evaluation and by outside personnel. Evaluations take place at regular intervals.

_____ 22. Intramurals are seen as an outgrowth of the physical education program. A wide variety of activities is offered for student participation.

_____ 23. The athletic program is seen as a separate entity and not as an end result of or goal for the physical education program.

_____ 24. Teachers separate physical education instruction and athletic coaching. Physical education is taught for the student body and athletics are offered for those students who excel.

Comments:

CURRICULUM ANALYSIS

1. The physical education program provides learning experiences to help each student attain the following:

_____ a. A personalized level of physical fitness and body conditioning.

_____ b. Specialized sport skills in a wide variety of activities.

_____ c. Knowledge of rules, techniques, and strategy related to individual, dual, and team sports.

_____ d. Desirable social standards and ethical behavior.

_____ e. Knowledge and practice of safety standards for self and others.

_____ f. Competence in activities that can be used for leisure pursuits.

_____ g. Knowledge and practice of concepts leading to human wellness.

FIGURE 3.6 Continued

_____ 2. Activities are progressively organized and adjusted to suit the maturity and skill levels of youngsters.

_____ 3. Students are treated with dignity and encouraged to participate in all phases of the program.

_____ 4. The program offers a variety of activities that will be attractive to all students. This includes skilled and unskilled, low-fit, and handicapped students.

_____ 5. Each daily lesson has a portion (10–15 min) of time devoted to physical fitness development.

_____ 6. An up-to-date library of physical education books, filmstrips, and related materials is available for students and teachers.

_____ 7. There is an aquatic program available in the school or community so all students have the opportunity to learn to swim.

_____ 8. Indoor and outdoor teaching stations are available for instruction.

_____ 9. The yearly curriculum is written. It is reevaluated each year, and modifications are made that facilitate attainment of objectives.

_____ 10. Units of instruction vary in length depending on the maturity and skill level of students. Block plans for each unit are developed and include skill instruction on a regular basis.

_____ 11. Lead-up games are taught to students in order to isolate and develop specific skills that need to be learned.

_____ 12. Student input is welcomed. Instruments designed to monitor student interests and desires are administered on a regular basis.

_____ 13. Students are allowed to make choices about the types of activity they want to learn.

_____ 14. Units that focus on self-assessment are offered during the freshman year. Results are used to help students find the types of activities they want to participate in for a lifetime.

Comments:

FACILITIES, EQUIPMENT, AND SUPPLIES

_____ 1. Maximum use of facilities for physical education instruction is apparent.

_____ 2. Outdoor facilities meet the basic acreage standard of 5 acres plus 1 acre for each additional 100 students.

3. Outdoor facilities include the following:

_____ a. Areas where different games and activities can be conducted without interference.

_____ b. Areas for court games.

_____ c. Backstops and goals for softball, soccer, and basketball, team handball, and field hockey.

_____ d. Suitable fencing for safety and control.

_____ e. Outdoor grassy areas that are free from rock, sprinkler heads, and other hazards that might cause injury.

4. Indoor facilities meet the following standards:

_____ a. They are clean, sanitary, and free from hazards.

_____ b. They are well lighted, well ventilated, heated, cooled, and treated for proper acoustics.

_____ c. They are surfaced with a nonslip finish and include painted game area lines.

_____ 5. Periodic inspection of all facilities and equipment, both indoor and outdoor, is conducted, and a written report sent to the appropriate administrators.

_____ 6. Storage facilities are adequate for supplies and portable equipment.

_____ 7. Adequate provision is made for off-season storage of equipment, apparatus, and supplies.

FIGURE 3.6 Continued

_____ 8. An office is provided for the physical education instructors that has a telephone for emergencies and clear vision into the locker room areas.

_____ 9. Basic supplies are sufficient for all instructional units. This includes a piece of equipment for each student when necessary.

_____ 10. Equipment necessary to teach units properly is available. This includes tumbling mats, basketball goals, volleyball standards and nets, gymnastic equipment, and so forth.

_____ 11. Personal storage lockers are available for students.

_____ 12. Adequate room is available for students for changing into proper physical activity attire.

_____ 13. Equipment and supplies necessary for the testing and evaluation program are available.

_____ 14. Tape recorders, record players, and records are available in sufficient number for the rhythmic program.

_____ 15. An adequate yearly budget is available for equipment repair, replacement, and development of new units of instruction.

Comments:

FIGURE 3.6   Continued

REFERENCES AND SUGGESTED READINGS

AAHPERD. 1987. *Basic Stuff Series*. Reston, VA: AAHPERD.

Bain, L. 1975. The hidden curriculum in physical education. *Quest* 24: 92–101.

Berliner, D. 1979. Tempus educare. In P. Peterson and H. Walberg (eds.) *Research on Teaching*, Berkeley, CA: McCutchan Publishing.

Corbin, C., and Lindsey, R. 1990. *Fitness for Life*. 3rd ed. Glenview, IL: Scott, Foresman & Company.

Darst, P., Beauchamp, L., and Thompson, L. 1989. What's going on in high school physical education: A descriptive study. Paper presented at the AAHPERD Convention, Boston.

Hellison, D. R. 1978. *Beyond Balls and Bats*. Reston, VA: AAHPERD.

Hellison, D. R. 1895. *Goals and Strategies for Teaching Physical Education*. Champaign, IL: Human Kinetics Publishers.

Jewett, A., and Mullan, M. 1977. *Curriculum Design: Purposes and Processes in Physical Education Teaching-Learning*. Reston, VA: AAHPERD.

Laban, R. 1963. *Modern Educational Dance*. 2nd ed., revised by L. Ullman. New York: Praeger Publishers.

Lindeman, L., Wardrop, D., and Leake, R. 1981. *Utah High School Physical Education Interests and Attitudes*. Utah State Office of Education, Salt Lake City, UT.

Mager, R. 1968. *Developing Attitude Toward Learning*. Belmont, CA: Fearon Publishers.

Metzler, M. 1979. The measurement of academic learning time in physical education. Doctoral dissertation, The Ohio State University.

Parker, M., and Steen, T. 1988. Outdoor pursuits and physical education: Making the connection. *Newsletter of the Council on Outdoor Education*. 30(1): 4.

Seidel, B., et al. 1980. *Sports Skills. A Conceptual Approach to Meaningful Movement*. 2nd ed. Dubuque, IA: Wm. C. Brown Group.

Siedentop, D. 1980(a). Physical education curriculum: An analysis of the past. *JOPERD* 51(7): 40–41.

Siedentop, D. 1980(b). *Physical Education — Introductory Analysis*. 3rd ed. Dubuque, IA: Wm. C. Brown Group.

Siedentop, D., Mand, C., and Taggart, A. 1986. *Physical Education — Teaching and Curriculum Strategies for Grades 5–12*. Palo Alto, CA: Mayfield Publishing Co.

Wilson, B., and Altieri, P. 1978. Complying with Title IX — Increasing participation through the elective program. *Arizona JOHPERD* 21(2): 6–7.

4 ADOLESCENCE AND THE JUNIOR HIGH SCHOOL CURRICULUM

There is a strong possibility that the junior high school curriculum may be the most important link in the chain of the total school curriculum. The junior high school years represent the first time students are able to make personal decisions about what they like and dislike. Decisions made are often irreversible and may last a lifetime. Unfortunately, this is often a time when students choose to avoid physical activity. If teachers and administrators know this is a critical time for youngsters, they should do everything possible to keep students excited about activity through a well-organized and expertly taught program. Unfortunately, it is often difficult to find a curriculum which is designed expressly for the adolescent student. Too often, the curriculum is a watered down high school curriculum or an extension of the elementary school curriculum. Neither program suits adolescents; they need a program that is designed to meet traits and characteristics that are unique to their stage of development.

THE CRITICAL YEARS OF ADOLESCENCE

Never again will youngsters have to experience as many major changes as they do during junior high school. Youngsters at this level want to be independent but still desire the security of authority. This places teachers in a situation where they are consistently challenged and questioned, but expected to exert their authority when necessary. It is important to understand the developmental characteristics of these youngsters in order to effectively teach them (see pp. 42–43). The following sections discuss characteristics and follow with a discussion of the implication of various traits.

Physical Characteristics

Rapid and Uneven Growth. Junior high school students go through a rapid and uneven growth spurt. Girls go through this spurt about 1.5 years earlier than boys and are usually taller and more mature early in this period. Once boys experience the growth spurt, they pass girls in height and weight. The final result is a wide range of physical maturity which had gone unnoticed in the elementary school years.

Implications. Teachers need to recognize the number of problems caused by the rapid and uneven growth. Girls will often be stronger, faster, and larger than boys. Boys may feel uneasy about this growth difference between the sexes as well as among themselves. More than ever, activities will have to be adjusted to account for the size and skill differences. Teachers can expect that boys who have not entered puberty will not be as strong and quick and will feel uneasy about competing in physical contact sports. Girls who are developmentally advanced or retarded may feel insecure and not want to participate in physical education activities. Teachers must take time to discuss this wide variation in maturity and help youngsters understand that they are normal. In addition, students must come to grips with the impact their physical size and development will have on their choice of participation in various physical activities.

Decreased Effectiveness to Learn Motor Skills. The range of motor ability broadens, and the skill level differences of students become increasingly apparent. Motor abilities are developing slowly due to the increase in growth velocity. Awkwardness, poor coordination, low strength, and low endurance are common during rapid growth spurts. As students go through puberty they develop secondary sexual characteristics. Boys experience facial hair, pubic hair, a voice change, and genital and shoulder development. Girls develop breasts, pubic hair, a widening of the hips, and an accumulation of body fat.

Implications. When growth velocity is high, the predisposition to learn motor skills is decreased. This makes the junior high school years a difficult time to teach new skills that are tough to master. Combined with an unwillingness to fail in front of peers, students soon learn to avoid activity or choose to avoid learning new skills in order to assure they are not embarrassed. A focus on individual and dual activities will minimize the risk of public failure. In addition, all units of instruction should start youngsters with success. This will prevent the tendency of adolescents to speak negatively (and loudly) about their dislike of the unit when they are failing. Finally, teachers must remember that students will develop musculature and add body fat which can change the body's center of gravity and perceptual awareness. Curriculum activities should allow students to relearn old skills and build on their past successes.

Modification of Physical Traits. Boys are stronger and may have more endurance than girls. Many girls have an advantage over boys in the areas of balance and flexibility. Posture is often poor due to social pressure. Ossification of the bones is usually not complete.

Implications. Physical performance differences between sexes become obvious to students. This increased awareness of physical differences demands that teachers discuss the differences and the importance of posture and lifetime fitness. An understanding of different body types and their impact on physical performance is important so students can begin to select activities that are well suited to their particular build and physique. Because of incomplete bone ossification, it may be a good time to avoid heavy physical contact sports in order to avoid permanent damage to the skeletal system. In addition, it is important to learn to participate in physical activities with others regardless of their ability levels. This is a time when students form cliques and choose to participate only with those who have similar capabilities. This can lead to a separation of sexes and friends with differing skill levels which is an undesirable outcome and may be self-limiting as students mature.

Social, Emotional, and Intellectual Development

Independence and Peer Groups. Students have a strong desire for independence. They believe that adults (authority figures) are old-fashioned. A desire to make decisions for themselves exists, and students are torn between adult and peer values. Peer groups, providing the standards for behavior, represent independence because of the absence of adults. Leaders, followers, and loyalty start to evolve from group dynamics. Fighting with parents and peers is common at this age, as is competitiveness.

Implications. Independence is an important trait that students *need* to learn. If students do not learn independence, they become liabilities to society since they cannot make decisions which contribute to the betterment of the community. Thus, it is important to provide situations that will allow youngsters to make decisions in a somewhat structured setting. They can learn the consequences of their decisions and behavior without finding themselves in a life-threatening situation. Teachers should allow opportunities for leadership skill development and help youngsters develop their decision-making skills. Participation in game and sport activities will help students understand the importance of rules in maintaining an environment which is acceptable to all participants.

Emotional Instability. Moods change quickly, for this is an emotional and unpredictable period. Students may be unstable, angry, fearful, and easily upset.

Implications. The moodiness of junior high school students is often precipitated by their rapid development and lack of experience in dealing with new social situations. Teachers must strive to be even-tempered and unruffled by students' consistent mood changes. It is interesting to note that students want great freedom to express their behavior and desires, but expect teachers to be perfect models. It is a time when teachers must display patience and direction without excessive force. In addition, teachers must be careful about avoiding double standards: expecting students to do as they are told regardless of the teacher's behavior. Generally, this is totally unacceptable to students in this age group and they will be quick to tell the teacher about such inconsistencies.

Social Awareness. Students are interested in improving themselves, especially in the physical area. Weight training, body building, and figure control or development are of special interest. Strong concerns about size and abilities are common. Grooming, clothes, and appearance become important since students are overly self-conscious about their bodies. Romantic interests begin at this age range and students try to impress each other in various ways. Girls are usually ahead of boys socially and may begin to date older boys. Social activities become important, and dances, movies, parties, and athletic events serve as social meeting places.

Implications. Teachers need to provide discussions about physiological changes. Acceptance of varying capacities and limitations is important to assure students begin to realize the importance of accepting individual differences. Allowing students to express themselves without ridicule or embarrassment is an important requisite for assuring that students learn to accept themselves. Finally, a number of social activities should be provided for students so they learn proper social behavior in a variety of settings.

Intellectual Development. Intellectual development continues throughout this period. Students can concentrate longer, are able to understand more complex concepts, and are better able to follow directions. An interest in the "why" of physical activity occurs. Daydreaming and fantasizing are lessening for many students. The variety of student activities decreases continually throughout this period and into adulthood. Students begin to make decisions about areas in which they want to specialize. This has strong implications for future sport and physical activity participation. A strong interest in risk, excitement, and adventure is common.

Implications. Intellectual development among students can be exciting for teachers since interaction can be meaningful and challenging. It becomes important to tell students why they are being taught certain activities rather than telling them to do it, "because I said so." It is important to help students become familiar with their physical abilities so they can make wise and thoughtful choices about activities that match their skills. Students in junior high school will often enjoy high-risk activities and will make poor decisions due to their desire to show off and impress others. It is important to assure that safety procedures have been thoroughly covered and that students understand the consequences of their behavior.

To summarize, the needs of students will probably be met if the teachers understand that junior high school students will display behavior which is unique to this age group. It should be expected, channeled into successful experiences, and managed by an understanding teacher. The following guidelines offer direction when presenting activities to students:

1. Arrange lesson presentations which assure that students will be successful. Avoid situations which embarrass or belittle students. Make failure a minor part of the program. Help students major in success!

2. Organize the presentation so individual differences are recognized and respected. Students need to feel that not all of them are expected to do the amount of activity regardless of ability level.

3. Keep all students active and involved in learning. Assure this occurs by providing individual assistance to all students. The best feedback is always given on a one-to-one basis; group instruction is always a compromise.

4. When necessary, group students by ability level. Most students learn best when they feel they have something in common with others. On the other hand, caution must be used with grouping to avoid the stigma of always being in the "slow group." A combination of homogeneous and heterogeneous grouping by skill level is probably the best answer.

5. Modify the activities to offer more success for more students. There is nothing sacred about playing the regulation game. Games were meant to be modified in order to provide the most enjoyment for participants. If this means lowering baskets, reducing distances, and changing rules, do it. Remember that student success is always more important than the integrity of the game.

SCOPE AND SEQUENCE OF THE JUNIOR HIGH SCHOOL CURRICULUM

Elementary school physical education approaches place emphasis on expanding the activity experiences of students. Youngsters enter kindergarten with similar skills. The physical education curriculum strives to offer a wide variety of activities to assure that students have the opportunity to experience success. In addition, a wide variety of activities assures that students will be involved in short units of instruction in order to minimize long bouts of failure. If units are short, students who don't like a certain activity or feel like failures know they will not have to continue the activity for long. In addition, the wide variety of short units assures that all students will find some activity they enjoy, increasing their opportunity to experience success.

In junior high school, it is important that this variety of units continue. In addition, the units should continue to be short to assure that students will not have to endure a unit of activity they dislike. It is important to assure that the **scope** of the curriculum is adequate. Scope refers to the breadth of activity at each grade level. A balanced curriculum places equal emphasis on all activities in the curriculum consistent with the program objectives and goals. Activities should meet the needs and interests of all learners. For example, a design that offers four or five team sports during the year will not meet the needs of students who do not like team sports, are uninterested in the sports offered, or prefer individual activities. Depending on the goals of the approach, activities should help students and instructors reach the desired outcomes. If skills for leisure are a goal, such activities need to be offered. Finally, balance should be a sole function of the physical education program. Balance is not achieved by integrating intramural and extramural programs into the overall program evaluation. The point here is that many students will choose not to participate in extracurricular activities; therefore a balanced curriculum should be a function of what happens in physical education regardless of outside activities.

Another important consideration in organizing the junior high school curriculum is the matter of **sequence**. Sequence is the order that units of instruction are presented on a year-to-year basis. Organized correctly, sequence should assure that students receive instruction in a progressive manner from kindergarten to graduation. Skills should be learned in a sequential manner, so that skills learned previously serve as the building blocks for new skills. Sequence is sometimes difficult to find in physical education curricula; teachers start youngsters in basketball in the first grade and continue a repetitious presentation of the sport until students leave school. This is similar to giving youngsters a calculus book in first grade, asking them to repeat the material for 12 years, and assuming that they have learned calculus.

Sequence in the junior high school years should ensure that the units of instruction are organized and designed expressly for this age level. At times, teachers will teach high school or elementary units to junior high school youngsters only to find that they are bored or failing. In addition, the sequence of activities should not place excessive emphasis on strategy and advanced skill. Students at this age are in a rapid growth curve which reduces the ability to learn motor skills. Asking students to split their concentration on skill performance and strategy reduces the odds that they will be successful. As an example, think back to learning to drive a car for the first time. It was difficult to concentrate on the fine motor skills involved in driving while thinking about the rules of the road. Frustration and fear can be the result of this type of overload. Until a skill is overlearned, it is important that students be allowed to concentrate solely on skill performance. When the skills have become overlearned, students can begin to concentrate on the cognitive side of skill performance. Techniques and game strategy should be emphasized after basic skills are refined. Remember that most junior high school students have not learned skills to the point that they are automatic and able to be performed without intense concentration.

Another consideration in scope and sequence is to understand that it is impossible to design a curriculum with a sequence that is perfect for all young-

sters. Students are always grouped (whether it be by grade, age, or developmental level) and every group is characterized by a range of differences. To expect students to strictly follow a written sequence is unrealistic. Effective teachers will have to modify the sequence depending on the capabilities of the student. As mentioned earlier, the best teaching is one-on-one, when activities and instruction are in line with the student's ability level. In summary it is important to remember that scope and sequence are important because they lend general direction to instruction. However, in order to meet the needs of all students, the scope and sequence will need to be modified.

JUNIOR HIGH SCHOOL CURRICULA: A REVIEW

Curricula for elementary school and high school students are abundant and specifically designed for the respective ages of participants. Unfortunately, plans for 7th and 8th grade students are practically nonexistent. In most cases, junior high school programs are adaptations of an elementary or high school curriculum. In many designs, virtually no consideration is given to the unique characteristics, abilities, interests, and developmental levels of students at this age. In fact, the physical education curriculum at the junior high school level has generated little professional attention. Siedentop (1980a) notes:

> Also, there is a continuing under-emphasis of the middle school curriculum, a fact that we can ill afford to ignore much longer, particularly in physical education where the developmental aspects of that period seem so susceptible to well-conceived, sensitively planned programs of physical education. (p. 41)

A number of 7th and 8th grade approaches have been patterned after the high school format. This arrangement is not the best situation for the majority of junior high students.

Schedule of Classes

Most junior high schools follow a block or traditional schedule with classes meeting every day for a constant length of time (45–55 min). Another common schedule pattern is called a 3/2 "swing" schedule. Physical education is paired with another subject area or a study hall, and the students attend class three days per week during the first semester and two days per week during the second semester. The students attend the study hall or the other subject area class (usually health) on the opposite days. The students "flip" their schedules at the end of the first semester from Monday, Wednesday, and Friday to

Tuesday and Thursday. Another common 7th and 8th grade schedule arrangement is to meet for physical education only twice a week all year long.

In a flexible schedule arrangement (see Chapter 3), classes might meet for varying lengths of time throughout the week. For example, one meeting might last for 45 min, and then two additional meetings would last for 90 min each. The flexible arrangement allows for lecture-laboratory approaches, travel time off campus, and better use of teachers and facilities.

Each of these arrangements offers some advantages and disadvantages for students, teachers, and school districts in terms of money and teaching-learning effectiveness. Curricula that schedule students for daily physical education class (as compared with class held every other day) cost more money in terms of teaching personnel but can provide more opportunities for successful involvement in physical activities. Teachers have a better chance to guide and counsel students when they interact with them daily. The effectiveness of the learning environment is reduced when teachers see a new group of students every other day. With a flexible schedule more money is spent on administrative maintenance, but the program can provide unique opportunities for exploring new learning environments (e.g., travel off campus to special facilities and activities such as scuba diving, skiing, or rock climbing that require larger time blocks).

Length of Instructional Units

There is great variance in the length of each unit in 7th and 8th grade curricula. Planners must remember that the number of class meetings per week is a key factor in deciding the length of a unit. A 3-wk unit that meets daily offers 15 sessions, while a 3-wk unit that meets twice a week allows only 6 sessions. Although both are 3-wk units, there is a big difference in what can be accomplished.

A common arrangement in the 7th and 8th grades consists of long units focused on seasonal athletic activities. Units are 6–9 wks and focus on a seasonal athletic sport. Students might take four to six activities in a year. The design would look similar to the following:

- First 9 wks — Flag football or soccer
- Second 9 wks — Basketball
- Third 9 wks — Wrestling
- Last 9 wks — Softball or track and field

The following is a design using 6-wk units:

- First 6 wks — Swimming
- Second 6 wks — Volleyball
- Third 6 wks — Basketball
- Fourth 6 wks — Gymnastics
- Fifth 6 wks — Track and field
- Last 6 wks — Softball

Another common design is to offer two units during each 9-wk grading period. One unit would be 5 wks and the other 4 wks. In this way, students take 8 units per year. Two examples of this approach are as follows:

Program A

- First 9 wks
    Soccer (5 wks)
    Flag football (4 wks)
- Second 9 wks
    Tennis (5 wks)
    Basketball (4 wks)
- Third 9 wks
    Volleyball (5 wks)
    Tumbling (4 wks)
- Last 9 wks
    Track and field (5 wks)
    Softball (4 wks)

Program B

- First 9 wks
    Field hockey (5 wks)
    Speed-a-way (4 wks)
- Second 9 wks
    Volleyball (5 wks)
    Dance (4 wks)
- Third 9 wks
    Basketball (5 wks)
    Gymnastics (4 wks)
- Last 9 wks
    Tennis (5 wks)
    Track and field (4 wks)

Another common arrangement uses short 2- and 3-wk units that offer students 12–18 different activities during the year. The following is an example:

Weeks	*Activity*
• 1–3	Swimming
• 4–6	Volleyball
• 7–9	Tennis
• 10–12	Flag football
• 13–15	Dance
• 16–18	Basketball
• 19–21	Badminton
• 22–24	Tumbling
• 25–27	Recreational games
• 28–30	Speed-a-way
• 31–33	Track and field
• 34–36	Softball

The designs discussed range from 4 units per year to 18 units per year. The students in the 4-unit approach will get an in-depth experience with 4 activities, while the students in the 18-unit approach will receive a shorter, broader experience with many different activities. The students involved in curriculum designs between these two extremes will find a compromise between breadth and depth. The issue of breadth versus depth continues to be a controversy among physical educators.

Bain (1980) states that junior high school units should be a minimum of 10–12 weeks with in-depth instruction available for those activities of interest to students. Benson (1982) also believes that short units (2–4 wks) only offer students an opportunity to do poorly and provide little change in skill level. The authors (Pangrazi and Darst et al., 1982) have argued previously for short units for this age group because of the developmental characteristics of junior high students. These youngsters, who are going through puberty, a rapid growth spurt, and a period of slow motor development, need successful experiences with a wide variety of activities. At a time when students find it difficult to tolerate failure, longer units can lock students into a frustrating or boring experience for a long period of time. Variety and novelty in a success-oriented atmosphere are important motivational keys for this age group. Students can find success in short units when emphasis is on exposure and on learning about one's personal strengths and weaknesses. Finally, because a majority of students are still trying to identify their strengths and weaknesses, it is important that they have the opportunity to experience a wide variety of activities. One-day units of instruction (see Chapter 19) offer greater variety and help maintain student interest. The junior high school years should not be a time of specialization and refinement, rather they should be a time of exploration.

Many teachers at the junior high school level claim that the learning environment is more productive when units are changed often. Students and teachers are more highly motivated when a new activity begins. Too often, long units turn into a prolonged class tournament without structured skill work. Students begin to expect physical education classes to consist of long units of tournament play and are forced into highly competitive situations without the opportunity to develop adequate skill level. This only adds to the frustration of the less-skilled students. Finally, one of the reasons some teachers advocate long units is to minimize their preparation duties. The fewer units taught, the less planning needed. This rationale is difficult to accept if the needs of students are not realized.

Types of Activities

The most common category of activity in the junior high school is team sports (e.g, flag football, basketball, volleyball, wrestling, track and field, softball). Many physical educators claim that these are the most popular activities with students and that they are the most economical activities in terms of facilities and equipment. More often than not, the truth is that they are popular with vocal students who are skilled in such sports. Less skilled students are often intimidated and afraid to admit that they don't like the sports for fear they will not be liked by their more skilled peers. In addition, sport units are economical (in terms of required equipment) when they are improperly taught. To teach basketball or softball with 3 or 4 balls assures that the majority of students will be standing rather than practicing skills in a semi-individualized manner.

Some teachers are beginning to teach lifetime sports such as tennis, badminton, bowling, and golf. These activities have more carry-over value for later life since they do not require a number of teammates for participation. Other schools have added units on popular activities such as aerobic dance, martial arts, jogging, and outdoor adventure activities like backpacking, canoeing, and rock climbing.

Innovative and successful approaches in schools develop a balance of team sports, lifetime sports, physical conditioning, dance, aquatic, and currently popular activities. Curricula that offer an activity balance in these various categories have a higher potential for positively affecting all students within the school. Certain students will find success with certain categories of activity, and schools with variety will provide more students with opportunities for success.

Physical Fitness Activities

A current concern in America is the decline of physical fitness among students. Few can debate the school's failure to provide enough activity to develop an adequate level of fitness among youth. Studies have consistently demonstrated that youngsters do not voluntarily engage in high-intensity activity (exercise heart rate above 160 beats per minute) during the school day. Secondly, since strength is an important requisite for learning and performing sport skills, it becomes an important ingredient for success in physical activities. This leads to the conclusion that schools may be shortchanging youth in the area of health and wellness by refusing to offer physical education programs that enhance their cardiovascular and strength development.

A balanced physical fitness program should offer the following to its participants:

1. Develop an understanding that maintenance of physical fitness is the responsibility of each student.
2. Provide an understanding of how fitness is developed.
3. Develop cognition of the importance of fitness as a part of wellness.
4. Provide a sound fitness development program that is part of each lesson.

Too often, there is not enough variety, progression, or challenge in the activities used. Progression is an important concept to remember when teaching fitness activities. The typical stereotype for physical fitness instruction has been the "daily dozen and run a mile" approach. This defeats everything known about individualized instruction. There is tremendous variation among students in terms of physical capacity. One of the most effective ways of turning youngsters off to exercise for a lifetime is to ask them to do more than they are capable of performing.

Programs that offer a variety of physical fitness activities and routines in a progressive and challenging manner will have a better chance of successfully influencing students. Junior high is an important time to have successful encounters with physical fitness activities. The learning sequences for this segment of the curriculum must be organized and planned for the entire year. Educators simply cannot justify the "three exercises and a lap" approach as a means to a lifetime of physical fitness.

One final word: These are the years in which students decide to "turn on" or "turn off" to physical activity. Just as there is no one way to live one's life, so there is no one way to achieve physical fitness that is meaningful for everyone. Emphasis should be placed on helping youngsters understand the different ways of maintaining fitness by exposing them to many fitness development activities. Exposure alone, however, is not enough. Students must develop knowledge and understanding of what works for them and why it works.

Requirements and Choice

Most junior high school physical education departments mandate students to take all of the activities that have been organized for the school year. Students usually do not have a choice. This arrangement is probably still the most common format regarding requirements.

A new trend, which started at the high school level and has filtered down to some junior high programs, allows students to choose activities in phys-

ical education. Classes may be open to both boys and girls, depending on their interests. Using this approach, male and female teachers work together and decide who is the better qualified to teach a specific activity. Each teacher can then develop two or three specialties and repeat teaching those specialties to different classes of students, rather than having to teach all activities to the same students.

This approach has been used in a segregated adaptation with male students grouped together and the females grouped together. The boys choose between several "boys' activities" and the girls select from different "girls' activities." A problem with this approach is that it narrows the available options. There are not as many choices as there would be if boys and girls chose from the same activities. For example, with two male teachers and two female teachers, the joint-curriculum design would provide four choices for all students, while the segregated approach would provide only two each for males and females. Another problem with the segregated design is that students may be denied access to certain activities because of sex stereotyping (e.g., boys excluded from dance or gymnastics, or girls excluded from weight training or flag football).

An example of alternating 4- and 5-week units in a coeducational curriculum with choices for students follows:

First Semester

- First 9 wks
  1. Volleyball, yoga, or soccer (4 wks)
  2. Flag football, archery, or tennis (5 wks)
- Second 9 wks
  3. Gymnastics, volleyball, or badminton (4 wks)
  4. Basketball, team handball, or field hockey (5 wks)

Second Semester

- Third 9 wks
  1. Aerobics, speed-a-way, or basketball (4 wks)
  2. Wrestling, orienteering, or volleyball (5 wks)
- Last 9 wks
  3. Softball, track and field, or badminton (4 wks)
  4. Swimming, Frisbee games, or yoga (5 wks)

Students can make four choices at the beginning of each semester. This design has been used coeducationally with males and females allowed to select any activity except a contact sport such as wrestling or flag football. If more than three teachers are available, students have the opportunity to make more choices.

The choice concept can be used with any length unit and any type of organizational schedule, and with either coeducational or segregated classes. This curriculum plan offers the following advantages:

1. More student motivation and enthusiasm and a desire to take more physical education because of a higher interest level.
2. Fewer problems with dressing, participation, and discipline.
3. Better use of teaching expertise and the development of specialists.
4. Improved instruction over a period of time.
5. Increased teacher motivation and enthusiasm.

A curriculum that increases the level of motivation of both students and teachers creates a positive environment for both teachers and students.

Some schools vary this approach by developing requirements by activity categories to ensure that breadth is provided. For example, students are required to take a certain number of team sports, lifetime sports, conditioning activities, dance units, aquatics, or recreational activities during the 7th and 8th grades. This concept is referred to as a **choice within a requirement**. Depending on the number of units offered, each student is required to take a specified number of activities from each category. If the program offers 24 three-wk units over a two-yr period, the requirements might include:

- 1 unit of wellness concepts
- 2 units of aquatics
- 2 units of dance
- 4 units of physical conditioning
- 6 units of lifetime sports
- 6 units of team sports
- 3 units of elective activities
- 24 units total

Coeducational Classes

The issue of coeducational classes continues to be a point of controversy. Some junior high schools have all physical education classes assigned with 50% boys and 50% girls. Other schools conduct a few coeducational units such as square dance, volleyball, or track and field, but offer the majority of units segregated by sex. Still other programs allow students to choose classes based on interest, so the class composition has no fixed gender percentage. In some schools, boys and girls are never taught together during physical education and are completely segregated. This is an unfortunate, illegal, and unacceptable situation, yet physical educators continue to take stands on both sides of the issue. A great deal has been written on the subject (Melograno, 1979; Blaufarb, 1978a, b) and many coeducational programs have been highly successful with boys and girls learning together.

Chapter 1 presents the issues and problems associated with Title IX and coeducational classes in physical education. The authors' experiences in this area have led to positive feelings about coeducational classes. Program objectives can be accomplished in a coeducational format. Students in grades K–6 are usually integrated in physical education classes, and there is reason to believe that they should be able to move into a coeducational format in the junior and senior high school programs.

Certainly, there are problems to be solved, such as dress, grading, puberty, comfort zones of teachers, attitudes, interest development, learning about individual differences, increasing activity choices, and improving instructional quality. Sensitive teachers working together can develop an exciting and challenging program for boys and girls. Wrestling or other contact sports are not advocated, but a balanced program that is based on the characteristics and interests of students can be effectively implemented. The complaints that many people espouse can be solved by teachers who have a strong desire to actually make the program work. The bottom line is this: regardless of the legality of the situation, teachers have a moral and educational obligation to offer coeducational classes. If both sexes do not learn to play together in a variety of activities at the junior high school level, they will undoubtedly never develop the necessary respect and understanding of differences required for successful participation.

A SUGGESTED CURRICULUM FOR GRADES 7 AND 8

The suggested curriculum discussed in this section is based on a developmental level approach. In short, a sequential arrangement of different physical activities should form the curriculum for students who are at various developmental stages. In other words, students should be involved at different levels of activity depending on their physical, social, emotional, and intellectual development. Curriculum planners must understand the characteristics, interests, and abilities of the student audience. Characteristics such as the wide range of skeletal age, the adolescent growth spurt, short attention spans, and low tolerance for failure dictate the development of junior high school curriculum. Studies (Gruelich and Pyle, 1959) have shown that a 5- to 6-year variation in skeletal age may be present among students in one grade level. Translated, this means that maturity of 11-year-olds in the 7th grade might vary in skeletal age from 8 to 14 years. Increased skeletal age usually correlates closely with success in the skilled positions in youth sport programs (Hale, 1956). This has important implications because students are usually grouped by similar chronological ages, yet students who are less mature physically are not ready to learn complex sport skills or receive in-depth instruction. To help immature students, multi-activity programs with short units and an emphasis on body management and basic movement skills can be utilized. Students who are physically advanced should be encouraged to seek opportunities outside of the school program (e.g., youth sports, YMCA leagues, city park and recreation programs, and private clubs).

Students should receive physical education daily or at least on a time basis equivalent to all other subject areas. The teacher-student ratio should be consistent with academic class ratios. Physical education is as important as math, science, and English, and the physical education schedule should be consistent with and analogous to other areas of the total school curriculum.

The daily lesson plan format for both 7th and 8th grades should include an introductory or warm-up activity (3–5 min), a physical fitness routine (10–15 min), and a lesson focus and game activity (25–30 min). (See Chapter 7 for details of the lesson plan format.) This format should be consistent and an outgrowth of the K–6 curriculum. A consistent instructional format within each class provides teachers and students with a measure of stability. The daily instructional format should be consistent in order to provide students with routine and structure. Each of the areas in the lesson plan should be planned on a yearly basis to assure that all activities will be taught. If activities are not planned, teachers will find that they forgot to include certain activities, or that they don't have enough activities for the remainder of the school year. In addition, trying to design scope and sequence is impossible if the activities are not in written format. How does one modify the curriculum when the activities presented cannot be recalled?

Introductory Activities

The introductory activity occupies 3–5 min of the total lesson format. The purpose of this is to prepare students physiologically for strenuous activity. An allied purpose is to psychologically ready students for activity. Students usually take a few minutes to become emotionally involved in activity after a day of sitting in classes. The introductory activity requires minimal organization and demands large muscle movement. It may be an integral part of the fitness routine or can be a separate entity. In either case, the introductory activity should raise the heart rate, warm up the body, and stretch the muscles in anticipation of the fitness development activity.

Teachers should change the introductory activity each week to add variety to the warm-up procedure. The 7th and 8th grade students can perform the same introductory activity. Figure 4.1 shows a recommended yearly sequence (36 wks). An in-depth discussion of introductory activities is found in Chapter 17.

Fitness Development Activities

The fitness development activity uses 10–15 min of the lesson, and its primary purpose is the development of physical fitness. Fitness routines should offer total fitness development to students. In other

Week	Activity
1	Orientation and simple games
2	Basic movements (e.g., start, stop, pivot)
3	Walk, trot, and sprint
4	Partner over and under
5	Run, stop, and pivot
6	Move, change direction, and pose on signal
7	European running
8	Flash drill
9	Marking and tag games
10	Quickness drills
11	Throwing and catching
12	Hula-Hoop movements
13	European running variations
14	File running drill
15	Manipulative skills
16	Follow-the-leader
17	Group over and under
18	New leader warm-up
19	Jumping and hopping skills
20	Walk, trot, and sprint
21	Leaping Lena
22	Rooster drill
23	Bend, stretch, and shake
24	Marking and tag games
25	Group agility drills
26	Shuffle drills
27	Running techniques
28	Partner movements
29	Fartlek running
30	Follow-the-leader
31	Throwing and catching on the move
32	Move, change direction, and pose on signal
33	Partner over and under
34	Seat rolls
35	Weave drills
36	Rubber band

FIGURE 4.1 Introductory activities for grades 7 and 8

words, an attempt should be made to develop and enhance major components of fitness, especially flexibility, muscular strength and endurance, body composition, and cardiovascular endurance. The activities should be demanding, progressive in nature, and of a type that students can utilize after graduation. Students must experience a wide variety of fitness routines so they can learn to select methods acceptable to them for a lifetime. They should leave school with the understanding that there are many ways to develop and maintain physical fitness, and the responsibility for doing so lies with them.

Students in grades 7 and 8 should stay with the same routine for at least four weeks in order to show gains in fitness development. Success in the fitness area helps motivate students and serves as a basis for future motor skill development. Students need to learn that success can be achieved in the fitness area through continued effort. The Fitnessgram System (1987) or the Physical Best Fitness Test (1988) can be used to monitor student progress in the fitness area, and a fitness report should be sent to parents at least once a year. Fitness testing does not take a great deal of time. Students can test themselves, and enter their raw scores in a microcomputer. A print-out reveals graphically the student's fitness profile. This entire self-testing process maintains the purpose of teaching students skills that they can use for a lifetime.

Fitness routines recommended for 7th and 8th graders are shown in Figure 4.2. An in-depth discussion and examples of these routines are found in Chapter 18.

Lesson Focus and Game

The lesson focus and game should last 25–30 min, depending on the length of the period. This is the instructional part of the lesson with major emphasis on skill development, cognitive learning, and enhancement of the affective domain. This phase of the lesson contains skills to be taught, drills, and

lead-up activities necessary for skill practice, all of which culminate in games and tournaments. The length of the activity units in the lesson focus should be short, in the range of 2–3 weeks if the classes meet daily. Three-wk units can be a combination of two activities such as flag football and Frisbee. The combination-type unit allows a daily alternation of the two activities. This combination can be an effective way to keep all students involved, that is, if they don't like football, they can always look forward to Frisbee the next day.

Students should have some choice as to which units they take. They should, however, be required to take at least one unit from each of the following categories: team sports, lifetime activities, physical conditioning activities, dance, and aquatics. Teachers need to decide which activities fit the various categories. The category requirement ensures a measure of activity breadth for each student. One way to expand the choice is to offer a number of activities taught by different teachers. Students can participate with their homeroom teacher in the introductory and fitness activities and then quickly transfer to the lesson focus activity they have chosen.

Students should also be required to take one short unit on self-testing procedures and wellness concepts (see Chapter 16). This unit should include formal guidance and counseling relevant to current and lifetime fitness. Students must have the opportunity to learn the fundamentals of personal fitness and health *before* they leave junior high school because many high schools do not require physical education. Each student will thus have five required general categories and one specific required unit. The remaining units are chosen by each student in any category. Students may repeat units or take advanced level units after meeting their requirements.

The specific activity units that are offered should be determined jointly by a student interest survey (see Chapter 3) and the physical education staff. Activity units must be used to accomplish program goals and should be changed from year to year, de-

Weeks	Grade 7	Grade 8
1–4	Teacher-leader activities	Teacher-leader activities
5–8	Stretching and running techniques	Stretching and running techniques
9–12	Four corner course	Weight training stations
13–16	Exercises to music	Exercises to music
17–20	Obstacle course and isometrics	Grass drills and partner resistance
21–24	Squad leader exercises	Squad leader exercises
25–28	Astronaut drills	Circuit training
29–32	Continuity drills	Rhythmic aerobic activity
33–36	Parachute activities	Parachute activities

FIGURE 4.2 Physical fitness routines

pending on the interests of students and the opinions of teachers. This approach should provide a balance of activities from the required categories.

A school with four physical education teachers might offer the curriculum design shown in Figure 4.3. During the first unit of each semester, students would make their eight choices based on the required categories and their personal interests. At that time, students would be reminded to select activities based on their interests and the curriculum requirements, rather than on the teacher or on who else is in the class. The composition of the class should be determined by interest and requirements rather than by gender of students. The only exceptions are contact activities such as wrestling, basketball, soccer, or flag football. These classes can be designated "males" or "females," or an alternative might be to allow both sexes in the same class and then separate them for competitive situations. With this alternative, however, a problem with numbers of students may arise in some activities such as soccer or flag football.

Previous learning is considered in the sequence of the horizontal or yearly curriculum. Activities that use common skills can be placed later in the year (e.g., team handball, speed-a-way, and floor hockey can build on basketball, volleyball, and soccer).

Within the vertical arrangement, the 7th grade curriculum should build on the K–6 program in terms of skills, cognitive learning, and class arrangement. The 8th grade curriculum should then build on the 7th grade. Increased knowledge, more in-depth strategies, and higher level skills are the focus of the 8th grade curriculum. Because of scheduling problems, some schools must put 7th and 8th grade students in the same class. This is acceptable but difficult because of the extremely wide range of developmental levels in these two grades. Teachers must be aware of developmental differences and provide a variety of learning activities for different levels within each unit.

Physical skill development within the units can be monitored with a series of performance objectives for each unit (see Chapters 7 and 10, plus the activity chapters). These objectives can be part of the motivation and evaluation schemes. Knowledge tests can be administered every 6 or 9 weeks, depending on the school's grading periods.

Implementation Options for the Recommended Curriculum

A junior high school that is different from the previous example in terms of philosophy, requirements, schedule, number of teachers, and so on, could still implement this curriculum design by modifying the different components to fit the existing framework. These are the basic options that might be implemented.

Weeks	Lesson Focus or Unit Choice
	First Semester (Weeks 1–18)
1–2	Self-testing and wellness concepts (required)
3–4	Swimming, volleyball, flag football, or Frisbee games
5–6	Swimming, tennis, badminton, or soccer
7–8	Weight training and wrestling (boys), basketball (girls), lacrosse, or tennis
9–10	Badminton, gymnastics, soccer, or Frisbee games
11–12	Basketball (boys), aerobic dance, lacrosse, or field hockey
13–14	Recreational games and orienteering, basketball (girls), team handball, and wrestling (boys)
15–16	Basketball (boys), aerobic dance, speed-a-way, or field hockey
17–18	Flag football, jogging, yoga, or team handball
	Second Semester (Weeks 19–36)
19–20	Coeducational dance—folk, square, and country (4 sections, required)
21–22	Recreational games and orienteering, speed-a-way, yoga, or jogging
23–24	Physical conditioning, volleyball, Frisbee games, or soccer
25–26	Gymnastics, badminton, tennis, or field hockey
27–28	Track and field, softball, physical conditioning, or volleyball
29–30	Modern dance, self-defense and juggling, jogging, or lacrosse
31–32	Track and field, softball, Superstars and new games, or team handball
33–34	Swimming, modern dance, recreational games, or flag football
35–36	Swimming, yoga, speed-a-way, or recreational games

FIGURE 4.3   Junior high curriculum model for a four-person department

Option 1. Students can be assigned to one teacher and could take a required unit from that teacher for every other unit. With 2-wk units, this ensures that students will have at least 9 units with the same teacher. A choice of activities would occur every other unit. Students would have 9 required units and 9 units with a choice of activity and teacher. This provides a balance of required and choice units. Students get to know one teacher well and have choices in the alternate units. The required units should be coeducational, and the choice units should be based on student interest.

Option 2. This option has students assigned to the same teacher all year in a coeducational setting. For every unit or every other unit, the teacher allows students to vote on several activity choices. A majority class vote determines which activity is to be taught. As previously described, some of the units could be required and some elective. Students would get to know one teacher very well and have a balance of chosen and required units. One problem with this option is the possible difficulty among the teachers in scheduling equipment and facilities. Another drawback is that teachers must be skilled in many areas and prepare for many activities. For example, three different classes may all choose basketball for the same unit, and the facility may accommodate only two basketball classes. In addition, if 2-wk units are used, a teacher has to prepare for and teach 18 different activities.

Option 3. This option has a set curriculum sequence with no student choice and the same teacher. Problems with facilities are eliminated because the sequence of activities can be coordinated before the year starts. Teachers are responsible for a variety of activities and are not able to specialize. Students have no choice of activities. Teachers get to know their students well because they are solely responsible for all instruction.

The different options provide a number of advantages and disadvantages depending on the situation and the teachers involved. All factors should be analyzed carefully to determine what is best for students and teachers, and compromises must be made in order to develop a quality program.

CURRICULUM ANALYSIS QUESTIONS FOR GRADES 7 AND 8

The existing curriculum approach needs to be thoroughly analyzed before improvements can begin to take place. The following curriculum analysis questions are offered for evaluating an existing program.

1. What is the physical education requirement?
2. What type of schedule exists? (Meetings per week and minutes per meeting)
3. What is the length of the activity units? (Breadth versus depth)
4. What types of activities are offered? (Variety)
5. Is there a balance of activity categories? (E.g., team sports, lifetime sports, aquatics, dance)
6. Is there an attempt to include currently popular activities?
7. Do students have any choice of activities?
8. Are coeducational classes available?
9. What types of fitness activities are offered?
10. Is there a variety of fitness activities included?
11. Are the fitness activities arranged sequentially throughout the year? (Progression)
12. Is there a monitoring system for fitness, physical skills, and knowledge?
13. Is there a system for reporting to parents on physical education specifically?
14. Is there a difference between the 7th and 8th grade curriculum? (Vertical articulation)
15. Do activities within the year build on previous learning? (Horizontal articulation)

PHYSICAL EDUCATION CURRICULA FOR GRADE 9

The 9th grade year is the last required unit of physical education in many schools. Consequently, it is important for 9th graders to leave with positive attitudes toward physical activity, a desire to return for additional physical education units, and a desire to pursue a lifetime of physical activity.

Ninth graders are usually in a transition state from junior high to senior high school. Some districts put the 9th graders with 7th and 8th graders, while other districts place them with 10th, 11th, and 12th grade students. Both arrangements have advantages and disadvantages, and decisions are usually based on such factors as class size, building space, and projected district growth. The 9th grade curriculum design usually resembles that of the other grades with which the students are grouped. The requirements, schedule pattern, length of units, types of activities, amounts of choice, class composition, adapted program, and other factors are frequently the same as those discussed in the junior high school section. The major difference is that the length of the 9th grade units tends to be longer than most 7th and 8th grade units. Some schools allow 9th graders to take longer, specialized units (9 wks or one semester) in subject areas such as dance, gymnastics, or weight training that are usually offered in a senior high school. Different levels of units may also be available for some 9th graders (e.g., beginning, intermediate, and advanced basketball).

A Suggested Curriculum for Grade 9

The grade 9 curriculum design for physical education needs to be especially attractive to students, because this may be their last required year of physical education. Making a curriculum attractive does not mean compromising educational objectives. The curricula must be designed with specific, valuable objectives in mind, and students should not be allowed to make all their curricular decisions in any situation.

A curriculum approach can be made both attractive and educationally sound by incorporating a number of factors. First, students should have some activity choices for each unit. At this grade level, they need continued opportunities to explore different activities. Second, the arrangement should incorporate organized self-testing, personal counseling, and a wellness orientation to give students additional information for making decisions about physical activity and their life-styles. Third, the choices of activity should include a wide variety of different categories of physical activity, especially new and popular units such as the martial arts, aerobics, outdoor adventure activities, and jogging. Fourth, the program must offer more depth in certain activities so students can develop higher skill levels. This means having different unit levels such as beginning, intermediate, and advanced, or at least an opportunity to repeat favorite units. Finally, efforts should be made to develop a positive learning environment so that students will enjoy learning and have a desire to return for additional learning.

Classes should meet daily and units can be increased to 3 wks in length. Students are still required to take units in the following categories:

- 1 unit of wellness concepts
- 1 unit of team sports
- 1 unit of lifetime sports
- 1 unit of dance
- 1 unit of aquatics
- 1 unit of physical conditioning
- 6 units of electives

This requirement ensures a measure of breadth. The electives can be used for greater depth in an activity, or for seeking additional breadth, depending on the interests of the student. Ninth graders should be able to repeat a class or take an intermediate-level class as part of their electives. Because students at this age have started to narrow their activity interests, they should be able to start specializing in favorite activities. Their developmental level will allow them to improve faster than the 7th or 8th graders in the motor skills area. Students who take 2 units of the same activity should demonstrate visible improvement in skill level development.

A short introductory or warm-up activity (3–5 min) is useful to prepare students for the physical fitness segment. These activities should be attractive and challenging. Low organization and large muscle activities should dominate this segment. An example is the popular "high five" activity in which football or basketball teammates slap their hands together with arms overhead after performing some feat of excellence. Ninth graders can be challenged to hit "high fives" after a 90-, 180-, or 360-degree turn to the left or right. This is a good way to prepare students for vigorous fitness activities.

The introductory activity should be changed at least every week. The yearly sequence suggested for grades 7 and 8 can be developed with the many additional examples offered in Chapter 17. For added interest, modified or new warm-up activities can be created, depending on the season, the type of fitness activity that follows (strength, endurance, flexibility), or the type of lesson focus activity that follows (basketball, golf, tennis).

A vigorous and demanding physical fitness routine (10–15 min) should follow the introductory segment. A different routine every 2 wks gives students a final chance to explore many different fitness activities. Emphasis should be placed on imparting knowledge to students so they understand which activities affect various parameters of fitness. Students need to be taught and encouraged to make decisions relative to physical fitness and their personal fitness routines. They should self-test twice during the year with the Fitnessgram System (1987) or Physical Best Fitness Test (1988). The results can be reported and interpreted for students and parents. A specific reporting system should be developed (see Chapter 12), and supplementary information provided so that parents and students understand the components of health-related fitness and how to develop and maintain fitness.

The 2-wk routines in Figure 4.4 are suggested for a 9th grade curriculum. Instructors should explain carefully and demonstrate progression and overload principles to students.

Results of a student interest survey combined with the opinions of teachers can be used to determine the activity units offered during the lesson focus segment (25–30 min). When feasible, the curriculum should be extended into the community to use nearby facilities such as bowling alleys, golf ranges, and ski slopes. Community resources can

Weeks	Physical Fitness Routines
1–2	Teacher-leader activities
3–4	Stretching-flexibility routines
5–6	Running techniques, drills, and procedures
7–8	Exercises to music
9–10	Weight training stations
11–12	Four corner courses
13–14	Continuity drills
15–16	Obstacle course and isometrics
17–18	File and interval running
19–20	Squad leader activities
21–22	Circuit training
23–24	Grass drills and partner resistance
25–26	Parachute fitness activities
27–28	Fartlek and random running
29–30	Astronaut drills
31–32	Rope-jumping activities
33–34	Student choice
35–36	Student choice

FIGURE 4.4 Two-week routines for a 9th grade curriculum

become an important part of the program both in terms of facilities and instructional personnel. Schools must begin working in concert with the evolving private sports industry.

Physical skills can be monitored with performance objectives for each unit. Educators can use a textbook, such as Dougherty's (1983) *Physical Education and Sport for the Secondary School Student*, to enhance the knowledge component of a curriculum. Students should take a written test every 9 wks after completing 3 units. Reading assignments, written work, and outside class projects should be given on a regular basis.

Instructors must take care to organize curriculum activities horizontally throughout the year and assure vertical articulation with the 8th grade program. Opportunities should be available to increase skill level in and knowledge of those activities included in previous years. The sequence of activity units in Figure 4.5 is suggested for a 9th grade curriculum with six teachers and appropriate facilities.

Weeks	Activity Unit Offerings	Weeks	Activity Unit Offerings
1–3	Wellness concepts and fitness testing (6 sections)		Badminton Lacrosse
4–6	Swimming I and II (2 sections) Flag football Badminton Dance I Recreational games	19–21	Soccer (2 sections) Dance I Tennis II Volleyball Team handball
7–9	Swimming I and II (2 sections) Flag Football Volleyball Dance I Physical conditioning and weight training	22–24	Gymnastics Basketball II (2 sections) Physical conditioning and weight training Orienteering and new games Field hockey
10–12	Dance II Frisbee games Speed-a-way Basketball Team handball Flag football	25–27	Gymnastics Basketball II Frisbee games Lacrosse Speed-a-way Tennis I
13–15	Dance II Tennis I Field hockey Basketball Wrestling Recreational games	28–30	Dance II Volleyball II Recreational games Wrestling II Softball (2 sections)
16–18	Aerobics and weight training (2 sections) Dance III Tennis I	31–33	Coed dance and fitness self-testing (6 sections)
		34–36	Swimming I and II (2 sections) Recreational games (2 sections) Superstars competition (2 sections)

FIGURE 4.5 Activity units for a 9th grade curriculum with six teachers

The curriculum options discussed in the 7th and 8th grade section are also possible for the 9th grade. Two different options discussed in that section could be implemented in the grade 9 structure.

CURRICULUM ANALYSIS QUESTIONS FOR GRADE 9 ———

Curriculum planners and student teachers should analyze the existing design carefully by answering the following questions.

1. What is the physical education requirement?
2. How often and how long do the classes meet each week?
3. How long are the units?
4. Do students have choice in selecting units?
5. Is there a variety and balance of units?
6. Is there opportunity for depth of instruction?
7. Is there an organized physical fitness component with variety and progression?
8. Is there an organized monitoring system for skills, fitness, and knowledge?
9. Is there a specific system for reporting to parents?
10. Are there any reading or written assignments?
11. How does the program articulate the vertical and horizontal components?
12. Are there any formal guidance and counseling aspects to the curriculum?
13. How are students prepared to make meaningful choices about physical activity for a lifetime?
14. How is the curriculum extended into the community?
15. On what basis are new activities added to the curriculum?

REFERENCES AND SUGGESTED READINGS

AAHPERD. 1988. *Physical Best Test Manual.* Reston, VA: AAHPERD.

Bain, L. 1980. Socialization into the role of participant: Physical education's ultimate goal. *JOPERD* 51(7): 48–50.

Benson, J. 1982. An alternative direction for middle school physical education. *The Physical Educator* 39(2): 75–77.

Blaufarb, M. 1978(a). *Complying with Title IX of the Educational Amendments of 1972 in Physical Education and High School Sports Programs.* Reston, VA: AAHPERD.

Blaufarb, M. 1978(b). *Title IX Sex-Integrated Programs That Work.* Reston, VA: AAHPERD.

Dauer, V. P., and Pangrazi, R. P. 1989. *Dynamic Physical Education for Elementary School Children.* 9th ed. New York: Macmillan Publishing Co.

Dougherty, N., (ed.) 1983. *Physical Education and Sport for the Secondary School Student.* Reston, VA: AAHPERD.

Gruelich, W., and Pyle, S. 1959. *Radiographic Atlas of Skeletal Development of the Hand and Wrist.* 2nd ed. Stanford, CA: Stanford University Press.

Hale, C. 1956. Physiological maturity of little league baseball players. *Research Quarterly* 27(3): 276–284.

Institute for Aerobic Fitness. 1987. *Fitnessgram User's Manual.* Dallas: Institute for Aerobic Fitness.

Melograno, V. 1979. *Designing Curriculum and Learning: A Physical Coeducational Approach.* Dubuque, IA: Kendall/Hunt Publishing.

Pangrazi, R., Darst, P., Fedorchek, S., and Coyle, K. 1982. The needed link: A physical curriculum designed exclusively for junior high students. *The Physical Educator* 39(2): 71–74.

Seaton, D. C., et al. 1983. *Physical Education Handbook,* 7th ed. Englewood Cliffs, NJ: Prentice-Hall, Inc.

Siedentop, D. 1980(a). Physical education curriculum: An analysis of the past. *JOPERD* 51(7): 40–41.

Siedentop, D. 1980(b). *Physical Education—Introductory Analysis.* 3rd ed. Dubuque, IA: Wm. C. Brown Group.

5 THE SENIOR HIGH SCHOOL CURRICULUM

Physical education can be an important concern of our high school administrators and parents, and a focus in serving the physical needs of high school students. High school students are interested in their fitness levels, in acquiring physical skills, and in experiencing risk, excitement, and adventure. Programs can gain the respect and support of the people involved. There are numerous examples of successful approaches that exist in Canadian and American high schools. Many factors affect the type of program used in each situation. Some of these factors are difficult to change in a short period of time (e.g., the state requirement for physical education; a school district requirement for physical education; the district philosophy on athletics, driver education, marching band; and the type of schedule the school utilizes). However, other factors that affect a curriculum can be quickly improved without dramatically disrupting the school routine and schedule.

Factors that affect the development of a curriculum can be implemented within the existing framework of a given situation. Because of the differences among states and among school districts, the degree of implementation may vary drastically. These factors include: types of activities, the balance of activities, the required activities, the length of units, the arrangements of units, the amount of student choice, the coeducational classes, the physical fitness sequences, the monitoring systems for fitness and skill development, the reporting system to the parents, and many others.

A small high school in upstate New York, a large urban high school in eastern Pennsylvania, or a medium-sized high school in central Arizona can all have a quality program within their existing frameworks. Certainly, some programs will have more students, more teachers, more facilities, and better equipment. Requirements, schedules, and administrative support may be quite different in each situation. Quality programs are not, however, a function of large facilities, abundant equipment, extensive physical education requirements, numerous teachers, or small class sizes. Outstanding high school programs are usually developed by a group of hardworking, dedicated professionals who are doing their best with the given resources. There is strong leadership and a central focus required of successful programs. A continual effort must be made to improve the program and to change those aspects that are detrimental to accomplishing goals. A sense of excitement must be found within the program. Teachers should have a purpose, and a commitment to that purpose. Curriculum developers should work positively within the present framework and try slowly to change the existing parameters that cause difficulties.

The first section of this chapter describes the developmental characteristics of high school students and implications for physical education programs in the high school, grades 10–12. This section is followed by a review of the current aspects of high school programs that currently exist, along with a discussion on the advantages and disadvantages of those situations. A suggested curriculum design with recommendations is presented followed by a series of curriculum analysis questions for these grade levels. These questions can help curriculum planners analyze existing curricula for grades 10–12. The answers to the questions provide planners with information about specific factors and components of an existing approach.

GROWTH AND DEVELOPMENT IN THE HIGH SCHOOL YEARS

The high school years offer the educational system an opportunity to polish and improve its product: students who can be productive individuals in society. To assure that the physical education program will contribute to this long-term objective, it is important to understand the growth and development of the students and the implication these characteristics have on a well-designed curriculum.

Physical Characteristics

Increases in Motor Ability and Coordination. Most students have finished their growth spurt and are approaching physical maturity. Bone growth and the ossification process are complete for most students. Sexual characteristics reach maturity for both boys and girls. Students are over the period of physical awkwardness and are much more comfortable with their physical abilities. Motor ability and coordination improve more quickly during this time period.

Implications. This is an excellent time for students to improve existing motor skills and to learn new skills. Students will not be as uneasy about trying new physical skills and performing in front of peers. Teachers can also move the students through instructional progressions at a much faster rate.

Modification of Physical Traits. There are continued increases in strength, endurance, and speed. Boys surpass the girls in these areas. The boys also surpass the girls in height and weight. Boys continue to develop muscularly while most girls level off in this area.

Implications. Teachers need to help students understand that physical differences among students will impact on skill performance. Students should continually be guided toward activities where they will be successful with their physical traits. Students should develop a sensitivity for participating with others at various ability levels.

Social, Emotional, and Intellectual Development

Social Awareness. Social activities such as dances, parties, athletic events, and clubs will dominate the lives of high school students. Students are much more concerned with dating, going steady, getting a job, marriage, and a career. Peer groups are very important and help to provide behavioral standards in areas such as dress, grooming, and interests. Peer groups give students experience with loyalty to a group yet independence from adults. Students still have a difficult time deciding between adult and peer values. Conflicts still exist between adults and students. Competition increases with an emphasis on grades, athletics, and dating. There is continued concern about size, strength, and physical ability. They are concerned about how their bodies look, but are more interested in cosmetic fitness rather than health-related fitness.

Implications. High school is not a time to force students into activities that do not interest them.

There should be many opportunities for choice. Dress requirements, time for changing clothes, and grooming time are important issues where students should have input into the physical education course requirements. Students should have opportunities to express their opinions and ideas with regard to various issues. Weight lifting, aerobics, body building, figure control, and other popular fitness activities should be available to these students.

Emotional Development. Most students have completed the puberty cycle and are more comfortable with their bodies and the direction of their lives. There are fewer mood swings and students seem to be more stable emotionally. Problems with fighting, extreme competitiveness, and arguing over issues start to diminish.

Implications. Students need additional experiences with emotional control. They need to understand the necessity of emotional control in physical education environments and in other aspects of life. Teachers need to be good models of emotional control so that students can witness acceptable behavior patterns. Teachers that talk about emotional control in class and behave quite differently during an interscholastic basketball game will have little credibility with their students.

Intellectual Development. Students are approaching their full intellectual potential. Their memories, and abilities to reason, concentrate, imagine, and think conceptually have improved and continue to develop. Students have experienced the knowledge explosion and changing American values. Many students have experienced broken homes, single-parent families, multiple moves, drugs, and sexual activity. Students are looking for risk, excitement, and adventure. They have a large base of knowledge and experience by the time they reach this period. Students have strong concerns about security, attention, affection, self-worth, and intellectual improvement. There is a continued narrowing of interests and an emphasis on specialization in activities where they perceive themselves as being competent.

Implications. Teachers need to be sensitive to the increasing intellectual abilities of their students. There must be a focus on the "why" of physical education and the objectives of the program. Students need to be able to choose the activities they want. Units should be longer to assure in-depth instruction. The curriculum should include units that incorporate risk, excitement, and adventure. Students also want to understand the cognitive concepts of activities as well as to improve their physical skills. Teachers should be enthusiastic and set high expectations for students.

The senior high school years are important in transforming adolescents into adults. Students must face the realities of the world and make decisions about education, careers, marriage, religion, politics, and life-styles. Teachers have a responsibility for imparting information, attitudes, and skills.

SENIOR HIGH SCHOOL CURRICULA: CURRICULUM DECISIONS

Senior high school physical education curricula vary greatly from state to state and from large urban schools with 10–15 physical education teachers to the small rural schools with 1 or 2 teachers. State requirements are different and some school districts allow a number of substitutions for physical education (e.g., marching band, choral music, health education, and athletics). The local school district and its faculty have the ultimate responsibility for developing the program within the state guidelines. Some districts have a 4-yr requirement, while others do not have any requirements. In other situations, districts may have a 3-yr requirement but allow substitutions such as cheerleading, athletics, orchestra, or pom-poms to fulfill the requirement. Yet another district may have a 2-yr requirement with a schedule allowing only 2 meetings per week.

Large, comprehensive high schools may have swimming pools, racquetball courts, a dance studio, and multiple weight rooms; the small school may have only an outdoor field and a single gymnasium. Nearby community facilities can also vary considerably and climate is another major factor. Schools in central Arizona, for example, can use tennis and racquetball courts year-round, but a school in northeast Ohio must keep students indoors for most of the winter. All these factors have a dramatic effect on the physical education program. Even when requirements, facilities, and weather conditions are similar, a significant difference may exist in the schedule, the length of units, the types of activities, the amount of choice, and the class composition.

Schedule of Classes

Most high schools follow a block schedule with classes meeting every day for the same length of time (45–55 min). In many other school districts, physical education only meets twice or three times a week all year long. Another common schedule pattern is called a 3/2 "swing" approach that was discussed in the junior high curriculum chapter. Physical education is paired with another subject and the students attend class 3 days per week during the first semester and 2 days per week during the second semester. Students attend the other subject area class (usually health or drivers' education) on opposite days. The students "flip" their schedules at the end of the first semester from Monday, Wednesday, and Friday to Tuesday and Thursday.

Some high school districts use a flexible schedule arrangement (see Chapter 3). This approach allows for classes to meet for varying lengths of time throughout the week, thus allowing for "flexibility." For example, one meeting might be a classroom lecture for 30 min and then two additional 90-min labs would be held on other days of the week. This arrangement allows for innovative instruction methods, travel time off campus, and better use of teachers' time. The advantages and disadvantages of these schedules has been discussed in Chapter 3.

Length of Activity Units

There is great variance in the length of units in the high school curriculum. The number of meeting days per week has an impact on the unit lengths. Districts that meet twice per week must have longer units whereas districts with daily physical education can use shorter units and offer more activities throughout a semester or a year. Generally, the length of high school units is longer than the junior high units because high school students need the opportunity for in-depth instruction. High school students should leave school feeling competent and confident, to assure they are willing to participate in public settings. High school students should be able to learn a few activities well, rather than having to experience many activities. Few adults will participate in an activity with friends unless they feel they are able to perform without embarrassment.

One of the most common high school designs consists of long units focused on the popular seasonal athletic activities. Units are 6- to 12-wks long and focus primarily on a team sport that is in season. Students take only 4–6 activities in a year. The approach might look similar to the following:

- First 10 wks — Flag football or soccer
- Second 10 wks — Basketball or volleyball
- Third 10 wks — Wrestling or badminton
- Fourth 10 wks — Softball or track and field

The following is a similar approach using 6-wk units:

- First 6 wks — Swimming, football, or tennis
- Second 6 wks — Volleyball, soccer, or field hockey
- Third 6 wks — Basketball, wrestling, or badminton

- Fourth 6 wks—Gymnastics, aerobics, or weight lifting
- Fifth 6 wks—Track and field, lacrosse, or rhythms
- Sixth 6 wks—Softball, superstars fitness, or speed-a-way

In states that use a 9-wk grading period, a common design offers 2 physical education units during that period. One unit is 5 wks in length and the other 4 wks. In this way, students take 8 units per year. An example of this approach follows:

- First 9 wks
  Soccer, golf, or orienteering (5 wks)
  Flag football, speed-a-way, or self defense (4 wks)
- Second 9 wks
  Tennis, team handball, or racquetball (5 wks)
  Basketball, wrestling, or rhythms (4 wks)
- Third 9 wks
  Volleyball, yoga, or soccer (5 wks)
  Gymnastics, badminton, or archery (4 wks)
- Fourth 9 weeks
  Track and field, racquetball, or field hockey (5 wks)
  Softball, badminton, or Frisbee (4 wks)

There are districts with a daily physical education format that use short 3-wk units and offer students 12–14 different units during a year. The following is an example:

Weeks	Activity
1–3	Swimming
4–6	Volleyball
7–9	Tennis
10–12	Flag football
13–15	Dance
16–18	Basketball
19–21	Badminton
22–24	Tumbling
25–27	Recreational games
28–30	Speed-a-way
31–33	Track and field
34–36	Softball

Many high schools have started offering specialized units that last one or two semesters. Common examples focus on popular activities such as weight training, aerobics, fitness for life programs, outdoor adventure programs, dance, archery, badminton, tennis, racquetball and gymnastics. These classes may meet every day or just twice a week.

The examples range from 1 to 12 unit activities per year. The students in the 1-unit design receive an in-depth experience while students in the 12-unit approach receive a broader experience of many different activities. Obviously, much less time is spent on each activity in the shorter units approach. This touches on the controversy discussed earlier in the junior high section on breadth and depth (see Chapter 4).

Types of Activities

Activities in high school physical education curricula have certainly changed over the past 20 yrs. Certainly the most common category of activity is athletic team sports (e.g, flag football, basketball, soccer, volleyball, wrestling, track and field, softball). These are popular with many students and with most physical education teachers because of their competency level. These activities are usually quite economical in terms of facilities and equipment.

In the late 1960s and early 1970s most schools started adding lifetime sports such as tennis, badminton, bowling, and golf. These activities were included because of the claims of more carry-over value for later life. The concept of lifetime sports has grown and now includes many activities such as racquetball, Frisbee, bicycling, and archery. Outdoor adventure activities have slowly been added to the high schools. Camping, backpacking, canoeing, rock climbing, and orienteering are popular activities in many programs nationwide. Self-defense and the various forms of the martial arts have also been added recently. The fitness boom has also impacted many school programs with new units on jogging, aerobics, weight training, and various combinations.

Quality high school approaches should try to offer a balance of fitness activities, team sports, lifetime sports, dance activities, aquatic activities, and the new activities. The physical education staff must keep in touch with the activity interests and trends of society in order to update the curriculum. It is also a good idea to try balancing the curriculum within these categories since the interests of high school students vary. To attract students, an interesting variety of activity categories must be offered. Certain students will be interested in certain categories of activity and arrangements with balance will provide more students with opportunities for success. For example, some students enjoy Frisbee, orienteering, and golf, while others prefer basketball, football, and baseball.

Physical Fitness Activities

Physical fitness is usually incorporated into the high school curriculum by one of four different approaches. These are as follows:

1. Separate specific units of physical fitness such as aerobics, weight training, jogging, and various combinations of activities are offered;
2. Regular daily physical fitness routines are used at the beginning of each class period throughout the entire year. Stretching-flexibility, strength development, and cardiovascular-respiratory-type activities usually dominate the fitness routines;
3. A lecture-lab concepts approach with an emphasis on fitness knowledge, self testing, and fitness program development is offered as a part of the physical education requirement;
4. Some type of a combination of the above is offered.

High schools that follow the first option are often criticized because fitness must be developed and maintained on a regular basis rather than by units that are intermittently included in the curriculum sequence. However, some schools offer fitness units to assure that the entire year focuses on regularity. Schools that use regular fitness routines for a short period of time each day are always criticized for not providing enough time to really impact fitness levels. The other side of the issue is that fitness would take up so much time that nothing else could be accomplished. Other critics point out the lack of variety, progression, and challenge in the fitness routines. The critics of the lecture-lab approach argue that there is too much time spent on cognitive activities which could otherwise be used for skill development.

Obviously, each approach has pros and cons. But remember that with current low levels of physical fitness in America, the school physical education curriculum must have a systematic plan to improve fitness levels of students. High school physical education classes may be the last time for many students to be influenced about the crucial aspects of physical fitness. Student success at this level is especially important to keep them interested and motivated. Physical fitness can be offered with a wide variety of activities, units, and routines in a progressive and challenging manner. Just as there is no best way to achieve physical fitness that is meaningful for everyone, there is no best way to get physical fitness into the curriculum. Strong emphasis should be focused on helping high schoolers to make wise choices regarding the different ways of developing and maintaining fitness.

Activities and Proficiency Levels

Many of the larger high schools are attempting to offer different levels of various activities. This implies sections for beginners, intermediates, and advanced levels for the most popular activities. Some high schools are using the following categories for their units:

1. Introductory units for the development of the basic skills and knowledge of the activity;
2. Team units for learning and practicing the basic team concepts of the activity;
3. Recreational units that allow the students to focus on competitive game activity.

This arrangement works nicely if students proceed through the first level before the second and the second before the third level. Students can skip a level if they are proficient at the earlier level. Grouping students by ability and experience allows for an efficient teaching and learning situation for teachers and students. Students are more comfortable with others who are near their ability level.

Requirements and Choice

Most senior high school physical education departments have a required core of units that all students must take. Students usually have little or no choice about what activities they will learn. Often the required units are traditional team sports and there is little opportunity to take activities of high personal interest. This arrangement is probably still the most common format regarding required classes. The following is an example of a required sequence for 10th graders that offers some variety and choice of activities:

Weeks	Activity
1–3	Physical fitness and wellness concepts
4–6	Racquetball or badminton
7–9	Flag football or soccer
10–12	Volleyball or basketball
13–15	Recreational games—Frisbee, horseshoes, table tennis, or shuffleboard
16–18	Weight training or tennis
19–21	Square dance
22–24	Badminton or team handball
25–27	Softball or racquetball
28–30	Tennis or speed-a-way
31–33	Track and field
34–36	Student's choice

A popular arrangement used by many high school districts gives students the opportunity to choose activities they want to take in physical education. This arrangement is used primarily for the elective or optional years of physical education, however, there are districts that are giving students choices even in the required program. The students are given a choice of several different activities for each unit.

The number of choices depends on the number of teachers and facilities that are available during each class period. Classes are usually open to both males and females depending on their activity interests. With this design, classes are taught by either a male or female teacher depending on qualifications and interests. Teachers can then develop teaching specialties and repeat teaching those specialties to different students throughout the year. This arrangement allows teachers to become experts with a smaller number of activities rather than being generalists who have to teach many different units to the same students.

Panama Central High School, a small high school in New York, offers a curriculum that gives students a choice of activities (Olsen, 1984). There is an emphasis on lifetime sports, team sports, self-testing activities, and aquatics. Classes for grades 9–12 are taught on a 3/2 swing schedule (3 days one semester, 2 days the second semester). The 40-wk school year is divided into four 10-wk physical education units. The teaching staff is able to offer 3 activities during each 10-wk period. Students choose their classes every 10 wks from the 3 different activities that are offered. At the end of each year, students will have completed 4 units and, at graduation, 16 units. Upper-class students are given priority for choices when the demand is too great for a selected activity. Figure 5.1 illustrates the 4-yr sequence offered at Panama Central.

This approach offers students a choice and has been used with males and females in both integrated and segregated class settings. The integrated design is excellent. It gives students more choices with better instruction because it is led by the most qualified teacher. The integrated curriculum moves away from "males" and "females" activities. Students should be free to choose and have access to the activities that they are truly interested in pursuing regardless of any previous gender identification it may have. This plan has been used with varying lengths of units and organizational schemes. As mentioned in the junior high chapter, the advantages of this scheme are increased motivation of teachers and students, fewer problems with participation and discipline, and better use of teachers' expertise. It seems wise for districts to consider some form of this curriculum because of the increased motivation level of both students and teachers.

A newer variation of this design involves stipulating requirements by activity categories such as team sports, lifetime sports, physical fitness activities, dance units, aquatic units, recreational activities, or adventure activities. Students choose units but they must meet the category requirements. This approach ensures that students receive a certain measure of breadth with activities. This plan is referred to as a **choice within a requirement**. Depending on the number of units offered, each student is required to take a specified number of units from each category. If the curriculum offered six 6-wk units over a 1-yr period, the requirements by category might include:

- 1 team sport unit
- 1 lifetime sport unit
- 1 swimming unit
- 1 physical fitness unit
- 1 adventure or recreational games unit
- 1 elective unit (student's choice)
- 6 units total

Coeducational Classes

The issue of coed high school physical education classes is still controversial. Practices within the senior high school still vary widely across Canada and the United States. Many schools have all coed classes while others keep males and females totally separate. Some schools offer several coeducational units, but the majority of units are still segregated by sex. Programs that allow students to choose classes end up with a mixture of boys and girls based on interest, so the class composition has no fixed gender percentage. Teachers and parents make various claims on both sides of this issue. The section in Chapter 1 on federal mandates presented the issues and problems associated with this controversial physical education area.

There is a wide variety of curricula in effect at various high schools. There are daily schedules, flexible schedules, and 3/2 swing schedules. Some schools have short units, others have 4- to 5-wk units, and still others offer specialized year-long units of modern dance, weight training, or gymnastics. Most programs are still dominated by team sports and lifetime sports; however, many have added aerobics, martial arts, yoga, bicycling, and other new activities. Some high schools give students a choice of activities while others have a set, required sequence. Coeducational classes are the rule in many schools, but others give high school students a choice of a coeducational or a segregated class. In some high schools, students have a choice of activities, and the consequent class composition is determined by interest rather than gender.

A SUGGESTED CURRICULUM FOR GRADES 10, 11, AND 12 _____

At this grade level, students are narrowing their range of interests in many areas, including physical education activities. Students are capable (and

Whenever and wherever possible, offer these courses on alternate years. However, unforseen circumstances may require changing the course sequencing.

Year 1	2	3	4
First 10 Wks			
A. Speedball	A. Golf	A. Speedball	A. Field Hockey
B. Field Hockey	B. Boating & Hunter's Safety	B. Archery	B. Running for Fitness–Aerobics
C. Archery	C. Soccer	C. Floor Hockey	C. Soccer
Second 10 Wks			
A. Basic Swimming	A. Recreational Swimming	A. Basic Swimming	A. Recreational Swimming
B. Volleyball	B. Recreational Games	B. Basketball	B. Bowling
C. Weights & Fitness	C. Weights & Fitness	C. Cross-Country Skiing	C. Weights & Fitness
Third 10 Wks			
A. Lifesaving	A. Competitive Swimming	A. Lifesaving	A. Synchronized Swimming
B. Gymnastics	B. Power Volleyball	B. Handball	B. Recreational Games
C. Weights & Fitness	C. Weights & Fitness	C. Weights & Fitness	C. Gymnastics
Fourth 10 Wks			
A. Bowling	A. Tennis	A. Golf	A. Tennis
B. Softball	B. Softball	B. Softball	B. Softball
C. Handball & Ping Pong	C. Basic Fishing	C. Squash	C. Camping

FIGURE 5.1 Panama Central Senior High School 4-year sequence (reprinted with permission from Gary M. Olson, Panama Central School. Panama, NY)

should be able) to choose the activities they want to pursue. According to Siedentop (1980b):

> Beyond the multi-activity program, students should gradually take over more and more responsibility for electing their own program of physical education. By the 10th grade, the program should be fully elective. Adolescence is no time to force students into certain activity settings as opposed to others. It is a time for growing independence, and physical education should reflect that developmental need, providing structure and guidance in an elective program. (p. 280)

The curriculum should be fully elective, with daily schedules that meet for 9 wks. All classes, except contact sports, should be open to both male or female students. 9-wk units allow for in-depth instruction and a high level of skill competency. High school students have the ability to persist at tasks for a longer period and can benefit from longer units of instruction. After 9 wks of instruction, students should have a sufficient level of skill and knowledge so that the reinforcing aspects of the activity will motivate them to continue outside the school environment. The curriculum should emphasize lifetime activities (e.g., tennis, racquetball, bicycling, and rock climbing), and offer many different levels of instruction to accommodate students' abilities.

Students switch lesson focus activities only after 9 wks of instruction and practice. They can repeat a lesson focus unit at a higher level if it is offered, or they can take 4 different units in 1 yr. Facilities, student interest, and faculty expertise will determine which activities are taught each 9 wks. Community facilities should be used as much as possible within such existing parameters as funds, travel arrangements, and legal liability. The community facilities might include rock climbing areas, parks for orienteering, ski slopes, rivers for canoeing or kayaking, bowling alleys, Nautilus equipment, or riding stables. A general physical activities handbook such as Seaton et al. (1983) or Dougherty (1983) should be used to supplement instructional activities found in each unit.

The physical fitness portion of the lesson (10–15 min) should also be elective in nature. Each available teacher coordinates a physical fitness activity at a different teaching station. Specific activities might include stretching, weight lifting, jogging, running intervals, exercising to music, rope jumping, bicycling, and various combinations. Students can attend their preferences on certain days of the week and then switch to different activities on alternate days. The only requirement is that students must maintain a balance of cardiovascular fitness and muscular strength/flexibility. This means they could participate in the cardiovascular activity 3 days a week and the strength/flexibility activity twice a week (or vice versa). If the class only meets twice a week, then students would have to alternate days with cardiovascular and strength/flexibility activities. After the fitness portion of the lesson, students move to their selected lesson focus with their original teacher. This allows them to select the type and variety of fitness activity they desire, as long as they maintain the balance described above.

A high school that has eight teachers available per period, and appropriate facilities could offer the following physical fitness stations:

1. Slow long distance running
2. Interval training (running)
3. Jump rope continuity drills
4. Weight training
5. Aerobic dancing—Beginning level routines
6. Aerobic dancing—Intermediate level routines
7. Stretching and flexibility activities
8. Obstacle course and isometrics

If facilities are limited and certain fitness activities are extremely popular (e.g., weight training, aerobic dancing), then a rotation schedule will have to be arranged and posted in the locker room. A rotation plan might allow students whose last names start with the letters A–M to participate on Monday and Wednesday, while those with names beginning with N–Z participate on Tuesday and Thursday. In this situation, teachers have to solve potential problems with attendance procedures for students who might ride a special bus to a ski slope or walk to a bowling alley. There may be times when these students would have to miss the fitness portion of the lesson due to the nature of their selected lesson focus. At least once or twice each year, all students should be involved in self-testing using the *Fitnessgram System* (1987) or *AAHPERD Physical Best Test* (1988) to monitor their personal fitness status.

Figure 5.2 shows the lesson focus units that could be switched from year to year, depending on attendance. Student interest surveys can help determine what units students will select. Teachers can become specialists in specific activities such as racquet sports, outdoor activities, or weight training and conditioning, and can thus improve the quality and level of instruction that students receive.

This format should help school programs compete with the growing private sports instruction industry for community dollars. A public relations program can communicate this information to the general public. The physical education profession can no longer afford to offer programs that show little or no concern for student preference.

Many options in this plan can be developed to fit the facilities, equipment, schedule, and philosophy of a particular high school. A school with 6-wk grading periods may want to have 6-wk rather than 9-wk units. A school with a 3/2 swing schedule may desire units that are longer than 9 wks. Students located in certain geographic locations may be especially interested in units on surfing, ice hockey, fishing, canoeing, or lacrosse. Certain communities have strong interests in specific activities such as golf, sailing, or horseback riding, and community facilities

Weeks	Elective Class Offerings
1–9	Golf and bowling combination Tennis Wellness concepts Orienteering and Frisbee Modern dance Weight training Swimming and diving Volleyball
10–18	Racquetball Tennis Basketball Gymnastics Modern dance Weight training Camping and backpacking Rock climbing
19–27	Golf Bowling Bicycling Badminton Modern dance Weight training Conditioning Yoga
28–36	Soccer Water sports Racquetball Orienteering and Frisbee Modern dance Weight training Sailing and canoeing Volleyball

FIGURE 5.2 Activity units for a high school curriculum with eight teachers

can then be an integral part of the school program. All of these factors need to be considered and incorporated into each specific situation.

CURRICULUM ANALYSIS QUESTIONS FOR GRADES 10, 11, AND 12

1. What is the physical education requirement?
2. What type of schedule exists?
3. How long are the units?
4. Do the students have any choice of units?
5. How many units are required?
6. Is variety, balance, and depth of units offered?
7. Is the fitness component organized with variety, progression, and overload principles in mind?
8. What type of monitoring system exists for physical skills, physical fitness, and knowledge?

9. Are there any self-testing procedures for students?

10. Are there any formal guidance and counseling procedures?

11. Are there any reading or written assignments for students?

12. Is the curriculum organized to consider both horizontal and vertical articulation?

13. How is the curriculum extended into the community?

14. Are community facilities or personnel used in the curriculum?

15. What information is used to add activities to and delete activities from the program?

ARTICULATING THE PROGRAM: KINDERGARTEN THROUGH GRADE 12

More often than not, physical education curricula are developed in parts. There is usually a curriculum for the elementary school level, one for junior high, and another for the senior high school. Each curriculum is written and organized independently of the others. A district-wide plan that considers factors such as state requirements, facilities, scheduling, and equipment is seldom developed. In many cases, elementary physical education specialists do not know junior and senior high school physical education teachers, let alone have an understanding of the curriculum at each level. Teachers often operate autonomously, without concern for or knowledge of what is done at other levels. This leads to a fragmented program that shows little connection between levels. Time, energy, and learning activities may be wasted, duplicated, or omitted in a curriculum that is not vertically articulated.

The curriculum for grades 10 through 12 presented in this chapter builds vertically on the 7 through 9 curriculum presented in Chapter 4 and on the K through 6 elementary curriculum developed by Dauer and Pangrazi (1989). It basically follows the same daily lesson plan format, and uses arrangements of learning activities appropriate for the developmental level of the students in a specific grade. The entire K through 12 sequence emphasizes individual success, physical fitness, exploration, guidance and counseling, self-testing, monitoring, physical skill development, requisite knowledge, wellness concepts, choice within requirement, and preparation for a lifetime of physical activity. Students are given requirements, choices, and activities as shown in Figure 5.3.

Chapters 4 and 5 provide school districts with a

Grades

| K | 1 | 2 | 3 | 4 | 5 | 6 | 7 | 8 | 9 | 10 | 11 | 12 |

Required units - - - - - - - - - Elective units
Variety and exploration - - - Specialized units
Balance and breadth - - - - - - - - - Depth
Physical fitness - - - - - - - Physical fitness
Required and varied - - - - - - Choice
Wellness concepts - - - - Wellness concepts
Required - - - - - - - - - - - - Choice

FIGURE 5.3 Kindergarten–12 curriculum components

sound, progressively arranged physical education curriculum that has been field-tested by the authors in many school districts. Options have been used depending on the specific factors involved. The curriculum is built on educational theory and research, as well as on practical factors influencing teaching-learning environments. It gives students many successful encounters with physical activity, so they will leave the physical education program with approach tendencies for learning in general and for physical activities in particular. Teachers develop expertise in specialized areas, which improves their motivational level and the quality of instruction. These are some of the advantages of a curriculum that has been developed through dialogue with teachers and experts in physical education.

REFERENCES AND SUGGESTED READINGS

AAHPERD. 1988. *Physical Best Manual*. Reston, VA: AAHPERD.

Bain, L. 1980. Socialization into the role of participant: Physical education's ultimate goal. *JOPERD* 51(7): 48–50.

Dauer, V. P., and Pangrazi, R. P. 1989. *Dynamic Physical Education for Elementary School Children*. 9th ed. New York: Macmillan Publishing.

Dougherty, N., (ed.) 1983. *Physical Education and Sport for the Secondary School Student*. Reston, VA: AAHPERD.

Olson, G. 1984. Physical education for the small school system. In R. P. Carlson (ed.) *Ideas II for Secondary School Physical Education*. Reston, VA: AAHPERD.

Seaton, D. C., et al. 1983. *Physical Education Handbook*. 7th ed. Englewood Cliffs, NJ: Prentice-Hall, Inc.

Siedentop, D. 1980(a). Physical education curriculum: An analysis of the past. *JOPERD* 51(7): 40–41.

Siedentop, D. 1980(b). *Physical Education—Introductory Analysis*. 3rd ed. Dubuque, IA: Wm. C. Brown Group.

Sterling, C. L. 1987. *Fitnessgram User's Manual*. Dallas, TX: Institute for Aerobics Research.

6 SECONDARY STUDENTS WITH DISABILITIES

The Education for All Handicapped Children Act (Public Law 94–142) was passed by the Congress of the United States in 1975. It was the 142nd act of legislation passed by the 94th Congress. This legislation introduced new requirements and vocabulary concepts into physical education programs across the United States. These concepts include individual education programs (IEP), mainstreaming, least restrictive environments, zero reject, and progressive inclusion. The purpose of the law was clear and concise:

> It is the purpose of this act to assure that all handicapped children* have available to them a free appropriate public education which emphasizes special education and related services designed to meet their unique needs, to assure that the rights of handicapped children and their parents or guardians are protected, to assist States and localities to provide for the education of all handicapped children, and to assess and assure the effectiveness of efforts to educate handicapped children.

In short, the law requires that all handicapped students, ages 3–21, receive a free and appropriate education that meets their particular needs. The law includes handicapped students in public and private care facilities and schools. Students with disabilities who can learn in regular classes with the use of supplementary aides and services must be educated with students who are able. Physical education is the only specific subject area mentioned in P.L. 94–142. The section in the law reads, the term special education "means specially designed instruction, instruction in physical education, home instruction, and instruction in hospitals and institutions."

To comply with P.L. 94–142, secondary schools must locate, identify, and evaluate all students who might have a disability. A screening process must be followed by a formal assessment procedure. An assessment must be made and an IEP developed for each student before placement into a special program can be made. The law states who will be responsible for developing the IEP and what the contents of the IEP will include.

The passage of the P.L. 94–142 shows that a strong commitment has been made to equality and education for all Americans. Prior to 1970, these students had limited access to our public schools. They certainly did not have an equal opportunity to participate in school programs. The government also assured that funding would be made available to assure quality instruction. The law authorizes a payment to each state of 40% of the average per-pupil expenditure in U.S. elementary and secondary schools, multiplied by the number of disabled youngsters who are receiving special education and related services. The federal mandate reveals the concern of the public for comprehensive education programs for all students regardless of handicap.

LEAST RESTRICTIVE ENVIRONMENT

P.L. 94–142 uses the term "least restrictive environment" to help determine the best placement arrangement of students with disabilities. This concept refers to the idea that not all individuals can do all of the same activities in the same environment. However, the concept of "zero reject" entitles everyone of school age to some aspect of the school program. No one can be totally rejected because of a disability. The focus should be on placing students into settings that offer the best opportunity for educational advancement. It is inappropriate to place a youngster in an environment where success is impossible. However, it would be debilitating to put a student in a setting that is more restrictive than necessary.

---

* The term *handicapped* is used in P.L. 94–142 to include youngsters who are mentally retarded, hard of hearing, deaf, speech impaired, visually handicapped, seriously emotionally disturbed, orthopedically impaired, other health impaired, deaf, blind, multihandicapped, or specific learning disabled. Currently, *disabled* is the term used to identify youngsters with handicapping conditions and will be used throughout this chapter.

Special educators speak about many experiences that offer a variety of opportunities from participation in regular physical education classes to physical education in a full-time special school. Figure 6.1 shows a series of options that might be available for physical education.

The least restrictive environment also varies depending on the unit of instruction and the teaching style. For example, for a student in a wheelchair, a soccer or football unit might be very restrictive, whereas in a basketball or Frisbee unit, the environment would not be as restrictive. For an emotionally handicapped student, the direct style of instruction might be the least restrictive environment, while a problem-solving method with group cooperation may be too difficult and would be more restrictive. Consistent and regular judgments need to be made, since curriculum content and teaching styles change the type of environment the student enters. It is shortsighted to place students into a situation and then forget about them. Evaluation and modification of environments need to be ongoing. The concept of "progressive inclusion" focuses on the idea that students make progress as a result of educational experiences. Thus, disabled students should have the opportunity to progress to the least restrictive environments and experience more and more of the mainstream of our schools and its programs.

MAINSTREAMING

Physical educators most often speak in terms of mainstreaming rather than least restrictive environments. Mainstreaming means that students with disabilities must have opportunities to integrate with other students in public schools. Prudent placement in a least restricted educational environment means that the setting must be as normal as possible (normalization), while ensuring that the student can fit in and achieve success in that placement. The placement may be mainstreaming but is not confined to this approach. There are several categories of placement relative to physical education classes.

1. Full Mainstreaming. Students with disabilities function as full-time members of a regular school routine. They go to all classes with able students. Within the limitations of their handicap, they participate in physical education with able peers. An example may be auditory-impaired students who with a minimal amount of assistance are able to participate fully.

2. Mainstreaming for Physical Education Only. Students with disabilities are not members of the regular academic classes in the secondary schools but can still participate in physical education with able peers. This setting may include emotionally disabled students who are grouped in the classroom and are seperated into regular physical education classes.

3. Partial Mainstreaming. Students participate in selected physical education experiences but do not attend on a full-time basis because they can be successful in only a few of the offerings. Their developmental needs are usually met in special classes.

4. Special Developmental Classes. Students with disabilities are in segregated special education classes.

5. Reverse Mainstreaming. Able students are brought into a special physical education class to promote intergroup peer relationships. The PEOPEL program is an example of this approach.

Segregation can be maintained only if it is in the best interests of the student. The purpose of segregated programs should be to establish a level of skill and social proficiency that will eventually enable the special student to be transferred to a less restricted learning environment. The goal of the process is the placement of the student in the least restrictive environment, where he or she can benefit most. Students with disabilities, working on their own, have often been denied opportunities to interact with peers and to become a part of the social and academic classroom network.

Students with disabilities should not lose contact with support personnel during mainstreaming. Even though the physical education teacher is responsible for the mainstreamed students during class time, these students still need access to special education teachers, school psychologists, and speech therapists. Support personnel should not view the situation as "getting rid of their students," but rather they should act as a source of information and support for the teacher in charge.

---

1. Regular physical education classes
2. Regular physical education classes with restricted class size (e.g., 15 able students per 1 child with disability).
3. Regular physical education classes with an aide or classroom teacher support.
4. Regular physical education classes plus part-time special education classes (e.g., 3 days regular, 2 days special per week).
5. Full-time special education class.
6. Full-time physical education in school for special education students only.

FIGURE 6.1 Physical education options, least to most restrictive environments

SCREENING AND ASSESSMENT ___

Every state is required to develop a plan for identifying, locating, and evaluating all students with disabilities. Generally, screening involves all students district-wide and is usually conducted at the start of the school year. Screening tests may include commonly used test batteries such as the Fitnessgram or AAHPERD Best Test. In most situations, screening tests may be administered without parental permission. They are used to make initial identification of students who may need special services.

Assessment is conducted after screening evaluations have been made. The appropriate students are referred to special education directors. Assessment is performed by a team of experts, which may include the physical education specialist. Due process for students and parents is important during formal assessment procedures. Due process assures that parents and students are informed of their rights and have the opportunity to challenge educational decisions that they feel are unfair or incorrect.

Due Process Guidelines

To assure that due process is offered to parents and students, the following guidelines must be followed:

1. Written Permission. A written notice must be sent to parents stating that their child has been referred for assessment. The notice must explain that the district requests permission to conduct an evaluation to determine if special education services are required for the child. Also included in the permission letter must be the reasons for testing and the tests to be used. Before assessment can begin, the letter must be signed by the parents and returned to the district.

2. Interpretation of the Assessment. The results of the assessment must be interpreted in a meeting with the parents. Persons who are knowledgeable of the test procedures must be present to answer questions parents may ask. At the meeting, parents must be told whether their child has any disabilities and what services will be provided.

3. External Evaluation. If parents are not satisfied with the results of the assessment, an evaluation outside of the school can be requested. The district must provide a list of agencies that can perform such assessments. If the results differ from the school district evaluation, the district must pay for the external evaluation. However, if the results are similar, parents must pay for the external testing.

4. Negotiation and Hearings. If parents and the school district disagree on the results of the assessment, the district is required to negotiate the differences. When negotiations fail, an impartial hearing officer listens to both parties and renders an official decision. This is usually the final review, however both parties do have the right to appeal to the state department of education, which must render a binding and final decision. Civil action through the legal system can be pursued should the district or parents still disagree. However, very few cases ever reach this level of long-term disagreement, and educators should not hesitate to serve the needs of youngsters with disabilities based on this concern.

5. Confidentiality. As is the case with other student records, only parents of the child or authorized school personnel can review the student's evaluation. Review by other parties can be done only after written permission has been given by the student's parents.

Procedures for Assuring Assessment Standards

P.L. 94–142 assures that assessment will be held to certain standards to assure fair and objective results. The following areas are specifically delineated:

Selection of Test Instruments. The test instruments used must be a valid examination of what they purport to measure. Thus, when selecting instruments, it must be clear to all parties how the tests were developed and how they will measure the area of disability. More than one test procedure must be used to determine the student's status. Both formal and informal assessment techniques should be used to assure that the results measure the student's impairment rather than simply reflect the student's shortcomings.

Unfortunately, youngsters must be labeled as disabled in order to reap the benefits of a special education program. The stigmatizing effect of labels and the fallibility of various means of testing students is a dilemma that must be faced. Although current pedagogical practices discourage labeling, it is double talk, since school districts must certify the handicap (to receive funding) by which the student is classified.

Administration Procedures. Many disabilities interfere with standard test procedures. For example, many students have communication problems and must be tested in a manner that assures testing of motor ability rather than communication skills. Many students have visual and hearing disabilities that prevent using tests that rely on these faculties.

A possibility of misdiagnosis and incorrectly classifying students as mentally retarded can occur with certain ethnic groups, such as native Americans, blacks, and Spanish speaking students. These young-sters, often victims of poor and impoverished living, may be only environmentally retarded and in need of cultural enrichment. It is subtle discrimination but it must be replaced with understanding that students differ because of culture, poverty, migrancy, and language. Many of the tests are based on white, middle-class standards. Minority students should be carefully assessed to determine the validity of the testing procedure.

Team Evaluation.   A number of experts should be used for assessment to help assure that all facets of the student will be reviewed and evaluated. Evaluation professionals must be well trained and qualified to administer the various tests. It is the responsibility of the school district to assure that this will occur.

DEVELOPMENT OF THE IEP

P.L. 94–142 requires that an individualized educational program (IEP) be developed for each disabled student receiving special education and related service. The IEP must be developed by a committee as stipulated by the law. Included on the committee must be the following members: a local education association representative who is qualified to provide and supervise the administration of special education, the student's parents, the teachers who have direct responsibility for implementing the IEP, and when appropriate, the student. Other individuals may be included at the discretion of the parents or school district such as an independent evaluator. This program identifies the student's unique qualities and determines educationally relevant strengths and weaknesses. A plan is then devised based on the diagnosis. The IEP must contain the following material:

1. Current status of the student's level of educational performance.
2. A statement of long-term goals and short-term instructional objectives.
3. A statement of special education and related services that will be provided to the youngster. Also, a report as to what extent the student will be able to participate in regular educational programs.
4. The dates for initiation of services and anticipated duration of the services.
5. Appropriate objective criteria for determining on an annual basis whether the short-term objectives are being reached.

Figure 6.2 is an example of a comprehensive IEP form.

Developing and sequencing objectives for the student is the first step in formulating the IEP. Short-range and long-range goals should be delineated, and data collection procedures and testing schedules established to monitor the student's progress. Materials and strategies to be used in implementing the IEP should also be established. Finally, methods of evaluation to be used are determined in order to monitor both the student's progress and the effectiveness of the program. (Computer assistance is helpful in relieving laborious hand recording.) Movement to a less restrictive environment should be based on achievement of specified competencies that are necessary in the new environment.

The IEP must contain a section determining whether specially designed physical education is needed. If not, the student should be held to the same expectations of his or her peer group. A student who needs special physical education might have an IEP with specified goals and objectives and might be mainstreamed in regular physical education with goals that do not resemble those of classmates.

Continued and periodic follow-up of the student is necessary. Effective communication between special and regular teachers is essential, because the student's progress needs careful monitoring. At the completion of the designated time period or school year, a written progress report should be filed along with recommendations for action during the coming year or time period. Here, again, the computer can be valuable. A summer program is often an excellent prescription to ensure that improvement is maintained. Records should be complete so that information about the youngster's problem and the effects of long-term treatment are always available.

CRITERIA FOR PLACEMENT OF STUDENTS

A difficult problem arises in determining the standards to be used for placing students into special programs. Several states have adopted criteria for determining eligibility of students for adapted physical education classes. State guidelines differ but should be followed closely if they exist. The standards are based on the administration of standardized tests for which norms or percentiles have been developed. This procedure helps to assure that objective guidelines are used, and avoids subjective judgment that may be open to disagreement and controversy. For example, criteria used by the State of Alabama are as follows:

1. Perform below the 30th percentile on standardized tests of
   a. Motor development
   b. Motor proficiency
   c. Fundamental motor skills and patterns

INDIVIDUALIZED EDUCATION PROGRAM

☐ Initial Placement
☐ Re-evaluation
☐ Change of Placement
☐ Review

A. **STUDENT INFORMATION:**
Student Name _____ (Last First Middle) Student No. _____ Home School _____
Date of Birth _____ Chronological Age ___ (M___ or F___) Present Placement/Grade ____
Parent/Guardian Name(s) _____ Receiving School _____
Home Address _____ (Street City/State Zip) Program Recommended _____
Home Phone _____ Work Phone _____ Starting Date _____
Emergency Phone _____ Three (3) Year Re-evaluation Due Date ___/___/___
Primary Language (Home) _____ (Child) _____ Interpreter Needed: Yes ___ No ___

B. **VISION SCREENING RESULTS:** Pass ___ Fail ___   **HEARING SCREENING RESULTS:** Pass ___ Fail ___
Date: _____ Comments: _____   Date: _____ Comments: _____

C. **REQUIRED OBSERVATION(S):** (All categories other than regular teacher)
___ Date(s) By: ___ Name(s) ___ Date(s) By: ___ Name(s) ___ Date(s) By: ___ Name(s)

D. **SUMMARY OF PRESENT LEVELS OF PERFORMANCE:**
Educational: _____

Behavioral: _____

E. Additional justification. See comments _____ Initial   See addendum _____ Initial

F. **PLACEMENT RECOMMENDATION INDICATING LEAST RESTRICTIVE ENVIRONMENT:**
Related services needed: Yes ___ No ___ (*List below.)

Placement Recommendation	Person Responsible	Amount of Time (Range)	Entry Date On/About	Review Reports On/About	Projected Ending Date	IEP Review Date
Primary:						
*Related Services:						

Transportation Needed? Yes ___ No ___ (If Yes, submit MPS Special Education Transportation Request Form.)

Describe extent student will participate in regular program: _____

Page 1 of ___

FIGURE 6.2   Example of an individualized educational plan

d. Physical fitness
e. Game/sport skills
f. Perceptual motor functioning
g. Posture screening
2. Exhibit a developmental delay of two or more years based on appropriate assessment instruments.
3. Function within the severe or profound range as determined by special education eligibility standards.
4. Possess social/emotional or physical capabilities that would render it unlikely for the student to reach his or her physical education goals without significant modification or exclusion form the regular physical education class.

If the student was determined not to be eligible for special education services, it may be beneficial to refer the student to programs for secondary students with special needs. These programs deal with areas that are not delineated by P.L. 94–142 such as obesity, physical fitness, and motor deficiencies. Unfortunately, few secondary schools offer such programs, and eligible students must survive in the

INDIVIDUALIZED EDUCATION PROGRAM

REPORT OF MULTIDISCIPLINARY CONFERENCE
Date Held _____

Student Name _____   Student No. _____

G. PROGRAM PLANNING:

Long-Term Goals: _____

Short-Term Objectives (Goals): _____

H. EVALUATION:

Evaluation criteria are described in the Individual Implementation Plan (IIP) which is available in the classroom file.

I. PLACEMENT COMMITTEE:

The following have been consulted or have participated in the placement and IEP decisions:

Names of Members	Position	Present (Initial)	Oral Report	Written Report	Signatures
	Parents/Guardian				
	Parents/Guardian				
	School Administrator				
	Special Ed Administrator				
	School Psychologist				
	Nurse				
	Teacher(s) Receiving				
	Teacher(s) Referring				
	Interpreter				

Dissenting Opinion: Yes _____ No _____ If Yes, see comments _____ See addendum_____ .
                                                                 Initial   Initial

J. PARENT (OR GUARDIAN) STATEMENT:

We agree to the placement recommended in this IEP. Yes _____ No _____

We give our permission to have our child counseled by the professional staff, if necessary. Yes _____ No _____

We understand that placement will be on a continuing trial basis and we will be contacted if any placement changes are contemplated. We are aware that such placement does not guarantee success; however, in order to help our child, we accept the responsibility to cooperate in every way with the school program. We acknowledge that we have been notified of and have received a copy of our due process rights pertaining to Special Education placement and have a basic understanding of these rights. We acknowledge that we have received a copy of the completed IEP Form.

_____   _____
Parent or Guardian Signature   Date

COMMENTS: _____

Page 2 of _____

FIGURE 6.2   Continued

---

regular programs. Physical educators must show concern for helping students with these problems since obesity and physical fitness are areas of strong concern among parents.

GUIDELINES FOR SUCCESSFUL MAINSTREAMING EXPERIENCES

The concern is not whether to mainstream, but how to mainstream effectively. The physical educator has to teach a number of students with disabilities and diverse impairments. Learning strategies that the instructor is familiar with and has been using successfully may not be appropriate for students with disabilities. Attitudinal change is important since the teacher must accept the student as a full-fledged participant and assume the responsibilities that go along with special education.

An important consideration when planning the IEP is whether the student is ready for mainstreaming. Many students with disabilities have severe developmental lags, that become insurmountable factors working against successful integration in normal classes. The student must be physically able to accomplish a portion of the program without much, if any, assistance. Placement should be limited to certain activities in which success can be achieved.

When a student is deemed ready for placement, consultation between the physical education teacher and the special education supervisor is of prime importance. In a setting where emotions and feelings can run high, it is important to assure that communication and planning occur on a regular basis. The reception and acceptance of the special students must not be left to chance. A scheduled plan should be instituted before the student is mainstreamed. Special and physical education professionals must discuss the needs of the student and develop realistic expectations. It is quite possible that the special education teacher may have to participate in the physical education class to assure a smooth transition. The thrust should center on what the student *can* rather than on what he or she *cannot* do. Any approach that treats students with disabilities as cripples is dehumanizing. Full information is due the physical education teacher before the student appears. This procedure should also be implemented when the student moves from one mainstreaming situation to another.

Both able and disabled students must have opportunities to make appropriate progress. The educational needs of students with disabilities must be met without jeopardizing the progress of other students. This does not rule out activity modifications so that those with disabilities can be included. Some adapted equipment may also be necessary.

The teacher is advised to help all students understand the problems related to being disabled. A goal should be to have students understand, accept, and live comfortably with persons with disabilities. They should recognize that students with disabilities are functional and worthwhile individuals who have innate abilities and can make significant contributions to society. The concept of understanding and appreciating individual differences is one that merits positive development and should concentrate on three aspects:

1. Recognizing the similarities among all people: their hopes, rights, aspirations, and goals.
2. Understanding human differences and focusing on the concept that all people are disabled. For some, disabilities are of such nature and severity that they interfere with normal living.
3. Exploring ways to deal with those who differ without overhelping, and stressing the acceptance of all students as worthwhile individuals. People with disabilities deserve consideration and understanding, based on empathy, not sympathy.

Students with disabilities should not be permitted to use their handicap as an excuse for substandard work. Youngsters should not be allowed to manipulate people into helping with tasks they are capable of doing. Coping skills need to be developed, because the disabled could encounter teasing, ignorance, and rejection.

Once the mainstreamed student, able students, and teacher have undergone preliminary preparation, consideration can be given to integrating the disabled youngster into the learning environment. Mainstreaming should allow the student to make commendable educational progress, to achieve in those areas outlined in the IEP, to learn to accept limitations, to observe and model appropriate behavior, to become more socially accepted by others, and in general to become a part of the real world. Some guidelines for successful integration of students with disabilities into physical education follow.

1. In addition to participation in the regular program of activities, it is important to meet the target goals specified in the IEP. This can involve resources beyond the physical education class, including special work and homework.

2. Build ego strength; stress abilities. Eliminate established practices that unwittingly contribute to embarrassment and failure.

3. Foster peer acceptance, which begins when the teacher accepts the student as a functioning, participating member of the class.

4. Concentrate on the student's physical education needs and not on the disability. Give strong attention to fundamental skills and physical fitness qualities.

5. Provide continual monitoring and assess periodically the student's target goals. Anecdotal and periodic record keeping are implicit in this guideline.

6. Be constantly aware of the students' feelings and anxiety concerning their progress and integration. Provide positive feedback as a basic practice.

7. Modify the regular program to meet the unique capacities, physical needs, and social needs of youngsters with disabilities.

8. Provide individual assistance and keep youngsters active. Peer or paraprofessional help may be needed. On-task time is important.

9. Consult regularly with the special education professional.

10. Give consideration to more individualization within the program so that youngsters with disabilities are smoothly integrated. The individualized approach must be based on the target goals of the IEP.

11. Consider using computer programs for recording data and generating meaningful reports.

TEACHER BEHAVIOR AND THE MAINSTREAMING PROCESS

The success or failure of the mainstreaming process depends largely on the interaction between the teacher and student with a disability. There is no foolproof, teacher-proof system. Purposes and derived goals are perhaps more important to students with disabilities than to so-called normal peers. Proper levels of organic fitness and skill are vital for healthful living. Such levels enable them to compete with peers. Teachers must accept responsibility for meeting the needs of students, including those with disabilities that permit some degree of mainstreaming. Teachers need to be able to judge when referral for special assistance or additional services is in order. Physical education specialists must be able to do the following: (1) analyze and diagnose motor behavior of the disabled, (2) provide appropriate experiences for remediation of motor conditions needing attention, and (3) register data as needed on the student's personal record.

Record keeping is important. A short period, perhaps the 5 min between classes, could be set aside to accomplish the task promptly. When time between classes is short, the teacher may want to use a portable tape recorder for recording evaluative comments during class time.

To work successfully with students with disabilities, teachers must know the characteristics of the specific impairment and how it affects learning. The teacher should also know how to assess motor and fitness needs, and how to structure remediation to meet those needs. Referrals should be minimal. Teachers should have alternative strategies in reserve in case the original method fails. Referral to the special education teacher then becomes a last resort.

Explanations and directions should be couched in terms that all students, including the retarded, can understand. Be sure that the students with disabilities understand what is to be accomplished before the learning experiences begin, especially when working with the hearing impaired. Concentrate on finding activities in which the student can excel. Try to find some activity through which they can achieve peer regard. In particular, these students should be expected to work to their full capacity. Do not accept a performance that is inferior in terms of the student's abilities.

Avoid placing disabled students in situations where they could easily fail. Give them opportunities that make the best use of their talents. Stress the special objectives of the disabled. Obvious increments of improvement toward terminal objectives are excellent motivators for both students and teachers. Let youngsters know that you as a teacher are vitally interested in their progress.

Apply multisensory approaches in teaching the disabled. Visual and auditory modes of learning may not reach slow learners. Manipulate the student through a given movement to communicate the correct "feel." Touch or rub the involved part of the body to provide tactile stimulation. Emphasis should be on helping students perform the skill, not doing it for them.

The presence of students with disabilities in the physical education class requires teachers to become more effective organizers. This ultimately results in an improved overall program. Ideally, all students in the class would have IEPs, so that the teacher could monitor the individual progress of each one.

Teachers should seek sources of information to aid them in dealing effectively with disabled students. Books about disabilities and suggested guidelines for dealing with special students are available. Workshops can be organized featuring knowledgeable individuals with successful programs who can help solve specific problems. Larger school systems may organize in-service education for physical education teachers.

FITNESS AND POSTURE FOR STUDENTS WITH DISABILITIES

The normalization process has directed attention to posture as a factor in peer acceptance. Since many junior high students with disabilities have low physical fitness levels, posture problems often occur in this group. One aim of mainstreaming is to make the special students less visible, hence the need to help them achieve acceptable posture. Values received from an attractive appearance include better acceptance by peers and more employment opportunities later.

Physical fitness is also important for these special students. To compete with and gain respect from peers, the goal of fitness, aside from personal values, is a justified thrust of the physical education program. Adequate physical fitness helps the student move through the school day, which may be complicated by a sensory deficit, a mobility problem, or a mental deficiency.

Special care must be given to students who have been excluded from physical education programs. Wheelchair students need special attention given to their cardiovascular development through activities that stimulate deep breathing. Arm development is important so that they can move in and out of the wheelchair easily.

It is crucial to correct an idiosyncratic gait or an appearance that gives the impression of deviance. These are often problems for mentally retarded youngsters. Early identification of a problem and inclusion of a posture correction program are important. The physical educator is often best qualified to initiate and supervise this program. Informal screening should include several tasks—walking, sitting, and stair climbing. Height, weight, and body type affect posture. Obesity may need to be considered in amelioration. Once identification is made, a more detailed analysis of the subject's posture can follow. The degree of postural abnormality governs whether referral is indicated. Videotaping can provide baseline data from which to monitor corrections. Achieving an acceptable posture is both a short-term (progress) and long-term (achievement) goal to be included in the student's IEP.

Exercise and physical conditioning procedures can be selected to help develop antigravity musculature and to provide flexibility training. These must be combined with comprehensive movement training so that the student learns to move as skillfully and gracefully as possible. Muscular relaxation techniques may help. A well-rounded physical education program is important and should be reinforced by corrective exercises.

Referral for severe conditions or for postural conditions that are difficult to correct should involve the support services of a physician or an orthopedic specialist. Braces may be needed, particularly for lateral curvature (scoliosis).

The psychosocial aspects of posture should be considered, with attention focused on the establishment of a good self-concept and effective social relations. Behavior management can focus on the motivation for better postural habits in standing, walking, sitting, lifting, and general movement. Proper posture should become a habit.

MODIFYING PARTICIPATION _____

Special education students may need additional consideration when participating in group activities, particularly when the activity is competitive. Much depends on the physical condition of the student and the type of impairment. Students like to win in a competitive situation, and resentment can be created if a team loss is attributed to the presence of a student with a disability. Equalization is the key. Rules can be changed for everyone so that the disabled student has a chance to contribute to group success. On the other hand, students need to recognize that everyone, including the disabled and the inept, has a right to play.

Be aware of situations that might devalue the student socially. Never use the degrading method of having captains choose from a group of waiting students. Elimination games should be changed so that points are scored instead of players being eliminated (this is an important consideration for all youngsters). Determine the most desirable involvement for students with disabilities by analyzing participants' roles in game and sport activities. Assign a role or position that will make the experience as natural or normal as possible.

Offer a variety of individual and dual activities. Disabled students need to build confidence in their skills before they want to participate with others. Individual activities give them a greater amount of practice time without the pressure of failing in front of peers. The aim of these techniques is to make the students with disabilities less visible so that they are not set apart from able classmates. Using students with disabilities as umpires or scorekeepers should be a last resort. Overprotectiveness benefits no one and prevents the special student from experiencing challenge and personal accomplishment. Avoid the tendency to underestimate students' abilities. The following sections offer ideas for modifying activities to facilitate integration of students with disabilities.

Modifications for Students Lacking Strength and Endurance

1. Lower or enlarge the size of the goal. In basketball, the goal can be lowered; in soccer the goal might be enlarged.

2. Modify the tempo of the game. For example, games might be performed using a brisk walk rather than running. Another way to modify tempo is to stop the game regularly for substitution. Auto-substitutions can be an excellent method for allowing students to determine when they are fatigued. They ask a predetermined substitute to take their place.

3. Reduce the weight and/or modify the size of the projectile. A lighter object will move more slowly and inflict less damage upon impact. A larger object will move more slowly and be easier for students to track visually and catch.

4. Reduce the distance that a ball must be thrown or served. Options are to reduce the dimensions of the playing area or add more players to the game. In serving, others can help make the serve playable. For example, in volleyball, other teammates can bat the serve over the net as long as it does not touch the floor.

5. In games that are played to a certain number of points, reduce the number required for a win. For example, volleyball games could be played to 7 or 11, depending on the skill and intensity of the players.

6. Modify striking implements by shortening and reducing their weight. Racquets are much easier to control when they are shortened. Softball bats are easier to control when the player "chokes up" and selects a lighter bat.

7. If possible, slow the ball by letting out some air. This will reduce the speed of rebound and make the ball easier to control in a restricted area. It will also keep the ball from rolling away from players when it is not under control.

8. Play the games in a different position. Some games may be played in a sitting or lying position, which is easier and less demanding than standing or running.

9. Provide matching or substitution. Match another student on borrowed crutches with a student on braces. Two players can be combined to play one position. A student in a desk chair with wheels can be matched against a wheelchair student. Permit substitute courtesy runners.

10. Allow students to substitute skills. For example, a student may be able to strike an object but may lack the mobility to run. Another student can be selected to run for her.

Modifications for Students Lacking Coordination

1. Increase the size of the goal or target. Increasing the size of a basketball goal will increase the opportunity for success. Another alternative might be to offer points for hitting the backboard near a goal. Since scoring is self-motivating, modification should occur until success is assured.

2. Offer protection when appropriate. The lack of coordination will make the student more susceptible to injury from a projectile. Use various types of protectors (such as glasses, chest protectors, or face masks).

3. When teaching throwing, allow students the

opportunity to throw at maximum velocity without concern for accuracy. Use small balls that can be grasped easily. Fleece balls and beanbags are easy to hold and release.

4. Use a stationary object when teaching striking or hitting. The use of a batting tee or tennis ball fastened to a string can offer the student an opportunity for success. In addition, a larger racquet or bat and "choking up" on the grip can be used.

5. Make projectiles easily retrievable. If a great deal of time is spent on recovering the projectile, students will receive few practice trials and feel frustrated. Place them near a backstop or use a goal that rebounds the projectile to the shooter.

6. When teaching catching, use a soft, lightweight, and slow moving object. Beach balls and balloons are excellent for beginning catching skills since they allow the student to track their movement visually. In addition, foam rubber balls eliminate the fear of being hurt by a thrown or batted projectile.

Modifications for Students Lacking Balance and Agility

1. Increase the width of rails, lines, and beam when practicing balance. Carrying a long pole will help minimize rapid shifts of balance and is a useful leadup activity.

2. Increase the width of the base of support. Students should be taught to keep the feet spread at least to shoulder width.

3. Emphasize use of many body parts when teaching balance. The more body parts in contact with the floor, the easier it is to balance the body. Beginning balance practice should emphasize controlled movement using as many body parts as possible.

4. Increase the surface area of the body parts in contact with the floor or beam. For example, walking flat-footed is easier than walking on tiptoes.

5. Lower the center of gravity. This offers more stability and greater balance to the youngster. Emphasis should be placed on bending the knees and slightly leaning forward.

6. Assure that surfaces offer good friction. Floors and shoes should not be slick or students will fall. Carpets or tumbling mats will increase traction.

7. Provide balance assistance. A barre, cane, or chair can be used to keep the student from falling.

8. Teach students how to fall. Students with balance problems will inevitably fall. Practice in learning how to fall should be offered so that they gradually learn how to absorb the force.

SPECIFIC TYPES OF DISABILITIES

To assist students with handicaps, an understanding of the disability and what it means to the student is essential. Basic information is provided here, and additional materials can be secured from special education consultants. The information provided here is just a starting point; students do not always fit into neat categories. These students need to develop strength and endurance as well as leisure and sport skills just like any able bodied student. National associations offer information about various disabilities and suggest ways of helping these special students.

Mental Retardation

The capacity of the mentally retarded student is deficient and does not allow the student to be served by the standard program. Deficient mental functioning is a question of degree, usually measured in terms of intelligence quotient (IQ). Mildly retarded students (with IQs ranging roughly from 50 to 75 or 80) are most often mainstreamed in both physical education and the regular classroom. Students with IQs below 50 usually cannot function in a regular classroom environment; they need special classes. These students are generally not mainstreamed and therefore excluded from the following discussion.

Academically, mildly retarded students (also termed "educable mentally retarded") are slower to understand directions, to follow directions, to complete tasks, and to make progress. Conceptually, they have difficulty pulling facts together and drawing conclusions. Their motivation to stay on task is generally lower. Academic success may have eluded them. These realities must be considered in the physical education setting. Improvement in these areas is a goal to be achieved.

Do retarded students differ physically from other students? In a study comparing 71 educable mentally retarded boys with 71 normal boys, aged 6–10 years, the following was noted. Differences between the retarded and the normal in respect to opportunities to be physically active tend to be substantial. Similarly, the motivation to be physically active may be less in the retarded, a reflection of their general motor ineptness. The relatively large proportion of subcutaneous tissue in the retarded is more than suggestive of a physically inactive life resulting in a corresponding low level of motor performance (Dobbins et. al., 1981).

In another study (Ulrich, 1983), a comparison was made of the developmental levels of 117 disabled and 96 educable mentally retarded youngsters with respect to criterion-referenced testing of 12 fundamental motor skills and 4 physical fitness skills. The investigation supports the findings of the previous study in that the educable mentally retarded students lagged 3.5 years behind normal students in motor skill development, as based on the researcher's selected criterion reference point. The investigator attributes this lag to a lack of opportunity for movement experiences at an early age. The disabled students were from special education classes, not from a mainstreaming situation.

Instructional Procedures

Studies of mildly retarded students support the assumption that they can learn, but at a slower rate and not to the depth of normal mentally functioning students. To help the mildly retarded develop their capacities so that they can become participating members of society, the learning process should concentrate on fundamental skills and fitness qualities. Unless this base is established, the retarded student faces considerable difficulty later in learning specialized skills. Minimizing skill and fitness lags can help ease the student into mainstream living.

The fitness approach involves motivation, acquisition of developmental techniques, and application of these to a personalized fitness program. The retarded student reacts well to goal setting, provided that the goals are challenging yet attainable. The pace of learning depends on the degree of retardation. Before a retarded student can learn, he needs to know what is expected and how it is to be accomplished. Common sense must govern the determination of progress increments. These should be challenging but within the performer's grasp. Often, past experiences have made retarded students the victims of a failure syndrome. The satisfaction of accomplishment must supplant this poor self-image.

Place emphasis on gross motor movement that is progressive in nature. Teach activities that are presented through demonstration rather than verbalization. Many of the skills may have to be accompanied by manual assistance to help student get the "feel" of the skill. To avoid boredom and frustration, practice periods should be short. Allow ample opportunity for youngsters to "show off" skills they have learned so that they can enjoy the feeling of accomplishment. Shaping behavior by accepting approximation of the skill will encourage the student to keep trying. Progress arrives in small increments and teachers must be sensitive to improvement and accomplishment, no matter how small.

Effort should be rewarded. Many of these youngsters are reticent to try a new activity. Instructions should be repeated a number of times. Safety rules must be followed since these students may not understand the risk of injury involved.

Epilepsy

Epilepsy is a dysfunction of the electrical impulses emitted by the brain. It is not an organic disease. It can happen at any period of life but generally shows up during early childhood. With proper care and medication, many people overcome this condition and live normal lives.

Epilepsy is a hidden problem. A student with epilepsy looks, acts, and is like other students except for unpredictable seizures. Unfortunately, epilepsy carries an unwarranted social stigma. A student with epilepsy meets with a lack of acceptance, even when adequate explanations are made to those around him her. A major seizure can be frightening—or even revolting—to observers.

Gaining control of seizures is often a long process, involving experimentation with appropriate anticonvulsive medication in proper doses. Fortunately, most epilepsy can be controlled or minimized with proper medication. One factor in control is to be sure that the student is taking the medication as prescribed.

Sometimes a student can recognize signs of seizure onset. If this occurs in a physical education class, the student should have the privilege of moving to the sideline without permission. A seizure may, however, occur without warning. The instructor should know the signs of a seizure and react accordingly. The teacher may be the first (even before the student) to recognize that a seizure is imminent.

Three kinds of seizures are identified. A *petit mal seizure* involves a brief period (a few seconds) of blackout. No one is aware of the problem, including the student. Sometimes it is labeled inattention and thus is difficult to identify. A *psychomotor epileptic seizure* is longer lasting (perhaps a few minutes) and is characterized by involuntary movements and twitching. The student acts like a sleepwalker and cannot be stopped or helped. The affected youngster does not respond when addressed and is unaware of the seizure. A *grand mal seizure* is characterized by complete neurological involvement. The student may become unconscious and lose control of the bladder or bowels, resulting in loss of urine, stool, or both. Rigidity and tremors can appear. The seizure must run its course.

Two points are important. First, throughout any seizure or incident, the teacher must preserve a matter-of-fact attitude and try not to exhibit pity. Second, the teacher must educate the other students to understand and empathize with the problem. Stress what the condition is and, later, what it is not. Explain that the behavior during a seizure is a response to an unusual output of electrical discharges from the brain. Everyone needs these discharges to function in normal living, but the person with epilepsy is subject to an unusual amount of the discharges, which results in unusual activity. The condition involves a natural phenomenon that gets out of control.

Students need to understand that the seizure must run its course. When the seizure is over, everyone can resume normal activity, including the involved student, although the student may be disoriented and uncoordinated for a brief period of time. Offer the student the option of resting or returning to activity. Proper emotional climate of the class is established when the teacher maintains an accepting and relaxed attitude.

Information about epilepsy should be a part of the standard health curriculum in the school, rather than a reaction to an epileptic seizure or to the presence of a student who may have seizures. Epilepsy can be discussed as a topic relevant to understanding the central nervous system. Certain risks are involved if the lessons have as their focus the problems of a particular student, because this may heighten the student's feelings of exclusion and place disproportionate attention on what might have been a relatively inconsequential aspect of his or her life. (This caution does not rule out helpful information being given to peers when a seizure has taken place.)

In the event of a grand mal seizure, some routine procedures should be followed. Have available a blanket, a pillow, and towels to clean up as necessary. Make the student comfortable if there is time. Do not try to restrain him or her. Put nothing in the mouth. Support the head on the pillow, turning it to one side to allow the saliva to drain. Remove from the area any hard or sharp objects that might cause harm. Get help from a doctor or nurse if the seizure continues more than 3 or 4 min, or if seizures occur three or more times during a school day. Always notify the school nurse and the parents that a seizure had occurred. Assure the class that the seizure will pass and that the involved student will not be harmed or affected.

Instructional Procedures

Recommendations regarding special modes of conduct and guidelines governing participation in school activities must come from the student's physician, since most epileptic students are under medical supervision. The instructor should stay within these guidelines while avoiding being overprotective.

Today's approach is to bring epilepsy into the open. A concerted effort should be made to educate today's students so that traditional attitudes toward the condition can be altered. Emphasize inclusion of the student rather than exclusion. If there is some doubt about control of the seizures, climbing and elevated activities should be eliminated.

Perhaps tomorrow's adults will then possess a better understanding. The student with epilepsy is a normal, functioning person except at the time of a seizure. Epilepsy is not a form of mental illness, and most people with epilepsy are not mentally retarded.

Visual Impairment

Mainstreaming for the visually impaired must be handled carefully and with common sense. The visually impaired designation includes those who are partially sighted as well as those who are legally blind. One has only to move about in a dark room to realize the mobility problems faced by a visually impaired student. This disability poses movement problems and puts limits on participation in certain types of physical activity. Total mainstreaming may not be a feasible solution.

There is a need to bring the student in contact with classmates, however, and to focus on the student's unique qualities and strengths. Empathy for and acceptance of the visually impaired student are most important. The task of monitoring movement and helping this student should be considered a privilege to be rotated among class members. If participation in the class activity selected is contraindicated, the monitor can help provide an alternate activity.

Instructional Procedures

Visually impaired students have to develop confidence in their ability to move freely and surely within the limits of their disability. Since limited mobility often leads to reduced activity, this inclination can be countered with a specialized physical fitness and movement program in which the lack of sight does not prove insurmountable. The student can participate in group fitness activities with assistance as needed. Exercises should pose few problems. Rope jumping is an excellent activity. Individual movement activities, stunts and tumbling, rhythms and dances (particularly partner dances), and selected apparatus activities can be appropriate. Low balance beams, bench activities, climbing apparatus, and climbing ropes may be within the

student's capacity. Manipulative activities, involving tactile senses, are not always appropriate. If the student has some vision, however, brightly colored balls against a contrasting background in good light can permit controlled throwing, tracking, and catching. Through the selection of activities, the sense of balance should be challenged regularly to contribute to sureness of movement. Since vision is limited, other balance controls also need to be developed.

The visually impaired student usually cannot take visual cues from other students or the teacher, so explanations must be precise and clear. Use a whistle or loud verbal cue to signal the class. For some situations, an assigned peer can monitor activity, helping as needed or requested. In running situations, the helper can hold hands with the visually impaired student. Another way to aid the student is with physical guidance until the feel of a movement pattern is established. This should be a last choice, however, occurring only after the student has had a chance to interpret the verbal instructions and still cannot meet the challenge. Touching a part of the student's body to establish correct sequencing in a movement pattern also can be of help.

Auditory Impairment

Auditory impaired students are those who are deaf or who must wear hearing aids. In physical education classes, these students are capable of performing most, if not all, activities that able students can perform. Since most instruction is verbal, a deaf student is isolated and often frustrated in a mainstreaming situation unless other means of communication are established. Accomplishing this while keeping the class functioning normally is a serious problem.

Some advocates for the deaf contend that implementing P.L. 94–142 with its emphasis on mainstreaming is not appropriate for deaf students and thwarts their development. Teaching the deaf is a challenging and specialized process, requiring different communication techniques. Many deaf students have poor or unintelligible speech and inevitably develop a language gap with the hearing world. Sign language, lip reading, and speech training are all important facets of communicative ability for the deaf. Integrating deaf students in the regular physical education class setting is a process that must be handled with common sense. The experience should be satisfying to the deaf student or it is a failure.

Instructional Procedures

Certainly, hearing-impaired students can perform physically and at the same level as students with normal hearing when given the opportunity. One successful approach to teaching both the hearing impaired and normal youngsters is to use contract or task card techniques. Written instructions can be read loudly by the teacher or monitor. Pairing students with severe hearing loss with other students can be a frustrating experience for both, but meaningful possibilities also exist. Such a pairing necessitates lip reading, the use of verbal cues, or strong amplification on a hearing aid. Visual cues, featuring a "do as I do" approach, can stimulate certain types of activity.

The deaf student should be near the teacher to increase the opportunities to read lips and receive facial cues. Keep the class physically active. Avoid long delays for explanations or question-and-answer periods. This becomes a blank time for the hearing impaired and leads to frustration and aggressive action. For rhythmics, some devices can be of benefit. Keep stereo speakers on the floor to provide vibration. Use a metronome or blinking light. For controlling movement patterns, hand signals should be developed for starting, stopping, moving to an area, assembling near the teacher, sitting down, and so on.

Static and dynamic balance problems are prevalent among hearing-impaired students. Focus on activities that challenge balance and insist on proper procedures. Have the student maintain the position or movement for 10 to 15 sec and recover to the original position, all in good balance.

Orthopedic Disabilities

Orthopedic disabilities in students encompass a wide range of physical ailments, some of which may involve external support items such as splints, braces, crutches, and wheelchairs. A few post-polio cases may be encountered. Generalizing procedures for such a wide range of physical abnormalities is difficult. Students with orthopedic problems usually function on an academic level with other students and are regular members of a classroom. As such, they appear with the class for physical education.

Instructional Procedures

Instructional focus must be on what the student can do and on the physical needs that are to be met. Mobility is a problem for most, and modification is needed if the class activity demands running or agility. Individualized programs are made to order for this group, because the achievement goals can be set within the student's capacity to perform.

Although volleyball and basketball are popular team sports, there will be few leisure opportunities for these individuals because of the difficulty of getting enough participants together for team play. Strong emphasis should be placed on individual and dual sports such as tennis, track and field, road rac-

ing, table tennis, badminton, and swimming. This allows the orthopedically impaired individual to play a dual sport with an able or disabled opponent or to participate individually in activities such as road racing and swimming.

For wheelchair students, certain measures are implicit. Special work is needed to develop general musculature to improve conditions for coping with the disability and to prevent muscle atrophy. In particular, wheelchair students need strong arm and shoulder musculature to transfer in and out of the wheelchair without assistance. Flexibility training to prevent and relieve permanent muscle shortening (contracture) should be instituted. Cardiorespiratory training is needed to maintain or improve aerobic capacity, since immobility in the chair decreases activity. From these experiences, the wheelchair student should derive a personal functioning program of activity that he or she can carry over into daily living.

Time devoted to special health care after class must be considered for students with either braces or in wheelchairs. Students with braces should inspect skin contact areas to look for irritation. If the student has perspired, a washcloth and towel will help him freshen up and remove irritants. Wheelchair students can transfer to a sturdy chair that is rigid and stabilized to allow the wheelchair to dry out. Provide adequate cushioning for any surface to which an orthopedically impaired person transfers, such as chairs, weight machines, and pool decks, to prevent pressure sores and skin abrasions. Adjust schedules so that time for this care is available. Scheduling the class during the last period before lunch or recess (or at the end of the day) allows this time.

Students with temporary conditions (fractures, sprains, strains) are handled on an individual basis, according to physician recommendations. Remedial work may be indicated.

Emotional Disorders

Emotionally disturbed students represent an enigma for mainstreaming. They have been removed from the regular classroom situation because they may cause a disruption and because they need psychological services. Physical education seems to be one area in which they can find success. Each case is different, however, and generalization is difficult. Some students may be withdrawn, loud, aggressive, mute, or rebellious.

Instructional Procedures

An important key when working with emotionally disturbed students is to establish a learning environment that is fair and consistent. The students need to know exactly what is expected and accepted in the instructional setting. In addition, rules must be clearly defined and nonpunitive in nature. Explanation of reasons for rules should be a regular topic of discussion since emotionally disturbed youngsters often feel that someone is making rules that are meant to punish them personally.

Disturbed students need a stable and organized environment that focuses on individual progress. They will become easily frustrated and quit if the activities are too difficult or cause embarrassment. Expect occasional outbursts, even when instructional procedures have been correct. If the unexpected is anticipated, teachers will not feel as threatened or hurt by the student's behavior.

Emotionally disturbed students need to know their limits of behavior. Set the limits and then enforce them consistently. Students must know who is in charge and what that person will accept. It may take a long time to develop confidence in the emotionally disturbed student, and vice versa. During this time it is important to build a sense of trust. Plan on problems and be ready to deal with them before they occur. A teacher who is patient and understanding can have a positive effect on students with this disability. Loving and forgiving teachers are most effective with the emotionally disturbed youngster.

Other Disabilities

A range of other disabilities may arise. These include cardiac problems, cerebral palsy, asthma, and diabetes.

Students with cardiac problems are generally under the guidance of a physician. Limitations and restrictions should be followed to the letter. The student should, however, be encouraged to work to the limits of the prescription.

An asthmatic student has restricted breathing capacity. The condition carries a warning against activities that can cause breathing distress. The student should be the judge of her physical capacity and stop when rest is indicated.

Cerebral palsy, like epilepsy, has strong negative social implications. Peer education and guidance are necessary. The signs of cerebral palsy are quite visible and, in severe cases, result in odd, uncoordinated movements and a characteristic gait. Medical supervision indicates the limits of the student's activities. Students with cerebral palsy are usually of normal intelligence; their chief problem is control of movement. An important goal is ensuring that they can achieve competency in performing simple movements. The excitability threshold is critical and must not be exceeded. Many need support services

for special training in both neural and movement control.

Occasionally, a diabetic student may be found in a physical education class. Diabetes is an inability to metabolize carbohydrates that results from the body's failure to supply insulin. Insulin is taken either orally or by injection to control serious cases. If the student is overweight, a program of weight reduction and exercise prescription are partial solutions. Diabetics are usually under medical supervision. Knowing that a diabetic student is in a physical education class is important because the student must be monitored to detect the possibility of hypoglycemia (abnormally low blood sugar level). The condition can be accompanied by trembling, weakness, hunger, incoherence, and even by coma or convulsions. The solution is to raise the blood sugar level immediately through oral consumption of simple sugar (e.g., skim milk, orange juice) or some other easily converted carbohydrate. The diabetic usually carries carbohydrates, but a supply should be available to the instructor. Immediate action is needed because low blood sugar level can be dangerous—even life-threatening. The diabetic probably has enough control to participate in almost any activity. This is evidenced by the number of diabetic professional athletes, who meet the demands of high activity without difficulty.

UTILIZING MICROCOMPUTER SERVICES

Microcomputers are becoming increasingly available in schools all over the country. The computer is a time-saving device that can take over the record-keeping chores required by the provisions of P.L. 94–142. Printouts of present and past status reports can be made available on demand. The computer can also provide comparisons with established norms, especially in physical fitness areas, and it can record progress toward the target goals set by the IEP. The computer minimizes the time necessary for recording student progress. In addition, computerized graphic compilations facilitate quick comprehension of progress reports. There are several computer programs available for writing and updating the IEP.

Another significant computer service is related to informational printouts. The due process regulations of P.L. 94–142 might be one such topic. Information concerning specific disabilities could be made readily available. Guidelines for formulating the IEP are another possibility. Long- and short-term objectives can be retrieved from a growing data bank.

Making relevant progress information available to students can be excellent motivation and stimulates a systematic approach to the attainment of specific achievements. The same information can also be the basis for reports to parents and other adults who are interested in the student. These reports can enhance parental cooperation.

PARENTAL SUPPORT

Having parents on the IEP committee spurs their involvement and establishes a line of communication between home and school. Home training or homework may be recommended for many students. If home training is indicated, parents must be committed in terms of time and effort. Their work need not be burdensome but must be done regularly in accordance with the sequenced learning patterns. Also, the school must supply printed and sequenced learning activities for a systematic approach to the homework. Materials should be understandable and goals clear. Parents should see obvious progress in their youngsters as assignments unfold.

Older students with disabilities may accept some responsibility for home training, relegating the parent to the role of an interested, encouraging spectator. Even if homework is not feasible, parental interest and support are positive factors. The parents can help their youngster realize what skills have been learned and what progress has been made.

RECRUITING AND TRAINING AIDES

The use of aides can be an effective way of increasing the amount of instruction and practice for students who are disabled. Volunteers are quite easy to find among various community organizations, such as parent–teacher, foster grandparents, and community colleges. High school students who volunteer have proven effective with junior high school students. An effective program, the PEOPEL project, was developed using trained student peers to teach students with disabilities in small classes.

An initial meeting with volunteer aides should explain the type of youngsters with whom they will work and clarify their responsibilities. Aides must learn how to be most effective in assisting the instructor. Training could include learning how to work effectively with individuals, recording data, and developing special materials and instructional supplies. In addition, the potential aides should receive experience in working with youngsters in order to see if they are capable and enjoy such work. Physical education specialists must also learn how to work with aides. In some cases, physical educators often find the task of organizing and supervising aides to be burdensome if they have not learned to supervise and organize.

There are many roles that aides can assume which increase the effectiveness of the instructional situation. For example, the aide may gather and locate equipment and supplies prior to the lesson. They may officiate games and assure that they run smoothly. Seasoned aides enjoy and are capable of offering one-on-one or small group instruction to youngsters. Aides should not reduce the need for involvement of the physical education instructor since they only implement instruction strategies that have been organized and developed by the professional educator. In addition, the physical educator must monitor the quality of the presentations made by the aide.

NATIONALLY VALIDATED PROGRAMS

For several years, nationally validated programs of proven practices in special education have been available. Portions of many of these programs are in or related to physical education. These programs are funded and endorsed by the U.S. Office of Education. Some deal with screening, assessment, and curriculum for students with special needs. Others feature management practices associated with special students. A number deal with early recognition and intervention so that the student can be fitted more successfully into the mainstreaming situation. Information pertaining to these programs can be secured from state departments of education or from the U.S. Office of Education. Four programs that have been recognized for outstanding contributions and have been identified as demonstration projects are described below.

Project ACTIVE (All Children Totally Involved Exercising)

Project ACTIVE provides direct service delivery to students with psychomotor problems through a competency-based teaching and individualized learning approach. A second component involves in-service training. Materials include a battery of tests and seven program manuals. Conditions addressed are low motor ability, low physical vitality, postural abnormalities, nutritional deficiencies, breathing problems, motor disabilities or limitations, and communication disorders.

Project Unique

Project Unique is a fitness assessment project designed to determine the best tests for measuring fitness in students with sensory (blind or deaf) or orthopedic impairments. Tests include AAHPERD Best items and others that can be administered in a mainstream setting.

Project I CAN (Individualize Instruction, Create Social Leisure Competence, Associate All Learnings, Narrow the Gap Between Theory and Practice)

Three separate programmatic systems make up Project I CAN, including preprimary skills, primary skills, and sport, leisure, and recreation skills. Each system includes an observational assessment approach, illustrative goals, objectives, instructional strategies, and program evaluation materials. Emphasis is placed on an achievement-based curriculum model.

Project PEOPEL (Physical Education Opportunity Program For Exceptional Learners)

Project PEOPEL is a peer-teaching model that pairs trained student aides with handicapped students in small mainstream high school classes. Aides must complete a one-semester training course. This model has been extensively field-tested and offers many advantages for students such as a high rate of feedback, individual attention, and additional instruction.

REFERENCES AND SUGGESTED READINGS

AAHPERD. 1988. *Physical Best Manual*. Reston, VA: AAHPERD.

Arnheim, D. D., and Sinclair, W. A. 1985. *Physical Education for Special Populations: A Developmental, Adapted, and Remedial Approach*. Englewood Cliffs, NJ: Prentice-Hall.

Dobbins, D. A., Garron, R., and Rarick, G. L. 1981. The motor performance of educable mentally retarded and intellectually normal boys after covariate control for differences in body size. *Research Quarterly* 52(1): 6–7.

Eden, A. 1975. How to fat-proof your child. *Reader's Digest* 107(December): 150–152.

Epstein, L. H., et al. 1984. The modification of activity patterns and energy expenditure in obese young girls. *Behavior Therapy* 15(1): 101–108.

Fait, H. F., and Dunn, J. M. 1984. *Special Physical Education: Adapted, Individualized Approach*. Philadelphia, PA: W. B. Saunders.

Foster, G. D., Wadden, T. A., and Brownell, K. D. 1985. Peer-led program for the treatment and prevention of obesity in the schools. *Journal of Consulting and Clinical Psychology* 53(4): 538–540.

Kalakian, L. H., and Eichstaedt, C. B. 1982. *Developmental Adapted Physical Education*. Minneapolis, MN.: Burgess.

Kneer, M. K. 1976. The role of student satisfaction in developing play skills and attitudes. *Quest* 26: 102–108.

Lohman, T. G. 1987. The use of skinfold to estimate body fatness on children and youth. *Journal of Physical Education, Recreation, and Dance* 58 (9): 98–102.

Miller, A. G., and Sullivan, J. V. 1982. *Teaching Physical Activities to Impaired Youth*. New York: Wiley.

Reid, G. 1981. Perceptual-motor training: Has the term lost its utility? *JOPERD* 52 (6): 38–39.

Seaman, J. A., and DePauw, K. P. 1982. *The New Adapted Physical Education*. Palo Alto, CA: Mayfield Publishing.

Sherrill, C. 1986. *Adapted Physical Education and Recreation*. Dubuque, IA: Wm. C. Brown.

Simon, J., and Smoll, F. 1974. An instrument for assessing children's attitude toward physical activity. *Research Quarterly* 45 (4): 407–415.

Sterling, C. L. 1987. *Fitnessgram System*. Dallas, TX: Institute for Aerobics Research.

Ulrich, D. A. 1983. A comparison of the qualitative motor performance of normal, educable, and trainable mentally retarded students. In R. L. Eason, T. L. Smith, and F. Caron (eds.) *Adapted Physical Activity*. Champaign, IL: Human Kinetics Publishers.

Wade, M. G. 1981. A plea for process-oriented tests. *Motor Development Academy Newsletter* (Winter): 1–4.

7 PLANNING FOR EFFECTIVE INSTRUCTION

A major objective of physical education is to improve skill performance. Students participate in physical education to become physically educated. If they go to a math class, they expect to learn math. Teachers owe students an educational experience rather than a recreational one. When developing a lesson plan, the following points should form the underlying foundation of the planning effort.

Is there a purpose to the lesson? The lesson should be designed to improve the skill performance of students. What is the purpose of the total program, the unit, and the lesson plan? If the lesson presentation does not contribute to the skill development of participants, it probably is difficult to justify. A teacher should always know why an activity is taught and how it fits into a developmental scheme designed for optimal student growth.

Is instruction part of the lesson? Instruction should be an observable action. There are many different methods for accomplishing instructional goals, but there must be instruction. Instruction can take many forms, such as working individually with students, evaluating a student's progress on a contingency contract, developing task cards, and conducting group instruction. Regardless of the method used, physical education instruction must be a regular and consistent part of the lesson. It is difficult to accept a program that concentrates only on recreational aspects. A major problem with the recreational approach is that often the rich get richer and the poor get poorer. For example, if "the ball is rolled out" for basketball games, skilled players will handle the ball more and dominate less-skilled players. Unskilled students are always under more pressure during competition and find it difficult to think about technique and proper performance when they are concentrating on performing their skills correctly. Therefore, recreational game situations usually benefit those students who have already learned the basic skills.

How does this lesson integrate with past and future instruction? It is important to know the types of experiences that students have had prior to a lesson. Secondary school teachers should know what youngsters did at the elementary and junior high school level so they can articulate their instruction with previous experiences of students in mind. Physical education teachers of all grades must work together effectively to reach common goals.

Make sure there is progression between lessons in a unit. It is critical to space skill development activities evenly throughout a unit so that instruction is sequential and regular. A poor, but common approach is to bunch all instruction into the first day or two of a unit. It becomes difficult for students to develop motor skills when there is little opportunity for instruction combined with skill practice.

The philosophy of the teacher often determines whether effective planning will occur. Does the teacher believe that youngsters must learn on their own and that the total responsibility for learning is the student's? Or does the teacher believe that student and teacher share the burden of learning in an environment where both are determined to reach educational goals? A teacher's plan for skill development will strongly affect student learning. If instructors do not assume responsibility for assuring that students learn new skills and refine old ones, who will?

ESSENTIAL ELEMENTS OF INSTRUCTION

Currently, emphasis is being placed on improving the quality of instruction. For many years, interest and energy were devoted to the development of better curricula, certainly a critical component of the educational process. However, educators are beginning to accept that regardless of the quality of the curriculum, if it is poorly taught the result will be lacking.

An educator who has had strong impact on improving the quality of instruction is Hunter (1982). She has published a number of articles and textbooks on the basic elements of instruction. Since physical educators are viewed by administrators as being part of the total school faculty, it is necessary that they participate in all faculty meetings and in-service sessions. The essential elements movement has been used in many schools nationwide, and physical educators have been expected to incorporate the essential elements of instruction into their lessons. Often, there is backlash from some physical education instructors who feel that the learning principles do not apply to their content area. Even though many of the constructs were designed for classroom teachers, the purpose of this section is to illustrate how the essential elements of instruction can be applied to physical education and utilized to improve the quality of teaching.

Setting Objectives

To many teachers, setting learning objectives seems to be a waste of time since they perceive the most important task to be designing sequenced content activities for students. There is little question that one of the most important challenges facing a teacher is the ability to keep students involved in many learning tasks. At first glance, objectives may seem to be a set of theoretical constructs that are removed from the instructional tasks at hand. However, the objectives of the lesson should be the focal point for all the learning activities presented. It is difficult to justify activities that do not help students reach desired outcomes. If teachers do not know why they are presenting specific activities, they will have little idea of what students are expected to learn.

Learning objectives should be characterized by the following points. First, they must be **observable**. The teacher and student must be able to tell when the objective has been reached. If it is not visible, neither party will know when it has been reached. In the physical education setting, this usually poses little problem since most activities are overt and easy to observe.

Second, the objective must **identify the content** to be learned. It must clearly and specifically delineate what is expected of the student. When both the teacher and student clearly understand what to do, both feel more comfortable about the learning situation. Problems arise when students try to guess what the teacher wants them to learn. They have a right to know what is expected of them and what they will have accomplished when the objective is reached.

Finally, the objective must **certify** that learning has taken place and that the learners know more than they did prior to accomplishing the objective. When objectives are ambiguous or nonexistent, students have no way of judging whether they have improved or learned anything. The following are examples of objectives that would meet the points listed above:

1. The student will demonstrate three ways to shoot free throws.
2. The student will show an understanding of soccer rules by explaining when a corner kick is awarded.
3. Using three juggling balls, students will be able to demonstrate cascading and reverse cascading.
4. The student will demonstrate knowledge and understanding of rhythmic gymnastic routines by diagramming a sample floor routine for balls.

Objectives set the focus for planning and make it easier to determine when students have learned. They also encourage teachers to look at the type of lead-up skills that students need to reach the desired goals.

Task Analysis

An ever-present challenge faced by physical education teachers is the question: "At what skill level do I begin instructing?" Selecting learning tasks at the correct level of difficulty for students is challenging since all classes contain students with a wide variety of skill development and maturation levels.

The first step in determining the proper entry level is to formulate a terminal objective (one that is beyond the grasp of the most skillful student in the class). Next, delineate the essential learning tasks that lead up to the objective in proper progression. At this point, expedient diagnosis for determining entry level takes place. If teaching a group, the teacher can begin by moving rapidly through the progression of learning steps until a number of students appear to have difficulty performing the activity. This approach serves two purposes: it offers a quick review of skills and a diagnosis of the student's ability level. When students progress individually and teaching is one-on-one, students can be instructed to perform two or three activities per episode to diagnose their skill level. When activities require a small group of students to share the same piece of equipment, a method of self-paced instruction can provide for review of skills already learned, as well as determine the correct entry level for individual students within each group. For example, when teaching balance beam activities, a list of movements down the beam can be posted on task charts. Students can move through the progression at their own rate, allowing them the opportunity to determine their correct entry level.

Instruction does not begin until the appropriate entry level for a student has been established. This requires thorough knowledge of the skill sequence for each unit of instruction, beginning with the lowest skill and progressing to the final objective.

Anticipatory Set

After objectives and learning strategies have been developed, the instructional process becomes the focal point. The anticipatory set is a simple idea; it is designed to get students to focus on the concept to be presented. For many teachers the most difficult part of the lesson is the opening sequence of instruction. Students have entered the gymnasium talking to their friends and seem to be more interested in socializing than learning. Before they are willing to learn, students must be "psychologically warmed up" so that they can focus their thoughts. The anticipatory set should be designed to accomplish this goal.

A key factor in an effective anticipatory set is to tie into students' past experiences or learning. For example, in a basketball unit, a teacher might ask students to think about some techniques effective players use when shooting. This focus could involve discussing hand placement, eyes on the basket, or keeping the elbow near the body. In any case, it is a key point which encourages the class to begin thinking about the task at hand.

Another value of the anticipatory set is to show the instructor the entry level of the students. Students might be asked, "How many of you can explain the fundamentals of the zone press?" The teacher might also show a videotape of a college team using the press to further stimulate student interest. The response of students who know the fundamentals of the zone press indicates their previous experience in the activity. This would affect the rate of presentation and the difficulty of the strategy covered in the opening lessons. When students learn quickly, it is often because they have had much experience in an activity. Therefore, knowing the entry behavior of students will be an indication of how fast and effectively learning will occur.

Within the anticipatory set, a teacher may share the learning objective (and rationale for such) with students. Prior to the actual presentation, students should be told exactly what they are expected to learn and why it is important. However, some caution should be used because the information may bore students or even confuse them if they have little previous experience. If learning is going to be effective, students must perceive that they have a need to learn. Very few people will make an effort to learn something if it does not seem to be important in their everyday mode of operation. Learning is enhanced when teachers tell students clearly and concisely **what** and **why** they need to learn. The more convinced students are about the importance of learning something, the more motivated they will be to participate. For example, teachers often talk with students about safety skills and warn them about "what not to do." However, if the students do not internalize the danger, cannot perceive the danger, or are just told not to do something, they will almost always fail to heed the warning. It is human nature to balk at doing something simply because someone demands it. Most individuals respond better to logic and clear explanation related to their personal experiences.

It is not always necessary to use anticipatory set, although there should be a sound reason for omitting it. If students are already set to learn, there is probably little value in using one. However, at the beginning of a lesson, after an interruption, or when choosing to move to a new objective, using an anticipatory set will be effective.

Some examples of anticipatory set are:

"On Monday, we practiced the skills of passing, dribbling, and shooting lay-ins. Yesterday, we put those skills into games of three-on-three. Take a few moments to think about the problems you or others in your game encountered while dribbling or passing, and be ready to discuss them (allow time for thought). Today, we are going to use some drills that will improve your passing and dribbling."

"Think of as many activities as you can that require upper body strength, and be ready to tell the class (allow time for thinking). This week we are going to learn and practice weight training. It is the most popular strength development activity in our country."

Input and Modeling

Input involves teaching. It is the process of giving information to students. There are a number of decisions that need to be made when presenting content. Information that should be given during input is: the definition of the skill, the elements or parts of the skill, and when and why the skill should be used. Some of the more cogent points involved in input follow:

1. Focus instruction on one or two key points. It is difficult for students to remember a series of instructions. During skill performance, it is common practice to tell students everything related to the skill performance, a practice that often leaves them baffled and overwhelmed. Most learners are capable of focusing on only one or two points when performing a skill.

2. Try to avoid lengthy skill descriptions. Once skill instructions go beyond 30–60 sec, students become listless and forget much of the material presented. Try to develop a pattern of short, concise presentations, alternated with practice sessions. This offers the instructor many opportunities to refocus class attention on the skill being practiced and to evaluate the effectiveness of skill learning sequences.

3. Present the information in its most basic and clearest form. If half the class does not understand the presentation, the teacher has failed, not the students. It is important to check for understanding (see the next section) to assure that the class is comprehending the material.

4. Offer the material through a number of different styles. Some students may learn best through lecture, whereas others must see a visual presentation. It is possible that many will learn from a peer discussion or through teacher-guided questioning. Students learn best utilizing different styles. Try to incorporate as many presentation styles as possible during the course of a unit of instruction.

The saying, "What you do speaks louder than what you say," relates closely to **modeling behavior.** If teachers are going to ask students to behave in certain ways, it is reasonable to think that they should act in a similar fashion. In physical education, one of the quickest and most effective ways to teach a physical activity is to demonstrate. Effective models should accentuate the critical points of performance. The teacher should verbalize key focal points so that students will know what to observe. Correct modeling involves two parts: **showing** the correct way to do a skill and **labeling** the correct way to do it.

Both teachers and students can model instructional activities. Regardless of who does the modeling, in the early stages of learning it is important that the demonstration is clear. Identify the aspect to be observed so that attention is drawn to the correct element of performance. If the teacher is having a student demonstrate, a narrative description of the activity by the instructor should accompany the performance. If possible, slow down the performance and try to present it in a step-by-step fashion. Many skills can be videotaped and played back in slow motion. The replay can be stopped at critical instances with students emulating the position. For example, in a throwing unit, the instructor might freeze the frame that illustrates the position of the arm. Students can practice imitating moving the arm into proper position based on the stop-action pose.

The following are examples of using modeling and input in tandem to assure an effective presentation:

Students are in partners spread out about 20 yds apart, with one partner having a football. "When kicking the football, take a short step with your kicking foot, a long step with the other foot, kick and follow through (model). Again, short step, long step, kick, follow through (label)."

"Listen to the first verse of this schottische music. I'll do the part of the schottische step we just learned starting with the second verse (model). Ready, step, step, step, hop (label). When I hit the tambourine, begin doing the step."

"Today we are going to work on developing fitness by moving through the challenge course. Move through the course as quickly as you can, but do your best at each challenge; quality is more important than speed. Travel through the course like this (model). Move under the bar, swing on the rope, and so on (label). When I say go, start at the obstacle nearest you."

Checking for Understanding

A most essential point of instruction is checking to see if students understand and comprehend the presentation. It is possible that a class may not understand any of the material being presented. In fact, students become very effective in displaying an exterior that says they understand even when they do not. One of the most common habits that teachers develop involves asking the question, "Does everybody understand?" Even though it appears that the teacher is checking for understanding, this seldom is the case. More often than not, the teacher does not even wait for a response. It takes a brave and confident student to admit to a lack of understanding in front of the class. In fact, many teachers are affronted when a student does venture a question. Therefore, the need for a quick and easy way to check for understanding without student embarrassment is important to effective learning.

The following are some suggestions for monitoring whether students understand:

1. Use hand signals. Examples might be: "Thumbs up if you understand," or "If you think this demonstration is correct, balance on one foot," or "Raise the number of fingers to signal which student you think did a correct round off." If the signals are given quickly and without comment, students will begin to understand that they can signal the teacher quickly and privately without embarrassment. Some teachers have used the method of closing the eyes and signaling if the situation is particularly touchy or embarrassing.

2. Ask questions that can be answered in choral response. Some students may mouth an answer even though they do not know the correct response. Therefore, the indicator for the instructor is the intensity of the group response. A loud response by the class usually indicates that the majority understand.

3. Direct a check to the entire class rather than to a specified student. For example, "Be ready to demonstrate the carioca step to me." This encourages all members of the class to focus on the activity knowing that they may be called upon to demonstrate. Even though it does not assure that everyone understands, it does increase the odds that more students are thinking about the skill check.

4. Use peer checking methods. Students can pair up and evaluate each other's performance using a teacher designed instrument. More than one evaluation can be made by different students to help assure the validity of the scoring.

5. Use tests and written feedback. Many situations in physical education require cognition of concepts. Use written tests asking students to diagram and explain the options of an offense or defense. Listing safety precautions for an activity would make the instructor aware of student understanding. Use written instruments judiciously since valuable time that could be devoted to skill practice can be absorbed by written assessment. Use these instruments when information cannot be gathered using more efficient methods.

In summary, when planning a lesson, be sure to include strategies for input and modeling. If specific activities are not listed on the lesson plan, they will probably be forgotten during the instructional process.

Guided Practice

The reason for offering guided practice is to assure that students are performing the skill correctly. It is a fallacy to assume that practice makes perfect. Correct practice develops correct skill patterns, whereas practicing skills incorrectly will develop imperfection. This leads to the first step in guided practice: moving the class through each step of the skill. During the early phases of guided practice, present small amounts of information clearly. Skills should build on previous skills learned so that the student begins to see the importance of prerequisite learning.

Practice should occur as soon as possible after students have performed the skill correctly. They should have a chance to get the "feel" of a skill as a whole before they begin to work on the parts. The opportunity to try the complete skill before practicing smaller components enhances the learner's ability to perceive how the parts fit together. The length

of practice sessions will vary depending on the experience of the youngsters. If it is an initial presentation and possibly the student's first experience with the material, the practice sessions should be massed. Massed practice involves allowing enough time for students to develop mastery of the material. When reviewing activities that teach basics, distributed practice sessions can be short and less frequent. All the theory in the world is useless when students are frustrated trying to learn a new skill. If frustration sets in, students will need to receive relevant information, guided practice, or a modification in the level of the skill expectation. If this does not work, the practice session may have to be terminated and practiced at a later time.

During guided practice sessions, monitor group responses and offer feedback to ease the pain of learning new activities. Some of the methods described in input and modeling could be used. The monitoring process should be overt and regular to assure that students understand and are on task. The feedback should be specific, immediate, and focus on the exact skill being practiced. It is not guided practice if students do not receive regular, meaningful feedback about their performance.

Finally, assure that all students receive the same amount of practice. If anyone should receive less practice, it should be the skilled performer. Too often, drills and lead-up activities result in the least-gifted student sitting on the sidelines. This only results in the gifted youngsters improving and less skilled students falling further behind.

Closure

The purpose of closure is to review the learning that has taken place during the lesson. Closure increases retention and allows students to review what they have learned. The discussion or activity should focus on the learning that has occurred rather than the activities practiced. It is not a recall of the activities that were completed, but rather a discussion of the type of skills and knowledge learned through practice.

Closure can increase the opportunity for transfer to occur since the discussion can focus on how the current movement patterns being learned are similar to those practiced earlier. Often, students may not realize that the movement pattern is parallel to one learned earlier unless questions from the teacher encourage students to perceive such relationships. Closure can encourage students to help each other. The discussion of what was learned can alert other students about what they should be learning through practice. A fringe benefit for the teacher is the opportunity to remind the class to tell their parents and others what they learned. How many times have parents asked, "What did you learn at school today?" only to hear the reply, "Nothing." In addition, a short closure session can reveal to the instructor which students have learned and which students need additional help.

The following are examples of how closure might be accomplished:

1. Have students describe two or three key components of skill performance to their partner.
2. Have students demonstrate skills in quick response to verbal cues given by the teacher or a peer.
3. Ask students to participate in a closing activity that requires use of the learned skills.
4. Perform an activity describing a key point in skill performance that was taught earlier.

PLANNING FOR QUALITY INSTRUCTION

The importance of lesson planning cannot be over-emphasized. Instructors at the junior and senior high school level have, at times, been criticized for their lack of planning. A cycle of not planning sometimes begins when student teachers observe master teachers doing little, if any, planning. The emphasis placed on developing meaningful lesson and unit plans in professional preparation courses seems unnecessary when a master teacher appears successful without the aid of thoughtful planning. The beginning teacher is unable, however, to meaningfully judge the effectiveness of the master teacher because of a lack of perspective and experience. The master teacher also may have taught the material for many years and may have evolved a method of presentation through trial and error. Obviously, it is possible to present a lesson without planning, but the quality of the lesson can, in almost all cases, be improved through research, preparation, and a well-sequenced plan.

A strong case for planning can be made if a teacher desires to be creative and develop the ability to interact well with students. Teachers, regardless of their experience and ability, have many elements to remember while teaching. When presenting a lesson, many situations occur that are impossible to predict. For example, dealing with discipline problems; the need to modify the lesson spontaneously; relating to students by name; offering praise, feedback, and reinforcement; and developing an awareness of teaching behavior patterns are difficult to predetermine. If the content of the lesson is planned, written, and readily available, the teacher can place

greater emphasis on other, equally important phases of teaching.

Lesson planning is unique to each teacher. The competency of the individual in various activities will determine to some extent the depth of the lesson plan. More research and reading will have to be done for a unit activity in which the teacher has little experience. If the teacher is unfamiliar with a unit and still refuses to plan, the quality of instruction will be poor. Too often the scope of a curriculum is limited by the competency of teachers who are unwilling to prepare and learn new skills and knowledge.

The purpose of planning a lesson is to increase the effectiveness of the instructor. Lesson plans should be designed for specific situations. Regardless of the content of the lesson, the general points below should be considered when developing a plan:

1. Learning physical skills demands practice and repetition. Each lesson should be organized to maximize the amount of meaningful participation and to minimize the amount of teacher verbalization and off-task student behavior.

2. Practice combined with instruction and meaningful feedback assures skill development. Instructional sequences and procedures to increase the amount of feedback can be written into the lesson plan. Key points to be learned may require regular and specific feedback to ensure that correct learning patterns occur.

3. Lesson plans must consider the ability level of the students. Build a range of activities into each lesson plan so that students can progress at varying rates, depending on their level of skill. The activities should be written in proper progression to enhance the rate of learning.

4. Necessary equipment should be noted in the lesson plan. This prevents the problem of being in the middle of a lesson only to find that needed equipment was not gathered. The initial placement of equipment and how it is to be distributed and put away are tasks that should be planned before teaching.

5. Minimize time needed for management activities with prior planning. The plan should list whether students are to be in small groups or partnered, the type of formation required, and how these procedures will be carried out.

6. List outcomes of the lesson. The direction of the lesson is assured when both instructor and students know where they are going. The outcomes can be written in brief form but should state clearly to students what they are expected to learn.

7. Since lesson plans are highly personal, they can be written in code. All information need not be written out in longhand. For example, effective teachers often write their lesson plan on 4 x 6 in. cards, which can be carried easily and used with minimal distraction. The important point is that the card contents reflect the instructor's thought and planning that have occurred before the actual teaching session.

8. Allot estimated time to various activities in the lesson. For example, the amount of time for roll call, warm-up activity, fitness development, and activities in the lesson focus should be estimated. The time schedule need not be inflexible, but it should be followed closely enough so that all planned activities are taught.

9. Planning is an important phase of teaching. Few teachers instruct for more than 4–5 hrs per day. If an 8-hr day is expected of other workers, instructors should expect that part of their remaining working time will be used for planning. Consider a comparison with coaching. All highly successful coaches spend a great deal of time planning, observing films, and constructing game plans. The game may not last more than an hour or two, but many hours of planning took place before the contest. Teachers of physical education should recognize the need to spend some time each day planning for 4–5 hr of daily teaching. The results of a well-planned lesson are rewarding to both students and teacher.

10. Planning should assure successful experiences for students. The plan should include enough challenge to motivate and enough variety to maintain interest. A balance of safety and challenge is required in the school setting.

EFFICIENT PLANNING: PROVIDING TIME TO LEARN SKILLS

Students can listen to an instructor, read books, watch gifted athletes, and still not improve their motor skill performance. Without practice activities and skill drills, participants will demonstrate little improvement in their performance level. American society has a fetish for buying books that discuss how to improve everything from aerobics to zen. Many people spend a great deal of money for private lessons and then never practice on their own. Obviously, students will not learn new skills if the lesson does not provide maximum opportunity for skill practice. Of all the elements that go into learning new skills, correct practice is the most critical and

necessary. Therefore, plan a lesson that assures necessary instruction and *maximizes* the amount of productive practice time for the learner.

There are reasons why students may not receive the maximum amount of time for practice in a lesson. It may be that there is a limited amount of equipment, and students have to wait to take their turn. Consider how much time can be wasted standing in line waiting for a turn. Contemplate the following example: Students are organized into groups of nine. They are to practice basketball shooting skills. Unfortunately, there is only one ball available for each group of nine students. Assume that it takes 20 sec to shoot 3 shots and recover the ball. That means that each student in the group will have to stand in line nearly 3 min before receiving a turn. If the drill continues for 15 min, each student will only receive a little more than 1 1/2 min of practice. Small wonder that students do not learn how to shoot correctly when such drills are used.

Another factor that may limit practice time is lack of space. This may force the instructor to rotate youngsters in and out of a game rather than organize two or more games. It is important to try and utilize activities that maximize participation and that avoid eliminating students. Often, the least gifted student is eliminated first and stands on the side waiting for a new game or activity. Students learn little, if anything, from standing in line or waiting to return to an activity.

There are times when a teacher may be unwilling to allow much practice time if the activity involves high risk. An example might be stunts and tumbling. In this case it might be necessary that students be tightly supervised on an individual basis. However, in most cases, activities taught in a physical education class are not high risk in nature and a lack of practice time is usually the result of poor planning.

Another criterion to remember when organizing lessons for maximum practice is the environment where the practice occurs. Whenever possible, drills should provide for private and sensitive practice settings. Too often, students are placed in a setting where they have to make mistakes in front of their peers. Not all of this can be prevented, but much can be done to enhance the quality of the setting. For example, students undoubtedly have friends who might accept their errors much more willingly than others. Many drills are best done with a friend in a one-on-one setting. It might be possible to assign individual homework, or to allow students to work at a personalized pace with the guidance of a contingency contract. Whenever possible, try to ease the burden of learning new skills by reducing the fear of failure and embarrassment.

Quality control within practice sessions is important if students are going to be expected to learn skills correctly. Drills in practice sessions must be related to the desired skill outcome. Too often, the drill actually causes skills to be learned incorrectly. For example, assume that we are teaching students to dribble a basketball. To teach dribbling in context, we organize the students into squads and have a dribbling relay that requires that they dribble the length of the floor, make a basket and return. Unfortunately, this drill will result in improper skill development since students will be concentrating on other things beside dribbling. Many of the students will be worrying about making the basket, others will be more concerned about speeding down and back, and others may be preoccupied with failing in front of their peers. Very few students will focus on dribbling the ball under control using proper form. The result is a situation in which very little effective and correct practice of dribbling takes place.

It is important when developing drills to eliminate distractions. What elements will prevent students from correctly practicing the skills? Is this drill designed to offer effective and productive practice, or is it just a way of keeping students busy? What stipulations could be made to assure that students will practice correctly? Does the drill provide a lead-in to actual use in an activity, or is it useful in and for itself? Examine each drill and modify it accordingly when it appears that desired skill outcomes are not being enhanced.

PLANNING FOR DEVELOPMENTAL LEVELS: IMPROVING STUDENT SUCCESS

The planned experience should be based on the developmental level and past experiences of students, to assure that what is offered can achieve educational goals. This boils down to designing drills and activities that are challenging but not threatening. An important key is understanding that whether an activity is challenging or threatening is based on the student's perception, not the instructor's. An activity is challenging when the learner believes that it is difficult but achievable. It is threatening when the learner perceives it to be impossible. It is obvious that the same drill could be challenging to some students and threatening to others. Trying to sort out how students perceive various activities makes teaching a difficult task.

The planned lesson must allow students to progress at different rates of learning. This does not always have to be done, since students can stand a certain amount of failure. On the other hand, if they are fed a steady diet of failure, they soon come to believe they *are* failures, leaving little reason for trying. The more opportunities offered for individual or partner practice, the greater the chance for self-paced learning.

Activities can and should be monitored, to offer the teacher a perception of how students are progressing. It might be possible to do a *placheck* (see Chapter 11) that would indicate the number of students on task. Usually when students find an activity too difficult, they will do anything to avoid it. The percentage of students off task increases quickly, offering the teacher some highly visible feedback. If students complain loudly, the activity should be carefully reviewed. Often, if given the opportunity, students will offer productive and effective modifications.

One of the strengths of pretesting or self-testing before the unit is that the instructor gains valuable feedback about the experience and capability of the class. It helps teachers avoid assuming that students know something, only to find out that their assumptions were incorrect. A caution must be offered here: It is very easy to get engrossed in evaluation to the point that it consumes too much instruction time. There must be a balance between completing sufficient diagnostic work for effective teaching and wasting too much time. Students learn little in an evaluation setting. They are only showing what they know. If the majority of class time is spent on evaluation, students will have little opportunity to develop new skills.

A final word on experience and skill levels. Students must succeed most of the time if they are expected to enjoy an activity for a lifetime. An instructor is in the position of being able to force (through punishment or embarrassment) students to do just about anything within the educational setting. If they are forced into activities that result in frequent failure, students will probably learn to dislike and avoid the activity forever. If teachers are concerned with giving students lifetime skills and attitudes, it is important to monitor and adjust their lessons regularly. Two serious errors committed by teachers are the loss of sensitivity to the learner's perceptions and feelings, and teaching without concern for each student as an individual.

PLANNING LESSONS THAT TEACH THE STUDENT AS A WHOLE PERSON

When learning experiences are being planned for students, it is important to remember that people learn as a whole. One does not learn a new skill in the psychomotor domain without developing some allied cognitive and affective outcomes. For example, if people are taught to dribble low and near the floor, they will wonder why it should be learned this way. They are integrating the activity cognitively into their total selves. At the same time, they are developing a related feeling about the skill (e.g., "I'm good at this skill" or "I'm never going to use this skill").

Teachers can enhance the effectiveness and duration of instruction by integrating educational goals in all domains. This point emphasizes the importance of telling students *why* they are learning new skills or performing them in a certain fashion. Learning in the cognitive area may involve knowing when to use a certain skill or how to correct errors in an activity. It involves decision making based on facts and information gathered from various sources. Cognitive development emphasizes the importance of helping students understand as contrasted to just "doing it because I told you to."

The performing arts (physical education, music, and drama) offer a number of opportunities for affective domain development. There are many occasions to learn to share, express feelings, set personal goals, and function independently. Teamwork, learning to be subordinate to a leader, as well as being a leader, can be learned. Teachers must realize the importance of teaching the whole person. It is sad commentary when one overhears teachers saying, "My job is just to teach skills. I'm not going to get involved in developing attitudes. That's someone else's job." Physical educators have an excellent opportunity to develop positive attitudes and values. The battle may be won but the war lost if teachers produce youngsters with good skill development but negative attitudes toward physical activity and participation.

Experiences can be enriched by encouraging students to discover ways of improving techniques or remedying problems they are having in skill performance. They can be given opportunities to help each other diagnose and improve techniques. Strategies for game situations can be developed through group discussions and planning. The point here is not to detract from skill learning and performance but rather to enrich and enhance learning situations so that the student is able to internalize them in a more personalized and meaningful manner. A golden rule does not have to be taught in every lesson, but little will be learned if teachers fail to offer integrated presentations on a regular basis.

Improving Cognitive Understanding

Cognitive development can be enhanced by involving students in organizing the content and im-plementation of the lesson. This is not to suggest that students will decide what, when, and how learning will take place, but that they will become involved in improving the structure of the learning tasks. There are many advantages to involving the learner in the instructional process such as:

1. Learners usually will select experiences that are in line with their ability and skill levels.
2. When learners help make a decision, they accept some of the responsibility for learning. It is easy to blame others for failure if a learner is not involved in some of the decisions. Personal involvement means accepting the responsibility to make decisions and see that they are implemented.
3. Most people feel better about an environment in which they have some input. Positive self-concepts are usually the result of a situation where learners help determine their destiny.
4. When lessons fail because incorrect decisions were made, the learner must shoulder some of the blame. This helps develop decision-making skills that must focus on personal responsibility.

Decision making and involvement in the learning process must be learned. People must have the opportunity to make decisions and be placed in a situation where they can realize the impact of their decisions. This means that the opportunity for making incorrect as well as correct decisions must be allowed. There is no decision making involved if only correct decisions are accepted and approved by the teacher. Soon, students begin to choose not to make decisions at all rather than risk making an incorrect choice.

Responsibility is learned. The stakes will be lower if students are allowed to begin making decisions at a young age. This involves allowing the learner to make decisions and to choose from alternatives. Allowing students to make choices should be done in a gradual and controlled manner by using some of the following strategies.

1. Present a limited number of choices. This allows the teacher to control the ultimate outcome of the situation, but offers students a chance to decide how the outcome will be reached. This may be a wise choice when learners have had little opportunity for decision making in the past. New teachers who have had little experience with their students should allow for student input using this model.

2. Allow students opportunity to modify an activity. In this setting, the learner is allowed to modify the difficulty or complexity of the skill being practiced. If used effectively, it will allow learners to adapt the activity to suit their individual skill levels. Involving them in this process can actually reduce the burden of the teacher who no longer has to decide about exceptions and student complaints that "it is too hard to do" or "I'm bored." It becomes the student's responsibility to personalize the task. Options allowed here could be to change the rules, the implement being used, the number of players on a team, or the type of ball or racquet. Some examples are:

a. Using the slower-moving family ball rather than a handball.
b. Increasing the number of fielders in a softball game.
c. Lowering the basket in a basketball unit.
d. Decreasing the length of a distance run or the height of hurdles.

3. Offer tasks that are open ended. This approach allows students the most latitude for deciding on the content of the lesson. In this situation, they are told the task and it is their decision how it will be reached. In this setting, the teacher decides the educational end while the student decides the means. As students become adept in using this approach, they learn to develop a number of alternatives. Examples that might be used at this level are:

a. "Develop a game that requires four passes before a shot at the goal."
b. "Develop a floor exercise routine that contains a forward roll, backward roll, and cartwheel."
c. "Develop a long rope jumping routine that involves four people and two pieces of manipulative equipment."

This approach is often called problem solving in that there is no predetermined answer (see Chapter 10). There is an unlimited number of answers, and students do not have to worry about making the wrong choice. This technique can be effective in helping students apply principles they have learned previously and to transfer previously learned skills to new situations. Ultimately, the problem is solved through a movement response that has been guided by cognitive involvement.

Enhancing the Affective Domain

Youngsters' feelings about a subject will determine their level of motivation to learn and will also affect the long-range effectiveness of the instruction. Very little is gained if students participate in a class yet leave hating it. It is possible to design experiences in a manner that will improve the opportunity for positive attitudes and values to develop. When developing the lesson plan, evaluate it in terms of the following points: Will the planned experience result in a positive experience for students? Few people

develop positive feelings after participating in an activity where they were embarrassed or failed miserably. Ponder some of the following situations and the attitudes that might result:

> Think of the situation where a teacher asks everyone to run a mile. Overweight students are obviously going to be last and make the rest of the class wait for them to finish. These students cannot change the outcome of the run even if they wanted to. Failure and belittlement occur every day. Small wonder they would come to dread class.
>
> How would students feel who have been asked to perform in front of the rest of the class even though they are unskilled? The added stress probably results in a poorer than usual response.
>
> What feelings would students have when asked to pitch in a softball game and be unable to throw strikes? Might they possibly do everything possible to avoid having this situation occur in the future?

Students need to know that teachers care about their feelings and want to prevent placing them in embarrassing situations. Sometimes, teachers have the idea that caring for students indicates weakness. This is seldom the case. Teachers can be firm and demanding as long as they are fair and considerate. To knowingly place students in an embarrassing situation is never justified and will result in the formation of negative attitudes.

It is difficult, if not impossible, to develop lesson plan content that will assure positive development of the affective domain. Attitudes and values are formed by students based in large part on how they are treated by teachers and peers. When enhancing the affective domain, *how* one teaches becomes more important than *what* one teaches. Students must be acknowledged as human beings with needs and concerns. They should be treated in a courteous and nonderogatory manner. Feelings should be discussed. If teachers fail to sense how students feel, they will not be able to adjust the learning environment in a positive direction. More often than not, the best way to discover how students feel is to ask them. The majority will be honest. If a teacher can accept student input without taking it personally, the result will be an atmosphere that produces positive attitudes and values.

THE LOGISTICS OF THE LESSON: PREINSTRUCTIONAL DECISIONS

Preinstructional decisions are basic to the success of the lesson. They are rather mundane, which causes many teachers to avoid thinking about them. However, they are every bit as important as planning the content of the lesson. In fact, if this phase of the lesson is not carefully thought out, it may be impossible to effectively present the content.

Determining the Instructional Format

How students are grouped for instruction is a decision that must be made early in the lesson-planning process. More than one arrangement can be used in a single lesson. The objectives and nature of the instructional experiences, plus the space and equipment available, determine the type of grouping. There are three basic schemes, with numerous variations and subdivisions.

Large Group Instruction

Large group instruction demands that all students respond to the same challenge, whether as individuals, partners, or members of a group. This format allows the teacher to conduct the class in a guided progression. The single-challenge format is convenient for group instruction and demonstration, because all students are involved in similar activities.

Pacing is a problem with no easy solution, since effective instruction must be personalized to meet each student's needs. Student differences are recognized, yet the assumption is made that a central core of activity is acceptable for students of the same age. Many of the instructional procedures already discussed involve the single-challenge format, and for this reason, no further elaboration is made here.

Small Group or Station Instruction

In the multiple-group (or station) format, the class is divided into two or more groups, each working on a different skill or activity. Some system of rotation is provided, and the students change from one activity to another.

Dividing a class into groups for station teaching is valuable at times, particularly when supplies and apparatus are limited. This arrangement can save time in providing apparatus experiences, because once the circuit is set, little change in apparatus is needed. The participants are changed, not the apparatus. Some system of rotation must be instituted, with changes either on signal or at will. Sometimes all stations are visited during a single class session, and in other cases, students make only a few station changes per session.

Class control and guidance may be a problem with the small group format, since stopping the class to provide instruction and guidance is not practical. Posting written guidelines at each station can help students be more self-directed. The instructions should include rearranging the station before moving

on. These measures preclude the teacher dividing his or her efforts over a number of stations. If a station has a safety hazard (e.g., rope climbing), the teacher may wish to devote more attention there.

Individual Skill Instruction

In the individual skill format, students select their skills from a variety of choices and rotate at will to new skills. They may get their equipment themselves or choose from pieces provided. The most effective format is when students work independently. It allows everyone to work on skills at a comfortable rate. In addition, it allows students to select a variety of skills and activities based on their competency level.

Use of Equipment

In many situations, equipment will be a limiting factor. Teachers need to know exactly what equipment is available and in working condition. By determining how much equipment is available, the teacher will know how to structure the lesson and group the students. For example, if there are only 16 paddles and balls for a class of 30, some type of sharing or station work will have to be organized.

How much equipment is enough? If it is individual-use equipment such as racquets, bats, and balls, there should be one per student. If it is group-oriented equipment such as gymnastics apparatus, there should be enough to assure waiting lines of no more than four students. Too often, teachers settle for less equipment because they teach the way they have been taught. For example, consider the teacher who is teaching volleyball and has plenty of balls. Rather than have students practice individually against the wall or with a partner, the teacher divides them into two long lines and uses one or two balls. Most of the time is spent waiting in line rather than practicing.

If equipment is limited, it obviously becomes necessary to adapt instruction. Teachers should be careful about accepting limited equipment without expressing their concern since many administrators believe that physical educators are always capable of "making do." Communicate with the educational leader regularly and explain the importance of equipment for effective instruction. Ask parent-teacher groups to help with fund raising to purchase necessary equipment. Remember, math teachers are not expected to teach math without a book for each student, and physical educators should not be expected to teach without adequate equipment. When teachers settle for less, they get less.

How can you get by with a dearth of equipment? The most commonly found solution is to teach using the small group format. This implies dividing students into stations where each group has enough equipment. For example, in a softball unit, some students might practice fielding, others batting, others making the double play, and so on. Another approach is to divide the class in half and allow one group to work on one activity while another is involved in an unrelated activity. For example, due to a shortage of paddles and balls, one half of the class could be involved in practice while the other half plays half-court basketball. This approach is less educationally sound and increases the demands made on the instructor.

Another approach is to use the peer review approach. While one student practices the activity, a peer is involved in offering feedback and evaluation. The two can share the equipment and take turns in practice and evaluation. The final approach is to do what is most commonly done: design drills that involve standing in line and waiting for a turn. In most cases, this is least acceptable from an educational standpoint.

The initial setup of equipment may depend on the focus of the lesson. For example, the height of the basket may be reduced to emphasize correct shooting form. The height of the volleyball net may be lowered to allow practice spiking. Nets may be placed at different heights to allow different types of practice. Remember that equipment and apparatus can be modified to best suit the needs of the learner. There is nothing sacred about a 10-ft basket or regulation-sized ball. If modifying the equipment will improve the quality of learning, change it.

Use of Time

There are a number of decisions related to time that need to be made prior to instruction. How the time allotted for the total lesson will be utilized is an important consideration discussed previously. The amount of time allowed for fitness and skill development will directly influence what is accomplished in a physical education program. For example, assume that a teacher decides to use 10 additional minutes per lesson for fitness development. The end result will be an increase of nearly 30 hr of time devoted to physical fitness during the school year. The use of time greatly affects whether or not program objectives are met.

Another advantage of programming the use of lesson time lies in accountability. Assume that physical fitness testing reveals that fitness levels of students are subpar. If a stipulated amount of time was not consistently apportioned for fitness development it would be difficult to ascertain whether lack of sufficient time was the reason for the low fitness levels.

The pace of the lesson is also directly related to time. Skillful teachers know when to terminate practice sessions and move on to new activities. For example, students will become bored and begin to display off-task behavior when practice sessions are excessively long. Knowing the right time to refocus their attention on a varied task is important. In most cases, it is better to err on the short side rather than allow practice to the point of fatigue and boredom, which could result in class management problems.

Timing the pace of the lesson is difficult since it involves a certain "feel" about the class. A rule of thumb might be to refocus or change the task when five or more students are off-task. At this point, the teacher has a few options for extending the length of the practice session:

1. **Refocus the class**. Ask the class to observe another student's performance, or explain the importance of the skill and how it will help their game-time performance.
2. **Refine or extend the task**. Stop the class and ask them to improve their technique by improving a phase of their performance, or to add a more difficult variation. This approach usually redefines the challenge and is a more difficult variation of the skill they were practicing.
3. **Stop and evaluate**. An effective approach can result in stopping the class and evaluating their performance. Students might work with a partner and check for key points. Emphasis is placed on evaluating and correcting the performance. Practice can resume after a few minutes of evaluation.

Pacing also depends upon whether the lesson is teacher or student directed. When teachers direct the pace, timing is controlled by the instructor and students are all expected to perform the same task at the same time. Determining whether a presentation should be teacher or student paced depends on the type of skill being taught. If the skill is closed in nature (only one way to perform or respond) then teacher pacing appears to be most effective. Teacher pacing can be accompanied by verbal cues and modeling behavior. It is effective in learning new skills because the cues and visual imagery help the learner develop a conception of the pattern to be performed. Student pacing allows learners to progress at their own rates. It is effective when open skills are being learned and a variety of responses are preferred or encouraged.

Use of Space

One of the first mistakes that a beginning teacher makes is to take a class to a large practice area, tell them the task, and fail to define the space. The class spreads out in an area so large that the teacher finds it impossible to communicate with and manage the class. The size of the space is dictated by the skills being practiced. Regardless of the size of the space, the practice area must be delineated. An easy way is to set up cones around the perimeter of the area. Chalk lines or natural boundaries can also signal restraining lines.

The amount of instruction offered also affects the size of the practice area. If students are learning a closed skill and need feedback and redirection regularly, it is important that they stay in close proximity to the instructor. An effective approach is to establish a smaller area where students move on signal for instruction and then return to the larger area for practice. If this approach is used, take care to prevent wasting time moving between areas.

Divide available space into smaller areas to maximize student participation. An example might be a volleyball game where only 10 students can play on the one available court. In most cases it would be more effective to divide the area to accommodate a greater number of students. A related consideration when partitioning spaces is safety. If the playing areas are too close together, it is possible that players from one area might run into those in the other area. Another example would be softball fields where the ball might hit a player in another area. In most cases, the safety of students can be ensured by careful planning.

Use of Instructional Devices

Instructional devices include a variety of materials, equipment, or people—any of which supplement, clarify, or improve certain instructional procedures. These devices can be used to present information, stimulate different senses, provide information feedback, restrict movements, control practice time, or aid in evaluation and motivation. The devices may be simple, such as targets taped on the wall or boun-

dary cones to dribble around in basketball (Figure 7.1), or they may be more sophisticated, such as loop films, movies, videotape recorders, or ball machines for tennis. Student leaders can also be useful as instructional aides.

It is the teacher's role to carefully plan instructional devices that will enhance the teaching-learning process. Because most public school environments have a large student-to-teacher ratio, teachers do not have enough time for each student. Instructional devices help the teacher impart more information and improve the motivational aspects of the class. A number of challenging and success-oriented activities can be developed using instructional devices. The following are examples:

1. In basketball, tape targets on a wall for various types of passes. Use a stopwatch to time students dribbling through a course of boundary cones. Pictures, diagrams, and handouts can provide students with graphic information on various skills and rules.

2. In volleyball, Hula-Hoops, jump ropes, or tape on the floor can be used as targets for setting, bumping (Figure 7.2), or serving. Extend a rope across the top of the net to help students hit serves above or beneath the rope to ensure height, accuracy, or velocity. Loop films are available to provide an excellent model for the various volleyball skills.

3. In tennis, empty ball cans are excellent targets for working on serves. A tennis ball suspended on a small rope that can be adjusted up or down on a basketball hoop will force students to get the "feel" of extending the arm for serves and overhead shots. A list of performance objectives for partners can control practice time and provide structure for a tennis class.

4. In track and field, a student leader might help run a station on low hurdles by timing heats and

FIGURE 7.1 Instructional devices

FIGURE 7.2 Volleyball bump against the wall

providing corrective feedback. Tie a string between two chairs to help students to attain more height in the long jump. Laminated posterboard diagrams of the release angle of the shot put combined with a discussion can give students important information before practice time begins (Figure 7.3).

5. In badminton, use targets to mark sections of the court. Suspend shuttlecocks on a rope, similar to the tennis ball example, for practicing overhand shots. A rope suspended on high jump standards will force students to get the proper height on clear shots. Loop films can serve as another learning station. Performance objectives tied to specific reinforcing events will motivate students to work on specific skills.

6. In flag football, a punting station can use the goal post for height and accuracy, boundary corners for placement accuracy, and a stopwatch for hang time. A swinging tire or a hoop suspended from a tree or goal post can be used for passing accuracy, and boundary cones for passing distance. Blackboards, magnetic boards, and overhead projectors are all useful for diagraming plays and defensive strategy. Student leaders can supervise each station, record the completion of various skills, and help provide corrective feedback for each student.

A creative teacher uses instructional devices in many different ways. These devices certainly do not replace the teacher, but they do help supplement the teaching-learning environment. Effective teachers are continually trying to add devices that motivate students, provide more feedback, or increase practice attempts. Teachers with a limited budget can still create instructional devices with such basic components as a roll of tape, several ropes, string, and

FIGURE 7.3 A poster explaining skills

hoops. An extensive budget does not always produce the best learning environments. A hard-working, ingenious teacher can develop effective instructional aids. Students seem to enjoy the challenge and success related to practicing with various types of instructional devices. Variety and novelty thus enhance the teaching-learning situation.

UNIT PLANNING

Units of instruction offer a meaningful method for organizing activities. Without units, teachers would have difficulty offering scope and sequence for various instructional activities throughout the year. Units are usually 2-, 3-, or 4-wk sequences of instruction dealing with the same activity or concept. Units can, however, be 5 wks or longer, depending on the type of curriculum developed.

Instructional units are developed from the curriculum model and the organizing center that is used in a specific curriculum. Most units focus on physical activity or movement forms such as team sports, lifetime sports, dance, or physical conditioning. On the other hand, some units have been developed to emphasize a concept or idea such as cardiovascular efficiency, body composition, flexibility, or strength. Other people have organized instructional units on students' motives or purposes such as achievement, appearance, and coping skills. Still others have planned units on analyzing movements with regard to time, space, force, and flow. A number of different organizing centers can be used for unit construction (see Chapter 3).

When unit plans are developed, a wide variety of sources is preferable to one textbook. The unit can reflect a range of activities gathered from different experts in the particular activity field. Another advantage of the unit plan is that it gives teachers a perception of how instruction should proceed. This prevents fragmentation. An instructor with a coherent unit plan does not simply teach from day-to-day, hoping that everything will somehow fit together in the end.

Elements of a Unit Plan

There are many different ways to write and organize units of instruction. Most plans contain the following elements, even though they may be titled differently or listed in a different order. Regardless of the organization method, the plan should contain the following information.

Objectives of the Unit

The objectives state what the students are expected to know on completion of the unit, and students should be made aware of what they are expected to learn. Objectives may be written in the three learning domains. For example, what cognitive understandings should students have, and are they to be tested in this area? What are the social and emotional concepts students should develop through participation in this unit? Finally, what skills, techniques, and game strategies should be learned on completion of the unit? Objectives must be written before organizing the activities and experiences, because the objectives will determine what is to be included in the unit.

Skills and Activities

This section is the instructional core of the unit and is organized according to unit objectives. Specific skills to be developed, drills to facilitate skill development, lead-up games to be taught, and culminating experiences are listed in this section. Scope and sequence are also developed in this section, which helps to assure a meaningful presentation. When activities are listed in proper sequence, instructionally sound and legally safe lessons are more easily written. The learning experiences may be listed as desirable student outcomes to assure simple translation by student and teacher.

Instructional Procedures

This plan area determines how the activities will be presented to assure the maximum amount of learning. Points to be included are instructional techniques, observations on the efficient use of equipment, necessary safety procedures, and teaching formations.

Equipment, Facilities, and Instructional Devices

Listing equipment and facilities allows the teacher to quickly see what is available and whether other teachers are using it for a unit being taught concurrently. If facilities or equipment need to be modified (for example, lowering goals or deflating balls), this should be listed also.

Culminating Activities

This section identifies how the unit might be concluded. A tournament between selected teams, an intraschool contest, or a school demonstration playday might result. In any case, the unit should finish with an activity that is enjoyable to students and leaves them with a positive feeling toward the unit of instruction.

Evaluation

The final plan section outlines how student progress is to be monitored. Monitoring can be carried out

by the instructor, or students can be given guidelines for self-evaluation. Written tests might be administered to evaluate the knowledge gleaned through the instructional process. Skill tests could be used to assess the level of performance and skill development. An attitude inventory might be administered to judge the impact of the unit on the affective area of learning.

Another phase of evaluation is asking students to comment on the unit and its method of presentation. This should be done in writing rather than verbally because some student comments may anger or belittle the teacher. Student evaluations can offer direction for modifying the unit and making it more effective in the future.

Suggested Weekly (Block Plan) Schedule

The purpose of a block plan is to distribute the activities of the unit into weekly segments. This gives the teacher a rough sense of timing and an indication of what should be taught and when. A block plan can help alleviate problems such as insufficient time to teach the desired activities, or insufficient activities to fill up the time frame. The weekly schedule need not be detailed. It eases the burden of writing lesson plans because the material to be taught has been identified and sequenced into a meaningful time frame. Daily lesson plans can then be developed easily from the block plan.

Figure 7.4 is an example of a 3-wk block plan for a unit on racquetball. A 3-wk block plan is included with many of the activities in Chapters 20–23.

Bibliography and Resources

The bibliography contains materials for both students and teacher. Students are given a list of materials that they can peruse if they desire more information. Location of materials should be identified. Teachers should have a separate list and collection of resources that they use for instruction. For example, pamphlets on nutrition or physical fitness, available films, bulletin board materials, and textbooks might be parts of the resource section.

The following outline offers a skeleton structure for designing detailed unit plans.

I. Title and grade level
II. Analysis and description of setting
   A. Previous experiences and exposure to activity
   B. Limiting factors: class size, class organization, mixed grades, facilities and equipment, period of day class meets
   C. Rationale for including the activity

Introduction What is racquetball? Grips—ready position Forehand stroke Backhand stroke Contract procedures Practice bounce and hit Rule of the day	**Review** Grip, forehand, backhand Equipment **Teach** Serves—Drive, Z Lob **Activities** Serves—practice Bounce and hit Rule of the day	**Review** Serves, rules **Teach** Backwall shots Hinders **Activities** Backwall practice Serve practice Rule of the day	**Review** Forehand, backhand **Teach** Court position Kill shots **Activities** Performance objectives or short game Rule of the day	**Review** Backwall shots **Teach** Ceiling shots Passing shots **Activities** Ceiling games One, two, or three shots
Review Problem rules Serve strategy Court coverage **Activities** Accuracy drills Drive serve Lob serve Backhand Backhand games One or two shots	**Teach** Cutthroat Doubles **Activities** Performance objectives Eight ball rally Rotation work up	**Review** Problem areas **Activities** Performance objectives Five and out Ceiling games	**Review** Rules **Activities** Performance objectives Regular game Cutthroat or doubles	**Review** Kill shots **Activities** Rotation work up
Activities Performance objectives Backhand games Regular game Tournament	**Review** Rules, strategy Shots, serves **Activities** Performance objectives Tournament games	**Written exam** **Activities** Performance objectives Tournament games	**Activities** Performance objectives Tournament games Cutthroat or doubles	Final performance objectives work Review course objectives Final games Return exam

FIGURE 7.4 Racquetball block plan

III. Objectives
    A. General unit objectives
    B. Specific behavioral objectives
        1. Psychomotor (physical performance) skills
        2. Knowledges, rules, and strategies
        3. Attitudes and values
IV. Organization
    A. Time (length of unit)
    B. Space available
    C. Equipment and supplies
    D. Basic grouping of students
    E. Number of groups
V. Content
    A. Introduction of the activity
    B. Rules
    C. Skills (diagram all drills)
    D. Activities and lead-up games
    E. Skill tests
    F. Written tests
    G. Block plan for entire unit
    H. Grading scheme
VI. References and resources

DAILY LESSON PLAN FORMAT

The suggested daily lesson plan has three major components (see Chapter 4): the introductory or warm-up activity, the fitness development activity, and the lesson focus (Pangrazi and Dauer, 1989). Each of these areas contains three columns of information: lesson content, instructional procedures, desired student outcomes, and notes and references. Figure 7.5 shows a sample lesson plan. A discussion of each of the parts of the sample lesson plan follows.

Lesson Content

The first column in the lesson plan identifies skills and activities. These are listed in correct progression, thus assuring that instruction will occur in line with the developmental capabilities of students. Progressive lessons assure that activities will be presented in a safe manner and that students will have a successful experience. The skills and related activities need not be written out in detail. The key point is that the instructor can quickly comprehend the activities when teaching. If more detail is needed, the notes and references column directs the teacher to a proper source.

Organization and Teaching Hints

A list of instructional procedures should be followed when presenting the activities, such as, how the equipment is organized, what formations to use, key points of instruction to share with students, and the specific feedback used. This column becomes more meaningful as the teacher gains experience. Newly discovered instructional procedures can be recorded and maintained for the next time the lesson is taught.

Expected Student Outcomes

Establish what students are expected to experience, learn, and perform. Specific physical skills should be listed. Various facts about physical fitness and sport participation, as well as expected values and attitudes that the class should discuss, are detailed in this section. With careful planning of expected student outcomes, teachers can offer a wide variety of experiences throughout the school year to help students develop in all domains—the psychomotor, cognitive, and affective.

ANALYZING THE LESSON PLAN

There are different approaches to writing lesson plans, but regardless of the style used, the plan should include the necessary elements for assuring effective instruction. The following questions can help teachers analyze a lesson plan to assure that it is both comprehensive and effective.

Have you included the following?

1. Title, length of lesson, and facility
2. A list of equipment, supplies, and instructional devices
3. Objectives of the lesson
4. References for further information

Does the instructional process do the following?

1. Provide for continuity with previous lessons
2. Review past material through lead-up activities
3. Communicate to students why the material is important for them to learn
4. Build motivational techniques into the presentation
5. Provide for students with varying interests and abilities
6. Include the special student

Does the lesson plan cover the following points?

1. Provide for warm-up, offer students a physical fitness activity, and include an instructional component
2. Outline new material clearly and with enough depth

Supplies and Equipment Needed:
Station 1: 2 batting tees, 4 balls, 2 bats
Station 2: 2 balls (can use whiffle balls)
Station 3: 4 bases (home plates), 4 balls
Station 4: 2 balls, 2 bats
Exercise task cards

Movement Experience — Content	Organization and Teaching Hints	Expected Student Objectives and Outcomes
Introductory Activity (2–3 min)		
Personal Choice Students select the type of introductory activity that they wish to use in order to warm up. They may use one they have previously learned in class, or they may create one of their own. Emphasis should be on a balanced approach that works all major muscle groups.	Encourage students to keep moving. It may be necessary to point out some activities to stimulate some of the youngsters.	PM. — The students will be able to create a warm-up routine that will physically warm them up for fitness activities.
Fitness Development (7–8 min)		
Squad Leader Exercises with Task Cards The squad leader takes his or her squad to a designated area and puts the group through exercises. The teacher gives the leader a task card listing the sequence of exercises and the number of repetitions. Variation: The squad leader can assign different squad members to lead various exercises. Suggested Exercises: 1. Sitting Stretch 2. Push-ups 3. Toe Toucher 4. Jumping Jack Variations 5. Body Circles 6. Crab Alternate — Leg Extension 7. Leg Extension 8. Treadmill Increase the number of repetitions by 10–20%.	Alternate 2–3 exercises with some running or rope jumping for development of the cardiovascular system. Distribute task cards to leaders before breaking into groups. Individual mats placed at each designated exercise area are helpful when performing abdominal exercises. Rotate leaders often so that all students have the opportunity to lead.	Cog. — Know why it is necessary to increase the number of repetitions (overload principle). PM. — The student will be able to perform all exercises at teacher established levels. Aff. — The students will demonstrate the self-discipline needed for independent group work.

FIGURE 7.5 Softball lesson plan

Movement Experience–Content	Organization and Teaching Hints	Expected Student Objectives and Outcomes
	Lesson Focus (15–20 min)	

Movement Experience–Content	Organization and Teaching Hints	Expected Student Objectives and Outcomes
Softball (Multiple Activity Station Teaching) Divide the class equally among the stations.	Squad formation. Have signs at each of the stations giving both direction and skill hints. Captain gathers equipment in designated spot before changing to next station.	Aff.—Willingness to cooperate at each station is crucial to the success of the lesson. Discuss and emphasize the importance of cooperation among peers.
Station 1 *Batting* 1. Weight on both feet. 2. Bat pointed over right shoulder. 3. Trade mark up on swing. 4. Elbows up and away from body. 5. Begin with hip roll and short step. 6. Swing level. 7. Follow through. 8. Eyes on ball. *Batting from Tee* 1. Stand back (3 ft) from tee, so when stepping forward, ball is hit in front. 2. Show three types of grips. *Fungo Hitting* 1. Students can be given this option instead of tee hitting. 2. Toss the ball up, regrasp the bat, and hit the ball.	Divide squad, with one batter, a catcher (next batter), and one or more fielders. Points to avoid: 1. Lifting the front foot high off the ground. 2. Stepping back with the rear foot. 3. Dropping the rear shoulder. 4. Chopping down on the ball (golfing). 5. Dropping the elbows. This is a higher level batting skill than tee hitting. Rotate batters, catchers, fielders.	PM.—The student will be able to meet the ball squarely on the tee. Cog.—The student will know the different points in good batting. Cog.—Strenuous exercise causes blood pressure to go up. This occurs because the heart beats faster and more blood is trying to push its way through the vessels. Why do some people have high blood pressure even at rest?

Station 2
Throwing and Catching
1. Show grips.
2. How to catch—Stress "give," eyes on ball.
 	
Practice Activity
1. Throw around the bases clockwise and counter-clockwise using the following throws:
  a. Overhand throw
  b. Sidearm throw
  c. Underhand toss
2. If enough skill, roll the ball to the infielders and make the throw to first. After each play, the ball may be thrown around the infield.
	This will be review for most students.
	Use "soft" softballs.
	Rotate infield positions, including the "ball roller."
	Set up regular infield staffed by a squad.
		PM.—The students will be able to increase their catching potentials and increase their accuracy in throwing (three styles).
		Cog.—The student will be able to define and recognize good points of throwing and catching.

FIGURE 7.5 Continued

Movement Experience– Content	Organization and Teaching Hints	Expected Student Objectives and Outcomes
Station 3 *Pitching Rules* 1. Face the batter, both feet on the rubber, and the ball held in front with both hands. One step is allowed and the ball must be delivered on that step. 2. Ball must be pitched underhand. 3. No motion or fake toward the plate can be made without delivering the ball. 4. No quick return is permitted, nor can the ball be rolled or bounced toward batter. 5. Practice both regular pitch and windmill.	Divide squad into two groups. Each has a catcher, pitcher, and "batter," who just stands in position. A home plate and teaching rubber are helpful. Stressed legal preliminary position before taking one hand off the ball to pitch. Rotate positions regularly.	PM.—The student will begin to pitch in observance with the rules. Cog.—The student will know the rules governing pitching. PM.—The student will be able to pitch 50% of the balls in the strike zone. Cog.—Softball is not a very effective sport for exercising the cardiovascular system. Most of the time is spent sitting or standing. Therefore, there is little, if any, aerobic activity.
Station 4 *Throwing or Batting Fly Balls* 1. Begin with high throwing from the "batter." 2. Have the fielders return the ball with a one-bounce throw to the "batter." 3. Show form for high and low catch. Show sure stop for outfielders. 4. After initial stages, allow fungo hitting of fly balls if the "batter" is capable.	Divide squad into two groups. Leave a bat at the station.	PM.—The student will begin to handle (catch) easy fly balls with confidence. PM.—The fielders will improve in estimating flight of the ball and getting under it in time.

FIGURE 7.5   Continued

3. Progress from simple to complex skill development
4. Progress from known activities to the unknown
5. Include notations for demonstrations and use of instructional devices
6. Include key questions and points that should be covered
7. Combine physical education activities with other academic areas when possible

Does the lesson plan meet the following criteria?

1. Readable and easily used by others
2. Usable during the actual instructional process
3. Designed for evaluation of curriculum effectiveness

In any case, formats used by teachers should cover the areas listed above. This will ensure that the les-son plan format reads easily, augments the instructional process, and provides for students of different abilities.

REFERENCES AND SUGGESTED READINGS

Hunter, M. 1982. *Motivation Theory for Teachers*. El Segundo, CA.: TIP Publications.

Hunter, M. 1982. *Reinforcement Theory for Teachers*. El Segundo, CA.: TIP Publications.

Hunter, M. 1982. *Teach for Transfer*. El Segundo, CA.: TIP Publications.

Hunter, M. 1986. *Mastery Teaching*. El Segundo, CA.: TIP Publications.

Pangrazi, R., and Dauer, V. 1989. *Lesson Plans for Dynamic Physical Education*, 9th ed. New York: Macmillan Publishing.

8 CREATING AN EFFECTIVE LEARNING ENVIRONMENT

Competent teachers create a learning environment where students want to learn and practice skills. Such an environment is characterized by a sensitive and caring teacher who uses a variety of techniques to foster learning in all students. It is a fallacy that teachers treat all students alike. More often than not, effective instructors have the ability to determine how students want and need to be treated. Some students may respond to subtle encouragement whereas others will require a more direct approach.

The focus of this section is to help teachers develop a repertoire of teaching skills which will allow them to meet the needs of all students in the class. Notice the word "all" in the previous sentence; many teachers can help students who want to learn, however only the best teachers are capable of motivating students who don't particularly like the subject matter. This is the challenge: teach all students regardless of their intrinsic desire to learn. A good place to begin is with the skill of listening. Few traits enhance the learning environment more than effective listening by the teacher. A student's self-worth is enhanced when a teacher listens and acknowledges his or her feelings and concerns.

DEVELOPING EFFECTIVE LISTENING SKILLS

For most teachers, listening skills are more difficult to learn than speaking skills. Instructors have been taught to impart knowledge to students and have practiced speaking for years. Many students have viewed teachers as people who teach you but do not care about your point of view. Poor communication is usually due to a breakdown in listening rather than speaking. There is a lot of truth in the adage, "People were given two ears and one mouth; to facilitate listening twice as much as they speak." The following points should be integrated into the teaching style of instructors.

1. Develop active listening skills. Good listeners convince the speaker that they are interested in what he or she is saying. Much of this is done through nonverbal behavior such as eye contact, nodding the head in agreement, facial expressions, and moving toward the speaker. Active listening shows students that their ideas and thoughts count and that they have some input into their destiny.

2. Try to determine what the student is trying to say. Many students are not capable of clearly expressing their feelings, particularly if they are deep concerns. The words expressed may not signal clearly what the student is feeling. For example, a teenager may say, "I hate P.E." In most cases, students do not hate all phases of physical education; rather it may be that something more immediate is the problem. An effective response might be, "You sound upset, are you having a problem you want to discuss?" This makes the student feel as though her feelings are important to the teacher, and also allows for an opportunity to clarify her concerns. It also prevents the teacher from internalizing the student's emotion and responding in a heated manner, such as "I don't care whether you like it or not, get on task!"

3. Practice paraphrasing what the student said. Paraphrasing is restating what was said to you, including the feelings detected, in your own words. For example, the teacher might respond, "Do I hear you saying that you are frustrated and bored with this activity?" If the paraphrasing is correct, it makes the student feel validated and understood. If the interpretation is incorrect, the student has an opportunity to restate the problem. In addition, it offers the teacher an opportunity to understand clearly how students perceive various situations.

4. Allow students to tell you how they feel. Teachers who listen to students learn more about their feelings. It is important to let students know that you will listen and then to practice doing so.

If you are a good listener, you may hear things that are not always positive. For example, students may tell you honestly which activities they enjoy and which they do not. They may tell you how you made them feel when you criticized them. This type of communication is constructive if it can be accepted by the teacher objectively. It gives the teacher consistent and ongoing evaluation. Even though it may not be a valid criticism of the program or procedures, it does offer opportunity for program and instructional improvement. A word of caution: If a teacher is insecure and finds it difficult to accept such communication, it is probably best to tell students this feeling. It may be necessary to avoid such interaction with students if it affects the confidence of the teacher.

5. Develop an awareness of situations that promote effective communication. Certain types of verbal interaction convince students that the teacher is unwilling to listen. Some of the more common examples are:

a. *Preaching or moralizing.* This is often manifested by telling others they "should know better than that!" Obviously, students make mistakes since they are young and learning. A big part of learning is making mistakes and knowing how to avoid such situations in the future. Teachers who expect such mistakes are not shocked by student misbehavior and are able to deal with it in a rational manner.

b. *Threatening.* Threats are often used to control students. They are usually ultimatums given to students to terminate undesirable behavior, even though the teacher knows that they will be impossible to carry out. For example, the threat, "If you do not stop that, I'm going to kick you out of class," is difficult to enforce. Most teachers are not in a position to expel students. If students hear enough idle threats, they soon learn to ignore and mock the teacher. As a reminder, it is not a threat if the misbehavior can and will be rectified consistently.

c. *Ordering and commanding.* If teachers appear to be bossy, students begin to think they are nothing more than pawns to be moved around the area. Try to develop patterns of communication that ask students to carry out tasks. Courtesy and politeness are requisites for effective teacher-student relationships. In addition, if teachers want to be treated with respect, they need to treat others similarly.

d. *Interrogating.* When there is a problem such as a fight between students, teachers often want to figure out who started the fight rather than deal with the feelings of the combatants. Very little is gained by trying to solve "who started it." Students will usually shirk the blame and suggest that it was not their fault. A much better solution is to begin by acknowledging feelings, "You know fighting is not accepted in my class, you must have been very angry to place yourself in this predicament." This allows students to talk about their feelings rather than place the blame on the other person. It also tells them that even when they do something wrong, the teacher cares about them.

e. *Refusing to listen.* This technique usually manifests itself by "Let's talk about it some other time." There are situations when this response is necessary. However, if it is always the case, students will begin to avoid interaction with the instructor.

f. *Labeling.* In this situation, the teacher tells students "Stop acting like fools," or "You're behaving like a bunch of animals." This is not only degrading, but it dehumanizes youngsters. In most cases, labeling is done because teachers think it will improve performance. In actuality, it is usually destructive and leaves a person with a negative feeling about the teacher.

REFINING COMMUNICATION SKILLS

The teaching-learning process involves the exchange of information between teachers and students. Communication must occur both ways: teachers with students and students with teachers. Communication behaviors can take many different forms. Different types of communication include a lecture on the strategy of a zone defense in basketball, directions for moving the class to four different stations for skill work, information feedback on a student's skill attempts, questions about the rules of a game, praise for lining up quickly at the end of class, or a smile for a well-executed lay-up. Communication forms can involve a number of sensory modes including the visual, verbal, and tactile. Visual cues involve demonstrations, loop films, and pictures. The teacher's gestures, facial expressions, or thumbs-up signs are a nonverbal type of visual communication. Indeed, some experts suggest that much of what students learn is picked up through nonverbal means (Galloway, 1971). Verbal communication involves lectures, discussions, directions, and other spoken words. Tactile communication encompasses physical contact such as manually manipulating a student's arms or legs for swimming instruction, or physically restricting a student's arm position in archery.

Effective teachers utilize efficient communication skills. Information is communicated in a minimum of time. Teachers should make sure that their information is clearly expressed in a vocabulary understood by the students. Use a variety of sensory modes, since students process information in different ways. Verbal information should be presented slowly so that students can comprehend, and the complexity of the information should be appropriate to the language development level of the students. Teachers should also encourage students to communicate with each other during physical education classes. Students can provide peers with important information for developing skills. Student communication can also be verbal, visual, or tactile.

Questions are an important communication form in the teaching-learning process. Teachers should use questions to evaluate the effectiveness of their lectures, demonstrations, or other types of instructional materials, including reading sheets, books, and pamphlets. They should also encourage students to ask questions since this fosters communication. The use of questions in a lesson must be planned carefully with an objective in mind. There are different categories of questions for specific goals (Siedentop, 1983). Recall questions focus on memory. Convergent and divergent questions require an analysis and a conclusion in a specific direction, such as problem-solving or guided-discovery styles. Value questions give students an opportunity to present an opinion that is neither right nor wrong.

IMPROVING COMMUNICATION BETWEEN TEACHER AND STUDENTS

The communication techniques that a teacher uses will have an impact on student motivation. Cheffers and Mancini (1978) found that few physical education teachers demonstrate sensitivity to students' feelings or ideas. Teachers who take a positive approach to communication with students and establish a warm, caring environment seem to be more effective (Medley, 1977). A positive approach to student motivation is recommended because of the long-term effects on both students and teachers. Both teaching and learning are more enjoyable when students and instructors can look forward to participating in a positive environment, and feel better about learning, teaching, and the overall school atmosphere at the end of the day. The positive approach seems to enhance the overall motivation of both teachers and students over a longer period of time.

Secondary school students often judge the quality of a teacher on attributes unrelated to the teacher's knowledge of subject matter. Various speech habits and the teacher's style of presentation can add to or detract from the instructional effectiveness. Students eventually tune out teachers who always shout commands, speak like drill sergeants, or repeat certain phrases. It is important to speak in terms consistent with the comprehension level and maturity of the students. Remember that students want to understand and to be understood. The following points will help facilitate the process of communication between student and teacher.

1. Describe specific behaviors rather than the person as whole. For example, "I can't understand why you do stupid things like that" judges the person as a whole and leaves the feeling of worthlessness. It is much more effective to suggest that "You need to listen when I am talking." This deals with behavior the student can improve and avoids undermining self-worth. In addition, most people will feel that you are interested in helping them improve rather than in belittling them.

2. Put yourself in the student's shoes. How would you feel if someone embarrassed you in front of the class? How do you feel when you are inept while trying to learn a new skill? These and other emotions often make listening difficult for youngsters. What conditions are necessary to make it easy for you to accept constructive feedback? Excessive feedback may actually stress the youngster and cause a reduction in performance. Offer feedback in small doses. If you are going to suggest ways to improve performance, try to do so on a personal basis and then leave the student to practice without scrutiny. To ask students to change and then stand over them until they do so may cause resentment and internal pressure.

3. What are your real feelings toward the student? At times teachers send mixed messages to students. They may be unhappy with the student because of a situation unrelated to class performance, yet unwilling to discuss the real issue. Instead, they respond with unkind feedback about a skill performance. Their negative feelings are then transferred to the youngsters regarding their performance in class. This was not the teacher's intent, but the result of pent-up feelings over an unrelated issue. Students will perceive negativity from a teacher. Take responsibility for communicating how you feel (albeit negative), but make sure that it is directed toward the undesirable behavior.

4. Accentuate the positive. When phrasing the instructional points of a lesson, stress the positive. For example, tell students to "Make a sharp cut," rather than saying "Don't round off your cut." An easy way to emphasize the *why* of an activity is to say, "Do this because...." If there are several different and acceptable ways to perform the movement patterns, be explicit. Show students the various ways, and discuss with them the reasons for the differences. Students like to know the correct technique, even if it is beyond their sphere of accomplishment. Explain only enough, however, to get the activity under way successfully.

5. Speak precisely. Limit the use of open-ended directives, and substitute those with precise goals. Instead of saying, "How many times can you . . . ?" or "See how many times you can . . . ," give student a definite target goal. Use directives like "See if you can . . . five times without missing," or "Show me five different ways you can. . . ." The teacher can ask the student to select a target goal. Using measurable and attainable goals is especially important when teaching slow learners or special education students.

6. Focus on repetition of correct performance. Doing an activity in many different ways or doing it many times is a first step in the learning process, not an ultimate goal. Ask students to pick the best way and to practice that skill. Students should be told to practice the skill until it is correct and then move on to something else. Students need to learn to assess when they are ready to move on; too often they move forward because they are bored or frustrated.

7. Optimize speech patterns. Certain teacher mannerisms may require attention and change. Avoid sermonizing at the least provocation. Excessive reliance on certain words and phrases—"okay," "all right," and the irritating "and uh"—are unappealing to students. Many adolescents will begin to listen for the repetitive speech patterns rather than listening to what the teacher is expressing. Acquire a broad vocabulary of effective phrases for indicating approval and good effort, and vary verbal patterns.

8. Conduct discussions in the classroom. Whenever possible, lengthy discussions should be held in the classroom for reasons of comfort and student expectations. Students expect to move in the activity area whereas they have learned to sit and interact cognitively in the classroom. Rules can be explained, procedures and responsibilities outlined, and formations illustrated on the blackboard. If discussions are going to last longer than 1 or 2 minutes, it is probably best to place students in a comfortable setting. It is expecting too much to ask students to sit and listen for a long period of time. In addition, if the discussion is lengthy, it will be more effective when instructional aides such as overheads, handouts, and films can be utilized.

9. Treat all responses to questions with dignity. The teacher should respect students' responses and opinions as long as he or she believes that they are sincere, and avoid humiliating a student who gives a wrong answer. Pass over inappropriate answers by directing attention to more appropriate responses. Or, tell students that they have offered a good answer but the question is not the right one. Remind them to save the answer and then go back to the students when it is correct for another question. Refrain from injecting personal opinion into the instructional question-answer process. At the end of the discussion, a summary of important points may be of value.

Do not be stunned, show surprise, or take offense if a student comments negatively in response to a query asking for candid opinions about an activity or procedure. When opinions are honest, some are bound to be negative.

IMPROVING INSTRUCTIONAL COMMUNICATION

Many words can be spoken, but little is accomplished if students do not understand what has been said. Communication implies more than words; it assumes that understanding has occurred. The following points can enhance the effectiveness of instruction.

1. Develop a stimulating speaking style. It is not necessary to be an outstanding speaker, yet it is important to be interesting and exciting. The chance for effective communication improves if students **want** to listen to a teacher. Use the voice effectively; alter the intensity, raise and lower the pitch, and change the speed of delivery. Use nonverbal behavior to emphasize important points. In addition, keep discussions short and to the point so that students are willing to stop what they are doing and listen.

2. Use a "tickler" to create interest. If a concept is somewhat difficult to comprehend, set the stage by briefly describing what is to follow and why it is important. This may mean repeating instructions if students are having trouble comprehending. An anticipatory set (Chapter 7) helps students prepare themselves for the upcoming dialogue. Quite often, students may miss the first part of the discussion before they realize what the teacher is expressing.

3. Build on previous learning experiences. Whenever possible, try to tie the discussion to previous skills and knowledge students have mastered. It can be effective to show students how a skill is similar (or dissimilar) to one learned earlier. Transfer of learning can be optimized if students understand the relationship to their previous experiences.

4. Present the material in proper progression. Skills should be taught in the sequence in which they will be performed. There are exceptions where a teacher may want to focus on a critical step first and then build around it. For example, in dance, a teacher may teach step patterns and then put them together to complete the dance. However, in most cases the progression should mimic the sequence of performance. Adolescents usually assume that the order in which activities are presented is the correct progression.

5. Model correct and incorrect examples. Most adolescents learn physical skills more quickly by observing rather than listening. This mandates modeling desirable and/or incorrect examples. For example, students will comprehend more quickly if they are shown the correct way to pivot and one or two incorrect examples of pivoting. Often, teachers try to talk students through all skills and movements. When possible, combine instruction with demonstration to improve the efficiency of the communication.

6. Check for understanding. Checking for understanding will help the teacher monitor the clarity of communication. A most efficient way is to ask a question and have students respond with an observable behavior. For example, "Raise your hand if you do not understand how to land correctly," or " See me if you do not understand how the game is played."

7. Separate management and instructional episodes. Much emphasis has been placed on maintaining short episodes of communication and focusing on cues that are easily understood. One more point deserves attention since it can be confusing. Teachers often combine management activities with instructional activities. For example, during a presentation of a new game, the teacher says the following. "In this game, we will break into groups of five. Each group will get a ball and form a small circle. On the command go, the game will start. Here is how you play the game. . . ." At this point, a lengthy discussion of game rules and conduct will follow. Most students will have forgotten the management strategies.

It is far more effective to move the class into the game formation and then discuss the activity. This serves two purposes: It reduces the length of the episode and makes it easier for the class to conceptualize how the game is played. In addition, it avoids the tendency of students to become unfocused, thinking about whom they want for a partner or on their team instead of listening to the rules. This points out the need to teach students one thing at a time.

Nonverbal Communication

Nonverbal communication is an important way of telling students what behavior is acceptable. Nonverbal communication is effective because it is interpreted by students and often perceived as more meaningful than words. For example, beginning teachers often have a difficult time keeping their feelings in line with their body language. They may be pleased with student performance, yet portray a less than pleased message (e.g., frowning or placing hands on hips). Another common example occurs when teachers want to assert themselves and gain control of a class. They often place their hands in their pockets, stand in a slouched position, and back away from the class. This nonverbal behavior signals anything but assertiveness and gives students mixed messages.

Many types of nonverbal behavior can be used to praise a class effectively: the thrust of a finger into the air to signify "number 1," thumbs up, a pat on the back, shaking hands, and so on. In contrast to the positive nonverbal behaviors, many negative signals can be delivered including some of the more common such as hands on the hips, finger to the lips, frowning, and staring. In any case, effective use of nonverbal behavior will increase the validity and strength of verbal communication.

When using nonverbal communication, consider the customs and mores of different cultures. It is the teacher's responsibility to learn how youngsters respond to different types of gestures. For example, Hmong and Laotian adolescents may be touched on the head only by parents and close relatives. A teacher who pats a student on the head for approval is interfering with the youngster's spiritual nature. The OK sign, touching thumb and forefinger, is an indication of approval in the United States. However, in several Asian cultures, it is a "zero," indicating the student is not performing properly. In many South American countries, the OK sign carries a sexual connotation. Teachers new to an area should ask for advice when expressing approval to youngsters from other cultures.

To make nonverbal behavior more convincing, teachers should view their behavior and then practice necessary modification. An effective method is to practice in front of a mirror and attempt to display different emotions. Another is to work with someone who does not know you well. If this person can identify the emotions demonstrated by the nonverbal behavior, they will be effective in a teaching situation. Using videotape recorders can be an effective tool for self-analysis. A teacher can self-analyze how he or she looks when under stress, when disciplining a student, or when praising.

IMPROVING SKILL PERFORMANCE WITH INSTRUCTIONAL CUES

Instructional cues are words that quickly and efficiently communicate to the learner proper technique and performance of skills or movement tasks. Adolescents learning skills need a clear understanding of critical skill points since motor learning and cognitive understanding of the skill must be developed simultaneously. Often, teachers will carefully plan skill and movement activities yet fail to plan for the instructional cues to be used during skill practice. The result may be a class that does not clearly understand technique and points of performance. When developing instructional cues, consider the following points.

Use Accurate Cues

If the cue is going to help the learner perform a skill correctly, it must be precise and accurate. It must also lead the learner in the proper direction and be part of a comprehensive package of cues. In other words, when the cues are considered as a package, they must direct the learner to correct accomplishment of the skill.

All instructors must teach activities that they know little about. Few, if any, teachers know everything about all activities. If accurate cues are going to be developed, the instructor must do some self-study. There are many textbooks and media aids for reference. These resources will almost always delineate the key points of the skill. Other options include asking other teachers who have strength in different activities, or videotaping an activity and analyzing points of performance where students have the most difficulty. In any case, cues are developed through study, practice, and experience. Even a beginning teacher should possess ample learning cues for teaching preliminary experiences. However, it is unexcusable not to prepare for each skill presentation and to consult a number of external resources.

Use Short, Descriptive Cues

Teachers often act in good faith when offering instructional cues. Unfortunately, they sometimes make the cues more comprehensive and lengthy than necessary. Many teachers teach as they were taught in high school. They remember a model where the teacher told the class everything they needed to know at the start of the unit and then let them practice without instruction for the rest of the period. This assumes that the students have comprehended a long list of instructions and are performing all the skills correctly. If this is not the case, students will spend the rest of the unit performing skills incorrectly. An incorrect motor pattern practiced for a long period will be very difficult to correct later.

To avoid confusing and overwhelming the learner, choose a small number of cues for each lesson. The cues should contain key words and should be short. They should help the learner focus on one phase of skill during practice. For example, when teaching batting, a cue might be: "Keep your head in and eyes on the ball." The purpose of this cue would be to avoid overswinging and pulling the head away from the path of the ball. Other examples of hitting cues might be:

- "Step toward the target."
- "Keep your elbows away from your body."
- "Shift weight from rear to front foot."

One way to examine the effectiveness of the cues is to see if they communicate the skill in total. Have all the critical points of batting been covered or is the skill being done incorrectly in certain phases? In most skills, the performance can be broken into three parts: preparing to perform, performing the skill, and follow through. Cues should focus on one phase at a time, because that is all most students can absorb. Descriptive words are most effective with adolescents, particularly if they have an exciting sound. For example, "**Snap** your wrists," "**Twist** the upper body during the follow through," or "**Explode** off the starting line." In other situations, the voice can strongly influence the effectiveness of the cue. For example if a skill is to be done smoothly and softly, the teacher can speak in a soft tone and ask students to "let the movement **flooooooow**" or to "move **smooooooothly** across the balance beam." Cues will be most effective when the teacher is able to use voice inflections, body language, and action words to signal the desired behavior.

Integrate Cues

Integrate cues to combine parts of a skill, and to utilize words that focus on the skill as a whole. These cues depend on prior cues used during the presentation of a skill and assume that concepts delineated in earlier phases of instruction were understood. Examples of integrating cues might be:

- "Step, rotate, throw"
- "Run, jump, and forward roll"
- "Stride, swing, follow-through"

Integrated cues are a set of action words that help students with the timing necessary in sequencing the parts of the skill. These cues are reminders of the proper sequence of skills and the mental images of the performance. Depending on the rhythm of the presentation, the cues can signal the speed and tempo of the skill performance. In addition, they can serve as a specialized language that allows the student and teacher to communicate effectively.

DEMONSTRATING AND MODELING SKILLS

Most students will want to see a demonstration of a skill or technique. The adage, "a picture is worth a thousand words," holds true in physical education. Demonstrations can illustrate variety or depth of movement, show something unique or different, point out items of technique or approach, illustrate different acceptable styles, and show progress. Another important reason for demonstrating is to help the teacher develop credibility with students. For example, many students may question whether a skill can be performed until they see the teacher or another student do it. Secondary school students are notorious for their "show me" attitudes; a demonstration will help show that the skill is in their range of ability.

The demonstration should increase the adolescents' understanding of the movements by encouraging them to observe critically and to analyze what they have seen. To this end, the demonstration should be followed by a period of practice and continued feedback.

Demonstration by the Teacher

Be sure that all the class can see and hear the performance. When explaining technique, the teacher should highlight key points of performance. The demonstration can show the proper starting position and then verbalize the instructions from that point on, or provide a more complete, point-by-point demonstration. The terminology should be clear, and the techniques demonstrated should be within the student's skill level. The more complex a skill is, the more demonstration needed. Questions can be raised during the demonstration, but the teacher should not allow the question-answer period to take up too much time.

Student Demonstration

The student demonstration is a most effective teaching technique, because it interjects the adolescents' own ideas into the lesson. As students practice and move, the class can be stopped for a demonstration.

If the demonstration is unsatisfactory, the teacher can go on to another student without comment or reprimand, saying only, "Thank you, Jessica. Let's see what Seth can do." Or the teacher might simply direct the adolescents to continue practicing.

Selecting several students to demonstrate their achievement is usually preferable, so that the others can observe varied approaches. If partner or small-group work is undertaken, the same principle holds.

Teachers Who Cannot Demonstrate

Because of physical and skill limitations, some teachers cannot demonstrate effectively. Few teachers can perform all physical activities well. Even the skilled teacher at times needs to devise substitutions for an effective instructor demonstration. Through reading, study, and analysis of movement, teachers can develop an understanding and a knowledge of the activities. Even if performing the activity is impossible, teachers must know how the activity is done. In addition, a number of visual aids and media can be used to offer meaningful orientation. Select skilled students to help demonstrate.

IMPLEMENTING EFFECTIVE INSTRUCTIONAL METHODOLOGY

Teachers need to develop an instructional environment that facilitates learning. A number of instructional behaviors can be demonstrated by the teacher to show that the activity area is safe and productive. Planning will assure students of an opportunity to learn skills in a positive setting. Each of the areas discussed below should be integrated into the lesson plan prior to the presentation of the lesson.

Create a Safe Environment

A safe environment is a requisite for effective teaching. Safety results from behaviors taught by the teacher. "Safety first and everything else second" should be the motto of every teacher. It is possible that a teacher will be removed from the teaching profession if accidents occur due to faulty planning and lack of foresight. Over half the injuries in schools occur in physical education classes; if they are due to poor planning and preparation, the teacher may be found liable and responsible for such injuries (see Chapter 13).

Teachers must foresee the possibility of hazardous situations that might result in student injury. Rules are only the beginning with students; safe and sensible behavior needs to be taught and practiced. For example, if students are in a gymnastics unit, they must receive instruction and practice in developing proper methods of absorbing momentum and force. It may even be necessary to practice safety, as in taking turns, spotting, and using the apparatus as directed.

Safety is assured when curricular presentations are listed in proper progression. Injuries are avoided when students perform only those activities for which they are prepared. The written curriculum can assure a safety committee or court of law that proper progression and sequencing of activities was used in the lesson presentation. In addition, proper progression of activities generates a feeling of confidence in students, since they feel they have the necessary background to perform adequately.

Safety inspections should be conducted at regular intervals. Apparatus that has not been used for a while should be inspected. Equipment such as tumbling mats, for example, should be kept clean to prevent the spread of disease. This assures that the teacher will not have to stop a lesson and try to fix the equipment, thus preventing unnecessary accidents.

In spite of the foregoing precautions, accidents do happen. Teachers should not refrain from using activities that have a certain degree of risk; in fact, this risk may be what makes the activity exciting. An important aspect of a physical education program is its ability to offer students an opportunity to take a risk and overcome fear. If students feel that adequate safety precautions have been taken, they will be less hesitant to learn new activities that involve risk.

Use Active Supervision

Observation of class performance is critical in assuring that students stay on task and practice activities correctly. This requires that the teacher supervise students in an active manner, that is, **positioning** oneself so that eye contact can be maintained with all students. Students have a tendency to stay on task if they know someone is watching. This mandates that the teacher stay out of the center of the area. It is quite common to observe teachers placing students in a circle and then standing in the center of the formation. Not only is it impossible to see all students, but it is difficult for youngsters facing the back of the teacher to hear. Since students cannot hear and there is little eye contact with half of the class, the teacher may not be aware of an accident or misbehavior.

Some teachers assume that you must move to the same location in the teaching area when giving instructions, or that students will listen only when the

teacher is on or near this spot. Not only is this incorrect, but it results in some rather negative consequences. Students who choose to exhibit deviant or off-task behavior will usually move far away from the instructor. Because the teacher's movement patterns are predictable, deviant students will be the farthest from the teacher and thus in a position that is difficult to observe. In addition, it is quite possible that the teacher may never move into certain areas, causing some students to believe that the teacher does not like them. Active supervision requires that the instructor move around the perimeter of the area. Another reason for moving in an unpredictable manner is to keep students on task. For example, when using a number of teaching stations, many teachers will move from station to station in a predictable manner. Some students will perform the tasks while the teacher is watching, but will move off task as soon as the teacher moves to the next station. If the teacher covers the stations in the same sequence on a regular basis, it is possible for the students to slack off while the teacher covers the other stations. The bottom line is: actively move in a random fashion so that students cannot anticipate who you will be observing next.

Active supervision demands movement and effective observation. If you develop a plan for reaching all students, they will more likely think you are concerned about them. In addition, it is important to place yourself in the optimum position to observe skill performance. For example, if you are observing kicking, stand to the side rather than behind the student. A judgment that needs to be made when observing performances is how long to stay with a single group or student. If you get overly involved with a student, the rest of the class may move off task. On the other hand, if contacts are short and terse, it is quite possible that the student will benefit from the interaction. Teachers must learn to pace instructional feedback. Probably the best approach is to give the student one or two pointers and then move to another student before returning to check progress.

Develop a Plan for Active Supervision

Experts who work with teachers are often amazed to see how they can "look at students but not see." In other words, teachers are looking at the class, but they are not seeing anything that will improve their instructional effectiveness. If teachers do not have a plan for actively supervising behavior, they usually will not be able to recall whether students exhibited the behavior. For example, if a teacher wants to keep all students on task, it is important he or she develop a plan for monitoring this behavior. A practical plan could involve scanning the class from left to right at regular intervals and observing the number of students who are performing the assigned task. When teaching a class of 25–35 students, it usually takes 4–6 sec to scan an entire class. If done faster, the teacher usually is not able to internalize the results of the scan. A number of variables can be evaluated through systematic observation: students responding to a start or stop signal (response latency), key points of skill performance, adherence to safety procedures, and on-task performance.

Design a plan for active supervision. This plan should include where to stand for observation, how long to stay with each student, and how to move through the instructional area. One approach to assure that all students have personal contact with the teacher is to check off the names of students who were addressed during the lesson. This can be done immediately after the lesson with a class roll sheet or at a later time if the lesson is recorded. Teachers will often find that they do not make regular contact with certain students and make excessive contact with others. This can lead to feelings of favoritism or concern that "the teacher does not like me." It is difficult to interact with all students in a single physical education lesson, however, in a 1- or 2-wk period, all students should receive feedback and attention.

The movement of the teacher should be planned since it affects supervisory effectiveness. To facilitate learning how to move throughout the area, divide it into four equal parts and make an attempt to move into each area a certain number of times. Instructions and reinforcement should be given from all quadrants. A student can chart the movement that will give the teacher evidence of goal achievement. (See Chapter 11 for an example an an observation recording chart.)

Maintain the Flow of the Lesson

An important phase of effective instruction is pacing the lesson to keep students interested, yet not frustrated. In addition, maintain the focus of the lesson so that the desired objectives are taught. The following points can aid the teacher in maintaining the flow of the lesson toward desired goals.

Minimize Verbalization and Increase Activity

It is easy to become engrossed in instruction and lose sight of student interest. Most students enter the class expecting to be involved in activity. If a teacher immediately spends 5 min with roll call followed by 5 or 10 min of lecture, students will lose interest and motivation. Often it is best to move the

class into activity first and give instructions later. This gives students the opportunity to get immersed in the activity, burn off a bit of energy, and be more receptive to listening.

Teachers can sometimes become angry about misbehavior and spend a few minutes talking about the need to be model students. Much of the "sermon" will be general in nature and reflect the instructor's anger. Lecturing students has little impact. If misbehavior has occurred, let the class start practicing, speak to the misbehaving students one-to-one, and resume instruction. Often, a whole class is lectured when only a few students were at fault. This forces the majority of students to listen to something that has little or no meaning to them. In addition, some students may think that the teacher is unfair for scolding the entire class. Remember that time spent talking to the entire class prevents meaningful skill practice. Minimize excessive talking and maximize productive and on-task practice.

Maintain the Focus of Instruction

It is easy to become derailed when an interesting event occurs in class. Lesson plans are designed to guide the instruction toward desired objectives. If teachers constantly allow students to "sidetrack" them to more interesting topics, it is doubtful that goals will be reached. Experienced teachers know that some students will intentionally try to move the teacher away from the tasks at hand in order to participate in activities they prefer. Effective teachers are able to maintain their momentum toward objectives and still show interest in student ideas. Sometimes it is necessary to deviate from planned objectives and take advantage of the "teachable moment." However, this should be the exception, not the rule. Students are well aware that the teacher is responsible for guiding the content of the lesson, and they expect it.

Maintain the Pace and Continuity of Instruction

Effective lessons flow in a consistent and well-planned manner. There are many transitions during a lesson: organizing students into groups, changing from one part of the lesson to another, and issuing and putting away equipment. It is important that students perceive the transitions as an integral part of the instruction. If a transition is excessively long, it interrupts the instructional momentum and students may begin to misbehave. Minimize time spent on transition; it detracts from accomplishing the lesson's goals.

Pace of instruction also affects the flow of the lesson. How often should a teacher break into practice sessions to clarify a point or refocus instruction?

In most cases there is a natural break in practice episodes when students become bored or fatigued and begin to move off task. This signals that it is time to refocus. If, after an instructional episode, most of the class are not performing the task correctly, stop and clarify the situation. However, if a teacher stops the class frequently without concern for the students' opportunity to learn, the result will be a lesson without flow and continuity. Students will become frustrated, feeling that they never have enough time to master a task.

Activity instruction demands continuity so that the learner understands the purpose of performing various activities. For example, most instructors break activities into parts, knowing how the skill as a whole is performed. Students also need to know how the various parts of a skill fit together. This should occur within the same lesson. It is expecting too much of students to have them practice parts for 1 or 2 wks and then put them together as a whole. Always integrate the activity or drill into the ultimate focal point: the accomplishment of the skill or activity.

Individualizing Instruction

One of the hardest tasks for a teacher is to meet the individual needs of students even though the majority of instruction is conducted as a group activity. It is obvious, even to the least experienced teacher, that the ability levels of students vary widely. As students mature, their range of ability increases, making it more difficult to meet all of their needs. In addition, many students participate in extracurricular activities such as baseball, basketball, and private tutoring in various sports. This range of experiences places greater responsibility on the instructor to modify tasks so that all students can find success. The following methods can be used to individualize instruction and keep students on task.

1. Modify the conditions. In this situation, the task is modified to help students find success. For example, it may mean moving partners closer together if they are learning tennis skills, using a slower-moving object such as a family soft ball, increasing the size of the target, changing the size of boundaries or goal areas, allowing students to toss and catch individually, or increasing the size of the striking implement. An optimum rate of error and success should be the goal of individualized instruction. When students find little success, they may exhibit off-task behavior to draw attention away from their subpar performance. This behavior is a clear indicator to the teacher that the error rate is too high and is preventing learning.

2. Increase the challenge through self-competition. When the success rate is too high, students will become bored and avoid continued practice. This calls for increasing the challenge by adding personal competition to the task. Challenge gifted students to see how many times they can perform without missing, break a personal record, or be allowed to use the skill in group competition. The challenge can be increased by asking gifted performers to use a faster-moving object, accomplish higher levels of performance, or increase the distance or size of the goal. Students respond best to challenges; a task is a challenge when it is slightly above their current skill level.

3. Offer different task challenges. Students do not have to be working on the same tasks simultaneously. It is desirable to have a number of tasks of varying complexity so that students of all skills can learn to develop personal challenges. Task cards or station teaching can allow students the opportunity to learn at an optimum rate. In cases where specialized sport skills are being learned, it is particularly important to offer different tasks. For example, students who have limited upper body strength would find inverted balances to be difficult, if not impossible. Balance activities utilizing the legs could be substituted, allowing all students to work on balance skills through different activity challenges.

4. Encourage higher levels of performance. Another solution for individualizing instruction is to refine the performance of skilled individuals. Fine points of technique can be used to offer greater challenge. For example, during throwing instruction, less gifted students may be learning proper footwork, whereas skilled throwers are working on distance, accuracy, or velocity of throws.

UTILIZING EFFECTIVE INSTRUCTIONAL FEEDBACK

Instructional feedback is used by effective teachers to assure student learning. Used properly, it can enhance a student's self-image, improve the focus of performance, result in individualized instruction, increase the rate of on-task behavior, and improve understanding. The following points offer direction for improving the quality of feedback used in the instructional setting.

Positive, Corrective, and Negative Feedback

Many teachers use corrective feedback to alter student performance. Unless a teacher utilizes a negative approach, little negative feedback (e.g., "That was a lousy throw") is used. Instead, they offer corrective feedback focusing on inaccurate phases of the performance (or related behavior). This is usually expected by students; however, if it is the only type of feedback offered, youngsters will begin to perceive it as negative. The danger of overusing corrective feedback is that it creates a climate where students worry about making errors for fear the instructor will embarrass or belittle them. In addition, excessive correction may cause youngsters to think that no matter what they do correctly, the teacher will never recognize their effort.

More effective is to focus on the positive points of student performance. This creates a positive atmosphere where students are willing to accept a challenge and risk error or failure. Teachers who use positive feedback usually feel better about their students since they look for strengths in performance and use this as a foundation for skill improvement. Most physical education instructors rely heavily on corrective feedback, and the observation has been made that many physical educators have a correction complex. Corrective statements are appropriate if the learning environment has a balance of positive and corrective feedback. Siedentop (1983) recommends that an educational environment should have a 3:1 or 4:1 ratio of positive feedback to corrective feedback. A higher ratio of positive feedback certainly enhances the overall positive atmosphere of the class. Since the use of corrective feedback comes easily for most teachers, it is usually necessary for them to practice increasing the amount of positive feedback used with students.

Use a Variety of Information Feedback

Information feedback is what students receive after they have completed a skill attempt. Feedback on the results of many skill attempts is obvious as, for example, in the case of golf swings, basketball shots, or baseball swings. It is inherent in the specific activity, and students know immediately the results of the skill attempt. Feedback on the form or topography of skill behavior is, however, difficult to attain. Teachers play an important role in providing students with useful information feedback on how well they are performing a skill.

A teacher usually gives feedback immediately after a skill attempt has been made. Teachers need to plan carefully for information feedback in classes. Planning for feedback should include determining the specific skill behaviors that a teacher is trying to foster. The feedback should be prescriptive in nature so that it helps to eradicate errors. Many different ways can be used to tell students that they

are performing at an acceptable level. Feedback statements can be general, specific, verbal, or nonverbal. Including a student's first name with the feedback is a meaningful way to make students realize that the teacher is aware of them and is sincere about their skill development. The following are some examples of different types of feedback:

Corrective or Prescriptive

- Get the shot put angle up to 42 degrees.
- Bend your knees more and uncoil.
- Adjust your grip by spreading your fingers.
- Accelerate through the ball.
- Keep your wrists stiff and start the action with your shoulders.
- Transfer your weight as you contact the ball.

Positive General

- Good job.
- Way to go.
- Nice defense.
- All right, Jim.
- Very nice hustle.
- Interesting question, Mike.
- OK, class.

Positive Specific

- Good angle of release.
- Perfect timing on the outlet pass.
- Way to hit the soft spot in the 1-3-1 zone.
- Great job looking off the undercoverage.
- That's the way to vary your serves. It keeps them off balance.
- Mike, good job keeping your head down.

Nonverbal Positive or Corrective

- Winking or smiling.
- Thumbs up or down.
- Pat on the back.
- Clapping the hands.
- Facial gestures.
- Making a "V" sign.
- Shaking the fist.

Plan a variety of feedback, including statements that use first names and give specific positive information, and nonverbal messages. Variety is necessary to avoid satiation and redundancy. Feedback should be directed at key points of the specific skill, and the terminology should be appropriate to the student's age and developmental level.

Offer Feedback to All Class Members

Teachers often have many students in class and must decide on the length of feedback episodes as well as the number of students to contact. It is a difficult decision and may depend on the skill being taught. For example, if it is a skill that students learn quickly, it is quite possible that the best model is to move quickly from student to student, assuring that there are no major dysfunctions. This might mean a systematic approach where all students are quickly observed, or a random approach of moving and looking for students having problems. This fast-moving approach will allow the teacher to come into contact with all students many times during the lesson. In addition, it will help keep students on task since they know the teacher is moving and watching the class regularly.

The drawback to this approach is that little opportunity for in-depth feedback occurs. If skills are complex and refinement is a goal, taking more time with students is usually more effective. This means watching a student long enough to offer highly specific and information-loaded feedback. The end result is high-quality feedback to a fewer number of students.

When giving feedback to students, avoid close scrutiny of the student at the completion of the episode. Many students will become tense if a teacher tells them how to perform a skill correctly and then watches to see if they do it exactly as instructed. Most students are willing to try new and risky ways of performing if they are allowed to practice without being closely observed by the teacher or class. In short, observe carefully, offer feedback, move to another student, and recheck progress at a later time.

Group or Individual Feedback?

In school settings, a large amount of feedback is group oriented. The most common method is stopping the class and offering feedback to all youngsters. This is the fastest method, but it also allows the most room for misinterpretation. Some students may not understand the feedback while others may not listen since it does not seem relevant to them. More effective is to direct the feedback (positive only) at a student so that the rest of the class can hear it. This allows the feedback to "ripple" through the class, offering instructional feedback to the rest of the class and a positive experience for the student identified. In addition, the student can demonstrate the skill and serve as a model for the rest of the class. Be careful to use this approach in a manner that avoids student failure in front of the rest of the class. An example of this approach would be, "Sarah is hitting the tennis ball at its peak when she serves."

In addition, feedback should focus on the desired task. For example, if students are asked to catch a batted ball in front of their body, it will cloud the issue if the teacher offers feedback on the quality of throw. If catching is the focus, feedback should be on catching so that students will continue to concentrate on that skill. An example of feedback in this setting would be, "Watch the way Michelle keeps her body in front of the ball when catching ground balls." A final clarification: it is not necessary to have students watch other students to accomplish the desired outcome. In fact, it is effective only if the performer is capable of showing the skill correctly. If this approach is used exclusively, less skilled (or shy) performers will never have an opportunity to receive feedback from the class. It can be just as effective to tell the class how well a student was doing and move on, for example, "Mike always keeps his head up when dribbling."

A final note about feedback: it should be offered to students as soon as possible after the performance. This is usually the case if a teacher is moving from student to student looking for feedback opportunities. If delayed feedback is offered, it should allow opportunity for immediate practice so that students can apply the information. Little is gained and much lost if students are told how to improve and then leave class without opportunity for practice. Few, if any, students will be able to remember the suggestions. If the end of class is approaching, it is probably best to limit feedback and work on situations that can be practiced immediately. Other problems can be solved at the next class.

DEFINING POLICIES AND PROCEDURES

The development and implementation of a high quality physical education program require that many policies and procedures are determined, communicated, and applied consistently to all students. Effective physical education programs have a well-developed set of written guidelines that are presented to the students on the first day of school and are reinforced continually throughout the year. Policies and procedures should be evaluated constantly to determine if they are actually contributing to program objectives. An excellent curriculum will not be effective without a well-developed set of policies and procedures, and an ongoing revision process.

Write these guidelines in a handbook or booklet available to all students, parents, and administrators. Discuss the information with students and require that students discuss the information with their parents. A form indicating that parents have read the guidelines should be signed and returned to the physical education teacher (Figure 8.1). Many students and parents have misconceptions about the nature of physical education, and clarifying all aspects of the program as soon as possible is important.

The physical education handbook should cover the following areas:

1. Philosophy of the program
2. Curriculum objectives
3. Program scope and graduation requirements
4. Uniform and dressing requirements
5. Showers and towels
6. Locks and lockers
7. Attendance and participation
8. Excuses and make-up procedures
9. Equipment
10. Grading procedures.

The handbook should be brief, clear, and succinct, and no more than 10 pages. A cover letter similar to Figure 8.1 should be enclosed, and include a return slip for the physical education teacher. Parents and students must be encouraged to question any aspect of the program that they find unclear or disagreeable.

Philosophy and Objectives

Communicating the department's views and objectives for the program is especially important. (Refer to Chapter 1 for a general discussion of physical education and program objectives.) Many people have varying views of physical education (e.g., strictly as a physical training program, or a training ground for the athletic program), and many adults have little information about the new approaches to physical education. A short 1-page discussion about the philosophy and objectives could help parents and students understand of the nature and importance of the program.

Program Scope and Graduation Requirements

Parents and students need to understand how physical education fits into the graduation requirements of the school. Many schools in each state require varying amounts of physical education for graduation. In some districts, physical education credit is

---

OVATION HIGH SCHOOL PHYSICAL EDUCATION DEPARTMENT
OVATION, AZ

Dear Parents:

   This booklet contains the policies and procedures of the physical education department. We would like you to read carefully and discuss the program regulations with your son or daughter. These policies and procedures are important for making the learning environment a pleasant experience for all students.

   We desire to have all students leave physical education classes with a positive attitude and the urge to be physically active throughout their lifetime. If you have any questions about the curriculum or the policies and procedures of the department, please call me at 925-4724.

   Please sign the slip at the bottom of the sheet and have your child return it to school.

   Thank you.

Sincerely,

_____

Physical Education Teacher

We have read the booklet and understand the policies and procedures.

_____   _____

Parent   Student

_____

Date

FIGURE 8.1   Letter to parent regarding policies and procedures

awarded for participation in athletics, cheerleading squads, marching band, ROTC, and driver education classes. These substitutions are a controversial topic that has been argued for years. Many physical educators have strong feelings on both sides of the issue as to what should be included in the scope of the physical education program.

The best way to answer the question of which activities should be awarded physical education credit is to examine the objectives of the program. If an activity fulfills the program objectives, then credit should be awarded for participation in that activity. If the activity does not fulfill the objectives, then physical education credit should not be awarded. Athletics, marching band, ROTC, and driver education are all important and valuable experiences for students, but in most cases, they do not fulfill the objectives of physical education. If a school board wants to award credit for participation in these activities, administrators should designate the credit appropriately, rather than labeling it physical education.

It is easy to understand why some people argue the physical benefits of the marching band or the skills developed while playing on a basketball team. These are, however, only a small portion of the objectives of a quality physical education program. Students need to experience success with a variety of lifetime sports and fitness activities, and to receive knowledge about health, exercise, and nutrition. This information is imparted to students and their parents through the physical education program. The program handbook is a starting point for developing parent and student awareness.

Another important aspect of the program scope relates to coeducational classes. Many parents will have had little or no experience with sexually integrated physical education classes, and convincing them of the benefits of coeducational classes may be difficult. Parents and students need time to slowly expand their comfort zones regarding this issue. The departmental handbook can begin "socializing" people to the idea of male/female classes.

Uniforms and Dress Requirements

Students should be strongly encouraged to change into active wear for physical education classes. The importance of comfort, safety, and hygiene must be emphasized. Many schools still require a specific uniform and enforce strict dress codes. Uniforms and dress codes can create many problems and continue to be a source of controversy. Students will often avoid physical education environments simply because of a dress code requirement, yet these same students will admit that they enjoy physical activities and would take a class if no dress code existed. The benefits of having all students dressed alike does not seem worth developing escape and avoidance behaviors in students.

Controversy over uniforms and dress codes should not develop into a critical issue. If the school favors a dress code, a student committee can be formed each year to select a new uniform. Clothing companies will provide several available options with school colors, emblems, or mascots. Students can then decide which uniform they desire, or they can be given the option of buying a different type of uniform. Several choices should be available. Adolescence is not a time to force students to wear the same clothes. It is, rather, a time of growing independence, and allowing students to select their physical education attire will not be detrimental to the accomplishment of program objectives (Figure 8.2).

In addition, each physical activity class is different and may require some type of specialized clothing that is appropriate for the activity. Rock climbing or horseback riding classes may require the wearing of long pants for safety. Aerobics, yoga, and the martial arts also necessitate specialized clothing for freedom of movement. Students certainly need warm attire for outdoor, cold weather activities.

Another problem is the legality of an imposed dress code. Some state laws stipulate that if a specific dress code is required, the school must purchase uniforms for those students unable to do so. Dress codes can also create problems for students with a specific religious belief that forbids wearing gym attire. Still other students may have physical deformities or embarrassing conditions that they wish to keep covered. For example, a student who has a severe case of acne on his back may not want to go swimming without a shirt and expose his upper body.

FIGURE 8.2 Participating in a variety of uniforms

These problems reveal why a flexible policy on uniforms and dress requirements is desirable. The perceived advantages of a strict dress code — developing discipline, school spirit, and cooperation; enhancing the identification of teams; reducing discrimination against poorer or wealthier students; and reducing unit cost of attire because of large orders — are debatable and hardly seem worth the problems generated. Teachers and students should both influence the decisions on dress requirements, and teachers should have the flexibility to make decisions that facilitate the learning process of each individual in each situation.

The department should have a policy regarding students who cannot afford a uniform or a change of clothes. Often, a special fund can be made available through candy or bake sales. The parent-teacher association may be able to provide funds through one of its projects. Sometimes used or unclaimed clothes can be cleaned and worn by students who cannot afford to buy a uniform.

Recommend a policy on the laundering of gymnasium clothes to students. Some schools require students to bring in clean clothes every Monday for the physical education teacher to inspect. The authors believe that this area should be one of personal choice, as is the laundering of regular street clothes. Depending on how often a class meets, teachers should encourage students to launder their gym clothes once or twice a week. If hygiene problems occur, students (and if necessary, parents) should be confronted. Getting students to develop personal management skills early in the physical education setting is important.

Junior high school students can be quite careless in keeping track of personal belongings. Students who wear similar uniforms must identify them with some type of permanent ink or name tag because of the numerous opportunities for mix-ups, losses, or pilferage.

Teachers need to be good models of appropriate attire for physical activities. An active teaching role is certainly enhanced by appropriate dress, and students are strongly influenced by the behavior of their teachers. It is difficult to defend teaching in blue jeans when students are not allowed to participate in similar attire. Educators must be careful to analyze personal policies and behavior. Many times, teachers fail to realize the inconsistencies they have developed in the learning environment. This is part of the hidden curriculum that was discussed in Chapter 3.

Attendance and Participation Policies

Teachers should work continually to create a positive environment. If students enjoy the experience, there will be fewer problems with attendance and participation. The overall curriculum and the instructional procedures will have more of an effect on students than will policies and procedures on attendance and participation. Many teachers spend so much time and energy on these latter concerns that they lose sight of the importance of curriculum and instruction. Students will be more enthusiastic about physical education if a quality curriculum and an effective instructional program exist.

Nevertheless, teachers do need to develop policies for attendance, participation, and excuses from class. A system that allows students to earn reinforcers (e.g., points, activity time, privileges) for attending and participating is an effective strategy. Too often, teachers use a negative or "chop" system by which students lose points or privileges or receive lower grades for inappropriate behavior. This approach creates a negative environment, while the positive approach has the opposite effect. Students can be awarded one point per day for attendance, one point for dressing, and points for participating, rather than subtracting or cutting points for not attending and participating. This award system allows students to earn points in a positive environment, and permits a daily measure of success.

All medical excuses and notes from parents should be presented to the school nurse at the beginning of the school day rather than during class time. Teachers should spend class time teaching rather than analyzing excuses. In addition, the nurse is more qualified than the physical educator to make decisions about medical problems requiring special attention. The nurse should make the final decision on participation, and should communicate with the physical education teacher both verbally and in writing. A form can be developed to facilitate this communication (Figure 8.3). Teachers must be aware of student differences. Some students will want to return to the activities too soon, while others may not want to return even when appropriate.

If students cannot participate for three consecutive days, they should be recommended to a physician. A physician's report form (Figure 8.4) should then be sent to the student's doctor. This type of form should help to improve communication between the school nurse, the physician, and the physical educator. Students need to understand that credit for physical education is not awarded to people who cannot participate in the class sessions.

Students who have minor problems such as being tired or having a sore throat, headache, or cramps should be handled on an individual basis. Some students can participate with these problems while others cannot. Teachers must become knowledgeable about the backgrounds and personalities of their

---

SCHOOL NURSE EXCUSE FORM

Student _____   Date _____

Please excuse the above named student from physical education class for the following day(s):

_____

The reason the student is excused is: _____

_____

_____

_____

Thank you,

_____
School Nurse

FIGURE 8.3   School nurse excuse form

students. A policy that treats all students the same is usually misdirected.

Religious beliefs relative to participating on various holidays or holy days often result in students' asking to be excused. This should be handled individually with each student and through the school administration. If any confusion arises about excuses due to minor illness or religious beliefs, students should be allowed to see the school nurse for illnesses and a guidance counselor or administrator about preferences and beliefs.

Remember that students also have bad days, headaches, cramps, family problems, and other concerns that will affect their daily performance. Sometimes students need a little extra encouragement to participate, and at other times they may need a day off. Effective teachers take the time and make the effort to get to know their students so they have some basis for judging individual situations. In contrast, some teachers believe that students are "cheating" on them if the student does not want to participate on a given day. Initially, students should be given the benefit of a doubt, because they may indeed have a problem. If the same student continues to have participation problems, the teacher will have to contact the parents or apply some alternative procedures.

Develop a policy for tardiness. Start each class at a precise time. Students need to know exactly what time the class begins, and excessive tardiness may have to be built into the make-up policies and procedures for grades.

Class Make-Up Policies and Procedures

All students should have the opportunity to make up missed classes because of excused absences. Try to focus the make-up work on the activities that were missed. Attending another physical education class or an extra class on the same activities is useful. Possibilities for make-up work can focus on knowledge activities, performance activities, or spectator activities. Depending on the objectives of the lessons missed, some activities will be more valuable than others. The following are examples that could be used in each area.

Make-Up Work—Knowledge Activities

The following alternatives might be offered to students who missed a knowledge activity. Students would be instructed to complete one of the following assignments and turn it in to the instructor:

1. Read an article in the sports section of the newspaper and write a 1-page analysis (form provided).

2. Read an article in any sports magazine and write a 1-page analysis (form provided).
3. Read a short biographical sketch about a noted sports figure and write a 1-page analysis (form provided).
4. List and define 15 terms from any of the following activities: basketball, field hockey, flag football, lacrosse, orienteering, physical conditioning, recreational games, running techniques, soccer, swimming, team handball, and volleyball.
5. List and explain 10 rules from any sport.
6. Diagram the playing area of any of the activities listed in activity number 4.
7. Read a book related to a sport and write a 1-page analysis (form provided).
8. Student choice (with teacher approval).

The form reproduced in Figure 8.5 can be used for student reports on these knowledge activities.

Make-Up Work—Performance Activities

Students who have missed performance activities might be told to participate in any of the follow-

---

PHYSICIAN'S REPORT FORM

Date _____

Dear Dr. _____

The following student, _____ , has requested that he/she be excused from physical education activities. We would like your help in designing a program that is appropriate for this student's physical condition. Our program offers a wide variety of physical activities. Please complete the following information to enable us to develop a personalized program.

Thank you for your time.

Sincerely,

_____

Physical Education Department Head

- -

1. Type of illness, injury, or handicap _____
_____

2. Restrictions _____
3. Activities to be avoided _____
4. Duration of restriction _____
5. Other important information _____
_____

6. Physician name _____
   Address _____ Phone _____
7. Signature _____ Date _____

Please send form to: Person _____
                      School _____
                      Address _____

FIGURE 8.4 Physician's report form

```
┌─────────────────────────────────────────────────────────────────────┐
│                          ARTICLE REPORT                               │
│                                                                       │
│     Name _____         │
│                                                                       │
│     Date _____         │
│                                                                       │
│     Publication _____          │
│                                                                       │
│     Author _____         │
│                                                                       │
│     Major idea of article:                                            │
│                                                                       │
│                                                                       │
│     Your opinion of the material:                                     │
│                                                                       │
│                                                                       │
│     What are the benefits of this material to you?                    │
│                                                                       │
│                                                                       │
│     Parent or guardian signature _____          │
│                                                                       │
└─────────────────────────────────────────────────────────────────────┘
```

FIGURE 8.5   Knowledge analysis sheet

ing activities and to write a 1-page analysis (form provided):

1. Run a mi. for time.
2. Run a parcourse.
3. Ride a bike for 30 min.
4. Attend an aerobics class.
5. Lift weights for 30 min.
6. Play 18 holes of disc golf.
7. Play one set of tennis.
8. Play two games of racquetball.
9. Play 18 holes of regular golf.
10. Engage in a workout at a health spa.
11. Student choice (approved by instructor).

The form in Figure 8.6 can be used for reports in the performance area.

Make-Up Work—Spectator Activities

Tell students to observe one of the following events and write a 1-page analysis (form provided). These events can take place at the junior or senior high school, community college, college, or professional level. Any of the following event activities is acceptable: football, soccer, cross country running, tennis, volleyball, basketball, softball, baseball, wrestling, track and field, swimming, and student choice (approved by instructor). Figure 8.7 is a form that can be used for reporting on spectator activities.

Showers and Towels

Students should be encouraged to shower after all vigorous activity sessions. Teachers must spend some time discussing hygiene and why showering

is necessary. Students need to understand the importance of developing lifetime health habits.

Showering, like the uniform issue, should not evolve into a polarizing conflict. Many physical educators have developed avoidance behaviors in students because of inflexible or poorly managed showering policies. For example, one teacher required students to shower after every class including golf, archery, riflery, and discussion sessions. Showering is surely not necessary after every physical education class. Other teachers have given students only 5–7 min to shower and change clothes. This is not enough time for students to fix their hair and clothes and prepare to return to the classroom. Students' caring about their appearance is an important aspect of personal development. Physical education teachers who overlook this fact often alienate students.

Teachers need to analyze carefully the nature of each lesson and the allotted time schedule. Swimming, for example, requires more preparation time at the end of class, and an archery activity does not necessitate showering. Showering policies should be flexible so teachers can make the appropriate time adjustments in lessons. Many students are uncomfortable showering in front of peers due to menstruation, underdeveloped bodies, acne problems, deformities, or various other problems. Private showers can help alleviate this concern. Teachers need to be sensitive to the fact that poorly planned and poorly administered showering and dressing procedures can turn students off to physical activity.

When students resist taking showers, teachers need to search for the underlying reason. Possibly an adjustment of times allotted can remedy the prob-

---

PERFORMANCE ANALYSIS

Name _____

Activity _____

Date _____

Explain the activity you participated in.

Explain the physical benefits of this activity.

What were your scores, time repetitions, and so forth?

Parent or guardian signature _____

FIGURE 8.6   Performance analysis sheet

SPECTATOR ANALYSIS

Name _____

Event _____

Date, place _____

Opponents _____

Final score _____

Type of offense and defense of each team:

How the scoring occurred:

Strengths and weaknesses of each team:

Your reactions to the event:

Parent or guardian signature _____

FIGURE 8.7   Spectator analysis sheet

lem, and if the activities are not vigorous, showering may not be necessary for all students.

Students should have a say in matters of personal health and cleanliness. If teachers make all of the decisions for students, little is learned about making decisions in later life. If students complain about peers who possess strong body odor, the matter should be discussed with the student and, possibly, with his or her parents. Some type of motivational system can be devised if necessary to encourage

students to shower (see "Behavior Games" in Chapter 9). Awarding points, activity time, or free time can be used to motivate showering behaviors. Teachers should try to avoid incorporating showering and dressing behaviors in the grading system, but it may be necessary in certain situations.

Students need to be reminded of the hazards in showering facilities. The shower room can be a dangerous area, and horseplay cannot be tolerated. Care must be taken when walking to and from the area, and absolutely no glass containers for food, drink, shampoo, or soap are allowed.

A policy on towels should also be determined. The simplest procedure is to have students bring towels from home along with their activity clothing. Students are then responsible for changing towels and uniforms on a regular basis. Mark names on the towels to minimize loss.

Some districts provide students with towels for physical education class. The towels can be purchased by the school and laundered on a regular basis in school facilities. This arrangement helps reduce mildew and odor problems created by students leaving wet towels in their lockers, and students are also motivated to shower because there are clean, dry towels available. The school must, however, purchase towels and laundering equipment, and hire someone to oversee the process. The towels need to be checked out and in each day, and a security system must be developed. This approach thus creates a number of additional management problems for teachers.

Still other schools use a towel service company that provides freshly laundered towels on a daily basis. This approach is usually more expensive but easier to manage. Funding for a towel service can come from the school's general budget, a student fee, a booster club project, or a physical education department project such as selling candy or painter hats, or sponsoring car washes. Each school district has fund-raising and budget procedures that need to be followed. The physical education staff needs to weigh carefully the advantages and disadvantages of each towel supply procedure before making a decision. It is also possible to try several methods before deciding on a specific procedure.

Locks, Lockers, and the Locker Room

Locker room procedures must be carefully organized to increase the efficiency of students moving to and from classes. Students need to know which doors to use at various times and for various activities. Classes will be coming and going all day, so the development of efficient traffic flow patterns to and from the locker room is a necessity.

Various types of locks and lockers are available. Most schools assign students a combination lock and a small wire basket or metal locker for their activity clothes. A longer, larger locker is usually available for street clothes during each activity period. The longer lockers commonly alternate with the shorter lockers throughout the locker room. This helps to spread students around and to use the entire area. The older students should be assigned the upper locker rows to ensure that students can reach higher

rows. The school usually provides the combination lock, and the teacher keeps a master list of combinations in his or her office. Students may be allowed to bring their own locks, but this can create problems for teacher access in emergency situations. Teachers must also keep a master list of which student occupies which locker. This can be done with a student locker assignment sheet (Figure 8.8). Problems such as forgotten combinations or misplaced locks can be readily solved when the teacher has a master list of combinations and the locker assignment sheet.

Supervision procedures for the locker room must be arranged to ensure safety and theft prevention. The room should be locked during class time to prevent thefts. Teachers should walk through the locker room regularly to check for unlocked lockers and clothes and towels that are left out by accident. This routine will also reduce the loss due to theft. In some situations, teacher aides can be hired to supervise the locker room, distribute towels, and help maintain the management policies.

Equipment

Proper types of equipment in adequate amounts are a must for implementing a high-quality program. Students cannot learn various physical skills without the proper equipment. Physical education departments need basketballs, tennis racquets, and Frisbees, just as math and reading departments need books, paper, and pencils. Students cannot learn to play tennis without a racquet, tennis balls, and the opportunity to practice on courts. In many instances, physical education departments are asked to get along without proper amounts of equipment. A class of 35 students needs more than 5 basketballs, 6 volleyballs, or 10 tennis racquets. Many administrators have to be shown that physical education is much more than one or two games of a specific activity.

Purchase

Funds from the general school budget should be used to purchase equipment for the physical education program, and the physical education budget and student-teacher ratio should be equal to those of other academic areas of the school. The physical education budget must be separate from the athletic budget. Some equipment can be shared, but a definite distinction should be made between the two budgets.

Equipment priorities should be determined by student interest surveys and the number of students who will be able to use the equipment. Certain activities are offered more frequently than others, and

STUDENT LOCKER ASSIGNMENTS

Teacher _____

Class period _____

Locker Number	Student's Name (Alphabetical Order)	Lock Number	Combination

FIGURE 8.8 Locker assignment sheet

equipment for these should be a higher priority. Certain types of equipment may receive lower priority because students are able to bring their own from home. This is a policy that must be determined by the department.

Order equipment from local dealers if possible. They are an important part of the community and will usually provide fast and efficient service for the local schools. In addition, they usually support the schools and will provide the best possible prices on equipment. Regional or nationwide companies may be able to provide reasonable prices on some equipment. Service, however, is often slower, and an order may not be filled for 1 to 6 months. Check with other teachers and schools on the reputation and reliability of specific companies before placing a large order. State and regional physical education conventions are attended by the equipment dealers in each area. This is a good opportunity to meet the dealers and discuss prices and new equipment.

The quality and price of equipment should be studied carefully before making a purchase. Check with other schools to see what experiences they have had with specific equipment. The cheapest price is not always the best deal. Durability and longevity are especially important. Equipment deal-

ers may not know how well certain equipment will hold up over a period of time. This is why talking with people who are currently using the equipment is important.

The concept of progression in buying equipment is useful in negotiating with budget committees or school boards when a large amount of capital is necessary for equipment. If several thousand dollars is needed to add equipment for a new activity, it may be possible to implement the activity in three phases over three years. The activity could be started with $800 to $1,000 for the first year, and more equipment could be added gradually over the next few years. A budget committee is usually more receptive to this approach.

Student interest and willingness to bring in personal equipment for particular activities is also an effective strategy for gaining administrative support for an activity. Offering a cycling unit with each student bringing in his or her own bicycle, or offering a golf class in which students use their own clubs are effective for generating student and administrative interest in new activities.

Another source of equipment is to have it constructed by the physical education staff, the maintenance department, or the industrial arts classes. Starting blocks, relay batons, soccer goals, team handball goals, and jump ropes are examples of equipment that can be constructed. Take care to ensure that all safety specifications have been met. There are several books and articles that describe how to make homemade equipment (Dauer and Pangrazi, 1989; Corbin and Corbin, 1983).

Physical education equipment can also be purchased jointly with other schools, city parks and recreation departments, and the athletic department. Many districts, for example, jointly purchase free weights and weight machines for the use of athletes, physical education classes, and adult community education programs. Joint purchases are an excellent way to share costs and involve the entire community. This method can be used for purchasing tennis, racquetball, badminton, volleyball, softball, basketball, and aerobic dance equipment.

Storage, Distribution, and Maintenance

An accurate equipment inventory should be completed at the beginning and the end of each school year. Records should be kept from year to year to determine the needs of the department and to facilitate the purchasing process. Documenting the type and amount of equipment lost each year will also provide information for improving the security and distribution procedures.

A storage area (Figure 8.9) that is easily accessible to both male and female teachers is desirable. It is also important for the storage area to be close to the teaching stations (i.e., the gym, fields, and courts). It is inconvenient to pick up and return equipment to an area far from the station. The storage area should contain labeled shelves, bins, and containers for all pieces of equipment. Every piece should have a designated space. All teachers, student leaders, and students who have access to the area need to cooperate fully in keeping the area clean and orderly. It is easy to become disorganized when many different people are sharing equipment.

Teachers need adequate methods for transporting equipment to and from the teaching areas. Various types of ball bags, shopping-type carts, and portable ball carts are available. These will reduce the amount of class management time expended on equipment transport. Students can be given responsibilities for the movement of equipment if they are trained properly.

Develop a system for using equipment that is not designated on the yearly master curriculum. A sign-up and check-out list should be posted in the storage area along with the yearly sequence of activities. The department head or equipment coordinator should then be notified if any changes are made in

FIGURE 8.9   Storage area

the schedule with regard to equipment. This will prevent problems with teachers not having the equipment necessary for their classes. Equipment should not be loaned to outside groups without following the designated procedures. If equipment is shared or loaned to other groups, it must be marked or identified with some regulation code to prevent losses or mix-ups with equipment from other sources.

Procedures should also be developed for repairing and maintaining equipment. Decisions on which equipment to repair and who will repair it must be made. If the repair work is minor and can be completed at school, then who will do the work and where will it be done? If equipment must be sent out for repair, then where and how will it be sent?

These decisions are all part of the ongoing process of implementing a quality physical education curriculum. Equipment is part of a program's lifeblood. Without adequate equipment, the effectiveness of the teaching-learning environment is greatly reduced, because students without equipment will become bored, unmotivated, and troublesome for the teacher. How can students learn to dribble, pass, and shoot a basketball when they must stand in line and take turns sharing a ball with five or six other students? The goal of a program should be to provide every student with a piece of equipment. The productive learning time can thus be greatly enhanced.

Grading Procedures

Grading is an important part of the policies and procedures described in the department handbook, and should be determined and discussed with students during the first week of classes. Parents should also be made fully aware of this area. Evaluation and grading recommendations are discussed in detail in Chapter 12.

REFERENCES AND SUGGESTED READINGS

Cheffers, J., and Mancini, V. 1978. Teacher-student interaction. In W. Anderson and G. Barrette (eds.) *What's Going on in the Gym. Motor Skills: Theory into Practice, Monograph 1.*

Corbin, D., and Corbin, C. 1983. Homemade Play Equipment. *JOPERD* 54(6): 35–38.

Galloway, C. 1971. Teaching is more than words. *Quest* 15: 67–71.

Medley, D. 1977. *Teacher Competence and Teacher Effectiveness.* Washington, DC: American Association for Colleges of Teacher Education.

Dauer, V. P., and Pangrazi, R. P. 1989. *Dynamic Physical Education for Elementary School Children.* 9th ed. New York: Macmillan Publishing.

Siedentop, D. 1983. *Developing Teaching Skills in Physical Education.* Palo Alto, CA: Mayfield Publishing.

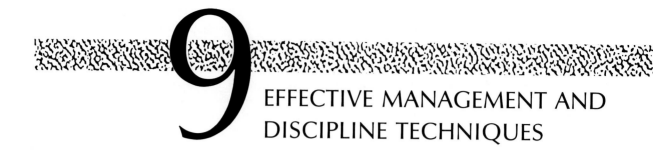

9
EFFECTIVE MANAGEMENT AND DISCIPLINE TECHNIQUES

Successful teachers use effective class management skills. The skills may vary among teachers in emphasis and focus, but the result is always quality teaching. Effective teachers take guidance from the following assumptions: that teaching is a profession, that students are in school to learn, and that the teacher's challenge is to promote learning. These assumptions imply a responsibility to a range of students, both those who accept instruction and those who do not. Teachers must believe that many students who have not yet found success will eventually do so. Instructing many students is relatively easy, but making appreciable gains among low-aptitude and indifferent students is the mark of an effective teacher.

THE EFFECT OF A TEACHER'S BEHAVIOR ON STUDENTS

The basic responsibility of the teacher is to direct learning toward target goals. Teachers should vary presentations and select instructional styles appropriate to the capabilities of students and the nature of activity sequences. How teachers teach, more than their teaching style, determines what students learn. No matter what the methodology or style, a diagnostic-prescriptive approach is superimposed on all teaching processes. The teacher observes critically the pace of instruction and adjusts the instruction based on the students' reaction.

Effective class management and organizational skills create a relaxed environment that offers students freedom of choice in harmony with class order and efficient teaching procedures. Management techniques include the mechanics of organizing a class, planning meaningful activities, and enhancing the personal growth of students. Effective teachers plan experiences to meet the needs of all students. Because skillful instructors have the ability to prevent problems before they occur, they spend less time

dealing with deviant behavior. In short, teachers who fail to plan, plan to fail.

Teachers must be aware of the impact of their behavior on students. In many ways, teaching reflects the personality, outlook, ideals, and background of the teacher. A successful teacher provides high-quality learning experiences and communicates a zest for movement that is contagious. Teachers must also appreciate personal habits and attitudes that may affect students negatively. Proper dress, a sound fitness level, and the willingness to participate with students reveal clearly how a teacher regards the profession and the subject.

A basic requisite for teachers is to model the behavior that they desire from students. This may mean moving quickly if they demand that students hustle. It may mean listening carefully to students or performing required fitness activities. Modeling desired behavior has a strong impact on students. The phrase "Actions speak louder than words" has significant implications for teachers.

Successful teachers communicate a belief that the students are capable, important, and self-sufficient. Stressing a positive self-concept and offering experiences to promote success are invaluable aids to learning. Students need to be reminded that the teacher enjoys seeing them achieve. They will appreciate the teacher's concern and usually respond with increased efforts.

Effective teaching occurs without sarcasm, ridicule, or threats. Teachers and students may become angry with one another in class. In some cases, teachers communicate that they do not like a student who misbehaves, and this lowers the student's self-esteem. Teachers should quietly (and privately) tell students that the misbehavior is unacceptable and that it must stop. At the same time, however, the instructor should communicate to the student that he or she is an acceptable person who is still cared for and appreciated.

CLASS MANAGEMENT SKILLS ____

Class management skills are a prerequisite to instruction. Moving and organizing students quickly and efficiently requires the teacher's comprehension of various techniques and the students' effective acceptance of those techniques. Observers of the teaching process agree that if a class is unmanageable, it is unteachable.

Instructing students in management areas should not be viewed as a negative or punishing proposition. Most students and teachers enjoy a learning environment that is organized, efficient, and that allows a maximum amount of class time for practicing an activity in a setting that encourages success and enjoyment. Teachers should remember that skills in management need to be practiced consistently throughout the school year.

Effective teachers are efficient managers of students. Teachers should strive to help students develop the ability to manage themselves. Management policies need to be planned carefully for every aspect of the learning environment. The term *management time* refers to the class time when no instruction or practice is taking place. The following are examples of management time activities:

1. Students dressing for class.
2. Teachers taking class roll.
3. Teachers explaining and directing the rotation format for skill work.
4. Students rotating from station to station.
5. Students picking up equipment and moving to a practice area.
6. Students forming a circle or an open formation for exercises.
7. Students returning equipment and returning to the locker room.

Management time usually has two phases involving both the teacher and students. The first is called "teacher talk time" on management. This includes the time it takes a teacher to explain the management procedures and give students the proper discriminative cues for action. An example would be when the teacher tells each of six squads to move to a designated spot and begin practicing. The second phase of management time refers to the students' response latency, or the time it takes students to respond and begin the appropriate activity. An illustration of response latency is the time elapsed while students pick up equipment and before they begin practicing their skills. Total management time is a combination of teacher talk time on management and the students' response latency.

Excessive management time reduces the time available for instruction and practice. Totally eliminating management time is impossible, but through effective planning, management time can be held to a minimum. Teacher talk time can be efficiently planned and student response latency can be practiced.

Teacher Talk and Efficient Management of Students

Teacher talk is a communication skill that should take a minimum amount of time, yet be clear to students. Students need to know where they are going and what they are supposed to be doing. Teachers should plan what they are going to say in order to move students efficiently. Directions must be given slowly and succinctly, using a limited amount of information. The language should be appropriate to the students' age level. In certain situations, directions can be enhanced with a diagram or a graphic display of the organizational scheme. Post the diagram in the locker room to be used concurrently with the explanation. The adage that a picture is worth a thousand words is appropriate in many situations.

Response Latency

Many variables affect a class's rate and speed of response. The nature of the activity, the students' motivational level, their feelings about the teacher, the time of day, and the weather are a few examples. The teacher is able to control some of these variables, while others are fixed. A positive, success-oriented atmosphere helps to improve the students' response time. Positive teacher reactions focused on appropriate student managerial behaviors are effective. Examples of such responses include:

1. Way to go class, everyone dressed and ready in 4 minutes.
2. Jim, great hustle back to your squad.
3. Thank you for getting quiet so quickly.
4. Look at squad one line up quickly.
5. Mary, excellent listening today, much better.
6. Way to stop on the whistle, nice work.

Another effective strategy is setting goals for management time (Darst and Pangrazi, 1981) and publicly posting the results. Reinforcing contingencies can be tied to the accomplishment of these goals (Siedentop et al., 1974). Activities like playing games, free time, or novelty activities are effective rewards for responsible management behaviors. The section on behavior games in this chapter can also be used to improve special management problems (Hamilton, 1974).

Rules and Roll Call

An effective method for taking roll each day helps reduce management time. One useful approach is to use squads and squad leaders. Each squad leader reports any absentees to the teacher orally or by filling out an attendance sheet. Another approach is to paint numbers on the floor and assign students numbers (Figure 9.1). The teacher or student leader glances quickly through the numbers and records the absentees while the students are exercising. Some teachers post a sign-in sheet for attendance, which students quickly initial. Yet another approach is to check attendance while students are beginning the first class activity. Regardless of the method used, the technique should save time and foster self-management qualities in students.

Instructional Delivery

A major goal of teachers is to have all students listening to directions given prior to activity. The instructions should be as specific and clear as possible. A teacher who talks longer than 30 sec during any single instructional episode will begin to lose control of the class. For this reason, alternate instructional episodes with periods of activity. Too often, teachers sit students down and explain many different technical points of skill performance. In a series of points, most people remember the first and last. This fact should help teachers understand the importance of giving students only 1 or 2 focal points when performing a skill. This reduces the length of the instructional episode and also eliminates the frustration of trying to remember too much.

Stopping the Class

A consistent signal should be established for stopping the class. It does not matter what the signal is, as long as it always means the same thing. Often, having both an audio signal (such as a whistle blast) and a visual signal (raising the hand overhead) is effective,

FIGURE 9.1 Students standing on numbers

since some students may not hear the audio signal if they are engrossed in activity. Regardless of the signal used to indicate a stop, it is usually best to select a signal different from the one used to start the class. Asking the class to freeze on signal is effective. To evaluate class effectiveness in responding to the stop signal, the teacher can time the latency of the response to the signal (see Chapter 11). If a class takes longer than 5 sec to stop and get ready for the next command, the situation should be discussed and the problem rectified.

Teachers must strive for 100% cooperation when students are asked to stop. If some students stop and listen to directions and others do not, class morale soon degenerates. The teacher can easily scan the class to see if all students are stopped and ready to comprehend the next set of directions. If the teacher settles for less than full attention, students will fulfill those expectations.

Organizing Students into Groups and Formations

Instructors should be able to quickly divide their classes into teachable groups. The drill toe-to-toe can be used to teach students to find partners. The goal of the game is to get toe-to-toe with a partner as fast as possible. Other challenges can be to get back-to-back or shoulder-to-shoulder or to look into the eyes of a partner. Students without a partner move quickly to the center of the teaching area and find someone else without a partner. Emphasis should be placed on rapid selection of the nearest classmate to prevent students from looking for a favorite friend or telling someone that he or she is not wanted as a partner.

Another effective activity for arranging groups is to alert the students with an audio or visual signal (whistle or fingers held high). When the whistle is blown a certain number of times, students form groups corresponding to the number of whistles and sit down to signify that they have the correct number in their group. Again, students who are not part of a group go to the center of the area and find the needed number of group members. Once this skill is mastered, students can move quickly into the proper-sized group depending on the number of whistle signals.

To divide the class into two equal groups, have students get toe-to-toe with a partner. One partner is asked to go to one area, and the other partner to another designated space. Other suggestions for grouping by partners are to ask students to find a partner with a birthday during the same month, with a phone number that has two similar numbers in it, and so on.

An effective technique for moving a class into a single-file line is to have students run randomly throughout the area until a signal is given. On signal, while continuing to move, they fall in line behind someone until a single line is formed. This exercise can be done while students are running, jogging, or walking. As long as students continue to move behind another person, the line will form automatically. The teacher or a student leader then leads the line into a desired formation or position.

Using Squads

Squad formations create a consistent procedure for starting and finishing each class period. They can be an effective means for arranging students for various class functions. Squads may meet at a designated spot in the gymnasium, at the pool, or on the playing field. Boundary cones are useful markers for assembling squads. Teachers should assign the squads and the squad leaders, and post the assignments in the locker rooms. Squads should be comparable in number of students and in physical size and ability levels of students. Squad leaders can be changed every 3 wks, and the entire squad composition should be changed every 9 wks.

Squad leaders should have specific opportunities to lead. The position carries extra responsibilities such as leading fitness activities, helping with equipment, taking attendance, setting up station work, or organizing team strategies. All students should get the chance to be a squad leader at some time throughout the year.

Teachers can help develop a certain esprit de corps within each squad by letting students select a squad name and by rewarding squads for good management behaviors. The best behaved squads might be allowed to select equipment first, receive extra play time, or participate in novelty activities. When employed properly, squad formation can be an effective means of arranging students. The following are guidelines for using squad formations to maximize teaching effectiveness.

1. Selection of squads or groups must never embarrass a student who might be chosen last. In no case should this be a "slave market" approach, in which the leaders look over the group and visibly pick those whom they favor.

2. A designated location should be used for assembling students in squad formation. When the teacher wants students in squads, students move to the predesignated area, with squad leaders in front and the rest behind.

3. Squads are effective in providing opportunities for peers to learn leadership and how to follow. The teacher should make maximum use of squad leaders, so that students regard being a leader as a privilege entailing certain responsibilities. Examples of leadership activities are moving squads to a specified location, leading squads through exercises or various introductory activities, and appointing squad members to certain positions in sport activities.

4. Squad leaders and the compositions of squads should be altered regularly. All students should have an opportunity to lead.

5. In most cases, an even number of squads should be formed. This allows the class to be broken quickly into halves for games. Having a class of 30 students divided into 6 squads of only 5 members each means a small number of students per piece of apparatus (and less waiting in line) in group activities.

6. A creative teacher makes the use of squads an exciting, worthwhile activity, not an approach that restricts movement and creativity. For example, cones can be numbered and placed in different locations around the activity area. When students enter the gym, they are instructed to find their squad number and assemble. This is an efficient way of moving students in position for circuit training or station teaching.

Using Equipment

Equipment should be distributed to students as rapidly as possible. When students wait for a piece of equipment, time is wasted. Often, teachers assign student leaders to get the equipment for a squad. This means that only the leaders are assigned a task, while others sit and wait (and may become discipline problems). Probably the easiest and fastest method is to have the leaders place the equipment around the perimeter of the area. Students then move on signal to a piece of equipment and begin practicing immediately. The reverse procedure can be used for putting equipment away. This contrasts with the practice of placing the equipment in a bag and telling students to "run and get a ball." This approach usually results in youngsters being knocked down or pushed, and an argument could ensue.

THE DEVELOPMENT OF SELF-DISCIPLINE SKILLS

Teaching students to incorporate self-discipline into their behavior patterns is an important goal. Self-discipline is behavior that will stay with students for a lifetime and impact the quality of their existence. A group of students is really a group of individuals, all of whom need to be treated and understood for their uniqueness. If management of behavior is going to be effective and meaningful, teachers will have to understand what reinforces each student.

Some teachers question the importance of discipline. The most basic reason for teaching self-discipline is that it allows students to learn effectively without encroaching on the rights of others. Our society is based on personal freedom hinged to self-discipline. Americans have tremendous freedom as long as they do not encroach on the rights of others. In similar fashion, students can enjoy freedom as long as their behavior is consistent with educational objectives and does not prevent other students from learning.

Most students cooperate and participate in the educational setting. In fact, the learner is largely responsible for allowing the teacher to teach. No one can be taught if they choose not to cooperate. Effective management of behavior means maintaining an environment where all students can learn. It is the teacher's responsibility to fashion a learning environment where all students can learn and feel comfortable. Students who are disruptive and off task infringe on the rights of others. If a teacher has to spend a great deal of energy working with youngsters who are disorderly, those students who want to learn are short-changed.

The focus of this section is to help teachers develop an action plan for modifying and maintaining good behavior. There are three phases to such a program: (1) increasing desired behavior, (2) eliminating undesirable behavior, and (3) maintaining desirable behavior. The focus of a discipline program should be on a positive and constructive approach designed to teach students to be responsible for their behavior.

Increasing Desired Behavior

When behavior is followed by appropriate positive reinforcement, that behavior is more likely to occur in the future. This principle should guide the teacher who wants to be an effective manager of students. The beauty of this simple principle is that it focuses on positive outcomes—desired educational outcomes. Key to implementing the principle is deciding what to use as reinforcers, which will effectively reinforce individuals, and how to use reinforcers.

Types of Reinforcers

Social reinforcers are the most commonly used by teachers. The teacher's behavior is used as the reinforcement for students when they perform desired behavior. Most students are familiar with social reinforcers. Parents use praise, physical contact, and facial expressions to acknowledge desired behavior in their children. The following are examples of reinforcers

that can be used for students in a physical education setting:

Words of Praise

Great job.	Nice going, Mike.
Exactly right.	I really like that job.
Perfect arm placement.	That's the best one yet.
Way to go.	Nice hustle.
Show the class your jump.	Excellent.

Physical Expressions

Smiling	Winking
Nodding	Clenched fist overhead
Thumbs up	Clapping

Physical Contact

Touching	Pat on the back
Hugging	Shaking hands
High Five	Arm around shoulder

Extrinsic Reinforcers

Many physical educators feel a need to offer some type of extrinsic reinforcer. Commonly, a system is used where students are given points when they are in uniform, on time, et cetera. If points are given to students to encourage desirable behavior, it is quite possible that students will choose to perform in the desired fashion solely for points. When the students find themselves in a setting without the opportunity to earn points, they may not behave in a desirable manner. Thus, the opportunity to teach self-discipline skills has actually been undermined. In addition, evidence shows that such extrinsic rewards may actually decrease a student's intrinsic motivation (Greene and Lepper, 1975). In most cases, it is best to use extrinsic reinforcers only if it appears that social reinforcers are ineffective.

Premack Principle

The Premack principle (Premack, 1965) is often used unknowingly by teachers on a regular basis. The principle states that any high-frequency behavior (preferred) that is contingent on a lower-frequency behavior (less-desirable) is likely to increase the occurrence of the lower-frequency behavior. This means that if the less-preferred behavior occurs, the student is then allowed to perform the more desirable behavior. In other words, an activity that students enjoy is used to increase the occurrence of an activity that students are reticent to perform.

Learning activities can be planned utilizing the Premack principle. This principle is sometimes referred to as Grandma's law, or "Eat your spinach, then you may have dessert." Teachers can arrange the environment so that students must spend a certain amount of time completing a certain number of attempts at a less popular activity before they can gain access to a preferred activity. For example, 7th grade students might have to complete the following performance objectives for basketball before they would be allowed to participate in a 3-on-3 class tournament.

Dribbling

1. Bounce (dribble) the ball 15 times consecutively with control (1 point).
2. Walk forward 25 ft while dribbling the ball with control (1 point).
3. Run forward 50 ft while dribbling the ball with control (1 point).

Passing (with a Partner)

4. Make 8 of 10 chest passes to a partner standing 10 ft away (1 point).
5. Make 8 of 10 bounce passes to a partner standing 15 ft away (1 point).
6. Make 6 of 10 overhead passes to a partner 15 ft away (1 point).

Shooting

7. Make 7 of 10 lay-ups from the preferred side (1 point).
8. Make 5 of 8 set shots from inside the key (1 point).
9. Make 4 of 8 set shots from the perimeter of the key (1 point).

In this situation, the 9 performance objectives are the less favorable activities, and the 3-on-3 tournament is the favorable activity.

Another example is to allow students to participate in basketball for 10 min after they have completed the fitness activities such as running or exercising. Select reinforcing activities that are within the realm of physical education. In some situations, however, when student motivation and interest are very low, teachers may have to use reinforcements outside the physical education area. These might include free time, playing cards, watching television, talking with peers, or playing pool. Such rewards are harder to defend educationally, but they may be necessary in extreme situations.

Access to novelty activities, competitive games, and class tournaments are usually effective reinforcing activities. Frisbee games such as golf, baseball, Guts, and Ultimate have been especially effective. Teachers need to analyze carefully the likes and dislikes of their students in order to plan learning activities that motivate. The goal of the Premack principle

is to get students to enjoy some type of physical activity.

The instructional devices discussed in Chapter 7 that communicate information to students about their skill attempts are good motivational devices and enhance learning activities. Targets on the wall or floor, ball machines, stopwatches, and obstacle courses provide students with a challenge, more practice attempts, feedback, and success with physical activity. With these elements in the teaching-learning process, most students are more motivated. Such devices add variety and novelty to learning activities and help keep students involved in a task. Effective teaching requires planning for a variety of instructional, motivational devices.

Selecting Reinforcers

A common question among teachers is: "How do I know what is reinforcing to students?" It is impossible to know what will reinforce a student until it is tried. However, there are a lot of things that most secondary students will respond to (e.g., praise, attention, games, free time, and special privileges). An easy way to identify effective reinforcers is to observe students, analyzing the things they enjoy doing during free time. Another simple solution is to ask them what they would like to do if they had a choice.

Using Social Reinforcers

When using social reinforcers, a teacher needs to work at praising and making positive statements. Many teachers feel uncomfortable when learning to administer positive reinforcement to adolescents because it makes them feel unauthentic. A common complaint when learning how to reinforce is "I do not feel authentic and students will think I'm a fake." Any change in communication patterns makes teachers uncomfortable. What is important is that the teacher learn to give sincere praise at appropriate times. Too often, the feedback becomes a speech pattern that is offered without thought and feeling.

Learning any new behavior will cause teacher discomfort. New patterns of communicating with a class require a period of adjustment. When learning new patterns of praise and reinforcement, the behavior will often seem contrived and insincere. There is no alternative unless a teacher plans to stay the same. Also, instructors who are unwilling to experience the uneasiness of learning will usually remain unchanged. They often assume that the patterns of speech learned as a student are effective in an instructional setting. The fact is that most teachers are made, not born, and have found success through hard work and dedication. If practiced regularly, new behavioral patterns will eventually become a natural part of a teacher's repertoire.

Praise is usually more effective when it refers to specific behavior exhibited by the adolescent. This contrasts with very general statements such as "Good job" or "You are an excellent performer." General and nonspecific statements do not tell the youngster what was done well (see Chapter 8). It leaves it up to the student to try and identify what the teacher has in mind. If the student's thoughts do not align with the teacher's intent, it is entirely possible that the wrong behavior will be reinforced. Try to describe the behavior that is to be reinforced rather than judge it. For example compare the following:

> **Describing:** "I saw your excellent forward roll, James; you tucked your head just right."

> **Judging**: "That's a poor job. I do not see why you cannot do better."

In the first example, the student is identified and the specific behavior performed is reinforced. In the second situation, it is impossible to identify what was poor or to whom the feedback was directed and the student feels as though he is a poor person. In most cases, if a question can be asked of praise or criticism (e.g., what was good, or why it was a poor performance), the feedback is nonspecific and open to misinterpretation. To increase the desired behavior, verbally or physically describe to the class or individual what makes the performance effective, good, or noteworthy. This reinforces the student and communicates to the rest of the class the type of behavior expected by the instructor.

Using Activity Reinforcers

Various, enjoyable activities can be used as reinforcement. Free time always ranks high among junior and senior high school students' preferences. Some examples of activities that might be used to reinforce a class are: free time to practice a skill, the opportunity to play a game, act as a teacher's aid, be a teacher in a cross-aged tutoring situation, or be a team captain. These are ideal opportunities for utilizing the Premack principle. Those students who complete the less desirable behavior get to participate in one of the more self-selected activities.

Prompting Desired Behavior

Prompts are used to remind students to perform desired behavior, and to encourage the development of new patterns of behavior. There are many ways to prompt students in the physical education setting. The most common are:

1. *Modeling.* The teacher performs the desired behavior to prompt students to respond in similar fash-ion. For example, the teacher will place his or her equipment on the floor when stopping the class to remind students to do likewise. Modeling is an effective prompt because many students will mimic the teacher.

2. *Verbal cues.* The most common method of prompting in secondary school classes is using verbal cues; use words such as "Hustle" and "Keep going." The purpose is to remind students of desired behavior. Usually, they are used to maintain the pace of the lesson, increase the intensity of the performance, or motivate students to stay on task.

3. *Nonverbal cues.* Teachers give many physical cues with their hands and related body language that communicate concepts such as "Hustle," "Move over here," "Great performance," or "Quiet down". In addition, when learning skills, youngsters can be physically prompted if moved into proper position, directed through the correct pattern, or have body parts properly aligned.

Consider the following notes concerning prompts. Do not use prompts to the point where students will not perform unless they are prompted. In fact, the goal is to remove the prompt so that behavior will be self-motivated. This process is called fading and implies a gradual removal of the prompts. It is most likely that teachers will use prompts at opportune times; however the major use of prompts is to implement new behavior patterns and increase the occurrence of desired behavior. Use the weakest (least intrusive) prompt possible to stimulate the behavior. For example, it would be possible to give students a long lecture about the importance of practicing the skill being taught. However, this approach is time consuming and overreactionary. It is not suited to multiple use and would be ineffective in the long run. Select a cue that is closely identified with the desired skill, and is short and concise.

In addition to these points, be sure that the prompt identifies the task being prompted. For example, if the teacher prompts the class to "hustle" and has not tied it to desired behavior, there may be confusion. Some students may think it means to perform the skill as fast as possible; others may see it meaning to stop what they are doing and hustle to the teacher. Tie the prompt to the desired behavior in a consistent manner and make sure that students clearly understand the meaning of your prompt.

Shaping Behavior

Shaping techniques can be used to build new and desired behavior. Shaping is used when the behavior does not exist in the student's repertoire. This technique involves the use of extinction and reinforcement. Shaping is slow and inefficient and should be used when prompting is not possible. Two principles are followed when shaping behavior.

1. Use differential reinforcement to increase the incidence of desired behavior. Reinforce responses that reach a predetermined criterion and ignore those that do not meet the criterion (extinction).

2. Increase the criterion that needs to be met for reinforcement to occur. Shift the criteria toward the desired goal. For example, if the desired behavior requires that the class become quiet within 5 sec after a signal has been given, it might be necessary to start with a 12-sec interval. Why the longer interval? In all likelihood, it is not reasonable to expect that an inattentive class will be able to quiet down quickly. If the 5-sec interval is selected initially, there is a good possibility that both teacher and students will be frustrated by the lack of success. In addition, this behavior will not be achieved very often, resulting in very few opportunities to praise the class. The end result may be a negative situation where both teacher and youngsters feel they have failed. This is the basis for gradually shifting the criteria toward the desired objective. In this case, start with 12 sec until the class performs as desired. Then, shift to a 10-sec interval and ask the class to perform to this new standard. The process is gradually repeated until the terminal behavior is reached.

DISCIPLINE: IMPROVING CLASS BEHAVIOR

Achieving discipline is similar to developing self-discipline. It is a process that leads students to appropriate behaviors in the teaching-learning situation. The process can take either a negative or a positive approach. Unfortunately, many teachers and administrators use a negative approach and extensive punishment. Many teachers are evaluated each year primarily on their ability to discipline (or punish) and keep students in line, rather than on the learning that takes place in their classes. There is no educational research to show that students disciplined by a negative approach learn more than students disciplined by a positive approach. Even if the negatively disciplined students learned a similar amount, they would probably leave physical education classes with a negative attitude toward activity.

Discipline is intertwined with motivation in the teaching process and should be developed through a positive and preventive approach. Students who are highly motivated will usually be highly disciplined. Teachers who are effective, positive motivators will have few problems with inappropriate student behaviors.

Clarifying Behaviors and Consequences

Teachers must make decisions about appropriate and inappropriate student behavior in their physical education classes. Sometimes students, parents, and administrators are also involved in deciding what is and is not appropriate. Appropriate behaviors are usually defined as those that contribute positively to the learning environment. In contrast, inappropriate behaviors detract from learning. These behaviors can be related either to physical skill development or to the development of social-emotional skills.

Appropriate behaviors usually include attending class, being on time, following directions, participating, cooperating with peers and teachers, and showing emotional control. Inappropriate, disruptive-type behaviors that detract from the learning environment include tardiness, profanity, obscene actions, defiance of authority, talking out of turn, and interfering with the rights of others. Certain schools and teachers will permit and accept a broader range of behaviors, while others might not permit the same behavior in a similar situation. A part of maturation is the student's learning to discern the behaviors accepted by each teacher.

All teachers have a perception of what they believe is appropriate and inappropriate behavior in their class. Many times, however, they do not write down the appropriate behaviors and do not effectively communicate these to students. An important step in behavior control is to decide exactly which behaviors are important and which behaviors are unacceptable. These can then be listed in a handout and discussed with students at the beginning of the year. The list should also be posted in the locker room and in the gymnasium, and sent to parents and administrators. All involved parties will then have a basic understanding of what the teacher considers appropriate and inappropriate behavior. This is the start of the process of students learning appropriate behaviors.

Teachers also need to develop strategies concerning the consequences for both appropriate and inappropriate behavior. Students and parents should understand the consequences involved and how they will be applied in various situations. An example of consequences for inappropriate behavior might include the following progression:

Step 1. An informal, private conference between the teacher and student focusing on the behavioral aberration. An agreement should be reached regarding the consequences of future behavior.

Step 2. A telephone call to the parents to discuss the problem and possible solutions.

Step 3. A conference with the teacher, parent, student, and principal or counselor to discuss the problem and develop a plan for changing the behavior. A written copy of the plan should be distributed to all people involved.

Step 4. Severe disciplinary actions
a. Loss of privileges: Privilege losses could include access to the library, cafeteria, clubs, athletics, or dances. Parents should be notified in writing about the procedures used.
b. In-school suspension: A school can have a designated area and a supervisor for in-school suspension. Strict rules and guidelines for school work, privileges, and procedures must be set for this program.
c. Short- and long-term suspensions: The school principal should have the power to suspend a student from school for 3 to 10 days, depending on the severity of the behavior and the student's history. Strict policies and procedures should be arranged and followed carefully. An appeal process must be available to students. Parents must be notified in writing as to the steps that have been followed.
d. Expulsion: The final step that may be used in extremely severe instances is expulsion. The principal usually initiates the action with a letter to the student and parents. An official action from the Board of Education may be required to expel a student. Due process and appeal procedures must be used and made available to the student.

Many secondary schools have some type of disciplinary referral form (Figure 9.2). This form is used to keep an accurate record of behavioral problems, and is a part of the communication process between students, teachers, parents, administrators, and counselors. The referral form can be an effective tool for controlling student behavior in certain situations. A disadvantage is that the approach is time consuming, and some teachers may be unwilling to use it. However, there are few shortcuts to a well-disciplined class.

Teacher Response to Student Behavior

Teachers' reactions to appropriate and inappropriate behavior are effective tools for increasing and decreasing specific behaviors. Verbal reactions can be positive in the form of praise, or negative in the form of scolds. Evidence shows that many teachers consistently use high rates of negative reactions and

relatively low rates of positive reactions (Boehm, 1974; Hamilton, 1974; Darst, 1976). A case was presented previously for the possible negative side effects of an environment based on coercion and punishment. Teachers need to focus their positive reactions on appropriate student behaviors. This is an effective preventive disciplinary strategy that enhances a positive and productive environment. Indeed, the evidence suggests that students learn more and feel better about learning in a positive environment.

Initially, teachers should display many positive reactions that give specific and immediate information when students are behaving appropriately. Examples include:

1. Thanks for getting dressed and ready to participate so quickly.
2. Squad three is listening well.
3. John, way to follow directions.
4. Good hustle between stations.
5. Sally and Sarah are working hard today.

Too often, teachers focus scolds on 1 or 2 students in the class, while 29 or 30 other students are receiving little teacher attention for behaving appropriately. Teachers should avoid repeating too many general positive statements like good job, good work, good hustle, way to go, and nice work, because students can become satiated with general statements and the positive statements will then lose their effectiveness. Teachers should also make sure that the intensity of their statements is commensurate with the behavior of the student. Students who are not behaving appropriately should not receive positive reactions from the teacher in an unqualified manner.

Scolds and other negative teacher reactions are necessary and useful from time to time in decreasing inappropriate behavior. Deliver scolds infrequently and with a certain amount of severity. Teachers should attempt to remain unemotional and to focus on the student's inappropriate behavior. Students must understand that the scold is not focused on them as people, but on their inappropriate behavior, and they must also understand exactly what the appropriate behavior is in the given situation. The appropriate behavior is usually obvious to students, but they may need to be reminded of the rules.

Another useful teacher reaction is called extinction. As mentioned above, this term refers to the technique of ignoring certain inappropriate behaviors that are not seriously disruptive to the learning environment. Many times, student behavior is maintained by the attention of the teacher and the peer group. For example, a student will misbehave, and the teacher will publicly scold the behavior. The friends of the student will laugh at the situation.

UNIFIED PUBLIC SCHOOLS

School _____

Phone _____

DISCIPLINARY REFERRAL:	Student's Name	Sex	Grade-Class	Date

1. The purpose of this report is to inform you of a disciplinary incident involving your son/ daughter.

2. You are urged both to appreciate the action taken by the teacher and to cooperate with the corrective action initiated.

Date of Incident	Time	Teacher's Signature

Parent's Name

Address

REASON FOR REFERRAL:

☐ Annoying to classmates   ☐ Rudeness, disrespect   ☐ Excessive talking

☐ Disturbing class   ☐ Profanity   ☐ Restless, inattentive

☐ Insubordination, disobedience ☐ Fighting   ☐ Ditching

☐ Smoking   ☐ Threatening, harassing others ☐ Truancy

☐ Other (State the problem) _____

_____

_____

_____

ACTION TAKEN PRIOR TO REFERRAL:

☐ Held conference with student ☐ Telephoned parent   ☐ Sent previous report home

☐ Consulted counselor   ☐ Held conference with parent ☐ _____

Do you desire to participate in a conference with Pupil _____ Parent _____ Guidance _____

Case referred to _____ Administration _____ Counselor for further action

Initial conference was held by _____

FIGURE 9.2 Disciplinary referral form

PRESENT DISPOSITION:

- ☐ Student regrets incident, cooperative
- ☐ Recurring incidents will be reported
- ☐ Student placed on probation

- ☐ Student placed on closed classes, which requires a Parent-Administrator conference
- ☐ Student suspended
- ☐ _____

- ☐ Parent is requested to call the school representative indicated _____
- _____

Additional Comments: _____
_____
_____

Logged |

1 ☐   2 ☐   3 ☐
4 ☐   5 ☐   6 ☐

COPIES: 1. Parent   2. Office   3. Admin.   4. Admin.   5. Counselor   6. Teacher

FIGURE 9.2 Continued

Unfortunately, peer laughter is reinforcing to the student, and the behavior will occur again. If the behavior is not seriously distracting, then ignoring it and showing a positive reaction to an appropriate behavior occurring later may be more effective. The teacher might also explain to the class that they, too, should ignore the student's inappropriate behavior. In this way, the student loses the attention of both teacher and peers. If the teacher feels a need to talk to the student, it should be done privately so he or she does not receive inadvertent reinforcement from the class.

Teacher reactions play a powerful role in controlling student behavior and establishing an effective, positive learning environment. Make careful plans regarding the use of these reactions. Teachers must think about the specific student behaviors that they will praise, scold, and ignore. A list of specific student behaviors and the accompanying teacher reactions should be developed by each teacher. An instructor's list might look like this:

Praise	*Scold*	*Ignore*
Listening	Fighting	Talking out
Following directions	Pushing	Raising a hand
Hustling	Disrupting others	Snapping fingers
Being on time	Cursing	Showing off
Proper dress	Obscene gestures	Constantly asking questions

Various situations may require still other reactions. Teachers should strive, however, to be consistent in their reactions, so students will know what to expect and will learn to behave accordingly.

Time-Out Procedures

In "time-out," the teacher removes the student from a positive or enjoyable situation (Martin and Pear, 1983). It is similar to the penalty box in an ice hockey game. If a student is behaving inappropriately, then the teacher can privately ask the student to go to the time-out area. The area should be far enough away from the class to avoid the ridicule of peers, but close enough to be within the supervision of the teacher. The area can be specifically designated in the gymnasium, or it can be an area in an outside field such as under a tree, on a bench, or in a baseball dugout.

Teachers need a consistent approach for dealing with undesirable behavior that occurs randomly on an individual basis. The time-out approach takes students out of the class setting and places them in a predesignated area when they misbehave. Being placed in the time-out area does not imply that the student is a "bad person," but rather that he or she has forgotten to follow the rules. Teachers should always communicate the feeling to students that they are acceptable individuals, but their misbehavior is unacceptable.

Being placed in time-out should communicate to youngsters that they have disrupted the class and must be removed so that the rest of the class can participate as desired. Students can also use the time-out area as a "cooling-off" spot that they can move to voluntarily if they are angry, embarrassed, or frustrated. If students have been placed in the time-out area for fighting or arguing, they should be placed at opposite ends of the area so that the behavior does not escalate. In addition, it can be mandated that they stay in their own half of the gymnasium until the next meeting of the class. This will prevent the possibility of continued animosity.

Discuss the plan with students, so that they know exactly what is acceptable and unacceptable behavior, and understand what actions will be taken if they exhibit undesirable behavior. Desired behavior, as well as consequences for unacceptable behavior, should be posted in the teaching area. Examples of desired behavior might be careful listening when the teacher is instructing, practicing the designated activity, and performing promptly the activities presented by the teacher. In most cases, the list of desired behaviors should number between 3 and 5 items. A larger number of behaviors will generate a negative atmosphere and make it difficult for students to remember all rules.

Remember that time-out does not stifle misbehavior if the youngster receives reinforcement. **Time-out means receiving NO reinforcement.** If class is a negative experience and the teacher does not reinforce students, taking them out of class is not a punishment and may be a reward. The class must be an enjoyable experience that is reinforcing to students. Too often, sitting a student out results in an experience that is reinforcing. For example, the student who is sent to the office gets to avoid activity while visiting with friends who come into the office. Notoriety can be achieved among peers for surviving the office experience and being able to tell others "It doesn't matter one bit what that teacher does to me." Sitting on the side of the gymnasium and watching peers participate may be more reinforcing than participating in class activities. Class participation must be an enjoyable experience; if not, all other efforts to improve behavior become much more difficult.

A possible set of consequences for unacceptable behavior might be as follows:

- **First misbehavior:** The student is warned quietly on a personal basis to avoid embarrassment. This could be a peer or teacher warning. At times, students are not aware that they are bothering others and a gentle reminder by a peer or teacher will refocus the youngster.

- **Second misbehavior:** The student is quietly asked to go to the time-out area for a predetermined time. The duration of the stay is usually 5 min.

- **Third misbehavior:** The student goes to time-out for the remainder of the period and loses free-time privileges. This can be enforced by serving time in detention. Detention is served during the student's free time in a study hall atmosphere supervised by teachers on a rotating basis.

These steps assume that the teacher will communicate with the student about the misbehavior and the expected behavior. If these consequences are ineffective, the last alternative is to call the parents for a conference with the principal and teacher. Students and parents must understand that participating in educational endeavors is a privilege and that people who choose to disrupt society ultimately lose their privileges (e.g., incarceration in reform school, prison, etc.).

A word to the wise: In most instances, the best way to handle misbehavior is to quietly reprimand the student. If the student is reprimanded publicly, he or she may rebuke the teacher and gain the respect of peers because of his or her outspokenness. In addition, teachers may become angry if students argue with them in front of other students. Anytime teachers become angry at students in class, they lose the respect of other students. If a student chooses not to follow a quietly issued command, it is best to deal with it after class.

Behavior Contracts

A behavior contract is a written statement specifying certain student behaviors that must occur in order to earn certain rewards or privileges. The contract is usually signed by the student and the teacher involved, and is drawn up after a private conference to decide on the appropriate behaviors and rewards. Letting the student make some decisions dealing with the contract is often useful.

The behavior contract may be a successful strategy for students with severe behavior problems. Make every attempt to use rewards that occur naturally in physical education class (e.g., Frisbee play, jump rope games, aerobics, basketball). In some cases, however, different types of rewards may have to be used. For example, a student who is interested only in rock music and motorcycles could be allowed to spend some time reading, writing about, or discussing one of these topics. As behavior improves and the student's attitude becomes more positive, the rewards should be switched to physical education activities. The contract is gradually phased out over a period of time as students gain control of their behavior and can participate in normal class environments.

Contracts can be written for a small group of students or for an entire class with similar problems, but teachers must be careful about setting up a reward system for too many students. The system can become too complex or time consuming to supervise properly. The contract is best used with a limited number of students in several problem situations. Examples of behavior contracts are given in Figures 9.3 and 9.4. The contract in Figure 9.3 can be used with an individual, a small group, or an entire class of students.

Behavior Games

Behavior games are an effective strategy for quickly changing student behaviors in the areas of management, motivation, or discipline. If a teacher is having severe disruptive problems in any of these areas, a well-conceived behavior game may quickly turn the situation around. These games can be packaged for a group of students to compete against each other or against an established criterion level. The goal of the game is to use group contingencies to develop behaviors that enhance the learning environment and eliminate behaviors that detract from it.

Various forms of behavior games have been used successfully by physical educators and athletic coaches (Darst and Whitehead, 1975; McKenzie and Rushall, 1973; Paese, 1982). Behavior games are effective with certain types of inappropriate behaviors: nonattendance, tardiness, nondressing, cursing, talking out, low practice rates, and high rates of management time. The following is an example of a behavior game that was used successfully with 7th graders in an effort to improve management behaviors:

1. The class is divided into four squads. Each squad has a designated color for identification. Four boundary cones with appropriate colors are set up as a starting area.

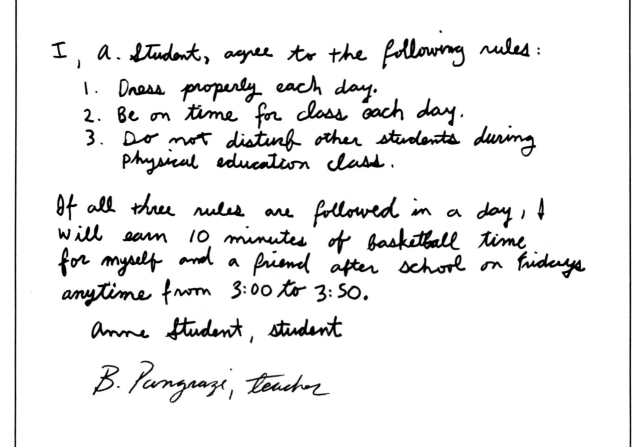

I, a. Student, agree to the following rules:

1. Dress properly each day.
2. Be on time for class each day.
3. Do not disturb other students during physical education class.

If all three rules are followed in a day, I will earn 10 minutes of basketball time for myself and a friend after school on Fridays anytime from 3:00 to 3:50.

Anne Student, student

B. Pangrazi, teacher

FIGURE 9.3   Individual behavior contract

```
                        BEHAVIOR CONTRACT

   I.Class Preparation          Points
     A. Attendance                 1
     B. On time                    1
     C. Properly dressed           1

  II.Social Behavior
     A. Showering                  1
     B. Lack of inappropriate      5
        behaviors
        Cursing                 9 points per day
        Fighting               (36 points per week)
        Disruption


During Friday's class, points may be exchanged for time in aerobics,
weight training, Frisbee, or basketball.

I agree to these conditions.


  _____

    Student


  _____

    Teacher
```

FIGURE 9.4 Group behavior contract

2. The rules of the game are as follows:
   a. Each squad member has to be dressed and in the proper place at a designated starting time. Reward: 2 points
   b. Each squad member has to move from one activity to another activity within the specified time (10, 20, or 30 sec) and begin the appropriate behavior. Reward: 1 point for each instance
   c. Each point earned is rewarded with 1 min of free activity time on Friday. Free activity time includes basketball, Frisbee, jump ropes, and flag football, or any other activity popular with students.
   d. The squad with the most points for the week earns a bonus of 5 points.
3. The teacher explains the allotted time for each management episode (10, 20, or 30 sec) and gives a "go" signal. At the end of the allowed time, the teacher gives a "stop" signal and awards points for appropriate behavior.
4. Squads that are successful are praised by the teacher, and the points are recorded on a small card. The unsuccessful squads are not hassled or criticized, just reminded that they did not earn a point.

5. On Fridays, the appropriate squads are awarded the special free-time activities, while the others continue work on the regularly scheduled class activities.
6. The game is slowly phased out as students begin to manage themselves better.

The results of the game were as follows:

1. The use of group contingencies and free-time activities reduced the overall class management time.
2. The free-time activities were within the physical education curriculum objectives and created a break from regular activities.
3. The free-time activities gave the teacher an opportunity to interact with students on a personal level.
4. The students enjoyed the competition and the success they experienced when they performed appropriate behaviors.
5. Students enjoyed the free time with novelty activities.
6. The positive approach of the game seemed to improve the overall teaching-learning atmosphere. The students were more attentive and cooperative.

7. The teachers felt that more time was available for instruction because of the reduction in management time.

With behavior games, all students or squads should be able to "win." Games do not have to have a winner and a loser. All participants in a behavior game should be able to win. Teachers must also be aware that sometimes one or two students may find it reinforcing to cause their team to lose the behavior game. They will try to break every rule to force their team to lose consistently. In these cases, the teacher should hold a special team discussion and possibly a team vote to eliminate those students from the team and from the game. The disruptive students could be sent to a time-out area or channeled into some special, alternative activity. They might even be asked to sit out from an entire day's activities. Again, caution is urged in exercising this option, because a time out may be exactly what these students had in mind as a final goal.

Another effective behavior game can be used to help students persist at learning activities in a station-type approach. Often, teachers will set up four or five learning stations for activities such as basketball, volleyball, soccer, or football. Performance objectives or learning tasks are posted at each station for the students to practice. Some of the students, however, are not motivated and do not use their time productively until the teacher rotates to their station. The teacher then prods the group, hassles a few students, and praises a few others. The overall environment is not very productive, and the teacher gets tired of hassling unmotivated students. A possible solution to this situation is the following game:

1. Divide the class into four or five squads. Let the students pick a name for their squad.
2. Set up the learning stations with the activities to be practiced. An equal number of squads and learning stations is necessary.
3. Program a cassette tape with popular music. The tape should have short gaps of silence for the duration.
4. Tell students that if everyone in their squad is properly engaged in practicing the appropriate tasks, a point will be awarded to their squad at each gap in the music. If one or more persons is not engaged, then no point will be awarded.
5. The points can be exchanged for minutes of free time for reinforcing motor activities such as Frisbee or jump rope. Fridays could be designated for reward time.
6. The music should be changed regularly, and the interval between gaps should be changed and slowly stretched until the gaps are eliminated. The music then serves as a discriminative cue for future practice time.

Many teachers have found that students enjoy exercising and practicing skills while listening to music. The music seems to enhance the motivational level of the environment. Students can be allowed to bring in their own music as a special reward for productive behavior. Teachers should be sure that the music is not offensive to others because of sexual, ethnic, or religious connotations.

Finally, the behavior game can be used as a challenge or change of pace and an enjoyable learning activity. The teacher may not have serious behavior problems in the class but may simply want to add an enjoyable learning activity. An example of this is the "burnout" game. It can be used in the following manner:

1. Fridays can be designated as "burnout" days. The last 5–10 min of the period can be used for the game.
2. To qualify for the "burnout" award, a student must have attended, been on time, dressed properly, and worked diligently all week.
3. On a rainy or nonparticipation day, each student submits a piece of paper with a written explanation of a "burnout" challenge activity that she or he would enjoy. Examples might include a stork-stand on one foot, one-arm push-ups, pull-ups, hanging on a rope for time, doing a headstand, or juggling without dropping an object. Students should be encouraged to select activities in which they excel. These challenge suggestions can be kept in a jar or hat for future choices.
4. A "burnout" award is made up and hung on a locker, posted on a bulletin board, announced over the morning news, or put in any similar, visible medium. A photograph of the "burnout" winner might be posted each week in the hall of fame.
5. On Friday, the teacher and the entire class try the burnout challenge to determine a winner. The winner might also receive several privileges like selecting the next activity from the jar or hat. The activity could be selected on Monday, and students might then practice during the week.
6. Teachers must make sure that the winner "qualified" for the award with the appropriate behaviors during the week.
7. Teachers can make the game enjoyable and something that students look forward to each week.

THE USE OF PUNISHMENT AND CRITICISM _____

Criticism is often used by teachers with the belief that it will improve the performance of students. Teachers find criticism and sarcasm to be their behavior control tools of choice because they give the impression that the results are effective and quick acting. Usually, the misbehavior is stopped immediately and the teacher assumes that the situation has been rectified. Unfortunately, this is not always the case, as will be described later. Criticism and punishment lend a negative air to the instructional environment, and that has a negative impact on both student and teacher. In most cases the person who is most affected by criticism or punishment is the teacher. The old saying, "It hurts me more than you," is often the case. The majority of teachers feel bad when they have to criticize or punish students. It makes them feel as though they cannot handle students and that the class is incorrigible. This feeling of incompetence can lead to a negative cycle in which the students feel negative about the instructor and the instructor negative about the class. The net result is that both parties finish the lesson feeling incompetent. In the long run, this may be one of the most debilitating effects of criticism and punishment.

As mentioned, another problem with criticism is that it does not offer a solution. In a study by Thomas et al. (1968), a teacher was asked to stop praising a class. Off-task behavior increased from 8.7% to nearly 26%. When the teacher was asked to increase criticism from 5 times in 20 min to 16 times in 20 min, more off-task behavior was demonstrated. On some days the percentage of off-task behavior increased to more than 50%. The point to be emphasized: When attention is given to off-task behavior and no praise is offered for on-task accomplishment, the amount of off-task behavior increases dramatically. What happens is that the teacher who primarily criticizes is reinforced by the students (they respond to the request of the criticism), but the students do not change. In fact, the students are reinforced (they receive attention from the teacher) for their off-task behavior. In addition, since their on-task behavior is not praised, it decreases. The net result is exactly the opposite of what was desired.

Punishment is another matter. It is a difficult decision to decide when to use punishment. Contrary to what many teachers think, punishment does work and is very effective at stopping undesirable behavior. In fact, just as reinforcement increases the occurrence of behavior, punishment will decrease undesirable behavior. The principles of reinforcement can be transferred to the use of punishment. Just as reinforcement should be given immediately, punishment should be administered as near the behavior as possible.

The question is whether or not punishment should be used in an educational setting. A consideration should be made about the long-term effects of the punishment. If the long-term effects of using punishment are more beneficial than not using it, it would be unethical not to use punishment. In other words, if the student is going to be in a worse situation from not being punished, it would be wrong not to use it. It may be necessary to punish a student for protection from self-inflicted harm (e.g., using certain apparatus without supervision). It may be necessary to punish students so that they learn not to hurt others. Punishment in these situations may cause discomfort to teacher and student in the short run, but may allow the student to participate successfully in society later.

Most situations in the educational setting do not require punishment since they are not as severe as those described above. A major reason for avoiding punishment is that it can have undesirable side effects. When students are punished, they learn to avoid the source of punishment. It forces them to be more covert in their actions. They spend time finding ways to be devious without being caught. Instead of encouraging students to discuss problems with teachers and parents, punishment teaches them to avoid these individuals for fear of being punished. Punishment also teaches students how to be aggressive toward others. Students who have been physically or emotionally punished by parents act in similar fashion with others. The result is a student who is secretive and aggressive with others, certainly a less than desirable trait. Finally, if punishment is used to stop certain behavior, as soon as the punishment stops the behavior will return. Little has been learned; the punishment has just caused short-term change.

If it becomes necessary to use punishment, remember the following points.

1. Be consistent and make the "punishment fit the crime." Students will quickly lose their respect for a teacher who treats others with favoritism. They will view the teacher as unfair if the punishment is extreme. In addition, peers will quickly side with the student who is treated unfairly causing a class morale problem for the instructor.

2. Offer a warning signal. This may prevent excessive use of punishment since students will often behave after receiving a warning. In addition, they will probably view the teacher as caring and fair.

3. Do not threaten students. Offer only one warning. Threats have little impact on students and cause them to feel that the teacher cannot handle the class. One warning gives students the feeling that you are not looking to punish them and are fair in your dealings. Follow through; do not challenge or threaten students and then ignore the same or similar behavior.

4. The punishment should immediately follow the misbehavior. It is much less effective and more often viewed as unfair when punishment is delayed.

5. Punish softly and calmly. Do not seek revenge or be vindictive. If responsible behavior is expected from students, teachers must reprimand and punish in a responsible manner. Studies (O'Leary and Becker, 1968) have demonstrated that soft reprimands are more effective than loud ones.

Try to avoid having negative feelings about the student and internalizing the student's misbehavior. In some cases, teachers become punitive in handling deviant behavior, and this destroys any chance for a worthwhile relationship. The misbehavior should be handled in a manner that contributes to the development of a responsible, confident student who understands that all individuals who function effectively in society must adjust to certain limits. Try to forget about past bouts of deviant behavior and to approach the student in a positive fashion at the start of each class. If this is not done, the student soon becomes labeled, making behavioral change difficult to accomplish and causing the student to live up to the teacher's negative expectations.

Make sure that only those students who misbehave are punished. Punishing an entire class for the deviant behavior of a few youngsters is not only unfair but may trigger undesirable side effects. Students become hostile toward those who caused the loss of privileges, and this peer hostility lowers the level of positive social interaction. If the group as a whole is misbehaving, punishing the entire group is appropriate.

EXPULSION: LEGAL CONSIDERATIONS

If serious problems occur, the physical education specialist should discuss the problems with the appropriate administrator. Many times, deviant behavior is part of a larger, more severe problem that is troubling a student. A cooperative approach may provide an effective solution. A group meeting involving parents, principal, counselor, and physical education specialist may open avenues that encourage understanding and increase productive behavior.

Legal concerns involving the student's rights in disciplinary areas are an essential consideration. While minor infractions may be handled routinely, expulsion and other substantial punishments can be imposed on students only after due process. The issue of student rights is complicated, and most school systems have established guidelines and procedures for dealing with students who have been removed from the class or school setting. Youngsters should be removed from class only if they are disruptive to the point of interfering with the learning experiences of other students, and all other means of altering behavior have failed. Sending a student out of class is a last resort and means that both teacher and student have failed.

REFERENCES AND SUGGESTED READINGS

AAHPERD. 1976. *Personalized Learning in Physical Education*. Reston, VA: AAHPERD.

Boehm, J. 1974. The effects of competency-based teaching programs on junior high school physical education student teachers and their pupils. Doctoral dissertation, The Ohio State University.

Canter, L., and Canter, M. 1976. *Assertive Discipline*. Santa Monica, CA: Canter and Associates.

Charles, C. M. 1981. *Building Classroom Discipline*. New York: Longman.

Cruickshank, D. R. 1980. *Teaching Is Tough*. Englewood Cliffs, NJ: Prentice-Hall.

Darst, P. 1976. The effects of a competency-based intervention on student teaching and pupil behavior. *Research Quarterly* 47(3): 336–345.

Darst, P., and Pangrazi, R. 1981. Analysis of starting and stopping management activity for elementary physical education teachers. *Arizona JOHPERD* 25(1): 14–17.

Darst, P. W., and Whitehead, S. 1975. Developing a contingency management system for controlling student behavior. *Pennsylvania JOPER* 46(3): 11–12.

Greene, D., and Lepper, M. R. 1975. Turning play into work: Effects of adult surveillance and extrinsic rewards on children's internal motivation. *Journal of Personality and Social Psychology* 31: 479–486.

Hamilton, K. 1974. The application of a competency-based model to physical education student teaching in high school. Doctoral dissertation, The Ohio State University.

McKenzie, T., and Rushall, B. 1973. Effects of various reinforcing contingencies on improving performance in a competitive swimming environment. Unpublished paper, Dalhousie University.

Martin, G., and Pear, J. 1983. *Behavior Modification— What It Is and How to Do It*. Englewood Cliffs, NJ: Prentice-Hall.

O'Leary, K. D., and Becker, W. C. 1968. The effects of

intensity of a teacher's reprimands on children's behavior. *Journal of School Psychology* 7: 8–11.

Paese, P. 1982. Effects of interdependent group contingencies in a secondary physical education setting. *Journal of Teaching in Physical Education* 2(1): 29–37.

Premack, D. 1965. Reinforcement theory. In D. Levine (ed.) *Nebraska Symposium on Motivation.* Lincoln, NE.: University of Nebraska Press.

Siedentop, D., Rife, F., and Boehm, J. 1974. Modifying the managerial effectiveness of student teachers in physical education. Unpublished paper, The Ohio State University.

Siedentop, D. 1983. *Developing Teaching Skills in Physical Education.* Palo Alto, CA: Mayfield Publishing.

Thomas, D. R., Becker, W. C., and Armstrong, B. 1968. Production and elimination of disruptive classroom behavior by systematically varying teacher's behavior. *Journal of Applied Behavior Analysis* 1: 35–45.

Wolfgang, C. H., and Glickman, C. D. 1980. *Solving Discipline Problems.* Boston, MA: Allyn and Bacon.

10 TEACHING STYLES FOR SECONDARY SCHOOL PHYSICAL EDUCATION

Different teaching styles have been discussed and applied successfully in various secondary school physical education classes (Mosston and Ashworth, 1986; Zakrajsek and Carnes, 1986; Rink, 1985; Harrison and Blakemore, 1989; Siedentop, 1983). Professionals have presented, labeled, and categorized these styles in many ways. Many of the terms overlap and can be confusing to the beginning teacher. A teaching style is an overall scheme for organizing the educational environment. The style provides direction for the specific involvement and role of the teacher and students in the process. The elements of the process are described, and a prediction is made about how the elements will affect student behavior.

A teaching style should provide direction for presenting students with information, organizing students for practice, providing feedback to students, keeping students engaged in appropriate behavior, and monitoring students' progress toward goals or objectives. Teaching styles should be analyzed in terms of the teacher's planning and setup of the environment, the teacher's behavior during the lesson, the student's behavior during the lesson, and student outcome variables. Teacher planning and setup includes any evidence of preplanning such as lesson plans, organizational arrangements, or instructional devices. The teacher's behavior includes instructions, questions, management cues, feedback, and demonstrating. Student behavior during the lesson includes activity time, waiting, receiving information, management time, and so forth. Student outcome variables include physical fitness levels, physical skills, knowledge, social-emotional behaviors, and attitudes toward physical activity. Analysis and evaluation strategies for these areas are discussed in Chapters 11 and 12.

In secondary school physical education, there is no best universal teaching style. Even though most educators will endorse their favorite approach, no evidence suggests that one strategy is more effective than another. Frymier and Galloway (1974) have concluded that there is no one best way of doing anything in education. Too many variables must be considered before an appropriate strategy can be selected. These variables include

1. The objectives of the lesson such as physical skills, physical fitness, knowledge, and social behaviors;
2. The nature of the activities involved such as tennis, volleyball, swimming, or fencing;
3. The nature of students, including individual characteristics, interests, developmental level, socioeconomic status, motivation, and background;
4. The total number of students in the class;
5. The equipment and facilities available, such as tennis racquets and courts; and
6. The abilities, skills, and comfort zone of the teacher.

Secondary teachers should develop a repertoire of styles that can be used with different objectives, students, activities, facilities, and equipment. Teachers who can implement a variety of approaches can use different combinations of styles to motivate both students and teachers.

Teachers need to make a conscious effort to maintain professional interest and enthusiasm. Too often, they become comfortable with a favorite teaching style. They may lose their enthusiasm because of large classes, inferior working conditions, low salaries, or problems with poorly motivated students. Teachers constantly complain about boredom, lack of new challenges, and burnout. Perhaps the use of a different teaching style in an appropriate setting could improve the environment for both students and teachers. A new or revised teaching style is certainly not a panacea for all the ills of every school environment or setting, and a teaching style should not be selected without considering all variables. Certain styles do, however, offer certain advantages in certain situations. A teacher who has developed a high-quality instructional program should consider different approaches with various teaching styles.

This chapter presents the characteristics of effective teaching-learning environments that have been documented. In addition, how to incorporate these characteristics into various teaching styles is discussed. The styles have been field-tested in many different secondary school environments, and various combinations of styles have been used to teach different activities. Teachers can use several different combinations in a lesson or unit plan; they do not have to adopt just one style at a time. In fact, many teachers are comfortable and effective using several styles in one lesson. Examples will be discussed with each style that follows.

Mounting evidence from teacher effectiveness research (Medley, 1977; McLeish, 1981; and Siedentop, 1983) indicates that, regardless of the teacher's instructional style, an educational environment will be more effective if it is characterized by the following points.

1. Students are engaged in appropriate learning activities for a large percentage of class time. Effective teachers use class time wisely. Little time is wasted on noncontent activities such as taking attendance, dressing, lunch tickets, or yearbook photos. Teachers plan carefully and insist on appropriate learning activities that deal with the subject matter. Students need time to learn and effective teachers make sure that students use class time to receive information and practice the skills. The learning activities are matched to students' abilities and are meaningful to the overall class objectives.

2. The learning atmosphere is success-oriented, with a positive, caring climate. The evidence clearly shows that teachers who develop a positive and supportive atmosphere are more effective in terms of student learning and student attitudes towards school (Berliner, 1979). The old idea of creating a harsh, negative, "tough guy" climate has proved not to be the best way to foster learning and positive attitudes toward physical activity. Appropriate social and organizational behavior needs to be supported by teachers. Students and teachers should feel positive about working and learning in the physical education environment.

3. Students are given clear objectives and receive high rates of information feedback from the teacher and the environment. Students need to know what they are going to be held accountable for in the physical education class. Class activities should be arranged so students spend large amounts of time on the required objectives. Activities should be meaningful with a clear cut tie to the class objectives. Positive and corrective feedback should be available from the teacher. Set up the environment so that students can receive feedback on learning attempts even when the teacher is not available. Peers and instructional devices can be used to provide feedback.

4. Student progress is monitored regularly and students are held accountable for learning in physical education. Students must be expected to progress on class objectives, and records need to be kept relative to various objectives. Students must know exactly what is expected of them and how the expectations are tied to the accountability system. Reward students for small steps of progress towards larger goals. If progress is not monitored regularly, then students cannot be held accountable and the environment will be less effective.

5. Low rates of management time and smooth transitions from one activity to another characterize the environment. Effective teachers are efficient managers of students. Students are moved from one learning activity to another smoothly and without wasting time. Time-saving procedures are planned and implemented efficiently. Students spend little time waiting during class transitions. Equipment is organized to facilitate these smooth transitions. Attendance procedures, starting and stopping procedures, and instructional procedures are all tightly organized with little wasted time.

6. Students spend a limited amount of time waiting in line or in other unproductive behaviors. Effective environments are characterized by high rates of time engaged in the subject matter. In physical education, this means high rates of time spent practicing, drilling, and playing. Physical education should be activity-oriented, and students should spend their class time doing the activity, not waiting for an opportunity.

7. Teachers are organized with high but realistic expectations for student achievement. Structure learning activities to challenge students. The activities must not be too easy or too difficult. Students need both success and challenge from learning activities. Expect students to learn and hold them accountable for their progress.

8. Teachers are enthusiastic about what they are doing and are actively involved in the instructional process. Students need to see an enthusiastic model—someone who has incorporated physical activity into his or her life-style. Active involvement means active supervision, enthusiasm, and high interaction rates with students. Teachers should keep these key characteristics in mind as they select, plan, and implement various instructional styles. These environmental characteristics can be present when using different strategies; they are more important than the teaching styles themselves in regard to student achievement and positive attitudes towards school and physical education.

DIRECT INSTRUCTION

Direct instruction is the most commonly used effective approach in secondary school physical education. The teacher is the central figure and is clearly in charge of the pace and direction of the class. Students spend most of the class time engaged in the appropriate subject matter. Goals are clearly presented to students and much time is devoted to practice. Students usually practice while the teacher actively supervises and provides frequent feedback. The teacher sets a positive, supportive tone for the students. The teacher makes decisions regarding objectives, content, materials, instruction, practice time, and evaluation procedures. The class is highly structured and there is little unsupervised student work time. A student's basic responsibility is to follow the directions of the teacher and work on skills.

A common scenario involving this style would begin with the teacher explaining and demonstrating the skills to be developed. Students are then organized into partners, small groups, or squads for practice. The teacher gives a signal for practice to commence on the specific skills and then moves around the area correcting errors, praising, scolding, encouraging, and so forth. The teacher gives a signal to stop, and the students gather around the teacher for a few final evaluative comments before moving on to the next class activity. The teacher serves as the major demonstrator, lecturer, motivator, organizer, disciplinarian, director, and error corrector.

A specific example of a direct-style lesson on basketball for 7th graders would follow this sequence: The teacher gives a lecture and demonstration on dribbling. He or she points out that students should use their fingertips, lower their center of gravity, watch the defenders, protect the ball from defenders with their bodies, and become proficient with both hands. There are enough basketballs for all students to practice dribbling in place. Students are then organized into 8 or 10 lines with 3 or 4 students in each line. A practice drill is explained and demonstrated. On the teacher's signal, the first student in each line dribbles the ball to midcourt with the right hand and back with the left hand. The remaining students wait in line for their turn. The teacher corrects a few students who are dribbling too high, praises a few for proper

form, scolds a few for horsing around in line, and reminds a few to change hands when they turn around to come back. Eventually, the teacher gives a stopping signal and makes a few general comments on how well or how poorly the class is performing. She then moves on to another dribbling drill or another basketball skill such as passing, shooting, or rebounding.

Students learn with this instructional strategy, and it offers a tightly controlled class environment that is safe for students. A common mistake of new teachers is to make students spend too much class time passively watching, listening to a lecture-demonstration, or waiting in line for a turn. Students consequently spend little time engaged in physical activity and become bored and frustrated waiting in line. Teachers need to constantly evaluate the teaching style they are using in regard to student practice time, management time, and waiting time. Overloading students with cognitive information will also be counterproductive to the overall goals of a program. Students need time to practice dribbling if they are expected to improve.

Another common problem with this approach is that many instructors primarily teach to the "norm" of the class. Higher skilled and lower skilled students are hindered because the learning activities are too easy and unchallenging, or too difficult and cause repeated failure or boredom. With this style, teachers rarely provide enough options for the various ability levels. If there is a wide range of basketball abilities, the teacher should provide several practice options for various student abilities (e.g., four different dribbling drills ranging from standing in place and dribbling to dribbling through a set of cones in 20 sec). The range of students' abilities is an important factor in selecting appropriate practice activities.

The direct instruction style of teaching has earned a poor reputation with some teachers because it was aligned with the command style of instruction. This style appears at the far end of Mosston's continuum of teaching styles (1986) and offers a limited amount of cognitive student involvement. Mosston's physical education model proposes several styles of teaching that move from a teacher-centered approach at one extreme to a student-centered approach at the other. As students move along the spectrum, there is more emphasis on cognitive involvement in a student-centered approach. Cognitive involvement is a noble goal for physical education, but it is certainly not the only goal. We suggest the continuum of styles in Figure 10.1 for secondary school instruction.

The direct instruction model has more flexibility and variations than the command style. Students do not have to be doing exactly the same things at the same time in the direct instruction approach. Re-

Direct	Task	Contract (individualized)	Guided discovery	Problem solving

Direct (teacher centered)   Indirect (student centered)

FIGURE 10.1   Continuum of teaching styles

search evaluating the direct instruction model (Rosenshine, 1979) has found it to be successful in terms of student achievement and positive student feelings about themselves and the school. This style of teaching has been researched mainly in elementary classroom situations, but the direct instruction model does appear to have merit in secondary school physical education settings because of the positive results of the strategy. This style should not be identified with the command style as defined by Mosston.

Direct instruction, like any other type of instruction, can be effective or ineffective depending on how it is used and administered. It can be an effective strategy for teaching physical skills, and is an especially important approach when activities present an inherent hazard or danger with immature students. Activities such as fencing, riflery, and rock climbing should be tightly organized and supervised with a teacher-directed format (Figure 10.2). Students should have little freedom until they understand the hazards of activity and demonstrate responsibility.

Overall, the direct style can be effective. The following points should be adhered to throughout the lessons:

1. Instructions and demonstrations should be brief, clear, and to the point. Many teachers talk too long and add too much detail for students to comprehend. Students need to get into the activity as quickly as possible.

2. Practice should be organized so that as many students as possible are kept active within the limits of the situation (i.e., equipment, facilities, and hazards).

3. The specific learning activities should fit the abilities of the students in the class. Activities that are too difficult will create frustration, and activities that are too easy will become boring. Teachers should encourage higher skilled students with challenges that are possible within the parameters of the situation. All students do not have to be doing the same activity at the same time.

4. Management time should be minimal, and transitions between activities should be smooth.

5. The environment should be positive, caring, and success-oriented, rather than negative and authoritarian.

6. Teachers should actively supervise students and provide frequent feedback to students during practice sessions.

Beginning teachers with new students, large classes, or situations that have had high rates of inappropriate student behavior should start with a highly structured, direct instructional approach. The direct instruction model can be varied according to the type of students and the nature of the activities taught. As teachers and students become comfortable with each other, teachers may want to vary the style or move to a different style.

TASK INSTRUCTION

The task style of teaching (Figure 10.3) focuses on specific learning tasks or performances. The teacher selects the tasks and the arrangement of the tasks for the students to practice. Tasks are usually set up in several learning areas or stations. Students rotate through each learning station and work on the assigned tasks. They usually have more freedom in this instructional strategy than in the direct approach, because they can work through the tasks at their desired speed and personal level of proficiency. At each station, students may have one or several tasks

FIGURE 10.2   Hazardous activity (reprinted from *Outdoor Adventure Activities for School and Recreation Programs* by P. W. Darst and G. P. Armstrong, 1980. Minneapolis, MN: Burgess, p. 86.)

FIGURE 10.3 Students practicing a task

to practice. They start and stop working on the tasks without specific teacher directions. For example, students may be given 5 min to work at each station that has 4 or 5 tasks. The teacher displays a rotation cue or signal after the time has passed.

This instructional style allows the teacher to move off center stage and away from being the central figure in the instructional process. The teacher can then become a better agent of feedback by visiting the various learning stations and by interacting with students who need help on the tasks. The teacher does not have to spend as much time directing and managing the entire group. This approach requires more preparation time for planning and designing tasks. Adequate facilities, equipment, and instructional devices are necessary to keep students productive and working on the appropriate tasks.

These general guidelines should be considered when selecting, writing, and presenting tasks for secondary school physical education classes:

1. Select tasks that cover all the basic skills of an activity.

2. Select tasks that will provide students with success and challenge. The tasks should be within the appropriate ability range of the students. Remember that the highest skilled student should be challenged and the lowest skilled student should be successful.

3. Avoid tasks that demand excessive risk and could cause injury.

4. For the station approach, tape task cards on the wall or to boundary cones, or place them on the floor if students can avoid stepping on them. Another alternative is to give students a copy of the tasks on a sheet of paper to take with them to each station. The task sheets can be stored at school in a locker and can be taken home to use for practice after school.

5. For 7th and 8th graders, write the tasks simply with a key word or phrase that students will understand. For 9th through 12th graders, the tasks can be written as performance objectives with the behavior, conditions, and criterion level identified. (See Chapters 20–23 for examples of performance objectives for various activities.)

6. Task descriptions should always use appropriate vocabulary for the age group involved. The tasks explain what to do and how to do it (see the examples in Figure 10.4). Be sure that students understand the tasks and are able to practice when unsupervised.

7. Present tasks verbally, and accompany them with a demonstration. Give students enough information to get started, not an in-depth lecture that takes an excessive amount of time.

8. Tasks should incorporate a combination of instructional devices that add feedback, variety, and a challenge to the environment. Examples of such devices include targets, cones, hoops, ropes, and stopwatches.

Figure 10.4 shows a list of basketball tasks with descriptions of what to do and how to perform each task. Task lists can be printed on one or two cards at each station.

The task style of instruction can be used with a variety of grouping patterns. Students may work alone, with a partner, or in a small group. The partner or reciprocal grouping pattern can be useful with large classes, limited amounts of equipment, or with certain skills in which the partner can time, count, record, or analyze the skill work. For example, one student can dribble through a set of cones while the partner is timing and recording. In another example with a group of three students, one student might bump a volleyball against the wall, another could analyze his or her form with a checklist, and the third student could count and record. Students enjoy the social aspect of being able to work on the tasks with a partner or friend.

Arrange tasks so that all students can find success and challenge in the physical education environment. Success and challenge can be built into the activities by offering a progressive arrangement of experiences from simple to complex with small steps along the way. Students should be able to progress at their own speed through the activities. As they build a backlog of success, learning activities should become more challenging.

An effective example of this instructional approach is the use of performance or behavioral objectives in a learning station arrangement. A performance objective is a statement of what students should be able to perform. Examples are as follows:

BASKETBALL UNIT

Dribbling Tasks (What to do)
1. Standing—right and left hand—25 times
2. Half speed—right and left hand—baseline to midcourt
3. Full speed—right and left hand—baseline to midcourt
4. Around the cones—25 sec

Dribbling Cues (How to do)
1. Finger tips
2. Lower center of gravity
3. Opposite hand in front
4. Eyes on opponents

Ball Handling (What to do)
1. Around head—left and right—5 times each
2. Around waist—left and right—5 times each
3. Around each leg—left and right—5 times each
4. Figure 8 around legs—10 times
5. Hand switch between legs—10 times
6. Bounce between legs and switch—10 times

Jump Shots (What to do)
1. 3 ft away—right angle, center, left angle
2. 9 ft away—right angle, center, left angle
3. 15 ft away—right angle, center, left angle
4. 20 ft away—right angle, center, left angle

Jump Shot Cues (How to do)
1. Straight-up jump
2. Wrist position
3. Elbow position
4. Slight backspin on ball
5. Follow through

Passing Skills (What to do)
Strike the target from 8 ft, 10 ft, 12 ft, 15 ft

1. Chest—10 times
2. Bounce—10 times
3. Overhead—10 times
4. One hand overhead (baseball)—10 times

Passing Cues (How to do)
1. Use your peripheral vision—do not telegraph.
2. Step toward target.
3. Transfer your weight to the front foot.
4. Aim for the numbers.

FIGURE 10.4 Basketball tasks

---

1. The student will complete 15 push-ups in 30 sec.
2. The student will run a mile in 8 min.
3. The student will hit 10 consecutive volleyball forearm passes up in the air at least 10 ft high.
4. The student will dribble the basketball through a set of 5 cones in 25 sec.
5. The student will punt the football at least 25 yd, 3 consecutive times within the boundaries.

The performance objective should contain the behavior to be performed, the conditions or setting, and the acceptable criterion level of performance. The following examples identify the three parts of a well-written performance objective:

Handball Example

Conditions	Behavior	Criterion
Standing 6 ft from the back wall in the middle of the court	bounce the handball against the back wall and hit the ball	3 of 4 shots below a red line

Standing 6 ft from the back wall in the middle of the court, the student will bounce the handball against the back wall and hit 3 of 4 shots below a red line drawn 3 ft above the floor of the court (right hand).

Volleyball Example

Conditions	Behavior	Criterion
Standing 5 ft from the bleachers	hit forearm passes against the bleachers	10 consecutive times at a height of at least 10 ft

Standing 5 ft from the bleachers, the student will hit 10 consecutive forearm passes against the bleachers at a height of at least 10 ft.

The key point is that students must be able to understand what they are expected to do in the activity. The specificity of the objective depends on the level of the learner. Students who are given clear-cut goals and a system for monitoring their own skill development will be more motivated to learn.

A learning station is a designated area in the gymnasium, on the soccer field, or in any appropriate area where students can practice specific learning activities such as performance objectives, viewing loop films, taking a rules test, or working with a partner. An effective instructional approach for soccer that combines performance objectives and learning stations might be organized as follows:

Dribbling Tasks

1. Dribble the soccer ball a distance of 20 yd 3 consecutive times, making each kick no more than 5 yd (1 point).
2. Dribble the soccer ball through an obstacle course of 6 pylons over a distance of 30 yd in 25 sec or less (1 point).
3. With a partner, pass the soccer ball back and forth 5 times while in a running motion for a distance of 50 yd 2 consecutive times (1 point).

Trapping Tasks

4. When the ball is rolled to you by a partner 10 yd away, trap it 4 of 5 times, using the instep method with the right and then the left foot (1 point).
5. Same as Task 4 using the sole of the foot (1 point).
6. With a partner tossing the ball, trap 4 of 5 shots using the chest method (1 point).

Kicking Tasks

7. Kick the ball to a partner, who is standing 10 yd away, 5 consecutive times with the right and left inside of the foot push pass (1 point).
8. Same as Task 7 using the instep kick. Loft the ball to your partner (1 point).
9. Kick 4 of 5 shots that enter the goal in the air from a distance of 20 yd (1 point).

Heading and Throw-In Tasks

10. Head 3 consecutive balls in the air at a height of at least 10 ft (1 point).
11. Head 6 consecutive balls back and forth with a partner (1 point).
12. Make 4 of 5 throw-ins from out-of-bounds into a Hula Hoop placed 15 yd away (1 point).

The soccer field practice area could be arranged as in Figure 10.5 with 4 learning stations, and the performance objectives could be written on a card at each station. Students could spend 3–5 min working on the objectives at each station and then rotate on to the next station. Arrange objectives so that students can experience success quickly and fre-

quently with the first few objectives and be challenged with later objectives. Objectives can be changed daily or repeated, depending on the progression of the class. Points earned through completion of the performance objectives can also help motivate many students. The points can be tied to other reinforcing activities.

The following format is used to teach volleyball. These performance objectives have been tested on secondary students in several different settings.

Forearm Pass (Bump)

1. Bump 12 consecutive forearm passes against the bleachers at a height of at least 10 ft (1 point).
2. Bump 12 consecutive forearm passes into the air at a height of at least 10 ft (height of a basket rim) (1 point).
3. Bump 10 consecutive forearm passes over the net with the instructor or a classmate (1 point).

Overhead Set Pass

4. Hit 15 consecutive set passes against the bleachers at a height of at least 10 ft (1 point).
5. Hit 15 consecutive set passes into the air at a height of at least 10 ft (1 point).
6. Hit 12 consecutive set passes over the net with the instructor or a classmate (1 point).

Serves

7. Hit 3 consecutive underhand serves into the right half of the court (1 point).
8. Hit 3 consecutive underhand serves into the left half of the court (1 point).
9. Hit 3 consecutive overhand serves into the right half of the court (1 point).
10. Hit 3 of 4 underhand serves into the left half of the court (1 point).

A gymnasium can be set up with volleyball stations similar to Figure 10.6.

Some teachers are not comfortable with the task style because there appears to be less order and control compared to direct instruction. With proper planning, organization, and supervision, however, teachers can effectively order and control the environment in task-style teaching. In many situations, teachers feel uncomfortable with this approach simply because they lack experience. Many professionals teach in the same way that they were taught in high school; since the direct style is most popular, many teachers have never experienced a different style of teaching.

Teachers and students need time to expand their comfort zones when experimenting with the task style. The task style can be effective in motivating

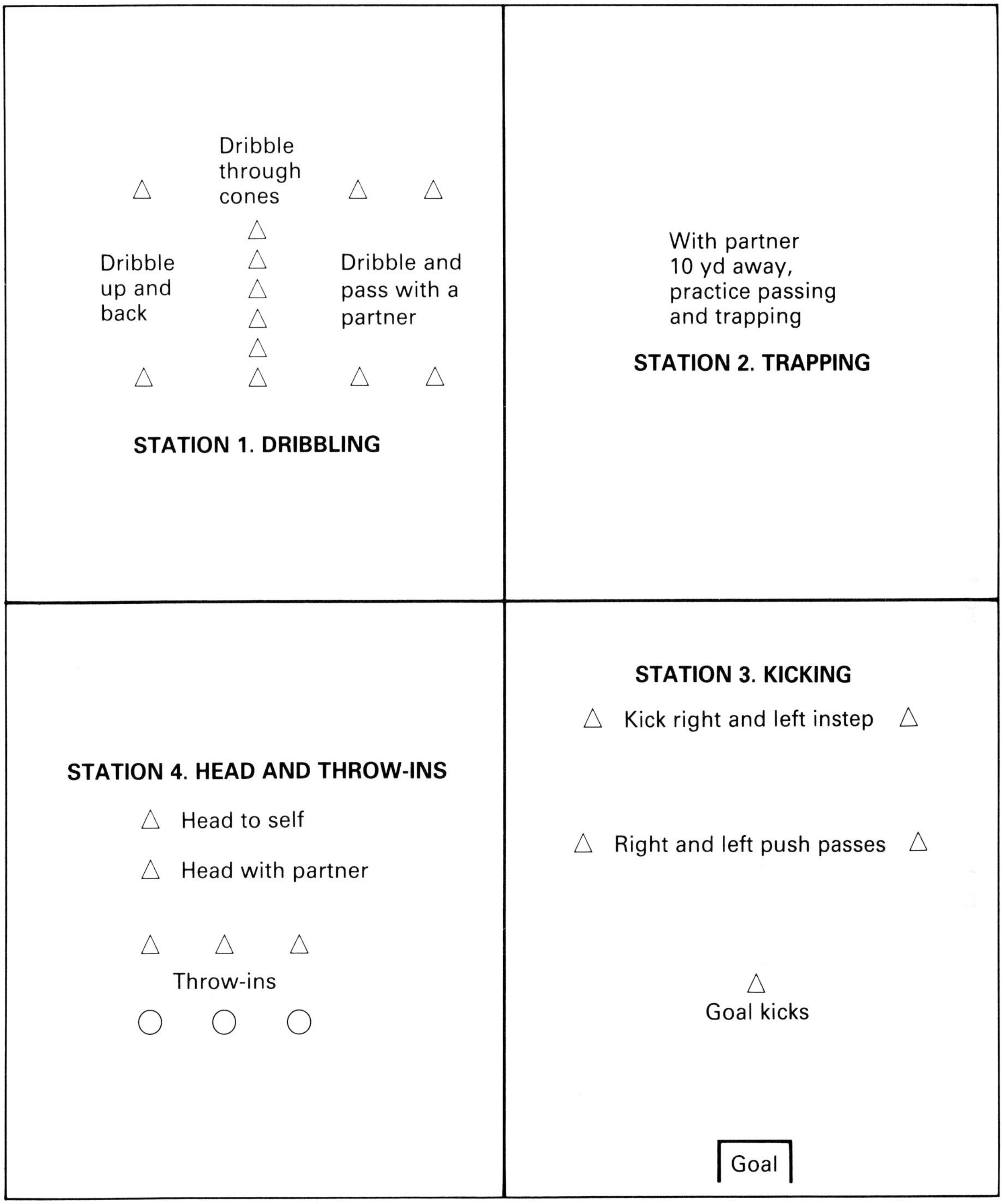

FIGURE 10.5   Soccer learning stations

students because of the variety and levels of learning tasks. Students may take some time to adjust to the increased freedom, flexibility, and opportunities to make decisions, but this gives them an opportunity to develop self-management skills since the teacher is not making every decision. Task teaching offers interesting challenges for both teachers and students.

CONTRACT (INDIVIDUALIZED) INSTRUCTION _____

Contract instruction is a more sophisticated form of task instruction. In the contract approach, a specific external reward system is attached to the ac-

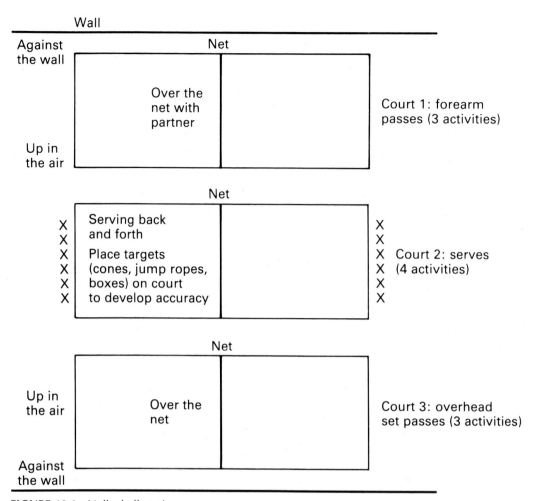

FIGURE 10.6 Volleyball stations

complishment of the tasks, and this arrangement increases the motivational level of the students. The students work on the tasks because they want to earn rewards that are tied to the tasks. Students are usually given several options concerning the tasks that can be completed. The tasks are arranged progressively so they increase in difficulty. Students can select tasks they are interested in completing. The teacher and students agree formally on what tasks will be completed and rewards earned. The contract approach is considered to be a form of individualized instruction because the teacher and the student can adjust objectives, learning activities, content, instruction, and evaluation to meet individual characteristics and interests.

Rewards in the contract system are usually tied to the grading scheme. Points are awarded for completing certain tasks, and the accumulation of more points means a higher grade. In situations where grades are not an effective reward, task completion can be tied to participation in a game activity. For example, students might have to complete 10 basket-

ball tasks before they could enter a 3-on-3 class tournament. In other situations, when students are not motivated by grades or by the game activity, they might be allowed to exchange points for a variety of predetermined reward activities such as exercising to music, jumping rope to music, playing Frisbee golf, or reading a sports article. These rewards can be activities that are not generally available to students. Contracts that use a variety of rewards have a better chance of motivating the majority of students in the class.

Contract instructional systems have been used successfully with many activities, including badminton, volleyball, soccer, tennis, racquetball, skin diving, and gymnastics (Darst, 1976; Darst and Darst, 1978; Claxton, 1981; Darst and Model, 1983). The approach has been used with upper elementary, junior high, senior high, and college-aged students. Junior and senior high students will work well in a contract system if they are gradually given opportunities to make decisions and control their practice behaviors. This type of instruction is especially effective with physical activities that require the development of individual skills (e.g., bumps, sets, forehands, backhands).

Guidelines for Developing Contracts

Rushall and Siedentop (1972) have suggested the following guidelines for developing contingency contracts in physical education:

1. Define the specific tasks or behaviors in observable, measurable terms (e.g., volleyball bumps, badminton clears, tennis serves, and soccer kicks, rather than vague, hypothetical terms such as positive attitudes, physical fitness, or self-concept).

2. Specify clearly the final performance for the end of the unit. Knowing the specific final goal will increase student motivation. Final goals such as bump 10 consecutive shots, serve 3 or 4 into a target area, or kick a goal in 3 of 4 shots will also serve as a competitive challenge for students.

3. Develop a monitoring and measuring system. This enables students to see daily improvement and set goals that progress toward the final, terminal objective. In addition to teacher assessment, peer assessment and self-assessment should be used in the monitoring system. This will aid in developing self-control.

4. Give rewards only for successful completion of the target performance. This can be speed, strength, endurance, accuracy, or a combination. For example, volleyball serves require a combination of speed and accuracy. An objective must therefore be set up that measures both parameters. Students could hit serves between the net and a rope strung 10 ft higher than the net. The serves must land inbounds and 10 ft or less from the backline. This would ensure both speed and accuracy. Many other physical skills, such as dribbling in soccer, pitching in baseball, or dribbling in basketball, require similar combinations.

5. Clarify the relationship between the performance and the reward.

6. The relationship between the performance and the reward should be fair for all students. The reward should be commensurate with a reasonable amount of effort and with the performance. It would be ineffective and unfair to demand a level of performance in a short time for a small reward.

7. Performances should be arranged in a progressive sequence so students can experience success quickly and frequently. As students build a backlog of success, the tasks should then become more difficult and challenging.

Figure 10.7 is a volleyball contract that uses grades as rewards. Such a contract is appropriate for upper-level high school students. The core objectives are required, and the students can choose from the optional objectives.

Figure 10.8 is a flag football contract that has been used with 7th and 8th graders. It follows the same format as the volleyball contract with points tied to a grading scheme, and core and optional performance objectives.

In many sections of Chapters 20 through 23, performance objectives are provided for the teacher's use. These can be arranged as part of a contract, or they can be used for motivation, instruction, and grading. The objectives will have to be modified according to the particular situation. They may be too difficult for certain students and too easy for others. It is important to assure that all students can find success and challenge with some of the objectives. Modification of the objectives requires some experimenting by the teacher.

Performance objectives that are listed focus primarily on physical skills rather than on cognitive activities. Certain teachers may want a specific combination of cognitive and physical skills to be built into the contract. The contract provides a framework for developing the type of objectives that a teacher wants to stress in a certain situation. For example, a contract could provide a balance of objectives related to attendance, participation, physical skills, and cognitive activities. The contract approach allows teachers to be flexible in the choice of objectives, and allows students flexibility in the selection of certain objectives and levels of performance (see "Contract Grading" in Chapter 12).

Applying and Administering Contract Instruction

Teachers need to explain the entire format so that students understand the objectives, rewards, learning activities, grading procedures, and other responsibilities. Contracts should be available to students so they can explain them to their parents, work on the objectives at home in their free time, or keep records of their performance at school. Students must understand how involvement in this strategy is different from other strategies. Some students will take longer to adapt and become comfortable with this instruction format.

Explain and demonstrate the performance objectives to students in the learning areas where they will be practicing. Introduce various instructional devices and targets. Students need a brief explanation and demonstration to get them started on the objectives. Arrange the gymnasium or playing field

VOLLEYBALL

Core Objectives

Forearm Pass (Bump)

1. Bump 12 consecutive forearm passes against the wall at a height of at least 10 ft (**1 point**).
2. Bump 12 consecutive forearm passes into the air at a height of at least 10 ft (**1 point**).
3. Bump 10 consecutive forearm passes over the net with the instructor or a classmate (**1 point**).

Overhead Set Pass

4. Hit 15 consecutive set passes against wall at a height of at least 10 ft (**1 point**).
5. Hit 15 consecutive set passes into the air at a height of at least 10 ft (**1 point**).
6. Hit 12 consecutive set passes over the net with the instructor or a classmate (**1 point**).

Serves

7. Hit 3 consecutive underhand serves into the right half of the court (**1 point**).
8. Hit 3 of 4 underhand serves into the left half of the court (**1 point**).
9. Hit 3 consecutive overhand serves inbounds (**1 point**).

Attendance and Participation

10. Be dressed and ready to participate at 8:00 A.M. (⅓ **point daily, 5 points for 15-day unit**).
11. Participate in 15 games (**1 point**).
12. Score 90% or better on a rules, strategies, and techniques test (2 attempts only) (**5 points**).

Optional Objectives

1. Standing 2 ft from the backline, bump 3 of 5 forearm passes into an 8-ft circle surrounding the setter's position. The height must be at least 10 ft, and the ball must be thrown by the instructor or a classmate (**1 point**).
2. Bump 3 of 5 forearm passes over the net at a height of at least 12 ft that land inbounds and not more than 8 ft from the backline (**1 point**).
3. Standing in the setter's position (CF), hit 3 consecutive overhead sets at least 10 ft high that land in a 5-ft circle where the spiker would be located. The ball will be thrown by the instructor or a classmate (**1 point**).
4. Hit 3 of 5 overhead passes over the net at least 12 ft high that land inbounds and not more than 8 ft from the backline (**1 point**).
5. Standing in the setter's position (CF), hit 3 of 5 back sets at least 10 ft high that land in a 5-ft circle where the spiker would be located. The ball will be thrown by the instructor or a classmate (**1 point**).
6. Volley 12 consecutive times over the net with the instructor or a classmate by alternating forearm passes and overhead passes (**1 point**).
7. Alternate forearm passes and overhead passes in the air at a height of 10 ft or more for 12 consecutive times (**1 point**).
8. Spike 3 of 4 sets inbounds from an on-hand position (3-step approach, jump, extended arm, hand contact) (**1 point**).
9. Spike 3 of 5 sets inbounds from an off-hand position (**1 point**).
10. Recover 3 consecutive balls from the net. Recoveries must be playable (8 ft high in the playing area) (**1 point**).
11. Hit 3 consecutive overhand serves into the right half of the court (**1 point**).
12. Hit 3 of 4 overhand serves into the left half of the court (**1 point**).
13. Hit 3 of 5 overhand serves under a rope 15 ft high that land in the back half of the court (**1 point**).
14. Officiate at least 3 games, using proper calls and signals (**1 point**).
15. Coach a team for the class tournament. Plan strategy, substitution, and scheduling (**1 point**).

FIGURE 10.7   Volleyball contract

16. Devise and carry out a research project that deals with volleyball. Check with the instructor for ideas **(1 point)**.

Grade Structure: C = 20 points
                   B = 28 points
                   A = 34 points

FIGURE 10.7   Continued

with learning areas for specific objectives, such as the dribbling area, passing area, shooting area, or ball-handling area. The objectives can be posted at each learning station, or students can carry a copy of the objectives with them.

A rotational scheme and grouping pattern can be organized, depending on the maturity and motivational level of students. One arrangement is to have students in equal-sized groups at each learning station and have them spend 3–5 min at each station before rotating to the next station. Another alternative is to allow students to rotate to a learning area whenever they are ready for specific objectives. The grouping patterns of practicing individually, with a partner, or with a small group can be used depending on available facilities, equipment, objectives, and student choice. Teachers need to consider the amount of freedom, flexibility, and choice that students can handle and still be productive. It is best to start with small amounts of freedom and gradually expand the choice options and program flexibility as students get used to the system. If students are given too much freedom too quickly, the results can be counterproductive.

The completion of performance objectives can be monitored by the teacher, student peers, student leaders from another class, or some combination of all three. If the class size is small and the number of objectives is small, the teacher may be able to do all of the monitoring. Otherwise, a combination of procedures is recommended. Teachers need to involve students, peers, and student leaders in the process. Students' involvement in the monitoring process should enhance their understanding of the objectives, and will also give students additional responsibility in the instructional environment.

Teachers or student leaders can use a performance chart to monitor objectives at each learning station, or they can carry a master list from station to station (Figure 10.9). This will depend on the number of objectives to be completed at each station. Another approach is to develop a performance sheet for each student that combines teacher and peer monitoring (Figure 10.10). This allows peers to monitor some objectives and the teacher to monitor more difficult objectives. A third system allows students to privately monitor themselves on the perfor-

mance objectives (Figure 10.11). Students then work alone on the objectives. Experiment with several monitoring approaches depending on the activity, the number of objectives, the students' abilities, the size of the class, and the equipment and facilities. Because of the various advantages of each approach, teachers should decide on the best one for their situation. For example, if teachers try to do all of the monitoring, they may become frustrated because little time is left for other teaching activities. If student leaders are involved, teachers must take time to train them properly. A problem with peer evaluation is that students are sometimes too lenient with the criterion levels of performances. A similar problem can occur with self-assessment. The teacher needs to spot-check any student monitoring procedure.

In some secondary schools, teachers use contracts as part of an individualized, independent study approach with a learning laboratory–resource center (Cottman, 1976). Students can select the level of an activity that they want to pursue. Learning packets with objectives, study guides, learning activities, and assessment procedures are available for a wide variety of activities. Students can work independently on objectives, view loop films, read books, and prepare for an assessment procedure. Assessment usually progresses from self, to peers, and finally to the teacher. This approach requires teachers to develop learning materials and procedures for supervising the distribution and return of those materials.

Overall, contract instruction can offer the following advantages in secondary school physical education programs, depending on how the instruction is planned, arranged, and monitored:

1. Students, parents, and administrators know exactly what is expected and accomplished by students.
2. The reward system enhances the motivational level of students.
3. Students at most competency levels can find success and challenge with objectives.
4. Students can progress through the objectives at their own rate.
5. Students have some choice of learning activities and the sequence of learning activities.

FLAG FOOTBALL

Core Objectives

Passing Tasks

1. Throw 10 passes to the chest area of a partner standing 10 yd away (**1 point**).
2. Throw 3 of 4 consecutive passes beyond a target distance of 20 yd (**1 point**).
3. Throwing 5 passes, knock over 3 targets from a distance of 10 yd (**1 point**).
4. Throw 4 of 6 passes through a tire from a distance of 10 yd (**1 point**).

Centering Tasks

5. With a partner 5 yd away, execute 10 over-the-head snaps to the chest area, using correct holding, proper rotation, and follow-through techniques (**1 point**).
6. Facing the opposite direction from a partner 5 yd away, execute a proper center stance with feet well spread and toes pointed straight ahead, knees bent, and two hands on the ball. Snap the ball back through the legs for 10 consecutive times (**1 point**).
7. Same as task 6 but move back 10 yd (**1 point**).
8. Center snap 4 of 6 times through a tire a distance of 5 yd away (**1 point**).

Punting Tasks

9. With a partner centering the ball, from a distance of 10 yd away punt the football using proper technique to another set of partners 15 yd away 3 consecutive times (**1 point**).
10. Same as task 9 but at a distance of 20 yd (**1 point**).
11. Punt the ball 3 consecutive times within the boundary lines of the field and beyond a distance of 20 yd (**1 point**).
12. Punt the ball 3 consecutive times for a hang time of 2.5 sec or better (use stopwatch) (**1 point**).

Catching Tasks

13. With a partner run a "quick" pass pattern and catch the ball 2 of 3 times (5–7-yd pattern) (**1 point**).
14. With a partner run a 10–15-yd "down and in" pass pattern and catch the ball 2 of 3 times (**1 point**).
15. With a partner run a 10–15-yd "down and out" pass pattern and catch the ball 2 of 3 times (**1 point**).
16. With a partner run a 5–7-yd "hook" pattern and catch the ball 2 of 3 times (**1 point**).

Attendance and Participation

1. Be ready to participate in football activities 5 min after the last bell rings each day (⅕ **point daily = 1 point weekly**).
2. Use proper locker room behavior (will be discussed or posted) at all times (⅕ **point daily = 1 point weekly**).
3. Score at least 90% on a written test (2 attempts only) (**5 points**).

Optional Objectives

1. Attend two football games (flag or regular) during the grading period (**1 point**).
2. Throw 3 of 4 passes through a tire from a distance of 10 yd (**2 points**).
3. Throw 3 of 4 passes through a tire from a distance of 15 yd (**3 points**).
4. Throw 3 of 4 passes through a moving tire from a distance of 10 yd (**3 points**).
5. Throw 3 of 4 passes through a moving tire from a distance of 15 yd (**4 points**).
6. Catch 2 passes in a game (**2 points**).
7. Intercept a pass in a game (**2 points**).
8. Write a one-page report on a fiction or nonfiction book related to the topic of football (**3 points**).

FIGURE 10.8   Flag football contract

9. Diagram a football field with all the dimensions and markings, and turn in your diagram to the instructor **(3 points)**.
10. Write up a list of at least 15 football terms with definitions, and turn in to the instructor a neat, finalized copy **(3 points)**.
11. Officiate at least 1 flag-football game during the class time, using correct calls and signals **(1 point)**.

Grade Structure: C = 22 points
                  B = 27 points
                  A = 32 points

FIGURE 10.8 Continued

PERFORMANCE CHART

Station 3							Parallel Bars								
Name	1	2	3	4	5	6	7	8	9	10	11	12	13	14	15

FIGURE 10.9 Performance chart for gymnastics

6. Students have some choice concerning the grouping arrangement of skill practice (e.g., alone, with a partner, or in a small group).
7. Students have to accept a certain amount of responsibility.
8. The contract form emphasizes student performance.
9. The contract format frees the teacher to give individual attention and become a better agent of feedback.
10. The contract format can provide students with large amounts of time spent engaged in the subject matter.

Problems that may need to be solved when using the contract approach include the following:

1. The performance objectives are time consuming to write and require constant revision.
2. A monitoring system needs to be developed that does not take up too much class time.
3. Instructional devices are necessary to provide variety and feedback. These increase the setup and take-down time of each class for the teacher.
4. Many teachers and students will need time to get used to the contract format. Both students and teachers are often more comfortable initially

PERFORMANCE OBJECTIVES: BEGINNING HANDBALL

Name _____

Instructor Checked	Class Member Checked	
____	____	1. Stand approximately 6 ft from the back wall and in the center of the court. Bounce the ball against the side wall and hit 3 of 4 shots below the white line with preferred hand.
____	____	2. Same as objective 1 but 3 of 5 with the nonpreferred hand.
____	____	3. Hit 3 of 5 power serves that land within 2 ft of the side wall and are otherwise legal.
____	____	4. Hit 3 of 4 lob serves within approximately 3 ft of the side wall that do not bounce out from the back wall more than 8 ft.
____	____	5. Stand approximately 6 ft from the back wall, bounce the ball against the back wall, and hit 3 of 4 shots below the white line on the front wall with the preferred hand.
____	____	6. Same as objective 5 but 3 of 5 with the nonpreferred hand.
____	____	7. Hit 3 of 4 diagonal or "Z" serves that hit the front, side, floor, opposite side, in that order. (The ball may hit, but need not hit the back wall for the serve to be effective.)
____	____	8. Hit 3 of 4 Scotch serves or "Scotch toss" serves that hit the front, side, floor, back, side, in that order. This is similar to the "Z" serve in execution, except that the ball hits the back wall after bouncing on the floor.
____	____	9. Return 3 of 4 serves hit to you by the instructor. (One of each of the following will be used: power, lob, diagonal, and Scotch.)
____	____	10. Execute 3 of 4 attempts at "3-hit drill." (Instructor will explain in detail.)
____	____	11. Execute 3 of 4 attempts at "4-hit drill." (Instructor will explain.)
____	____	12. Hit 3 of 5 ceiling shots with preferred hand. The ball will be thrown or hit by instructor and must be returned to the ceiling, front wall, and floor, in that order.

Note: Entry into ladder tournament is contingent on completion of any 8 of the 12 objectives. To receive a grade of A for the class, you must exhibit proficiency in all 12 objectives.

Objectives 1–8 may be checked by a class member, however, the instructor may spot-check any objectives at his or her discretion.

Objectives 9–12 will be checked by instructor. Performance objectives may be tested in courts 1 and 4.

FIGURE 10.10   Performance objectives—handball

SKIN DIVING CONTRACT—NUMBER 1

Use of FACE MASK

Mark the date that each performance objective is met.

_____ 1. Adjust face mask strap to your head size.

_____ 2. Apply saliva to face mask—rub all around face plate, <u>do not rinse</u> (fog preventive).

_____ 3. Vertical tilt: Fill mask with water and hold to face without strap. In chest-deep water, go under in vertical position and by tilting head backward, away from chest, push against upper edge of mask and exhale gently. Completely clear mask 3 of 5 attempts.

_____ 4. Horizontal roll: Fill mask with water and hold to face without strap. While in a horizontal position, roll onto left shoulder, push gently with right hand against side of mask, and exhale gently. Completely clear mask 3 of 5 attempts.

_____ 5. Repeat objective 3 with strap around back of head.

_____ 6. Repeat objective 4 with strap around back of head.

_____ 7. In 6 ft of water, submerge to bottom of pool by pinching nostrils and gently exhaling into mask until you feel your ears equalize. Successfully equalize pressure in 4 of 5 attempts.

_____ 8. In 9 ft of water repeat objective 7.

_____ 9. Repeat objective 3 in deep water.

_____ 10. Repeat objective 4 in deep water.

_____ 11. Throw mask into shallow water, submerge, and put mask on. Complete vertical tilt clear in one breath, 4 of 5 attempts.

_____ 12. Throw mask into shallow water, submerge, and put mask on. Complete horizontal roll clear in one breath, 4 of 5 attempts.

_____ 13. Same as objective 11 in 6 ft of water.

_____ 14. Same as objective 11 in 9 ft of water.

_____ 15. Same as objective 12 in 6 ft of water.

_____ 16. Same as objective 12 in 9 ft of water.

FIGURE 10.11   Skin diving contract

with the familiar teacher-centered approach. Changing to a contract format will require some time for adjustment.

INQUIRY INSTRUCTION _____

The inquiry model of instruction is process-oriented, rather than product-oriented. A student's experience during the process is considered more important than the final product, or solution. Students experience learning situations in which they have to inquire, speculate, reflect, analyze, and discover. They must be cognitively active in this type of instruction.

The teacher guides and directs students, rather than commanding or telling. Students must discover their own answers and solutions.

The teacher is responsible for stimulating the students' curiosity about the subject matter to enhance their involvement. The teacher uses a combination of questions, problems, examples, and learning activities to lead students toward one or more final solutions. The steps involved must follow a sequence and be arranged logically so that students can move from one step to the next after a certain amount of thinking. The steps should not be too small or too large to prevent students becoming bored or frustrated. The instruction environment must be one of open communication. Students are comfortable experimenting and inquiring without fear of failure.

Some physical educators believe that inquiry methods of instruction should have a more prominent place in educational methodology (Schueler, 1979). Students need opportunities to inquire, solve problems, and discover, instead of experiencing only those approaches that heavily emphasize listening, absorbing, and complying. Arguments have been made to expand the focus of physical education methodology to include the inquiry style. Proponents of this style believe that it enhances students' ability to think, improves creativity, creates a better understanding of the subject matter, enhances self-concept, and helps develop lifelong learning patterns. Some educators argue that students who do not experience inquiry methods are dormant, unchallenged, and unused. These are broad and dramatic claims that are not supported by research findings.

Critics of the inquiry method point out the following problems with the approach: too much time is spent on one subject or topic, a focus is on trivial or nonessential learning, most motor skills have one best solution that should be quickly explained, secondary students already know the answers, and the instruction is difficult to plan because each class has a wide range of knowledge and ability.

These methods offer some advantages when learning about certain physical education activities and issues. The methods should be used in those situations to give teachers yet another teaching tool in their repertoire of skills.

Guided Discovery or Convergent Style

The inquiry method in physical education is generally characterized by two approaches called guided discovery or convergent styles and problem-solving or divergent styles (Mosston and Ashworth, 1986). Teachers using the guided discovery style lead students through a series of experiences in the hope that students will discover the one planned solution. The teacher has a best, specific answer that she or he wants students to discover.

Various types of learning activities can guide students to discover the following:

1. Court coverage strategies in tennis, badminton, racquetball, and handball;
2. Angles of release for distance throwing with the shot put, discus, football, and softball;
3. Batting stance and foot pattern alterations for hitting the baseball or softball to various fields;
4. Ready position for basketball, baseball, football, and tennis;
5. Specific passes in basketball for various situations

depending on the defenders and the type of defense;
6. Dribbling techniques in soccer used to fake a defender and move the ball up field;
7. The need for a specific type of pass or hand off in certain situations to advance the ball in a game of team handball;
8. The role of a person's center of gravity and momentum in performing activities in gymnastics such as the balance beam or the side horse.

Teachers can set up the learning environment for these activities in many different ways. For example, students can be asked a series of questions and can then be given several learning activities to perform. Students can then participate in these activities after which a brief discussion can take place privately or in a group to see if students have discovered the proper solution. This approach can be a small portion of the lesson that is completed quickly or it can be a major portion of class time.

In basketball, students could analyze and determine the best offensive solution when a defender is playing very tight defense. The best solution probably is to fake a shot and then drive to the basket. If the defender is playing loose defense, then the offensive player should probably take a shot. Students should have the opportunity to practice playing tight and loose defense as well as the opportunity to try the offensive position with a tight and loose defender on them. This will give them a chance to discover the best solution. In soccer, students could experiment with long and short passes with defenders in certain positions. Long, high passes are necessary to get the ball over a defender, whereas quick, short passes that stay on the ground are necessary to keep the defender from intercepting, and the quick passes are easier for a teammate to receive and trap. In the shot put and discus throws, students could experiment with various release angles to see how it affects the flight and distance of the throws. Students should discover the best angle of release for maximum distance.

Problem-Solving or Divergent Style

The problem-solving method involves a divergent approach, rather than converging on one solution. Students are put through a series of experiences and are helped to devise as many acceptable solutions to the problem as possible. The teacher encourages students to be creative and to develop unique solutions. Students must analyze the pros and cons of each solution. This style can be useful for discussions and assignments dealing with values, social issues, wellness concepts, and controversial topics related to sport and physical education. Honesty in sports, cooperation with teammates, competition, violence in sports, amateur versus professional sports, athletes taking drugs to improve performance, arguing with officials, women participating in sports, and masculine and feminine roles are examples of topics that could be researched, explored, discussed, or debated in a physical education class.

Wellness is a curriculum area that lends itself to the problem-solving approach. Many different approaches and methods can be used for maintaining an optimum fitness level. Students can learn to solve their personal fitness problems with physical activity programs that are personalized to meet their needs. Problem-solving approaches are also useful in resolving the issues of proper diet and weight control. Stress reduction, alcohol and drug abuse, and tobacco use are areas that can be addressed effectively with problem-solving techniques.

The teacher is responsible for creating an open environment where students can explore all aspects of these controversial topics. Books, articles, movies, interviews, questions, and discussions are possibilities for accumulating and sharing information. Students should be encouraged to gather information and to weigh carefully all alternatives before making a decision. The teacher should remember that his or her opinion must not carry more weight or emphasis than student opinion. An effective strategy for starting the problem solving is called a "trigger story." The following are examples:

> You and your partner are involved in a tightly contested golf match with another twosome. Your partner hits his drive into the woods. While you are getting ready for your second shot, you turn and see your partner kick his ball out of the woods into an area where there is a clear shot to the green. His kick was not visible to either of your opponents. What would you do in this situation?

> You are playing a Pop Warner football team. During the game, you make an aggressive, yet legal tackle on your opponent's best running back. The running back receives a leg injury as a result and has to be carried off the field. Your teammates cheer and praise you for injuring the star player. Your coach also praises you when you come off the field. What should you do?

> At a bicycle motocross race, you hear the father of a 5-year-old criticizing his daughter for losing the championship race. The daughter is crying. You hear the father say to the mother: "She has to learn to compete. That's what life's all about." How do you react?

> You are coaching a 9th grade girls volleyball team. The game is close and everyone is excited. The mother of a member of your team is being obnox-

ious. She yells mean things at players on both teams, at the coaches, and at the officials. During a time out, the referee comes over and says, "Can't you do something about her?" What would you do?

> Your team is warming up when the referee walks in. Everybody recognizes him. He refereed your last game that you lost because he called a foul every time you moved. A member of your team loudly says, "Not him again!" What would you say?

> Right after the fourth game of the season, which your team just lost by 4 points, you are walking out of the locker room when you hear a parent say to a player on your team, "Boy, did you embarrass me tonight. You were terrible!" How would you react in this situation?

A problem-solving approach can be a useful teaching method in some physical skill areas, particularly when skills can be performed or developed in more than one way. Teachers can allow students to experiment briefly with these skills to determine which approach would be most effective for them. In many cases a skill can be adapted for certain situations. Some examples are the batting stance in baseball, golf grips and swing, putting grip and stroke, starts for sprints, high jumping technique, and training methods for distance running. A problem-solving style can also be used when developing routines for gymnastics including the many different ways to correctly perform on pieces of apparatus. Students can experiment with many ways to mount the equipment, to make various turns, to make various swings, to travel across the equipment, and to perform various dismounts. In team sports, students can figure out several offenses that will work against a particular defense and several defenses that will work against a specific offensive strategy. In basketball, a defender needs to experiment with options against a taller or quicker player. Students can also determine their options against opponents in various individual sports. In racquetball, there are several serves that will counter an opponent's strong forehand or extreme quickness. If a lob serve does not work, maybe a power serve, or a Z serve will be more effective.

Students could work on these skills in small groups and then report the findings to the class. The teacher can control the discussion and lead students to several acceptable solutions. In some cases, all solutions may not be acceptable, because they may be dangerous, illegal, or ineffective in certain situations.

The inquiry instruction model offers an interesting alternative for secondary school physical educators and should be used at certain times with certain activities.

REFERENCES AND SUGGESTED READINGS

Berliner, D. 1979. Tempus educare. In P. Peterson and H. Walberg (eds.) *Research on Teaching: Concepts, Findings, and Implications.* Berkeley, CA: McCutchan.

Claxton, D. 1981. A tennis contract for college students. Unpublished paper, Department of Physical Education, Grand Canyon College.

Cottman, G. 1976. *A Guide to Contract Teaching in Physical Education.* Westover, MD: Georganna S. Cottman.

Darst, P. 1976. Volleyball contracting—An effective tool for learning. *Arizona JOHPERD* 20(1): 14–16.

Darst, P., and Darst, C. 1978. Individualizing skin diving teaching and learning. *Foil Fall Issue*: 22–27.

Darst, P., and Model, R. 1983. Racquetball contracting—A way to structure your learning environment. *JOPERD* 54(7): 65–67.

Frymier, J. D., and Galloway, C. M. 1974. Individualized learning in a school for tomorrow. *Theory into Practice* 13(2): 65–70.

Harrison, J. M., and Blakemore, C. L. 1989. *Instructional Strategies for Secondary School Physical Education,* 2nd ed. Dubuque, IA: Wm. C. Brown.

McLeish, J. 1981. Effective teaching in physical education.

Victoria, B.C.: Department of Education, University of Victoria, mimeo.

Medley, D. 1977. *Teacher Competence and Teacher Effectiveness.* Washington, DC: American Association for Colleges of Teacher Education.

Mosston, M., and Ashworth, S. 1986. *Teaching Physical Education.* 3rd ed. Columbus, OH: Merrill Publishing.

Rink, J. E. 1985. *Teaching Physical Education for Learning.* St. Louis: Times Mirror/Mosby College Publishing.

Rosenshine, B. 1979. Content, time and direct instruction. In P. Peterson and H. Walberg (eds.) *Research on Teaching: Concepts, Findings, and Implications.* Berkeley, CA: McCutchan Publishers.

Rushall, B., and Siedentop, D. 1972. *The Development and Control of Behavior in Sport and Physical Education.* Philadelphia: Lea & Febiger.

Schueler, A. 1979. The inquiry model in physical education. *The Physical Educator* 36(2): 89–92.

Siedentop, D. 1983. *Developing Teaching Skills in Physical Education.* 2nd ed. Palo Alto, CA: Mayfield Publishing.

Zakrajsek, D., and Carnes, L. 1986. *Learning Experiences—An Approach to Teaching Physical Education.* Champaign, IL: Human Kinetics Publishers.

11

IMPROVING INSTRUCTION SYSTEMATICALLY

Few professionals question the need for trying to improve instructional effectiveness. Most young teachers want to be respected for their ability to impart knowledge and change behavior patterns of their students. University classes in teacher education strive to impart teaching skills to students. Those students who become effective instructors have one thing in common: They are motivated to improve and excel. It is not enough, however, to be motivated. Motivation without proper teaching skills leaves teachers in a predicament. They want to change and grow, but do not know what needs to be changed and learned. Therefore, a systematic approach for evaluating instruction is advocated so teachers can assess when they are improving or need to improve.

DEFINING EFFECTIVE INSTRUCTION

This is a broad and general term that can be defined many ways. Simply put, effective instruction probably is best measured by what students learn through their contact with a teacher. The goal of an instructor is to teach new skills, refine previously learned skills, change attitudes, and leave students with a positive feeling about what they have learned. If students do not learn, instruction has not occurred. Some teachers feel they are successful if they teach students all the key points of skill performance. If, in spite of the presentation of key points, students do not perform differently than they did prior to the skill analysis, instruction was ineffective.

A common saying in education is "students learn when teachers teach." This is probably true if teachers are effective in their teaching methods. On the other hand, learning is not guaranteed. Teaching effectively demands that positive changes in behavior occur. The changes may be attitudinal, skill oriented, or knowledge based. Regardless of the learning domain affected, learning occurs and teaching is effective only when observable changes result.

Think about it: If there are no noticeable changes in students, how can teachers say they have taught effectively? This leads us to the need for systematic evaluation of instruction. If teachers are going to be valued for their contributions to the lives of students, there must be observable and measurable results. Being accountable means being able to show change in student behavior.

IMPROVING TEACHING SKILLS

Teaching is learned just like any other skill. If you want to learn to play racquetball, you practice racquetball. Most people who have learned sport skills have followed the process of setting goals, diagnosing their problems, prescribing methods for improving, and evaluating their progress. This approach is needed to improve teaching skills as well. To learn to teach, you must practice teaching, diagnose your weaknesses, prescribe changes, and evaluate your progress. It is not enough to listen to professors, read books, and observe other teachers. Active participation in teaching is necessary.

The second part of improving teaching skills requires that teachers do more than teach. Many experienced teachers have taught the same thing for years without changing. They have not incorporated new skills and ideas into their teaching methods. This results in a teacher who is stagnant and unchanging. What would you think of athletes who never tried to change or use newly discovered techniques? Quite likely they would not remain competitive. This same problem occurs in the teaching profession and causes the public to believe that some teachers do not care about being effective.

Practice and improvement should go hand in hand. Teachers need to evaluate their performances so they know whether they are improving or becoming stagnant. Ask teachers you know whether they are better teachers this year as compared to last year. If they say yes, ask them to prove it. If they can't give you anything more than a belief that they are better, you have found teachers who have never utilized the process of systematic instructional improvement.

THE NEED FOR GOALS AND FEEDBACK

Teachers need goals aimed at improving their teaching effectiveness. However, establishing goals without evaluation is like driving down a highway without a map. How can you know when you have reached your goals if you do not establish some method of evaluation? Therefore goals and feedback need to be developed concurrently. For example, assume you want students to learn to set a volleyball more effectively. It will be necessary to have an objective way of evaluating whether they have improved. This is feedback: information gathered to modify future responses.

Feedback about teaching can be used to guide improvement in instructional methods. Assume you have a goal of improving your class's volleyball skills. For comparative purposes, you want to try teaching the volleyball set using a reciprocal teaching method for instruction. You allow half the students to teach a friend the set while you teach the other half of the class using a teacher-centered, direct style of instruction. After a week of practice, you evaluate the ability of the class to perform the volleyball set. Comparing the half of the class which used the reciprocal style versus the half which was taught using the direct style would generate feedback about the effectiveness of the teachers and the method. This offers feedback about the effectiveness of a teaching style and feedback related to the improvement of student performance on the volleyball set.

This example illustrates that a goal was set and data gathered related to goal accomplishment. This is the key to instructional improvement. Later in the chapter, systematic approaches for improving instruction will be offered. All the approaches involve setting goals and establishing a data base of information to see if they were accomplished. Learning to collect meaningful data about teaching is mandatory if teachers are going to seek improvement and be aware of progress.

THE NEED FOR SYSTEMATIC EVALUATION

Instruction has most often been evaluated using inexact and insensitive methods such as intuition, checklists, rating scales, and observation. Over the years, these methods have proved to be relatively ineffective in improving the quality of instruction. The use of an evaluator's intuition relies on the expertise of a supervisor, who observes the instructor and then recommends changes and reinforces specific practices. Supervisors who have the exact background as the teacher are, unfortunately, hard to find and often unable to follow up on their evaluations. Improvement is difficult to identify because the evaluation offers little or no quantification. It is quite possible that the supervisor will forget what the quality of the first lesson was compared with the present teaching episode. In this situation, evaluating whether or not improvement has occurred is next to impossible.

Checklists and rating scales are often used as evaluation tools and give the appearance of an objective, quantified method (Figures 11.1, 11.2, 11.3). The ratings are unfortunately unreliable and become more so when the number of choice points is increased. The scales and checklists are open to a wide spread of interpretation depending on who is performing the evaluation. Most of the evaluation done using checklists and rating scales is subject to the impressions and opinions of the evaluator rather than from objective data.

This indicates the need for a systematic method of observing teachers that quantifies the teaching effectiveness. Siedentop (1983) is a recognized leader in developing systematic methods for teacher evaluation and research. His techniques have led to much educational research in the area of pedagogy. The focus of this chapter is the use of methods that are systematic in nature and feasible for self-evaluation of instructional effectiveness.

Methods advocated here emphasize using systematic observation for self-improvement. If the reader chooses to conduct research projects and to study this area in-depth, the Siedentop text *Developing Teaching Skills in Physical Education* (1983) should be used as a primary resource. Another useful text for learning about observation instruments and evaluation techniques is *Analyzing Physical Education and Sport Instruction* (Darst et al., 1989). The authors strongly subscribe to the methods advocated in these texts, and this chapter will show how these methods can be easily applied and implemented in the typical school setting by physical education teachers.

EVALUATING EFFECTIVE TEACHING

What should be evaluated in the teaching process? Teachers need to know where to start the process of systematic evaluation. There are three major areas

Student _____ Activity _____ Grade _____

	5	4	3	2	1	Comments
1. Use of language						
2. Quality of voice						
3. Personal appearance						
4. Class management						
5. Presentation and teaching techniques						
6. Professional poise						
7. Enthusiasm, interest						
8. Adaptability, foresight						
9. Adequate activity						
10. Knowledge of subject						
11. Appropriate use of student help						
12. Demonstration (if any)						
13. Progression (if applicable)						
14. General organization						

General evaluation
    5–Superior
    4–Above average
    3–Average
    2–Below average
    1–Poor

Evaluating Teacher

_____

Date _____

FIGURE 11.1   Example of a rating scale

which can be observed and evaluated. The first is **teacher behavior**. This includes evaluation of areas such as teacher movement, giving instructions, the praise to criticism ratio, use of first names, and the length of instructional episodes. This area focuses on the performance of skills which are managed by the teacher. The responsibility for performing behaviors in this category rests solely with the teacher. Often, for beginning teachers, this is a good starting point because they can begin to improve their in-structional behavior rather than blame others for their problems. Unfortunately, performing adequately in the teacher behavior category does not assure learning, although it increases the probability.

The second category of observable behavior is **student behavior**. Examples of student behavior which could be analyzed are the rate of deviant behavior, the amount of time students stay on task, the number of students on task, and the number of practice trials students receive. These variables can

NAME: _____														
(Last) (First) (Middle)														
SUBJECT OR GRADE LEVEL: _____														

Type (X) in space that indicates your appraisal of the student teacher:	Superior	Above Average	Average	Below Average	Unsatis-factory	Not Known		Superior	Above Average	Average	Below Average	Unsatis-factory	Not Known
Appearance							Innovativeness						
Mental alertness							Communication skills						
Poise and personality							Lesson planning ability						
Enthusiasm							Rapport with students						
Health and energy							Classroom control skills						
Emotional stability							Student motivation skills						
Tact and judgment							Teaching skills						
Desire to improve							Provides for individuals						
Dependability							Understands students						
Professional attitude							Knowledge of subject						
Cooperation							Potential as a teacher						

ADDITIONAL COMMENTS:

(Give this completed and signed form to the student teacher)

Name _____   (Supervising Teacher)   Date _____

Name _____   (College Supervisor)   Date _____

FIGURE 11.2 Example of a rating scale

be evaluated through direct observation and link more closely to student learning than teacher behavior variables. Note that these behaviors are *process* oriented. Emphasis is placed on increasing or decreasing the occurrence of student behavior rather than measuring the actual performance of a skill.

The best indication of learning is the evaluation of **student skill performance**, fitness levels, knowledge levels, and attitudes toward physical education. Chapter 12 provides many ideas and examples for looking at these areas. This third category focuses on the *product* of learning. Little thought is given to *how* students learned: *if* they learned is the con-

---

EVALUATION FORM

Activity _____   Date _____

Student Teacher _____ Elementary _____ Secondary _____

College Supervisor _____ Cooperating Teacher _____

This evaluation of student teaching serves as a tangible basis for discussion among the cooperating teacher, the college supervisor, and the student. The following symbols will be used: Plus (+) indicates a positive feature of the student teacher's work; minus (−) indicates a need for improvement.

TEACHING COMPETENCIES

☐	Appearance	☐	Planning and organization
☐	Use of language	☐	Execution of lesson-teaching technique
☐	Voice	☐	Knowledge of subject
☐	Enthusiasm	☐	Demonstration of skills
☐	Poise	☐	Appropriate progression
☐	Creativeness	☐	Provisions for individual differences
		☐	Class management-control
		☐	Adaptability, foresight
		☐	Appropriate choice of activity

COMMENTS:

FIGURE 11.3 Example of a checklist

---

cern. On the surface, this seems to many teachers to be the only important evaluative area. Either students learn the skill or they don't. If they learn the skill, teachers have taught. However, things are not so simple. It may be that students have learned the skills but leave physical education with a negative attitude toward activity. What would be gained if students learned skills they never wanted to use again? What about unskilled students? Would they ever find any type of success in physical education classes?

The best evaluation system would probably include behavior from all three categories. It is important to look at one's teaching behavior. It is also necessary to evaluate how students behave in a class setting. If both teachers and students are demonstrating effective behavior patterns, the evaluation of skill performance will be appropriate. All three areas are interrelated and all three need to be evaluated regularly.

METHODS FOR SYSTEMATICALLY OBSERVING INSTRUCTION

Instruction can be systematically observed using a variety of methods to gather information. These instruments are easy to use. The major problem arises in defining the area to be evaluated and then making decisions about the data. Most importantly definitions should be written and then followed consistently if the data are to be meaningful. The methods require little more than pencil, paper, tape recorder, and stopwatch. A videotape recorder can add another dimension, but is not a necessity.

Event Recording

In simplest terms, event recording involves noting how many times an event occurs during a specified time period. Event recording identifies the frequency with which certain behavior occurs. It measures the quantity of events, not the quality. For example, the event recording might be defined as the number of times the teacher interacts with students, or the number of times a positive statement is made. A teacher might tally the number of practice attempts students receive after a skill has been introduced, or the number of times the class is asked to stop and come to attention. Event recording results are usually divided by the number of minutes in the evaluation session to give an event rate per minute. This enables the teacher to compare lessons that involve different content or teaching styles.

To lessen the time needed for analysis, use a sampling technique. For example, if the lesson is 30 min long, 4 bouts of recording, each lasting 2 min at evenly distributed points in the lesson, would reduce the burden of recording and would still yield representative results. Any observable behavior of teachers, students, or between teachers and students can be recorded when the behavior has been clearly defined.

Duration Recording

While event recording offers insight into the frequency of certain behavior, duration recording reveals how long the behavior takes in terms of minutes and seconds. Time is the measure used in this type of recording. As with event recording, duration recording does not have to be done for an entire lesson. Use representative sampling techniques so that 3 or 4 bouts of observation, 3 min per bout, can be used to generalize about the entire session.

These data are usually converted to percentages so comparisons can be made from lesson to lesson. This is done by dividing the entire observation time into the amount of time devoted to the specific observed behavior. For example, if 20 min of observation took place and if the student was observed to be in activity for 10 of the 20 min, the result would be 50%. This would be expressed as "50% of the total time was spent in activity." This approach is recommended for identifying the duration of certain behaviors, such as practice, managerial, or instructional behaviors.

Interval Recording

Interval recording is used to record behavior patterns for short periods of time. In interval recording, the intervals should be 6–12 sec, with one interval for observing and the other for recording. If a teacher used 6-sec intervals during a 1-min session, 5 intervals would be for observing and 5 for recording the results. According to Siedentop (1983), it is important to have at least 90 data points (observe-record = 1 point) to establish the validity of the

technique. It would be possible to generate 100 data points in 20 min using 6-sec intervals.

The data generated from this technique are usually converted to a percentage of the data points in which the behavior occurred. If, for example, the behavior occurred in 40 of 100 data points, the figure would be 40%. The percentages are then compared from lesson to lesson. A simple way to keep track of intervals is to wear a recorder headset that "beeps" every 6 sec. The observer can alternate observing and recording with each signal. This technique is reliable, particularly when the intervals are short, and can be used to record the amount of instructional time, managerial time, academic learning time, and other types of observable behavior.

Placheck Recording

Placheck (Planned Activity Check) recording is similar to interval recording in that behavior is observed at different intervals, but this technique is used to observe group behavior. At regular intervals during a lesson, the observer scans the group for 10 sec. The scan should begin at the left side of the instructional area and move to the right side, taking note of which students are not on task. The observer makes only 1 observation per student, and does not go back or change the decision, even if the student changes behavior during the 10-sec interval.

The technique is used to identify student effort, productive activity, and participation. It is usually best to record the less frequently occurring behavior to ease the burden of counting. For example, if the teacher is interested in identifying the percentage of students involved in the assigned activity, recording the number of students who are *not* participating might be easier. The intervals should last for 10 sec and should be spaced randomly throughout the lesson. There should be 8 to 10 observation intervals. Again, signals to observe can be recorded on a tape recorder at random intervals to cue the observer. This technique will yield information concerning the behavior of the group.

SYSTEMATIC OBSERVATION FOR SELF-IMPROVEMENT

Each teacher has different strengths and weaknesses and different concerns for improvement. The approach used for systematic observation directed at self-improvement may vary greatly from teacher to teacher. Instructors need to decide which variables they want to evaluate, and determine the best possible way to record and monitor the data.

Evaluating one area at a time is usually best at

the start. Trying to record more than one variable at a time may frustrate and confuse. It may also confound the picture by making it difficult for the teacher to decide how to change the teaching behavior in question.

After the teacher decides which behavior needs to be changed, a plan for meaningful evaluation must be developed. This means identifying the behavior that affects the desired educational outcome, and deciding which method of observation is most appropriate. At that point, a coding form must be developed to facilitate recording the data.

Coding sheets should be specific to each situation and suited to the teacher. Areas on the sheet should provide for recording the teacher, the date, the focus and content of the lesson, the grade level and competency of the students, the duration of the lesson, and a short description of the evaluation procedure. The sheets should be consistent for each type of behavior so the instructor can compare progress throughout the year.

Deciding what behavior will be recorded depends on the instructor's situation. For example, can the data be gathered by students who are not participating? Can another teacher easily gather the data? Can the data be gathered from an audio tape or is a video tape necessary? Is the instructor willing to let others gather the information, or does the teacher believe that it is important to keep the data confidential? These and other questions will determine what areas the teacher is able to evaluate. The authors find that in most cases the teacher is least threatened by self-evaluation techniques and is more willing to change when it is not required by outside authorities. Another advantage of self-evaluation is that teaching behavior changes least in the absence of outside observers. Self-evaluation techniques thus reveal the actual patterns exhibited in day-to-day teaching.

Many areas that can be evaluated are discussed later in this chapter along with coding forms. These are only examples which can be easily modified to meet the specific needs of the instructor. The important point is that teachers make self-evaluation an ongoing and integral part of the teaching process. Teachers should think continually about ways to improve. Teachers never stay the same; they either improve or slack off.

IMPROVING THE QUALITY OF INSTRUCTION

Quality instruction results when an effective teacher implements a well-planned lesson. Many successful teachers have learned how to do this over a period of years through the ineffective method of trial and error. Sheer experience does not, unfortunately, guarantee that one will grow into an outstanding teacher. Witness the fact that there are many experienced yet mediocre teachers. The key to improving teaching ability is experience coupled with meaningful feedback about the teacher's performance.

Teachers often have difficulty finding someone capable of offering evaluative feedback. Principals and curriculum supervisors may be too busy to evaluate teaching regularly, or they may not possess the skills necessary for systematically observing teaching behavior. This only accentuates the importance of learning to self-evaluate. Without regular and measurable means of evaluation, improving the quality of teaching becomes next to impossible. Teachers have long been told to talk less, move more, praise more, learn more names, and increase student practice time—primarily without documented methods of measurement. This section shows the many phases of teacher behavior that are observable and therefore measurable. The data can be gathered by the teacher, by teaching peers, or by selected students.

The authors' evaluation emphasis is on the do-it-yourself approach. Feedback that is gained in the privacy of one's office is easier to digest and less threatening. Teachers may set personal goals and chart their performance without others knowing. When teachers choose to evaluate their teaching procedures, they are usually willing to change. This attitude is often in contrast to the teacher's resistant attitude when principals or department heads impose external evaluation. Instructors rarely see a need for such evaluation, doubt the validity of the process, and thus refuse to change.

Instructional Time

An educational process requires that teachers instruct. The throw-out-the-ball approach is nothing more than leisure time activity in a school setting. Instructors should be aware of the amount of instruction they offer students. Instructional time refers to initial demonstrations, cues, and explanations to get students started on an activity. This time deals directly with physical education content. (See Chapter 7 for elements of instruction.)

It is important to find a meaningful balance between instruction and practice. An observer can tally the number of instructional episodes and the length of each episode occurring in a daily class. At a later time, the average length of instruction can then be evaluated, as well as the proportion of the lesson that was used for instruction. Instructional episodes should generally be short and frequent, with an attempt made to limit episodes to 45 sec or less.

How To Do It

1. Design a form for duration recording.
2. Have a colleague or a nonparticipating student turn on the stopwatch every time an instructional episode begins, and stop the watch when instruction ends. Record the episode on the form, clear the watch, and be ready to time the next instructional episode. An alternative method would be to record the lesson using an audio tape recorder, and then rerun the tape at the end of the day and time the instructional episodes. Be sure to establish a criterion for identifying the difference between instructional and management episodes. (For a description of management episodes, see Chapter 9.)
3. Total the amount of time spent on instruction.
4. Convert the amount of time to the percentage of lesson time devoted to instruction by dividing the length of the lesson into the time spent on

instruction. The average length of an instructional episode can be determined by dividing the total instructional time by the number of instructional episodes. Figure 11.4 is an example of a form that might be used.

Class Management Episodes

Effective teachers are efficient managers of students. Management time is when no instruction or practice is taking place. Management occurs when students are moved into various formations, when equipment is gathered or put away, and when directions are given about these areas. It also includes taking roll, keeping records, recording fitness scores, and changing clothes (see Chapter 9 for a description of management skills). Figure 11.5 is an example of a form that can be used to evaluate the amount of management time. This form involves duration recording using a stop watch.

INSTRUCTIONAL TIME

Teacher _Charlene Darst_   Observer _B. Pangrazi_

Class _1st period_ Grade _10_ Date and time _3/22 – 9:05_

Lesson focus _Golf_   Comments _1st class meeting of unit_

Starting time _9:15_ End time _10:00_ Length of lesson _45 min_

15	10	8	35	17	1:03	31	9	8
14	21	10	21	43	7	3:19	25	

Total instructional time _8 min 56 sec_

Percent of class time devoted to instruction _19 %_

Number of episodes _17_ Average length of episode _31.5 sec_

FIGURE 11.4 Sample form for instructional analysis

MANAGEMENT TIME

Teacher _Don Hicks_ Observer _Connie Pangrazi_

Class _5th period_ Grade _7_ Date and time _11/7 – 2:05_

Lesson focus _Frisbee_ Comments _____

Starting time _2:13_ End time _2:50_ Length of lesson _37 min_

55	10	21	1:15	19	18	55	33	16
43								

Total management time _5 min 45 sec_

Percent of class time devoted to management _15%_

Number of episodes _10_ Average length of episodes _34.5 sec_

FIGURE 11.5 Sample form for management time

Understanding the amount of time being used for class management, and the length and number of episodes, can be meaningful to teachers. The number of episodes and the length of each can be recorded by an observer. These data are useful for analyzing how much lesson time is devoted to the area of management. A high percentage of management time can indicate to instructors an inefficient organizational scheme or students' slow response to explanations.

How to Do It

1. Design a form that gathers the data desired (Figure 11.5).
2. Record the lesson with an audio tape recorder. Time the length of each management episode, and record each episode in a box on the form.
3. Total the amount of management time and divide it by the length of the period to compute the percent of management time during the lesson.
4. Total the number of episodes and divide this number into the amount of time devoted to management to find the average length of a management episode.

Response Latency

Response latency is the amount of time it takes a class to respond to commands or signals. Response latency may occur when instructions are given to begin practicing an activity or to stop an activity. An observer can thus evaluate the amount of time that elapses from the moment a command is given to start or stop an activity to the moment when the students actually begin or stop. The amount of time that elapses is the response latency and is wasted time. An accompanying criterion needs to be set for the percentage of students who are expected to be on task. It is not unreasonable to expect 100% of the students to respond to the command. If less than 100% of the class is expected to respond, a gradual loss of class control may occur. The average amount of response latency can be calculated, so the instructor can then set a goal for improving student behavior. A certain amount of response latency should be expected. Few groups of students stop or start immediately, and most instructors have a strong feeling about the amount of latency that they are willing to tolerate. After more than a 5-sec response latency, teachers usually become uneasy and expect the class to stop or start.

How to Do It

1. Develop a form for gathering the data (e.g., Figure 11.6).
2. Have a nonparticipating student or colleague time the response latency each time the class is asked to stop (start). The clock should run from the time the command to stop is given until the next command is given, or until the class is involved in productive behavior. For example, the teacher gives the command to stop the activity and return to squads (watch is started). The students stop the game and slowly return to squads. The teacher waits until all students are sitting quietly before giving the next direction (watch is stopped). Remember that starting and stopping response latency are two separate behaviors and should be recorded separately.
3. Identify the number of response latency episodes and divide this number into the total amount of time logged for response latency to calculate the average.

Practice Time (Time on Task)

For students to learn physical skills, they must be involved in meaningful physical activity. Physical education programs deal with a finite amount of scheduled time per week. Practice time, or time on task, has also been identified by some as ALT-PE (Metzler, 1979). This is an acronym for *Academic Learning Time-Physical Education*, and is defined as activity in which students are practicing skills in a setting that enables them to experience accomplishment. Instructors need to gather data about the amount of time students are involved in productive, on-task activity. In one well-regarded school district, the authors found that the average amount of activity time per 50-min period was only 9–12 min. One

might certainly question whether much learning could take place in this program.

To evaluate practice time, duration recording is most effective. A student or fellow teacher can observe a lesson and time the intervals when students are involved in practicing skills. The chart in Figure 11.7 is an example of the results of a duration recording for practice time.

The teacher's goal should be to increase the amount of time that students spend on skill practice. A teacher might therefore choose to increase the amount of practice time by using more equipment, selecting only drills that require a minimum of standing in line, or streamlining the amount of verbal instruction.

How to Do It

1. Design a form for collecting the data (Figure 11.8).
2. Have a nonparticipating student or colleague identify students who will be used for the evaluation. These are the students the evaluator will observe to see when they are involved in practice and for how long.
3. Turn on the stopwatch when the students are engaged in practice activity, and record the interval of practice.
4. Total the amount of time for student practice (in minutes) and divide it by the length of the lesson. This will compute the percent of practice time in a given lesson.

Student Performance

Some classes will have a greater percentage of students performing at optimum levels than others. Reasons for this will vary. A class may be poorly motivated, have difficulty understanding instructions, or be out of control. In any case, instructors should evaluate the percentage of students who are performing in a desired manner. This can be accomplished by using the placheck (Planned Activity Check) observation technique (Siedentop, 1983). The placheck can be used to identify a range of behavior. The instructor must determine the area of evaluation. Examples of areas that could be evaluated are students performing the stipulated activity, productive behavior, effort, and interest in the activity. Once the baseline data are gathered, teachers can begin to increase the percentage of students involved in the desired observable behavior.

How to Do It

1. Design a form for recording the desired data. Figure 11.9 is an example of a form that can be

RESPONSE LATENCY

Teacher _____Paul Darst_____ Observer _____Reid Wilcox_____

Class _____5th period_____ Grade ___9___ Date and time _2/5 – 12:45_

Lesson focus _Team Handball_ Comments _____

Starting time _12:50_ End time _1:33_ Length of lesson _43 min_

Starting Response Latency

3	12	17	5	5	11	18	9	7
11	3	5	6	14				

Stopping Response Latency

12	13	8	18	5	5	14	12	11
3	10	19	18	17				

Total amount of starting response latency _2 min 6 sec_

Percent of class time devoted to response latency _4 %_

Number of episodes _14_ Average length of episode _9 sec_

Total amount of stopping response latency _2 min 45 sec_

Percent of class time devoted to stopping response latency _6 %_

Number of episodes _14_ Average length of episode _11.8 sec_

FIGURE 11.6 Sample form for response latency

Teacher: Debbie Massoney School: Jason Junior High		
Parts of the lesson	Practicing	Inactive, off task, listening
Introductory activity	2.5 min	1.0 min
Fitness development	11.5 min	2.5 min
Lesson focus	15.0 min	7.5 min
Total	29.0 min	11.0 min

FIGURE 11.7   Results of duration recording for practice time

PRACTICE TIME

Teacher _Eugene Petersen_   Observer _P. W. Darst_

Class _2nd period_ Grade _8_ Date and time _11/15 — 9:15_

Lesson focus _Basketball_ Comments _week two_

Starting time _9:25_ End time _10:00_ Length of lesson _35 min_

35	10	2:04	25	29	1:39	17	55	34
43	1:55	1:01	33	10	10	18	1:17	4:50
24	39	31	34					

Total practice time _20 min 13 sec_

Percent of class time devoted to practice _57.8 %_

Number of episodes _22_ Average length of episodes _55.1 sec_

FIGURE 11.8   Sample form for collecting data on practice time

STUDENT PERFORMANCE

Teacher _Bob Pangrazi_ _____   Observer _Norma Pike_ _____

Class _2nd period_ _____ Grade _12_ _____ Date and time _1/26 — 9:20_ _____

Lesson focus _Weight Lifting_ _____ Comments _____

Starting time _9:28_ ___ End time _10:12_ _____ Length of lesson _44 min_ _____

Active/inactive

On task/off task

5	4	12	7	8	5
9	2	1	8		

Effort/noneffort

Number of Plachecks _10_ _____

Total number of students in class _33_ _____

Average number of students not on desired behavior _6.1_ _____

Percentage of students not on desired behavior _18%_ _____

FIGURE 11.9 Placheck observation of student performance

used for placheck observation. The example can be used to identify three different areas of student performance.

2. Place 8–10 audio signals (whistle) at random intervals on a tape recorder to signal when a placheck should be conducted.
3. Scan the area in a specified and consistent direction from left to right every time the tape-recorded signal sounds. The class is scanned for 7 to 10 sec while the number of students who are not engaged in the desired behavior is recorded.

4. Convert the data to a percentage by dividing the total number of students into the average number of unproductive students and multiplying the result by 100. Eight to ten plachecks spaced randomly throughout a class period will yield valid information about the conduct of the class.

Instructional Feedback

The type of feedback that teachers offer to students will strongly influence the instructional presentation.

It is possible for instructors to analyze their interaction patterns and to set meaningful goals for improvement. Both students and teachers often assume that teaching is an art and that one is born with the necessary qualities. Developing useful patterns of communication is therefore unnecessary. Nothing could be further from the truth. Developing successful communication skills is an uncomfortable process that all teachers must accept if they want to be effective. Few teachers enter the profession with the ability to communicate with warmth and clarity. The process of changing communication behaviors will create discomfort and concern but will ultimately pay rewarding dividends. Evaluation in the following areas can offer feedback for creating useful change.

Praise and Criticism

When students are involved in activity, teachers give a lot of feedback dealing with student performance. This feedback can be positive and constructive, or negative and critical. It is easy to ask a student or peer to record or tally the occurrences of praise and criticism. The occurrences can be tallied and evaluated at the end of the day. The teacher should calculate the number of instances and the ratio of positive to negative comments. Using these data, the instructor can then begin to set goals for increasing the number of comments per minute and modifying the ratio of positive to negative comments. A teacher can expect to average 1 to 2 comments per minute with a positive to negative ratio of 4:1.

General versus Specific

Feedback given to students can be specific or general. Comments like "Good job," "Way to go," and "Cut that out" are general in nature. General feedback can be either negative or positive; it does not specify the behavior being reinforced. In contrast, specific feedback could identify the student by name, mention the actual behavior being reinforced, and might be accompanied by a valuing statement. An example would be, "Michelle, that's the way to keep your head tucked! I really like that forward roll!"

To evaluate this instructional area, teachers can tally the number of general and specific feedback instances. Since both types of feedback can be negative or positive, this can also be counted. Using first names personalizes the feedback and directs it to the right individual. Total the number of times that first names are used. The number of valuing statements can also be monitored. Divide the totals in all of the categories by the length of the lesson (in minutes) to render a rate per minute. Figure 11.10 is an example of a form that can be used to tally the feedback behaviors described in this section.

Positive feedback should be specific whenever possible so that students know exactly what it was they did well. An instructor might say, "Your throw to second base was exactly where it should have been!" This type of feedback creates a positive feeling in a class and thus is important. Sometimes, however, teachers use this type of feedback to such an extent that it becomes a habitual form of communication (i.e., "good job, nice serve"). These comments do not identify the specific desirable behavior and may be ignored by students. It is also possible that an undesirable behavior may be reinforced when feedback is general.

Corrective Instructional Feedback

Effective teachers are usually excellent at coaching students to higher levels of performance. This involves giving performers meaningful corrective feedback. Corrective feedback focuses on improving the performance of the participant. Teachers should try to ignore poor performances if students are already aware of them.

Corrective instructional feedback is specific whenever possible, so performers know what it is they must correct. An example of corrective instructional feedback might be, "Your throw to second base was too far to the left of the base! Try to throw the ball directly over the base." This type of feedback tells the student what was incorrect about the skill attempt and how the skill should be performed.

Nonverbal Feedback

Much performance feedback can be given nonverbally. This is certainly meaningful to students and may be equal to or more effective than verbal forms of communication. Examples of nonverbal feedback that could occur after a desired performance are a pat on the back, a wink, a smile, a nod of the head, the thumbs up sign, and clapping the hands. Nonverbal feedback can also be negative: a frown, shaking the head in disapproval, walking away from a student, or laughing at a poor performance.

It is possible to tally the number of positive and negative nonverbal behaviors exhibited by a teacher. Either a student or another instructor can do the tallying. Students are often better at evaluating the instructor in this domain, because they are keenly aware of what each of the instructor's mannerisms means.

How to Do It

1. Design a form to collect the data. Figure 11.10 is an example of a form that can be used.
2. Audio tape a lesson for playback and evaluation at a later time.

INSTRUCTIONAL FEEDBACK

Teacher _____ Observer _____

Class _____ Grade _____ Date and Time _____

Lesson Focus_____Comments_____

Starting Time_____End Time_____Length of Lesson_____

Interactions unrelated to skill performance	+								
	−								
General instructional feedback	+								
	−								

Specific positive instructional feedback

Corrective instructional feedback

First names

Nonverbal feedback	+								
	−								

Ratio + to −/nonskill related _____

Ratio + to −/skill related _____

FIGURE 11.10 Sample form for tallying teaching behaviors

3. Record the data to be analyzed. It is usually best to take one category at a time when beginning. For example, analyze the use of first names during the first playback, and then play the tape again to evaluate corrective feedback.
4. Convert the data to a form that can be generalized from lesson to lesson (i.e., rate per minute, rate per lesson, or ratio of positive to negative interactions).

Active Supervision and Student Contact

When instructors are involved in the teaching process, they are in constant contact with students. Contact means that they are moving among and offering personalized feedback to the students. Count the number of times an instructor becomes personally involved with a student. This type of feedback differs from total class interaction and demands that the instructor have keen insight into each student's behavior and particular needs.

Related to this area is teacher movement and supervision. Instructors often have a particular area

in the gymnasium from which they feel comfortable teaching. Before instruction can begin, the teacher moves back to this area. The teacher's movement pattern causes students to drift to different areas, depending on their feeling about the activity or the instructor. Students who like the instructor will move closer, whereas students who dislike the teacher or are uneasy about the activity may move far away. This results in a configuration in which the good performers are always near the instructor and the students who may be somewhat deviant in performance are farther away and thus more difficult to observe.

These problems can be avoided if the instructor moves throughout the teaching area. Teacher movement can be evaluated by dividing the area into quadrants and tallying the number of times the instructor moves from section to section. A tally is made only if the teacher speaks to a student or to the class as a whole. Do not make a tally when the teacher merely passes through a quadrant. Evaluate the amount of time spent in each quadrant. Spend approximately the same amount of time in each area.

When students cannot predict where the teacher will be next, they have a greater tendency to remain on task.

The most accurate recording is of the amount of time a teacher stays in a quadrant. The length of time can be recorded on the form in relationship to where the teacher stands. At the end of the lesson, analyze the amount of time spent in each quadrant. Another technique is to code the type of teacher behavior that occurs each time the instructor moves into a new quadrant. For example, an "M" might signify management activity, an "I" instructional activity, and a "P" practice time. This tally reveals the amount of time the instructor spent in each area and also where the teacher moved to conduct different types of class activities.

How to Do It

1. Develop a coding form similar to the one in Figure 11.11.
2. Ask a nonparticipating student or a colleague to record the desired data on teacher movement. A better alternative is to videotape the lesson and evaluate it later.
3. Evaluate the data by calculating the number of moves per lesson and the number of moves during instruction, management, and practice.

COMBINATION SYSTEMS FOR OBSERVING TEACHERS AND STUDENTS

After practicing with these observation systems that focus primarily on one or two fairly simple teaching behaviors, you may want to try a more sophisticated combination system that focuses on multiple teaching or multiple student behaviors. Some of these systems include the simultaneous observation of teacher and student behaviors using the same system. Many instruments have been field-tested in junior and senior high school settings for research purposes. Use these only after successful use of the simpler, single behavior-type recording forms. The more sophisticated systems require more practice time in order to code data that are valid and reliable.

Flow of Teacher Organizational Patterns (FOTOP)

FOTOP is an instrument that describes the way that a teacher uses organizational patterns while teaching physical education (Johnson, 1989). This system fo-

cuses on the sequential behavior patterns of the teacher, not the student. It uses a 15-sec interval recording technique. The organizational behavior patterns of the teacher are divided into teaching and nonteaching categories. The 5 teaching categories include the following:

1. Cognitive Structuring—The teacher speaks directly to the entire class such as in lecturing, demonstrating, or asking questions. The students are passively standing or sitting while listening.
2. Mass Activity Instruction—The entire class is involved in activity that is controlled by the teacher. The teacher directs instruction toward the entire class such as drills, scrimmage or controlled game situations.
3. Small Group Instruction—The teacher is instructing a small group of two or more students but not the entire class as in station teaching or circuit training.
4. Individual Instruction—The teacher is working with one specific student.
5. Testing—Any formal evaluation procedure such as written tests or skill tests.

The five nonteaching categories involve the following:

1. Managerial Functions—Administrative duties such as taking attendance, passing out equipment, moving the class to various teaching areas, or giving management directions.
2. Supervision Functions—The teacher watches the class without giving any instruction. Students are playing or practicing on their skills.
3. Officiating—The teacher performs the role of an official or referee.
4. Participating—The teacher participates in the activity but not for instructional purposes.
5. Other—Any other behavior or function that does not fit into any other category.

The FOTOP recording sheet (Figure 11.12) has five 2-min intervals across the top of the form and the specific behavior categories down the left side. The observer enters the number 1 in the appropriate category slot after observing the first 15 sec. Then, the number 2 is entered after the next 15 sec and the number 3 after the next 15 sec and so forth until number 8 is entered after the last 15 sec of the 2-min interval. Each 2-min column will have numbers 1–8 entered. If more than one behavior pattern occurs during the 15-sec interval, the observer must decide which behavior dominated the interval.

After all five 2-min segments are recorded, the time can be converted to minutes and seconds for each category. Each number entered on the form

TEACHER MOVEMENT

Teacher _Danny Marcello_   Observer _Ellen Colleary_

Class _5th period_   Grade _9_   Date and time _3/17 — 1:05_

Lesson focus _Volleyball_   Comments _____

Starting time _1:15_   End time _2:01_   Length of lesson _46 min_

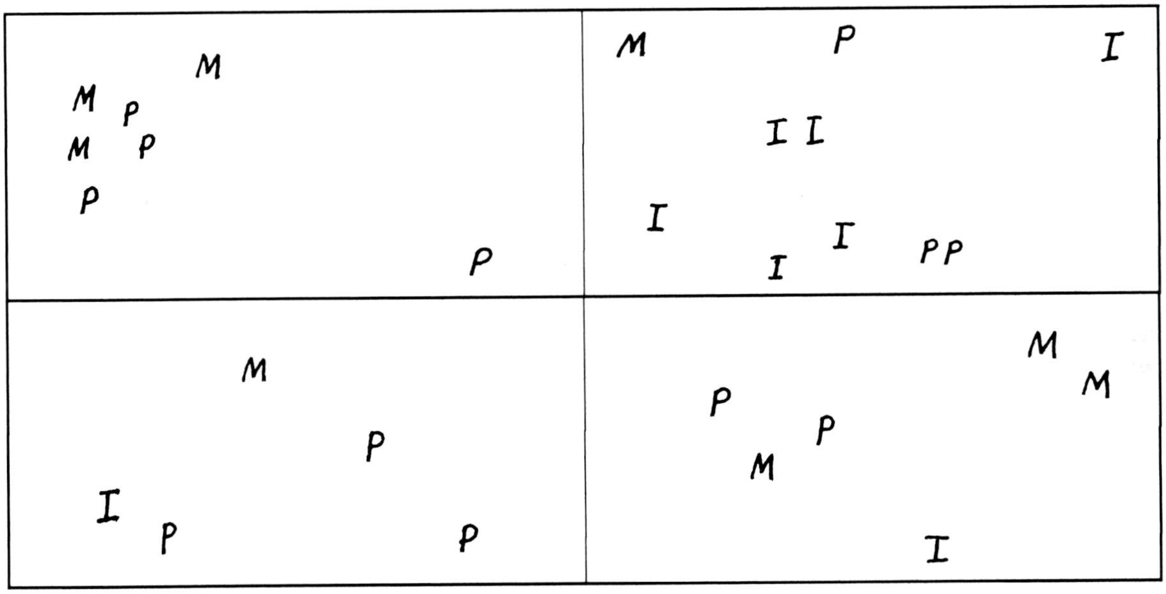

Total number of moves _28_

Number of moves (I) _8_   (M) _8_   (P) _12_

Average number of moves per min _.6_

FIGURE 11.11   Sample form for recording active supervision and student contact

represents 15 sec. This time can then be converted to a percentage of total observed time as shown in Figure 11.12. Using this data from the FOTOP instrument, teachers can make decisions and set goals for changing their behavior patterns.

Arizona State University Observation Instrument (ASUOI)

The ASUOI is an observation system that focuses on 14 categories of teacher behavior (Lacy and Darst, 1989). The system has been expanded and modified several times to create an instrument that is especially sensitive to the instruction category of be-

havior. The system can be used with event or interval recording. A computer software package has been developed for the system and is available from Pandau Media, Tempe, Arizona.

The teacher behaviors include the following:

1. Use of first name—Using a student's first name or nickname.
2. Preinstruction—Information that is given to students prior to participation such as explaining a skill, drill, or strategy.
3. Concurrent instruction—Specific instructional cues or prompts given during practice or playing time.

Instructor ___Instructor A___ Date ___10/14___

Observer ___Observer A___ Activity ___Volleyball___ Teaching station ___Gym 203___

Class beginning time ___10:00___ Ending time ___10:50___

Coding beginning time ___10:00___ Ending time ___10:10___

Teaching	2 min 1	2 min 2	2 min 3	2 min 4	2 min 5	Total time min:sec	% of total time
Cognitive structure	5, 6, 7, 8	1, 2, 3				1:45	17.5
Mass activity instruction		4, 5, 6, 7, 8				1:15	12.5
Group instruction							
Individual instruction				(5, 6)	1, 2	1:00	10
Testing							
Nonteaching							
Managerial functions	1, 2, 3, 4					1:00	10
Supervising				7, 8	3, 4	1:00	10
Officiating			1, 2, 3, 4, 5, 6, 7, 8	1, 2, 3, 4		3:00	.30
Participating					5, 6, 7, 8	1:00	10
Other							

Instructions: Record by placing Numbers 1-8 in the appropriate category and time module every 15 sec. To find percentage, convert time to seconds and divide by 600.

Comments: (Use back of sheet if necessary.)

FIGURE 11.12 Completed FOTOP recording sheet (from *Analyzing Physical Education and Sport Instruction* by P. Darst, D. Zakrajsek, and V. Mancini (Eds.), 1989. Champaign, IL: Human Kinetics. Copyright 1989 by P. Darst, D. Zakrajsek, and V. Mancini. Reprinted by permission of Human Kinetics).

4. Postinstruction—Information or feedback that is given to students after a skill attempt.

5. Questioning—Questions that are asked about skills, strategies, or assignments.

6. Physical assistance—Manually moving a student's arms or legs to get them into the proper position or to move through the proper range of motion.

7. Positive modeling—The teacher demonstrates the correct way to perform a skill.

8. Negative modeling—The teacher demonstrates the incorrect way to perform a skill.

9. Hustle—Teacher statements that are intended to intensify the efforts of the students.

10. Praise—Verbal or nonverbal compliments or statements of acceptance.

11. Scold—Teacher behaviors that express displeasure with the students. These can be verbal or nonverbal.

12. Management—Teacher behaviors that focus on organizational aspects of a class such as lining up, taking attendance, rotating from stations, et cetera.

13. Uncodeable—Behavior that does not fit into the remaining categories.

14. Silence—Used with interval recording, and focusing on periods of time where the teacher is monitoring without any verbal interactions.

The event recording procedure involves placing a tally within a behavior category as the behavior occurs. Figure 11.13 is an example of a completed

Arizona State University Observation Instrument (ASUOI)

Date _11-15_ Coach _Darst_ Sport _Basketball_ Observer _Lacy_

Categories	Time _____	Time _____	Total	RPM	Percentage
Use of first name	HH HH IIII	HH HH HH I	30	1.5	15.5
Preinstruction	HH	II	7	.35	3.6
Concurrent instruction	III	I	4	.2	2.1
Postinstruction	HH HH HH HH HH HH HH II	HH HH HH HH HH HH HH HH IIII	81	4.05	41.2
Questioning	IIII	II	6	.3	3.1
Physical assistance	II		2	.1	1.0
Positive modeling	III	IIII	7	.35	3.6
Negative modeling	II	I	3	.15	1.5
Hustle	HH HH	HH III	18	.9	9.3
Praise	IIII	HH I	10	.5	5.2
Scold	III	IIII	7	.35	3.6
Management	HH HH HH HH HH II	HH HH HH IIII	46	2.3	23.7
Uncodable	II	I	3	.15	1.5
Total	102	92	194	9.7	

Comments _Preseason Practice - 20 minutes total observation_

FIGURE 11.13 Completed ASUOI event recording sheet (from *Analyzing Physical Education and Sport Instruction* by P. Darst, D. Zakrajsek, and V. Mancini (Eds.). 1989. Champaign, IL: Human Kinetics. Copyright 1989 by P. Darst, D. Zakrajsek, and V. Mancini. Reprinted by permission of Human Kinetics).

event recording sheet for a basketball session. The behaviors can be totalled, a rate per minute established, and a specific percentage for each behavior calculated.

Figure 11.14 is an example of an interval recording sheet for ASUOI. A 5-sec interval can be used and the appropriate number assigned to the behavior can be entered in the block. If a student's first name is used with a behavior, then a 1 is entered with the number of the other behavior such as 1/10 to show a first name with a praise. The number of intervals for each behavior can be tallied and a percentage determined (see Figure 11.15).

Teachers can use the feedback from this instrument to analyze and set goals for their teaching behaviors in the various categories. Examples of behavior teachers may want to analyze include the use of the various instructional categories, praise to scold ratios, management procedures, or hustle behaviors.

Self-Assessment Feedback Instrument (SAFI)

SAFI was designed for use as a simple self-assessment system for teachers and coaches (Mancini and Wuest, 1989). It focuses primarily on how feedback is given during instruction. The categories developed are a modification of the Cheffers' Adaptation of Flanders' Interaction Analysis System (CAFIAS). SAFI gives teachers an event recording system that is easy

Arizona State University Observation Instrument (ASUOI)

12	14	14	7	4	13	4	14	10	1/12	4	3	14	5	14	5	14	14		
12	14	14	12	4	13	10	14	1/10	11	4	14	14	14	14	14	14	14		
12	14	14	12	6	12	14	14	14	9	6	14	14	14	14	4	11	14		
13	14	14	11	4	12	14	14	14	2	4	1/3	14	4	13	4	4			
12	14	1/3	1/3	7	12	1/10	14	14	2	5	4	14	4	14	10	4			
12	3	5	4	14	12	9	14	14	14	14	4	12	14	14	4	4			
1/5	4	14	6	14	2	9	14	14	14	14	5	12	14	14	14	14			
2	4	14	4	14	2	6	14	Rest	14	5	14	12	1/9	14	14	14			
2	14	4	4	14	2	7	14	1/10	14	14	14	12	14	1/2	14	10			
2	14	4	14	14	14	7	14	14	14	10	9	14	14	2	14	4			
7	14	4	14	14	14	3	1/3	14	14	14	4	1/4	14	14	14	4			
2	1/10	9	14	14	14	4	14	12	14	14	7	4	1/6	3	14	14			
7	9	7	14	14	1/11	4	14	12	1/4	14	14	8	4	14	1/10	14			
1/5	10	8	14	14	4	14	14	12	1/4	14	14	7	4	4	14	14			

Coach _Claxton_ Date _4-15_ Observer _Lacy_

School _Grand Canyon H.S._ Sport _Tennis (varsity boys)_

Comments _Record (10 min.) – Rest (2 min.) – Record (10 min.)_
Mid-Season – Day after match.

Behavior codes

1. Use of first name
2. Preinstruction
3. Concurrent instruction
4. Postinstruction
5. Questioning
6. Physical assistance
7. Positive modeling
8. Negative modeling
9. Hustle
10. Praise
11. Scold
12. Management
13. Uncodable
14. Silence

FIGURE 11.14 Completed ASUOI interval recording sheet (from *Analyzing Physical Education and Sport Instruction* by P. Darst, D. Zakrajsek, and V. Mancini (Eds.). 1989. Champaign, IL: Human Kinetics. Copyright 1989 by P. Darst, D. Zakrajsek, and V. Mancini. Reprinted by permission of Human Kinetics).

to learn for recognizing various sequences of teaching behavior. This system is best used with an audio tape or videotape of a class.

The system focuses on the following 11 behaviors:

1. **Praise**—Teacher praise or encouragement directed toward student efforts such as "Way to hustle, Seth."
2. **Praise/Reinstruct**—Teacher praise followed by useful information for future behavior such as "Good hit, try to extend your arms for more power."
3. **Acceptance**—Teacher accepts and builds on student ideas.
4. **Questions**—Teacher asks questions about skills, class materials and requires students to answer.
5. **Instruction during performance**—Teacher provides information while students are practicing skills, drill, or scrimmage. An example would be: "Don't forget to block out for rebounding."
6. **Directions**—Teacher gives directions for students to follow such as "Set up the figure 8 drill."
7. **Hustle**—Intense directions or orders that increase the enthusiasm or motivation of the students.
8. **Criticism**—Teacher expresses displeasure with students by using criticism, anger, or sarcasm. An example is "That's not good enough."
9. **Constructive criticism**—Teacher displeasure that is aimed at improving students' skills or behaviors. An example is "Almost, but it still is not quite correct."

Arizona State University Observation Instrument (ASUOI)

Categories	Number of intervals	Percentage of intervals
1. Use of first name	18	7.5
2. Preinstruction	11	4.6
3. Concurrent instruction	8	3.3
4. Postinstruction	34	14.2
5. Questioning	8	3.3
6. Physical assistance	4	1.7
7. Positive modeling	8	3.3
8. Negative modeling	2	0.8
9. Hustle	8	3.3
10. Praise	12	5.0
11. Scold	8	3.3
12. Management	19	7.9
13. Uncodable	4	1.7
14. Silence	114	47.5
Total	240	100

FIGURE 11.15 Completed ASUOI recording worksheet (from *Analyzing Physical Education and Sport Instruction* by P. Darst, D. Zakrajsek, and V. Mancini (Eds.). 1989.Champaign, IL: Human Kinetics. Copyright 1989 by P. Darst, D. Zakrajsek, and V. Mancini. Reprinted by permission of Human Kinetics).

10. **Criticism/Reinstruct** — Criticism that is followed by information for improvement. For example, "You dingbat, keep your weight back or you will never have any power."
11. **Constructive criticism/Reinstruct** — Constructive criticism with additional information. "Almost correct, but you still need to shorten the length of your stride another 3–5 in."

As the observer watches the videotape, a tally is made in the proper behavior category during the 10-min segment that is under observation (see Figure 11.16). The tallies are totalled and converted to a percentage of the total and a rate per minute. These data provide the teacher or coach with objective information about the type and frequency of feedback provided to the students. After a teacher establishes a normal pattern of behavior, decisions for changes and specific goals can be established for future lessons. Goals are usually expressed as target percentages or rates per minute.

REFERENCES AND SUGGESTED READINGS

Darst, P. W., Zakrajsek, D. B., and Mancini, V. H. (eds.). 1989. *Analyzing Physical Education and Sport Instruction*. 2nd ed. Champaign, IL: Human Kinetics.

Johnson, T. W. H. 1989. Flow of Teacher Organizational Patterns (FOTOP). In P. W. Darst, D. B. Zakrajsek, and V. H. Mancini (eds.) *Analyzing Physical Education and Sport Instruction* (pp. 173–177). Champaign, IL: Human Kinetics.

Self-Assessment Feedback Instrument (SAFI)

Directions: Classes or practices are divided into 10-minute segments for ease of observation.
During each 10-minute segment, place a tally next to the appropriate behavior category each time this
behavior occurs. The use of various behaviors may be calculated in terms of percentage of total behaviors or
as rate per minute.

Name_____ Date_____

Class/practice no._____ Length_____

Category	0-10	11-20	21-30	31-40	41-50	Total	Percent or Rate
Praise (2)							
Praise/reinstruct (2-5)							
Acceptance (3)							
Questions (4)							
Instruction during performance (8-5, 8\-5 or 9-5)							
Gives directions (6)							
Hustle behavior (6H)							
Criticism (7)							
Constructive criticism (7-2)							
Criticism/reinstruct (7-5)							
Constructive criticism/ reinstruct (7-2-5)							
Other behavior of interest							
Total							

FIGURE 11.16   SAFI recording sheet (from *Analyzing Physical Education and Sport Instruction* by P. Darst, D. Zakrajsek, and V. Mancini (Eds.), 1989. Champaign, IL: Human Kinetics. Copyright 1989 by P. Darst, D. Zakrajsek, and V. Mancini. Reprinted by permission of Human Kinetics).

Lacy, A., and Darst, P. 1989. The Arizona State University Observation Instrument (ASUOI). In P. W. Darst, D. B. Zakrajsek, and V. H. Mancini (eds.) *Analyzing Physical Education and Sport Instruction* (pp. 369–377). Champaign,IL: Human Kinetics.

Mancini, V., and Wuest, D. 1989. Self-Assessment Feedback Instrument (SAFI). In P. W. Darst, D. B. Zakrajsek, and V. H. Mancini (eds.) *Analyzing Physical Educa-tion and Sport Instruction* (pp. 143–147). Champaign, IL: Human Kinetics.

Metzler, M. 1979. The measurement of academic learning time in physical education. Doctoral dissertation, The Ohio State University.

Siedentop, D. 1983. *Developing Teaching Skills in Physical Education.* 2nd ed. Palo Alto, CA: Mayfield Publishing Co.

12

STUDENT EVALUATION AND GRADING

Evaluation needs to be twofold. The first concern is to evaluate students in order to give them an indication of what and how well they are learning. The second is evaluation of the program and its objectives. This is most commonly done by evaluating students, looking at group statistics, and then determining whether objectives such as fitness and skill development have been accomplished. Regardless of how evaluation is managed, the emphasis on accountability has continued to place more importance on this area. No longer are school boards willing to support a program that does not document its impact on students. Similarly, students are much less willing to accept a grade in physical education if it is not grounded on principles similar to those in academic areas.

It is sometimes difficult to determine why evaluation takes place. For example, when fitness testing is conducted, is it for the purpose of assigning grades to students, reporting their personal progress, or evaluating the fitness component of the program? Evaluation of students can in fact serve many different purposes, all of which are important. This means that the instructor should consider carefully what results are desired before beginning evaluation. Since evaluation results can be used for more than one purpose, no attempt is made here to separate grading and program evaluation. The instructor's task is to determine how the results will be applied.

EVALUATION—DIFFERENT VIEWPOINTS

There are many different ideas as to the best way to evaluate students. This section examines the different approaches, offers insight into each, and leaves readers with the responsibility of selecting the approach that works best for their needs.

Educational Objectives versus Administrative Tasks

Most physical educators generally agree that physical education should help students achieve in four areas: skill development, physical fitness, personal values, and cognitive development. Some grading systems attempt to assign weight to each of the areas when compiling a grade. Regardless of the amount of emphasis given to each area, the final grade depends on accomplishment in each area. This contrasts with grading of administrative tasks through which students earn a part or all of their grade by showering, attendance, participation, promptness, and wearing the proper uniform. This approach allows students to earn a grade that has little to do with accomplishment and progress toward the objectives of physical education.

A problem occurs when students receive a grade that is earned in a manner completely different from the rest of the school curriculum areas. For example, if a student misses some classes in math, forgets to bring a pencil, and is tardy, teachers may be concerned and ask parents and a school administrator to help rectify the problem. The teacher would seldom think of flunking the student, however, if all tests were passed with an A grade. In other words, the student has earned a grade based on the accomplishment of educational goals. The reverse situation is important to examine. If a student fails all examinations in math, a grade of F in the course would undoubtedly be the result, even if the student had attended every day, was never tardy, and carried out other administrative tasks demanded by the teacher. If grades in other curricular areas of the school are earned through accomplishment of educational objectives, it is probably wise to follow suit in the physical education area.

Administrative tasks are usually enforced through school or district-wide regulations. For example, most districts have procedures for dealing with excessive absences or tardiness. The teacher need not further penalize a student through a grade reduction. Sometimes students are graded on participation, which is similar to receiving a grade just because one is physically present in class. On the other hand, students should be able to choose not to participate in class only when they are excused by the administration or by the school nurse (i.e., for sickness or injury). Participation alone should not be used as a factor in assigning grades. Rather, all students should be expected to participate unless excused by administrative edict.

If a student does not attend class, it is certainly defensible to ask the student to repeat the class. This is usually done by assigning a failing grade. Because instructors would do this in other academic areas, excessive absences are an acceptable criterion for failing the student. The point here is that the grading system in physical education should be in line with the grading system in other subject-matter areas. When physical educators choose to grade otherwise, the grade soon becomes meaningless to other teachers and students. In some school districts, the physical education grade is no longer calculated in the overall grade point average, or it does not figure in graduation requirements. When this occurs, it becomes easy to say that physical education should no longer be required of all students since the grade is meaningless. The bottom line is to grade in a manner that is compatible with other subject-matter areas.

Process versus Product

Another area of concern when evaluating is whether the process or the product of education is more important. Those who emphasize the process of education stress the importance of students leaving school with warm and positive feelings toward physical education. They state their beliefs in the following manner: "I am not concerned about how many skills my students learn, I just want them to walk out of my class with positive feelings about physical education." The assumption is that students who feel positive about physical education will be willing to participate physically throughout their lifetime. These teachers assign grades based on how hard a student tries (effort), and are willing to give a higher grade to a less skilled performer who tries hard than to a skilled performer who exhibits low effort.

The people who reside in the product camp focus only on student accomplishment and see effort as something that is laudable, but not a part of the grade. They often state their philosophy as follows: "I don't really care whether students like me or physical education. What is ultimately important is their performance. After all, the students who are best in math earn the highest grades, so why should it be any different in physical education?" This usually means that the teacher will give the highest grade to the best performer, regardless of other factors. It also means that some students, no matter how hard they try, will never receive an above-average grade.

This is a difficult problem to resolve and is always hotly debated. One point is that students should learn how society works from the grading system. People are not rewarded in life based on how hard they try, but rather, on their performance. For example, if real estate agents try hard but never sell a house, they will not make any money. The payoff is for selling houses, not for trying hard to sell houses.

Another problem lies in the area of developing competency in various physical skills. Research shows (AAHPERD, 1954) that 78% of all hobby interests are established before the age of 12. Interests are established based on competency in different areas. A relatively low percentage of adults select new hobbies in areas in which they feel incompetent. If this is the case, then school physical education programs are going to have to graduate students whose skill competencies allow them to feel comfortable in public view. This is a strong point in favor of developing a grading system that focuses on skill development and performance.

The best solution is to develop a grading system that rewards performance and to present the program in a positive manner. Much is to be said for developing a positive attitude in one's students toward activity, and attitude development usually depends largely on how the teacher presents the material rather than on the grade received. Instructors should help students understand that they perform differently from each other in math or science and receive a respectively higher or lower grade. Physical education is similar to academic subject areas in that those who perform best will be entitled to the highest grade. The bottom line is that society rewards performance rather than effort, and the grading system should be a prelude to adjusting to societal demands.

Relative Improvement

Many physical educators believe that effort, or "just doing the best that you can," is the most important factor in assigning grades. In an attempt to reward effort, they then base student grades on the amount a student improves. This usually involves pretesting and posttesting to determine the amount of progress made throughout the grading period. This approach contrasts sharply with basing the grade on absolute performance, and may mean that the best performer in the class does not receive the highest grade because of lack of improvement.

Grading on improvement is time-consuming and requires that the same test be given at the beginning and end of the semester or unit. The test may or may not be a valid reflection of what should be learned in the class, and may not be sensitive enough to reflect improvement made by both poor and outstanding performers. Testing at the beginning of a unit can also be discouraging and demoralizing if a student performs poorly in front of peers. It can also be hazardous in some activities, such as gymnastics or archery, which require intensive instruction to prevent accident or injury.

Another problem that becomes apparent is the issue of performing for a grade. Students learn quickly that if they perform too well on the pretest, they will be penalized at posttest time. It is thus important to perform at a low level in order to demonstrate a higher degree of improvement on the posttest. A related problem is that improvement is sometimes easier at lower levels of skill than at high levels of performance. Most teachers are aware of the rapid improvement beginners make before reaching a learning plateau. A skilled performer may be at a level where improvement is difficult to measure. In this case, the skilled performer receives a lower grade than the poor performer.

Finally, grading on improvement is not compatible with society or with other subject areas in the school setting. Society does not pay people for improvement, but rather for performance. Teachers in other academic areas do not give a higher grade to the student who has improved the most, regardless of where he or she started. The bottom line is that grading on improvement is difficult and time consuming, and results in a system that may at times reward lack of effort and low ability.

Grading on Potential

Some teachers choose to grade on potential rather than on the present state of performance. In other words, a grade may be boosted by a teacher who believes the student is a good athlete who can perform all of the skills. This policy is unfortunately a double-edged sword and may result in students being penalized for not having ability or for lacking potential.

The approach depends on the teacher's feelings about the student in question. It is based on intangibles, and may result in a grade being assigned because the student is "just like her brothers." When grades are based on the teacher's subjective beliefs rather than on criteria that can be measured and evaluated, the grades become difficult to defend. The bottom line is that a grading system should be based on tangible data that can be recorded from observable behavior and performance.

Negative versus Positive Grading Systems

In an attempt to make the grading system defensible and concrete, many teachers have started using point systems. In most point systems, both performance objectives and administrative factors are listed as grade components. A student may be able to earn a grade through performance, attitude, and knowledge. Unfortunately, point systems can become a negative influence when handled incorrectly. For example, some teachers give all students 100 points at the start of the semester and then "chip off" points for various unsatisfactory levels of performance. A student may lose points for not trying, not performing, or not knowing answers on a test. Students soon realize that energy should be spent on avoiding any behavior that loses points.

This contrasts with a system that rewards positive behavior. When the student performs well, points are assigned and the student can earn the grade desired through self-direction. In a negative system, the teacher makes all the judgments about points lost and receives in turn the negative feelings of the student. When positive behavior is rewarded, students feel as if the teacher cares about their welfare and growth.

Sometimes when a negative system is used, the teacher begins to focus on what students cannot do, rather than on what they can do. Energy is spent on "policing" students and threatening to take away points if they do not behave. Most students do not respond well to this approach, since a loss of points does not require an immediate change in behavior and a redirection. Note also that the loss of points will result in a reduction of the final grade, a consequence that may be 6–9 wk away. Few students will respond positively to grade leverage of this type. In fact, the only students who usually care about their grades are those performing well in the first place. Threatening to lower the grade of a student who does not like physical education or school in general only further alienates the student and is based on an ineffective system of negative reinforcement. Ultimately, the grading system should be a positive situation, which encourages students to perform.

Pass–Fail versus Letter Grades

Another approach to grading concerns the issue of whether letter grades should be assigned to students or whether the course should be offered on a pass-fail basis. Pass-fail has become more common today because of the push to avoid having physical education grades count in the academic grade point average. This approach prevents students from receiving a low grade in physical education while earning high grades in subject matter areas. Problems are unfortunately inherent in this approach.

With a pass-fail grading system, there is no method for rewarding the outstanding performer. The student who earns a grade of C or D receives the same final grade as the top performer in the class. This approach thus reinforces making a minimal effort to accomplish goals, because differing levels of performance are not rewarded. The pass-fail system also does little to show students that they have improved. For example, if a student is performing at the C level and then earns a B by the end of the next quarter, the pass grade reflects no change in performance. Grading systems should reward improved standards of performance.

Some teachers endorse pass-fail grading because it eases the burden of evaluation. They no longer have to worry about bookkeeping chores, because the grade is only grossly indicative of student progress. Recording anything more than the minimum performance required for passing the class becomes meaningless. Some teachers therefore support this grading system because of ease of implementation.

When the grading system in physical education differs from those in other subject matter areas, defending the program in the school setting becomes difficult. If physical education does not require grading integrity, the subject probably should not be counted in the grade point average. The problem lies in the final outcome. If the physical education department chooses to operate autonomously from the rest of the school system, it then becomes vulnerable to nonsupport and abandonment. Physical education should be considered an integral part of the school system and should be graded in a manner consistent with other subject matter areas.

METHODS OF GRADING

There are many approaches to grading in junior and senior high schools. Realistically, none of the schemes solves all problems or results in an ideal reporting system. Grading methods are chosen because of the school philosophy, the teacher philosophy, and the desires of parents. For example, if parents are unhappy with the grading system, they will complain to the school administration. If these dissatisfactions are expressed regularly and by a relatively large number of parents, the superintendent may take the matter under advisement. This results in scrutiny of the overall program, the objectives of the program,

the philosophy of the teachers, and the feelings of students. An instructor cannot, therefore, take a teaching position and begin a grading program without first considering the school district policies and the desires of fellow teachers.

All grading systems have strengths and weaknesses. These need to be weighed in terms of how closely the system meets the needs of students and the concerns of parents, as well as the goals of the teachers. A number of evaluation approaches will be offered in this section, and some may be better suited than others to the reader's situation. Remember, however, that all of these approaches have worked at one time or another because of various school parameters.

Subjective Observation Systems

Many teachers have used observation systems at different times. Much evaluation takes place by observing students and making a subjective judgment about their performance. One of the drawbacks of the observation system is that it is not completely reliable; two different teachers may differ dramatically in their assessment of the same student. On the other hand, observation can be done with a minimum of effort, requires little time, and gives students immediate feedback.

The observation system can be improved by using a check sheet or scorecard. Criteria are listed and can be ranked on a scale of points. Even though using the check sheet will increase the reliability of the data, the overall approach is still basically subjective.

A score sheet like the one in Figure 12.1 can be used to evaluate what a teacher may believe is student attitude. This type of score sheet can also be used to evaluate skill development. For example, teachers select the types of skills they believe a student should learn in a basketball unit. While the unit is underway, the teacher observes individual students and assigns a score. Grades can then be awarded on the basis of various areas evaluated, with students who accumulate the most points receiving the highest grade.

Personal Interviews

The interview system can be used to monitor students. In this approach, the teacher questions individual students about their knowledge, as well as monitoring their skill levels. The strength of the approach lies in the relationship that the teacher develops with students. The personal interview can make students feel wanted and cared for, since few students have the opportunity to share with an instructor how much they have learned in a class. The weaknesses of the approach are in the areas of time

ATTITUDE CHECK SHEET

Assign 0 to 5 points during each observation with 5 being the highest score. A number of observations should be made during the semester in order to reveal consistency and improvement.

Student _____ Date _____ Lesson Focus _____

	0	1	2	3	4	5
1. Tries all activities	0	1	2	3	4	5
2. Is on time	0	1	2	3	4	5
3. Consistently gives a maximum effort	0	1	2	3	4	5
4. Shows concern for others	0	1	2	3	4	5
5. Listens to and applies criticism	0	1	2	3	4	5
6. Shows enthusiasm	0	1	2	3	4	5
7. Participates with all students	0	1	2	3	4	5
8. Shares ideas with teacher and class	0	1	2	3	4	5
9. Demonstrates leadership	0	1	2	3	4	5
10. Volunteers to help others	0	1	2	3	4	5

FIGURE 12.1   Student attitude check sheet

and objectivity. For example, a teacher who comes in contact with a large number of students would find it impossible to talk individually with each one. The approach is also highly subjective and may result in a grade being assigned on the quality of the interview rather than on the knowledge and performance of the student. The interview system can be made somewhat more objective if checklists of questions and skill evaluations are developed and followed with each student.

Even if this approach cannot be used on a broad scale, interviewing can be a useful tool for evaluating the effectiveness of the program and the instruction. Teachers can select key students to interview to see how well they are learning, how they feel about the instructional approach, and what they might like to have added to the program. Seldom do teachers sit down and discuss the wants and concerns of students. This approach can enhance an important phase of instruction.

Self-Evaluation

If one of the important phases of evaluation is to teach students how to assess their performances,

then a self-evaluation scheme can be a useful component of a grading system. Some teachers believe that grading students destroys their respect for the teacher, and undermines their belief that the teacher is concerned about them.

The most common approach is to teach students to set goals, to develop strategies for reaching the goals, and to evaluate their performance. When student self-evaluation is used, the instructional approach is closely related to evaluation technique. This is because of the amount of time required to teach students to set meaningful goals and strategies and to apply evaluation techniques. In most cases, teachers who use this approach also evaluate the students. The final grade is then a composite of student and teacher evaluation.

Another variation of the self-evaluation approach is to allow the class to develop goals that they want to achieve. The class decides democratically what they wish to accomplish, and the teacher then decides how best to accomplish the goals. At the end of the instructional session, both students and teacher evaluate the progress made and the final grade.

Some teachers like to add a third phase to the

evaluation process by having students evaluate students. This results in a three-pronged evaluation scheme: teacher, student, and self-evaluation. One of the strongest reasons given for using this approach is that it makes students feel more involved in the educational process. Students are more likely to believe that the grading system is fair when it manifests itself through teacher, peer, and self-evaluation.

For these systems to function smoothly and effectively, goals and objectives must be written in outline form. Students need a checklist of activities couched in behavioral terms. This helps to rule out personality conflicts and maintains skill accomplishment as the primary focus. Teachers will sometimes find a large discrepancy between their assigned grades and the students'. This may reveal a personality conflict between student and teacher. A useful idea for checking the reliability of the grades is to calculate the correlation between the three sets of scores. The three groups will be closely related if adequate guidelines were developed for conducting the evaluations.

Contract Grading

Contract grading is a student-paced grading approach that allows students to progress at differing rates. All students can achieve well using this approach, because emphasis is placed on mastery rather than time. For example, gifted students may progress faster than less skilled students. The less skilled can, however, practice at home, receive extra help, and ultimately achieve the same level of accomplishment.

Contract grading specifies the performance and criteria that a student has to accomplish to earn a specific grade. The performance objectives are written in approximate order of difficulty with both the quantity and quality of the performance spelled out. It then becomes easy for students to assess their performances and to determine what is necessary to earn their desired grade.

This approach eliminates a lot of subjective evaluation, and also reduces student concern about grades, since students follow their own progress and are keenly aware of how well they are doing. Another plus is that students can choose different methods of learning necessary skills. Each of the objectives is graded as no credit or pass. A student is either capable of accomplishing the performance objective or must continue to practice, without penalty, until it is learned. Some teachers do not allow students to proceed to a new objective until the previous one has been reached. In theory, this seems to be a sound approach since each objective is supposed to be based on skills learned prior to the present objective. In practice, however, the approach is usually unwise. Experience has shown that students who cannot perform some objectives will be able to easily accomplish others that follow later in the sequence. This occurs because it is impossible to determine exactly how an individual learner will progress, and because an exact science of sequencing skill development is presently unavailable.

A difficulty in using contract grading is writing performance objectives that are neither too easy nor too difficult to accomplish. For example, if students cannot accomplish the objectives, they will become discouraged and view the process as unfair. On the other hand, if the objectives are too easy, students will not be challenged to learn new skills and may become bored. Initially, the units have to be written based on the experience of the teacher and then modified from year to year to find the correct level of difficulty.

Another possible problem is that of evaluation and determining which students have mastered the objectives. For example, if a teacher has a class of 30 or more students, evaluation can become a full-time task. If instructors are determined to be the sole evaluator, they will have little time to instruct. A compromise is usually a reasonable solution. Students can evaluate themselves or have a peer evaluate them for the duration of the unit, then 2 or 3 days at the end of the unit can be designated for instructor evaluation. Since all of the skills cannot be evaluated by the teacher in this amount of time, randomly selected performance objectives can be tested to check the reliability of the peer and self-evaluation process.

Figure 12.2 is an example of performance objectives that can be used for a 3-wk unit on lacrosse. Twenty points are possible. A checklist (Figure 12.3), with the objectives listed across the top of the paper and student names down the side, can be used to record student accomplishment as they pass the various objectives.

For the sake of discussion, students could then earn their grades by accumulating points. Assume that three 3-wk units are taught during a quarter grading period. A total of 60 points would be possible (20 per unit), and the following scale could be used to assign grades:

- A = 55 or more points
- B = 50–54 points
- C = 45–49 points
- D = 40–44 points

When students know exactly what they must accomplish in a class and how their grade is determined, they bear more of the responsibility for learning. This can result in an increase in motivation.

LACROSSE

Core Objectives (1 point each)

1. With a crosse, throw an overhand shot 4 of 8 times through a target from a distance of 10 yd.
2. Throw an underhand shot 4 of 8 times through a target from a distance of 10 yd.
3. Throw a sidearm shot 4 of 8 times through a target from a distance of 10 yd.
4. Using any throw technique mentioned above, throw the ball through a target 3 of 5 times from a distance of 10 yd.
5. With a partner, catch the ball with an overhand catch 3 of 5 times from a distance of 10–15 yd.
6. Catch the ball with an underhand catch 3 of 5 times from a distance of 10–15 yd.
7. Catch the ball with the backhand catch and reverse pivot 3 of 5 times from a distance of 10 yd.
8. With a partner rolling the ball from a distance of 10 yd, use the side retrieve technique 5 of 10 times.
9. Using the cover retrieve technique, scoop a "dead" ball up 5 of 10 times.
10. Defend 4 of 8 shots taken by a partner from a distance of 10 yd.

Optional Objectives (2 points each)

1. With a partner passing the ball from a distance of 20 yd, use a running side retrieve technique 5 of 10 times.
2. Using the cover retrieve technique, scoop up a "dead" ball 5 of 10 times.
3. With a crosse, throw an overhand shot 4 of 5 times through a target from a distance of 15 yd.
4. Throw an underhand shot 4 of 5 times through a target from a distance of 15 yd.
5. Score 1 of 3 shots past a goalie from a distance of 10–15 yd.

FIGURE 12.2   Lacrosse contract

Name	Core Objectives										Optional Objectives				
	1	2	3	4	5	6	7	8	9	10	1	2	3	4	5

PERFORMANCE OBJECTIVE MONITORING FORM

FIGURE 12.3   Performance objective monitoring form

Global Grading

For want of a better title, global grading is defined as assigning points or percentages for the different domains of learning. As discussed previously, this is a common approach that has been used often and is criticized frequently. The approach attempts to assign a grade to categories such as attitude, physical skill development, physical fitness, and knowledge. The areas are weighted, depending on the desires of the individual teacher. Figure 12.4 summarizes a global grading plan.

It becomes apparent that teachers using this system are making many subjective judgments. The weakness of the approach lies in the fact that a student with high skill may receive a failing grade, whereas a low-skilled student can receive an above-average grade. With this approach, students have difficulty determining how they are being graded and when they are making progress. Since the teacher makes many subjective judgments about attitude and skill application, it is possible for students to feel that the situation is out of their control.

Some teachers view the opportunity to reward students for effort and participation as a strength of this approach. As discussed earlier, many teachers believe that attending and trying are reason enough to earn a grade.

The grading system is thus a reflection of the instructor's philosophy and must be chosen carefully. Teachers should not allow the students' fear of a grade reduction to be the reason for including attitude and administrative elements in the grading scheme. The instructor is responsible to motivate students to perform administrative tasks and to participate. It is a questionable practice, at best, to assume that students will perform because of the threat of receiving a lowered grade, which will not be reported in some cases for weeks.

EVALUATING THE COMPONENTS OF PHYSICAL EDUCATION

The method of grading to be used influences the choice of areas to be evaluated. For example, if fitness is considered an important component of physical education, then the teacher is likely to choose to evaluate this area. The evaluation will demonstrate the students' progress and indicate whether the program is accomplishing fitness goals as desired. Evaluation is an important phase of the instructional process. Teachers must be watchful, however, of the amount of time spent on this area. It is easy to use 4–6 wk of the school year for evaluation if one does not identify what is necessary as opposed to esoteric. Little learning takes place during testing, and

Area	% of Grade	Evaluative Process
Attitude Attendance Punctuality Proper dress Participation	20%	Attendance records and teacher observation
Physical skill Proper form Application Consistency Effort	30%	Performance objectives and teacher observation
Physical fitness CV endurance Leg strength Arm-shoulder strength Trunk strength Flexibility Body fat	30%	Fitness testing
Knowledge Tests Work search Crossword puzzles	20%	Written tests, crossword puzzles, and word searches

FIGURE 12.4   Global grading plan

it can be an uncomfortable and unproductive time for students.

Wellness Evaluation

A wellness evaluation should be undertaken annually to identify and assess factors that, if untreated, could result in later health problems. Often, the data are gathered at different places in the school setting by school nurses and physical education teachers. The information should be collated and made available to teachers, students, and parents. The wellness profile results should be interpreted for students and sent home to parents. The wellness profile does not diagnose disease, but offers basic measurements of health status. If results of the measurements give cause for concern, parents can decide if the student should see a doctor.

The wellness profile (Figure 12.5) should consist of two parts. The first is a listing of the data gathered, and the second a description of what each item measures and why it is important to sound health. If a battery of professionals is brought together, the profile information can be gathered quickly. With the help of school nurses, physical education instructors, and clerical aides, it is usually possible to gather all the data in one period, with the exception of the distance run. Data other than those in Figure 12.5 can also be included in the wellness profile (e.g., visual screening, auditory screening, posture checks, and immunization and medical examinations).

Physical Fitness Evaluation

A battery of physical fitness tests is available. There is much to be said, however, for using a standardized test that is administered to many students. It is difficult to evaluate how fit a student is if the test items are not checked for reliability and validity. The items are measuring something, but it may not be physical fitness. Many states have developed physical fitness tests. Teachers may find the state test more meaningful if they wish to compare their students with others in the state. Two of the most popular fitness tests are the Fitnessgram System and the AAHPERD Physical Best Program.

Fitnessgram System

The Fitnessgram System* consists of a 5-item test battery, software for reporting results, and an awards

system based on participation in fitness activities. In addition, an instructor's package filled with information and educational activities for students, a videotape, and software are available to teachers.

The Fitnessgram is a report card which is computer printed after test results are input. Test results are criterion referenced to a minimum required fitness level. A unique facet of the Fitnessgram System is that it provides 3 awards to youngsters. This award system is based primarily on exercise behaviors rather than an attempt for the student to demonstrate that he or she is the "best." The Fitnessgram awards program acknowledges and commends performance, however it places its highest priority on the development and reinforcement of health-related behaviors that are attainable by all students. Following is a brief description of each of the awards.

1. "Get Fit" Award. This award is offered to youngsters who have demonstrated commendable exercise behavior by completing the 6-wk "Get Fit" development program. Each participating student completes an exercise log as evidence of completion of the activities and returns the log to the instructor. The "Get Fit" program is designed to condition students for the Fitnessgram test. The program consists of activities from 4 areas: Warm-Up, Strength Development, Aerobic Activity, and Cool-Down. To qualify for the award, students must participate and record their activity at least 3 days a week for a 6-wk period.

2. "I'm Fit" Award. The "I'm Fit" award recognizes students who have achieved the acceptable health standard on at least 4 of the 5 Fitnessgram test items. To qualify for the award, students must also satisfy a prerequisite verifying that they have qualified for the "Get Fit" award or have participated recently in a sustained exercise program.

3. "Fit for Life" Award. The Fitnessgram "Fit for Life" award is designed to recognize individuals who have displayed commendable exercise behavior. *It rewards regular participation in vigorous activities.* An exercise log and point values for specific activities are provided to help record achievement. Participants earn points through regular participation in an activity or activities of their choice, and complete an exercise log in order to receive an award. The log is signed by a verifier before the award is issued. Some of the items included in the "Fit for Life" awards are biker's caps, T-shirts, backpacks, wristwatches, and duffel bags. A wide range of activities for participation is offered, including basketball, calisthenics, cycling, dance aerobics, fitness walking, gymnastics, ice hockey, jogging/running, rope jumping, skating, soccer, swimming, and weight training.

* Material is reprinted by permission of The Institute for Aerobic Research. The Fitnessgram software is available free when 200 Fitnessgram report cards are ordered. To order the software and report cards, write to Fitnessgram, Institute for Aerobic Research, 12330 Preston Road, Dallas, TX 75081.

WELLNESS PROFILE

It is important to understand your personal health. As an ongoing component of the physical education program, you recently participated in the health screening. Listed below are the results and corresponding percentile scores for a person in your age group. An explanation of the items included in this screening is listed below.

HEALTH COMPONENT	SCORE	ACCEPTABLE/ UNACCEPTABLE
Skinfold	_____ % body fat	_____
Sit and reach test	_____ centimeters	_____
Sit-ups (1 min)	_____ repetitions	_____
Aerobic field test (run-walk 1 mi)	_____ minutes: seconds	_____
Height	_____ inches	_____
Weight	_____ pounds	_____
Blood pressure Systolic	_____ mm Hg	_____
Diastolic	_____ mm Hg	_____

Dental and oral inspection _____

The profile is not meant to diagnose disease, but to indicate basic measurements of health. If you are concerned or uncertain, please take this form to your doctor or clinic. Please feel free to contact the school nurse if you have any questions.

EXPLANATION OF WELLNESS PROFILE ITEMS

Skinfold: This measurement relates to the amount of fat a person carries. People who have too much fat are more likely to have problems such as diabetes (excessive sugar in the blood) and high blood pressure.

Sit and reach: The sit and reach test measures flexibility of the lower back and hamstring (back of thigh) muscle group. A lack of flexibility often contributes to low back pain.

Sit-ups: Sit-ups measure the strength and endurance of the abdominal muscle group. Strength in this area is important for proper posture and to prevent low back pain.

Aerobic field test: The aerobic field test consists of running or walking a mile in the least amount of time possible. This test is the best single indicator of cardiorespiratory endurance, which is important in preventing heart disease.

Height and weight: These are general measurements of a child's growth. It is important that children's growth be observed regularly to assure that the body is developing normally.

Blood pressure: Blood pressure is recorded using two values. The top number (systolic) represents the pressure in the arteries when the heart is pumping blood. The

FIGURE 12.5 Wellness profile

bottom number (diastolic) is the pressure in the arteries when the heart is at rest. High blood pressure increases the risk of heart disease.

Dental and oral inspection: An inspection of the gums and teeth is conducted to visualize noticeable inflammation, sores, and cavities.

Interpreting the results:
  Results are in two categories. The first is the raw score, which is your actual performance. The second column checks whether your scores are acceptable or unacceptable for a minimum fitness level needed for a healty life-style.

FIGURE 12.5 Continued

Fitnessgram Test Battery

The Fitnessgram test battery consists of the following items that are described in detail in the *Fitnessgram User's Manual* (1987). The Fitnessgram recommends desirable health standards for children by age and sex. These standards have been established by a panel of experts and represent minimum levels of performance that most often correlate with health. Students are not compared to each other (percentile norms), as in traditional youth fitness testing, but to standards that indicate health. This approach is used because it is often argued that the reference could be fit or unfit. The meaningfulness of percentile ranking in fitness testing is directly linked to the fitness status of the group; therefore, scores offer no indication of health level.

One Mile Run/Walk.   The one mile run/walk item tests aerobic capacity relative to body weight, and is considered to be the best indicator of a person's overall cardiorespiratory capacity.

- **Equipment needed:** A flat running course and stopwatch.
- **Testing procedures:** Students are instructed to run a mile as fast as possible. As students cross the finish line, elapsed time is called to participants (or a partner).

Sum of Skinfolds.   The sum of the skinfolds is used to evaluate body composition. Teachers have been shown able to obtain reliable and objective results after training and practice using this method. The calf and triceps are used as sites for measurement since they are noninvasive and predict total body fatness as well as or better than other skinfold locations. As an alternative, the Fitnessgram offers a body/mass index if skinfold scores are not available.

- **Equipment needed:** A skinfold caliper is necessary to perform this measurement. The major requirement for a caliper is that it produce

a constant pressure of 10 g/mm^2 throughout the range of skinfold thickness. Both expensive and inexpensive calipers have been shown to be effective with teachers who have had training and sufficient practice.

- **Testing procedures:** The triceps skinfold is measured over the triceps muscle of the right arm at a point midway between the elbow and the acromion process of the scapula. The midpoint is best located by a measuring tape or string with the elbow flexed at 90 degrees. The midpoint between the elbow and shoulder is marked on the side of the arm and then extended to the back at the same level (Figure 12.6). The skinfold site should be parallel to the longitudinal axis of the upper arm. It is important that the skinfold be measured at the midpoint and on the back of the upper arm. Pinching the fold slightly above the midpoint will ensure that the fold is measured right on the midpoint.

  The calf skinfold is measured on the inside of the right leg at the level of the maximal calf

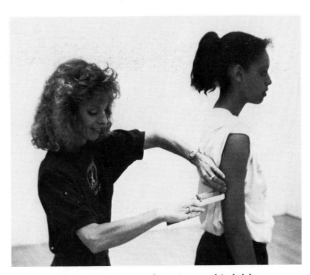

FIGURE 12.6 Measuring the triceps skinfold

girth. The right foot is placed flat on an elevated surface with the knee flexed at a 90-degree angle (Figure 12.7). The vertical skinfold is grasped just above the level of the maximal girth and the skinfold is measured at the maximal girth.

The skinfolds are read to the nearest millimeter after the caliper pointer stops. The skinfolds should be measured three times and the median of the three measurements taken as the student's final value. The two scores in millimeters are then entered into the computer, interpreted, and reported in a percent body fat score.

Sit and Reach. The sit-and-reach test item is used to evaluate the lower back.

- **Equipment needed:** A box approximately 12 in. high with a measuring scale placed on top of the box with the 9 in. mark even with the near edge of the box.
- **Testing procedures:** The student sits at the box with the shoes off, knees fully extended, and feet shoulder width apart. The feet are placed flat against the end of the box. The arms are extended forward over the measuring scale with the hands placed one on top of the other. With palms down, the student reaches directly forward with both hands along the scale 4 times, and holds the position of maximum reach on the fourth trial. This position must be held for

FIGURE 12.7 Measuring the calf skinfold

at least 1 sec. The score is the most distant point reached with the fingertips of both hands on the fourth trial, measured to the nearest ½ in.

Modified Sit-Up. The modified sit-up is used to evaluate abdominal muscular strength and endurance. Optimal functioning of these muscles is an important factor in preventing lowback pain.

- **Equipment needed:** Tumbling mats and stopwatch for timing.
- **Testing procedures:** The student lies on his or her back with the knees flexed and the soles of the feet flat on the floor. The heels are placed about 15 in. from the buttocks. The arms are crossed on the chest with the hands on the opposite shoulders. During the test, the feet are held by a partner to keep them in contact with the testing surface. Arm contact with the chest must be maintained throughout the movement. The chin should remain tucked forward on the chest. A sit-up is completed when the elbows touch the thighs. The student then returns to the starting position until the midback makes contact with the testing surface. The student performs as many sit-ups as possible during a 60-sec interval. The score is recorded as the number of correctly executed sit-ups performed within the 60 sec.

Pull-Up and Flexed-Arm Hang. This item is used to measure upper body strength and endurance. It is important because of its possible relation to bone growth and health, and its importance in daily functioning and maintenance of proper body alignment. The Fitnessgram test uses either the pull-up or flexed arm hang to test upper body strength. Both boys and girls may take either test. Students who possess sufficient strength to perform pull-ups should do the pull-up test. All other students should be tested using the flexed-arm hang.

Pull-Up

- **Equipment needed:** A horizontal bar that allows a student to hang fully extended.
- **Testing procedures:** The student assumes a hanging position on the bar with an overhand grasp (palms facing away from the body). The student then uses the arms to pull the body up until the chin reaches over the bar without touching it. The body is lowered and the exercise repeated as many times as possible.

  Interpretation: One pull-up for both boys and girls is the minimum level of performance.

Flexed-Arm Hang

- **Equipment needed:** A horizontal bar and stopwatch.

- **Testing procedures:** The student uses an overhand grip as described in the pull-up test. The student is raised by spotters off the floor to a position where the chin is above the bar, the elbows flexed, and the chest close to the bar. A stopwatch is started as soon as the student takes this position. The position is held as long as possible. The watch is stopped when the student's chin touches the bar, or the head tilts backward to keep the chin above the bar, or the chin falls below the bar. The score is recorded in the number of seconds the student hangs correctly.

AAHPERD Physical Best Program

The AAHPERD Physical Best program focuses on helping all children achieve health-related physical fitness. The approach is multifaceted in that it encourages participation in activities that are conducive to health, emphasizes the process of fitness motivation, and includes a participation-based award system. The program also recognizes the need to assist practitioners in understanding the philosophy of the program as well as implementation procedures.

The Physical Best Program Manual offers an educational approach designed to motivate all children to attain fitness. An accompanying educational kit includes lesson plans, contracts, wall charts, report cards, and other educational materials designed to help teachers motivate students to make a commitment to personal fitness. An important phase of the Physical Best program is asking students to develop personalized activity logs to stimulate pride in accomplishment. The *AAHPERD Physical Best Program Manual* can be purchased from AAHPERD Publications, P.O. Box 704, Waldorf, MD 20601.

The Physical Best program offers three awards to students.

1. Fitness Activity Award. The Fitness Activity award recognizes those students who participate in regular physical activity beyond the regular physical education program. Students must maintain a log of their exercise and physical activity. The physical education teacher determines who receives the award.

2. Personal Fitness Award. Individuals progress toward achievement of their health fitness through a total approach: values, knowledge, and physical ability. Students must be motivated to develop and maintain their personal best.

3. Health Fitness Award. The Health Fitness award recognizes the mastery of health fitness standards. Students must attain a minimum level of physical fitness on all items of the AAHPERD Physical Fitness Test Battery.

Physical Best Test Battery

Sum of Skinfold Fat. The purpose of the test is to evaluate the level of fatness or body composition.

- **Equipment needed:** Skinfold calipers are necessary. The inexpensive plastic calipers are suitable substitutes.
- **Testing procedures:** Two skinfold fat sites (triceps and subscapular) are measured easily and correlate well with total body fat. The triceps skinfold is measured over the triceps muscle of the right arm halfway between the elbow and the acromion process of the scapula with the skinfold parallel to the longitudinal axis of the upper arm. The subscapular site (right side of the body) is ½ in. below the angle of the scapula and in line with the natural cleavage lines of the skin.

  The recommended testing procedure is

  1. Firmly grasp the skinfold between the thumb and forefinger and lift up.
  2. Place the contact surfaces of the caliper ½ in. above or below the finger.
  3. Slowly release the grip on the calipers to exert their full tension on the skinfold.
  4. Read skinfold to nearest 0.5 mm after needle stops (1–2 sec after releasing grip on caliper).

Modified Sit-Up. The purpose of the sit-up* is to evaluate abdominal muscular strength and endurance.

- **Equipment needed:** Mats can be used to create a comfortable surface, and a stopwatch is necessary to time the test.
- **Testing procedures:** The student lies on his or her back with knees flexed and feet flat on floor, with the heels 12–18 in. from the buttocks. The arms are crossed on the chest with the hands on opposite shoulders. The feet are held by a partner to keep them in touch with the testing surface. The student curls to the sitting position. Arm contact with the chest must be maintained. The chin should remain tucked on the chest. The sit-up is completed when the elbows touch the thighs. To complete the movement, the student returns to the down position in which the midback makes contact with the testing surface.

  The number of correctly executed sit-ups performed in 60 sec is the score. Rest is allowed

---

* We prefer the term "curl-up" for this movement, but use the term "sit-up" here because this is AAHPERD terminology.

between sit-ups, and the student should be aware of this before starting. The goal is to perform as many sit-ups as possible.

Sit and Reach.   The purpose of the sit-and-reach test is to evaluate the flexibility of the lower back and posterior thighs.

- **Equipment needed:** The test apparatus consists of a sit-and-reach box that can be constructed or purchased. Detailed instructions for constructing the box are illustrated in the AAHPERD *Health-related Physical Fitness Test Manual* (1980). If it is not possible to construct a box, a measuring stick ruled in centimeters can be taped to a box or bench. The rule should extend beyond the bench (toward the sitting person) so that the 23-cm line is exactly in line with the vertical panel against which the feet of the subject are placed. In other words, 0–23 cm of the measuring stick hangs over the feet of the person being tested.
- **Testing procedures:** Students remove their shoes and sit down at the test apparatus with knees fully extended and the feet shoulder width apart. The feet should be flat against the end board of the box. The arms are extended forward with one hand placed on top of the other to perform the test. The student reaches directly forward, palms down, along the measuring scale four times and holds the position of maximum reach on the fourth trial. The position of maximum reach must be held for 1 sec.

Distance Runs.   The purpose of the distance runs is to measure maximal functional capacity and cardiorespiratory endurance.

- **Equipment needed:** Either of the two distance run tests can be administered on a 440-yd or 400-meter track, or on any other flat, measured area. A stopwatch is needed for timing the runs.
- **Testing procedures:** Norms are available for each of the two distance runs. They are the 1-mi run for time and the 9-min run for distance. The decision as to which of the two tests to administer should be based on facilities, equipment, time limitations, administrative considerations, and personal preference of the teacher.

1. **One-mile run.** Students are instructed to run 1 mi as fast as possible. As they cross the finish line, elapsed time should be called to the runners (or their partners). Walking is permitted, but the objective is to cover the distance in the shortest possible time.
2. **Nine-minute run.** Students are instructed to run as far as possible in 9 min. The students continue to run until a whistle is blown when 9 min have elapsed. They then stand in place until their distance has been recorded. The distance that each student runs is recorded to the nearest 10 yd or 10 meters. Walking is permitted, but the objective is to cover as much distance as possible during the 9 min.

Pull-Up and Modified Pull-Up.   Pull-ups measure upper body strength and endurance, which is important because of its possible relation to bone growth and health, and in daily functioning and maintenance of proper body alignment. The AAHPERD test battery uses either the pull-up or modified pull-up to test upper body strength. Both boys and girls may take either test. Students who possess sufficient strength to perform pull-ups should do the pull-up test. All other students should be tested using the modified pull-up.

Pull-Up

- **Equipment needed:** A horizontal bar that allows a student to hang fully extended.
- **Testing procedures:** The student assumes a hanging position on the bar with an overhand grasp (palms facing away from the body). The student then uses the arms to pull the body up until the chin is over the bar without touching it. The body is lowered and the exercise repeated as many times as possible.

Modified Pull-Up

- **Equipment needed:** An adjustable pull-up bar and elastic band that is suspended across the uprights and parallel to and about 7–8 in. below the bar.
- **Testing procedures:** The youngster is positioned on his back with the shoulders directly below the bar that is set at a height 1 or 2 in. beyond the child's reach. The youngster assumes the starting position with the buttocks off the floor, the arms and legs straight, and only the heels in contact with the floor. An overhand grip (palms away from the body) is used and the thumbs are placed around the bar. A modified pull-up is completed when the chin is hooked over the elastic band. The movement should be accomplished using only the arms. The body must be kept straight.

Sport Skill Evaluation

The majority of time in physical education is spent on skill-oriented activities. Most physical educators believe that students should be held accountable for skill development, but instructors seldom monitor students' progress. It is possible to evaluate both general motor development and sport skill development, but because the general motor development may not predict success in sports, monitoring performance in the sport skill area is usually best.

The sport skill tests can be used to evaluate the effectiveness of instruction in physical education classes. Achievement can be measured objectively and the results used for assigning grades to students. Skill tests contain activities that are important to effective functioning in sports and are thus applicable to skill practice and development. They can help students objectively chart improvement in skill development over a long period of time. Lastly, the skill tests can diagnose weak points of performance and can help the instructor create individual skill development assignments.

Many sport skill tests have been designed by experts in physical education. Tests have been developed for baseball, basketball, football, golf, gymnastics, handball and racquetball, soccer, swimming, tennis, and volleyball. This list is not inclusive, as tests for other sports can be found. A useful source of standardized tests is the text by Johnson and Nelson (1979). The following is an example of a standardized test for evaluating performance in handball.

Cornish Handball Test

The test consists of five test items: the 30-sec volley, the frontwall placement, the backwall placement, the service placement, and the power test. When the tests were analyzed for validity, however, the power test and the 30-sec volley alone predicted handball performance almost as effectively as all five items together. To conserve time, it is therefore recommended that only the two items be used.

Equipment. Several handballs are required. The service line is the only marking necessary for the volley test. For the power test, a line is drawn on the front wall at a height of 6 ft. Lines are also drawn on the floor as follows: the first line is 18 ft from the front wall; the second line is 5 ft behind the first; the third, fourth, and fifth lines are each 5¾ feet apart. These lines form 6 scoring zones. The area from the front wall to the first line scores 1 point, as does the first of the 5 zones behind. The 2, 3, 4, and 5 zones score two, three, four, and five points, respectively. A stopwatch is needed for the volley test.

Power Test Directions. The subject stands in the service zone and throws the ball against the front wall. Subject lets the ball hit the floor on the rebound before striking it. The subject then hits the ball as hard as possible, making sure that it strikes the front wall below the 6-ft line. Subjects must throw the ball against the wall before each power stroke. Five trials are given with each hand. A retrial is allowed for an attempt in which the subject steps into the front court or fails to hit the wall below the 6-ft line. *Scoring*: The value of the scoring zone in which each trial first touches the floor is recorded. The subject's score is the total points for the 10 trials.

Thirty-Second Volley. The subject stands behind the service line, drops the ball, and begins volleying it against the front wall for 30 sec. The subject should hit all strokes from behind the service line. If the ball does not return past this line, the subject is allowed to step into the front court to hit the ball, but must then get back behind the line for the succeeding stroke. If the subject misses the ball, the instructor hands over another ball, and volleying continues. *Scoring*: The score is the total number of times the ball hits the front wall in 30 sec.

Bear in mind that tests evaluate components of a sport only and can never completely evaluate actual performance under competitive pressure. Skill tests can also become so complex that the teacher may find them unacceptable in the instructional setting. Some tests require a large number of trained personnel for administration, which may not be feasible. Regardless of these restrictions, however, an instructor should arrange to conduct some skill evaluations. It is important that students know they are responsible for learning specific skills.

Constructing a Skill Test

If the teacher finds that the available tests are not satisfactory, developing one's own test that is feasible and valid may be possible. (In this case, the test would measure what it purports to measure, namely, ability in the specific sport.) Designing a test is a demanding process and requires quite some time. The following steps are mandatory for developing a skill test.

1. The sport must be analyzed to determine which skills appear to be necessary for successful performance. The test writer must be able to isolate the skill in order for it to be used as the basis for a test.

2. Standard procedures to be used when testing must be written and followed carefully during trial testing. This ensures that the test will be administered in the same manner every time.

3. The test should be administered to a selected group of students. Include in the trial group some outstanding performers as well as some less-skilled students. The purpose of the trial testing is to see if the test is capable of predicting who the better performers are.

FIGURE 12.8 Taking a knowledge test

should score higher than the less-skilled performers on both the test and in the tournament situation.

6. To check the reliability of the test, retest one group to see if the results are similar to the first test period. If results are similar, then the test is reliable and gives similar results in a test-retest setting.

The procedure is time consuming, but this approach ensures that the test is valid and reliable, and assures the teacher that it measures the desired outcome. When possible, finding a test that someone else has developed and implementing it in the school setting is easier.

Knowledge Evaluation

Knowledge tests can be given to assess the students' understanding of the rules, strategy, and history of a sport or activity (Figure 12.8). The tests should be developed according to the ages of the students involved at the different grade levels. Test questions can be multiple choice, true-false, completion, or essay. To minimize the amount of time necessary to complete the test, avoid essay questions. This will also reduce the amount of grading time. Figure 12.9 is an example of a test that might be administered

4. If the test appears to be somewhat predictive of the best through the poorest performers, then it is valid. To check the validity, rate all of the performers in the trial group and compare the completed group rating with the results found using the test. This comparison would involve computing a correlation coefficient for validity.

5. A tournament could be conducted to see if the test accurately predicts performance in the game situation. The best performers in the tournament

---

HANDBALL EXAM

I. In the blanks below, fill in the name of the area of the court designated by each letter. (10 points)

```
                                    C
                                  ┌────┐
     D                    B       │    │  A      E
                                  └────┘
```

A _____ Line
B _____ Line
C _____
D _____ Court
E _____ Court

FIGURE 12.9 Knowledge test

II. In the following diagrams, draw an arrow to indicate the path that the ball is most likely to follow. None of these shots has hit the floor. The (X) indicates the point of origin of the shot. (6 points)

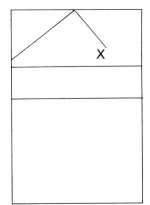 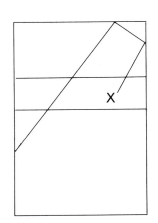 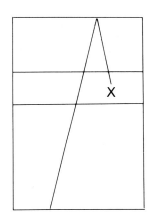

III. In the spaces at the left, place a (+) if the statement is <u>True</u>; place a (0) if the statement is <u>False</u>. (60 points)

_____ 1. A game consists of 15 points

_____ 2. Only the server may score a point.

_____ 3. The server may either bounce the ball before serving, or hit it straight out of her hand.

_____ 4. Only one foot need be in the service zone when serving.

_____ 5. In doubles, the partner with the better left hand usually plays the left side.

_____ 6. The choice for the right to serve is decided by the toss of a coin, and the side winning the toss starts the first and third games.

_____ 7. If a player swings and misses on the serve, he is given only one more chance.

_____ 8. A legal serve must bounce in the back court on a fly or after touching one side wall.

_____ 9. In doubles, only one person serves in the first and second service. After that, both players on each team serve.

_____ 10. A player is out if he is hit with his own shot on the fly, but it is a hinder if his own shot hits him on one bounce.

_____ 11. It is common courtesy to alternate serves to each court, but in tournament play there is no such rule.

_____ 12. The more walls that a shot hits, the deader the rebound will be.

_____ 13. When playing a "lane shot," it is usually best to hit the ball underhand.

_____ 14. It is good to use the side wall when using the "lob serve."

_____ 15. The "kill shot" should be attempted when the ball is chest high.

_____ 16. The most advantageous court position is just behind the short line.

_____ 17. It is often wise to let a waist-high shot bounce off the back wall so that it can be returned from a lower height.

_____ 18. In doubles, a player may call a hinder when she is obstructed from hitting the ball by her partner.

FIGURE 12.9 Continued

_____ 19. In doubles, the server's partner must lean against the side wall until the ball passes the service line.

_____ 20. The ball should be contacted at the junction between the fingers and the palm.

IV. In the spaces at the left, place the letter of the answer that best completes the statement. (24 points)

_____ 1. Which of the following is <u>not</u> a serve?
A. Scotch toss serve
B. Ceiling serve
C. Power serve
D. Z serve

_____ 2. All of the following concerning body position for hitting the "kill shot" are correct <u>except</u>:
A. Bend the knees and waist.
B. Weight transfer is from the front foot to the rear foot.
C. Contact should be at shin level or lower.
D. The forearm should be parallel to the floor.

_____ 3. All of the following are "shorts" <u>except</u>:
A. Hitting the side wall and then the front wall.
B. Hitting the front wall and then having the ball bounce in front of the short line.
C. Hitting the front wall and then the two side walls.
D. Hitting the front wall and then the ceiling.

_____ 4. All of the following statements concerning receiving the serve are true <u>except</u>:
A. The receiver must be behind the short line while the ball is being served.
B. The receiver may return the service on either the volley or the first bounce.
C. A short may be returned if so desired.
D. The receiver does not have the option of returning the service on a foot fault.

_____ 5. How many bounces are permitted on the serve?
A. 2
B. 3
C. 4
D. unlimited amount

FIGURE 12.9 Continued

to junior high school students at the completion of a unit on handball.

Sometimes an acceptable alternative is to give students a crossword puzzle or a word search in place of a written test. (See units on archery, badminton, and bowling in Chapters 21 and 22 for examples of puzzles and word search.) Teachers can check students' knowledge using both of these approaches, and the students seem to enjoy the activities more than a conventional test.

REFERENCES AND SUGGESTED READINGS

AAHPERD. 1954. *Children in Focus*. Reston, VA: AAHPERD.

AAHPERD. 1988. *Physical Best Program Manual*. Reston, VA: AAHPERD.

Johnson, B. L., and Nelson, J. K. 1979. *Practical Measurements for Evaluation in Physical Education*. Minneapolis, MN: Burgess Publishing Co.

Sterling, C. L. 1987. *Fitnessgram User's Manual*. Dallas, TX: Institute for Aerobic Research.

13 LIABILITY AND SAFETY

Physical education is a high-risk activity. Teachers entering the profession assume that there will be more opportunity for accidents than in other academic areas. Over 50% of all accidents in the school setting occur in physical education. Facilities and equipment such as swimming pools, gymnastics apparatus, diving boards, and playground equipment can all be sources of injury. Activities in the curriculum also offer ample opportunity for accidents and personal injury. Football, wrestling, archery, gymnastics, pole vaulting, high jumping, and weight lifting have a record of higher accident rates than other activities. These statistics are not presented to alarm teachers, but to increase awareness of the situation. The teacher's responsibility is to create a safe environment for students where risk and the opportunity for injury are minimized.

All students have a right to freedom from injury caused by others or due to participation in a program. Courts have ruled that teachers owe their students a duty of care to protect them from harm. Teachers must offer a standard of care that any reasonable and prudent professional with similar training would apply under the given circumstances. A teacher is required to exercise the teaching skill, discretion, and knowledge that members of the profession in good standing normally possess in similar situations. Lawsuits usually occur when citizens believe that this standard of care did not exist.

Liability is a responsibility to perform a duty to a particular group. It is an obligation to do a particular thing that is required by law and enforced by court action. Teachers are bound by contract to perform their duties in a reasonable and prudent manner. Liability is always a legal matter. It must be proved in a court of law that negligence occurred before one can be held liable.

TORT LIABILITY

Tort liability is a lawsuit for breach of duty. It is concerned with the teacher-student relationship and is a legal wrong that results in direct or indirect injury to another individual or to property. The following is the legal definition of a tort as stated in *Black's Law Dictionary* (1968):

> A private or civil wrong or injury, other than breach of contract, for which the court will provide a remedy in the form of an action for damages. Three elements of every tort action are: existence of legal duty from defendant to plaintiff, breach of duty, and damage as proximate result.

In tort liability, the court can give a monetary reward for damages that occurred. The court can also give a monetary reward for punitive damages if a flagrant breach of duty can be established. The court usually rewards the offended individual because of negligence of the instructor or another responsible individual.

NEGLIGENCE AND LIABILITY

Liability is usually concerned with a breach of duty through negligence. Lawyers examine the situation that gave rise to the injury to establish if liability can be determined. Four major points must be established to determine if the teacher was negligent.

Duty. The first point to examine is that of duty owed to the participants. Did the school or teacher owe students a duty of care that implies conforming to certain standards of conduct? When examining duty or breach of duty, the courts always look at reasonable care, which is exemplified by the actions of a member of the profession in good standing. In other words, to determine a reasonable standard, the court uses the conduct of other teachers as a standard for comparison.

Breach of Duty. The teacher commits a breach of duty by failing to conform to the required duty. After a required duty is established, it must be proved that the teacher did not carry out this duty. Two situations can result: (1) The teacher did something that was not supposed to have been done (e.g.,

221

put boxing gloves on students to solve their differences); or, (2) The teacher did not do something that should have been done (e.g., failed to teach an activity using proper progressions).

Injury.   An injury must occur if liability is to be established. If no injury or harm occurs, there is no liability. It must also be proved that the injured party is entitled to damages as compensation for financial loss or physical discomfort.

Proximate Cause.   The failure of the teacher to conform to the required standard must be the cause of the injury. It must be proved that the teacher's breach of duty caused the injury. Proving a breach of duty is not enough; it must be shown simultaneously that the injury was a direct result of the teacher's failure to provide a reasonable standard of care.

Foreseeability

A key to the issue of negligence is foreseeability. The courts expect that a trained professional should be able to foresee potentially harmful situations. Was it possible for the teacher to predict or anticipate the danger of the harmful act or situation, and to take appropriate measures to prevent it? If the injured party can prove that the teacher was able to foresee the danger involved in an activity or situation (even in part), the teacher will be found negligent, that is, failing to act in a reasonable and prudent manner.

All activities, equipment, and facilities need to be examined for possible hazards and sources of accidents. For example, a common game played in the school setting is bombardment or dodge ball. During the game, a student is hit in the eye by a ball and loses her vision. Was this a foreseeable accident that could have been prevented? Were the balls being used capable of inflicting severe injury? Were students made aware of rules that might have prevented this injury? Were the abilities of the students fairly equal, or were some students capable of throwing with such velocity that injury was predictable? These types of questions would be considered in court in an attempt to prove that the teacher should have been able to predict an overly dangerous situation.

TYPES OF NEGLIGENCE

Negligence is defined by the courts as conduct that falls below a standard of care that is established to protect others from unreasonable risk of harm. The types of negligence are categorized as follows:

Malfeasance.   This occurs when the teacher does something improper. The act would be ruled unlawful and wrongful and without legal basis. This type of negligence is illustrated by the following incident: A male student misbehaved on numerous occasions. In desperation, the teacher gave the student a choice of punishment—a severe paddling in front of the class or running many laps around the field. The student chose the former and suffered physical and emotional damage. Even though the teacher gave the student a choice whereby he could have avoided the paddling, the teacher is still liable for any harm caused.

Misfeasance.   This type of negligence occurs when the teacher follows the proper procedures but does not perform according to the required standard of conduct. Misfeasance is based on an action that was not up to a required standard. It is usually the subpar performance of an act that might otherwise have been lawfully done. An example would be a teacher's offering to spot a student during a gymnastics routine and then not doing it properly. If the student is injured due to a faulty spot, the teacher can be held liable.

Nonfeasance.   If a teacher fails to perform an act or to carry out a duty or procedure, negligence can be proven. Nonfeasance is based on lack of action and failure to perform a duty. It is usually an act of omission. The teacher knows the proper procedures, but fails to follow them. Teachers can thus be negligent if they act or fail to act. In contrast to the previous example, the teacher guilty of nonfeasance would know that it is necessary to spot certain gymnastics routines, but would fail to do so.

The courts have expected teachers to behave with more skill and insight than parents (Strickland et al., 1976). Understanding and performing proper procedures and duties in a befitting manner is essential, because teachers are expected to have a high standard of professional training.

Contributary Negligence.   The legal situation is different when the injured student is partially or wholly at fault. Students are expected to exercise sensible care and to follow directions or regulations to protect themselves from injury. This responsibility is always directly related to the maturity, ability, and experience of the student. Improper behavior by the injured party as cause of the accident is contributory negligence, since the injured party contributed to the resulting harm. To illustrate contributory negligence, assume that the teacher has explained the shot put and all of the safety rules. As students begin to practice, one of them runs through a restricted area that is well marked and is hit by a shot. There is a strong possibility that this student will be held liable for his actions.

Comparative or Shared Negligence. Under the doctrine of comparative negligence, the injured party can recover damages only if found to be less negligent than the defendant (the teacher). Where statutes apply, the amount of recovery is generally reduced in proportion to the injured party's participation in the activity leading to the injury.

Common Defenses against Negligence

Clearly, negligence must be proved in a court of law. Undoubtedly teachers are often negligent in performing their duties, but the injured party does not always take the case to court. When the teacher is sued, some of the following stands may be taken in an attempt to show that the teacher was not the primary cause of the accident.

Contributory Negligence. Contributory negligence attempts to convince the court that the injured party acted in a manner that was abnormal. In other words, the injured individual did not act in a manner typical of students of similar age and maturity. The defense would attempt to demonstrate that the activity or equipment in question had been used for years with no record of accident. A case would be made for the teacher's manner of presentation, that students were taught to act in a safe manner, and that the injured student acted outside the parameters of safe conduct. A key point in this defense is whether the activity was suitable for the age and maturity level of the participants.

Act of God. The act of God defense puts the cause of injury on forces beyond the control of the teacher or school. The case is made that it was impossible to predict that an unsafe condition would occur and that through an act of God, the injury occurred. Typical acts would be a violent gust of wind that blew over a volleyball standard, a cloudburst of rain that made a surface slick, or a flash of lightning that struck someone on the playing field. Even the act of God defense, however, is used only in cases in which the injury might not have occurred had reasonable and prudent action been taken.

Proximate Cause. In an attempt to prove that the accident was not caused by the negligence of the teacher, the proximate cause defense is used. To prove negligence, a close relationship must exist between the breach of duty by the teacher and the injury. Proximate cause is common in cases dealing with proper supervision. The student is participating in an activity supervised by the teacher. When the teacher leaves the playing area to get a cup of coffee, the student is injured. The defense will try to show that the accident would have occurred regardless of whether the teacher observed it directly or not.

Assumption of Risk. Clearly, physical education is a high-risk activity when compared with most other curriculum areas. According to the assumption of risk defense, the participant assumes the risk of an activity when choosing to be part of that activity. The assumption of risk defense is seldom used by physical education teachers, because students are not often allowed to choose to participate or not participate. An elective program that allows students to select desired units of instruction might be more defensible on these grounds than a totally required program. Athletic and sport club participation is by choice, and players do assume a greater risk in activities such as football or gymnastics.

AREAS OF RESPONSIBILITY

Teachers need to be keenly aware of areas in which they may be found negligent in fulfilling their responsibilities. These areas most often lead to lawsuits when teachers fail to conduct themselves in a reasonable, prudent, and careful manner.

Supervision

Teachers have a responsibility to supervise students in all school settings and are accountable for this duty. The two types of supervision are general and specific. General supervision refers to always being physically present in the gymnasium or field. It also means that the teacher will be immediately available to any student who needs assistance or aid. A common general supervision situation occurs when a student is injured. The teacher must sometimes take the student to the nurse while leaving the rest of the class unattended. If an accident occurs while the class is unattended, the teacher is usually found negligent. Either another student must attend the injured party, or another teacher must be secured to attend the class.

When conducting general supervision duties, the teacher must be able to see all participants. A plan of rotation (written, if necessary) should provide for contact with all students. Discipline in the supervised area is a necessity. If the court finds that the injury occurred because of lack of student control, the teacher may be held liable.

Specific supervision requires the instructor to be with a certain group of students. An example would be the need to spot students who are performing difficult gymnastics activities. If certain pieces of apparatus require special care and proper use, the teacher should have rules and regulations posted near the apparatus.

The following guidelines will help ensure that proper supervision occurs:

1. Never leave a class unsupervised, regardless of the situation. The teacher may have to answer a telephone call, go to the bathroom, secure more equipment, or discipline a student privately. Before doing any of these, another qualified supervisor must be secured. A class should never be split and sent to different areas if both areas cannot be supervised simultaneously.

2. Be aware of any possible dangers in the area. If the playing field has sprinkler heads that could cause injury, mark them off with cones. If broken glass or other debris is on the field, the area should be marked off and avoided. It is the responsibility of the supervisor to be aware of these situations and to keep students from them.

3. Post safety rules in the area. Students should be made aware of the posted rules, and receive instruction and interpretation of the rules when necessary. If rules are modified, rewrite them in proper form. There is no substitute for documentation when defending one's policies and approaches.

4. Arrange and teach your class so that all students are always in view. This probably means supervising from the perimeter of the area. A teacher who is at the center of an area with her or his back to some students cannot supervise properly.

5. Do not leave equipment and apparatus unsupervised at any time if it is accessible to other students in the area. An example would be leaving equipment on the playing field between classes. If other students in the area have easy access to the equipment, they may use it in an unsafe manner, and the teacher will be found liable if an injury occurs.

6. Do not consent to supervise activities in which you are unqualified to anticipate possible hazards. If you are assigned to supervise such an activity, send a written memo to the department head or principal stating your lack of insight and qualification for such supervision.

7. The number of supervisors should be determined by the type of activity, the size of the area, and the number and age of the students.

Instruction

A very important consideration is whether or not the student received adequate instruction before or during participation. Adequate instruction means a statement of how to perform the activity correctly, a statement of necessary safety precautions, and a statement of proper equipment and apparatus use. If instructions are given, they must be correct, understandable, and include proper technique, or the instructor can be held liable. The risk involved in an activity must also be communicated to the learner.

The age and maturity level of the student plays an important role in the selection of activities. Younger students require more care, instructions that are easy to comprehend, and clear restrictions in the name of safety. Students often have a lack of fear and caution concerning some activities, and the teacher must be aware of this in discussing safety factors. Youngsters have little fear and a great deal of faith in the instructor. This places a greater responsibility on the teacher to give adequate instruction.

Careful planning is a necessity. Written curriculum guides and lesson plans offer a well-prepared approach that is subject to examination by other teachers and administrators. Lesson plans should be developed that include proper sequencing and skill progression. Teachers are on defensible grounds if they can show that the progression of activities was based on presentations made by experts and was followed carefully. District and state guidelines enforcing instructional sequences and restricted activities should be closely checked.

Proper instruction demands that students are not forced to participate. If youngsters are required to perform an activity against their will, the teacher may be open to a lawsuit. In a lawsuit dealing with stunts and tumbling (Appenzeller, 1970), a student claimed that she was not given adequate instruction in how to perform a stunt called "roll over two." The teacher was held liable because the student claimed that she was forced to try the stunt before adequate instruction was offered. Gymnastics and tumbling are areas in which lawsuits are prevalent due to a lack of adequate instruction. In addition to presenting oral instruction, post the proper sequence of skills and lead-up activities to assure proper presentation. Teachers need to tread the line carefully between helpful encouragement and forcing students to try new activities.

Because the use of punishment is a part of the instructional process for many teachers, the consequences should be examined carefully before implementation. Certainly physical punishment that brings about permanent or long-lasting damage is indefensible. The punishment used must be in line with the physical maturity and health of the student involved. The practice of having students perform laps when they misbehave may have gone unchallenged for years, but what if an asthmatic student or a student with a congenital heart disease is asked to run and suffers an attack? What if the student is running unsupervised and is injured by a fall or suffers from heat prostration? It would be difficult to defend such a punishment practice. The authors would also add that it is difficult to defend making students perform physical activity for misbehavior under any circumstances. In any case, if a child is injured while performing a physical punishment, the teacher is usually liable and is held responsible for the injury.

The primary point to remember about instruction is that the teacher has a duty to protect others against unreasonable physical or mental harm, and a duty to avoid any acts or omissions that might produce such harm. The teacher is educated, experienced, and skilled in the area, and should be able to predict situations that might be harmful.

The following points can help the teacher plan meaningful and safe instruction:

1. Sequence all activities in a unit of instruction and develop a written lesson plan. Most problems occur when snap judgments are made under the pressure and strain of the teaching situation.

2. Eliminate high-risk activities. If in doubt, discuss the activities with other experienced teachers and administrators.

3. Never force students to do an activity. The activities used in the curriculum must be within the developmental limits of the students. Since the range of maturity and development within a given class may be wide, some activities may be beyond the ability levels of various students.

4. If the students' grades are based on the number of activities in which they participate, some students may feel forced to try all activities. Teachers should tell students clearly that the choice to participate belongs to them. When they are afraid of getting hurt, they can elect not to do an activity.

5. Include in the written lesson plan the necessary safety equipment. The lesson plan should state clearly how the equipment is to be arranged, the placement of mats, and where the instructor will carry out supervision.

6. Activities should be selected for the curriculum based on the contribution they will make to the growth and development of the students. Including activities "for the fun of it" or "because students liked it" are not considered valid reasons in a court of law. The activities included should be based on the constructs of the curriculum and the consensus of experts.

7. If a student states that he or she is injured, or brings a note from parents stating that the student is not to participate in physical activity, the teacher must honor the request. These excuses are almost always given at the start of the period when the teacher is busy with many other duties (e.g., getting equipment ready, taking roll, and opening lockers). It is impossible to make a thoughtful judgment at this time. The school nurse is qualified to make these judgments when they relate to health and should be consulted about such matters. If a student continues to bring in excuses over a long period of time, the teacher can have a conference with the parents to rectify the situation.

8. Make sure the activities included in the instructional process are in line with the available equipment and facilities. An example would be the amount of space available. If a soccer lead-up activity is brought indoors because of inclement weather, it may no longer be a safe, appropriate activity.

9. If spotting is required for the safe completion of activities, it must always be done by the instructor or by trained students in the class. Teaching students how to spot is as important as teaching them physical skills. Safe conduct must be taught.

10. Have a written emergency care plan posted in the gymnasium. This plan should be approved by health care professionals and should be followed to the letter when an injury occurs.

EQUIPMENT AND FACILITIES

The equipment and facilities used in the physical education program must allow safe participation in all activities. The choice of apparatus and equipment should be based on the growth and developmental levels of the students. For example, letting elementary school children use a horizontal ladder that was designed for high school students may result in a fall that causes injury. Hazards found on playing fields need to be repaired and eliminated. The legal concept of an "attractive nuisance" should be understood. This implies that some piece of equipment or apparatus, usually left unsupervised, was so attractive to children that they could not be expected to avoid it. When an injury occurs, even though students may have been using the apparatus incorrectly, teachers and the school are often held liable, because the attractive nuisance should have been removed from the area when unsupervised.

Develop a written checklist of equipment and apparatus, and make inspections regularly. The date of inspection should be recorded to show that it was done at regular intervals. If corrective action is needed, notify the principal or appropriate administrator in writing. Telling them verbally is not enough, for this approach offers little protection for the teacher. If a potentially dangerous situation exists, rules or warnings should be posted so students are aware of the risk before participating.

Proper installation of equipment is critical. Climbing equipment and other equipment that must be anchored should be installed by a reputable firm that guarantees their work. When examining an apparatus, it is important to inspect the installation at the same time.

Maintenance of facilities is also important. Keep grass short and inspect the grounds for debris. Fill holes in the ground and remove loose gravel. Proper types of finish that prevent excessive slipping should be used on indoor floors. Shower rooms should have a roughened floor finish applied to prevent falls when the floors are wet.

The facilities should be used in a safe manner. Often, sidelines and end lines of playing fields for football, soccer, or field hockey are placed too close to walls, curbings, or fences. Even though the size of the playing area may be reduced, the boundaries should be moved to allow adequate room for deceleration. In the gymnasium, do not ask students to run to a line that is close to the wall. Another common hazard is baskets positioned too close to the playing area. The poles that support the baskets must be padded.

The proper use of equipment and apparatus is important. Regardless of the state of equipment repair, if it is misused, it may result in an injury. Students must be instructed in the proper use of equipment and apparatus before it is issued. All safety instruction should be included in the written lesson plan to ensure that all points are covered.

Athletic Participation

When students are involved in extracurricular activity, teachers or coaches are still responsible for the safe conduct of activities. A common area giving rise to lawsuits involves students who are mismatched either on the basis of size or ability. Just because the competitors are the same sex and chose to participate in the same activity does not absolve the instructor from liability if an injury occurs. The question the court examines is whether the teacher tried to match students according to height, weight, and ability. The courts are more sensitive about mismatching in the physical education setting than in an athletic contest, but mismatching is a factor that should be considered in any situation.

Participants in extracurricular activities should be required to sign a responsibility waiver form. The form should explain the risks involved in voluntary participation and discuss briefly the types of injuries that have occurred in the past during practice and competition. Supervisors should remember that waiver slips do not waive the rights of participants, and that teachers and coaches can still be found liable if injuries occur. The waiver forms do communicate clearly the risk involved, however, and may provide a strong assumption of risk defense.

Participants should be required to have a medical examination before participating. Examination records should be kept in the files and identified prominently in cases of any physical restriction or limitation. Students should not be allowed to participate unless they purchase medical insurance, and evidence of coverage should be kept in the folders of athletic participants.

Preseason conditioning should be undertaken in a systematic and progressive fashion. Starting the season with a mile run for time makes little sense if students have not been preconditioned. Coaches should be aware of guidelines dealing with heat and humidity. For example, in Arizona, guidelines are to avoid strenuous activity when the temperature exceeds 85°F and the humidity exceeds 40% (Stone, 1977). When these conditions occur, running is curtailed to 10 min and active games to 30 min. Drinking water should always be available and given to students on demand.

Whenever students are transported, teachers are responsible for their safety both en route and during the activity. Use licensed drivers and school-approved vehicles, and be sure travel plans include official approval from the appropriate school administrator. If a group of students transport each other in their own cars, the instructor has a responsibility to assure the safety of the vehicles. The cars should not be overloaded, and the instructor must lead the caravan and maintain proper speed. The group should go and return together. One special note: If the driver receives expenses for the trip, the possibility of being held liable for injury increases dramatically. Many insurance policies do not cover drivers who receive compensation for transporting students. If a teacher is transporting students and receiving reimbursement, a special insurance rider that provides liability coverage for the situation should be purchased.

SAFETY

The major thrust of safety should be to prevent situations that cause accidents. It is estimated that over 70% of the injuries associated with sports and with physical activity in general could be prevented through the use of proper safety procedures. On the other hand, accidents do occur, and proper emergency procedures should be established to cope with any situation. A comprehensive study of injuries in sport and related activities was conducted by the Consumer Product Safety Commission (1975). This study involved a network of computers in 119 hospital emergency rooms that channeled injury data to a central point. The sports and activities that produced the most injuries were, in order, football, touch football, baseball, basketball, gymnastics, and skiing. The facility that produced the most disabling injuries was the swimming pool.

Learning to recognize potential high-risk situations is probably the most important factor in preventing accidents. Teachers must clearly understand the hazards and potential dangers of an activity before they can establish controls. One cannot assume that participants are aware of the danger and risk involved in various activities. Students must be told of the danger and risk before participation begins.

Guidelines for Safety

1. In-service sessions in safety should be administered by the most experienced and knowledgeable teachers. Department heads may be responsible for the training, or outside experts can be asked to undertake the responsibility. Giving in-district credit to participating teachers is a strong indication of a district's desire to nurture proper safety techniques.

2. Review medical records at the start of each school year. Students who are atypical or handicapped should be noted and identified within each class listing. It is important to identify these individuals before the first instructional day. If necessary, the teacher or school nurse can call the doctor of a handicapped or activity-restricted student to inquire further about the situation and any special needs.

3. At the beginning of the semester, conduct a safety orientation. This should include a review of potentially dangerous situations, shower-room and class conduct, and rules for proper use of equipment and apparatus. Teachers must urge students to report any condition that might cause an accident.

4. Discuss safety rules for specific units of instruction at the onset of each unit. Post rules and bring them to the students' attention regularly. Posters and bulletin boards can promote safety in an enjoyable and stimulating manner.

5. If students are going to act as instructional aides, they should be trained. It is important that aides understand the techniques of spotting and offering proper instruction if they are going to be part of the educational process.

6. If equipment is faulty, remove it completely from the area until it is repaired. Along the same lines, do not modify or use equipment for anything other than its original purpose.

7. An inventory of equipment and apparatus should include a safety checklist. At the end of the school year, send equipment in need of repair to the proper agents. If the repair cost is greater than 40% of the replacement cost, discarding the equipment or apparatus is usually advisable.

8. Purchase equipment on the basis of quality and safety as well as potential use. Many lawsuits occur because of unsafe equipment and apparatus. The liability for such equipment may rest with the manufacturer, but it will have to be so proved. This means that the teacher should state, in writing, the exact specifications of the desired equipment. The substitution of a lower priced item may result in the purchase of less-safe equipment. If the teacher has specified the proper equipment, however, the possibility of the teacher's being held liable for an injury will be reduced.

9. Report and file the occurrence of injuries. The injury report should be filed by type of injury (e.g., all ankle sprains in one folder, all broken arms in another). The report should list the activity during which the injury occurred and the conditions surrounding the injury. At regular intervals, analyze the reports. The analysis may show that injuries are occurring regularly in a specific activity or on a certain piece of equipment. This process can provide direction for creating a safer environment or for defending the safety record of a sport, activity, or piece of equipment.

Safety Committee

A safety committee can meet at regular intervals to establish safety policies, to rule on requests to allow high-risk activities, and to analyze serious injuries that have occurred in the school district. This committee should develop safety rules that apply district-wide to all teachers. It may determine that certain activities involve too great a risk for the return in student benefit. Acceptable criteria for sport equipment and apparatus may also be established by the committee.

The safety committee should include one or more high-level administrators, physical education teachers, health officers (school nurse), parents, and students. Remember that school administrators are also usually indicted when lawsuits do occur, because they are held responsible for program content and curriculum. Their representation on the safety committee is therefore important. In addition, students may be aware of possible hazards, and parents may voice concerns often overlooked by teachers.

Safety should be publicized throughout the school regularly, and a mechanism should exist that allows students, parents, and teachers to voice concerns about unsafe conditions.

Assessing the Health Status

Periodic health examinations do not uncover every problem related to participation in physical activity. Some conditions may appear only after exercise. In other instances, the condition may have developed after an examination and may have an important bearing on the health status of the student.

The task of screening children who respond poorly to exercise is not difficult; it involves identifying certain conditions that are indications of an abnormality. The Committee on Exercise and Fitness of the American Medical Association lists these observable signs, which may accompany or follow exercise and may be indications for referral to a physician. In any case, if the teacher identifies some of these symptoms, the school nurse should be notified and asked to examine the student. Teachers should never attempt to make medical decisions, regardless of their experience and expertise.

- **Excessive Breathlessness.** Some breathlessness is normal with exercise, but if it persists long after exertion, it is cause for medical referral.
- **Pale or Clammy Skin.** Pale or clammy skin or cold sweating following or during exercise is not a normal reaction to physical activity within the usual temperature ranges of the gymnasium or playing field.
- **Unusual Fatigue.** Excessive fatigue, as evidenced by unusual lack of endurance or early failure to maintain moderate activity, suggests the need for medical referral. Attributing such reactions to lack of effort is unwise until possible organic causes have been ruled out.
- **Persistent Shakiness.** Unusual weakness or shakiness that continues for more than 10 min following vigorous exercise is cause for concern.
- **Muscle Twitching or Tetany.** Muscular contractions such as twitching or tetany, whether localized or generalized, sometimes occur as an unusual reaction to exercise, and are cause for referral.

In addition, such medical symptoms as headaches, dizziness, fainting, broken sleep at night, digestive upset, pain not associated with injury, undue pounding of the heart or irregular heartbeat, disorientation, or personality change are contraindications of nor-

mal functioning. The committee cautions that an occasional episode need not alarm the instructor, but recurring or persisting patterns of any of these symptoms, particularly when related to activity, indicate the need for medical review.

PLANNING FOR EMERGENCY CARE

Establishing procedures for emergency care and for notification of parents in case of injury are of utmost importance in providing a high standard of care for students. To plan properly for emergency care, all physical education teachers should have first aid training. First aid is the immediate and temporary care given in an emergency before the physician arrives. Its purpose is to save life, prevent aggravation of injuries, and alleviate severe suffering. If there is evidence of life-threatening bleeding or if the victim is unconscious or has stopped breathing, the teacher must administer first aid. When already-injured persons may be further injured if they are not moved, then moving them is permissible. As a general rule, however, an injured party should not be moved unless absolutely necessary. If there is any indication of back or neck injury, the head must be immobilized and should not be moved without the use of a spine board. Remember the purpose of first aid—to save life. The emergency care plan should consist of the following steps:

1. Administration of first aid to the injured student is the priority. Treat only life-threatening injuries. If a school nurse is available, she or he should be called immediately to the scene of the accident. Emergency care procedures should indicate whether the student can be moved and in what fashion. It is critical that the individual applying first aid avoid aggravating the injury.

2. Unless the injury is so severe that the student must be taken directly to the hospital emergency care unit, the parents should be notified. Each student's file should list home and emergency telephone numbers where parents can be reached. If possible, the school should have an arrangement with a local emergency facility, so a paramedic unit can be called immediately to the scene of a serious accident.

3. In most cases, the student can be released to a parent or a designated representative. Policies for transportation of injured students should be established and documented.

4. A student accident report should be completed promptly, while the details of the accident are clear.

Figure 13.1 is an example of an accident report form that covers the necessary details. The teacher and principal should both retain copies and send additional copies to the administrative office.

Personal Protection: Minimizing the Effects of a Lawsuit

In spite of proper care, injuries do occur, and lawsuits may be initiated. Two courses of action are necessary to counteract the effects of a suit.

Liability Insurance. Teachers may be protected by school district liability insurance. Usually, however, teachers must purchase a policy. Most policies provide for legal services to contest a suit and will pay indemnity up to the limits of the policy ($300,000 liability coverage is most common). Most policies give the insurance company the right to settle out of court. If this occurs, some may infer that the teacher was guilty even though the circumstances indicate otherwise. Insurance companies usually settle out of court to avoid spending a lot on legal fees to try to win the case in court.

Record Keeping. The second necessary course of action is to keep complete records of accidents. Many lawsuits occur months or even years after the accident, when memory of the situation is fuzzy. Accident reports should be filled out immediately after an injury. The teacher should take care to provide no evidence, oral or written, that others could use in a court of law. Do not attempt to make a diagnosis or to specify the supposed cause of the accident in the report.

If newspaper reporters probe for details, the teacher should avoid describing the accident beyond the basic facts. When discussing the accident with administrators, only the facts recorded on the accident report should be discussed. Remember that school records can be subpoenaed in court proceedings. The point here is not to dissemble, but to be cautious and avoid self-incrimination.

A Safety and Liability Checklist

The following checklist can be used to monitor the physical education environment. Any situations that deviate from safe and legally sound practices should be rectified immediately.

Supervision and Instruction

1. Are teachers adequately trained in all of the activities that they are teaching?
2. Do all teachers have evidence of a necessary level of first aid training?
3. When supervising, do personnel have access to a written plan of areas to be observed and responsibilities to be carried out?
4. Have students been warned of potential dangers and risks, and advised of rules and the reasons for rules?
5. Are safety rules posted near areas of increased risk?
6. Are lesson plans written? Do they include provisions for proper instruction, sequence of activities, and safety? Are all activities taught listed in the district curriculum guide?
7. When a new activity is introduced, are safety precautions and instructions for correct skill performance always communicated to the class?
8. Are the activities taught in the program based on sound curriculum principles? Could the activities and units of instruction be defended on the basis of their educational contributions?
9. Do the methods of instruction recognize individual differences among students, and are the necessary steps taken to meet the needs of all students, regardless of sex, ability, or disability?
10. Are substitute teachers given clear and comprehensive lesson plans so that they can maintain the scope and sequence of instruction?
11. Is the student evaluation plan based on actual performance and objective data rather than on favoritism or arbitrary and capricious standards?
12. Is appropriate dress required for students? This does not imply uniforms, only dress (including shoes) that ensures the safety of the student.
13. When necessary for safety, are students grouped according to ability level, size, or age?
14. Is the class left unsupervised for teacher visits to the office, lounge, or bathroom? Is one teacher ever asked to supervise two or more classes at the same time?
15. If students are used as teacher aides or to spot others, are they given proper instruction and training?

Equipment and Facilities

1. Is all equipment inspected regularly, and are the inspection results recorded on a form and sent to the proper administrators?
2. Is a log maintained recording inspection, the equipment in need of repair, and when repairs were made?
3. Are "attractive nuisances" eliminated from the gymnasium and playing field?
4. Are specific safety rules posted on facilities and near equipment?
5. Are the following inspected periodically?
   a. Playing field for presence of glass, rocks, and metal objects

STUDENT ACCIDENT REPORT

_____ **SCHOOL**

In all cases, this form should be filed through the school nurse and signed by the principal of the school. The original will be forwarded to the superintendent's office, where it will be initialed and sent to the head nurse. The second copy will be retained by the principal or the nurse. The third copy should be given to the physical education teacher if accident is related.

Name of Injured _____ Address _____

Phone _____ Grade _____ Home Room _____ Age _____

Parents of Injured _____

Place of Accident _____ Date of Accident _____

Hour _____ A.M. P.M. Date Reported _____ By Whom _____

Parent Contact Attempted at _____ A.M. P.M. Parent Contacted at _____ A.M. P.M.

DESCRIBE ACCIDENT, GIVING SPECIFIC LOCATION AND CONDITION OF PREMISES _____

_____

NATURE OF INJURY _____
(Describe in detail)

CARE GIVEN OR ACTION TAKEN BY NURSE OR OTHERS _____

_____

REASON INJURED PERSON WAS ON PREMISES _____
(Activity at time—i.e., lunch, physical education, etc.)

STAFF MEMBER RESPONSIBLE FOR STUDENT SUPERVISION AT TIME OF ACCIDENT _____

IS STUDENT COVERED BY SCHOOL-SPONSORED ACCIDENT INSURANCE? ____ YES ____ NO

MEDICAL CARE RECOMMENDED ____ YES ____ NO

WHERE TAKEN AFTER ACCIDENT _____
(Specify home, physician, or hospital, giving name and address)

BY WHOM _____ AT WHAT TIME _____ A.M. P.M.

FOLLOW-UP BY NURSE TO BE SENT TO CENTRAL HEALTH OFFICE.

REMEDIATIVE MEASURES TAKEN _____
(Attach individual remarks if necessary)

FIGURE 13.1 Sample student accident report form

| School _____ | Principal _____ |
| Date _____ | Nurse _____ |

On the back of this sheet, list all persons familiar with the circumstances of the accident, giving name, address, telephone number, age, and location with respect to the accident.

FIGURE 13.1 Continued

b. Fasteners holding equipment such as climbing ropes, horizontal bars, or baskets

c. Goals for games, such as football, soccer, and field hockey, to be sure that they are fastened securely

d. Padded areas such as goal supports

6. Are mats placed under apparatus from which a fall is possible?

7. Are playing fields arranged so participants will not run into each other or be hit by a ball from another game?

8. Are landing pits filled and maintained properly?

Emergency Care

1. Is there a written procedure for emergency care?

2. Is a person properly trained in first aid available immediately following an accident?

3. Are emergency telephone numbers readily accessible?

4. Are telephone numbers of parents available?

5. Is an up-to-date first aid kit available? Is ice immediately available?

6. Are health folders maintained that list restrictions, allergies, and health problems of students?

7. Are health folders reviewed by instructors on a regular basis?

8. Are students participating in extracurricular activities required to have insurance? Is the policy number recorded?

9. Is there a plan for treating injuries that involves the local paramedics?

10. Are accident reports filed promptly and analyzed on a regular basis?

REFERENCES AND SUGGESTED READINGS

Appenzeller, H. 1970. *From the Gym to the Jury.* Charlottesville, VA: Michie Company Law Publishing.

Arnold, D. E. 1983. *Legal Considerations in the Administration of Public School Physical Education and Athletic Programs.* Springfield, IL: Charles C Thomas.

Baley, J. A., and Matthews, D. L. 1984. *Law and Liability in Athletics, Physical Education, and Recreation.* Boston, MA: Allyn and Bacon.

Black's Law Dictionary. 4th ed. 1968. St. Paul, MN: West Publishing.

Blucker, J. A., and Pell, S. W. 1986. Legal and ethical issues. *Journal of Physical Education, Recreation, and Dance* 57: 19–21.

Dougherty, N. J. (ed.) 1987. *Principles of Safety in Physical Education and Sport.* Reston, VA: AAHPERD.

Kaiser, R. A. 1984. *Liability and Law in Recreation, Parks, and Sports.* Englewood Cliffs, NJ: Prentice-Hall.

Stone, W. J. 1977. Running and running tests for Arizona school children. *Arizona JOHPERD* 21: 15–17.

Strickland, R., Phillip, J. F., and Phillips, W. R. 1976. *Avoiding Teacher Malpractice.* New York: Hawthorn Books.

Law Division, Institute for the Study of Educational Policy. 1986. *School Athletics and the Law.* Seattle, WA: University of Washington Press.

U.S. Consumer Product Safety Commission. 1975. *Hazard Analysis of Injuries Relating to Playground Equipment.* Washington, DC: U.S. Government Printing Office.

INTRAMURALS, SPORT CLUBS, AND ATHLETICS

Intramural sport programs are rarely priority items in junior and senior high schools. In a study (Maas, 1978) of programs in Ohio and Iowa, approximately two-thirds of the schools did not sponsor an organized intramural program, for reasons always related to the athletic program. In most school districts, the athletic program is the number one after-school activity, and therefore gets the facilities, the money, and the qualified personnel. In contrast to the athletic program, a well-developed intramural program can serve the needs of many students, while offering activity and recreation in a school sanctioned-setting.

A study in Michigan (Seefeldt, 1976) revealed that as many as 80% of students who participate in athletics in elementary school drop out or are eliminated during the secondary school years. This would not be such an alarming figure (considering that athletic programs are for the elite) if there were other avenues for students to enjoy sports. One of the best and most economical programs is the intramural program. If, however, the school district does not hire proper personnel to administer it, the program soon becomes second-rate and fails to attract participants. The ensuing discussion offers direction for developing a quality intramural program that is based on student interest and conducted through student input and energy.

INTRAMURALS

What, Who, and Why of Intramural Programs

What is an intramural program? It is organized activity for students that is an extension of the physical education program. Student attendance and participation are voluntary, and the program is limited to the boundaries of a specific school. The intramural program can be a laboratory for using the skills and knowledge gained in the physical education program. In terms of supervisory personnel, equipment,

and facilities, the intramural program should be funded by the school district. In some cases, fees are required if the activity involves private facilities such as bowling alleys, skating rinks, and horseback riding stables.

When a broad variety of activities is offered in the intramural program (Figure 14.1), physical education teachers can delegate more class time to instruction, because the opportunity to play the sport can occur in the intramural setting. The intramural program can also be a social meeting ground for students. Youngsters have the opportunity to participate in an activity that they may enjoy and use throughout their lives.

Who participates in an intramural program? Hopefully, every student in the school. The program should offer something of interest to all students and should also provide appropriate competitive experiences for students of all sizes, shapes, and skill levels. All students should have ample opportunity to find success and enjoyment in the program, regardless of their physical stature or ability level.

Why have an intramural program? An intramural program offers students an opportunity to develop interest and competence in a wide range of recreational activities. The program also gives students an

FIGURE 14.1 Intramural racquetball

FIGURE 14.2 Intramural lacrosse

opportunity to develop and maintain a reasonable level of fitness. Evidence has shown that if people do not develop competence and confidence during their school years in their ability to participate in recreational activities, they seldom participate in later life. In the intramural program, students learn to compete against and cooperate with each other in an environment that has little at stake in terms of winning and losing. The program can be a setting for developing lifelong friendships.

The intramural program can also be a place to learn leadership and followership skills. Students learn to compromise and assert themselves. Through these programs, students, parents, and teachers often become closer friends. Finally, the program offers students a place to spend some of their out-of-school time in a supervised setting (Figure 14.2), rather than walking the streets with nothing to do. Few programs for youth offer so many benefits at such a low cost to society.

Recreation versus Competition

Since a successful intramural program should attract all types of students, the question arises as to whether competition or recreation should be featured. If competition is the overriding concern, then tournaments that identify champions and reinforce winners are featured. Competition emphasizes practicing as much as possible, only playing participants who are the best, and avoiding mistakes as much as possible.

If recreation is featured, emphasis is placed on participation and playing all teams an equal number of times. Tournament and league standings are avoided or not posted, and students play each game as an entity in itself. Rewarding recreation emphasizes attendance and participation, and all students are expected to play the same amount. Awards and trophies are not offered, but in some cases, certificates of participation are given.

Which direction should the intramural program

take? As usual, there is no easy answer, but there are some points to be considered. Because many students may have been cut from an athletic program, they may still want to compete. However, many of the participants may not have participated on an athletic team after the elementary school years, and they may simply desire a positive experience. In a survey by Fagan (1979), 581 students in a public high school were asked if they would like to have a competitive program, a recreation-oriented program, or a mixture of both. The results indicated that 9% preferred a competition-oriented program, 9% wanted a recreation program only, and 82% desired a combination of recreation and competition. This is not surprising, since one of the elements of a game is the opportunity to match skill and wits with an opponent in a competitive setting. The survey result also points out that students want to have an opportunity to relax, play, and communicate with peers. The best programs probably offer students a balance of competition and recreation.

Activities

The types and varieties of activities offered to students are at the heart of the intramural program. There should be activities to meet the desires of all students. In some cases, the intramural program has been an outgrowth of the athletic program rather than of the physical education program and has been directed by athletic coaches. The result is probably a program that is conducted in a manner similar to the athletic program. In most cases, this type of program is doomed. The scope of intramural activities should be unlimited and dictated by students. If students are expected to participate in the program in their free time, it is going to have to cater to their desires and wants. Never should the intramural program be regarded as "minor" league for athletes who might make the varsity team at a later date.

A student survey is a good idea to see where student interests lie and to establish the magnitude of those interests. Copies of the survey can be given to homeroom teachers to be returned when they are completed. Compilation of results should then be posted, so students can clearly see that the activities offered are a result of their expressed interests. The survey is a strong tool when bargaining with the administration for program facilities and equipment. When principals understand that many students desire certain activities, the physical educator then has some leverage to gain program support. Figure 14.3 is a sample of the type of survey that could be administered. The survey will also indicate to students the number and variety of activities that can be offered.

HUMERUS HIGH SCHOOL INTRAMURAL SURVEY

Student name _____ Class standing _____

1. Would you participate in the intramural program if activities were offered that interest you? Yes _____ No _____ If no, why not?

2. What do you like most about the present intramural program?

3. What do you like least about the present intramural program?

4. If you choose not to participate, would you be willing to help out in the program in other roles? Check those ways in which you could offer your aid. Officiating _____ Publicity _____ Secretarial _____ Scorekeeping _____ Other (identify) _____

5. It is possible to develop a program that emphasizes competition, recreation, or a combination of both. Which would you desire? Competition _____ Recreation _____ Both _____

6. What days and what time of the day would be best for your participation?

Day	Time
Monday _____	_____
Tuesday _____	_____
Wednesday _____	_____
Thursday _____	_____
Friday _____	_____
Saturday _____	_____

7. Should awards be given to winning participants? Yes _____ No _____ Please justify your answer.

8. Please list any other points that would make the program better suit your needs.

9. The following is a list of activities that might be offered. Please circle 5 that you would most like offered in the intramural program. If an activity that you want is not offered, please write it in the blank at the end of the form.

Archery	Checkers	Flickerball	Lacrosse
Badminton	Chess	Floor hockey	Lawn bowling
Bait and fly casting	Cooperative games	Frisbee golf	Marbles
Basketball	Croquet	Golf	New games
One on one	Cross country	Driving	Orienteering
Two on two	Darts	Putting	Paddle tennis
Other	Decathlon	Gymnastics	Relays
Free throw shooting	Deck tennis	Handball	Riflery
Billiards	Fencing	Horseshoes	Roller hockey
Bowling	Field hockey	Ice hockey	Roller skating
Box hockey	Figure skating	Judo	Shuffleboard
Cards	Flag football	Kite flying	Skiing

FIGURE 14.3 Sample high school intramural survey

Soccer	Speed-a-way	Tetherball	Volley tennis
Softball	Steeplechase	Track and field	Water basketball
Fast pitch	Swimming	Tumbling	Water polo
Slow pitch	Table tennis	Volleyball	Weight lifting
One pitch	Tennis	Two player	Wrestling

Others _____

10. Do you know of any experts who could teach and help organize any of the activities designated above? If so, please describe how they can be contacted.

FIGURE 14.3 Continued

After the survey has been administered and compiled, information about the activities most desired, times when the program will be offered, and possible experts to help with instruction are identified. A program in line with student interests is much easier to develop if a diagnostic instrument similar to the one in Figure 14.3 is administered.

Leadership

Leadership of an intramural program is a joint obligation. The school district should fund personnel to supervise the program and to minimize liability programs. However, students also have a responsibility to organize committees and to implement a successful program. They should develop the policies, rules, and procedures that guide the program.

A most effective way of ensuring student input and energy in implementing the intramural program is to develop an intramural council. The council can consist of 6–10 students and should be balanced by sex and grade level. This body makes the final decisions about the wide-ranging aspects of the program. Committees that report to the council should be developed and maintained with productive students. Some of the following committees might be organized to serve the intramural council:

Activity Development. The activity development committee is responsible for selecting intramural activities as well as facilities, equipment, and personnel necessary for implementation.

Rules and Regulations. The rules and regulations committee develops guidelines for administering the program. This committee is also the enforcement body when rule infractions occur.

Scheduling and Statistics. The scheduling and statistics committee schedules games and contests, maintains school intramural records and league standings, and oversees other related matters.

Referees. The officiating committee recruits referees, trains them, and interprets and makes rulings dealing with protests.

Public Relations. The public relations committee develops all materials for promoting the program; seeks funding from private organizations; and sponsors car washes, raffles, and other fund-raising activities.

Safety. The safety committee develops an approved list of procedures for first aid and emergency situations, and provides a trained student capable of administering first aid and able to be present at activities.

The formation of the student intramural council should not supersede the need for qualified adult personnel, and the school district should be willing to hire adequate help. Without district funding, there is usually little administrative commitment to the program, and a lack of administrative commitment leads ultimately to program failure.

Motivating Students to Participate

There are many methods for promoting intramural programs and encouraging participation. Regardless of the method used, to have the program work, students must see the benefits of participating. The program must exude a spirit and be an "in" thing to do. Some of the following suggestions have been used with success in varying situations and can be modified to meet the needs of a particular school.

Intramural Bulletin Board. Bulletin boards, located throughout the school, display schedules, standings, and future activities. Pictures of champions can also be posted and labeled.

Patches. Winners are awarded arm patches with a school designation, the year, and activity. Some successful programs have awarded patches for participating in a certain number of activities regardless of winning or losing.

T-shirts. T-shirts can be given to winners or participants. The school can hold a T-shirt day on which teachers and participants wear their shirts to school.

Point Total Chart. Points are given for winning first, second, third, or fourth place in an activity, or points can be awarded simply for participation. The points may be awarded to homeroom teams or on an individual basis. The point total chart keeps a running tally throughout the year.

Trophies. Trophies are awarded to homerooms based on point totals at the end of the school year. An excellent idea is to award an "outstanding participant trophy" to those who earned the most participant points.

Newspaper Reports. These articles are written by students and are placed in the school or local newspaper. They motivate best when they explicitly name students.

Field Trips. Field trips are awarded to all participants at the end of the activity. For instance, at the end of the basketball tournament, all participants might attend a college or professional game together.

Extramural Competition. A playday activity can be organized between one or more schools that have similar activities. The participants meet at one school on a Saturday and compete against each other. These students would be a group of nonathletes, and the playday provides an opportunity for them to compete in a setting similar to athletic competition.

Two schools of thought are involved in promoting intramural programs. One awards notoriety and trophies to winners, while the other offers awards and equal publicity to all participants. A case can be made for both approaches. A consideration is that winners receive a great deal of reinforcement, but others of lesser accomplishment may need additional positive strokes, which makes equal publicity for all students important in the implementation of a successful program.

Facilities and Equipment

Without proper facilities and equipment, an intramural program has little chance for success. A major concern is the conflict between athletics and intramurals. Much time and money has been poured into athletic programs, and athletics can be expected to take priority in terms of facility use. At best, the programs should compromise on the use of facilities at opportune times, such as during the final game of the intramural tournament.

Another way to work through the facility problem is to schedule program activities out of season. For example, intramural basketball programs could be scheduled in the fall or spring, and this would alleviate the conflict. Or, schedule intramural activities during low-demand times such as before school, during noon hour, and later in the evening. Community facilities such as churches, the YMCA or YWCA, and city park and recreation areas can be used at times to increase the number of participants who can be accommodated. Scheduling becomes paramount in assuring that facilities will be available. The scheduling committee should work with the athletic director and staging director to avoid conflicts.

Equipment should be provided mainly by the district. Some successful programs have been funded by student activities such as car washes or raffles, but in general, when the district chooses not to give funding, the program is held in low esteem. If the program involves private facilities (e.g., bowling alleys, golf courses, or skating rinks), club members will usually receive reduced rates.

Having an equipment committee that determines how and when money will be spent is a good idea. The committee also becomes responsible for maintaining and repairing equipment. The school should provide a storage area for intramural equipment that is used solely by intramurals. It usually does not work well to use physical education program equipment for the intramural program. When equipment is lost or damaged, hard feelings result and program support is lost.

Officials

Critical to the success of any athletic endeavor is the quality of the officiating. The intramural program should be officiated by students. It is unrealistic to think that teachers will be willing to work ball games. A sound approach is to develop an officiating committee that has the responsibility of acquiring and training officials. Many students who do not play competitively are willing to officiate and enjoy being an integral part of an event.

Students should be recruited as soon as possible so they can acquire experience and work confidently with experienced officials. They should be trained in rules and game mechanics prior to a tournament and should be allowed to practice with as little pressure as possible. The word of the officials is absolute. If a disagreement arises, it is filed and resolved through proper protest channels.

Scheduling officials and being sure that they make their assignments is crucial. Turner (1978) proposes an excellent plan that is easy to implement. Figure 14.4 is a chart showing who is assigned to officiate.

Intramural Department
Flag Football Officiating Assignments
(For Week of October 1–5)

FIELD	Oct. 1 MONDAY	Oct. 2 TUESDAY	Oct. 3 WEDNESDAY	Oct. 4 THURSDAY	Oct. 5 FRIDAY
1	____ Williams	_TK_ Kelley	_JB_ Bell	_TT_ Tucker	_FG_ Gordon
	____ Robbins	_CM_ Morton	_JG_ Goodall	_MN_ Nagel	____ Jackson
2	____ Nagel	_SG_ Geltman	_MG_ Gallagher	_DA_ Andrews	_jh_ Houle
	____ Horton	_EC_ Chapin	____ Jackson	_MK_ Keene	____ Turner
3	____ Andrews	_jh_ Houle	_FG_ Gordon	____ Bent	_SG_ Geltman
	____ Sullivan	____ Stinson	_SK_ Kenton	____ Chapin	_GR_ Robbins
	____ ____	_Bent_	_AN_ Williams	_FG_ Gordon	_EC_ Chapin
	____ ____	_Bell_	____ Houle	_SG_ Geltman	_CM_ Morton
	____ ____	_Williams_	____ Andrews	____ ____	_Bent_
	____ ____	____ ____	____ Jackson	____ ____	_Bell_

FIGURE 14.4 Chart of officials' assignments (reprinted with permission from the *Journal of Physical Education, Recreation, and Dance,* February, 1978, p. 42)

The initials to the left of the typed name indicate that the individual has read and accepted the assignment. Blank lines are provided for the names of people who are willing to officiate, if needed. If an official has accepted an assignment, but then cannot carry it out, he or she must contact the first person who has signed up for that day. When a replacement has been found, the person who cannot make the appointment notifies the intramural office.

Officials can be given points for the number of games they work; they can also be awarded patches, T-shirts, and trophies for their accomplishments in a fashion similar to participants. Without some recognition, students have little motivation for carrying out the thankless obligations of officiating.

Equating Competition

All participants should know that they have an opportunity to succeed in the intramural setting. Students seldom continue to participate if they foresee a constant diet of losing or other negative experiences. Grouping by ability has both advantages and disadvantages. It can be awkward to have skilled and unskilled players together when the activity demands a great deal of progression and skill performance. In those cases, having similarly skilled students play together and compete against teams of similar ability is probably better. However, placing less-skilled athletes with skilled athletes may improve the perfor-mance level of the unskilled students and enhance their confidence. It also provides opportunities for skilled persons to aid the less skilled.

When grouping for teams, try the following methods. Homerooms can compete against homerooms. This is the most heterogeneous method of grouping. Students of varying skill levels will then play on the same team. Grouping by homeroom may be effective if students are randomly placed there. Another method is to use divisions of competition. Depending on the activity, students can be grouped by ability, size, or age. Homerooms could sponsor two or more teams of different ability that would play in different leagues. The advantage of homeroom sponsorship lies in the camaraderie developed among students and the possibility of enhancing the classroom relationships. Probably the best solution is to equalize the competition regardless of homeroom assignments or other segregating factors. Choosing teams that are somewhat equal can be done in the following ways:

1. Leaders are elected by the students. The leaders then choose teams in a private session held away from the rest of the participants.
2. Students are arranged by height or weight. The names of students within a certain range are put in one box, and a different range of heights in another box. Teams are then selected by drawing the names of an equal number of students of similar size for each team.

Whatever method is used to form teams, the supervisor should be sensitive to maintaining a balance of competition and preventing embarrassing situations. Teams should never be selected in such a fashion that the poorest player is chosen last. The intramural experience should be a positive experience that all students anticipate with enthusiasm. If the program is to succeed, participants are needed, and should be treated as important and meaningful people.

Tournaments

A variety of tournaments can be organized to carry out the intramural program. The type will depend on the number of entries, the number of sessions or how many days the tournament will continue, the facilities and equipment available, and the number of officials, scorers, and other helpers on hand. The following types of tournaments are often used with success.

Round Robin Tournament

The round robin tournament is a good choice when adequate time is available for play. In this type of tournament, every team or individual plays every other team or individual once. Final standings are based on win-loss percentages. To determine the amount of time the tournament will take, the following formula can be used:

$$\frac{TI(TI - 1)}{2}$$

where TI = number of teams or individuals. For example, if there are five teams in a softball unit, $5(5 - 1)/2 = 10$ games are to be scheduled.

To arrange a tournament for an odd number of teams, each team should be assigned a number (number the teams down the right column and up the left column). All numbers rotate, and the last number each time draws a bye. An example using seven teams follows:

Round 1	Round 2
7	6
6 — 1	5 — 7
5 — 2	4 — 1
4 — 3	3 — 2

Round 3	Round 4
5	4
4 — 6	3 — 5
3 — 7	2 — 6
2 — 1	1 — 7

Round 5	Round 6
3	2
2 — 4	1 — 3
1 — 5	7 — 4
7 — 6	6 — 5

Round 7	
1	
7 — 2	
6 — 3	
5 — 4	

To arrange a tournament for an even number of teams, the plan is similar, except that the position of Team 1 remains stationary and the other teams revolve around it until the combinations are completed. An example of an 8-team tournament follows.

Round 1	Round 2
1 — 2	1 — 8
8 — 3	7 — 2
7 — 4	6 — 3
6 — 5	5 — 4

Round 3	Round 4
1 — 7	1 — 6
6 — 8	5 — 7
5 — 2	4 — 8
4 — 3	3 — 2

Round 5	Round 6
1 — 5	1 — 4
4 — 6	3 — 5
3 — 7	2 — 6
2 — 8	8 — 7

Round 7	
1 — 3	
2 — 4	
8 — 5	
7 — 6	

Ladder Tournament

A ladder format can be used for an ongoing tournament that is administered by a teacher or informally by students. Competition occurs by challenge and is supervised minimally. Various arrangements are possible, but participants usually challenge only those opponents who are two steps above a participant's present ranking. If the challenger wins, she or he changes places with the loser. The teacher can establish an initial ranking, or positions can be drawn out of a hat. Figure 14.5 shows an example of a ladder.

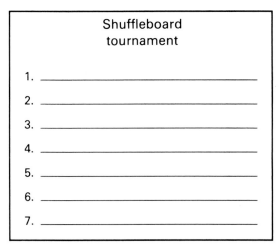

FIGURE 14.5   Ladder tournament chart

FIGURE 14.7   Elimination tournament chart

Pyramid Tournament

A pyramid tournament is similar to a ladder tournament, but more challenge and variety are possible because there is a wider choice of opponents (Figure 14.6). In the pyramid tournament, players may challenge any opponent one level above their present ranking. In another variation, players must challenge someone at their level and beat that person before they can challenge a person at a higher level.

Elimination Tournament

The disadvantage of the elimination tournament is that the poorer teams are eliminated first and do not get to play as many games as the more proficient teams. The skilled thus get better, and the less skilled sit out without the opportunity to improve. The advantage of the elimination tournament is that it can be completed in a shorter amount of time than, for example, the round robin tournament. Double-elimination tournaments are somewhat better than single elimination, because two losses are required before

a team is relegated to the sidelines. Remember that students come to intramurals to play rather than to sit on the side and watch others play. Figure 14.7 is an example of a simple single-elimination tournament with six teams.

SPORT CLUBS

Sport clubs are filled with students who are bonded by their common interest in some sport or activity. The concept originated in Europe and has become more common in the United States, largely because of the inability of school districts to fund a wide variety of activities. The clubs are for students, are run by students, and are often funded by the students. They offer young people the chance to organize a club that meets the specific needs of a group and the opportunity to socialize with friends.

Sport clubs are sometimes administered by guidelines set by the intramural director in a school district. The clubs can be an outgrowth of either the intramural or athletic program. The types of sport

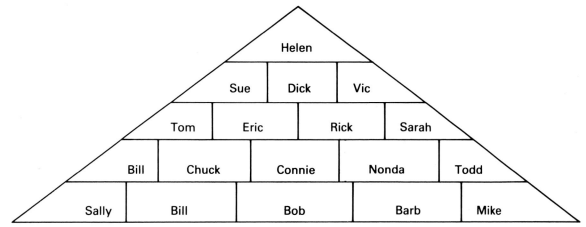

FIGURE 14.6   Pyramid tournament chart

clubs to be developed are usually dictated by students. The following steps are typical of a system for developing a sport club network in the school setting.

Determine the Interests of Students.   A survey instrument (Figure 14.3) can be used to determine student interests in and concerns for sport clubs. It is usually best to develop one or two clubs first to demonstrate the effectiveness of this approach to the district administrators.

Meet with Interested Students.   Before the meeting with students, find a faculty member or some other person to serve as the club's advisor. The advisor should have a keen interest in the area and a minimal amount of expertise. For example, it would be foolish to appoint a teacher as an advisor to the backpacking club if he had never backpacked. During the first meeting, the dues necessary for conducting club activities should be discussed. If the cost is prohibitive, many students may choose not to participate. Students should also discuss the joys and dangers of participating in the activity. School guidelines for clubs can be discussed so students understand clearly the parameters involved.

Develop a Constitution.   After the initial meeting, students who are still interested will meet again to develop a constitution. This document should delineate membership requirements, the function and selection of officers, and meeting dates. An outline form can be used to aid in the development of similar club constitutions.

Establish Rules and Regulations.   Clubs need to determine the scope of their organization and the requirements of club members to retain active membership. If competition with other clubs is involved, travel funding and housing requirements should be explicitly outlined. The need for adult chaperons and drivers, and the need for a waiver of responsibility signed by parents should be a part of the rules network. The basic premise of the rules is to eliminate misunderstandings and to encourage a safe, liability-free club setting.

Seek Funding, Facilities, and Equipment.   With the help of the advisor, students should determine what facilities and equipment are available and when they can be scheduled. Seeking outside funding from private organizations and service clubs is also important. In some cases, school time may be given for clubs to conduct meeting and planning sessions. Appropriate facilities such as bowling alleys or swimming pools need to be contacted to see if 1 or 2 hr per week can be reserved for club activities.

Conduct a Periodic Evaluation.   The clubs should be evaluated on a regular basis to see if interest is waning, whether the needs of students are being met, and whether the manner of club conduct needs to be modified. Sometimes when clubs are developed based on the interests of students, that interest can decrease to such an extent that the club should be discontinued. New student interests may also develop and result in new clubs. A periodic evaluation may result in a new club advisor, better ways to facilitate club goals, or an attempt to stimulate renewed interest in the club.

Implementing a Club Sport

The following areas should be considered when developing a club sport. They are considerations that school district personnel need to be aware of if a successful program is to be implemented.

Liability

Students who participate in the club should have liability insurance. Depending on the activity, the regular school insurance may cover the student during participation. However, if the activity is exceptionally risky (e.g., skiing, rugby), supplementary insurance may be needed. Parents must certify that the student is covered by their insurance policy if students choose not to purchase insurance offered by the district's carrier.

A signed parental responsibility waiver form is necessary for participation in club activities. Even though the form does not waive the student's right to sue and seek redress, a signed form communicates to the school district that the parents approve and are aware of their student's participation in the program.

Instructors and advisors to the program must be competent to administer the activity. If the school district advisor lacks proper training, experts outside the school should be secured. These may be parents or interested community volunteers. In most cases, the responsibility for supplying a safe environment falls on the school district.

Procedures for handling injuries are important and may involve having a physician on call. Written procedures should be available and understood by all club members in case an accident occurs. For example, what steps will be taken if someone is injured on a backpacking trip? Accidents do happen, and there is much less trouble if proper emergency procedures have been planned for such an occurrence.

Budget

It would be ideal if the school district funded sport clubs. In some cases, student fees are assessed at the start of the school year and distributed on an equal basis to all clubs. This provides a financial foundation, but almost all clubs require additional funding. The most common methods used are cake sales, car washes, rummage sales, sales of old and outdated equipment, candy sales, and donations.

When travel and lodging are necessary, students are usually expected to absorb the cost. School districts will often provide a bus if the activity is scheduled when buses are available. Travel by private car is the least acceptable method of transport due to the possibility of an accident and subsequent liability problems.

Many clubs have an equipment bank in which equipment is stored for use year after year. The club thus develops an adequate source of equipment over a period of years. Used equipment from local colleges and high school athletic programs can sometimes be secured to augment the equipment bank.

Coaching

Qualified coaches and other school-affiliated advisors are usually involved in administration of the athletic and intramural programs. This means that club advisors and coaches may have to be selected from the community. Some type of screening should be undertaken by the school district to see that the advisors are properly qualified. The club programs will have to be conducted at a time when these people are available since many potential advisors are employed during the school day. If the activity is recreational in nature, then interested parents may carry out the supervisory responsibilities. All adults involved should be approved by the school district and required to sign a form agreeing to abide by district policies.

Facilities

Facilities usually have to be scheduled at low-use times. Sport clubs are often last in line for facilities, after the athletic and intramural programs. Facilities need to be found in the community if the clubs involve sports that are offered interscholastically. For example, city parks have softball fields that can be used. Some school districts choose not to approve clubs dealing with sports that are offered at the intramural and interscholastic level. The philosophy behind this ruling is that club sports should offer opportunities that are not available through other avenues. If that is the case, then most sport club programs will be conducted in private facilities such as bowling alleys, swimming pools, ski areas, skating rinks, riflery and archery ranges, and racquetball clubs.

Achievement Clubs

Many of the activities suggested in the intramurals section for motivating students can also be used with club sport activities. In addition, some clubs can be formed for which students are eligible only after they have met predetermined standards of achievement. Examples might be a push-up club, jogging club, bike-riding club (Figure 14.8), distance swimming club, and a weight lifting club. In each case, students can join the club and be a part of the group only after they have met the minimum standards.

INTERSCHOLASTIC ATHLETICS

The interscholastic athletic program usually stands at the top of the pyramid in terms of attention, time, and money focused on the program. Sports in the school setting should contribute to the educational purposes of the institution. There are many arguments as to whether the athletic program is a negative or positive influence on students. In this chapter, the authors will not attempt to pass judgment on the athletic program, but rather to examine both sides of the issue, identify guidelines for a quality program, and suggest various screening methods for teachers who choose to coach. Athletics should not be considered either inherently good or bad. How the athletic program is conducted makes it a positive or negative experience for participants. It is entirely possible to create a positive experience for students through a competitive sports program, but the program should not be the "tail that wags the dog."

FIGURE 14.8 Achievement club poster

Values of an Athletic Program

A strong athletic program can develop a sense of belonging among the participants. Students like to see what they can accomplish by themselves and with the help of peers. Team sports teach them that goals can be reached only if teammates are willing to cooperate. It becomes quickly apparent that cooperation precedes competition. Conducting a competitive game is impossible when teammates do not cooperate and follow the established rules.

Athletics often teach students that the journey is more important than the destination. The work done to reach a goal is the essence of an athletic experience, and students learn that after the victory, continued hard work is still necessary. This lesson may carry over to adult life and help the participant continue to succeed.

Athletics give students something to talk about and something to do. Many of the problems of youth arise because of boredom and little to do when the school day is over. Athletics give status to participants and make them feel that they are important to others. The program also allows students to share their positive accomplishments with others and to learn to appreciate the accomplishments of friends.

The athletic program serves as a laboratory for gifted students. It can offer students a chance to perfect their skills to a high level with the aid of a knowledgeable coach. Students who are athletically gifted are appreciated and rewarded for their accomplishments. Society offers few opportunities to practice with proper facilities and to receive coaching at little or no cost. The athletic program also brings a community of people together for a common cause. Parents and business people begin to develop pride in their community and find a common ground for communication. The athletic team can be a unifying factor that brings together people of all backgrounds.

Participation in athletics can teach students how to maintain a level of physical fitness and to care for their bodies. They learn about the need for self-discipline when one desires to reach a goal. The importance of sacrifice, following training rules, and practicing regularly become an attitudinal set of participants. Sportsmanship and self-control must be practiced if students are to find success. Rules and regulations become an integral part of sport participation and illustrate to students the importance of following predetermined rules. Students also learn that they are penalized when rules are broken, and those unwilling to cooperate are seldom welcome to participate. Finally, the athletic program can show students how highly regarded and important excel-lence is to people. Athletics should try to embody excellence and the Olympic ideal. Students set goals and make sacrifices in an attempt to achieve excellence without any guarantee of success.

Athletics can motivate students to stay in school. Studies have shown that the dropout rate among athletes is less than among nonparticipating students. The athletic program can be the incentive that offers students an important reason for continuing their schooling.

Detrimental Effects of an Athletic Program

The athletic program mobilizes large amounts of time, energy, and money to aid a relatively small number of participants. This sometimes leads to neglect of the less-skilled performer. In contrast, an athlete who receives special attention can develop the attitude that athletes are better than others and are eligible for personal favors and special attention. This can lead to a situation whereby student athletes develop a value set that is detrimental when their playing days are over.

Participation in athletic programs often interrupts the educational environment. Athletes leave school to go on trips, or receive released time to practice. The athlete may begin to believe that it is more important to be a successful athlete than a competent student.

Another possible effect of the athletic program is a loss of personal identity. Athletes are told when to eat, when to practice, when they can have free time, and when to study. They may soon begin to wonder if they can make any important decisions for themselves and whether they have the right to live their own lives.

Increased aggression and violence are sometimes the result of an athletic program. The intense rivalry between schools can encourage groups of students to perform violent and destructive acts. One theory of aggression states that it is a learned behavior and that athletics strongly encourage aggressive acts. Whether or not the theory is correct is less important than making sure that students are coached to do their best without hurting or maiming others. If athletes are encouraged to "kill the bum," it is quite possible that aggressive tendencies may be stimulated.

The pressures of coaching are apparent to all who have filled a head coaching position in a major sport. This pressure is often unjust and can lead to unacceptable coaching behavior. Athletic coaching is a good example of holding an individual accountable for the end result (winning) regardless of how that individual reaches the goal. When this occurs, students often suffer from the coach's lack of concern and caring about personal problems and injuries. Until an equal emphasis is placed on the process of coaching as well as on the product, the athletic setting will be less than a positive and developmental experience.

At times, parents and community members can become so deeply involved in the athletic program that they apply pressure on students to win at all costs. Student athletes begin to feel that if they do not win, they will not be accepted as an integral part of the community. The athletic program then becomes an incessant effort on the part of students to achieve the adults' goals. In these situations, the adults have forgotten that the athletic program was developed for students in an effort to contribute to the youngsters' personal growth. When the program becomes instead an adult program with adult goals, students cannot separate what is important from what is not.

Another concern for athletes is injury. All participants assume the risk of injury through involvement. If the desire to win exceeds the desire to provide a safe environment, then some students may be ordered to play with an injury or may receive injuries due to lack of proper care and treatment. Concern for the health of participants is the paramount program goal.

Developing a Quality Athletic Program

Depending on how it is organized and presented, an athletic program can be a positive or negative experience for students. The following guidelines, if heeded, should help to ensure meaningful experiences for participants. All districts will have to interpret the guidelines based on their specific situation, but it is difficult to imagine that a worthwhile program will result if the guidelines are deviated from to a large degree.

1. The athletic program should be voluntary. All students who choose to participate should have an opportunity to compete. All athletes should have the opportunity to play if they have practiced and disciplined themselves. Cutting players from a squad is an accepted practice, but there should be another arena in which those players can compete. This may mean a junior varsity, C squad, or strong intramural or sport club program. If athletics is regarded as an educational experience, all students have the right to receive that experience.

2. The program should be based on the maturation level of participants. This is particularly important at the junior high school level, because these students exhibit a wide range of development. Group-

ing by age, ability, or size may be necessary if the program is to be meaningful.

3. The athletic program should be an after-school program. The practice of giving a period of school time for practice is discriminatory and runs counter to the established rule that an academic education is the school's priority. Along the same lines, excusing athletes from physical education is also difficult to justify. If the program is educational, then all students, regardless of background, should be able to benefit from it.

4. The athletic program should offer a broad spectrum of activities for participants; the fewer activities offered, the fewer participants. The program should also be balanced in offering activities to all groups — skilled and unskilled, boys and girls, able-bodied and handicapped.

5. Organization of the athletic program should meet the needs of students. The concerns of the spectators should be met only after the program has been developed. Many sports are being dropped because they are not drawing large numbers of spectators and are therefore not making money. If this unfortunate trend continues, football and basketball could conceivably represent the total athletic program.

6. The program should require that all participants be certified medically healthy by a physician. The program should be evaluated regularly in terms of safety practices to ensure that proper procedures are being conducted.

7. Procedures to be followed should an accident occur must be written, posted, and sent to parents. Most districts ask that parents sign a waiver of responsibility form before a student can participate. This is an opportune time to explain the safety and first-aid procedures being followed. Insurance for all participants is a must.

8. As idealistic as it may sound to many coaches, the program should emphasize enjoyment and participation over winning. Skill development and a positive experience are a heritage that students can take with them after graduation. One might well question what has been gained if students win most of their games but lose the desire to participate in sports once they leave school.

9. Physical conditioning should be an important phase of the program. Preconditioning is essential to the safety and welfare of players, and should precede intense, early-season practice sessions.

10. Facilities should be shared by all facets of the athletic, intramural, and sport club programs. It is understandable that athletics expect to take priority, but someone needs to direct the situation so that all programs are given acceptable use of the facilities and equipment.

11. Awards, trophies, and other incentives used to identify outstanding achievement should be minimized. This is not to avoid rewarding excellence, but to encourage proper discretion. If awards are given in excess, they become meaningless.

12. The athletic program should be constantly evaluated. In some cases, the program is seldom scrutinized until an infraction occurs. Periodic evaluations by the athletic director, principal, and coaching staff can aid in preventing problems. Evaluation can serve to improve offerings for both boys and girls, upgrade scheduling efficiency, and show the need for in-service training.

The Athletic Council

To help assure that a quality athletic program is maintained, many school districts are developing an athletic council. The council is generally a district-wide body comprised of the superintendent (or a representative), principals, the athletic director for the district, coaches from each of the schools, and student representatives from each school. All schools, sports, and sexes should be equally represented.

The athletic council can help plan and evaluate the total district program and can help deal with problems such as finance, facilities, and personnel. The council can promote the athletic program and serve as a screening body when outside parties become involved with the program. This body may also be responsible for evaluating coaches and hearing grievances. Sometimes, for example, parents have a concern but are hesitant to approach the coach involved. The council could hear such cases confidentially without revealing the plaintiff's identity.

The council can enhance the image of the coaching community. It can be a place where coaches work together to achieve the highest ideals and to reach common goals. In summary, the council should be a valuable asset for coaches, administrators, and athletes.

Securing Qualified Coaches

Qualified coaches are the cornerstone of a sound athletic program. Most coaches are highly motivated and dedicated. In most cases, they have to be motivated by their enjoyment of sport rather than by the financial remuneration, for coaching is one of the lowest paid professions. An athletic director recently calculated that assistant coaches were receiving about 50 cents per hour. Most coaches enter the profession because they were successful athletes and found positive experiences in the athletic program. Being an outstanding athlete seldom guarantees success in coaching, however. Coaches need to have a wide range of abilities. The following attributes are representative of the characteristics of successful coaches:

Strong Character. The coach should be a model for athletes to emulate. How the coach relates to others, the individual's physical appearance, honesty, integrity, and other personal qualities often teach students more about athletics than the actual participation experience. Many administrators find cause for concern when coaches swear, drink, or smoke excessively, and most students cannot deal with the double standard of a coach who advocates team fitness but does not practice fitness, who tells them to be respectful but yells when a mistake is made, who preaches honesty but shows them how to foul without being caught. Many athletes remember their coach much longer than they remember the actual playing experience.

Knowledge of Growth and Development Patterns. The coach must have a strong background in motor development and motor learning. Understanding the physical limits of athletes is as important as understanding their capabilities under pressure. The coach should also have some knowledge of psychology and the emotional development of secondary-level students. Knowing when to reinforce, when to scold, and when to praise are key components of a successful coaching career.

Knowledge of the Activity. Coaches should know the fundamentals of the sport that they are coaching and the best ways to present and teach the basic skills. A good coach understands strategy and knows when to use various types of game plans. The coach must be an excellent teacher, and in many cases, the best coaches are also regarded as the best teachers. Concurrent with a knowledge of the sport is the ability to plan carefully. Both teaching and coaching demand a high degree of planning to succeed. Effective coaches always attempt to account for every minute of practice time so that idle or wasted time is minimized.

Coaching Certification

The need for certification in the coaching profession is great. The belief is still widely held that anyone can coach—regardless of background or training. Unfortunately, almost anyone can find the opportunity to coach due to the lack of certification requirements and standards.

Noble and Sigle (1980) found that 34 states allowed nonteachers to coach on a regular or emergency basis. Twenty states had no minimum requirements other than age, and only eight states required a teaching certificate.

Training in many areas is necessary for coaches to be productive and motivating. The AAHPERD Task Force on Certification of High School Coaches identified the following aspects as essential in the training of coaches:

1. Medical aspects
2. Sociological and psychological aspects
3. Theory and techniques
4. Kinesiological foundations
5. Physiological foundations

Coaching is an impressive responsibility, and regardless of certification, coaches should make an attempt to seek the best possible training.

The Teaching-Coaching Conflict

A personal conflict often occurs when teachers choose to coach. Particularly in physical education, a teacher who is required to coach long hours has a difficult task. Many physical education instructors are not hired for their expertise in teaching, but rather for their ability to coach more than one sport. This policy can result in a situation where teaching takes second place to coaching, and most of the teacher's planning and energy are dedicated to the coaching assignment.

Teachers who also coach often end up working 10 to 12 hr days. The pay is low, but the rewards can be great. Coaching ability is scrutinized regularly in terms of the winning and losing record, and teachers may become caught up in the pressure of trying to be a winning coach for fear of losing their position. In this situation, it takes a strong and gifted person to place equal emphasis on teaching and coaching. Physical educators should not lose sight of the fact that about 90% of their salary comes from teaching and the remaining 10% from coaching. Many more students are affected by the outstanding teacher than by the effective coach. The ability to perform well in both roles is a difficult challenge, particularly when the majority of contingencies apply to the coaching role.

REFERENCES AND SUGGESTED READINGS

Fagan, K. 1979. Intramural survey, Arcadia High School. Unpublished report.

Maas, G. M. 1978. Promoting high school intramurals. *JOPERD* 49(2): 40–41.

Noble, L., and Sigle, G. 1980. Minimum requirements for interscholastic coaches. *JOPERD* 51(9): 32–33.

Seefeldt, V. 1976. Joint legislative study on youth sports programs: Agency sponsored sports phase I. State of Michigan, November.

Turner, M. 1978. Scheduling student officials. *JOPERD* 49(2): 42.

15 PUBLIC RELATIONS

Public relations activities are vital to the future of the physical education profession. The public's current interest in physical fitness, health, wellness, and nutrition offers the profession unique opportunities. The increasing concern for preventive medicine and the emphasis on maintaining wellness make this time an opportunity for significant growth within the physical education profession. Nothing is more important than the health and vitality of an individual. Unfortunately, most people do not associate physical education with learning how to make the most of one's health. In the past, the emphasis in physical education was on participation in team sports. Little information was presented on why and how certain activities could be healthful.

Physical educators have been hesitant to advertise and promote their programs. For many years, it was considered unprofessional to advertise and tell others about the merits of using the services of doctors, lawyers, or teachers. Today, however, all professional fields are using promotion. Witness the advertisements on television and in newspapers for various hospitals, doctors, and lawyers. Even churches are erecting billboards in an attempt to increase the size of their congregation, but seldom does one see an advertisement promoting physical education as a profession.

For years, people have associated physical education with athletics. When physical education teachers tell the public in what area they teach, many will ask which sport they coach. No one can question the exposure athletics receive through parental support and the media. The critical point is that few parents and community members understand that physical education emphasizes preparation for a lifetime of involvement in activity.

When the public does not understand the educational value of a profession, they find it easy to do without. For example, driver training is taught in most schools, and statistics have shown that such training reduces the number of accidents and deaths. A lower insurance rate is therefore given to those who have participated in driver education. If the public looks to physical education and sees little payoff in terms of life-style and the quality of life, then many become advocates of making the program elective or doing away with it altogether. When money is in short supply, which areas are scrutinized first? Physical education is usually at the head of the line. Why? Because the public has decided that it is of little value. This is the bottom line of public relations. A program must offer something of lifetime value to participants, and the public must come to understand that. Nothing sells physical education like a sound program.

Another point of concern is trying to reach the public. Teachers often do an adequate job of reaching parents and telling them about the program, but many people who pay taxes and help support education never receive any information about the schools. It is not enough to reach the parents. Colleagues, people without children in school, and other students should receive attention and concern. This large group of people will not support physical education programs if physical education professionals have not kept them informed.

GUIDELINES FOR PUBLIC RELATIONS

The public relations program should be based on a number of points because many factors are involved in developing a strong program of publicity and exposure. The following points should be considered:

1. Explain to students why they are in physical education. If you are attempting to influence their lives, they have a right to know why you are asking them to do various activities. In most cases, understanding why one is doing something is more important than actually performing an activity.

2. Encourage students to explain to their parents why they are experiencing various activi-

246

ties and learning episodes. An effective public relations agent is an excited student telling Mom and Dad all about a unit in physical education.

3. Share your program with colleagues and administrators. It is important that they understand innovations and the new activities presented. Many times, physical educators need the support of colleagues to reach goals, and administrators are seldom informed about physical education programs. What do they tell complaining parents, and how do they defend a program if they are not aware of it?

4. Inform the community media of newsworthy happenings. For example, when a new unit of instruction is being presented, send a note to the television, radio, and newspaper organizations. Over a period of time, they have a need for material and may make contact. Maintaining an ongoing program of news releases is important. Large public relations firms often send out news releases with the expectation that not many will be used. They operate on the law of averages, that sooner or later the media will need some of the material.

5. Find the friends of physical education. Many people who are not associated with the profession are strong advocates. They can speak forcefully for physical education in the schools without having a vested interest. Develop a physical education booster group that is invited to visit the program regularly. They need to know what is going on if they are expected to share the program with others. Another way to communicate with the group is through a "friends of physical education" newsletter that describes the various aspects of the program. Remember that the athletic program has used booster groups to strong advantage for years. There is no reason why the physical education program cannot be as successful.

6. How one acts and communicates with others has a great impact on the profession. Some teachers become disenchanted with teaching and start to communicate these feelings to students, parents, and the public. Teachers are walking billboards for their chosen professions. Students respect teachers who are enthusiastic and positive about the work they perform. Examining carefully why one chose to enter the teaching profession and explaining those reasons to others is important.

7. Communicate to others how the program influences the lives of participants. Parents and students have a right to know the benefits of a sound physical education program. Send home with the students brochures or newsletters that explain the

impact of physical education on youth, and tell parents how they can help their children become more proficient in physical activity. Figure 15.1 is an example of a short booklet that communicates the what, why, and how of physical fitness to parents in simple terms.

8. Become actively involved in professional organizations such as the state, local, and national associations of health, physical education, recreation, and dance. Professionals sometimes forget the old adage, "United we stand, divided we fall." A professional organization is for teachers and gives them a chance to pursue and establish professional goals. Physical education has suffered from teachers deciding to get along without paying dues to an organization. Certainly one can get along without an organization, but who listens to one lonely voice? Unfortunately, physical educators who are only interested in coaching have sometimes weakened these organizations by their lack of interest. They become so involved in coaching that they believe there is not enough time to participate. Some of the most dynamic and respected teachers are also coaches; these people would add a great deal to a professional organization.

The best known professional organization for physical education is the American Alliance for Health, Physical Education, Recreation, and Dance (AAHPERD). Its membership consists of teachers and professors from all levels and professional backgrounds throughout the United States. Each state has an AAHPERD organization related to the national organization. Both organizations have political advocacy groups that work for bettering the standing of the physical education profession.

9. Reach out to experts in other physical activity areas. For example, there are many capable people in specialized areas such as yoga, fencing, martial arts, and gymnastics, who could conduct special workshops or help students begin a unit. They can add new and exciting curriculum activities that might not be strong competency areas for the physical educator. When these people are used, all prosper. Students receive sound instruction, and teachers make good friends and advocates for their program.

10. Teach and emphasize lifetime skills and activities. When students and parents see that the skills they learn will be used throughout their lives, they are more likely to become strong advocates of a program. Few people participate in team sports after age 25, yet most want to participate in some type of activity. If competency in lifetime sport skills is

AEROBIC?   HEART RATE?   FITNESS?

CARDIOPULMONARY?

MENTAL TOUGHNESS?   OVERLOAD?

EXERCISE?

What do all these words mean and how can they affect the growth of your youngster? A good place to start is to find out what you know about **fitness** and the **physical growth** of YOUR children.

The following are a series of questions to test your knowledge in the area of **fitness**.

ANSWERS TO THE FOLLOWING APPEAR AFTER QUESTIONS

MULTIPLE CHOICE (There is only one correct answer)
CIRCLE CORRECT ANSWER

1. According to doctors the most important type of **physical fitness** involves:

   A. Arm strength
   B. Abdominal muscles (stomach)
   C. Leg muscles
   D. Heart and lung system
   E. All of the above

2. **Cardiopulmonary** fitness can be developed by:

   A. Jogging
   B. Swimming
   C. Sit-ups
   D. Roller skating
   E. A, B, and D

3. **Aerobic** activities:

   A. Are exercises in which one must completely leave the floor at one point
   B. Are similar to acrobatic activities
   C. Are activities that involve the prolonged use of air
   D. Involve the use of balloons
   E. None of the above

FIGURE 15.1   Physical fitness booklet (modified from a booklet by Clayre Petray, Long Beach State University)

TRUE-FALSE (The statement must be **entirely true** to circle T)

T F   4. Children don't need regular daily activity like adults do because they can become physically fit during recess periods at school.

T F   5. Parents do not have to worry about heart disease and their child.

T F   6. One advantage of a student's being overweight is that he or she will become more respected because of his or her size.

T F   7. A physically fit person has better digestion than one who is not.

T F   8. There is no need for concern if a child under 5 years is fat.

T F   9. Studies show that by ages 8–12, children decide what physical activities they will pursue during their free time in later life.

T F 10. Youngsters have smaller bodies and hearts than adults. They should therefore **not** be **encouraged** to push themselves past the point of being tired.

T F 11. Youngsters should be encouraged to "clean their plates" at each meal to ensure proper diet and nutrition.

T F 12. To become physically fit, students must exercise for 30 min continuously 5 days per week.

T F 13. To get in shape, it is necessary to join a health spa so that you have access to a variety of equipment.

T F 14. Although exercise makes you stronger, it also makes you more tired.

T F 15. When you begin breathing hard while exercising, this shows that you are pushing yourself hard enough to strengthen your heart muscle.

T F 16. One of the best ways to ensure that your youngster will become physically fit is to enroll her or him in competitive sports such as baseball or tackle football.

T F 17. Although a person's heart rate increases while she or he is exercising, the result is a decrease in her or his resting heart rate.

T F 18. The best way for an overweight student to lose weight is to increase his or her amount of daily activity.

T F 19. Exercise in most cases will not increase appetite.

ANSWERS!!!!!

1. **D—HEART AND LUNG SYSTEM.**
Strengthening the heart and lung system (known as **cardiopulmonary fitness**) can prevent the onset of heart disease, the killer of almost 1,000,000 people each year.

2. **E—A, B, and D (JOGGING, SWIMMING, AND ROLLER SKATING).**
Cardiopulmonary fitness involves the development of the heart (cardio) and lungs (pulmonary). The heart and lung system can be strengthened by activities that involve **continuous** movement of the whole body. Sit-ups build the stomach, but do not strengthen the heart muscle.

3. **C—ARE ACTIVITIES THAT INVOLVE THE USE OF AIR.**
Aerobic activities are those in which air is utilized, and through which the heart and lungs

FIGURE 15.1 Continued

become more efficient (**cardiopulmonary fitness**). Aerobic activities can increase the size of, as well as strengthen, both the heart and blood vessels.

4. **False.** Although youngsters have the opportunity to be active at recess, studies show that they stop at the first sign of tiring. To increase the level of cardiopulmonary fitness, activity must be nonstop for 15–30 min.

5. **False.** Signs of heart disease have been found in children as young as 2 years.

6. **False.** Overweight students cannot move as quickly in game situations and therefore are usually chosen last as team members. Peer pressure and ridicule are great among children.

7. **True.**

8. **False.** The widely held belief that "baby fat" disappears is a **myth.** "Baby fat" most often turns into "adult fat."

9. **True.** If children are competent at using their body in a variety of movements at an early age, they will be more likely to continue to use their body throughout their life. A person's activity level is also established early. **Active** young people tend to be **active** older people: **activity** is the best means to prevent obesity.

10. **False.** The heart of young children, barring any medical complications, is stronger and proportionately larger than at any other time in life. Youngsters need to learn to be **mentally tough** so that they can push themselves past the first signs of tiring.

11. **False.** Eating habits, like activity levels, are established early. The nutritional value of a meal is determined more by the composition of the foods than by the amount.

12. **True.** Once the desired level of physical fitness is attained, 3 days per week will maintain the desired level.

13. **False.** Health spas do offer a variety of equipment, but very little of it is designed to work the **heart** for an adequate time period. For exercise to benefit the **heart,** it must be done continuously for 15–30 min. Aerobic activities such as bike riding, swimming, roller skating, and jogging can be used effectively to develop **cardiopulmonary fitness.**

14. **False.** People who are physically fit are more energetic, sleep better, and seem to enjoy life more.

15. **False.** To strengthen the heart muscle and thus develop cardiopulmonary fitness, exercise must be strenuous enough to elevate the heart rate to approximately 150 beats per min. The pulse can be taken from the wrist (with index finger), during or immediately following exercise. By counting the number of beats for 10 sec and multiplying by 6, the heart beats per minute during exercise can be determined. The pulse must be taken **immediately** upon completion of the exercise.

16. **False.** Bone growth occurs at an uneven rate until approximately age 12. A contact sport such as tackle football can cause permanent bone injuries. Baseball requires excessive throwing, which sometimes impairs bone growth in young children. Neither of these sports involves 15–30 min of continuous activity for any of the players.

17. **True.** The resting heart beat of the average person is between 70 and 80 beats per min. Through strenuous exercise, cardiopulmonary fitness is increased, and the heart muscle and blood vessels are thus strengthened and enlarged. The heart then works more efficiently, that is, moving the same amount of blood in fewer beats. A person who increases his or her cardiopulmonary fitness may lower the resting heart rate by as much as 10 beats per min.

FIGURE 15.1 Continued

18. **True.** Research studies have shown that increasing a person's amount of daily activity is the most successful approach to weight loss. For example, consider the fact that there are **3500 calories in 1 lb.** For a person to lose 1 lb, he or she must burn 3500 calories. Jogging or walking burns approximately 100 calories per mi. If a person takes no more than 15 min and jogs or walks 1 mi per day, without any change in diet, he or she will lose an average of **1 lb per month.** Diet, when combined with exercise, can speed up the process of weight loss.

19. **True.** Unless a person is in an extensive training program (the equivalent of running 10 mi per day or more), regular exercise will not, in most cases, increase his or her appetite.

PHYSICAL FITNESS: WHAT IS IT?

Physical fitness is a term that people of all ages should know. There are a great variety of interpretations of the meaning of this widely used term. In this booklet, the term **physical fitness** refers to the level of efficiency of the **heart and lung system,** that is, **cardiopulmonary fitness.**

The body has many important muscles, all of which need to be used or exercised regularly. The **heart and lung system,** however, is considered by most physicians to be the key to the prevention of heart disease, the number one killer in America today. Through the right type of exercise, the chances of contracting heart disease can be lessened. The heart is a muscle and reacts to exercise as do the muscles in other parts of the body. Continuous vigorous exercise has the effect of strengthening the heart muscle and can result in an increase in the size of the heart. Besides increasing the **size and strength** of the heart muscle, continuous vigorous exercise also increases the **size and number** of blood vessels in the heart and lung area. Blood is thus pumped more efficiently as the level of **cardiopulmonary fitness** increases. These important effects of vigorous exercise on the heart and lung system decrease the chance that heart disease will occur.

Your **cardiopulmonary fitness** level affects how you look and how you feel. A person who has a high level of fitness performs her or his daily work without getting overtired. When a full day's work is done, the physically fit person has energy left over for leisure time activities: a walk to the park, a bike ride, a game of ball, or a refreshing jog around the block.

As stated previously in the question and answer portion of this booklet, habits and attitudes are established at an early age. It is therefore essential that young children be taught the meaning and implications of **physical or cardiopulmonary fitness.** Such simple experiences as putting the hand on the heart muscle after vigorous activity, to "feel the heart pumping blood fast," begins to increase their awareness of this important muscle.

NOW THAT I KNOW WHAT
CARDIOPULMONARY FITNESS IS:
How Do I
Help My Son or Daughter
Become More Fit?

The **heart** is a muscle and thus can be increased in **size and strength** through exercise, **but what kind of exercises build the heart?**

FIGURE 15.1   Continued

1. For an exercise or activity to benefit the heart, **it must be continuous.** Activities such as jogging, walking, swimming, roller skating, or bike riding should be continued for a minimum of 5 min. Any type of aerobic activity that can be performed continuously for 5 min can be beneficial.

2. Not only must an activity be **continuous,** but it must be **vigorous. How vigorous?** Activity must be vigorous enough to increase the heart rate to 150 beats per min. To find out if your child is involved in adequate vigorous activity, take her or his pulse **immediately** following exercise. By placing your index finger on the front of the neck, you can find the pulse (from the carotid artery). Count the number of beats for **10** sec and multiply by **6** to find the number of heart beats in 1 min during exercise. If there is any delay (even 15–30 sec) in taking the pulse following exercise, it will **not** be an accurate count.

HELPFUL HINTS

There are many ways in which parents and family members can help youngsters to get added activity time throughout the week. One of the best ways to increase the amount of time that children spend in activity is to join them in the activity. Daily brisk walks or jogs to the park are great.

Bicycle riding is another fun activity that promotes fitness. Swimming as well as roller skating are terrific ways for students to have fun and keep fit. Another way is to take a soccer ball or large rubber ball to the park and run and kick it around for a half hour or so.

Other fitness ideas that you might try are kite flying, jumping rope, jogging in place, or dancing to a record. Take a few minutes to find out what students are doing actively and then see if you can increase the amount of time they spend at the activity. With a little enthusiasm and a little extra time put aside each day, your son or daughter can be on the road to cardiopulmonary fitness.

The **"fitness experience"** maintains health, keeps a person in good shape, helps prevent heart attack, and builds muscles.

FIGURE 15.1   Continued

not developed, few people will have the desire to participate in later life. Those who can look back and give credit to physical education will become forceful believers and backers of physical education programs in the schools.

11. Expressing appreciation to those who have participated and supported the program is important. Students often choose to cooperate and participate in a program. Giving them credit for their support is important. Administrators make a quality program possible through their support for equipment, facilities, scheduling, et cetera. They need to be shown appreciation regularly. When a demonstration program is sponsored, thank parents for their support. Working with students becomes difficult if parents tell them that the program or the teachers are poor. Cooperative students usually have supportive parents. Thank them.

WHAT DOES THE PUBLIC NEED TO KNOW?

An important step in designing the public relations program is to determine what information should be shared with the public. It is a procedure similar to planning a lesson or drawing up a game plan in that it gives direction and goals to the public relations program. Information can then be released to the public in a meaningful progression and through different media. Some of the following points are useful in sharing the philosophy and workings of the physical education program with the public. They are areas that are sure to stimulate interest in the program.

1. Discuss the impact of the program on the physical growth and development of students. This area

should be promoted extensively because exercise has so many beneficial effects that contribute to the wellness of an individual. Parents and the public should hear about the effect of regular aerobic exercise on the cardiovascular system, the impact of weight lifting on the development of the skeletal system, and how conditioning programs improve various fitness attributes.

2. Emphasize the importance of physical education and of regular activity in developing a strong, positive self-concept (Pangrazi, 1982). Physical fitness and the performance of motor skills affect how one feels personally. This can lead to renewed confidence in one's self.

3. Explain how the program is organized to help all students improve and develop, not just skilled athletes. The majority of students are not skilled athletes but the program must meet their needs. Parents are concerned about whether the program is designed to aid their child.

4. Share the rationale, aims, and objectives of the program with the public. When most people are asked about the goals of a physical education program, few understand that the program is different from an interscholastic athletic program. This misunderstanding is due largely to a lack of communication about the program.

5. The public should know that a sound physical education program provides an opportunity for all students to participate and compete. Explain that the program is allied with intramurals and sport clubs and that students are helped to find a place, become involved, and interact with others.

6. Convince others of the need to offer students organized leisure-time activities. Physical education is the only area in school where students are offered a chance to be physically active.

7. Reinforce the importance of health as a top priority. People seldom take time to maintain their health status. Physical education teaches students how to maintain wellness for a lifetime. When one's health is lost, working, playing, and sharing with others is difficult. Nothing is more important than good health. Sell this fact.

ESTABLISHING AN ADVISORY COUNCIL

A public relations advisory council can be most helpful in disseminating information about the program. The advisory council should consist of people such as a school board member, an administrator,

teachers, interested parents, community media personnel, students, and any other key members of the community. The purpose of the committee is to determine how the program can be promoted, what program components should be shared, and how the information can be disseminated. The committee is not involved in curriculum development, but in analyzing the program and determining how it can be promoted.

The council should develop a working policy for bringing information to the public. This usually consists of the following steps:

1. Survey a representative sample of the public to see what they know and do not know about the program. This prevents the sharing of information that is common knowledge. The survey can be a simple tool that is designed by the council to diagnose areas they deem important.

2. Develop a public relations policy to begin disseminating information to the public in areas they know little about.

3. Determine how the facts should be presented to make them interesting and informative.

4. Perform a cost analysis to see what needs to be acquired in terms of supplies, equipment, and related materials in order for the council to function.

5. Assign tasks such as fundraising, writing copy, and disseminating information to different members of the council.

The council should search out people who are friends of physical education. The council composition should be balanced with people who have different abilities. For example, some people may have media contacts, other council members may know people who are willing to be benefactors, and still others may possess expertise in writing copy.

IMPLEMENTING THE PUBLIC RELATIONS PROGRAM

The public relations program can be implemented in different ways. All methods should help the public better understand the operation of a program. Regardless of the method used, selling an inferior program is impossible. People will refuse to endorse and accept a program that does not benefit its participants. Therefore, begin with a quality program, for nothing sells like quality. When students tell parents about their accomplishments in the program, public relations benefits are being accrued. Strong planning, excellent teaching, and concern for students are the cornerstones of a physical education program that will be well accepted.

Personal Conduct

Many people still imagine physical educators as being slightly obese, carrying a bat in one hand, wearing a whistle around the neck, and being outfitted in baggy sweat pants. This stereotype yells at people to hustle, seldom exercises, and is often in poor physical condition. The point here is that the teacher's dress and actions will be scrutinized by the public and will continue to be a point of reference long after the image has changed. Teachers must model the behavior they desire in others. They must stay fit, exercise regularly, and use up-to-date methods of dealing with people. A physical education teacher who behaves in a professional manner does more to sell physical education than any public relations ploy.

The School Setting

Developing a meaningful relationship with students is important. Students must understand why various activities are being taught and how they benefit from participation. Remember that students who dislike the program communicate their dislike to parents, and parents often know little about the program other than what their youngsters tell them. If most of the messages are negative, parents will share negative comments with other parents. Students ultimately grow up to become school board members, teachers, and administrators. If their experience was negative, they may be unwilling as adults to support physical education.

Teachers in other areas need to know about the program. In too many cases, the physical educator stays in the gymnasium and seldom mingles with other teachers. This can create an atmosphere of animosity, particularly when physical educators are coaches and choose to miss faculty meetings and related social functions. Behaving in a manner consistent with the rest of the faculty members is politic.

Some physical educators have had excellent success with a faculty fitness program offered one day a week for faculty members. During this time, they demonstrate various skills and activities that can be performed during the week. Another related program is a faculty recreation program. Faculty members can gather after school or in the evening to participate in volleyball, badminton, basketball, and other desired activities. Administrators can be invited to participate too, which offers personal contact in an informal setting.

Another activity that develops goodwill toward the physical education program is a school playday.

Students participate together in an activity that is lighthearted and enjoyable. Teachers also become involved and participate with students in this recreational setting. An example of a playday would be sponsoring "loony" contests such as the water balloon throw, the trike ride, three-legged race, pie-eating contest, pit-spitting contest, and any other novel activities. The emphasis is on friendly competition and participation.

Announcements can be placed regularly in the school newspaper. Tell the school about upcoming units, about registering for the playday, when special speakers are scheduled, and about happenings in the intramural program. The school newspaper can be a source of strong public relations with students. Along the same lines, the school district newsletter that is sent to parents should be used. For instance, the grading system could be explained, or the results of fitness testing published.

Communicating with Parents

The more parents understand about the educational nature of the program, the more willing they may become to support it. Since many parents do not distinguish between an athletic program and a physical education program, the public relations thrust must be to help clarify the differences.

Parents can be involved actively as program participants or passively as spectators. A parents' night can be scheduled when different activities are taught by instructors to both students and their parents. This gives parents a first-hand experience with the instructional nature of the program. If parents are not asked to participate, a wide variety of student demonstrations can be planned to show the broad spectrum of skills that are taught. In either case, demonstrations should illustrate the features and organization of the program.

The physical education booster group can be used to help interpret the program to parents. Discussions and panel representations at parent-teacher organizations can be conducted, and interpretive booklets distributed. Slides of program highlights might be shown to enhance the presentation. The use of outside experts is also effective in dealing with controversial issues. Parents should be given the opportunity to ask questions and resolve points of concern.

Another way to involve parents is to use them as teacher's aides. They can help with fitness testing projects and thus begin to understand how students function in the physical education setting. Projects should also be scheduled on Saturdays or evenings so parents working outside the home can be involved.

Brochures and handouts explaining the program

can be sent home with students. Parents should be encouraged to follow up and help their students practice skills at home. Surprisingly, few parents receive calls from teachers at the junior and senior high school level unless something is wrong. Parents should also be called when their son or daughter has accomplished something positive and has performed well. Parents will begin to support a program when they hear positive messages about their youngsters.

A source of public relations with parents that sometimes goes unheeded is grade reporting. The wellness profile (see Chapter 12) is an excellent tool for communicating the status of the student's health to parents. The profile can forewarn parents of possible health problems that need medical attention. Programs are now available for students to enter their fitness test results in the computer. The data are analyzed and the computer prints out a personalized report for the student. Some districts now use these data to maintain files that follow students from kindergarten through high school. Comparative data that describe a youngster's growth and development can be sent to parents at regular intervals. When parents understand that the school is helping to maintain the wellness of their youngster, positive feelings result.

PRACTICAL IDEAS FOR PUBLIC RELATIONS PROMOTIONS

The following ideas are possibilities for increasing the exposure of the physical education program. All of these suggestions can be modified and are offered simply to initiate ideas.

Bulletin Boards, Displays, and Posters

In the school setting, visual displays serve to advertise and promote the program. They show the rest of the faculty that physical educators are active and proud of their accomplishments. The art teacher will sometimes help to develop posters that require special artistic ability, and students with artistic skills are often willing to work on the media products. The following are some suggestions:

1. A schedule bulletin board shows what will be done in the program 3–4 weeks in advance. On it are listed special events, activities to be taught, and testing days.
2. A special announcement board can be used to post special events such as intramural games, interscholastic games, guest speakers, and film screenings.

3. Visual displays at opportune times can reach a wide variety and large number of people. Examples of such times are open houses, just before school closes for the summer, prior to Christmas vacation or spring holidays, and before school opens in the fall. At these times, parents are visiting the school and forming their opinions of the program.

Hints for Making Bulletin Boards

First, select a bulletin board that is located where the largest number of people will see it. A bulletin board in the main hall of the school will remind students who are not involved in physical education of important and exciting happenings in the program. The bulletin board should attract and hold the attention of observers. The message should be apparent to viewers and should stimulate interest. Do not put too much detail on the bulletin board.

Print or write in large letters. Visibility from 20–25 ft is a good guideline. To attract attention, use catchy titles such as Quiz, Mystery Pictures, or Unusual Facts, or use humor. The bulletin board should give specific dates and times, who to contact, and the names of program directors. Clippings and photographs are always interesting to students. Brightly-colored paper, colored yarn, cut-out letters, and three-dimensional designs are also effective in catching the eye of the observer.

Bulletin boards and posters should be changed often (at least every 4–6 weeks). If they go unchanged, they go unobserved after a while. Make sure that student accomplishments are displayed on the bulletin boards from time to time. In summary, make sure the bulletin boards list the five Ws: who, what, why, when, and where.

Parent Involvement

Invite parents to a physical education awards assembly or banquet. This is a good time to present physical fitness achievement awards. Another award that can be issued is the improvement award. This award would be within reach of all students and could be based on percent improvement. For example, if activities are listed on a contract basis, students could be pretested to see which skills they performed at passing standards. Criteria could then be set, such as "Increase the number of skills you know by 25%." Awards would be given to those students meeting the criteria. Figure 15.2 is a letter that could be sent to parents of students who earn the award.

Community Relations

Community organizations are interested in school instruction, and it is important that information

Dursthill Junior High School
850 Fairview Avenue
Picante, AZ

Dear Dad and Mom,

It may surprise you to learn that I have won an achievement award. This award will be given to me during the awards banquet (assembly) on Friday, November 21, at 7:00 P.M. I hope you will be able to attend, as this historic occasion deserves your presence.

The cost for the banquet is $4.00 per person. This is a small amount to spend on such a fine daughter.

Come on, Dad and Mom! Jog out of the house and contribute to character development.

Your daughter,

FIGURE 15.2   Letter to parents announcing award winner

about physical education be included in the programs and meetings of these organizations. Examples of such community organizations are coordinating councils, service clubs, youth clubs, and parent-teacher groups. These groups are always looking for speakers for luncheon meetings. The program chair should be contacted and given an explanation of the type of physical education curriculum offered. A short description of the program can then be forwarded, along with a form such as the one in Figure 15.3. After all arrangements have been made, it is most important to deliver a well-planned and well-executed presentation that focuses on the learning accomplished through the physical education curriculum.

Writing to Newspapers

The local newspaper can be the physical education program's best friend. The types of skills performed in the program are visual and will create an impact in the newspaper. Local newspapers are often looking for articles that will fill in pages and stimulate interest. The following are guidelines to help make the news release more acceptable to the news editor.

Type all articles double-spaced on white paper with wide margins. Some room should also be left at the top of the page for editing. Be sure to include a name and telephone number so the editor can easily reach the contributor if a question arises. Keep paragraphs to 5 or fewer typewritten lines, 1–3 sentences per paragraph, and 10–20 words per sentence.

Report facts, and if you are unsure about any facts, verify the information. Begin the article with a lead sentence or paragraph that gives the who, what, why, when, where, and how of the story. Place the single most important point of the article in the lead paragraph, and arrange the rest of the facts in descending order of importance. Make the last few paragraphs short so they can be cut without affecting the story significantly. Try always to make the story emphasize the educational value of the physical education program.

When possible, include photographs with the news release. The pictures should be close-ups that show faces and emotion. Photographs should also be action-oriented and illustrate phases of the program. Type captions and attach them to the photos. Indicate who is to receive credit for the photo (e.g., "Photograph by . . . ").

PHYSICAL EDUCATION PROGRAM REQUEST

1. Name of organization _____

2. Location _____
            Place   Address   Room

3. Time: _____ From _____ To _____
         Day   Date   Time of Program

4. Topic preferred _____

5. Type or program desired (speaker, films, etc.) _____

6. Questions and answers, if desired: Yes ____ No ____ (Please check)

7. Background or interests of group _____

8. Chairperson introducing _____

9. Estimated size of audience (circle): 1–15, 16–20, 50–100, over 100

10. If film is involved: Can room be darkened? _____

    Is screen available? _____ Size and type of screen _____

    Type of projector _____ Microphone available _____

    Other facilities _____

11. Other factors, requests, suggestions _____

    _____

    _____

    _____

    Name of person making request _____

    Position in organization _____

    Address _____

    Telephone _____

Please telephone in request and follow up by forwarding this form to:

Name _____

Address _____

Phone _____

FIGURE 15.3   Request form for a physical education program

PHYSICAL EDUCATION PUBLIC INFORMATION (PEPI)

The Physical Education Public Information (PEPI) project is a continuing project of the AAHPERD. It identifies coordinators in every state who are responsible for interpreting the profession through the media. The focus of PEPI is to tell the public about the positive benefits of physical education. The organization has attempted to communicate such benefits as the contribution of physical activity to academic achievement, the effectiveness of regular exercise as low-cost health insurance, and the importance of developing skills that will last a lifetime. PEPI regularly sends advertisements to coordinators for insertion in journals, brochures, and newspapers.

DEMONSTRATION PROGRAMS

Demonstration programs can attract a large number of parents. The activities should illustrate the attainment of the program objectives and also be typical of the experiences that occur regularly. If rehearsal is going to take place, it should only be to keep the program moving smoothly. A demonstration program need not offer perfect performances. In fact, the spontaneous and natural appearance of a program will usually stimulate more response and appreciation from parents.

As many students as possible should be included in the program. Parents will usually not attend if their youngster is not included. Specialty numbers can be integrated in the program to show off outstanding performances. A printed program that includes all of the names of participants is desirable and makes all of the students feel important. If possible, ask someone unrelated to the program, such as the principal, to open the demonstration and welcome parents. The program should be fast moving and take 45–60 min. Parents are interested primarily in seeing their youngster perform and will not sit for much longer than 1 hr.

It is usually wise to omit competitive contests that cause some to be declared losers. Focus instead on educational performances that show skill development. Since all students can perform physical fitness activities, including this type of activity in the program is meaningful.

REFERENCE AND SUGGESTED READING

Pangrazi, R. P. 1982. Physical education, self-concept, and achievement. *JOPERD* 53(9): 16–18.

16 WELLNESS FOR A LIFETIME: ACTIVITIES FOR INSTRUCTION

The need for teaching students how to maintain personal wellness for a lifetime becomes apparent when one examines the skyrocketing costs of minimal health care. Health insurance policies cost 5–10% of an individual's gross income. A short stay in the hospital may incur a bill for thousands of dollars, yet in spite of runaway costs, Americans continue to pay and put little or no effort into maintaining a healthy life-style.

Human wellness is a state of health that allows an individual to participate fully in life. Having the energy and enthusiasm to undertake activities of all types after a full day's work is characteristic of people who are well. An individual who is well is not only free of sickness or other malady, but is happy, vibrant, and able to solve personal problems.

Teaching students how to achieve a lasting state of wellness lends credibility to the physical education profession. For many years, physical educators were seen solely as teachers of physical skills who had little concern for the knowledge and comprehension involved in physical performance. The various personalities and unique needs of the student participants were often ignored by teachers who appeared to be concerned only about the product (i.e., "Learn the skill or else!"). The age-old argument of product versus process can be moderated by teaching the process of developing physical wellness, for wellness is a process. There are no trophies or other extrinsic rewards for achieving it. Wellness is personal. When it is achieved, the individual is directly rewarded by an enhanced life-style. Teachers can no longer ignore the importance of teaching students the what, why, and how of maintaining a healthy profile. Maintaining wellness must be considered a primary objective of secondary school physical education.

Why teach wellness in the physical education setting? Teachers are often skeptical about teaching material other than physical skill activities, yet the ability to develop and maintain personal wellness will remain with an individual for a lifetime. This is one of the few long-lasting gifts teachers can offer to students. Achieving wellness is unique and personal. What is useful to one person may be superfluous to another. Teachers must therefore teach students how to search for wellness and then maintain it once found.

At present, the credibility of the physical education profession is strained. Teachers often offer students skills and activities that they will never use again. For example, students may spend 9 wks each year from junior high through the sophomore year of high school involved in football. This is equivalent to 36 wks of football, or one entire school year. The possibility is strong that few of these individuals will play football after graduation from high school. Few, people play football after age 25, yet one year of physical education was spent playing and learning a sport that becomes literally useless in maintaining a healthy life-style in adulthood. Small wonder that many adults believe that they learned little in physical education to help them after graduation. The authors are not belittling football or asking for elimination of the sport. The point is that physical education programs have often shown an inadequate concern for teaching students the skills that are useful after they leave school.

Teaching students how to maintain a state of wellness makes activity purposeful. Students begin to understand why certain activities and games are selected in place of others. Selection of activities for a lifetime of physical involvement can only occur after students have been exposed to a wide range of instructional units. A systematic approach to curriculum development is critical in assuring that students know the many alternatives and pathways to personal fitness and health.

INTEGRATING WELLNESS INSTRUCTION INTO THE PROGRAM

Paramount to all instruction dealing with wellness is an emphasis on self-responsibility for maintaining a healthy life-style. Regardless of what students are taught, if an emphasis is not placed on teaching students how to make personal decisions, little will have been gained. Most students will do what is asked of them when they are in school. The critical point is teaching students the problem-solving skills that will enable them to make meaningful decisions throughout life, when teachers are no longer present.

At the secondary school level, teachers should take a multifaceted approach to developing units of instruction dealing with wellness. The first step is to ensure that students understand how the body functions. This involves understanding the anatomy of the body, the physiological functioning of the body during exercise, and the mechanical principles involved in movement. It is beyond the scope of this text to list all the information that students should digest and comprehend. An outline and an instructional unit in each of these areas will be offered. References are listed at the end of the chapter for instruction in greater depth.

Students may receive instruction about the systems of the body in health education classes. In most cases, however, material covered in those classes does not deal with exercise and the impact it has on the body. Learning how the body reacts and adapts to exercise is of utmost importance, and students probably will not receive this information anywhere else.

The second step in presenting units of instruction dealing with wellness is to delineate which concepts students need to understand. This provides direction for both teacher and students. The concepts should give students a general idea of what is important and what areas must be understood to achieve proper functioning. The concepts should help the instructor organize the material to be presented. Students should be given an outline that they can follow. The concepts, when taken as a whole, offer a framework to help students make personal decisions about health maintenance. This approach contrasts with giving students a set of objectives that must be learned and that leave little room for student input and inquiry.

The third step in organizing units of instruction in this area is to present mini-laboratory experiences that apply the concepts and bring them to life. These learning activities can be used to add substance to the instructional concepts. The laboratory experiences are simple, yet illustrate clearly how the body functions in different settings. Many of these experiences can be done in 5 or 10 min by a whole class. They are excellent rainy day activities, or students can do them as homework. Students should be encouraged to develop a notebook of activities and lab experiences that they can use for a lifetime.

The authors have offered varying curriculum models for grades 7–12 in Chapters 4 and 5. Each model contains a unit of instruction on wellness and self-testing. This approach should be analyzed carefully and considered when developing a comprehensive physical education curriculum. It is strongly recommended that instruction be offered at each grade level in this important area. The instruction should be clearly devoted to developing wellness for a lifetime, and should receive instructional emphasis on a par with other units in the physical education curriculum.

INSTRUCTIONAL STRATEGIES FOR TEACHING WELLNESS

Physical education enhances fitness and skill levels of students, allowing them opportunities for developing an active life-style. A program goal should be helping young people to make responsible decisions about wellness and its impact on their lives. Throughout life, people are faced with many decisions that may have a positive or negative impact on their level of wellness. The ability to make responsible choices depends on a wide range of factors: understanding one's feelings and personal values, the ability to cope with stress and with problems in general, the impact of various factors on health, and practice in using decision-making skills.

DEVELOPING AWARENESS AND DECISION-MAKING SKILLS

The focus should be on helping students to view themselves as total beings. Stability occurs when all parts fit together in a smooth and consistent fashion. When a problem occurs, the balance of physiology, thinking, and function is disrupted. Individuals must then use their knowledge, coping ability, and decision-making skills to restore the equilibrium associated with personal stability. Teachers can try to help students understand their feelings, values, and attitudes, and the impact that all of these have on coping and decision-making ability. Each of these areas will be discussed.

Self-Concept

Self-concept is defined as the total perception an individual has of self. Self-concept is enhanced when the individual has a strong, positive feeling of belonging and a sense of worth. These attitudes can be fostered by providing activities that focus on themes that help a person to

1. Recognize that there are many individuals, yet that each of us is unique.
2. Feel loved and able to love.
3. Be able to recognize and cope with feelings and emotions.
4. Function in a group, yet also be comfortable alone.
5. Like to and be able to do many things.
6. Relate successfully to others.

A student who has a healthy self-image will be better able to make a decision in the presence of peer pressure. Individuals who feel positive about themselves are less influenced by peer pressure than those with poor self-concepts.

Through the process of education, each student should be made to feel important and worthwhile. Youngsters will realize that they are not perfect and that change is desirable. The identification of personal strengths and weaknesses can offer direction for self-growth and for understanding personal limitations. When dealing with areas of self-concept and personal worth, students should be comfortable to express feelings. They should feel free to ask questions without fear of ridicule or embarrassment. Discussions should be positive and criticism constructive. As students develop more positive feelings about themselves, their ability to make responsible decisions will improve. They will be prepared to make decisions in everyone's interests, including their own.

Coping Skills

Coping is the ability to deal with problems successfully. Learning to cope with life's problems is dependent on and interrelated to knowledge of self, decision-making skills, and the ability to relate to others. Specific skills that deal with coping include the following:

1. Admit that a problem exists and face it. It is impossible to cope with a problem if the problem is not recognized.
2. Define the problem and who "owns" it. Individuals must identify what needs to be faced and decide if the problem is theirs or belongs to others.
3. List alternative solutions to the problem. A basic step in decision making, problem solving, and coping is to identify the alternatives in a given situation.
4. Predict consequences for oneself and others. After the alternatives are identified, weigh the potential consequences of each, and then rank them in order of preference.
5. Identify and consult sources of help. All sources should be considered. In order to do this, teachers should introduce students to some of the resources available and explain how to locate helpful sources.
6. Experiment with a solution and evaluate the results. If the decision did not produce satisfactory results, another alternative can often be tried. Evaluation of results also allows people to keep track of their ability to discover satisfying solutions.

Decision-Making Skills

Youngsters are faced with many situations that require decisions. Making decisions is something everyone does every day, often without thinking. Because it is a common process, it receives little attention until a person is faced with an important decision that has long-term consequences.

Although the schools attempt to help students learn how to make personally satisfying decisions, a major portion of a teacher's time involves developing information or supplying it to students. Obtaining information, although extremely important, is only one segment of the decision-making process. A question that should be asked is "If you are going to provide information to others, what do you want them to do with that information?" Students should be given the opportunities to put information to use.

Decision making is defined as a process in which a person selects from two or more possible choices. A decision does not occur unless there is more than one course of action, alternative, or possibility to consider. If a choice exists, the process of deciding may then be used. Decision making enables the individual to reason through life situations, to solve problems, and, to some extent, to direct behavior.

Often there are no "right" answers or outcomes of the decision-making process. The decision is instead judged on the effective use of a process that results in satisfying consequences. This distinguishes decision making from problem solving. Problem solving usually identifies one best or correct solution for everyone involved.

When making decisions, it is important for students to consider each of the following steps:

1. Gather information. If meaningful choices are going to be made, gathering all the available information is important. Information should be gathered from as many sources as possible. Students generally consider information valid when they see that it comes from many different sources and that they are allowed to view both sides of an issue. Teachers too often present students with information that supports only one point of view.

2. Consider the available choices. The next step is to consider all the available choices. This is an important step if students are to realize that they have many different possibilities from which to choose and that their choices will influence the direction of their lives. It does not make sense to consider possibilities that students have no chance of selecting. Many choices have been made for students in the school setting, and they sometimes come to believe that others will make all the decisions for them and that they, in turn, bear no responsibility for their successes or failures.

3. Analyze the consequences of the choices. When the various choices are delineated, students must consider their consequences. If the consequences are ignored, an unwise choice may be made that is detrimental to one's health. Making wise decisions about wellness demands that students be made aware of consequences. They should understand some of the reasons why people may choose to smoke or drink, even though the consequences are negative. The most important role of the teacher is helping students understand positive and negative consequences without moralizing or telling students how to think.

4. Make a decision and implement it. When all of the information has been gathered, students must make decisions and implement them in their lifestyles. The decisions will be personal to each student and need not be revealed to others.

Skillful decision makers have greater control over their lives because they can reduce the amount of uncertainty surrounding their choices and limit the degree to which chance or their peers determine their future.

Two individuals may face a similar decision, but because each person is different and places differing values on the outcomes, each decision will be unique. Learning decision-making skills increases the possibility that each person will achieve what he or she most values.

Decisions also have limits. Each decision is necessarily limited by what a person is capable of doing, by what a person is willing to do, and by the environment in which the decision is being made. Impor-

tant to the development of these skills is the environment in which they are practiced. A nonjudgmental atmosphere is most productive. Since there is no "right" answer, the person making a decision should be free to select from any of the available choices and be willing to accept the probable consequences and results.

LEADING DISCUSSION SESSIONS

The success of discussions depends on how effectively the teacher is able to establish and maintain the integrity and structure of the lesson and the students' psychological freedom. Integrity and structure mean that all students are dealing with the same issue in a thoughtful and responsible way. Psychological freedom means that individual students participate to the degree that is most comfortable for them, such as: choosing to comment or to refrain; responding to directed questions or choosing to pass; agreeing or disagreeing with what has been said; or deciding what data is needed, and requesting that data. This demands certain teacher behavior to establish a meaningful environment. A brief description of necessary teaching behaviors follows.

Structuring

Structuring is used to create a climate that is conducive to open communication by all parties. This is accomplished by outlining expectations and role relationships for both teacher and student. Structuring includes any of the following:

1. Establish a climate at the beginning of the lesson by explaining what the student and teacher will be doing and how they will work together.
2. Maintain the established lesson structure by forbidding students to be pressured to respond or to be put down for their ideas.
3. Add to or modify the lesson structure established at the beginning of the lesson. For example, this may involve changing to small-group sessions, rather than a total class discussion.

Focus Setting

The purpose of focus setting is to establish an explicit and common topic or issue for discussion. Because this teaching behavior is used in different circumstances, the behavior can be formulated by the following methods by the teacher:

1. Presenting a topic, usually in the form of a question, to the group for discussion.

2. Using focus setting to restate the original question or to shift to a new discussion topic because students have finished discussing the original question.

3. Using focus setting to bring the discussion back to the topic when a student unknowingly shifts to a new topic.

4. Use focus setting to label a discussion question presented by a student as a new topic and to allow discussion of it.

Clarifying

Clarifying teaching behavior is used to invite a student to help the teacher better understand the substance or content of the student's comment. Whenever possible, the clarifying teaching behavior should give the student some indication of what it is that the teacher does not understand. In addition, the behavior should be formulated in a way that puts the burden on the teacher for not being able to understand, rather than implying that the student was unclear or inadequate in any way. Clarifying is used only when the teacher does not understand. The teacher does not assume the responsibility of clarifying for the students.

Acknowledging

Acknowledging teaching behavior is used to let a student who is talking to the teacher know that the teacher understands what has been said and that the student has made a contribution to the discussion. Unlike most other teaching behaviors, this one can be implemented through nonverbal as well as verbal means.

How an acknowledging teaching behavior is worded and when it is and is not used must be considered carefully. This behavior is intended to be a nonjudgmental way of saying, "I understand." To use acknowledging only when the teacher understands and agrees, but to do something else when the teacher understands and disagrees, is a serious misinterpretation of the purpose and function of this teaching behavior.

Teacher Silence

The purpose of teacher silence is to communicate to students through nonverbal means that they are responsible for initiating and perpetuating the discussion. Teacher silence is used only in response to student silence. It protects the students' rights and responsibility to make their own decisions about the topic being discussed. In one sense, this teaching behavior is a nonbehavior.

UNDERSTANDING THE MAJOR SYSTEMS OF THE BODY————

A basic understanding of how the body functions is important if students are to learn how to maintain a healthy organism. The three major systems discussed here are the skeletal, muscular, and cardiorespiratory system. A brief discussion of each is provided with concepts and suggested learning activities offered to enhance student understanding.

The Skeletal System

The skeletal system is the framework of the body. The bones act as a system of levers and are linked together at various points called joints. The joints are held together by ligaments, which are tough and unable to stretch. In a joint injury when the bones are moved beyond the normal limits, it is the ligaments that are most often injured.

Joints that are freely movable are called synovial joints. Synovial fluid is secreted to lubricate the joint and reduce friction. A thin layer of cartilage also reduces friction at the ends of the bones. A disk, or meniscus, forms a pad between many of the weight-bearing joints and absorbs shock. When the cartilage is damaged, the joint becomes less able to move easily, and arthritis often occurs.

Muscular activity increases the stress placed on bones. The bones respond to this added stress by increasing in diameter, becoming more dense (and more resistant to breakage), and by reorganizing their internal structure, which offers more bone strength (Rarick, 1973). The bones act as a mineral reserve for the body and can become deformed as a result of dietary deficiency. The bones also can change shape due to regular stress. This may give athletes, whose skeletal systems are conditioned, a mechanical advantage in performing certain skills. The skeletal system is not a static system, but changes and adapts in response to the demands placed on it.

The bones are connected to make three different types of levers, with the joint acting as the fulcrum (Figure 16.1). The muscles apply force to the joints, while the body weight or an external object provides the resistance. The levers are classified as first-, second-, or third-class levers. Examples of third-class lever actions are the movement of the biceps muscle to flex the forearm at the elbow joint, the sideways movement of the upper arm at the shoulder joint by the deltoid muscle, and the flexion of the lower leg at the knee joint by the hamstring muscles. A second-class lever occurs where the gastrocnemius muscle raises the weight of the body onto the toes.

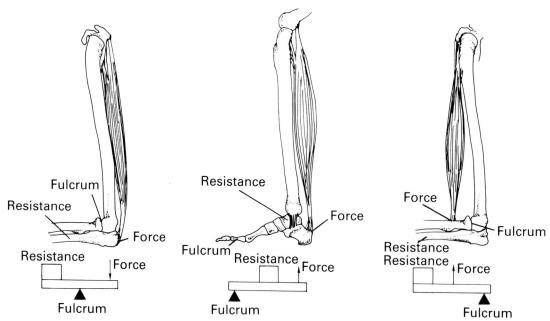

FIGURE 16.1 Types of levers in human joints

The forearm is an example of a first-class lever when it is being extended at the elbow joint (fulcrum) by the triceps muscle.

Basic Concepts

1. The skeletal system consists of 206 bones and determines the external appearance of the body. This network of bones is somewhat malleable and can be reshaped, made denser, and stronger.

2. Joints are where two or more bones are fastened together by ligaments to allow movement that is restricted by the range of motion. The range of motion at various joints can be increased by regularly performing flexibility exercises. The most flexible people have the greatest range of motion at a combination of joints.

3. Bones are held together by ligaments and muscle tissue. The stronger the muscles become, the stronger the ligaments and tendons become in response. This makes a stronger joint, which is more resistant to injury.

4. Attractive posture occurs when the bones are in good alignment. Alignment depends on the muscular system to hold the bones in correct position. Poor posture occurs when the muscles are weak and increased stress is placed on the joints.

5. The bones meet at joints to establish levers. Movement occurs when muscles apply force (by contraction only) to the bones.

6. The attachment of the muscle to the bone deter-

mines the mechanical advantage that can be gained at the joint. Generally, those muscles that attach farther from the joint can generate more force. There is, however, a trade-off. When the attachment is farther from the joint, the amount of speed that can be generated is less, and vice versa.

7. The human body has three types of lever arrangement. These are classified by the fulcrum, force, and resistance. The majority of levers in the body are third-class levers, in which the point of force (produced by the muscles) lies between the fulcrum (joint) and the point of resistance (the weight of the object to be moved).

Suggested Learning Activities

1. Identify and locate the bones of major significance in movement. (Approximately 167 bones are capable of moving.) Some that can be assigned are:
a. Arm-shoulder girdle—radius, ulna, humerus, scapula, and clavicle
b. Back-pelvis—spinal column, pelvis, coccyx
c. Thigh-leg—femur, tibia, fibula, patella
d. Chest—sternum, ribs

2. Identify the type of movement possible at selected joints. Use various terms to identify the movements (e.g., extension, flexion, adduction, abduction, pronation, supination, plantar flexion, etc.).

3. Diagram and list the types of levers found in the body. Illustrate the force, fulcrum, and resistance points. Identify muscle attachments and the impact of such in terms of generating force or speed in movement.

4. Obtain animal bones and analyze the various parts of the bone. Identify the bone marrow, growth plates, epiphyses, ligaments, tendons, muscle origins and attachments, and cartilage.

5. Study outdated X-ray films of children to see the different rates of ossification. Note differences in bone shape and structure between individuals.

The Muscular System

The muscular system (Figure 16.2) is complex. Muscles apply force to the bones to create movement, and always create movement through contraction. When one set of muscles contracts, the other set relaxes. Muscles are always paired. The muscle (or group of muscles) that relaxes while another set contracts is called the antagonistic muscle. The muscles located on the anterior side of the body are flexors and reduce the angle of a joint while the body is standing. Muscles on the posterior side of the body produce extension and a return from flexion.

People are born with two types of muscle fiber. These are commonly referred to as slow twitch and fast twitch fibers. Slow twitch fibers respond efficiently to aerobic activity, while fast twitch fibers are suited to highly demanding anaerobic activity. This explains, in part, why people perform physical activities at varying levels. People are born with a set ratio of fast and slow twitch fibers. Those with a higher ratio of slow twitch fibers are better able to perform in endurance activities; those with a greater percentage of fast twitch fibers might excel in activities of high intensity and short duration.

Strength gains are made when muscles are overloaded, and overload occurs when people do more work than they performed previously. This means that more weight must be lifted on a regular basis if gains are to occur. Exercises should overload as many muscle groups as possible in order to ensure total body development. Both the flexors and extensors should receive equal amounts of overload exercise so a proper balance between the two muscle groups is maintained. Muscular strength appears to be an important factor in performing motor skills.

Muscular exercises should apply resistance through the full range of motion in order to maintain maximum flexibility. Strenuous exercise such as weight lifting should be done every other day so that the muscles have an opportunity to heal and regenerate. Maintaining muscular strength throughout life is important. If exercises are not done to maintain strength, atrophy will occur rapidly. It has been shown that the average American will gain 1 lb of additional weight per year after age 25. This can result in 30 lb of excess weight by age 55.

During the same period, the bone and muscle mass decreases by approximately 0.5 lb per year, which results in a total gain of 45 lb of fat (Wilmore, 1977).

Basic Concepts

1. Muscles contract and apply force by pulling only. They never push. When movement in the opposite direction is desired, the antagonistic muscles must contract.

2. A reduction in joint angle is called flexion; an increase in the joint angle is extension. Generally, the flexor muscles are on the anterior side of the body, and the extensors are on the posterior side.

3. Exercises should focus on developing the flexors and extensors equally if proper posture and joint integrity are to be maintained.

4. Muscles can be attached directly to the bone. A tendon, such as the Achilles, can also be the source of attachment. The origin of the muscle is the fixed portion of the muscle; the insertion is the moving part of the muscle.

5. Progression involving gradual overloading of the muscles is necessary to increase muscular strength and endurance. Males find that regular exercise can cause an increase in the girth of a muscle. Females rarely attain similar results from strenuous exercise. This is because the male hormone testosterone is responsible for the increase in muscle size and is present in greater quantity in males.

6. Different types of training are necessary for developing muscular strength and muscular endurance. Larger amounts of weight and fewer repetitions will cause a greater increase in strength; less weight and more repetitions will enhance muscular endurance.

7. There are different types of muscular contractions: isometric (without movement), isotonic (with movement), and eccentric (movement that lengthens the muscle from a contracted state). The contraction most commonly used for developing strength and endurance is the isotonic.

8. Static stretching can increase flexibility. Flexibility (the range of motion at a joint) increases due to a lengthening of connective tissue that surrounds the muscle fibers.

9. Muscle soreness occurs when the work load is applied too intensely. The soreness probably results from muscle tissue damage. Static stretching will alleviate the pain somewhat and will help prepare the body for continued activity.

10. The principle of specificity is important in developing muscular strength. Only those muscles that

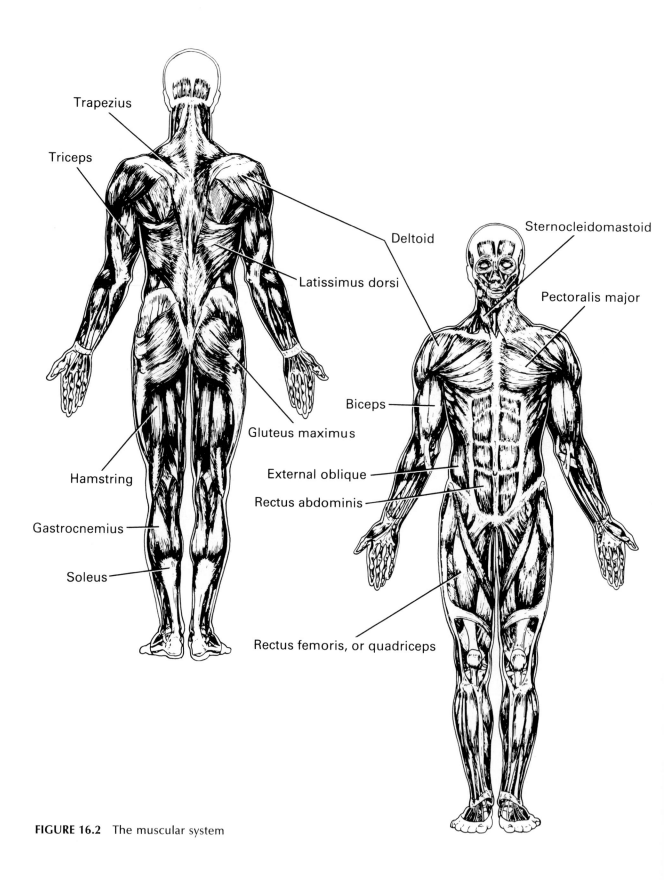

FIGURE 16.2 The muscular system

are exercised will develop. If the goal is stronger leg muscles, they must be exercised. There is no carry-over from other muscle groups (i.e., strengthening the arms will not cause an increase in leg strength).

Suggested Learning Activities

1. Identify major muscle groups and their functions at the joints. Discuss the origins and insertions of the muscles.

2. Study muscles from animals under a microscope. Show stained biopsies of human muscle fiber that reveal fast and slow twitch muscle fibers.

3. Perform some skill-related activities that might reveal which individuals appear to be endowed with more fast twitch than slow twitch fibers. Examples might be the standing long jump, vertical jump, and an endurance activity such as the mile run.

4. Develop a personal strength profile for students. Measure the strength of various muscle groups using a dynamometer and set goals for well-rounded strength development.

5. Perform an action research project. As an example, pretest students for strength and divide them into equal groups. Have one group train for 12 wks using muscular endurance techniques while the other trains for 12 wks using muscular strength techniques. Retest and compare the results of the two groups after training.

6. Identify various sports and games, and determine what type of training will achieve maximum results.

7. Discuss certain exercises that should be avoided, such as straight-leg sit-ups and deep-knee bends.

8. Have students identify why backache occurs in over 70% of Americans. Prescribe a program of exercise that could remedy the majority of these back problems.

The Cardiorespiratory System

The cardiorespiratory system consists of the heart (Figure 16.3), lungs, arteries, capillaries, and veins. The heart is a muscle that pumps blood throughout the circulatory system—arteries, capillaries, and veins. The coronary arteries bring the heart a rich

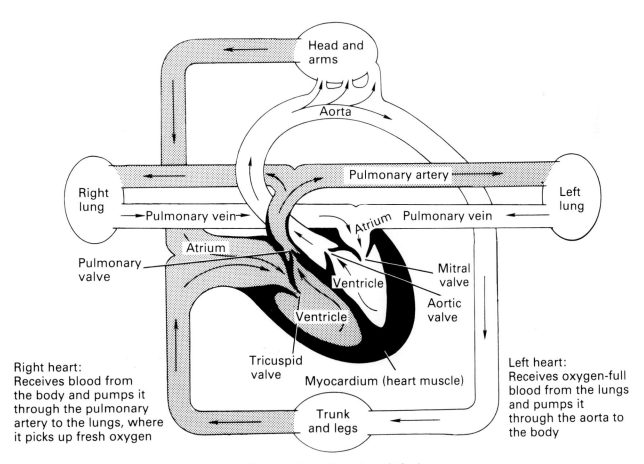

FIGURE 16.3   Structure of the heart (after the American Heart Association)

supply of blood. Heart disease occurs when fatty deposits block or seriously impede the flow of blood to the heart.

The heart has two chambers and is, in effect, divided in half with each side providing different functions. The left side of the heart pumps blood carrying nutrients and oxygen to the body through the arteries to the capillaries, where the nutrients and oxygen are exchanged for waste products and carbon dioxide. The waste-carrying blood is returned through the veins to the right side of the heart, from which the blood is routed through the lungs to discharge the carbon dioxide and pick up oxygen. This oxygen-renewed blood returns to the left side of the heart to complete the circuit.

Each time the heart beats, it pumps blood through both chambers. The beat is called the pulse; its impact travels through the body. Pulse is measured in number of beats per minute. A pulse rate of 75 means that the heart is beating 75 times each minute. The cardiac output is determined by the pulse rate and the stroke volume, which is the amount of blood discharged by each beat.

The pulse is measured by placing the two middle fingers of the right hand on the thumb side of the subject's wrist while the subject is seated. Taking the pulse at the wrist is usually preferable to using the carotid artery, because pressure on the carotid can decrease blood flow to the brain.

The respiratory system includes the entryways (nose and mouth), the trachea (or windpipe), the primary bronchi, and the lungs. Figure 16.4 shows components of the respiratory system.

Breathing consists of inhaling and exhaling air. Air contains 21% oxygen, which is necessary for life. Inspiration is assisted by muscular contraction, and expiration is accomplished by a relaxing of the muscles. Inspiration occurs when the intercostal muscles and the diaphragm contract. This increases the size of the chest cavity, and expansion of the lungs causes air to flow in as a result of reduced air pressure. When the muscles are relaxed, the size of the chest cavity is reduced, the pressure is increased, and air flows from the lungs.

The primary function of the lungs is to provide oxygen to the cells on demand. The amount of oxygen needed will vary depending on activity level. When an individual exercises strenuously, the rate of respiration increases in order to bring more oxygen to tissues. If the amount of oxygen carried to the cells is adequate to maintain the level of activity, the activity is termed *aerobic*, or *endurance exercise*. Examples are walking, jogging, and bicycling for distance. If, because of high-intensity activity, the body is not capable of bringing enough oxygen to the cells, the body will continue to operate for a short

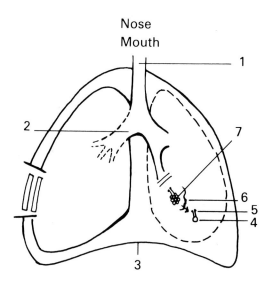

1. Trachea
2. Bronchus
3. Diaphragm
4. Alveolus
5. Respiratory bronchiole
6. Alveolar sacs
7. Terminal bronchiole

FIGURE 16.4 The respiratory system

time without oxygen. This results in an oxygen debt, which must be repaid later. In this case, the activity is termed *anaerobic exercise.*

The respiratory rate will return to normal after exercise. The recovery rate will be faster if the oxygen debt incurred during exercise was small. An individual has recovered from the exertion of exercise when blood pressure, heart rate, and ventilation rate have returned to preexercise levels.

Basic Concepts

1. The heart is a muscular organ that must be exercised like other muscles to maintain maximum efficiency. The most effective heart exercise is activity of low intensity and long duration, which is aerobic in nature.

2. Pulse rate varies among individuals. It does slow down at rest, however, as a result of aerobic training. Resting pulse rate is sometimes used as an indicator of the state of training.

3. Cardiorespiratory training appears to decrease the susceptibility of individuals to heart disease. The younger one begins maintaining fitness, the better the opportunity to retard the onset of cardiovascular disease.

4. Aerobic endurance activities (jogging, brisk walking, bicycling) appear to change the chemistry of the blood and lower the cholesterol level. There are two types of lipoproteins, high density (HDL) and low density (LDL), and exercise appears to increase the ratio of HDL to LDL. This is important, because HDL seems to prevent harmful plaque from building up in the arteries.

5. Hypokinetic diseases are somewhat influenced by gender, heredity, race, and age. Many of these diseases can be prevented, however, by controlling factors such as smoking, obesity, inactivity, improper diet, and high blood pressure.

6. The heart rate must reach the training state if cardiorespiratory benefits are to be realized. (See Suggested Learning Activities, below, item 7 for calculating the training zone.)

7. The heart grows stronger and larger when the body is involved in aerobic activity (30 min or more). A larger and stronger heart results in a greater stroke volume per beat.

8. If weight control is a concern, maintaining muscle mass is important. Severe dieting often results not only in a loss of fat cells, but in a loss of muscle tissue as well. Since muscle tissue burns twice as many calories as fat tissue, it is important in weight control as well as for cosmetic and performance reasons.

9. The vital capacity of the lungs can be increased through regular aerobic exercise. This makes the oxygen exchange system more efficient.

Suggested Learning Activities

1. Discuss the acronym DANGER in regard to cardiovascular disease.

   D on't smoke.
   A void foods high in fat and cholesterol.
   N ow control high blood pressure and diabetes.
   G et medical examinations at least every other year.
   E xercise moderately each day.
   R educe and lose weight if carrying excess fat.

2. Compare resting pulse rates among students. Look for differences between sexes, ages, and states of training. Try taking the resting pulse rate in different positions.

3. Examine the impact that exercise has on heart rate. Record the resting heart rate. Have each person run in place for 1 min. Take the pulse rate immediately and record it. Continue taking the pulse rate at 2-min intervals 3–5 times to demonstrate recovery rate. Discuss individual differences in maximum heart rate and recovery heart rate.

4. Teach students how to take blood pressure. Exercise for 1 min as described above and monitor the effect that exercise has on blood pressure.

5. Demonstrate the effects on the cardiovascular system of carrying excess weight. Identify two students who weigh the same, are of the same sex, are in similar training states, and who do not carry excess weight. Monitor their resting heart rate before starting. Ask one person to perform the upcoming task while carrying two 10-lb weights. Set two markers 20 yd apart, and have both students run back and forth between the cones ten times. Immediately after they finish, monitor their heart rate and recovery rate as described above. Discuss the fact that excessive body fat is merely dead weight that must be moved, and note how the excess weight decreases physical performance.

6. Compare heart rates after 2- or 3-min bouts of different types of exercise. Experiment with walking, jogging, sprinting, rope jumping, bicycling, and calisthenics. Discuss the differences.

7. Calculate the heart rate zone that should be maintained to achieve the training effect and to ensure that the individual is not under- or over-exercising. To do this, first determine the estimated maximum heart rate by taking 220 minus the student's age, then multiply the difference by 60% and 80%. An example for a student who is 15 follows:

- $220 - 15 \quad = 205$
- $60\% \text{ of } 205 = 123$
- $80\% \text{ of } 205 = 164$

The heart rate training zone for this student would be a heartbeat (or pulse rate) between 123 and 164. Have the class try different modes of exercise and see if they raise their heart rate into the training zone.

8. Identify resting respiratory rates. Have students try different types of exercise and compare the effects each has on the respiratory rate.

ROADBLOCKS TO WELLNESS

The following areas are important for students to understand. Wellness involves knowing what activities to avoid as well as what to do. Teaching about these activities should not be done by preaching and telling students what they should or should not do. Emphasis should be placed instead on showing students the pros and cons of various practices and the consequences of making certain decisions. The ultimate decision and responsibility rest with the student, not the teacher.

In this section we will discuss stress, nutrition and weight control, substance abuse, and personal safety. All are areas in which behavior can be modified to enhance the quality of life. Students will make decisions in these areas that may dramatically affect how they live and, sometimes, whether they will live. They should become well versed in the knowledge that concerns each area.

Stress

Stress is the body's reaction to certain situations in life. Everyone experiences some stress. Stress, by itself, is probably not harmful, but handling stress is critical in determining the impact it will have on one's life. It is important for teachers to remember that students may be under a great deal of stress. Often, students are seen as carefree and without worries. Quite the opposite is usually the case. Students live under the stress of other's expectations, peer pressure, sexual mores, and the necessity of becoming an independent being. If teachers appreciate that students are subject to stress, they can begin to deal with them in ways that alleviate possible stressors and allow for stress release. In this way, teachers can have an impact on the students' self-concept and their world view.

Psychologically, stress may take the form of excitement, fear, or anger. Physical changes also accompany psychological stress. For example, heart rate increases, blood pressure rises, ventilation rate increases, perspiration increases, body temperature may rise, and the pupils may dilate. This response to stress once aided human beings in survival and is labeled the "fight or flight" syndrome. When a situation arises that may cause one harm, the body's endocrine system prepares it to fight or to flee the situation. People often speak of the "adrenaline flowing" when they are scared or worried about upcoming situations.

Unfortunately, our society and schools offer few opportunities to relieve tension through activity, and few individuals find the motivation to do so. The resulting tension and stress that build up cause individuals to expend a great deal of energy in unproductive ways. People often feel fatigued when they are unable to release stress. Many nervous habits, such as constant movement while sitting, playing with an item in the hands, and various facial twitches, are the body's attempts to relieve tension.

The ultimate question when dealing with stress might be: "What does it matter if I'm under stress? All people are." It matters because excessive stress has many detrimental effects on the body. It increases the risk of heart disease and can lead to insomnia and hypertension. Indigestion is common in stressed individuals, as is constipation. Many backaches and general body aches originate through

stress. Doctors are diagnosing more and more "psychosomatic" diseases that have no physical prognosis and appear to be caused by stress. Another serious problem associated with unrelieved stress is the tendency of individuals to try to cope by using substances such as alcohol, tobacco, and drugs.

Individuals who exhibit Type A behavior (Friedman and Rosenman, 1974) are much more likely to suffer from the ill effects of stress. Type A behavior is characterized by some of the following patterns:

1. Moving everywhere rapidly, even when it is unnecessary.
2. Feeling bored and impatient with classes and how things are being done by others.
3. Trying to do two or more things simultaneously. (This is referred to as polyphasic thought or action.)
4. Having to always feel busy and feeling uneasy when time is taken to do nothing or to do something relaxing.
5. Needing to do everything faster and more efficiently than everyone else.
6. Exhibiting many strong gestures such as clenching the fists, banging a hand on the table, or dramatically waving the arms.

Students need to learn to identify Type A behavior and to understand various methods of modifying it to achieve more productive patterns.

Learning to cope with stressful situations is important. The first step involves developing an awareness of what types of situations cause stress. Sharing situations with others often releases the tension and allows students to feel that they are "normal" and are maturing properly. In the physical education setting, emphasis should be placed on the role that activity can play in stress reduction. Involvement in enjoyable and success-oriented physical activities can decrease tension. This involvement has a side-effect, because the required concentration will provide a diversion from worries and stressors. Note, however, that if the activity is not enjoyable and if the student consistently fails to find success, the level of stress may actually increase.

Some experts believe that exercise applies stress to the body in a systematic fashion and thus prepares the individual to deal with other stressful situations. One goal of teachers should be to provide a variety of activities and to help students select activities that will be productive and meaningful ways of relieving tension.

Another beneficial strategy is to teach various relaxation techniques that help relieve general body stress. These are discussed in a later section in this chapter.

Basic Concepts

1. Stress affects all individuals to varying degrees. Some stress is necessary to stimulate performance and increase motivation.

2. The amount of stress one is able to cope with depends on how it is perceived. Positive self-concepts help people accept threatening situations in a less stressful manner.

3. When people have difficulty dealing with stress through productive methods, such as exercise, relaxation activities, and talking with friends, they often attempt to relieve stress through unhealthy and potentially dangerous means, such as alcohol, tobacco, and drug usage.

4. Stress causes changes in perceptible bodily functions. An awareness of these changes is necessary if students are to recognize when they are under stress and need to cope with its effects.

5. Stress appears to increase susceptibility to many diseases and causes psychosomatic illnesses.

6. Exercise is an excellent way to relieve stress and tension when the activity is perceived as enjoyable and success-oriented.

7. Stress is a critical risk factor that influences the onset of heart disease. Type A behavior is accompanied by an increased risk of heart disease.

8. There are different ways of relieving stress, among them are exercise, expressing feelings to friends, developing problem-solving skills, and performing accepted relaxation techniques.

Suggested Learning Activities

1. Hold an isometric contraction at the elbow joint. With the other hand, feel the contraction in the biceps and triceps. Repeat the activity with other muscle groups. Discuss how stress causes generalized body tension that can result in tensed muscles and an increase in general body fatigue. Learning to recognize muscle tension is a desired outcome of this discussion.

2. Discuss the concept of "choking" under pressure. How does this relate to athletic performance? What happens when stress is greater than the individual's ability to cope with it? Discuss how some stress increases performance, while too much decreases it.

3. Discuss the importance of perception in stressful situations. How is stress perceived? Should students face up and admit it when they are worried or scared? Is it better to be "tough" and not tell anyone

how they feel? Is it better to keep emotions inside or to share feelings with others?

4. Discuss the importance of finding activities in which students believe they are successful. How are positive self-concepts developed? Why are some people able to cope with failure and losing better than others?

5. Discuss situations in physical activity settings that give rise to increased stress, such as failing in front of others, not being selected for a team, being ridiculed for a poor performance, or losing a game that was personally important. How could these situations be handled differently?

6. Discuss the parameters of Type A behavior patterns. How can they be modified through activity and changes in behavior? Why do people develop Type A behavior? Are Type A behavior patterns productive?

7. Identify physical activities that seem to relieve tension and stress. Discuss the relationship between involvement in activity and the reduction of stress.

8. Identify and discuss unproductive attempts to relieve stress such as drinking, smoking, and drug abuse. Why are these methods chosen rather than exercise, discussions, or relaxation activities?

9. Discuss the many effects of stress on bodily health. Give students a stress inventory to see how much stress they are under, and discuss ways of reducing this pressure.

10. Teach relaxation techniques such as deep breathing, progressive muscle relaxation, and personal meditation. Emphasize the importance of taking time for these activities daily. Just as brushing the teeth is necessary for healthy dentition, relaxation is necessary for a healthy body and mind.

Nutrition and Weight Control

Proper nutrition is necessary if students are to expect a high level of physical performance from their body. An important area of concern deals with the balance between caloric intake and expenditure in order to maintain proper weight control. Students should understand the reasons and methods for maintaining an optimum level of body weight. Discuss the impact of empty calories through excessive ingestion of junk foods. Explain the importance of a balanced diet to help the body grow and develop. Point out that the role of exercise in weight control and muscle development is as important as a balanced diet.

Students should understand the elements of a balanced diet. The body needs fats, carbohydrates, proteins, minerals, and vitamins. A balanced diet draws from each of the four basic food groups: milk and milk products; meat, fish, and poultry with nuts and legumes as supplements; fruits and vegetables; and breads and cereals. The usual recommendation is that carbohydrates make up a little more than 50% of the daily diet, with fats contributing 30% and proteins about 12%. The impact of various vitamins and minerals on body functions should be understood, as well as which foods are sources of the specific nutrients.

Foods high in cholesterol and fat should be consumed moderately. Some cholesterol and fat are necessary for proper body function. When too much fat is ingested, however, cholesterol and triglyceride levels in the blood plasma increase. This increase is probably detrimental to the body, for many studies have shown a relationship between high cholesterol and triglyceride levels and coronary heart disease. To travel in the bloodstream, fats must combine with water-soluble protein molecules called lipoproteins, which have an important effect on cholesterol and triglyceride levels. Some of these compound molecules are of a type called high-density lipoproteins (HDL), which are associated with a decreased risk of cardiovascular disease. Because polyunsaturated fats appear to increase HDL levels, the general recommendation is to include some polyunsaturates in the diet. Students should know which foods are high in saturated and unsaturated fats, and should be encouraged to have their cholesterol levels monitored by a physician.

Depending on the criteria used, anywhere from 30–50% of students are overweight, meaning that their body weight is over the accepted limits for their age, sex, and body build. It is important for students to begin to develop an awareness of the caloric content of foods as well as the nutritional value. They can then begin to count calories and practice consistency in the amount of calories they ingest. Coupled with this awareness should be some comprehension of the number of calories expended through various types of physical activity (Figure 16.5). Students need to understand that when caloric intake exceeds caloric expenditure, obesity results. A well-documented and common cause of obesity is inactivity. Most experts believe that obese students do not eat more than normal weight students; rather, they exercise less.

Obesity is a roadblock to wellness. Life insurance companies view overweight people as poor risks because of their shorter life expectancy. Excessive body fat makes the heart work harder, increases the chance of having high blood pressure, and lowers the possibility of recovery from a heart attack. Even

Activity	Calories per Hour
Moderate activity	**200–350**
Bicycling (5½ mph)	210
Walking (2½ mph)	210
Gardening	220
Canoeing (2½ mph)	230
Golf	250
Lawn mowing (power mower)	250
Lawn mowing (hand mower)	270
Bowling	270
Fencing	300
Rowboating (2½ mph)	300
Swimming (¼ mph)	300
Walking (3¾ mph)	300
Badminton	350
Horseback riding (trotting)	350
Square dancing	350
Volleyball	350
Roller skating	350
Vigorous activity	**Over 350**
Table tennis	360
Ice skating (10 mph)	400
Tennis	420
Water skiing	480
Hill climbing (100 ft/hr)	490
Skiing (10 mph)	600
Squash and handball	600
Cycling (13 mph)	660
Scull rowing (race)	840
Running (10 mph)	900

FIGURE 16.5 Caloric expenditure (source: adapted from material from the President's Council on Physical Fitness and Sports, Washington, D.C.)

more detrimental to students is the psychological impact that obesity has on self-concept development. Students of normal weight find it much easier to perform physical tasks, because strength in relationship to body weight is a critical performance factor. Overweight students are often punished more severely than normal weight students for the same type of deviance and may receive lower grades for a similar quality of work.

Basic Concepts

1. Diet should be balanced and contain foods from each of the four basic groups. This ensures that the body will receive essential nutrients.

2. Caloric expenditure (body functions plus exercise) and intake (eating) must be balanced to maintain a healthy weight. A weight-reducing program should include a reduction in caloric intake and an increase in daily exercise.

3. Activities vary in the energy they require. Individual needs must be considered in the selection of activities to promote weight control and physical fitness maintenance.

4. Junk foods add little if any nutritional value to the diet and are usually high in calories. Foods such as sugar, margarine and butter, oils, and alcohol are high in calories but make little or no contribution in terms of nutrition.

5. Excessive weight makes performing physical tasks difficult. This results in less success and in less motivation to be active, thus increasing the tendency toward obesity.

6. Obesity increases the risk of heart disease and other related diseases such as diabetes.

7. A majority of obesity cases are caused by inactivity, or lack of sufficient activity. The majority of overweight students do not consume more calories than normal weight students; they are simply less active.

8. Vitamins are not nutrients, but are catalysts that facilitate metabolic processes. Certain vitamin deficiencies can produce various diseases.

9. Various foods are excellent sources of specific nutrients. Students should be able to identify which foods to ingest to provide a balance of the needed nutrients, vitamins, and minerals.

Suggested Learning Concepts

1. Post a list of activities and their energy demands on the bulletin board. Discuss the need for selecting activities that will burn enough calories to balance caloric intake.

2. Maintain a food diary. Record all the foods eaten daily and the amount of calories in each. Compare the amount of calories ingested with the amount of calories expended.

3. Maintain a nutritious-food diary. Record all the foods eaten daily and categorize each by food group. Determine the percentage of carbohydrates, proteins, and fats in relation to all the food ingested during each day.

4. Develop a desirable and practical balanced diet that can be followed for one week. Arrange with parents to facilitate the diet within their budget restrictions.

5. Calculate the Recommended Daily Allowance (RDA) for various nutrients. Compare a daily intake

with the recommendations for various minerals and vitamins.

6. Bring various foods to class that have labels offering nutrition information. Determine which foods are good buys for desired nutrients.

7. Develop an activity diary. For one week, record all activity over and above maintenance activities. Calculate the number of calories burned per day.

8. Discuss and analyze the ways in which society rewards physically fit individuals. Contrast these with the ways in which obese people are discriminated against in various situations.

Substance Abuse

Substance abuse is defined as the harmful use of alcohol, tobacco, or drugs. It is common in today's schools as students seek different ways to explore an expanding world. If students are expected to make wise and meaningful decisions in this area, they must understand the impact of various substances on their physical and psychological being. Facts, both pro and con, should be presented in a nonjudgmental environment, without moralizing and preaching. It is difficult for students to make personal decisions if most of the information they receive is from peers or moralizing adults.

Alcohol, tobacco, and drugs deter wellness and are usually detrimental to total health. The use and misuse of these substances should be discussed objectively with students, because much of the information they receive is from biased sources, such as parents, peers, and various media formats. The physical education teacher can promote unbiased discussions and fact-seeking sessions that relate to wellness. Many times, the physical educator is the only person oriented to wellness promotion. As mentioned earlier, however, if the instructor feels strongly that an issue has only one acceptable point of view, then discussions should be avoided. Telling students only the reasons why *not* to do something can result in a strong polarization in the opposite direction.

Alcohol has both short-term and long-term effects. Short-term effects vary as a result of the depressant effect that alcohol has on the central nervous system. Some people become relaxed, others become aggressive, and some become active in differing degrees. Ultimately, a lack of coordination and confusion occur if a great deal of alcohol is ingested.

The long-term effects of alcohol abuse may be liver damage, heart disease, and malnutrition. The greatest concern surrounding long-term drinking is the possibility of alcoholism. Most agree that alcoholism has the following components: loss of control of alcohol intake; presence of functional or structural damage (physical and psychological); and dependence on alcohol to maintain an acceptable level of functioning.

Students usually drink for any of the following reasons: curiosity; desire to celebrate with parents; peer pressure; to be like adults and appear more mature; to rebel against the adult world; because their models or admired adults drink; or because they are alcoholics. Students are often ambivalent about alcohol. They know its detrimental effects, and yet they see many of their friends and role models using it. The problem is a difficult one, and an understanding of both moderate use and abstinence is needed. An understanding of how to cope with peer pressure to drink alcohol is also needed, and is discussed in the next section on basic concepts.

Tobacco use is common among junior and senior high students. Smoking increases significantly the possibility of heart attacks, strokes, and cancer. Chronic bronchitis and emphysema are diseases prevalent among smokers. A recent study revealed that the average life-span of long-term smokers is seven years shorter than that of nonsmokers.

Students need to understand the impact of smoking on a healthy body. Along with this knowledge, they should examine why so many people choose to smoke. Today, the fastest growing segment of the smoking population is young girls and women. Students will make the final decision for their individual behavior, but before they do so, they need to understand thoroughly the ramifications of smoking.

The use of marijuana and of hard-core drugs should also be discussed. Outside agencies are often most helpful in discussing substance abuse in an objective manner with students. The use of steroids, "pep pills," and pain relievers in athletics should also be debated. In each case, the intent should be to enhance students' awareness so they know the alternatives and consequences. Substance abuse is contrary to the whole concept of physical wellness. Physical educators need to accept the challenge of increasing student understanding and knowledge in these areas.

Basic Concepts

1. The earlier one begins to smoke, the greater the risk to functional health.

2. People smoke for psychological reasons.

3. Young people may choose substance abuse out of curiosity, for status reasons, or from peer pressure.

4. Choosing a life-style independently of peers requires great courage.

5. Decisions about substance abuse are poor decisions if they are based on a dearth of knowledge. Wise and purposeful decisions can be made only when all of the alternatives and consequences are understood.

6. Substance abuse is often an attempt to cope with stress-related problems. Exercise and relaxation are much more productive, healthy methods of coping.

7. The use of alcohol, tobacco, and drugs always carries the risk of addiction. When people are addicted, they are no longer in charge of their life-styles. All people, to some degree, are subject to addiction; no one is immune.

8. Spending time and effort on developing personal competencies is more productive than substance abuse. Personal competency in many areas reduces the need to "be like everyone else," and contributes to a positive self-concept.

9. The use of harmful substances frequently reduces the pleasure one can receive from experiencing the world. Physical performance is often reduced because of substance abuse.

10. A person can drink and smoke and still excel at athletics, but maximum performance levels may be reduced and the ultimate effect on the athlete will be harmful. Students see many professional athletes who smoke and drink. They need to be aware that this happens, but they should understand that the choice is undesirable from a wellness standpoint.

Suggested Learning Activities

1. Identify and discuss the reasons why people choose or choose not to become involved in substance abuse.

2. Discuss the importance of making personal decisions based on what is best for you. Why do we follow others and allow them to influence our decisions, even when those decisions are not in our best interest?

3. Develop a bulletin board that illustrates the many ways used by the tobacco, alcohol, and drug industries to try to get young people to buy their products. Reserve a spot for advertisements (if any can be found) that admonish and encourage students to abstain or moderate the use of various substances.

4. Students often see professional and college athletes smoking and drinking on television while hearing from teachers and coaches that these habits impair performance. Discuss why these athletes can perform at a high level even though they may drink or smoke.

5. Students often choose to be part of a peer group at any cost. Discuss how our society often respects and honors individuals who have the courage to go their own way. Examples might be Columbus, Helen Keller, Braille, and so forth.

6. Identify and discuss the ways in which people in our society choose to relieve and dissipate stress. Discuss productive releases of tension such as recreation, hobbies, and sports.

7. Bring in speakers who are knowledgeable about the effects and uses of alcohol, tobacco, and drugs. If necessary, bring in a pair of speakers who might debate both sides of an issue.

8. Develop visual aids that identify the various effects that alcohol, tobacco, and drugs have on the body.

Safety and First Aid

Safety and first aid have often been part of the physical education program because more accidents occur in physical education than in any other area of the school curriculum. Safety is an attitude and a concern for one's welfare and health. An accident is an unplanned event or act that may result in injury or death. Often, accidents occur when they could have been prevented. The following are the most common causes of accidents: lack of knowledge and understanding of risks; lack of skill and competence to perform tasks safely, such as riding a bike or driving a car; false sense of security that leads people to think that accidents happen only to others; fatigue or illness that affect physical and mental performance; drugs and alcohol; and strong emotional states (e.g., anger, fear, or worry) that cause people to do things they might not otherwise do.

Traffic accidents are one area in which many deaths could be prevented. Wearing seat belts reduces the risk of dying by 50%. Drinking alcohol while driving increases the risk of an accident twentyfold compared to not drinking. Another factor that has reduced the number of traffic deaths is the 55 mph speed limit. Since students are going to drive, driver education and an awareness of the possibility of serious injury should be a part of the wellness program.

Bicycles are another source of numerous accidents. Automobile drivers have difficulty seeing bicycles, and the resulting accidents are often serious. Students need to learn bicycle safety. The physical education setting is often the only place where this training occurs. Classes in bicycling for safety and fitness are usually well received by junior and senior high school students.

Swimming-related accidents are the second leading cause of accidental death among young adults. More than 50% of all drownings occur when people unexpectedly find themselves in the water. Another major cause of death from drowning is alcohol ingestion. Swimming and drinking do not mix well. Physical education programs should encourage all students to learn to swim and to learn water safety rules at sometime during their school career.

Physical education and sports are sources of injury in the school setting. Proper safety procedures should be taught, as well as first-aid techniques. Students should know how to stop bleeding, treat shock, and administer mouth-to-mouth respiration and cardiopulmonary resuscitation (CPR). Many physical education programs now include a required unit of instruction dealing with these topics. It is estimated that 100,000–200,000 lives could be saved by bystanders if they knew CPR.

Basic Concepts

1. Accidents are unplanned events or acts that may result in injury or death. The majority of accidents could be avoided if people were adequately prepared and understood the necessary competencies and risks involved.

2. Wearing seat belts and not drinking alcohol while driving will dramatically decrease the risk of death by automobile accident.

3. Bicycles are often not seen by car drivers. Bicycling safety classes can help lower the number of bicycle accidents.

4. Swimming-related accidents are the second leading cause of accidental death among young people. Drownproofing programs and avoiding alcohol will dramatically decrease the risk of death by drowning.

5. Many thousands of lives could be saved if all people knew how to perform CPR.

6. All students should know how to stop bleeding, and how to administer mouth-to-mouth respiration and CPR.

7. Basic first aid procedures to prevent further injury to victims are competencies that all students should possess.

Suggested Learning Activities

1. Discuss the causes of different types of accidents and how many accidents could be avoided.

2. Identify the types of accidents that happen to different age groups and why this appears to be the case.

3. Identify the role of alcohol and drugs in causing accidents. Why are these substances used in recreational settings?

4. Develop a bulletin board that illustrates how to care for shock victims. Practice the steps in a mock procedure.

5. Have an "accident day" when various types of accidents are staged that demand such treatments as stopping bleeding, mouth-to-mouth respiration, and CPR.

6. Outline the steps to follow in case of a home fire. Discuss how many fires could be prevented.

7. Conduct a bicycle safety fair. Have students design bulletin boards and displays that explain and emphasize bicycle safety.

ENHANCING STUDENT WELLNESS

It is apparent that the wellness of students can be seriously impaired when safety issues are dealt with incorrectly. However, proper nutrition, avoiding substance abuse, and practicing proper safety when bicycling or driving a car can enhance the wellness of participants. The purpose of this section is to help students further advance their wellness status through positive action, rather than by simply avoiding various foods, substances, and situations. This section takes a three-pronged approach: (1) physical fitness and activity; (2) stress reduction; and (3) self-evaluation. None of the areas will be covered in its entirety since there are many in-depth sources. A highly recommended source for helping students develop lifetime fitness is the text by Corbin and Lindsey (1990).

Physical Fitness and Activity

There are two types of physical fitness that are generally identified (Corbin and Lindsey, 1983). The first is skill-related physical fitness and the other is health-related fitness. Skill-related fitness contains many elements that deal with sport performance, among them are balance, coordination, reaction time, agility, power, and speed. Skill-related fitness has less impact on the wellness of an individual and will not be further discussed in this section.

Health-related fitness is directly related to the wellness of individuals and is generally defined as consisting of cardiovascular fitness, strength, muscular endurance, flexibility, and body fatness. Each of these items is defined briefly as follows:

Cardiovascular fitness is the most important phase of fitness for wellness. Cardiovascular fitness is a complex concept, but, simply put, involves efficient functioning of the heart, blood, and blood vessels in order to supply oxygen to the body during aerobic activity.

Strength refers to the ability of a muscle or muscle group to exert force. Without strength, a low standard of performance can be expected, because muscles will fatigue before an individual can perform well.

Muscular endurance refers to the ability of a muscle or muscle group to exert effort over a period of time. Endurance utilizes strength and postpones fatigue so the effort can be expended for long periods. Cardiovascular fitness also plays a key role in how long people can perform an activity.

Flexibility is a person's range of movement at the joints. It allows freedom of movement and ready adjustment of the body for various movements.

Body fatness refers to the percentage of body weight that is fat. People who are physically fit generally have a lower percentage of body fat than those who are unfit. For males in secondary school, 11–15% fat is a reasonable range, while 20–25% is acceptable for females (Corbin and Lindsey, 1990).

It is important to help students develop a health-related fitness plan that they can use to monitor themselves throughout their lives. The basic steps for such a plan are as follows:

1. Identify present areas of fitness and weakness by pretesting. Many tests can be used to evaluate the five components of health-related fitness.

2. Identify the present activities that the students are performing by having them fill out a survey, which lists a wide variety of activities. Post a chart that shows the components of health-related fitness enhanced by each activity. A good source for surveys and lists of activity benefits is *Fitness for Life* by Corbin and Lindsey (1990).

3. Select some activities that will build the health-related fitness components that each student needs, as identified in Step 1. Each student will begin to have a personalized plan that is meaningful only to him or her.

4. Plan a week-long activity program that contains activities that are enjoyable and help alleviate weaknesses in various component areas. Evaluate the week-long program and develop a month-long program in order to provide longer range goals. In the program, delineate the frequency of exercise, the intensity, and the amount of time to be spent exercising.

Stress Reduction

Many methods are recommended for learning to cope with stress. Only the most popular and acceptable in the school setting are covered here. An excellent text devoted entirely to this topic is *Human Stress: Its Nature and Control* (Allen, 1983).

In an earlier section, exercise was discussed as an excellent method of controlling stress. It appears to allow negative feelings to dissipate and positive feelings to replace them. The relaxed feeling that occurs after an exercise bout is championed by many as the best part of activity.

Many deep-breathing exercises are available. The relaxation response advocated by Benson (1975) is supposed to replicate the effects of transcendental meditation (TM). Individuals sit comfortably and quietly and breath deeply through the nose. The word "one" is said each time the person exhales. Twenty-minute bouts, once or twice a day, are recommended.

Another popular method is progressive relaxation as developed by Jacobson (1968). In this technique, a muscle or muscle group is first tensed and then relaxed slowly and smoothly. All the major parts of the body are in turn relaxed as one works down from the head to the toes.

Regardless of the activity choice selected for relaxation, students should be taught the importance of taking time to relax. People are often told that they are wasting time if they are not busy scurrying here and there. It can be an important learning situation to take 4 or 5 min at the end of a class to sit down and relax. This communicates to students that relaxation is indeed important since the instructor allows time for the activity.

Self-Evaluation and Behavior Self-Control

Self-Evaluation

The final step in maintaining wellness is being able to evaluate oneself on a regular basis. Individuals ultimately answer to themselves, and thus students need not share the results of their evaluations. Many surveys can help people evaluate their level of wellness.

Many other inventories, such as drinking and smoking scales, are available from various governmental agencies. Students can begin to see the extent of a problem and whether they have a problem or are improving.

Finally, teach students to evaluate their own levels of physical fitness. Each of the health-related fitness items can be evaluated easily. If students are not given time in the physical education program to evaluate their own fitness levels, they will probably not take the time for evaluation once they leave school. One of the best techniques is to give each student a self-testing card that has room for recording four or five different testing episodes. Allow students to self-test themselves with a friend and record their performances. Instructors can file the cards and return them when it is time for another testing period. This system allows students to monitor their physical fitness gains or losses.

Behavior Self-Control

Students should be taught how to improve their self-control by altering their behavior. Attitudes can be changed by changing behavior patterns. Behavior self-control is a systematic approach to solving problems. It involves keeping records of behavior in order to understand the positive and negative variables that influence behavior. The following steps can be taught effectively to students to help them learn to manipulate their behavior.

1. Maintain behavior records. Students can learn to monitor their exercise patterns and record the performances on personal charts. They can then begin to observe their patterns of exercise, the duration of the exercise, and the intensity of effort. Such observation becomes self-reinforcing when, for example, students see clearly that they are exercising only two days per week and showing little gain, or when they observe rapid improvement after exercising five days per week for several weeks. Another advantage of recording behavior is that the routine act of recording reminds the performer that the behavior must be done. This routine reinforcement causes the behavior performance to improve.

2. Develop a priority schedule. If students want to exercise regularly, they must schedule the activity and make it a high-priority item. In other words, exercise must be done before other less important tasks are performed. Scheduling the activity for a certain number of days at a specified time is most effective.

3. Analyze restrictive factors. Even after behavior has been analyzed and priorities are set, students may find that desired behavior patterns are not being followed. The reasons for this must then be analyzed and other changes effected to increase the probability of carrying out the behavior. For example, the time of exercise may have to be changed, or the length of the bout. Exercising for two shorter periods per day, instead of one long period, might be the answer. Exercising with a friend or changing the mode of exercise would be other possible solutions.

4. Establish rewards. To continue the activity over a long period of time, it can be helpful to establish personal contingencies that are available after performing the desired behavior. For example, students might relax and watch television immediately after exercise, or take a long, hot shower. Regardless of the reward, it must be meaningful and worthwhile to the individual. Verbalizing internally after each exercise routine is also effective as a contingency. One might say to oneself, "I feel better and look stronger after every bout of exercise." In any case, if students can identify something positive that occurs because of or after the exercise bout, they will have a tendency to continue on the path of wellness.

REFERENCES AND SUGGESTED READINGS

Allen, R. J. 1983. *Human Stress: Its Nature and Control.* Minneapolis, MN: Burgess Publishing Co.

Benson, H. 1975. *The Relaxation Response.* New York: William Morrow & Co., Inc.

Corbin, C., and Lindsey, R. 1990. *Fitness for Life.* 3rd ed. Glenview, IL: Scott, Foresman Co.

Friedman, M., and Rosenman, R. H. 1974. *Type A Behavior and Your Heart.* New York: Alfred A. Knopf, Inc.

Jacobson, E. 1968. *Progressive Relaxation.* 2nd ed. Chicago, IL: University of Chicago Press.

Rarick, G. L., ed. 1973. *Physical Activity, Human Growth and Development.* New York: Academic Press.

Wilmore, J. H. 1977. *Athletic Training and Physical Fitness.* Boston, MA: Allyn and Bacon, Inc.

17

INTRODUCTORY ACTIVITIES

Introductory activities are used during the first part of the lesson as preparatory exercises. They require minimal instruction and allow for a maximum amount of movement. Starting a lesson is difficult, but the task is eased when instructors can begin with activity and little verbal interaction. Most students desire immediate activity when they arrive for class. The introductory activities can meet this need.

Introductory activities are vigorous in nature and revolve around large muscle activity. An objective of introductory activities is to develop a high level of skill in movements basic to sport and leisure pursuits. Students should understand how the activities can be applied to their personal activity interests.

Involvement in introductory activities helps prepare students for strenuous activity. They serve as a psychological and physiological warm-up for the fitness portion of the lesson. During the introductory activity, teachers can work on reaction drills in which students freeze in response to a signal. This helps refocus class management skills and reinforces the need for stopping on signal.

Introductory activities should be selected with the interests and developmental levels of the students in mind. Junior high school students, because of their rapid growth spurt, need activities that emphasize body control, coordination, and agility. Senior high school students need to understand how introductory activities will affect sport and dance performance and other activities in which they have developed competency and interest.

Use vocabulary and jargon appropriate to the maturity level of the students when introducing activities. Effective teachers possess some acting skills when presenting introductory activities. Capitalize on popular movies and television series, and on famous people and news items. This adds enthusiasm and motivation to the learning environment.

To minimize unproductive time, use students as leaders. They need opportunities to lead, and to learn not to always depend on teachers to make decisions. Inform the class of the goal and the desired accomplishment. Students can perform signals that are necessary for some of the day's lesson activities.

Students should learn to develop introductory activities suited to their needs. As long as the activities are vigorous and emphasize large muscle movement, they can be used in this part of the lesson. It is also entirely possible that the introductory activity may place demands on the cardiovascular system and can be used for this purpose after the fitness portion of the lesson. As usual, a large variety of introductory activities should be taught and presented to show students that there are many acceptable methods for preparing for activity.

AGILITY ACTIVITIES

Seat Roll

Students are on all fours with head up, looking at the instructor. When the teacher gives a left- or right-hand signal, students respond quickly by rolling in that direction on their seat. Seat rolls can be alternated with running in place or with rope jumping to increase the challenge.

Arkansas Flip

Begin in the same position as the seat roll. Students flip over to the left or right, without touching their seats to the floor, so they are in a crab position (half flip). The flip should be a quick, continuous movement. Students can wait for the next signal in the crab position or, if the teacher designates, can continue over to all fours position with the head up (full flip).

Quarter Eagle

Students are in a ready position with the head up, arms flexed in front of the body, knees slightly bent, feet straight ahead and shoulder width apart. The instructor gives a hand signal left or right. The class responds by making a quarter turn in that direction and returning to the starting position as quickly as possible.

A variation involves having participants move on a verbal signal such as "go." The students then make a quarter turn to the left or right, and wait for the next signal. They continue to make quarter turns on each signal.

Wave Drill

In the wave drill (Figure 17.1), students are in ready position. They shuffle (without a crossover step) left, right, backward, or forward on signal. A useful variation is to place an obstacle (boundary cone) for students to shuffle over.

Variation 1. Same as original, except use a crossover step.

Variation 2. Same as original, except that students are on all fours.

Variation 3. Students stand between two cones or bags stuttering the feet (rapid running in place). On a hand signal to the left or right, the performer steps over the obstacle in the corresponding direction and moves the feet in place while waiting for the next signal.

Variation 4. Same as variation 3 except that students move left or right with both feet together (ski hop). Emphasis is on watching the signal and moving quickly.

Log Roll (Three-Person Roll)

Students are in groups of three and on all fours to start the log roll. The instructor gives a signal left or right. The middle person rolls in that direction, while the person on that side rolls up and over the top of the middle person. The drill continues with each person rolling several times. The objective is to roll straight, get up quickly, and not touch anybody while rolling over them.

FIGURE 17.1   Wave drill

FIGURE 17.2   Rooster hop drill

Square Drill

The class forms several 10-yd squares with boundary cones. Students stand in the middle of each side of the square and face the center. On signal, they shuffle around the square to the left or right, depending on the signal of the teacher. A student can be in the center of the square to give a direction signal.

Lateral Shuffle

Place two cones about 5 yd apart. A student stands in the middle and shuffles quickly back and forth between the cones, touching the cone each time. Students try to touch as many cones as possible in 15 sec. Set up enough pairs of cones so all students can participate simultaneously.

Rooster Hop Drill

Students hop 10 yd on one leg in the following sequence: 1. left hand touching the right toe, which is on the ground; 2. right hand touching the left toe on the ground; 3. right hand touching the right toe on the ground; 4. left hand touching the left toe on the ground. (See Figure 17.2.) Students can be challenged to develop different combinations and tasks.

Weave Drill

The weave drill (Figure 17.3) is similar to the wave drill, except that students shuffle in and out of a series of obstacles such as cones, blocking dummies, or boards. A shuffling step is used rather than a crossover step.

Running Weave Drill

Students run through the maze with a regular running stride. (See Figure 17.4.) A stopwatch can challenge students to improve their time, and the maze can be arranged in many different ways. Let students

FIGURE 17.3   Weave drill

FIGURE 17.5   All fours circle

set up the maze and time each other. A variation could be done using the carioca step.

Leaping Lena with a Forward Roll

Students stand in a ready position stuttering the feet quickly. On the first command, students leap forward as far as possible and begin moving the feet again. Two more leaps are repeated and then a forward roll is performed. Students return to the end of the line when finished.

Burpee-Flip Drill

The burpee-flip can be done in small groups or in unison with the entire class. The teacher calls out the number, and students yell the number while performing the movement. The sequence is as follows:

1. Standing position
2. Bend the knees, hands on the floor or ground
3. Legs kick back into an all fours position, head up
4. Half flip right to a crab position
5. Half flip right to an all-fours position

This drill can also be done with a left flip or with two flips, one left and one right, and so forth. Let students try this drill with a small group. Challenge them to stay together and to continue enlarging the group. Participants must call the numbers for their group.

Another variation is to put a push-up in before the flip. Step 4 would be the down motion and Step 5 would be the up motion. Use caution to ensure that students are far enough apart in case one student flips the wrong way.

All Fours Circle

Students lie on their stomachs with heads close together and legs extended outward like the spokes of a wheel (Figure 17.5). One person starts by placing the hands in the center and moving around the circle over the other students without touching anyone. The last person who is passed is the next participant. The drill can be done with 4–12 people.

Coffee Grinder Square

With the coffee grinder square (Figure 17.6), students start at one corner of the square, run to the next corner, and perform a coffee grinder on the right arm (arm extended on the ground, supporting the body weight, while the feet walk 360 degrees around the arm). At the next corner, they put their left arm down and do another coffee grinder. This continues through the four corners. The square should be made with something flat, such as beanbags or bases. Students should move in the same direction around the square.

FIGURE 17.4   Running weave drill

FIGURE 17.6   Coffee grinder square

FIGURE 17.7   Flash drill

Flash Drill

Students stand in a ready position facing the teacher (Figure 17.7). The teacher exclaims "feet," and students stutter the feet quickly. The teacher then "flashes" the following hand signals:

1. Hands up: Students jump up and return to stuttering feet.
2. Hands down: Students move to the floor and return to stuttering feet.
3. Hands right: Students shuffle right.
4. Hands left: Students shuffle left.
5. Hands make a circle: Students do a forward roll and get up stuttering.

SPORT MOVEMENT CHALLENGES

The following activities can be done with sport movements such as sliding, leaping, running, and jumping. The locomotor movement is then combined with a challenging activity that is used in sport such as a pivot, stop, or change of direction.

Move and Change Direction

Students run in any direction, and change direction on signal. The change in direction can be specified or student selected. If specified, the commands might be to reverse, right angle, 45 degrees, or left turn. The change in direction should be made quickly in pivotlike fashion.

Move and Change Speed or Level

Students move throughout the area. On signal, they are challenged to move close to the floor or as elon-

gated as possible. They can be challenged to touch the floor or give a "high five" while moving. Combinations of changing the level (as well as changing the speed of the movement) can be developed.

Move and Change the Type of Locomotion

Students move using a specified locomotor movement. On signal, they change to another type of movement. Challenges can be given to do the movements forward, backward, sideways, or diagonally.

Change Move and Quickly Stop

Students move throughout the area and quickly stop under control. Emphasis should be placed on stopping using proper technique. Students should lower the center of gravity, widen the base of support, and place one foot in front of the other to absorb the force.

Move and Perform Athletic Movement

Students move and stop on signal. They then perform an athletic skill move, such as a basketball jump shot, leaping football pass catch, volleyball spike, or soccer kick. Students should place emphasis on correct form and timing. A variation of the activity is for students to move with a partner and throw a pass on signal, punt a ball, or shoot a basket. The partner catches the ball or rebounds the shot.

Move, Stop, and Pivot

Students move under control throughout the area. On signal, they stop, pivot, and resume moving. Emphasis should be placed on making a sharp pivot and a rapid acceleration. The skill is similar to running a pass pattern in football.

Move and Perform a Fitness Task

The class moves throughout the area. When a signal is given, students perform a predesignated fitness task. Examples of tasks are push-ups, sit-ups, squat thrusts, and crab kicks. The fitness tasks can be written on a card and flashed to the class to signal the next challenge.

Move and Perform a Stretch

The class is challenged to run throughout the area. On signal, they stop and perform a designated stretching activity. (See Chapter 18 for a comprehensive list of stretching exercises.) A list of stretches that covers all body parts can be posted, and students can perform a different stretch after each signal.

INDIVIDUAL ACTIVITIES _____

Number Challenges

Students are challenged to move and perform to a set of three to four numbers. For example, the given set of numbers might be 25, 10, 30. The first number would signify some type of locomotor movement, the second number a set of stretching exercises, and the last an activity with equipment. Implemented, this challenge might be 25 running steps, 10 repetitions of a stretching activity, and 30 rope-jumping turns.

Four Corners

A square is marked using four boundary cones. Students spread out around the perimeter of the square. On signal, they move in the same direction around the square. As they pass a corner, they change the locomotor movement they are doing. Other challenges would be to move on all fours, in crab position, or using a frog jump.

Gauntlet Run

Students line up at one end of a football field or area of similar size. Challenges are placed every 10 yd. Examples of challenges might be to jump over benches, crawl through hoops, run through tires, long-jump a certain distance, hop backwards, high-jump over a bar, do a forward roll, or perform an animal walk. Students can begin at different challenges so the activity does not become a race. Emphasis should be placed on warming up and achieving quality movement.

Rubber Band

Students begin from a central point with the instructor. On signal, the students move away from the instructor using a designated movement such as a jump, run, hop, slide, carioca, or walk. On the second signal, students sprint back to the instructor's position where the activity originated. The cycle is repeated with different movements. As a variation, students can perform one or two stretching activities when they return to the teacher.

Rope Jumping

Each student has a jump rope. On the first signal, they begin jumping rope. On the second signal, they drop the rope and perform a stretching activity. A third signal can be used to designate performing a light, easy run. Emphasis should be placed on preparing students for fitness activity rather than offering a severe workout.

Milk Carton Kicking

Half-gallon paper milk cartons filled with newspaper, or gallon-size plastic milk containers can be used for this introductory activity. Each student has a carton and dribbles or kicks it throughout the area. Students can also work with a partner and dribble the container back and forth. The carton is a medium for encouraging movement. All kicking and dribbling should be done on the move.

Ball Activities

Each student has a ball and dribbles it throughout the area while moving. On signal, students stop and move the ball behind the back, around each leg, and overhead. Emphasis is on learning to handle the ball as well as on moving. A variation is to drop one ball on signal and play catch with a partner until the signal to resume dribbling is given.

Beanbag Touch and Go

Spread different colored beanbags throughout the area. On signal, students run to a beanbag, touch it, and resume running. To increase the challenge, the color of the beanbag can be specified and the touch must be made with a designated body part. An example might be, "Touch 6 yellow beanbags with your left hip." Students can also move to a beanbag, perform a pivot, and resume running.

Vanishing Beanbags

Spread beanbags throughout the area to allow one per student. Students move around the area until a signal is given. On the signal, they find a beanbag and sit on it. The instructor then signals for the class to move again, and one or more beanbags are removed during this interval. Now when students are signaled to find a beanbag, some will be left without one. A challenge is offered to not be left out more than five times. Locomotor movements and different body parts can be specified to add challenge and variety.

Rolling Hoops

Each student has a Hula-Hoop and rolls it alongside while running. On signal, the hoops are dropped, and students are challenged to move in and out of 15 hoops. The number and color of hoops to move in and out of can be specified, as well as the type of activity to perform. When the task is completed, the student picks up the hoop and resumes rolling it.

Animal Walks

Two parallel lines marked with boundary cones are placed 10–20 yd apart. Half of the class lines up on one line and the other half on the opposite line. On signal, students animal-walk from one line to the other. Examples of walks that can be done are the dog walk, seal walk, crab walk, rabbit jumps, bear walk, and walrus walk.

PARTNER AND SMALL GROUP ACTIVITIES

Marking

Marking is an excellent activity for learning to elude an opponent and also for learning to stay defensively near someone. Partners are selected, and one elects to chase the other. On the first signal, the challenge is to stay as close as possible to the partner who is attempting to get away. When a second signal is given, both partners must immediately freeze. If the chaser can reach out and "mark" the partner, the chaser scores a point. Roles are reversed each time a signal is given.

Pentabridge Hustle

To start the Pentabridge hustle (Figure 17.8), students form groups of five. They spread out as far as possible in the playing area and form individual bridges that another person can move under. On signal, the first person in the group of five moves under the other four bridging students and runs ahead and forms a bridge. The next person in sequence moves under the four bridges. This becomes a continuous movement activity. Activity success depends on making sure that students form bridges that are quite a distance apart so that enough running occurs to ensure warm-up.

Over, Under, and Around

Students find a partner. One person gets in position on all fours while the other stands alongside, ready to begin the movement challenge (Figure 17.9). The challenge is given to move over, go under, and run around the partner a certain number of times. For example, move over your partner 5 times, go under 8 times, and run around 13 times. When the task is completed, partners change positions and the challenge is repeated. To increase motivation, the challenge can be made to move over, under, and around different students. For a more difficult challenge, the persons on all fours can move slowly throughout the area.

FIGURE 17.8   Pentabridge hustle

New Leader

Students work in small groups. The task is to continuously move in a productive fashion that will warm up the group. One person begins as the leader. When a signal is given, a new leader steps up and leads the next activity.

Pyramid Power

Students move throughout the area. On signal, they find a partner and build a simple pyramid or partner stand (Figure 17.10). Examples are the hip-shoulder stand, double-crab stand, double-dog stand, and shoulder stand. Students should be cautioned to select a partner of similar size and to stand on the proper points of support.

Leapfrog

Students work in groups of four or five. All students in the group move into the leapfrog base position with the exception of the last person in line. On signal, the last person leapfrogs over the others and moves into a base position. The next person now leapfrogs over the others, and the activity becomes one of continuous movement. Activity success depends on maintaining a large distance between each of the leapfrog bases.

FIGURE 17.9   Over, under, and around

FIGURE 17.10   Examples of pyramid power

FIGURE 17.11 Mirror drill

Tag Games

A variety of tag games can be used to motivate students to move. They are excellent for teaching students to elude and chase each other. Examples of tag games are:

1. Balance tag. To be safe, balance in a stipulated position.
2. Push-Up tag. Assume the push-up or other designated position to avoid being tagged.
3. Snowball tag. Two people begin by being "it". When they tag someone, they hold hands. As a number of people are tagged, the chain of people becomes long, and only those at the end of the chain are eligible to tag.
4. Frozen tag. When tagged, the person must freeze with the feet in straddle position. To be able to resume play, three people must move under and through a "frozen" person's legs.
5. Spider tag. Students stand back-to-back with a partner with the elbows hooked. A pair of people are "it" and chase the other pairs. If a pair is tagged (or becomes unhooked), they are "it".
6. Triangle plus one tag. Three students hold hands to form a triangle. One person in the triangle is the leader. The fourth person outside the triangle tries to tag the leader. The triangle moves around to avoid getting the leader tagged. Leader and tagger are changed often.

Follow-the-Leader

Students are grouped by pairs. On signal, the leader performs all types of movements to elude his or her partner. Zigzags, rolls, 360-degree turns, and jumps are encouraged. Partners switch after 30 sec. The same drill can be done with one leader and two or more followers.

Hoops on the Ground

Students run around the area where hoops are spread. When the teacher calls a number, students must get that number of students inside one hoop in 5 sec or less.

Mirror Drill in Place

Each student faces a partner (Figure 17.11). One person is the leader and makes a quick movement with the hands, head, legs, or body. The partner tries to be a mirror and perform the exact movement. The leader must pause briefly between movements. Leader and partner exchange places after 30 sec.

Formation Rhythmic Running

The class begins in circular formation. Students move to a drumbeat or other steady beat. They attempt to run rhythmically to the beat, lifting the knees and maintaining a formation or line with even spacing between students. Challenges can be added, such as clapping hands on the first beat, stamping the feet on the third beat, and thrusting a hand into the air on the fourth beat of a four-count rhythm.

As students become experienced at maintaining the formation and rhythm of the activity, they can be led into different formations such as a rectangle, square, triangle, or line. Students can also "wind up" and "unwind" the line, and can learn to cross in front of each other to "break a line."

PHYSICAL FITNESS

All students have the right to develop a meaningful level of physical fitness. Physical education programs that do not make time for fitness development indirectly teach students that fitness is not important for a healthy life-style. At the secondary school level, students should have the opportunity to experience and select fitness routines that are useful and motivating to them personally. Physical fitness activity should be offered as a positive contribution to total wellness. It should be something that benefits those who participate, and not something to be used as punishment for misbehavior.

PHYSICAL FITNESS AND WELLNESS

Secondary school students need to know the payoffs of developing a high level of fitness. They must understand the impact that fitness can have on their state of wellness. If a need for fitness is not demonstrated to students, teachers cannot expect them to choose to stay physically fit when school is over. The following points highlight the importance of wellness and the role played by physical activity in a healthy life-style.

Heart Disease

Heart disease afflicts 500,000 to 2 million people, depending on the statistics one examines. It is a killer of young people as well as adults. Many think of it as a geriatric disease, yet symptoms have been found in as many as 70% of American youth. In an Iowa study (Glass, 1973), 5,000 youngsters between ages 6 and 18 were examined over a two-year period. Seventy percent had one or more positive risk factors, such as high cholesterol levels, high blood pressure, or obesity.

On examining the development of arteriosclerosis in humans, Dr. Kenneth Rose (1973) wrote: "The first signs appear around age two and the disease

process is reversible until the age of nineteen. At nineteen, the process of the disease appears to be irreversible, and from then on, it inexorably progresses until it becomes clinically manifest, usually in the forties."

Students need to be aware of the heart disease risk factors and how they can modify each of them. The primary risk factors are high blood pressure, cigarette smoking, and high cholesterol levels. Secondary risk factors are less strongly associated with heart disease, but are still important. These are obesity, lack of exercise, stress, and heredity. As an example of how risk factors increase the possibility of heart attack, consider that if one smokes and has high blood pressure and high cholesterol levels, the risk of heart attack is increased fivefold.

Cholesterol Levels

Exercise, or lack of it, is linked to cholesterol levels. Regular aerobic exercise appears to reduce cholesterol levels. How cholesterol travels in the blood may be more important than the serum cholesterol level. High-density lipoproteins (HDL) appear to cleanse the body of cholesterol in contrast with low-density lipoproteins (LDL), which carry cholesterol to be deposited at the cellular level. The critical point in terms of cardiovascular disease is the ratio of HDL to LDL. Exercise appears to increase the ratio of HDL to LDL and to increase lean body weight (Gilliam et al., 1978).

Stress

Exercise appears to reduce stress levels. The tranquilizer effect of exercise has been compared with the effect of the common tranquilizer meprobamate (deVries and Adams, 1972). Five treatments were given and studied using 36 anxious patients. One treatment was the tranquilizer, another was a placebo, the third was walking at a heart rate of 100 for 15 min, the fourth was 15 min of walking at a heart rate of 120, and the fifth was a controlled comparison with resting. The results showed that 15 min of walking caused a 20% to 25% reduction in muscular activity, which in turn reduced anxiety. The tranquilizer had no impact on the subjects.

Even though this study was done with elderly subjects, it bears out the point that even moderate exercise can bring about a reduction in anxiety and stress levels. Teenagers must deal with stress. They are constantly under pressure and are expected to perform well in relation to peers. Since exercise is a stressor, it can prepare the body to cope and resist other types of stress in life (Miller and Allen, 1982). The impact that stress has on an individual's state of health may thus be reduced through exercise.

Smoking

Smoking one pack of cigarettes per day increases the risk of heart disease threefold. It is difficult, if not impossible, to justify the use of tobacco. Secondary school students, however, have many motivations for smoking, and a blatant "Don't do it!" serves little purpose. Perhaps the most effective strategy is to conduct valuing sessions in which students analyze both sides of the issue. The emphasis is on making a personal decision based on each individual's unique parameters. Materials dealing with smoking and related hazards are available from the Department of Health and Human Services, Rockville, MD 20852.

Bone Structure and Flexibility

Exercise affects skeletal development. Vigorous activity causes increased stress on the bones, which results in an increase in bone diameter and improved internal structure. Osteoporosis, or loss of bony tissue through demineralization, is the result of inactivity. This condition causes bones to be more susceptible to breaking. Exercise can reverse the process and develop bones that are highly mineralized and resistant to fracture.

Flexibility and joint mobility can be maintained through exercise, because exercise increases the elasticity of the muscles, tendons, and ligaments. Flexibility results in fewer injuries, better posture, and improved sport performance.

Musculature

Exercise causes an increase in strength, and strength is an important factor in learning motor skills (Rarick and Dobbins, 1975). Strength is also important in reducing sport injuries to joints. For these reasons, weight lifting is used in athletic training regardless of the activity.

A loss of strength is often associated with increas-ing age. In fact, loss of strength is usually a result of inactivity instead of physiological changes. In a study (Petrofsky and Lind, 1975) examining grip strength in 100 men who worked in a machine shop, no change in grip strength was found from age 22 to 62. Regular exercise is thus essential to maintain an adequate level of strength throughout life.

Obesity

Excess weight is found in over 30% of all schoolchildren. Obesity decreases the motor performance of students because of the reduction in strength to body weight ratio. In many teenagers, obesity is unfortunately due to a decrease in muscular activity. As weight increases, the impulse for physical exertion decreases. As students become more obese, the cycle becomes uncontrollable, so that many overweight youngsters see no point in trying to control their weight.

Lack of activity appears to be a critical factor in cases of obesity. This heart disease risk factor not only affects the health status of individuals, but takes a psychological toll as well. In diet comparisons of obese and normal weight students, no substantial difference in caloric consumption was found. In a study of high school girls (Johnson et al., 1956), obese female students were found to eat less than normal weight girls, but they also exercised two-thirds less (in total time). Movies taken of normal and overweight youngsters (Corbin and Fletcher, 1968) demonstrated a wide difference in activity levels of the two groups, but their diets were similar.

Obesity is measured by the percent of body fat an individual carries. Body fat can be measured easily using skin calipers, and this measurement can be converted to give an estimate of the percent of body fat an individual carries in relation to total body weight. If an individual carries more than 20% fat, the person is carrying excess fat.

Exercise can have a strong impact on weight reduction. The two ways of reducing body fat are through exercise and diet. Diet is more often chosen because it seems less difficult. Permanent weight losses seldom occur through diet manipulation, however. The best answer for most individuals is usually a combination of moderate dieting and increased activity.

A close look at dieting reveals the relative effectiveness of the process. It is necessary to burn approximately 3,500 calories to lose 1 lb of fat. A person fasting completely would still lose only 1 lb per day. Most people can easily maintain their weight on 2,000–2,800 calories per day, which reveals the difficulty of weight control by diet alone. Most of the rapid weight losses boasted by different diets are due to the loss of body fluids, not body fat. In fact, during the first 2 or 3 wks of crash dieting, 60–70% of the weight lost is lean body tissue that includes body fluids (Wilmore, 1980). The loss of lean body tissue is undesirable because of the loss of body strength and the effect on physical appearance.

What is the maximum amount of weight that can be lost using a starvation diet? If a female who normally consumed 2,000 calories to maintain body weight went on a starvation diet, one might estimate that she would lose about 0.6 lb of fat per day. When food intake is reduced to starvation levels (Wilmore, 1980), however, the body reduces its energy needs by 25–30%. The amount of calories burned per day is therefore reduced to 1,400–1,500, and the amount of fat lost is only about 0.4 lb per day. Under these severe restrictions, the dieter would be able to lose about 3 lb per week, at most.

Examine the impact of exercise on weight loss. Approximately 3,500 calories must be burned to lose 1 lb. Depending on the size of the individual, approximately 120 calories can be burned per mile of movement. If 1 mile of running or pace walking were done everyday, 840 calories would be burned per week. At the end of a month of exercise, 3,600 calories would be expended. If the individual's caloric intake were maintained, a pound of weight would still be lost. At the end of a year, 12 lb of weight would be lost. Exercise is a slower way to lose weight, but it carries many health-related benefits and the weight loss is often permanent. Remember that weight is gained slowly over a period of days, weeks, and years. Individuals should not expect to lose it in a period of one or two weeks.

Longevity

If one wants to live longer, consider the results of a study done using 7,000 subjects in California (Nelson, 1979). Seven health habits were examined: eating regularly and not snacking between meals; eating breakfast; getting eight hours of sleep; maintaining normal weight; not smoking; not drinking, or drinking in moderation; and exercising regularly. Men who observed all seven of the healthy living practices were shown to live an average of 11 yr longer than men observing only one or none of the habits. Women who observed the practices lived an average of seven years longer than those who did not. Men who participated in active sports had the lowest mortality rate.

The relationship of exercise to human wellness is becoming increasingly clear. The responsibility for good health resides with the individual to foresee and prevent health dysfunctions. Students need to relate exercise and activity with a healthy body in much the same way that they have learned to associate brushing the teeth with dental health.

A LIFETIME OF FITNESS ACTIVITY

Students often leave school with little insight into fitness and how it can be a part of their daily lifestyles. The following points give students a framework for developing an approach to lifetime fitness. The points are general in nature and should help most students feel that they are capable of maintaining physical fitness.

1. Perform activity you enjoy. If it is going to be a part of your life-style, it should be enjoyable and rewarding.

2. Do not overdo it. When exercising, stop if fatigue sets in. Make the exercise pleasant—take along your dog, pick some flowers, talk to friends. Tie the routine to something enjoyable. If the experience is overly painful, most individuals will discontinue it. Rewards must occur in one form or another, such as improved appearance, weight control, or feeling less stressed.

3. Make it personal. Many adults choose fitness activities that can be done individually. Jogging, walking, and calisthenics are possible choices.

4. Make it a top priority in life. Nothing should be a higher priority than one's personal health. Without health, it is impossible to work, play, and fulfill other responsibilities.

5. Make exercise an important part of the daily routine. Exercise must be as important as work, health habits, and leisure-time activities. If it does not get equal billing, it does not get done when time is short. Allow 30 min a day for exercise.

6. Exercise at any time during the day. The only exceptions are the 1–2 hr after a meal, and when the weather is too hot and humid.

7. If you like to monitor personal improvement, do so, but do not get drawn into a competitive situation that reduces spontaneity and enjoyment of the activity.

8. There is some evidence (Glasser, 1976) that if the following activity conditions are met, exercise will become positively addicting and a necessary part of one's life.

a. The activity must be noncompetitive; the person chooses and wants to do it.

b. It does not require a great deal of mental effort.

c. The activity can be done alone, without a partner or teammates.

d. The participant believes in the value of the exercise for improving health and general welfare.

e. The participant believes that the activity will become easier and more meaningful if they persist. To become addicting, the activity must be done for at least 6 mo.

f. The activity is accomplished in such a manner that the participant is not self-critical.

THE BROAD PROGRAM OF PHYSICAL FITNESS

There is much more to acquiring physical fitness than just providing physical fitness routines. The components of a broad program are as follows:

1. Teach students to assume responsibility for their personal fitness development. This includes helping students set personal goals that have meaning. It implies an extension of fitness development beyond recess and free time in school, as well as application to the home and community environment.

2. Provide an understanding of how fitness is developed. This implies an explanation of the value of the procedures followed in class sessions so that students understand the purpose of all fitness developmental tasks. In addition, it requires teaching students the basic components of a personal fitness program for life.

3. Develop cognition of the importance of fitness for wellness. Students should understand how to perform fitness activities and why these activities should be performed. They need to know the values derived from maintaining a minimal fitness level.

4. Provide a sound fitness development program that is part of each lesson. This is the culmination—the "show me how"—procedures that embody the first four program points.

Teachers should examine how the physical education program and accompanying instruction communicate the importance of fitness to students. Too often, the area deleted from physical education instruction is physical fitness. This communicates to students that fitness is the least important aspect of physical education. In fact, values shared with students should develop the comprehension that physical fitness is the foundation of skill performance, personal health, and wellness.

COMPONENTS OF PHYSICAL FITNESS

Although it is generally agreed that physical fitness is an important part of normal growth and development, a general definition of its precise nature has not been universally accepted. Through research and scholarly inquiry it is becoming increasingly clear that the multidimensional characteristics of physical fitness can be divided into two areas: health-related physical fitness and skill-related physical fitness. This clear differentiation between *physical fitness related to functional health and physical performance related primarily to athletic ability* has come about after much discussion and debate. Although this definition has curricular implications, classifying fitness into two categories should not lessen the importance of either in the total growth and development of youngsters. Understanding the distinctive features of health-related physical fitness and skill related physical fitness should help educators develop objectives and goals for elementary physical education.

Health-Related Physical Fitness

Health-related physical fitness includes those aspects of physiological function that offer protection from diseases resulting from a sedentary life-style. It can be improved and/or maintained through properly directed physical activity. Specific components include cardiovascular fitness, body composition (ratio of leanness to fatness), abdominal strength and endurance, and flexibility. These components can be measured using the *Fitnessgram System* (Sterling, 1987) or the *AAHPERD Physical Best Program* (1988) and are essential in developing and maintaining the physical health and well-being of students. The following are the components of health-related fitness.

Cardiovascular Fitness

Aerobic fitness is important for a healthy life-style and may be the most important element of fitness. Cardiovascular endurance is the ability of the heart, the blood vessels, and the respiratory system to deliver oxygen efficiently over an extended period of time. To develop cardiovascular endurance, activity must be aerobic in nature. Activities that are continuous and rhythmic require that a continuous supply of oxygen be delivered to the muscle cells. During aerobic exercise, oxygen the body uses in a given period of time is called the maximum oxygen uptake and is the best indicator of cardiovascular endurance. Activities that stimulate development in this area are paced walking, jogging, biking, rope jumping, aerobic dance, swimming, and continuous movement sports such as basketball or soccer.

In contrast to aerobic activity is anaerobic exercise, an activity that is so intense that the body cannot supply oxygen at the cellular level. The body can therefore continue the activity for a short time only. Examples of anaerobic activity are sprinting, running up stairs, or an all out effort in any sport.

Body Composition

Body composition is an integral part of health-related fitness. Body composition is the proportion of body fat to lean body mass. After the thickness of selected skinfolds has been measured, the percentage of body fat can be calculated by using formulas that have been developed using other more accurate methods of measuring body fat. The conversion of skinfold thickness to percent body fat is sometimes inaccurate but is easier to communicate to parents.

Attaining physical fitness is difficult when an individual's body composition contains a high amount of body fat. An understanding of caloric intake and expenditure (see Chapter 16) is important for weight control. It is possible to eat enough to gain weight regardless of the amount of exercise performed. Since the wellness status of individuals is dependent on body composition, students must learn about concepts and consequences in this area.

Flexibility

Flexibility is the range of movement through which a joint or sequence of joints can move. Inactive individuals lose flexibility, whereas frequent movement helps retain the range of movement. Through stretching activities, the length of muscles, tendons, and ligaments is increased. The ligaments and tendons retain their elasticity through constant use. Flexibility is important to fitness; a lack of flexibility can create health problems. People who are flexible are less subject to injury in sport, usually possess sound posture, and may have less lower back pain. Many physical activities demand a wide range of motion to generate maximum force.

Two types of stretching activity have been used to develop flexibility. Ballistic stretching (strong bouncing movements) was the most commonly used until recently, but has come under scrutiny since it may initiate the stretch reflex. This reflex is an involuntary response to a stimulus (stretch) and causes the muscle to contract. The reflex may cause muscle soreness and strain and may not develop an increased range of motion.

Static, controlled stretching, without bounce, is effective because it does not induce the stretch reflex. It involves gradually increasing the stretch to the point of discomfort, backing off slightly to where the position can be held comfortably, and maintaining the stretch for an extended time. Static stretching is safer and less likely to cause injury. This method of stretching can be used to reduce muscle soreness or to prepare for strenuous activity. The length of time to hold the stretch can be started at 5–10 sec and increased gradually up to 30–45 sec.

Muscular Strength and Endurance

Strength is the ability of muscles to exert force; it is an important fitness component for learning motor skills (Rarick and Dobbins, 1975). Most activities in physical education do not build strength in the areas where it is most needed: the arm-shoulder girdle and the abdominal region.

Muscular endurance is the ability to exert force over an extended period. Endurance postpones the onset of fatigue so that activity can be performed for lengthy periods. Most sport activities require that muscular skills, such as throwing, kicking, and striking, be performed many times without fatigue.

When muscular strength is a desired training outcome, it is necessary to lift or move near-maximum work loads with minimal repetitions. Strength development is accompanied by muscle hypertrophy, an increase in the number of muscle fibers recruited, and an increase in oxygen use capacity. The hypertrophy of muscle fibers occurs only in adolescents and adults since the hormone, testosterone, triggers this growth. Children and females usually do not have high enough levels of the hormone to cause a substantial increase in muscle fiber size.

To develop muscular endurance, a low-resistance, high-repetition work load is suggested. For most athletes, a balance of the two work loads is probably most useful. Usually, muscular strength and endurance workouts should be conducted three days per week. This gives the muscles a chance to recover from the exercise stress.

Skill-Related Physical Fitness

Skill-related fitness includes those physical qualities that enable a person to perform in sport activities. Synonymous with skill fitness is athletic fitness or motor fitness. In addition to the health-related aspects that are important to sport performance, specific components making up skill-related fitness are agility, balance, coordination, power, and speed. Most skill-related fitness components can be measured with the AAHPERD Youth Fitness Test (1987). Some of the components of skill-related fitness are described in the following sections.

Agility

Agility is the ability of the body to change position rapidly and accurately while moving. Wrestling and football are examples of sports that require agility.

Balance

Balance refers to the body's ability to maintain a state of equilibrium while remaining stationary or moving. Maintaining balance is essential to all sports but is especially important in the performance of gymnastic activities.

Coordination

Coordination is the ability of the body to perform smoothly and successfully more than one motor task at the same time. Needed for football, baseball, tennis, soccer and other sports that require hand-eye and foot-eye skills, coordination can be developed by practicing repeatedly the skill to be learned.

Power

Power is the ability to transfer energy explosively into force. To develop power a person must practice activities that are required to improve strength, but at a faster rate involving sudden bursts of energy. Skills requiring power include high jumping, long jumping, shot putting, throwing, and kicking.

Speed

Speed is the ability of the body to perform movement in a short period of time. Usually associated with running forward, speed is essential for the successful performance of most sports and general locomotor movement skills.

SKILL-RELATED OR HEALTH-RELATED FITNESS?

For years, the only available fitness test for teachers was the AAHPERD Youth Fitness Test (1987). This test is also known as the President's Council on Physical Fitness and Sports Youth Fitness Test. It is a skill-related test that offers an award to youngsters performing at the 85th percentile or better in all test items. Because skill-related fitness is closely allied to one's natural or inherited traits, it is difficult for all students to achieve. Skill-related fitness is closely related to athletic ability. The traits of speed, agility, coordination and so on, form the basis of the ability to excel in sports. Unfortunately, only those students who have been blessed with exceptional

athletic ability are able to win the fitness award. Results of the National School Population Fitness Survey funded by the President's Council on Physical Fitness and Sports showed that only $\frac{1}{10}$ of 1% of boys and $\frac{3}{10}$ of 1% of girls could pass 6 tests at the 85th percentile, the standard used for earning the Presidential Fitness Award over the years. This high failure rate does not motivate the youngsters to participate in fitness activity. In fact, it often discourages youngsters who need to be motivated the most: the poor performers.

Teaching health-related fitness should be a top priority in the physical education lesson. The beauty of health-related fitness is that *all* students can improve their performance through regular and progressive exercise. This is one of the few areas in physical activity where a teacher can say with confidence and integrity, "If you are willing to practice and put forth an effort, you will improve." This contrasts with skill-related fitness, that is based on genetic traits and abilities. The other reason it is important to teach health-related fitness is that it will develop exercise patterns that give students the ability to maintain cardiovascular and postural health for a lifetime.

Skill-related fitness components are useful for performing motor tasks related to sport and athletics. The ability to perform well depends on the genetic skill of the individual. Where it is possible for all students to perform adequately in health-related fitness activities, it is difficult, if not impossible, for a large number of youngsters to excel in this area of fitness. Asking youngsters to "try harder" only adds to their frustration if they lack native ability, since they see their more skilled friends perform well. When skill-related fitness is taught, it should be accompanied by an explanation of why some students can perform well with a minimum of effort whereas others, no matter how hard they try, never excel. There are many examples that can be used to illustrate the situation such as the differences in speed, jumping ability, strength, and physical size in individuals.

This strong concern to assure health-related fitness for all students has led to the formation of the *Fitnessgram System* (Sterling, 1987) and the *AAHPERD Physical Best Program* (1988). These new physical fitness evaluation programs are comprehensive in that they are concerned about developing habitual and lifelong patterns of fitness activity. They offer award systems that contrast sharply with the President's Council on Physical Fitness and Sports Test in that they reward the process of consistent and regular activity rather than the product of a one-time testing trial. The awards can be won by students who are willing to exercise regularly and consistently for an extended period of time. Most fitness experts agree that if youngsters become involved in the daily process of exercising, the product will take care of itself.

Another important concept emphasized by both of the new fitness programs is that of criterion standards. In the past, fitness tests have asked students to compare their performance to that of other students, regardless of the many complicating factors, such as body type, genetic makeup, and age differences. Youngsters have been compared on percentile charts that showed what percentage of the students ranked above and below them. For students who performed poorly, this is demoralizing. The new tests establish minimum levels of performance as acceptable standards. Performance in excess of the minimum is certainly laudable, but not required. This approach helps students understand that it is critical to achieve a minimum level of fitness rather than compare oneself with others. In addition, self-improvement becomes more important than trying to improve for the purpose of doing better than someone else. These new fitness evaluation programs emphasize self-improvement through regular activity programs.

Fitnessgram System

The Fitnessgram System* consists of a 5-item test battery, software for reporting results, and an awards system based on participation in fitness activities. In addition, an instructor's package filled with information and educational activities for students, a videotape, and software is available. The software is discussed later in this chapter in the section on microcomputer applications.

The Fitnessgram is a report card, which is computer printed after test results are input. Test results are criterion referenced to a minimum required fitness level. A unique facet of the Fitnessgram System is that it provides three awards to youngsters. This award system is based primarily on exercise behaviors rather than an attempt for the student to demonstrate that he or she is the "best." The Fitnessgram awards program acknowledges and commends performance, however, it places its highest priority on the development and reinforcement of health-related behaviors that are attainable by all students. For a detailed discussion about administration of the Fitnessgram test items see Chapter 12.

*Fitnessgram material is reprinted by permission of The Institute for Aerobic Research. The Fitnessgram software is available free when 200 Fitnessgram report cards are ordered. To order the software and report cards, write to Fitnessgram, Institute for Aerobic Research, 12330 Preston Road, Dallas, TX 75230.

AAHPERD Physical Best Program

The AAHPERD Physical Best Program focuses on helping all students achieve health-related physical fitness. The approach is multifaceted in that it encourages participation in activities that are conducive to health, emphasizes the process of fitness motivation, and includes a participation-based award system. The program also recognizes the need to assist practitioners in understanding the philosophy of the program as well as implementation procedures.

The *Physical Best Program Manual* offers an educational approach designed to motivate all students to attain fitness. An accompanying educational kit includes lesson plans, contracts, wall charts, report cards, and other educational materials designed to help teachers motivate students to make a commitment to personal fitness. An important phase of the Physical Best program is asking students to develop personalized activity logs in order to stimulate pride in accomplishment. The *AAHPERD Physical Best Program Manual* can be purchased from AAHPERD Publications, P.O. Box 704, Waldorf, MD 20601. See Chapter 12 for an explanation of all test items.

DEVELOPING PHYSICAL FITNESS

The following points deal with enhancing students' fitness level. Students should leave a physical education program keenly aware of these basic principles and able to apply them to a personal fitness program.

Overload

To increase one's present level of physical fitness, the body must be overloaded beyond the normal activity level. To ensure that systematic overloading occurs, students should be able to prescribe their own work loads. Frequency, duration, and intensity are the variables involved in arranging the amount of exercise necessary. These variables are interrelated, so changing one may require a change in another.

Frequency is the number of exercise sessions an individual performs per week. Three to five workouts are necessary for benefits to accrue. In cardiovascular endurance exercise, a strenuous and demanding workout is usually followed the next day by mild exercise. As mentioned, strength training demands a day of complete rest between workouts. To maintain an acceptable level of fitness, a minimum of three workouts per week is usually required.

Duration is the length of each exercise bout. For

developing cardiovascular endurance, the minimum amount of aerobic exercise should be 20–30 min. The intensity of the exercise will have an impact on the duration of the fitness session. For most individuals, monitoring the duration of the activity instead of the intensity is best. An example would be the jogger who is torn between monitoring the amount of time spent jogging versus timing the speed (intensity) at which the distance can be run.

To measure **intensity** in aerobic activity, monitor the heart rate. A productive intensity requires that the heart rate reach the training state, which is 60–80% of the maximum rate possible. Duration and intensity can also be monitored in strength development. Most strength-inducing activities are high intensity and therefore require longer duration through an increased number of set, or repetitions.

Progression is important to maintain motivation and reduce the chance of injury. Work loads should be compounded gradually by increasing the intensity and duration of exercise. Teachers can sometimes be overly enthusiastic about developing fitness in a short amount of time. Remember that achieving fitness is an ongoing process that needs to occur throughout a lifetime. The important point is to stimulate and then maintain the students' desire to exercise. A reasonable progression during the school year will help ensure that this occurs.

Training Heart Rate

Heart rate can be used to determine the intensity of exercise. It gives an indication of whether the work load should be increased or decreased. To monitor heart rate, palpate at the wrist or carotid artery. When palpating the pulse at the wrist, place the index and middle finger near the joint on the thumb side (Figure 18.1). If the pulse is to be found at the carotid artery, first find the Adam's apple, then slide the index and middle finger to either side. Apply only slight pressure at either site to allow blood flow to continue.

To count the heart rate, begin the count within 5 sec after stopping exercise. The count should start

at zero, be taken for 10 sec, and multiplied by 6 to give the heart rate per minute. The heart rate should decrease to less than 120 beats per min after exercise has been terminated for 5 min. This is called the recovery heart rate and gives a rough indication of fitness level.

For exercise to enhance the level of cardiovascular endurance, the heart rate must be elevated to the training state. Using the following formula, the heartbeat range that should be maintained during exercise can be calculated.

1. Determine the estimated maximum heart rate by taking 220 minus the individual's age.
2. Multiply the difference by 60% and 80%.

The two results give the range of heart rates per minute that should be maintained while exercising. For example, assume that a student is age 16. Subtract 16 from 220, which equals 204. Multiply 204 by 60% and 80%. According to these results, a heart rate between 122 and 163 beats per minute should be maintained during exercise to reach the training state.

Once the training heart rate has been determined, the exercise routine can be undertaken. At the conclusion of the workout, monitor the heart rate. If it is above the beats per minute allowed by the formula, reduce the intensity of the workout. However, if the heart rate is too low, increase the intensity of the aerobic exercise.

Warming Up and Cooling Down

Warm-up activities should be conducted before an intense workout. Secondary school students probably have a lesser need for warm-up routines than older adults since they have little cardiovascular degeneration. It is important, however, that students learn that warming up and cooling down are necessary phases of exercising.

Warm-up activities should cause a gradual increase in the heart rate and body temperature. They should consist of flexibility exercises that stretch all the major muscle groups. Light-paced jogging can also prepare the heart muscle for the oncoming workout.

After the workout, cool down by walking for a few minutes. This can help prevent soreness the next day by massaging the waste products of exercise into the circulatory system. When a person stops exercising, the heart continues for a time to pump blood to the muscles at a vigorous rate. If no cooling down activity is done, there is little action to send the blood back to the heart, and it will pool in the veins. This pooling may cause light-headedness, which can be prevented by proper cooling down.

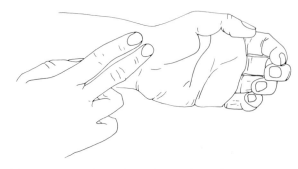

FIGURE 18.1   Taking the pulse at the wrist

The walking might be followed with stretching exercises to undo the tightening of muscle groups that occurs from strenuous activity.

Specificity of Exercise

Physical conditioning should match the demands that a sport or activity makes on an individual. Specificity infers that all skills and activities are unique and require specialized training. The implication of specificity is that if only a certain part or component of the body is exercised, only that part develops. A consideration of specificity emphasizes the importance of a balanced approach to fitness. For example, if one chooses only to jog for fitness, the cardiovascular system will be developed. Flexibility, however, will decrease in the lower back and hamstrings, and abdominal strength will decrease. Muscular power, as revealed by the vertical jump, will decrease also. A balanced approach to fitness includes flexibility, strength development, and cardiovascular endurance activity in an exercise regimen.

EXERCISES FOR DEVELOPING PHYSICAL FITNESS

Exercises in this section are divided into four groups. The first group consists of warm-up and flexibility activities. The following groups of exercises primarily develop muscular strength and endurance in these areas: upper body, midsection, and lower body. When exercise routines are planned, they should contain a balance of activities from all groups. The following instructional procedures (and exercises to avoid) should be considered carefully when developing exercise routines.

Instructional Procedures

1. When a new exercise is introduced, it should be demonstrated, broken into components, and its value should be explained. It should be practiced at a slower-than-normal pace and then speeded up. Emphasize proper form.

2. Work load depends on the number of repetitions or duration of effort. The instructor should start at a minimal work load and gradually increase the amount. Lesson plans should reflect the desired work load so it is a matter of record.

3. When isometric or partner-resistance exercises are used, teach students to make a maximum effort for 8–12 sec. Students must learn to monitor the duration of their efforts and perform the activities in sets.

4. At times, allow students to set their own limits for exercises. For example, they can be given a "challenge week" during which they establish their own work load. This can be the start of self-direction and personalizing fitness development.

5. In the early stages of learning rhythmic exercises, develop a means for starting the activities. For example, "one, two, ready, begin" could be used to start activities, and "one, two, and halt" to stop them. This helps emphasize for students the parts of an exercise.

6. Proper form is important when performing exercises. For instance, in exercises requiring the arms to be held in front of the body or overhead, the abdominal wall needs to be contracted to maintain proper positioning of the pelvis. The feet should be pointed reasonably straight ahead, the chest should be up, and the head and shoulders in good postural alignment.

7. Exercises in this section are not adequate for developing cardiovascular endurance. Additional aerobic activity is necessary to enhance this important fitness component. Furthermore, vary the aerobic activity. Too often, such activity consists of everybody running a lap. This practice is not only boring, but does little to meet the personal needs of all students. Exercise substitutes for running might be interval training, rope jumping, obstacle courses, grass drills, astronaut drills, brisk walking, rhythmic aerobic exercise, and parachute movements.

Avoiding Harmful Practices and Exercises

Consider the following points when offering fitness instruction.

1. For developing abdominal strength, use the sit-up with the knees bent instead of the straight-leg sit-up. When the legs are bent at the knee, the abdominal muscles are isolated from the psoas muscle group. This concentrates development on the abdominals rather than on the lower back area, and avoids development of an excessive lower back curve. Sit-ups should be performed with a smooth curling movement with the chin tucked. This prevents the common bouncing and jerking motions.

2. During stretching exercises, apply a smooth, constant pressure. Students should stretch to the point of discomfort, then back off slightly and hold the position. Avoid bouncing to further the range of motion because it actually decreases the level of flexibility. Stretching exercises must be done in a controlled, slow, and sustained manner.

3. If forward flexion is done from a sitting position in an effort to touch the toes, bend from the hips, not the waist.

4. Avoid straight-leg raises from a supine position because they may strain the lower back. This problem can be alleviated by placing the hands under the small of the back.

5. Avoid deep-knee bends (full squats), because they may damage the knee joints. Note that deep-knee bends have little developmental value as an exercise. It is much more beneficial to flex the knee joint to 90 degrees and then extend the joint.

6. Do not hyperextend the knees in stretching exercises performed from a standing position. The knee joint should be relaxed rather than locked. In all stretching activities, participants must judge their own range of motion. Expecting all students to be able to touch their toes is an unrealistic goal, particularly in the early stages of exercising.

7. Use caution when placing stress on the neck. Examples of activities in which caution should be used are the inverted bicycle, wrestler's bridge, and the sit-up performed with the hands behind the head. Most of these activities can be avoided, or work loads can be carefully adjusted to the capacity of the student.

Flexibility and Warm-Up Exercises

The exercises in this section increase the range of motion at various joints. They also prepare the body for more strenuous activity, which may follow. In the beginning, the stretching positions should be held for approximately 10 sec. As flexibility increases, the stretches can be held for up to 30 sec.

Lower Leg Stretches

Lower Leg Stretch.   Stand facing a wall with the feet about shoulder width apart. Place the palms of the hands on the wall at eye level. Walk away from the wall, keeping the body straight, until the stretch is felt in the lower portion of the calf (Figure 18.2). The feet should remain flat on the floor during the stretch.

Achilles Tendon Stretch.   Stand facing a wall with the forearms on it. Place the forehead on the back of the hands. Back 2–3 ft away from the wall, bend, and move one leg closer to the wall. Flex the bent leg with the foot on the floor until the stretch is felt in the Achilles tendon area. The feet should remain flat on the floor as the leg closest to the wall is flexed. Repeat, flexing the other leg.

FIGURE 18.2 Lower leg stretch

Balance Beam Stretch.   Place one foot in front of the other, about 3 ft apart. The feet should be in line as though one were walking a balance beam. Bend the forward leg at the knee, lean forward, and keep the rear foot flat on the floor (Figure 18.3). Repeat with the opposite leg forward. The calf of the rear leg should be stretched.

Upper Leg Stretches

Bear Hug.   Stand with one leg forward and the other to the rear. Bend the forward knee as much as possible while keeping the rear foot flat on the floor. Repeat the exercise with the other foot forward. *Variation*: Different muscles can be stretched by turning the hips slightly in either direction. To increase the stretching motion, look over the shoulder and toward the rear foot.

Leg Pick-Up.   Sit on the floor with the legs spread. Reach forward and grab the outside of the ankle with one hand and the outside of the knee with the other. Pick the leg up and pull the ankle toward the chin. The back of the upper leg should be stretched. Repeat the stretch, lifting the other leg.

Side Leg Stretch.   Lie on the floor on the left side. Reach down with the right hand and grab the ankle. Pull the ankle and upper leg toward the rear of the body. Pull the ankle as near to the buttocks as pos-

FIGURE 18.3   Balance beam stretch

sible and hold, stretching the front of the thigh (Figure 18.4). Repeat with the other side of the body.

Hurdler's Stretch.   Sit on the floor with one leg forward and one to the rear as though moving over a hurdle. The forward leg should be straight, and the rear leg bent and tucked in toward the buttocks. Lean gradually forward, bending at the hips and tucking the head. This stretches the back of the thigh. Next, lean backward, away from the forward leg, to stretch the top of the thigh. Repeat, reversing leg positions.

Groin Stretch.   Sit on the floor with the legs spread as far apart and kept as straight as possible. Slowly

lean forward from the hips and reach with the hands. Do not bend at the neck and shoulders, because that puts pressure on the lower back. Stretch and hold in three positions: left, right, and directly ahead.

Lower Back Stretches

Back Bender.   Stand with the feet about shoulder width apart. Bend the knees slightly and gradually bend the lower back starting at the hips. Relax the arms and neck and let the upper body hang. If more stretch is desired, gradually straighten the legs.

Ankle Hold.   From a standing position with the knees bent, reach down and hold both ankles with the hands. Gradually straighten the legs, applying stretch to the lower back.

Sitting Toe Touch.   Sit on the floor with the legs straight and together. Reach forward and grab the lower legs. Gradually walk the hands down the legs toward the ankles; continue to walk the hands down and touch the toes. Remember to bend from the hips, not the upper back.

Feet Together Stretch.   Sit with the knees bent and the soles of the feet touching. Reach forward with the hands and grasp the toes. Gently pull on the toes and bend forward from the hips, applying stretch to the inside of the legs and lower back. To increase the stretching effect, place the elbows on or near the knees and press them toward the floor.

Cross-Legged Stretch.   Sit on the floor with the legs crossed and tucked toward the buttocks. Lean forward with the elbows in front of the knees. To stretch the sides of the lower back, lean forward to the left and then the right.

Body Twist.   Figure 18.5 shows the body twist. Sit on the floor with the right leg straight. Lift the left leg over the right leg and place it on the floor outside the right knee. Move the right elbow outside the

FIGURE 18.4   Side leg stretch

FIGURE 18.5   Body twist

upper left thigh and use it to maintain pressure on the leg. Lean back and support the upper body with the left hand. Rotate the upper body toward the left hand and arm. Reverse the position and stretch the other side of the body.

Table Stretch.   Stand facing a table, chair, or similar platform. Place one leg on the table while maintaining the weight on the other leg. Lean forward from the hips to apply stretch to the hamstrings and lower back. Repeat with the other leg on the table. *Variation*: Stand with the side of the body facing the table. Place one leg on the table and bend toward the table to stretch the inside of the leg. Repeat with the other side of the body facing the table.

Back Stretches

Back Roller Stretch.   Curl up by holding the lower legs with the arms. Tuck the head gently on the knees. Tip backward and then roll back and forth gently. The rolling action should be slow and should stretch the length of the back. *Variation*: Perform the same stretch but cross the legs and tuck them close to the buttocks.

Straight-Leg Roller.   In a sitting position, roll backward and allow the legs to move overhead. Support the hips with the hands to control the stretch. The legs can be straightened and moved to different positions to vary the intensity and location of the stretch.

Squat Stretch.   Begin in a standing position with the legs shoulder width apart and the feet pointed outward. Gradually move to a squatting position, keeping the feet flat on the floor if possible (Figure 18.6). If balance is a problem, the stretch can be done while leaning against a wall.

Side of the Body Stretches

Wall Stretch.   Stand with one side toward the wall. Lean toward the wall and support the body with the hand. Walk away until the feet are 2–3 ft from the wall. While supporting the weight in the leaning position, bend the body toward the wall, stretching the side. Reverse and stretch the other side.

Elbow Grab Stretch.   In a standing position with the feet spread, raise the hands above the head. Grab the elbows with the hands. Lean to the side and pull the elbow in that direction. Reverse and pull to the opposite side.

Standing Hip Bend.   Stand with one hand on the hip and the other arm overhead. Bend to the side with the hand resting on the hip (Figure 18.7). The arm overhead should point and move in the direc-

FIGURE 18.6   Squat stretch

tion of the stretch with a slight bend at the elbow. Reverse and stretch the opposite side.

Sitting Side Stretch.   Sit on the floor with the legs spread as far apart as possible. Lift the arms overhead and reach toward one foot. Reverse and stretch in the opposite direction. Try to maintain an erect upper body.

FIGURE 18.7   Standing hip bend

Arm and Shoulder Girdle Stretches

Arm and Shoulder Stretch.   Standing, extend the arms and place the palms of the hands together. Move the arms upward and overhead. Lift the arms as high as possible over the head.

Elbow Puller.   Bend the right arm and place it behind the head. Reach to the right elbow with the left hand. Pull the elbow to the left to stretch the triceps and the top of the shoulders. Reverse the positions of the arms and repeat.

Elbow Pusher.   Place the right arm over the left shoulder. Push the right elbow toward the body with the left hand and hold. Repeat in the opposite direction.

Wishbone Stretch.   Move the arms behind the back and clasp hands. Keep the arms straight and raise the hands toward the ceiling to stretch the shoulder girdle (Figure 18.8). *Variation*: Stand near a wall (back toward the wall) and place the hands on it. Gently bend at the knees and lower the body while keeping the hands at the same level.

Exercises for Upper Body Development

Push-Ups.   The basic push-up is done from the front leaning rest position. Only the hands and toes

FIGURE 18.8 Wishbone stretch

FIGURE 18.9 Push-ups

are on the floor, and the body is kept as straight as possible (Figure 18.9). The exercise is a two-count movement, as the body is lowered by bending only at the elbows and then returned to the starting position.

As the body is lowered, only the chest touches the floor before the return to starting position. The push-up should be done with controlled movement. The arms can be adjusted together or apart, depending on the desired muscles to be exercised. As the arms are moved closer together, greater demands are placed on the triceps. Spreading the arms beyond shoulder width increases the work load on the muscles across the chest (pectorals). *Variation:* If it is difficult to perform a full push-up, the half (knee) push-up is excellent. Movement is the same as the push-up, but the body is supported by the hands and knees.

Inclined Wall Push-Ups.   This exercise can be done with either the feet or the hands on the wall (Figure 18.10). The hands version is easier and should precede the push-up with feet on the wall. In the hands version, the hands are placed on the wall while the feet walk as far from the wall as possible. The farther the performer's feet move from the wall, the more inclined and difficult the push-up will be.

When the student is able to do the inclined push-up with the hands on the wall, the feet-on-the-wall version can be attempted. This exercise is similar to doing a push-up in the handstand position and demands a great deal of strength. As the hands are walked closer to the wall, the incline becomes less, and a greater demand is placed on the shoulder girdle muscles.

Reclining Partner Pull-Ups.   Students find a partner of similar strength. One partner assumes a supine position on the floor while the other stands in a straddle position at chest level. Partners use a wrist-lock grip with both hands. The standing partner

FIGURE 18.10 Inclined wall push-ups

stands erect while the partner in supine position attempts to do a reclining pull-up (Figure 18.11). The upward pull is done completely by the person in supine position bending at the elbows. The standing person's task is to remain rigid and erect.

It is helpful for the person in supine position to start this exercise with the feet against a wall. This will prevent the person from sliding and will keep the focus of the activity on upper body development.

FIGURE 18.11 Reclining partner pull-ups

Rocking Chair. The exerciser moves to prone position on the floor. With the arms out to the sides of the body, the back is arched in an attempt to raise the upper body off the floor. While the upper body is elevated, different activities and arm positions can be attempted. For example, arm circling, waving, clapping hands, or placing the hands behind the head can add challenge to this upper back and shoulder development activity. *Variation:* The lower body can be elevated instead of the upper. Various movements can then be done with the legs. In either exercise, a partner may be required to hold the half of the body not being moved.

Crab Walk. This activity can be modified in several ways to develop trunk and upper body strength. The crab position is an inverted walk on all fours. The stomach faces the ceiling with the weight supported on the hands and feet. Crab-walking can be done in all directions and should be performed with the trunk as straight as possible. *Variations:* The crab kick can be executed from this position by alternating forward kicks of the left and right leg. The double crab kick is done by kicking both feet forward and then backward simultaneously.

Midsection Exercises

Rowing. Students begin in supine positions with the arms above the head. Rowing is a controlled two-count exercise. On the first count, the arms are moved toward the feet as the person moves to a sitting position; the knees are pulled simultaneously to the chest (Figure 18.12). On the second count, the person returns to starting position.

Modified Sit-Up. Starting position is on the back with the knees flexed, feet on the floor, and the heels 12–18 in. from the buttocks (Figure 18.13). Arms are crossed on the chest with the hands on opposite shoulders. The student curls to a sitting

FIGURE 18.12 Rowing

FIGURE 18.13   Modified sit-up

FIGURE 18.14   Alternate knee touch

position while keeping the arms touching the chest. The first count of the sit-up is completed when the elbows touch the thighs. The student then returns to the down position with the midback making contact with the testing surface.

V-Seat.   Starting position requires students to sit on the floor. Arms are held parallel to the floor at shoulder height in front of the body. The exercise is performed by leaning slightly back, lifting the legs from the floor, and touching the feet with the fingertips. The body should form a "V". The V-seat can be repeated a set number of times or can be held for a set period of time.

Partial Curl-Up.   Begin the exercise in supine position with knees bent and feet flat on the floor. Arms should be folded across the chest. The exercise is performed by smoothly tucking the chin and curling the shoulders forward and off the floor. The lower back should remain on the floor throughout. Complete the activity by lowering the shoulders to the floor. The head should not touch the floor since the chin is tucked into the chest.

Alternate Knee Touch.   Use the same starting position as described for the partial curl-up, but place the hands behind the head. The exercise is done by contracting the abdominal muscles and lifting both the legs and shoulders off the floor (Figure 18.14). Hold this position and alternately touch the right elbow to the left knee and vice versa before returning to the starting position.

Upper Body Twist.   Lie flat on the back with arms folded across the chest. Keep the buttocks on the floor while lifting the right shoulder and touching the right elbow to the floor near the right hip (Figure 18.15). Alternate from side to side. Hold the position for 3–5 sec on each contraction.

Hip Walk.   Begin in sitting position with the legs straight and together. Keep the abdominal muscles

contracted while moving the buttocks forward by alternately "walking" the hips. Practice moving backward as well as forward.

Lower Body Exercises

Squat Jumps.   Begin in squatting position with one foot slightly ahead of the other. Assume part of the weight with the hands in front of the body. Jump as high as possible and return to the squatting position. Taking some of the body weight with the hands is important to avoid stressing the knee joints.

Treadmill.   Begin on all fours with one foot forward and one behind. Rapidly alternate foot positions while taking the weight of the body on the arms. The movement of the feet can be varied by moving both feet forward and back simultaneously or by moving the feet apart and together.

Jumping Jacks.   Begin in standing position with the arms at the sides and feet together. Simultaneously lift the arms overhead and spread the legs on the first count. On the second count, return arms and legs to the starting position. *Variations*: Feet and arm movements can be varied. The arms can be moved in front of the body, behind the body, and in different patterns. The legs can be split for-

FIGURE 18.15   Upper body twist

FIGURE 18.16   Side leg flex

ward and backward, crossed in front of each other, and swung to the front of the body.

Running in Place.   Running in place is most beneficial when the upper leg is lifted parallel to the floor. The thighs can touch the hands held slightly above the parallel line to encourage the high lift.

Side Leg Flex.   Lie on your side side on the floor. Rest the head in the right hand and place the left hand along the side of the body. On the first count, lift the left leg and arm and point them toward the ceiling (Figure 18.16). Return to the starting position on the second count. Rotate to the other side of the body after performing the desired number of repetitions. *Variation*: The double side leg flex is an exercise that demands more effort. Both legs are lifted simultaneously as far off the floor as possible.

Front Leg Kick.   From standing position, alternately kick each leg forward and as high as possible. This exercise should be done rhythmically so that all movement occurs on the toes. When the leg is kicked upward, the arm on the same side should be moved forward in an attempt to touch the toe of the lifted leg.

ACTIVITIES AND ROUTINES FOR DEVELOPING FITNESS

The following are methods of organizing exercises and aerobic activities to develop total body fitness. All of the routines should enhance muscular strength and endurance, as well as cardiovascular endurance.

Teacher and Student Leader Exercise Routines

During the first part of the school year, teachers should lead and teach all exercises to ensure that they are learned correctly. It is also important that teachers stay involved in fitness activities throughout the year to demonstrate their willingness to do the activities that they are asking students to perform. In some cases, teachers ask students to exercise and maintain fitness while they choose not to do either. Pushing others to be fit is difficult if the teacher does not make a similar personal commitment.

When a wide repertoire of exercises has been learned, students can begin to lead the exercise routines. Leading not only means starting and stopping the exercises, but includes designing well-balanced routines that offer total body development. Students can be guided in the desirable number of repetitions and how to count exercises as they are being performed. In any case, students should not be forced to lead the exercises; leading should be a personal choice.

More than one student leader can be used at one time. For example, if four leaders are selected, they can be thinking of the exercises to choose when it is their turn. Leaders can be placed on four sides of the class (Figure 18.17), with the class rotating one-quarter turn to face a new leader after each exercise. If a leader cannot think of an appropriate exercise, the class can be asked to volunteer one. In any case, emphasis should be placed on learning to weave together a set of exercises that offers total body development. Continuous movement activity should also be added to the exercise routines to assure cardiovascular endurance development.

Squad Leader Exercises

Squad leader exercises offer students the opportunity to develop fitness routines without teacher intervention. Squad leaders take their squad to a designated area and put the squad through a fitness routine. It is helpful if a blank exercise card is given to each squad leader a few days before the student will lead. The leader can develop a routine and write down the exercises and repetitions or duration of each.

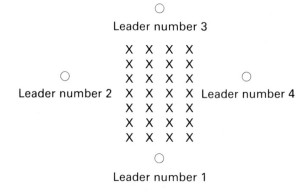

FIGURE 18.17   Student-led exercises

Squad leaders can also assign members of the group to lead or to offer certain activities. A number of exercises can be specified to develop a particular area of the body. For example, ask leaders to develop a routine that has two exercises for the arm-shoulder girdle area, two for the abdominal region, one for the legs, three for flexibility, and 2 min of continuous movement. The responsibility for planning a fitness routine that is balanced and developmental should shift gradually from the teacher to the students.

Exercises to Music

Without question, music increases the motivational level of students during exercise. While there are many commercial exercise-to-music records on the market, they all suffer from one major problem. They seldom meet the specific work-load requirements of different groups of students, and they cannot provide the necessary systematic overload. Teachers therefore need to develop their own homemade exercise-to-music tapes that can be tailored to meet the needs of a specific class or grade.

Homemade exercise tapes can be developed using a record player and a tape recorder. Music that is currently popular can be combined with exercises that students have already learned. Avoid music that might affront some members of the community. Either the teacher or a group of students can make the tapes. When students do the taping, they have control over the selection, sequence, and number of exercises and repetitions. The routines can be adapted to particular needs and characteristics of the group. Procedures for starting and stopping exercises can be incorporated easily in the taping.

Continuous Movement Activities

Jogging

Jogging is running at a slow pace. It is faster than walking, but slower than sprinting. Jogging is an excellent conditioner for the cardiovascular system and can be done by virtually all students. It does not require specialized equipment or specialized skill.

Any one of three approaches can be used to develop a jogging program. The first is the jog-walk approach, which emphasizes the amount of time that one is involved in continuous movement. Students determine how far they can jog before they need to slow down and walk. Walking is continued until the exerciser is again ready to jog. The goal is to decrease the length and time of the walking episodes and to increase the jogging.

A second approach to increasing endurance through jogging is to set up definite and measured intervals. An example would be setting up cones to mark jogging intervals of 110 yd and walking intervals of 55 yd. As the fitness level increases, the length of the jogging interval is increased and the walking interval decreased.

Finally, the work load can be increased by increasing either the duration of the jog or the pace of the jogging. The goal is either to maintain a constant pace and to increase the distance run, or to run the same distance at an increased pace. Increasing the speed is usually the less desirable alternative, because the intensity of the exercise may discourage students.

Jogging is performed in an erect body position with a minimal amount of leaning. Excessive leaning is less efficient and demands a greater amount of energy. The elbows should be bent and the arms carried in a relaxed manner. Most joggers strike the ground with a flat foot. This allows the force of impact to be absorbed over a larger surface area, which seems to be more desirable. Some joggers land on the heel and then rotate to the toe. In either case, trying to change a jogger's foot action is often ineffective.

Jogging should be a noncompetitive activity. Students should be encouraged to look for self-improvement instead of comparing their performance with others. An enjoyable technique is to ask students to jog with a partner who has similar ability. They should be encouraged to talk and visit while they jog. Point out that if they find it difficult to talk while jogging, they are probably running too fast.

Endurance and continuous activity should be rewarded. Teachers sometimes have a tendency to ask students to run a certain distance and then they reward those students who complete the distance first. This is discouraging to the majority of the joggers. Students should be permitted to run in any direction they desire until a certain amount of time has elapsed. This prevents the situation in which a few gifted runners finish first and have to sit and wait for the rest of the class to complete a given distance.

A general rule of thumb for beginning a jogging program is to ask students to walk and jog continuously for 5 min. Increase the amount of time 1 min per week up to 15 min. Individuals can increase the total amount of time while they also try to reduce the amount of walking.

Ideas for an instructional unit on jogging can be found in Chapter 21.

Walking

Walking is an activity that almost all people can do. The disadvantage of walking compared with jogging is that it must be done for a longer period of time to receive similar cardiovascular benefits. Walking has the advantages, however, of not requiring any special equipment and of having a low injury rate. Walking, probably more than any other activity, will be done by students when they reach adulthood.

Rope Jumping

Rope jumping is a demanding activity that requires little equipment. For some participants it can be a valuable approach to cardiovascular fitness. The energy demands of rope jumping are similar to jogging. Rope jumping can be performed for a specified amount of time or for a specified number of jumps.

A variety of activities can be done with a jump rope to help avoid the monotony and excessive fatigue of continuous jumping. The rope can be turned at fast or slow speeds while different foot steps are performed. If rope jumping is used for the fitness portion of the lesson, it should be alternated with stretching activities to give students an opportunity to recover from aerobic demands.

See Chapter 21 for ideas on developing a unit of instruction on rope jumping.

Four Corners

A large rectangle is formed using four cones as markers. Students move continually around the perimeter of the rectangle. At each corner, a different movement is performed. Examples of activity alternatives that can be performed on the long sides of the rectangle are jogging, skipping, sliding, jumping, and hopping. On the short sides of the rectangle, movements on all fours (e.g., bear walk, crab walk, seal crawl) can be performed. Another interesting variation is to use tumbling activities, or use tires and challenge students to go over, around, and through them. The need for continuous movement should be emphasized, and the rectangle should be large enough to provide a challenging work load for the cardiovascular system.

Interval Training

Interval training involves carefully controlling the work and rest intervals of the participant. Intervals of work (exercise) and rest can be measured in distance, repetitions, or time. Interval training is done by monitoring the heart rate. The student first needs to get the heart rate up to 120–140 beats per min by warming up. Strenuous activity is then performed to push the heart rate into the 170–180 beats per min range. At this point, the runner begins the rest interval (usually walking) until the heart

rate returns to 120–140 beats per min. Theoretically, the amount of time it takes for the heart rate to return to 120–140 beats per min should not exceed 90 sec. The major advantage of interval training is that endurance can be increased markedly in a short period of time.

Interval training can be used with various locomotor movements. For example, the following work and rest activities can be alternated. Intervals can be measured in either distance or time.

Work Activities	*Rest Activities*
Brisk walking	Slow walking
Jogging	Walking
Sprinting	Jogging
Rope jumping	Walking
Jumping in place	Walking

Rhythmic Aerobic Exercise

At present, this type of activity is extremely popular throughout the United States. Aerobic dance is the basis for many variations of rhythmic exercise now implemented. These routines develop a high level of cardiorespiratory fitness, as well as strength and flexibility. Popular music is used to increase the activity enjoyment.

Rhythmic aerobic exercise consists of a mixture of fundamental movements—dance steps, swinging movements, and stretching exercises. Routines are developed to music that has a definite and obvious beat.

The activities and routines should ease the burden of learning. If the movement patterns are too difficult, students become self-conscious and discouraged. Use the following points as guidelines when teaching new aerobic exercise routines.

1. Use movements that are organized in units of 4, 8, or 16 counts. When phrases in the music are repeated, it may be desirable to repeat the same or previous steps.

2. Alternate the strenuousness of the activities. This allows interval training to be built into the routines. Stretching movements can be alternated with demanding locomotor movements.

3. Routines motivate more students when they appear not to be dance activities. The challenge is to develop demanding routines that will increase the endurance level of all participants. All students should be comfortable performing the routines.

4. Follow-the-leader activities work well with students after they have developed a repertoire of movements. Each student can be responsible for leading one activity.

5. Energetic and positive teachers strongly influence the success of the presentations. Students need to see teachers enjoying fitness activities.

Basic Steps

The basic steps and movements can be used to develop a wide variety of routines. The majority are performed to four counts, although this can be varied, depending on the skill level of the students.

Running and Walking Steps

1. **Directional runs** can be done forward, backward, diagonally, sideways, or turning.
2. **Rhythmic runs** integrate a specific movement (e.g., knee lift, clap, jump, jump-turn) on the fourth beat.
3. **Runs with stunts** are performed while lifting the knees, kicking up the heels, or slapping the thighs or heels. Runs can also be done with the legs extended, such as the goose step.
4. **Runs with the arms in various positions** can include the arms on the head, straight up or down, or on the hips.

Movements on the Floor

1. **Sit-ups or curl-ups** can be used in many ways. For example, use four counts: 1. up to the knees; 2. touch the floor; 3. back to the knees; 4. return to the floor. A V-seat can be held for two counts and rested for two counts.
2. **Side leg raises** can be done with a straight leg on the side, or with bent knees on the back extending the lower leg.
3. **Alternate leg raises** are performed in supine position with one leg raised to meet the opposite hand. Repeat using the opposite leg or both legs.
4. **Push-ups** can be done in two- or four-count movements. A four count would be: 1. halfway down; 2. touch chest to floor; 3. halfway up; 4. arms fully extended.
5. **Crab kicks and treadmill** can be performed to four-count movements.

Standing Movements

1. **Lunge Variations.** To perform a lunge (Figure 18.18), step forward onto the right foot while bending at the knees and extending arms into the air (counts 1 and 2). Return to starting position by bringing the right foot back and pulling arms into a jogging position (counts 3 and 4). Vary the exercise by changing the direction of the move, or the depth and speed of the lunge.
2. **Side Bends.** Begin with the feet apart. Reach overhead while bending to the side. This move-

FIGURE 18.18 Lunge variations

ment is usually done to four beats: (1) bend, (2) and, (3) hold, and (4) return.
3. **Reaches.** Alternate reaching upward with the right and left arms. Reaches can be done sideways also and are usually two-count movements.
4. **Arm and Shoulder Circles.** Make arm circles with one or both arms. Vary the size and speed of the circles. Shoulder shrugs can be done in similar fashion.

Jumping Jacks Variations

1. **Arms Alternately Extended.** Jump with the arms alternately extended upward and pulled into the chest.
2. **Side Jumping Jacks.** Use regular arm action while the feet are kept together for jumping forward, backward, and sideways.
3. **Variations with Feet.** Try forward stride alternating, forward and side stride alternating, kicks or knee lifts, crossing the feet, and a heel-toe step.

Bounce Steps

1. **Bounce and Clap.** The step is similar to the slow-time jump rope step. Clap on every other bounce.

2. **Bounce, Turn, and Clap.** Turn a quarter- or half-turn with each jump.

3. **Three Bounces and Clap.** Bounce three times and then clap and bounce on the fourth beat. Turns can be performed using the four counts.

4. **Bounce and Rock Side to Side.** Transfer weight from side to side, and forward and backward. Add clapping or arm swinging.

5. **Bounce with Body Twist.** Hold the arms at shoulder level and twist the lower body back and forth on each bounce.

6. **Bounce with Floor Patterns.** Bounce and make different floor patterns such as a box, diagonal, or triangle.

7. **Bounce with Kick Variations.** Perform different kick variations such as knee lift, kick, knee lift, and kick; double kicks, knee lift, and slap knees; kick and clap under the knees. Combine the kicks with two or four count turns.

Activities with Manipulative Equipment

1. **Jump Ropes.** Using the jump rope, perform basic steps such as forward, backward, slow, and fast time. Jump on one foot, cross arms, and jump while jogging. Swing the rope from side to side with the handles in one hand and jump over it.

2. **Beanbags.** Toss and catch while performing various locomotor movements. Challenge students using different tosses.

3. **Hoops.** Rhythmically swing the hoop around different body parts. Perform different locomotor movements around and over hoops.

4. **Balls.** Bounce, toss, dribble, and add locomotor movements while performing tasks.

Sample Routine

1. March, moving arms in large circles (8 counts).
2. Hold side lunge position and circle right arm (8 counts). Reverse circling with left arm (8 counts).
3. Bounce forward twice, slapping thighs; then bounce backward twice, thrusting arms in the air. Repeat four times (16 counts).
4. Bounce and clap turn. Perform a quarter-turn on every second bounce. Repeat four times clockwise (8 counts) and four times counterclockwise (8 counts).
5. Repeat numbers 3 and 4.
6. Grapevine step with clap on fourth beat. Repeat to the left. Repeat sequence four times (32 counts).
7. Jumping jack variation extending arms up and out (8 counts). Repeat four times (32 counts).
8. Bounce and twist (8 counts).

9. Side jumping jacks, two-count version. Repeat eight times (16 counts).
10. Bounce, bounce, bounce, clap—four-count movement. Repeat four times (16 counts).
11. Rhythmic running with clap on fourth beat. While running, move to a circle formation (16 counts).
12. Bounce and twist (8 counts).
13. Side leg raises (2 counts). Perform four on each leg (16 counts).
14. Rhythmic running with a clap on every fourth beat (16 counts).

Resistance Training

Most coaches use strength development through resistance training. Physical education programs should instruct students in the use of weights and weight machines for proper development with an emphasis on safety. Using resistance training as an instructional unit is often difficult because of lack of equipment and facilities.

Resistance training routines should develop all major body parts. This prevents the excessive development of specific body parts, which may lead to postural or joint problems. Exercises should be performed through the full range of motion. If training is being done for a specific sport, it may be important to analyze the sport and develop exercises that replicate the range of motion it utilizes.

Resistance exercises should be performed at a speed similar to the movements performed in various physical activities. If a student is involved in an activity requiring speed, then the exercises should be performed at a similar speed. Similarly, if a student is involved in activities demanding high levels of endurance, then exercises should be designed to increase this attribute. If the sport or activity demands strength, the training program can be geared to develop muscular strength. In each case, the student should understand the program differences and how to develop a personal program.

Safety

Students should know and practice necessary safety precautions. The following points should be clear to all students and should be reinforced regularly. The instructor is wise to post safety rules as a further reminder and to avoid the consequences of possible lawsuits.

1. Perform warm-up exercises before intense lifting. These may be a set of calisthenics or a set of resistance exercises at a lower level.

2. Correct form is necessary to prevent injury as well as to develop strength. When a heavy weight

is lifted from the floor, the lift should be done with bent knees, straight back, and head up.

3. Spotters are absolutely necessary when near-maximum weight is being lifted. Exercises such as the bench press, squats, and declined presses should always have two students present to spot.

4. Weights should be checked by the instructor before each period and by students each time they use them. Collars should be tightly fastened, cables checked, and bolts on machines periodically tightened.

5. Wide leather practice belts should be used when heavy lifting is performed. This prevents injury to the lower back and abdominal wall.

6. All exercises should be explained in class before implementation. This means that proper form, points of safety, and necessary spotting are discussed before students participate.

Repetitions and Sets

There is wide variation in the proper number of repetitions and sets that need to be performed to achieve optimum results. Repetitions are the number of times a participant performs an exercise to make a set. Each set, in turn, consists of a specified number of repetitions of the same exercise. Determining the proper number of repetitions or sets is difficult. Literally dozens of experts have researched this area without agreement. For the physical education setting, a middle-of-the-road approach is probably best. This means that three sets of ten repetitions should be performed for each exercise.

Strength or Endurance?

Muscular strength and endurance are developed using different methods. If maximum strength is desired, the exercise program should emphasize heavy resistance and fewer repetitions. If endurance is the desired outcome, the program should emphasize a high number of repetitions with less resistance. Some strength and endurance will be developed regardless of the type of program, but major gains will depend on the selected emphasis.

Frequency and Rest Intervals

Frequency is usually discussed as the number of workouts per week. The most common pattern suggested is to lift every other day, three days per week. The day-long rest between workouts allows the muscle tissue to recover and waste products to dissipate. Some participants alternate by exercising the upper body and the lower body on different days. This results in a six-day program while retaining the day of rest between workouts.

The rest interval between repetitions and sets can be timed carefully to increase the intensity of the workout. By organizing the exercises in a circuit stressing different muscle groups, the amount of time needed for a total workout can be reduced. In other words, recovery time is not needed between sets if the next exercise places demands on a different group of muscles.

Planning a Unit

Chapter 21 contains several ideas and activities for a unit on resistance training that can be modified or augmented to meet the needs of the instructor, the students, and the physical education program.

Circuit Training

Exercise stations are organized into a circuit for the sake of fitness development. Each of the stations should contribute, in part, to the total fitness of the participant. The components of fitness—flexibility, muscular strength and endurance, and cardiovascular endurance—should be represented in the circuit.

Developing a Circuit

1. If the circuit is to be used as a group activity, it should contain activities that all class members are capable of performing.

2. Organize the stations so that different muscle groups or fitness components are exercised. In other words, consecutive stations should not place demands on the same area of the body.

3. Students should know how to perform all of the activities correctly. Proper form is important. Instruction can be done verbally or descriptive posters can be placed at each station.

4. Distribute students evenly among the stations at the beginning of the exercise bout. A rotation plan ensures that students move to the correct station.

5. Measure dosage in time or repetitions. Students can move on their own to the next station if they have completed the required number of repetitions. If a time criterion is used, the class moves as a whole when students have exercised for a specified amount of time.

6. To increase the demands on the cardiovascular system, one or two of the stations can include rope jumping or running in place. Another alternative is to have students run around the circuit a certain number of times before moving to the next station.

7. The circuit should generally contain no fewer than ten stations. The result of participation in the circuit is a total body workout.

Timing and Dosage

If the work load at each station is based on time, dosage can be carefully controlled. Signals to start exercising, stop exercising, and to rotate to the next stations are given. This allows precise timing of intervals. A reasonable expectation for beginning circuit training is 30 sec per station.

The amount of rest between stations can also be monitored to increase or decrease the work load. An effective way of timing the circuit is to use a tape recording of popular music that students enjoy, with signals to stop and start activities interspersed at proper intervals. The music is motivational, and the intervals are precisely timed.

Another approach is to rotate when a specific work load has been performed at a station. Students rotate when they have completed the task. Different work loads at the same station can be offered as a way of making the circuit meet the specific needs of students. For example, work loads could be labeled bronze, silver, and gold. The bronze workout would require the lowest number of repetitions or duration, whereas the gold would be the most demanding. Students would then exercise at their level of capability. Post signs stating the number of repetitions required for each level.

Figure 18.19 is an example of a circuit that might be developed for junior high school students.

Astronaut Drills

Astronaut drills are continuous movement activities that combine various exercises with walking and jogging. Students move randomly throughout the area or follow each other in a circle formation. The drills begin with brisk walking. On signal, the teacher or selected students lead the class in exercises or stunt activities. If a movement is not developed immediately, the class runs in place.

Combinations of the following activities can be arranged to develop a demanding routine:

1. Various locomotor movements such as hopping, running, jumping, leaping, skipping, and running on the toes
2. Moving throughout the area on all fours in the crab position, and using various animal walks such as the seal walk, dog walk, and rabbit walk
3. Performing exercises, such as arm circles, body twists, and trunk and upper-body stretches, while moving around the area
4. Performing stationary exercises, such as push-ups, sit-ups, and jumping jacks, to stress development of the upper body and abdominal wall

Students move throughout the area and perform as many exercises as possible. They can also develop individual routines that control the amounts of time allotted for movement activity and stationary activity.

The following is an example of an astronaut drill that might be implemented. Note that the duration of the movements can be timed or the repetitions counted. These mechanics can be determined by the students or the instructor. In either case, the drill enables overload and progression to be built into the routine.

1. Walk throughout the area.
2. Run and leap.
3. Stop, perform push-ups.
4. Walk and do arm circles.
5. Crab-walk.
6. Stop, find a friend, and perform partner resistance exercises.
7. Hop for a period of time on each foot.
8. Walk on all fours.
9. Run, with the knees lifted as high as possible.
10. Stop, perform treadmill.
11. Repeat the above steps.

Nine-Station Course

1	2	3	4
Rope jumping	Push-ups	Agility run	Arm circles
8	7	6	5
Windmill	Treadmill	Crab walk	Rowing

9 Hula-Hooping (or any relaxing "fun" activity)

FIGURE 18.19 Circuit training stations

Continuity Exercises

The continuity exercises can be done in open squad formation or in scatter formation. Since each student has a jump rope, students must have plenty of room to avoid hitting each other. Performers alternate between rope jumping and two-count exercises. Rope jumping is done for timed episodes and should be performed fast-time. Music with the proper rhythm can be used to help maintain the rhythm. At the signal to stop rope jumping, students quickly drop the rope and move into position for the exercise. Selected exercises should be performed in a down position and be two-count in nature. A leader says "Ready" and the students respond "One-two," while performing the exercise. For each repetition, students wait until the command "Ready" is given.

The following is an example of a routine:

- **First signal:** Begin rope jumping.
- **Second signal:** Stop jumping, drop ropes, and move to the push-up position. On each command of "Ready," do one push-up to a two-count cadence.
- **Third signal:** Resume rope jumping.
- **Fourth signal:** Drop ropes and move into supine position on the floor with the arms overhead, preparatory to doing the rowing exercise. On the command "Ready," perform the exercise to the two-count cadence.
- **Fifth signal:** Resume rope jumping.
- **Sixth signal:** Drop the ropes, and move into crab position. Prepare to do the double crab kick. On the signal "Ready," both feet are extended forward and back in a two-count movement.
- **Seventh signal:** Resume rope jumping.
- **Eighth signal:** Move into position for the side leg flex exercise. On the command "Ready," lift the upper leg and return it to starting position for a two-count movement.
- **Ninth signal:** Resume rope jumping.
- **Tenth signal:** Move into position for the reclining partner pull-up. On signal, pull the body up on count one, and return to the floor on count two. Switch positions with partner after the proper number of repetitions has been performed.

The number of repetitions and the duration of the rope-jumping episodes should be determined by the fitness levels of the students. More exercises can be added to the routine above. Instructors can use a tape recorder to signal the start and finish of the rope-jumping episodes.

Continuity exercises are an example of interval training. The rope jumping stresses the cardiovascular system, while the exercises develop strength and allow the performer to recover.

Grass Drills with Partner Resistance Exercises

Grass drills require performers to move alternately from a rapid running-in-place position to a down position on the grass or floor. The activities are strenuous and are performed in quick succession at top speed. Work load progression is developed by increasing the duration of the bouts. Since grass drills are quite demanding, they should be alternated with partner resistance exercises. This type of interval training allows participants to rest the cardiovascular system while developing strength in the partner resistance exercises.

Grass Drills

Basic grass drills involve moving rapidly from one of three basic positions to another on the commands "Go," "Front," and "Back." "Go" tells students to run in place at a rapid pace on the toes, raising the knees, and pumping the arms. "Front" signals students to drop quickly to the floor in prone position with the hands in push-up position. The head should point toward the center of the circle or the front of the room. When "Back" is stated, students move into a supine position with the arms alongside the body and palms down. The head-to-leg position is opposite that of the "Front" position.

Grass drills can be done in two ways:

1. Continuous Motion. When "Front" or "Back" commands are given, the student moves to the corresponding position and immediately returns to the "Go" phase without the command being issued.

2. Interrupted Motion. The performer stays in position until the "Go" command is given. This allows a number of variations to be built into the drills. For example, push-ups, sit-ups, crab-kicks, and various movements on all fours can be executed prior to issuing the "Go" command.

Partner Resistance Exercises

Partner resistance exercises are enjoyable for students because they offer variable work loads and a chance to work with a partner. Partners must be matched in size and strength so they can challenge each other. The exercises should be performed throughout the full range of motion at each joint and should take 8–12 sec each to complete. The partner providing the resistance gives the "Begin" command and counts the duration of the exercise.

Three sets of each exercise are done by each student as they alternate the exercise and resistance roles.

The following are examples of exercises that can be performed. Students should be challenged to invent their own partner resistance exercises, with emphasis placed on developing a set of exercises that strengthens all body parts.

Arm Curl-Ups. The exerciser keeps the upper arms against the sides of the body, bends the elbows, and turns palms up. The partner puts fists in the exerciser's palms. The exerciser then attempts to curl the forearms upward to the shoulders. To develop the opposite set of muscles, push down in the opposite direction, starting with palms at shoulder level.

Forearm Flex. The exerciser places the hands, palms down, on the partner's shoulders. The exerciser attempts to push the partner into the floor. The partner may slowly lower the body to allow the exerciser to move through the full range of motion. Try the exercise with the palms up.

Fist Pull-Apart. The exerciser places the fists together in front of the body at shoulder level. The exerciser attempts to pull the hands apart while partner forces them together with pressure on the elbows. Reverse this exercise and begin with the fists apart. Partner tries to push them together by grasping the wrists.

Butterfly. The exerciser holds the arms straight, forming a right angle with the side of the body (Figure 18.20). The partner attempts to hold the arms down, while the exerciser lifts with straight arms to the sides. Try the activity with the arms above the head; move them down to the sides against partner's effort to hold them up.

Camelback. The exerciser is on all fours with the head up. The partner sits or pushes on the exerciser's back while the exerciser attempts to hump the back like a camel.

Back Builder. The exerciser spreads the legs and bends forward at the waist with the head up. The partner faces the exerciser, and clasps the hands together behind the exerciser's neck. The exerciser then attempts to stand upright while the partner pulls downward.

Swan Diver. The exerciser lies in the prone position with arms out at the sides and tries to arch the back while the partner applies pressure to the calf and upper back area (Figure 18.21).

Scissors. The exerciser lies on one side while partner straddles him or her, and holds the upper leg down. The exerciser attempts to raise the top leg.

FIGURE 18.20   Butterfly

The exercise is reversed and performed with the other leg.

Bear Trap. Perform as in the Scissors, but spread the legs first and attempt to move them together while partner holds them apart.

Knee Bender. The exerciser lies in prone position with legs straight, arms ahead on the floor. The partner places the hands on the back of exerciser's ankle. The exerciser attempts to flex the knee while the partner applies pressure. Reverse legs. Try this exercise in the opposite direction with the knee joint at a 90-degree angle.

Resistance Push-Up. The exerciser is in push-up position with arms bent so that the body is halfway

FIGURE 18.21   Swan diver

up from the floor. The partner straddles or stands alongside the exerciser's head and puts pressure on the top of the shoulders by pushing down. The partner must judge the amount of pressure to apply in order to prevent the exerciser from collapsing.

Isometric Exercises

Isometric exercises are done without movement. They are performed solely for the purpose of developing strength. The amount of time needed to exercise the major muscle groups in this way is minimal. A complete isometric exercise can usually be done in 5 min or less. These exercises do not require equipment, do not cause a high level of fatigue, and can be performed easily in a small space or office.

The disadvantage of isometric exercise is that it appears to raise the blood pressure of the individual. This may be a problem for someone who has heart disease. Other disadvantages are that isometric exercise does not benefit cardiovascular endurance and only builds strength at the joint angle at which the exercise is performed. Finally, many individuals receive little feedback from their isometric performance in terms of perspiration, increased muscle size, or healthy fatigue. They therefore see little point in continuing the activity.

To achieve results, the contractions must be maximal in nature. They should be held for 8–12 sec, and should be performed at various joint angles to develop strength throughout the total range of motion. An isometric routine should be performed a minimum of three days a week and should contain 10–15 exercises. The following is a sample routine that might be used to develop overall body strength. All of the exercises should be held at maximum contraction for 8–12 sec.

Handhold.   The exerciser makes a fist of one hand and holds it with the other hand. The hand holding the fist attempts to squeeze the fist as hard as possible.

Pull and Push Hands.   The exerciser locks both hands together and attempts to pull them apart. To push, the palms are placed together and pressure is applied.

Neck Developer.   To develop muscles in the back of the neck, the hands are clasped and placed behind the head. The head attempts to move backward while the hands pull forward. For the front of the neck, place the palms on the forehead and push backward while the head pushes forward. This exercise can be modified by placing a hand on the side of the head and applying force.

Arm Curl.   Hold the forearm at waist level in front of the body. Place the palm of the other hand into the hand of the flexed arm. Attempt to curl the flexed arm upward while applying downward pressure with the other hand. Switch hand positions.

Knee Hold.   Sitting on the floor, spread the knees approximately 12 in. apart. Put the hands on the inside of the knees and apply outward pressure, while simultaneously applying inward pressure with the knees. Switch the hand position to the outside of the knees and reverse the force application.

Knee Lift.   Sit on the floor with one leg extended and the other flexed. Place the palms of the hands on top of the flexed knee. Lift the knee upward while applying downward pressure to the knee. Switch to the other knee.

Body Tightener.   In a standing position, contract and hold the following muscle groups: shoulders forward, shoulders back, shoulders upward, abdominals toward the spine, lower back muscles, lower leg muscles by standing on tiptoe, lift toes as high as possible, and turn the upper body as far as possible and hold, then reverse the direction of body twist.

Ankle Hold.   Sitting on the floor, cross the legs at the ankles. Lift the lower leg while applying downward pressure with the leg on top. Reverse the positions.

Leg Squeeze.   Sit on the floor with the knees bent and near the chest. Reach around the legs with both arms and clasp hands. Attempt to pull the lower legs toward the seat while applying outward pressure with the legs.

Many isometric exercises can be developed with a partner or by using jump ropes or cut inner tubes to make large rubber bands. The partner resistance exercises described earlier can be performed as isometric exercises.

Obstacle Courses

Obstacle courses, or parcourses, are popular throughout the country. Different stations are developed and the participants move from station to station as they cover the course. The type of movement done between stations can also place demands on the participants' body systems.

Courses can be run for time, or repetitions can be increased to ensure balanced fitness development. Courses should be developed to exercise all parts of the body. A variety of activities, such as stretching, vaulting, agility runs, climbing, hanging and chinning, and crawling, can be included to place demands on all aspects of fitness. Figure 18.22 repre-

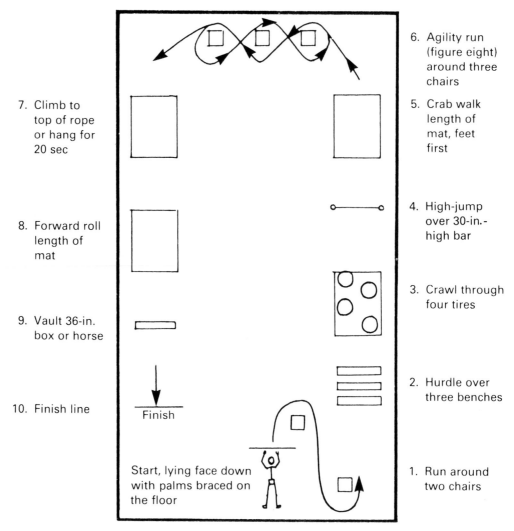

FIGURE 18.22   Obstacle course

7. Climb to top of rope or hang for 20 sec

8. Forward roll length of mat

9. Vault 36-in. box or horse

10. Finish line

6. Agility run (figure eight) around three chairs

5. Crab walk length of mat, feet first

4. High-jump over 30-in.-high bar

3. Crawl through four tires

2. Hurdle over three benches

1. Run around two chairs

Finish

Start, lying face down with palms braced on the floor

sents an indoor obstacle course that might be constructed for students.

Parachute Exercises

The parachute can be used to develop fitness activities that are exciting and challenging. Through these activities, students work together to enhance their fitness level. They should be encouraged to develop unique, new group activities. The following are examples of exercises that use the parachute.

Toe Toucher.   Sit with the feet extended under the parachute and hold the chute taut with a two-hand grip, drawing it to the chin. Bend forward and touch the grip to the toes. Return the chute to the stretched position.

Curl-Up.   Extend the body under the parachute in curl-up position, so the chute comes up to the chin when held taut. Do curl-ups, returning each time to the stretched position. Encourage students to work

together and snap the chute tight each time they recline.

Dorsal Lift.   In prone position, lie with the head toward the chute. Grasp the chute with the arms extended overhead. On signal, raise the chute off the floor while simultaneously raising the head and chest. Encourage students to lift the chute high enough so they can "see a friend" across the way.

Sitting Leg Lift.   In a sitting position with the legs under the chute, lift the legs on signal while holding the chute taut, and lift the chute off the floor. Hold the position for 6–10 sec. Try to keep the legs straight. As a variation, start in a supine position with the legs under the chute and do a V-seat.

Sitting Pulls.   Sit with the back to the parachute. Grasp the chute and raise it overhead. On signal, try to pull the chute down to the knees. Other variations are done facing the chute and raising it above the head, lowering it to eye level, and to waist level.

Emphasis should be placed on using the arms and shoulder girdle to apply force, rather than leaning.

All Fours Pulls. Get on the floor in a crab-, bear-, or seal-walk position. Grasp the chute with one hand. On signal, pull and hold the contraction for 6–10 sec. Repeat using the other hand and different positions.

Isometric Exercises. A wide variety of isometric exercises can be done using the parachute. Various body parts can be exercised by applying pressure to the chute. The exercises should be held for 6–10 sec. Encourage students to develop new isometric techniques.

Rhythmic Aerobic Activity. The parachute is excellent for stimulating aerobic activity. For example, students can do various locomotor movements while holding onto the chute. A sample routine with the chute follows:

1. Sixteen skips clockwise
2. Sixteen skips counterclockwise
3. Sixteen jumps to the center of the parachute
4. Sixteen hops backward and tighten the chute
5. Eight-count parachute lift overhead
6. Eight-count lower parachute to toes
7. Four-count parachute lift overhead
8. Four-count lower parachute to toes
9. Repeat steps 5–8
10. Thirty-two running steps clockwise with the chute held overhead
11. Thirty-two running steps backward with the chute held at waist level
12. Perform a 16-count dome
13. Repeat steps 10–12
14. Finish with a parachute lift and release the chute

Running Activities and Drills

A number of running drills and activities can be used to improve running techniques, agility, and fitness levels, depending on how they are administered. These are useful activities for the fitness portion of the lesson.

Form Running

This drill works well on a football field using the yard lines as markers. A squad of students lines up on the boundary line at the goal line, 10-yd line, 20-yd line, 30-yd line, and so forth. The teacher stands on the hash mark closest to the students, on about the 25-yd line. On signal, the first student in each line runs across the field on the respective yard line. The teacher continues to give a starting signal for each wave of students until all of the students are on the opposite boundary line. The teacher then moves to the opposite hash mark and starts the students running back across the field. Each time the students run across the field, they should be told to concentrate on one aspect of their running form. The following aspects can be emphasized:

1. Keep the head still—no lateral or turning movements. Eyes should be focused straight ahead. Keep the chin down.
2. Relax the hands. Place thumb on the first pad of the index finger. Put hands in the front pocket as they move backward.
3. Bend elbows approximately 90 degrees, and move the arms straight forward and back with no lateral movement across the chest. Arms gently brush the sides of the body.
4. Align feet straight ahead. Knees drive straight ahead rather than upward. High knee action can be used as another variation, although it is not necessary for good running form. The heel of the foot should come close to the buttocks.
5. Align the foot, knee, and hip. The body tilts forward about 5 degrees from the feet, not from the hips.
6. The length of the stride is usually shorter for longer runs (i.e., a longer stride for sprinting and a shorter stride for distance running).

Give students only one aspect of running form to concentrate on during each trip across the field so that they can emphasize and overlearn each point. Beginning slowly and increasing the speed gradually works best. Start the drill at half-speed, then proceed to three-quarter speed, and finally, full speed.

This same drill format can also be used with other running activities.

1. Backwards Running. Stay on the line. Roll the shoulders forward and keep them forward while running. Emphasize the arm movement forward and back. Pull that arm through with each step.

2. Crossover Step Backward. The teacher stands on the boundary line and the first wave of students moves 5 yd out on their respective yard lines facing the teacher. The teacher gives a left- or right-hand signal. The students start backward with a crossover step. When the teacher changes the direction signal, students rotate their hips and crossover step on the opposite side. Students must keep their eyes on the teacher and concentrate on rotating their hips and staying on the line.

3. Crossover Step Forward. As students run forward, they concentrate on stepping across the line with each step. It is important to start slowly and to increase the speed gradually.

4. Carioca. Students stand sideways on the line with their arms held out, parallel to the ground. On a signal, the students move sideways down the line by using a crossover step in front and a return step, a crossover step in back, and finally another step. This process is repeated for the length of the field. Students should make sure that they lead with both the right and left shoulder.

5. Shuffle Sideways. Students stand sideways on the line in a ready position (i.e., feet shoulder width, knees bent, head up, arms flexed in front of the body). On signal, students shuffle down the line without a crossover step. Students should also lead with both the left and right sides. A variation is to have students spread out down the line and face the teacher, who is standing in front of the entire group. The teacher gives a left- or right-hand signal to start the group moving.

All of the form running drills can also be done without lines if necessary. Boundary cones can be used to mark the beginning and end of each running section. Another variation is to place cones at one-third and two-thirds of the distance and ask students to vary their speed in each third. For example, students could jog the first third, sprint the second, and ease to three-quarter speed during the last third. Or, change the type of running during each third. The following combinations might be used:

1. Jog, shuffle right, and shuffle left
2. Carioca, shuffle, and sprint
3. Backward run, crossover left, and crossover right
4. Form run, crossover front, and form run
5. Carioca left, carioca right, and sprint

File Running

Divide the class into two or three groups according to cardiovascular fitness level: high, medium, and low. Each group lines up single file and begins to jog around a given distance, such as a quarter-mile track, a field, or a set of boundary cones. Students should keep a 2–3-yd distance between each person. The last person in line sprints past the file and becomes the leader. When the new leader is in place, the new last person begins to sprint past the file. This procedure continues for a given distance or a given number of minutes. The high fitness group will cover more distance in a given time.

Walk–Jog–Sprint

This is a continuous movement activity in which the teacher controls the speed of movement with a whistle signal. Three whistles mean sprint, two mean jog, and one signal, walk. The students start by walking

Times for 40- and 100-Yard Dashes

To run 1 mi in:	You would have to run the 40-yard dash 44 times, with each dash run in:	Or run the 100-yard dash 17.6 times, with each dash run in:
3.48 min (world record time)	5.18 sec	12.95 sec
5:00 min	6.81 sec	17.04 sec
6:00 min	8.18 sec	20.45 sec
7:00 min	9.55 sec	23.87 sec
8:00 min	10.90 sec	27.25 sec
10:00 min	13.62 sec	34.08 sec

FIGURE 18.23   Pace chart—1

around a given area (track, field, or boundary cone). The teacher then alternates the periods of jogging, sprinting, and walking for a number of minutes or for a given distance. It is important to progressively build up the time or distance.

Pace Work

Students need to practice running at an even pace for a given distance, such as a 6-, 8-, or 10 min mi. Pacing can be practiced by running shorter segments of the distance at the correct speed.

Figures 18.23 and 18.24 show the required time for covering certain distances in order to maintain correct pacing. It is easiest to use a marked track, but a workable track can be developed through placement of boundary cones. Using a rectangle is helpful for ease of measurement. Students are divided into groups and challenged to run distances at a given time. For example, the fast group might work on a 6-min-mile pace: 110 yd in 22.5 sec, 220 yd in 45 sec, and 440 yd in 90 sec. The medium group could work on an 8-min pace, and the slow group could focus on a 10-min-mile pace. It is interesting to have students calculate a world record pace for a given distance and then try to run a small segment of that distance at the record pace. For instance, have them run 50 yd at a 4-min-mile pace, or 440 yd at a 2.5-hr marathon pace.

Another strategy for teaching students about pace is to set up a square, 50 yd on a side. Place a cone at every corner and in the middle of each side. Put an equal number of students at each cone. Calculate

Interval	To run 1 mi (1760 yd) in:								
	4:00	*5:00*	*6:00*	*7:00*	*8:00*	*9:00*	*10:00*	*11:00*	*12:00*
¾ (1320 yd)	3:00	3:45	4:30	5:15	6:00	6:45	7:30	8:15	9:00
½ (880 yd)	2:00	2:30	3:00	3:30	4:00	4:30	5:00	5:30	6:00
¼ (440 yd)	1:00	1:15	1:30	1:45	2:00	2:15	2:30	2:45	3:00
⅛ (220 yd)	:30	:37½	:45	:52½	1:00	1:07½	1:15	1:22½	1:30
¹⁄₁₆ (110 yd)	:15	:18¾	:22½	:26¼	:30	:33¾	:37½	:41¼	:45

FIGURE 18.24 Pace chart for a 1 mi run—2

the 25-yd time for various speeds (e.g., a 6-, 8-, or 10-min mile. Have students try to run at a given speed, and blow a whistle each time they should have completed a 25-yd run. The students should be at a cone each time the whistle sounds. They can tell if they are going too fast or too slow.

Random Running

Random running is a simple and effective way to improve cardiovascular fitness (Pangrazi and Wilcox, 1979). The emphasis is on long, slow, distance (LSD) running. Students are allowed to run randomly throughout the area at a pace that is comfortable for them. They are encouraged to find a partner and to talk while jogging.

Students who need to walk because of their subpar level of fitness can do so without experiencing the stigma of finishing last during a run. The distance each student runs is not charted. Effort is acknowledged, rather than speed or distance-running ability. Emphasis is placed on being active, involved, and moving during the entire episode, rather than on seeing how far one can run or jog.

Students can begin with a 10-min random running episode three times per week. The duration of the run can be increased 1 min per week until a maximum 20-min episode is achieved. This allows the majority of students to increase their work load in a gradual and palatable manner.

Fartlek

Fartlek is a form of training that was developed in Sweden in the 1930s and 1940s. The training is aerobic in nature and entails hard, but untimed, long distance efforts over topographic challenges. The hilly terrain is run at varied tempos. (The term Fartlek translates to "speed play.")

Fartlek is usually done on soft surfaces. A typical workout for an athlete in training might be as follows:

1. Five to 10 min of easy jogging
2. Steady, intense speed for 1–2 km
3. Five min of rapid walking
4. Easy running broken by 50–60 meters of accelerated runs that cause moderate fatigue
5. Easy running with 2–5 intermittent swift strides every 100 meters to moderate fatigue
6. Full uphill effort for 150–200 meters
7. One min of fast-paced running on level ground
8. Easy running for 5–10 meters.

This workout illustrates the variation involved in fartlek. Students can be given a workout that might last 10–20 min and encompasses the many different tempos and geographic features described. The run challenges can be written on cards, and students select runs of varying difficulty (e.g., easy, moderate, difficult, strenuous).

REFERENCES AND SUGGESTED READINGS

AAHPERD. 1988. *Physical Best Manual.* Reston, VA: AAHPERD.

AAHPERD. 1987. *Youth Fitness Test Manual.* Reston, VA: AAHPERD.

AAHPERD. 1980. *Lifetime Health Related Physical Fitness Test Manual.* Reston, VA: AAHPERD.

Corbin, C. B., and Fletcher, P. 1968. Diet and activity patterns of obese and non-obese elementary school children. *Research Quarterly* 39(4): 922–928.

deVries, H. A., and Adams, G. M. 1972. Electromyographic comparison of single doses of exercise and meprobamate as to effects on muscular relaxation. *American Journal of Physical Medicine* 51: 130–141.

Gilliam, T. B., et al. 1978. Blood lipids and fatness in children age 7–13. *Canadian Journal of Applied Sport Science* 3: 65–69.

Glass, W. 1973. Coronary heart disease sessions prove vitally interesting. *CAHPER Journal*, May–June issue.

Glasser, W. 1976. *Positive Addiction.* New York: Harper & Row, Publishers, Inc.

Johnson, M. L., Burke, B. S., and Mayer, J. 1956. The prevalence and incidence of obesity in a cross-section of elementary and secondary school children. *American Journal of Clinical Nutrition* 4(3): 231–38.

Miller, D. K., and Allen, T. K. 1982. *Fitness: A Lifetime Commitment*. Minneapolis, MN: Burgess Publishing Co.

Nelson, D. O. 1979. *Dynamic Fitness*. Logan, UT: Utah State University.

Pangrazi, B., and Wilcox, R. 1979. RRP—An effective approach to cardiovascular fitness for children. *Arizona JOHPERD* 22(2): 15–16.

Petrofsky, J. S., and Lind, A. R. 1975. Aging, isometric strength, and endurance, and cardiovascular responses to static effort. *Journal of Applied Physiology* 41: 91–95.

Rarick, L. G., and Dobbins, D. A. 1975. Basic components in the motor performances of children six to nine years of age. *Medicine and Science in Sports* 7(2): 105–110.

Rose, K. 1973. To keep people in health. *Journal of the American College Health Association* 22: 80.

Sterling, C. L. 1987. *Fitnessgram User's Manual*. Dallas, TX: Institute for Aerobics Research.

Wilmore, J. H. 1980. Physical fitness guidelines for adults. In *Proceedings of the National Conference on Physical Fitness and Sports for All*. Washington, DC: The President's Council on Physical Fitness and Sports, 39–48.

19

ONE-DAY UNITS OF INSTRUCTION

The units in this chapter offer students and teachers a change of pace in instruction. The units are personally challenging and allow students to develop new skills and to work closely with classmates. They are presented easily, and should motivate students and offer them a variation in the instructional process. Many are useful for rainy days, shortened period days, or for introductory activities.

The units require equipment that is rarely used in typical physical education programs. They are meant to be presented for one or two days without worry about continuity of instruction. Most of the units are noncompetitive and focus on learning and on performing novel tasks. Since variation in student ability makes little difference in the presentation of these activities, they can be offered as challenge activities to students. For example, the proper progression of juggling activities can be taught. After the rudimentary skills are learned, some students will progress to more challenging tasks, whereas others remain at a lower level.

An excellent way to use the one-day units is to present them on a Tuesday or Thursday to break up a longer unit of instruction. Students should be encouraged to help each other master the tasks, with emphasis placed on cooperation rather than competition. This creates a different environment that may be more meaningful for some students. The low-key instructional approach is also an inviting variation for instructors.

INDIVIDUAL AND DUAL UNITS OF INSTRUCTION

Units in this area include juggling, beanbags, wands, hoops, stunts, tumbling, and combatives. They focus on individual skill development and allow each student to progress at an optimum rate of development. Many modifications of the units can be made, and students can develop new and different challenges that the rest of the class can try.

Beanbags

The following are challenges that can be taken in any order. The best size beanbag is usually 6 in. × 6 in., because it can be balanced on various body parts and used for many challenges. The advantage of the 4 in. × 4 in. beanbags is that they can be used for juggling activities as well as for many of the challenge activities listed here. Students should try to master the stunts with both the right and left hands.

1. Toss the beanbag overhead and catch it on the back of the hand. Try catching on different body parts such as shoulder, knee, and foot.
2. Toss the beanbag, make a half-turn, and catch it. Try making a different number of turns (e.g., full, double, and so forth).
3. Toss, clap the hands, and catch. Try clapping the hands a specified number of times. Clap the hands around different parts of the body.
4. Toss, touch various body parts or objects. For example, toss, touch the toes, shoulders, and hips before catching. Specify objects to touch, such as the wall, the floor, or a line.
5. Toss, move to various body positions, and catch the beanbag. Suggested positions are sitting, kneeling, supine or prone position, and on one's side.
6. Reverse no. 5 by tossing the beanbag from some of the suggested positions and then resuming the standing position.
7. Toss and perform various stunts before catching the beanbag, such as heel clicks, heel slaps, jump and perform a full turn, and push-up.
8. Toss the beanbag from behind the back and catch it. Toss overhead and catch it behind the back.
9. Toss, move, and catch. Cover as much ground as possible between the toss and catch. Move forward, backward, and sideways, using different steps such as the carioca, shuffle, and slide.
10. Toss the beanbag with various body parts (feet,

knees, shoulders) and catch it with the hands or other body parts. Try to develop as much height on the toss as possible.

11. Perform some of the stunts with a beanbag in each hand. Catch the bags simultaneously.

12. Play a balance tag game. Specify a body part that the bag must be balanced on while moving. Designate who is it. If the beanbag falls off or is touched with the hands, the player must freeze and is subject to being tagged.

13. Try partner activities. Play catch with a partner using two or three beanbags. Toss and catch the beanbags using various body parts.

Hoops

Hoops are useful for offering various challenges to students. A 42-inch-diameter hoop is usually the best size choice. This is a large enough hoop to move through and over and to use for Hula-Hoop activities. Students should try to master the activities with both sides of their body. Emphasis can be placed on creating new routines with the hoops. The following are suggested ideas:

1. Spin the hoop like a top and see how long the hoop will continue to spin. While the hoop is spinning, see how many times it can be jumped.

2. Hula-Hoop using various body parts (waist, knees, ankles, neck, wrist). Hula-Hoop from the neck to the knees and back up to the neck. Hula-Hoop on a wrist and then change to the other wrist. Pass the hoop to a partner while Hula-Hooping.

3. Try many of the Hula-Hooping challenges while using two or more hoops. Hula-Hoop with a hoop on two or more body parts.

4. Play catch with a partner while Hula-Hooping. Catch more than one object and Hula-Hoop with more than one hoop.

5. Jump or hop through a hoop held by a partner. Vary the challenge by altering the angle and height of the hoop. Try jumping through two or more parallel hoops without touching them.

6. Roll the hoop like a spare tire. Change direction on signal. Roll two or more hoops at the same time.

7. Use the hoop in place of a jump rope. Jump the hoop forward, backward, and sideways. Perform various foot stunts like toe-touching, rocker step, and heel-and-toe while jumping.

8. Roll the hoop forward with a reverse spin. The spin should cause it to return to the thrower. As the hoop returns, try some of the following challenges: Jump the hoop, move through it, kick it up with the toe and catch it, and pick it up with the arm and begin hooping it.

9. Play catch with the hoop with a partner. Use two or more hoops and throw them alternately as well as simultaneously.

10. Employ the hoop relay. Break into equal-size groups. Join hands and place a hoop on a pair of joined hands. The object is to pass the hoop around the circle without releasing the hand grip. The first group to get the hoop around the circle is declared the winner.

Juggling

Juggling offers a challenge to secondary school students. If the majority of students have not mastered basic juggling skills, juggling scarves should be purchased. They are lightweight, sheer scarves that move slowly and allow students to master the proper arm and hand movements. Once the movement pattern is learned, beanbags, jugglebags (small round beanbags), and fleece balls can be used before proceeding to balls, rings, and clubs.

Juggling with scarves does teach students the correct patterns of object movement, however, it does not transfer automatically to juggling with faster-moving objects such as fleece balls, tennis balls, rings, and hoops. Therefore, two distinct sections for juggling are offered: a section on learning to juggle with scarves, and a section explaining juggling with balls. Juggling with scarves will bring success to a majority of the class while youngsters who have mastered the scarves can move to balls and other objects.

Juggling with Scarves

Scarves are held by the fingertips near the center. To throw the scarf, it should be lifted and pulled into the air above eye level. Scarves are caught by clawing, a downward motion of the hand, and grabbing the scarf from above as it is falling. Scarf juggling should teach proper habits (e.g., tossing the scarves straight up in line with the body rather than forward or backward). Many instructors remind students to imagine that they are in a phone booth to emphasize tossing and catching without moving.

Cascading

Cascading is the easiest pattern for juggling three objects. The following sequence can be used to learn this basic technique.

1. One scarf. Hold the scarf in the center. Quickly move the arm across the chest and toss the scarf with the palm out. Reach out with the other hand

FIGURE 19.1   Making a figure-8 motion with scarves

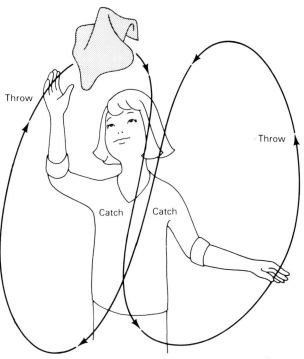

FIGURE 19.2   Reverse cascading

and catch the scarf in a straight, downward motion (clawing). Toss the scarf with this hand using the motion and claw it with the opposite hand. Repeat the tossing and clawing sequence. The scarf should move in a figure-eight pattern as shown in Figure 19.1.

2. Two scarves. Hold a scarf with the fingertips in each hand. Toss the first one across the body as described in Variation 1. When it reaches its peak, look at it, and toss the second scarf across the body in the opposite direction. The first scarf thrown is caught (clawed) by the hand throwing the second scarf and vice versa. Verbal cues such as toss, claw, toss, claw, are helpful.

3. Three-scarf cascading. Hold a scarf in each hand by the fingertips. Hold the third scarf with the ring and little finger against the palm of the hand. The first scarf to be thrown will be from the hand that is holding two scarves. Toss this scarf from the fingertips across the chest as learned earlier. When scarf one reaches its peak, throw scarf two from the other hand across the body. As this hand starts to come down, it catches scarf one. When scarf two reaches its peak, throw scarf three in the same path as that of scarf one. To complete the cycle, as the hand comes down from throwing scarf three, it catches scarf two. The cycle is started over by throwing scarf one with the opposite hand. Tosses are

always alternated between left and right hands with a smooth, even rhythm.

Reverse Cascading

Reverse cascading involves tossing the scarves from waist level to the outside of the body and allowing the scarves to drop down the midline of the body (Figure 19.2).

1. One scarf. Begin by holding the scarf as described in the Cascading section. The throw goes away from the midline of the body over the top, so the scarf is released and falls down the center of the body. Catch it with the opposite hand and toss it in similar fashion on the opposite side of the body.

2. Two scarves. Begin with a scarf in each hand. Toss the first as described in Example 1. When it begins its descent, toss the second scarf. Catch the first scarf, then the second, and repeat the pattern in a toss, toss, catch, catch manner.

3. Reverse cascading with three scarves. Think of a large funnel fixed at eye level directly in front of the juggler. The goal is to drop all scarves through this funnel so that they drop straight down the center of the body. Begin with three scarves as described above for three-scarf cascading. Toss the first scarf from the hand holding two scarves.

Column Juggling

Column juggling is so-named because the scarves move straight up and down as though they were inside a large pipe or column and do not cross the body. To perform three scarf column juggling, begin with two scarves in one hand and one in the other hand. Begin with a scarf from the hand that has two scarves, and toss it straight up the midline of the body overhead. When this scarf reaches its peak, toss the other two scarves upward along the sides of the body (Figure 19.3). Catch the first scarf with either hand and toss it upward again. Catch the other two scarves and toss them upward continuing the pattern.

Showering

Showering is more difficult than cascading because of the rapid movement of the hands. There is less time allowed for catching and tossing. The scarves move in a circle following each other. It should be practiced in both directions for maximum challenge.

Start with two scarves in the right hand and one in the other. Begin by throwing the first two scarves from the right hand. Toss the scarves in a large circle away from the midline of the body and overhead as high as possible. As soon as the second scarf is released, toss the scarf across to the left hand and throw it in the same path with the right hand. All scarves are caught with the left hand and passed to the right hand.

Juggling Challenges

1. While cascading, toss a scarf under one leg.
2. While cascading, toss a scarf from behind the back.
3. Instead of catching one of the scarves, blow it upward with a strong breath of air.
4. Begin cascading by tossing the first scarf into the air with a foot. Lay the scarf across the foot and kick it into the air.
5. Try juggling three scarves with one hand. Do not worry about establishing a pattern, just catch the lowest scarf each time. Try both regular and reverse cascading as well as column juggling.
6. While doing column juggling, toss up one scarf, hold the other two and make a full turn. Resume juggling.
7. Try juggling more than three scarves (up to six) while facing a partner.
8. Juggle three scarves while standing side by side with inside arms around each other. This is easy to do since it is regular three-scarf cascading.

Juggling with Balls

Juggling with balls requires accurate, consistent tossing, and this should be the first emphasis. The tosses should be thrown to the same height on both sides of the body, about 2–2.5 ft upward and across the body, since the ball is tossed from one hand to the other. Practice tossing the ball parallel to the body; the most common problem in juggling is that the balls are tossed forward and the juggler has to move forward to catch them.

The fingers, not the palms, should be used in tossing and catching. Stress relaxed wrist action. Encourage students to look upward to watch the balls at the peak of their flight, rather than watching the hands. Focus on the where the ball peaks, not the hands. Two balls must be carried in the starting hand, and the art of releasing only one must be mastered. Progression should be working successively with one ball, then two balls, and finally three balls.

Recommended Progression for Cascading

1. Using one ball and one hand only, toss the ball upward (2–2½ ft), and catch it with the same hand. Begin with the dominant hand, and later practice with the other. Toss quickly, with wrist action. Then

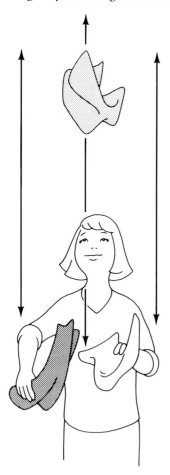

FIGURE 19.3 Column juggling

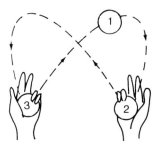

FIGURE 19.4   Cascading with three balls and two hands

handle the ball alternately with right and left hands, tossing from one hand to the other.

2. Now, with one ball in each hand, alternate tossing a ball upward and catching it in the same hand so that one ball is always in the air. Begin again with a ball in each hand. Toss across the body to the other hand. To keep the balls from colliding, toss under the incoming ball. After some expertise has been acquired, alternate the two kinds of tosses by doing a set number (4 to 6) of each before shifting to the other.

3. Hold two balls in the starting hand and one in the other. Toss one of the balls in the starting hand, toss the ball from the other hand, and then toss the third ball. Keep the balls moving in a figure-eight pattern (Figure 19.4)

Recommended Progression for Showering

1. The showering motion is usually counter-clockwise. Hold one ball in each hand. Begin by tossing with the right hand on an inward path and then immediately toss the other ball from the left directly across the body to the right hand. Continue this until the action is smooth.

2. Now, hold two balls in the right hand and one in the left. Toss the first ball from the right hand on an inward path and immediately toss the second on the same path. At about the same time, toss the ball from the left hand directly across the body to the right hand (Figure 19.5).

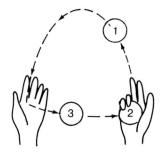

FIGURE 19.5   Showering with three balls and two hands

3. A few students may be able to change from cascading to showering and vice versa. This is a skill of considerable challenge.

Stunts and Combatives

This unit should emphasize personal challenge and brief competitive episodes. Students enjoy the chance to pit their strength and coordination skills against others. The combatives should be between opponents of approximately the same skill level and size. Partners should be switched often so there is little chance for animosity to develop. The contests start and stop by mutual agreement, with either party able to terminate the contest immediately. There is little point in running tournaments to see who is the class champion in a specific combative. Instead, emphasize enjoyment, learning one's strengths and weaknesses, and being able to contest a number of opponents.

Stunts, on the other hand, require that students work cooperatively to accomplish them successfully and are an excellent way to help students learn more about their peers.

Suggested Individual Stunts

Leg Dip.   Extend both hands and one leg forward while balancing on the other leg. Lower the body until the seat touches the heel and then return to the standing position. This must be done without the aid of the arms and without losing balance.

Behind the Back Touch.   Start in a standing position with the arms extended behind the back and hands clasped. Squat slowly and touch the floor with an extended finger, then return to the standing position.

Knee Jump.   Kneel on the floor with the seat on the heels and the toes pointing backward. In one continuous motion, swing the arms forward and jump to the feet. If accomplished, try to perform a half-turn during the jump.

Wall Climb.   Take a push-up position with the feet against the wall. Walk up the wall with the feet to a handstand position and then return to the push-up position.

Popover.   While in push-up position, propel the body upward and do a half turn to the inverted push-up position. Popover to the regular push-up position.

Double Heel Click.   Jump upward and click the heels twice. If accomplished, try to perform a triple heel click before landing.

Push-Up Inversion. Begin in push-up position. Push strongly off the floor and bring the legs through the arms in one smooth motion—assuming the inverted push-up position. Return to the original position with a strong movement backward.

Jump Through. Hold the left toe with the right hand. Jump the right foot through without losing the grip on the toe. Try the stunt with the other foot.

Sitting Lift-Off. Sit on the floor with the legs extended forward. Place the hands on the floor somewhere between the hips and knees, depending on the balance point. Lift the entire body off the floor in a balanced position. The stunt can be learned in stages—first with the heels remaining on the floor, then with the heels held off the floor by a friend.

Jumping Toe Touch. Begin in a standing position with the hands held in front of the body, shoulder-width apart, palms down. When ready, jump up and bring the feet quickly forward so the toe tips touch the hands in front of the body. The attempt should be to bring the hands to the feet, lifting the feet as high as possible.

Leg Circling. In a squatting position with both hands on the floor, place the left knee between the arms and extend the right leg to the side. Swing the right leg forward and under the lifted right arm, under the left leg and arm, and back to starting position. Perform several circles in succession. Try circling with the other leg.

Suggested Partner and Group Stunts

Leapfrog. One student forms the base by standing stiff-legged, bending over, and placing the hands on the knees. The other student runs and leaps over the base by performing a light push-off on the back of the base. A number of students can form bases to create a series of leaps for the moving student.

Wheelbarrow. One partner is in push-up position with the legs spread. The other person walks between the legs and grasps and lifts the partner's lower legs. The partner in push-up position then walks the arms while the other person moves forward, backward, or sideways (Figure 19.6). A double or triple wheelbarrow can be performed with students extending their legs over the back of the student in push-up position and placing their hands on the floor.

Caterpillar. One student is on hands and knees, acting as the support. Another student, facing the same direction, places the hands about 2 ft in front of the support's hands (Figure 19.7). The second student's legs are then placed on top of the support and locked together at the ankles. Five to six stu-

FIGURE 19.6 Wheelbarrow

dents can continue this process and then begin walking when everyone is in place.

Knee Stand. The base student is in crab position. The other student stands on the knees of the base. A spotter may be necessary to help the second student come to a balanced position.

Cooperative Scooter. Two students face each other and sit with toes under the seat of the other. The arms are joined by holding the other student's arms at the wrist or above (Figure 19.8). Students scoot forward or backward by cooperatively lifting the feet when the other lifts the seat. Progress is made by alternately flexing and extending the knees and hips.

Spider Walk. The base student is in a sitting position with the back against a wall. The next student backs up and sits lightly on the knees of the base. More students can be added in similar fashion. The hands should be placed around the waist of each person in front. Walking is done by moving the feet on the same side together (Figure 19.9).

Triple High Jump. Students form groups of three and join hands. One of the students is designated as

FIGURE 19.7 Caterpillar

FIGURE 19.8   Cooperative scooter

FIGURE 19.10   Spotting the back balance

the performer and jumps over the joined arms of the other two. The performer is assisted in the jump by an upward lift from the others. The hands to be jumped over should be clasped lightly and released if the jumper does not gain enough height.

Octopus.   Eight to 12 students work together to develop this activity. Half of the students form a circle with hands joined, while each student in the other half finds a pair of joined hands to lean backward on, placing the weight on the heels. Each of the leaners then join hands behind the backs of the others, thus creating two separate groups with joined hands. The octopus begins moving slowly around the circle, taking small side steps. The stunt is brought to a climax by moving as fast as possible.

Double Bear Walk.   The base student is on hands and knees. The top student assumes the same position with the hands on the shoulders and the knees over the hips of the base. They move slowly throughout the area without losing balance.

Double Crab Walk.   The bottom student moves into crab position. The top performer straddles the base and also assumes the crab position with the hands on the shoulders and the feet on the knees of the base. They move slowly throughout the area.

Back Balance.   Students work with a partner. One partner lies in supine position and becomes the base. The base bends the knees, and the balancer places the small of the back on the soles of the base's feet. The balancer then lies back and balances in a layout position (Figure 19.10).

Sitting Balance.   The base assumes a supine position on the floor. The balancer straddles the base so that they are looking at each other. The balancer sits on the soles of the base's feet while the base holds the ankles of the balancer (Figure 19.11). The legs of the balancer should be extended as much as possible.

Abdominal Balance.   The base assumes a supine position on the floor, then raises the legs and positions the feet so the soles are parallel to the floor. The balancer faces the base and places the abdomen on the soles of the base's feet. The base grasps the hands of the balancer and extends the legs to move the performer into a balanced position. The balancer should attempt to arch the back, raise the head, and extend the arms to the sides.

Seat Press.   The base lies on the floor with the knees bent and the feet flat on the floor. The balancer straddles the base facing the feet of the base. The two join hands, and the top partner sits on the joined hands supported by the base (Figure 19.12). The balancer's legs are placed on the knees of the base.

FIGURE 19.9   Spider walk

FIGURE 19.11 Sitting balance

FIGURE 19.12 Seat press

FIGURE 19.13 Minipyramids

Minipyramids. Students can work in groups of three to five to develop various types of pyramids (Figure 19.13). Some examples are shown in the figure. Students should be encouraged to develop different types of pyramids and allowed time to share them with the rest of the class.

Combatives

There are many types of combatives. This list should give insight into the many variations but is certainly not exhaustive.

Arm Wrestling. This popular activity can be done lying on the floor or sitting at a table. The right hands are clasped, and the elbows are bent and rest on the floor or table. When ready, the goal is to force the opponent's hand down to the floor or table surface. The elbows cannot be lifted from the surface.

Leg Wrestling. Opponents are side by side and supine on a mat with their heads in opposite directions. They lock the near elbows and prepare for action. On signal, they lift the inside leg vertically two times before hooking the legs on the third count. They then try to roll the opponent over backwards.

Standing Hand Wrestle. Contestants place the toes of their right feet together and grasp right hands in a handshake grip. The left foot is moved to the rear for support. The goal is to force the opponent to move either foot.

Finger Wrestle. Opponents stand on the right foot and hold the left foot with the left hand. The index fingers of the right hand are hooked, and opponents attempt to push each other off balance.

Flag Grab. Contestants have a flag tucked in the belt and attempt to keep others from pulling it out. At the same time, opponents try to collect as many flags as possible.

Palm Wrestle. Contestants face each other, standing 12 in. apart. The palms of the opponents are placed together and must remain so for the duration of the contest. The goal is to push the opponent off balance.

Push-Up Breakdown. Opponents are in push-up position and attempt to break down the other's position. It is a fall when one of the opponents is brought down from the push-up position to the ground.

Crab Breakdown. This is similar to the push-up breakdown, except that the opponents are in crab position. As a variation, try getting the opponent to touch the seat to the floor while keeping the hands and feet on the floor. The takedown must occur through jostling and pushing the opponent.

Toe Dance. Contestants begin by placing their hands on the opponent's shoulders. The goal is to step on top of the toes of the opponent. A variation can be to see how many toe touches can be accumulated in a specified time.

Seat Pull-Up. Opponents sit on the floor, facing each other, with the knees bent, and the soles of the contestants' shoes together. Players bend forward, grasp hands firmly, and attempt to pull their opponent's seat off the floor. The winner must be sitting upright in position when the opponent is lifted from the floor, or the contest is a draw.

Back-to-Back Takedown. Contestants sit back to back and lock elbows. The feet are widely spread to form a broad base of support. Both players attempt to pull the other to the left and touch the opponent's shoulder (or elbow) to the floor. As a variation, attempt the contest by pulling in the opposite direction.

Tug-of-War Activities

Tug-of-war activities can be conducted in pairs. Partners should be changed often so students have a chance to compete with many others and are not subjected to constantly losing or to seldom being challenged. Tug-of-war ropes are easily made from 10 ft of ⅜-in. nylon rope and two sections of ⅝-in. garden hose 2 ft long. The rope is threaded through the garden hose, which serves as a handle, and tied with a bowline knot so there is a loop at each end of the rope.

Partner Pulls

Partners can have contests using some of the following suggested positions and activities:

Different Positions. Facing, back to back, side to side, one handed, two handed, crab position with the rope hooked over the foot, push-up position, and on all four are a few suggested variations.

Balance Pulls. Students begin in a stationary position. The goal is to cause the opponent to move the feet or lose balance.

Pick-up Contest. Place Indian clubs or bowling pins behind the contestants. The goal is to pull and move backward in order to pick up the clubs.

Multiple Rope Pulls. Ropes can be twisted together so four to six students can become involved in the contest.

Pick-up and Pull. The ropes are laid on the floor between two contestants. On signal, the two opponents run to the rope, pick it up, and the tug-of-war ensues.

Team Tugs-of-War

Small groups and classes can have contests with the large commercially available tug-of-war ropes. Most are 50 ft in length and at least 1 in. in diameter. Many of the ropes have large loops on the end so students can stand inside of them. Caution must be used with the loops, however, because students cannot easily release the rope when the other team gains momentum.

A suggested manner for conducting team tugs-of-war is to tie a marker in the middle of the rope. Two parallel lines are drawn 10–20 ft apart. The pull starts with the marker in the middle of the two lines. The goal is to pull the marker over your team's line. Variations for different types of pulls are to try pulling with the rope overhead, having opponents pull with their backs to each other, pulling with one hand on the ground or in the air, or pulling from a seated position.

Wands

Wands provide challenge through balance and flexibility activities, which can be performed individually. Wands are usually made from ⅝-in. or ¾-in. dowels and should be 42 in. long. They can be painted, and rubber tips can be placed on the ends to soften the noise they make when falling on the floor.

Wand Whirl.   Stand a wand in front of the body, and balance it with one finger. Release the wand, perform a full turn, and catch the wand. Try the activity in both directions. Try catching with one finger on top of the wand.

Thread the Needle.   Hold the wand in both hands near the ankles. Without letting go of the wand, step over the wand and through the space between the arms. Return to the starting position. Try passing the wand under the feet side to side, one foot at a time, with the wand held in front and behind the body.

Thread the Needle (Jumping).   Virtually the same stunt as the previous activity, except that the stick is jumped over and passed under the feet simultaneously.

Wand Kickover.   Balance the wand in front of the body with one hand. Release the wand, kick a leg over, and catch the wand. Try kicking in both directions using both legs. Try catching the wand with one finger.

Walk Under.   Grasp the wand with the right hand. Twist under the right arm without letting go of the wand, without taking it off the floor, and without touching the knee to the floor. Try using the left arm also.

Broomstick Balance.   Balance the wand vertically in one hand. Begin by walking while balancing and then attempt to balance the wand in a stationary position. Try walking in different directions, using both hands, and balancing the wand on different body parts.

Wand Walkdown.   Start in a straddle stance, with legs straight. Hold a wand near one end, with the other end of the wand above the head and pointed toward the ceiling. Bend backward, place the wand on the floor behind, and walk the hands down the wand. Return to standing position. If the wands do not have rubber tips, a spotter may have to stabilize the wand end on the floor.

Partner Exchange.   Partners face each other, balancing a wand in front of them. On signal, each runs to the other's wand and catches it before it hits the floor. Challenge can be added by increasing the distance, using two wands, and performing stunts such as a full turn or heel click before catching the wand.

Reaction Time.   One partner holds the wand horizontally. The other partner places one hand directly above the wand, palm down. The wand is dropped and the person must try to catch the wand before it hits the floor. This can also be tried holding the wand vertically. The other person forms a "V" with the thumb and fingers and is challenged to catch the wand. Marks can be placed on the wand, and students challenged to catch the wand on certain marks.

Wand Wrestle.   A wand is held in the vertical position by two opponents. The goal is to move the wand to the horizontal plane. One person is designated to move the wand horizontally while the other resists the attempt. Roles are reversed after each bout.

Wand Release.   Players sit facing each other with the legs straight and the soles of the feet together. Together, they hold a wand horizontally at chest level. A win occurs when one person causes the other to release the grip on the wand. Neither player is allowed to leave or modify the starting position.

Isometric Exercises.   Wands are a useful instrument for performing isometric exercises. Examples are attempting to twist the wand, to stretch the wand, to compress the wand, or to pull against different body parts. Many stretching activities can also be done using the wands.

LOW-ORGANIZATION GAMES

The following activities are enjoyable for students because they demand few specialized skills yet require teamwork. The games help develop camaraderie among students, and teams can be reorganized periodically to equalize the competition. Rules listed are only starting points; students and teachers can modify any and all of the rules as they desire.

Cageball Games

Cageballs come in many different sizes. The most common size is 2 ft in diameter, which is an easy size to store and inflate. The next size is 4 ft in diameter, which makes the games more interesting at the high school level. Drawbacks to the larger size are storage, expense, and inflation time. The largest cageballs, often termed earth balls, are 5 or 6 ft in diameter. These can be kicked, batted, and tossed. Students should not be allowed to mount the ball and roll it, however, since falls in those circumstances are common.

Crab Cageball. Students are divided into four teams. Cones can be used to delineate the corners of a square. One team forms one side of the square, so a different team makes up each side. All players sit with hands behind them for support. Each team is numbered from right to left beginning with the number one. The cageball is placed in the middle of the square. The instructor or another student calls out a number and one member from each team (with the number called) crab-walks to the center and attempts to kick the cageball over the other teams. A team has a point scored against it when: (1) the ball is kicked over or through the team, (2) a team member touches the ball with the arms or hands, or (3) a player stands to block or stop the ball. The team with the fewest points is declared the winner.

Long Team Cageball. Players are divided into two teams. The teams move into sitting position in two lines facing each other 10–15 ft apart. The teacher rolls or throws a cageball between the two lines. The object is for one team to kick the ball over the other team. A point is scored against a team when the ball goes over or through a line. The team with the fewer points wins. Again, a point is awarded if a player stands or touches the ball with the hands. More than one cageball can be used simultaneously.

Cageball Football. The game is played on a large playing field. The class is divided into two teams. The object of the game is to carry the cageball across the goal line. The only way the ball can be advanced, however, is when it is in the air. Whenever the ball is on the ground, it can only be moved backwards or sideways. This game is best played with a 4-ft or larger cageball.

Cageball Target Throw. The cageball is used as a target in this game. Divide the class into two teams and place them on opposite sides of the gym. A center line divides the area in half, and teams are restricted to movement in their half. Use cones to mark the goal line near the ends of the playing area. Center the cageball between the teams. Each team is given a number of playground balls or volleyballs for throwing at the cageball. The object is to move the cageball across the opponent's goal line by hitting the cageball with the volleyballs. The cageball cannot be touched by any player. If it is touched, regardless of intent, the point goes to the other team.

Scooter Cageball Soccer. Each player is given a scooter. The ball may be advanced by using the feet only. The object is to score a goal in a fashion similar to soccer. Penalty shots are awarded for rough play, touching the ball with the hands, and leaving the scooter.

RECREATIONAL ACTIVITIES

Many recreational activities can be used as one-day units. Rules and regulations usually accompany the activities and are specific to the situation. The authors have had success with some of the following activities:

- Shuffleboard
- Deck tennis
- Tennis volleyball
- Table tennis
- Pillow polo
- Sacket
- Horseshoes
- Tetherball
- Lawn bowling
- Global ball
- Hocker
- Pickleball

Frisbee, bowling, and orienteering are three excellent recreational activities that are covered in depth in later chapters. They can also be used as short one-day activities.

RELAYS

When they are not overused, relays are enjoyable activities for students. To keep the atmosphere vibrant and the students motivated, the teams should be changed often to equalize the ability of various groups. If the same team wins every bout, the outcome is predetermined and the rest of the class will not be motivated. Another motivator is frequent changing of the relay. The relay can be run once to show students how it is to be conducted, and then one to three times for competition.

All relay teams should have the same number of persons on each squad. It is wise to change the order of the squads, so different people get a chance to run starting and finishing legs. Define the signals to start the relay, and tell students what position they must assume when finished (i.e., sitting, kneeling, or some alternative position).

Potato Relays.   Potato relays have been played for years. A small box to hold the objects (potatoes) is placed in front of each squad. Four circles (hoops can be used) are placed 10–15 ft apart in front of each squad. The goal is for the first runner to pick up an object from the box and carry it to one of the hoops, come back, pick up another object, and place it in another hoop. This is done until all the hoops are filled. The next person picks up the objects one at a time from the hoops and places them back in the box. The pattern is repeated until all members of the squad have had a turn.

Wheelbarrow Relay.   Use the wheelbarrow position described earlier in the chapter as the means of locomotion. All members of each squad must participate in both the carrying position and the down formation.

Bowling Pin Relay.   Four bowling pins per squad are used. They are evenly spaced in front of each squad in a fashion similar to the potato relay. The first person in line lays all of the pins down, and the next person stands them up. Only one hand can be used.

Over and Under Ball Relay.   Each team is spread out in open squad formation so players are 10–15 ft apart. The first person in line passes the ball backward overhead to the nearest teammate. That person throws it backward between the legs to another teammate, and the pattern repeats. When the ball gets to the end of the squad, that person runs to the front of the squad and passes the ball backward. The process is repeated until all players have had a turn at the end and front of the squad.

Stepping Stone Relay.   Two small carpet squares are used per squad. The first person in line is the mover and helps the next person in line move down and back. The only way to advance in this relay is by standing on a carpet square and moving to another. It is illegal to move or stand on the floor. The mover picks up the rear carpet square and moves it in front of the advancing player so the next step can be taken. All players must play both roles before the relay is completed.

Pass and Squat Relay.   Players are spread out so they are 10–15 ft apart. The first person in line turns around, faces the rest of the squad, and throws a volleyball or soccer ball to the first person in line, who returns the throw and squats. The leader now throws the ball to the next person until all members

have received a throw and have squatted. When the ball is thrown to the last player, that person dribbles the ball to the front of the squad and repeats the pattern.

Fetch Relay.   Squads line up and place one member at the other end of the playing area, 10–20 yd away. This person runs back to the squad and fetches the next person. The person who has just been fetched in turn runs back and fetches the next person. The pattern continues until all members have been fetched to the opposite end of the playing area.

Snowball Relay.   This relay is similar to the fetch relay, except that after one person has been fetched, both players run back and pick up another player. The pattern continues until the majority of squad members are running back and forth, picking up the remaining members. This relay can be exhausting for the first few people in line and should not be run too often.

Sport Skill Relays.   Many sport skills can be used for relays. For example, dribble the basketball down the court, make a basket, and return. The problem with relays of this type is that success is predicated on the skill level of the participants. If some students are less skilled in basketball, the relay can be a source of embarrassment, causing these students to bear the brunt of losing the relay. An instructor who uses sport skill relays is wise to include a wide variety of skills and to develop many different types of relays.

Spread Eagle Relay.   Break the class into groups of 8–10 students. They lie down on the floor and form a circle with their heads toward the center. They join hands and spread the legs (Figure 19.14). Participants in each squad are numbered, beginning with one through the number of squad members. When a number is called, that person stands up, runs around the circle, and then resumes the prone position on the floor. The runner must place both

FIGURE 19.14   Spread eagle relay

feet between each pair of legs. The first person to return to the starting position earns a point for that squad. The squad with the most points wins.

COOPERATIVE ACTIVITIES

Cooperative activities require students to work together. They can be used early in the year as mixers in an attempt to help students get to know one another. Emphasis is on enjoyment and accomplishment.

Group Games

Mass Stand Up. Start with two people sitting back to back. Lock elbows and try to stand up. Increase the number to three people, then four, and so forth. See how many people can stand up simultaneously.

Butt Tug. Stand in two lines back to back. One line moves to the left one step. Bend over, cross the arms between the legs, and grasp the hand of two different people from the other team. Now begin tugging. Try forming two teams in the described position and have a race while maintaining the hand grips.

Circle Sit. Have students form a circle and hold hands. Close the circle so shoulders are touching. Move the right side of the body toward the center of the circle and move inward, eliminating gaps. Now sit on the knees of the person behind. Try walking in this position when everyone has assumed the sitting position. Put the left side toward the center and sit on a new partner's lap.

Animal Sounds. Students all close their eyes. Someone is designated to move throughout the group and assign animal names to the players. The number of animals assigned will determine the number of groups formed. This is a useful way to organize groups. When the command is given, the only noises that can be made are those that resemble the animals. Students must keep their eyes closed and move throughout the area in search of another person who has been assigned the same animal. For example, people assigned to be cows search for their counterparts by making a mooing sound and listening for others mooing.

Entanglement. Divide the class into two or more groups. Each group makes a tight circle with their arms pointing toward the middle. In each group, students hold someone's hand until everybody is holding hands. Each person must hold a hand of two different people. On signal, the two groups race to see which can untangle first without disjoining hands. The group may end up in either one large circle or in two smaller, connecting circles. People can be facing different directions when finished.

Bulldozer. Students lie in prone position side by side and as close as possible on the floor. The end person rolls on top of the next person and on down the line of people. When that person gets to the end of the line, the next person starts the roll. Two teams can be formed and a relay race conducted.

Zipper. Players make a single-file line. Each student bends over, reaches between the legs with the left hand, and grasps the right hand of the person to the rear. This continues on down the line until all hands are grasped. On signal, the last person in line lies down, the next person backs over the last person and lies down, and so forth until the last person lies down, and then immediately stands and reverses the procedure. The first team to zip and unzip the zipper is declared the winner.

Addition Tag. Two are selected to be "it." They must hold hands and can tag only with their outside hands. When they tag someone, that person must hook on. This continues and the tagging line becomes longer and longer. Regardless of the length of the line, only the hand on each end of the line is eligible to tag.

SUGGESTED READINGS

Darst, P., and Armstrong, G. 1980. *Outdoor Adventure Activities for School and Recreation Programs.* Minneapolis, MN: Burgess Publishing Co.

Fluegelman, A., ed. 1976. *The New Games Book.* Garden City, NY: Doubleday and Co.

Orlick, T. 1982. *Cooperative Sports and Games Book.* New York: Pantheon Books.

Rohnke, K. 1977. *Cowstails and Cobras.* Hamilton, MA: Project Adventure.

Simpson, B. 1974. *Initiative Games.* Butler, PA: Encounter Four, Butler County Community College.

20 TEAM SPORTS

The goal of Chapters 20–23 is to offer beginning level units in a wide variety of instructional activities. An environment that is safe, success-oriented, and challenging for students is a desired outcome of the units. Rating scales, performance objectives for contracts, station work ideas, block plans, crossword puzzles, and rainy day activities are some of the ideas presented in this section. It is important that teachers try new ideas as they strive to improve the instructional process. A variety of learning activities helps motivate both students and teachers.

The various units should be used by teachers as a framework for developing their instructional units. These units are not all inclusive, but starting points that stimulate and encourage a wide range of instructional approaches. The ideas can be adapted and shaped into a unit that is unique to each teacher and meets the particular needs of students in different areas. This allows the teacher to retain control in planning and developing instructional sequences.

Lead-up activities and skills are presented in detail for unit subjects about which a dearth of resource materials exists. Some units are highly complex and demand in-depth, specialized instruction. In these cases, we have not attempted to cover the area, but rather offer resources that seem particularly effective and comprehensive. For this reason, the reader will note that outside resources are listed for the areas of gymnastics, track and field, aquatics, and rhythms. It would be somewhat presumptuous to assume that one could put all of the necessary instructional elements in a text of this nature, when others have written complete books about the various subjects.

BASKETBALL

Basketball is a popular game played on schoolyards by many participants. It was invented in 1891 at Springfield College by Dr. Naismith, who used peach baskets and a soccer ball. The game offers reinforcement to participants when a basket is made, and is one of the few team sports requiring skills that can be practiced individually. The game demands great cardiorespiratory endurance and fine motor development.

Basketball instruction should focus on developing skills and competence so students leave school with the ability to participate in recreational games later in life. At the junior high school level, emphasis should be on lead-up games that allow all students to find success and enjoyment. As students develop the skills necessary to play the game well, instruction during the high school years can concentrate on strategy and teamwork. Highly skilled and interested students should be offered additional opportunities to play through intramural programs, recreational leagues, or interscholastic competition.

Sequence of Skills

One of the attractive components of basketball is that little equipment is necessary for participation. Students should be required to wear a gym shoe made for the activity. Running shoes are a poor substitute for basketball shoes because they often leave black marks on the floor, do not offer adequate support, and wear out quickly.

The following skills are basic to the game of basketball. Students never learn these skills to perfection, so offer time for regular practice. For example, players can always make a better pass, develop more efficient dribbling skills, or shoot a higher percentage of baskets.

Passing

Regardless of the pass used, certain points should be emphasized. The ball should be handled with the fingertips. As the ball makes contact with the hands, the elbows should bend and the hands move toward the body in order to "give" with the ball and absorb the force. The passer should step forward in the direction of the receiver. The ball is released with a quick straightening of the elbows and a snap of the wrists. The arms and fingers are fully extended with the palms turned outward for the follow-through after the ball has been released. Passers should anticipate where their teammate is going to be when the ball reaches the receiver. Many of the passing drills should therefore focus on passing while moving.

Chest Pass.   The chest pass is used frequently in basketball for passes up to 20 ft. The ball is held at chest level with the fingers spread on both sides of the ball. One foot is ahead of the other in stride position. The elbows remain close to the body, and the ball is propelled by extending the arms, snapping the wrists, and stepping toward the target (Figure 20.1).

Bounce Pass.   The bounce pass is used to transfer the ball to a closely guarded teammate. It is directed to a spot on the floor that is closer to the receiver than the passer. The ball should rebound to waist level of the receiver. Passing form is similar to the chest pass.

Flip Pass.   This pass is used for a close-range exchange. The ball is flipped somewhat upward to a teammate. It is used often as a pass to a player cutting to the basket for a lay-up shot.

Two-Handed Overhead Pass.   This pass is used against a shorter opponent, usually in back court. The passer is in a short stride position with the ball held overhead. The momentum of the pass comes

FIGURE 20.2   Dribbling under control

from a forceful wrist and finger snap. The upper arms remain relatively in place.

Catching

For effective catching, it is important to keep the eyes on the ball, follow the ball into the hands, and concentrate on the catch before beginning the next task. The receiver should move toward the ball and reach for it with the fingers spread. When the pass is at waist level or above, the thumbs should be pointed in and the fingers up. When the ball is to be caught below waist level, the thumbs are out and the fingers down. The hands should "give" and move toward the body to absorb the force of the throw and thus make the ball more catchable.

Dribbling

Dribbling requires bent knees and crouching. The forearm of the dribbling hand is parallel to the floor, and the ball should be pushed toward the roll, rather than slapped. The ball is controlled with the fingertips. Most of the force supplied to the ball should be from the wrist, so arm movement is minimized. Emphasis should be placed on controlling the ball (Figure 20.2).

FIGURE 20.1   Throwing a chest pass

Shooting

Certain points are common to all shooting. The body should be squared up with the basket whenever possible. The ball is held with the fingers spread, and the elbow of the shooting hand should always be directly behind the ball. The eyes are fixed on the rim, and the ball is shot with a slight backspin on it. The arm is extended on follow-through with the wrist flexed.

Lay-Up Shots

For a right-handed lay-up, the player approaches the basket from the right side at an angle of about 45 degrees. The ball is released with the right hand and the weight on the left foot. As the body is elevated off the floor by the left foot, the ball is released 12–18 in. above the basket on the backboard. For a left-handed shot, the sequence is the opposite. The shooter should always reach toward the spot on the backboard with the shooting hand, and students should practice shooting with each hand.

FIGURE 20.3   One hand set shot

One-Hand Push Shots.

The push shot is used primarily for shooting free throws (Figure 20.3). Few people shoot a one-hand shot from a set position. The ball is held at shoulder level in the nonshooting hand. The shooting hand is behind the ball, the fingertips touching the ball, and the wrist is cocked. The legs are shoulder width apart and the knees slightly bent. To shoot, straighten the legs and push forward with the forearm and wrist. The wrist should be bent over on follow-through and the arm straight.

Jump Shots

The jump shot is the most popular shot in basketball because it is difficult to block. The hands are in the same position as described for the one-hand push shot. After the shooter jumps, the ball is placed just above and in front of the head. The elbow must be kept under the ball so the shooting hand moves in a straight line toward the basket. The wrist snaps on release. The shot should be performed using a jump in an upward plane. Leaning forward, sideways, or backward will make the shot much less consistent. The jump shot is sometimes difficult for junior high school students. They often learn the wrong motor pattern of throwing the ball instead of shooting it. If this is the case, use a smaller ball, a lower basket, or both to develop the correct pattern.

Ideas for Effective Instruction

Drills used in basketball should simulate game conditions as closely as possible. There are few situations in basketball where players are standing still. Passing drills should therefore include player movement, shooting drills should require movement and pressure, and drills for dribbling under control should include looking away from the ball.

Baskets can be lowered to 8.5–9 ft to increase the amount of success. This will also help develop better shooting patterns in the weaker, smaller players. Note that almost all students will select the lower basket when they have a choice of a basket at regulation height and another, lowered basket. Most people are motivated by being able to dunk the shot and thus shoot a higher percentage.

The program should concentrate on skill development and include many drills. Basketball offers endless drill possibilities, and using many drills gives variety and breadth to the instructional program. The drills should offer each student as much practice as possible in a stipulated amount of time. Lining up a squad of eight players to take turns makes little sense. Use as many balls as possible. In some cases, students may be willing to bring one from home for class use. More baskets and balls mean that more students will have an opportunity to practice and learn skills.

There are many basketball drills to enhance passing, dribbling, and shooting, but the lead-up games that follow in the next section encourage skill practice while introducing competition and game play. When possible, therefore, isolate skills and practice them in lead-up games to maintain a high level of student motivation.

Lead-Up Games and Learning Activities

Keepaway

The essence of the game is to make as many consecutive passes as possible without losing control to the opposite team. Teams may consist of 5–10 players. Use pinnies so players can identify their teammates. The game is started with a jump ball, and the goal is to maintain control. Each defensive player must stay with a designated opponent, rather than the defensive team swarming in a zone defense. As soon as possession is lost, counting of passes is started by that team. The team that makes the most consecutive passes within a designated time is the winner.

Five Passes

This game is similar to keepaway, but the object is to make five consecutive passes. As soon as these have been made, the ball is turned over to the other team. Students are not allowed to travel with the ball. Two or three dribbles may be allowed between passes. Players may hold the ball for only 3 sec.

Dribble Tag

Divide the playing area into two equal parts. All players begin dribbling in one half of the area. The object of this game is to maintain a continuous dribble while avoiding being tagged by another player. If tagged or if control of the ball is lost, the player must move to the other half of the playing area and practice dribbling without the pressure of competition.

Dribble Keepaway

The area is divided into two equal parts. All players start in one half of the area and begin dribbling. The goal is to maintain control of the dribble while trying to disrupt the dribble of an opponent. If control of the ball is lost, the player moves to the other side of the area and practices.

Around the World

Shooting spots are marked on the floor with tape (Figure 20.4). Players are in groups of three. A player begins at the first spot and continues until a shot misses. The player can then wait for another turn or take a second "risk" shot. If the risk shot is made, the player continues "around the world." If the shot is missed, the player must start over on the next turn. The winner is the player who goes around the world first. A variation is to count the number of shots that players take to move around the world. The person who makes the circuit with the fewest shots is the winner.

Twenty-One

Players are in groups of three or four. Each player receives a long shot (distance must be designated) and a follow-up shot. The long shot, if made, counts two points, and the follow-up shot one point. The follow-up shot must be taken from the spot where the ball was recovered. The first player to score twenty-one points is the winner. A variation is to play team twenty-one in which the first team of players to score twenty-one is declared the winner.

Horse

Players work in groups of 2–4 and shoot in a predetermined order. The first player shoots from any place on the court. If the shot is made, the next player must make the same type of shot from the same position. If the shot is missed by the next player, that player receives an "H", and the following player can shoot any shot desired. No penalty is assigned for a missed shot unless the previous player has made a shot. A player is disqualified if the letters

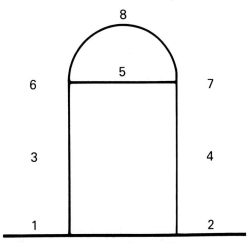

FIGURE 20.4   Around the world

spelling HORSE are accumulated. The winner is the last remaining player.

Sideline Basketball

The class is divided into two teams, each lined up along one side of the court, facing the other. The game is played by three or four active players from each team. The remainder of the players standing on the sideline can catch and pass the ball to the active players, but they may not shoot or enter the playing floor. They must keep one foot completely out of bounds at all times.

Active players play regular basketball with one variation, they may pass and receive the ball from sideline players. The game starts with the active players occupying their own half of the court. The ball is taken out-of-bounds under its own basket by the team that was scored upon. Play continues until one team scores or until a period of time (2 or 3 min) elapses. The active players then take places on the left side of their line, and three new active players come out from the right. All other players move down three places in the line.

No official out-of-bounds on the sides is called. The players on that side of the floor simply recover the ball and put it into play without delay by a pass to an active player. Out-of-bounds on the ends is the same as in regular basketball. If one of the sideline players enters the court and touches the ball, it is a violation, and the ball is awarded out-of-bounds on the other side to a sideline player. Free throws are awarded when a player is fouled. Sideline players may pass to each other and should be well spaced along the side.

Half Court Basketball

Teams of two to four work best for this variation. The game is similar to regulation basketball with the following exceptions: When a defensive player recovers the ball, either from a rebound or an interception, the ball must be taken back to midcourt before offensive play can begin. After a basket is made, the ball must again be taken to midcourt. For out-of-bounds and ball-handling violations, the ball is awarded to the opponents out-of-bounds at a spot near the place where the violation occurred. The ball, in this case, does not have to be taken to midcourt. If a foul occurs, the ball is given to the offended team, or regulation foul shooting can be done.

Three on Three

There are many lead-up games in which the number of players on a team varies. The advantage of playing half court basketball with only two or three players on a team is that each player gets to handle the ball more. Regulation rules are followed.

Three on three can be played with four or five teams. An offensive team of three stands forward of the midcourt line while another team is on defense. The other teams wait behind midcourt for their turn. A scrimmage is over when one team scores. The defensive team then goes on offense, and a new team comes in to play defense. The old offensive team goes to the rear of the line of waiting players. The game can be varied so that the winning team stays on after a basket is scored. Caution must be used with the winner-stay-on approach as it sometimes means that the better players get much more practice than the less skilled performers. Make the teams as equal as possible so all have a chance to win.

Suggested Performance Objectives

The following are examples of performance objectives that might be used in a beginning basketball class. The standards may have to be adjusted, depending on the skill level and age of the students.

Core Requirements

Dribbling Tasks

1. In a stationary position, execute a right-hand dribble 10 consecutive times (1 point).
2. Same as task 1 except use the left hand (1 point).
3. Using a reduced speed, dribble the ball with the right hand from the baseline to the midcourt line without losing control (1 point).
4. Using a reduced speed, dribble the ball with the left hand from the midcourt line to the baseline without losing the dribble (1 point).

Passing Tasks

5. Standing 10 ft away from the target on the wall, throw 10 consecutive two-hand chest passes (1 point).
6. Standing 10 ft away from a partner, execute 8 of 10 consecutive two-hand passes (1 point).
7. Standing 10 ft away from the target, throw 10 consecutive two-hand bounce passes (1 point).
8. Standing 10 ft away from a partner, execute 8 of 10 consecutive bounce passes (1 point).
9. Standing 10 ft away from the target, throw 10 consecutive two-hand overhead passes (1 point).
10. Standing 10 ft away from a partner, execute 8 of 10 consecutive two-hand overhead passes.

Shooting Tasks

11. Starting from the right side about 20 ft from the basket, dribble the ball toward the basket and make 4 of 6 lay-ups using the backboard (1 point).
12. Same as task 11, but start from the left side (1 point).
13. Standing 6 ft from the basket (right side), make 4 of 6 bank shots (1 point).
14. Same as task 13, but use the left side (1 point).
15. Standing at the free-throw line, make 5 of 10 consecutive set shots (1 point).
16. Standing 10 ft from the basket, make 5 of 10 jump shots (1 point).

Rebounding Tasks

17. Standing with the feet shoulder width apart and with both hands at shoulder level, jump up and touch the target on the wall 3 consecutive times using both hands (1 point).
18. Standing 2–3 ft away from the basket, toss the ball off the right side of the backboard and rebound with both hands 5 consecutive times (1 point).
19. Same as task 18, but use the left side (1 point).
20. Standing 2–3 ft from the basket, toss the ball off the right side of the backboard, rebound using both hands, and pivot right using the overhead pass or chest pass to a partner. Repeat 5 consecutive times (1 point).
21. Same as task 20, but use the left side and pivot left (1 point).

Optional Requirements

1. Officiate at least one regulation game during class time, using correct calls and signals (1 point).
2. Write a one-page report on the game of basketball (3 points).
3. Make a list of 15 basketball terms and define them (3 points).
4. Write a one-page report on Coach Wooden's book, *They Call Me Coach* (3 points).
5. Perform a figure-eight ball-handling technique by weaving the ball around one leg and then around the other leg—forming a figure eight—successfully for 10 sec (2 points).
6. Make 8 of 10 bank shots from anywhere outside the foul lane (2 points).
7. Make 9 of 10 free throws (2 points).

Grading Structure

A = 35 points; B = 28 points; C = 20 points

Rainy Day Activities

The test in Figure 20.5 might be a useful rainy day activity. It can give rise to discussions of rules and rule interpretations.

Suggested Readings

AAHPERD. 1966. *Basketball Skills Test Manual for Girls.* Reston, VA: AAHPERD.
AAHPERD. 1966. *Basketball Skills Test Manual for Boys.* Reston, VA: AAHPERD.
Barnes, M. 1973. *Women's Basketball.* Boston, MA: Allyn and Bacon, Inc.
Ebert, F., and Cheatum, B. 1977. *Basketball.* Philadelphia, PA: W. B. Saunders Co.
Lindeburg, F. A. 1967. *How to Play and Teach Basketball.* 2nd ed. New York: Association Press.
Moore, B., and White, J. 1980. *Basketball: Theory and Practice.* Dubuque, IA: Wm. C. Brown Group.
Richards, J. 1971. *Treasury of Basketball Drills from Top Coaches.* West Nyack, NY: Parker Publishing Co.
Wooden, J. 1966. *Practical Modern Basketball.* New York: Ronald Press Co.

QUIZ 1. RULES AND TERMINOLOGY

True or False. Place a **T** or **F** to the left of the statement, depending on whether the statement is true or false.

_____ 1. The key is the area that separates the midcourt from the back court.

_____ 2. The outside roll is a maneuver used by a defensive player who is guarding the player with the ball.

_____ 3. When performing the jump shot correctly, the shooting elbow should be away from the body in order to give greater accuracy to the shot.

_____ 4. The 3-sec line is contained within the key.

FIGURE 20.5 Basketball rules quiz

_____ 5. It is permissible to drag the pivot foot a short distance, as long as that foot maintains contact with the floor.

_____ 6. A feint is a deceptive motion in one direction when a player desires to move in another direction.

_____ 7. A dribbler must keep the eyes locked on the ball while dribbling in order to maintain control.

_____ 8. It is a violation for a defensive player to remain in the 3-sec lane for longer than 3 sec.

_____ 9. In most instances, the cardinal rule for a defensive player is to stay between the offensive player and the basket.

_____ 10. A player should jump off the right foot when shooting a right-handed lay-up.

Multiple Choice. Circle the correct answer.

11. The main idea in the game of basketball is to:
    a. Keep the ball as long as possible
    b. Score more points than the other team
    c. Receive fewer team violations

12. A good way to learn the game of basketball is by learning the easier skills first, then moving on to learn more difficult skills, and finally using all of the skills in a game situation. This way of learning is called:
    a. Progression
    b. Regression
    c. Retrogression

13. A basketball player can become better by:
    a. Practicing the correct way to dribble, shoot, and pass
    b. Reading books written by experts and viewing films
    c. Both a and b

14. Basketball is played best when all members of the team cooperate with and help one another. This cooperation and helping is sometimes called:
    a. Intramurals
    b. Teamwork
    c. Progression

15. Before playing in a regular basketball game, a player should:
    a. Know the exact size of the playing area
    b. Learn the basic skills of the game
    c. Be able to jump up and touch the rim

16. The penalty for most violations is loss of the ball or the other team's receiving the ball out-of-bounds near the place of the violation. Some violations that incur loss of the ball as a penalty are:
    a. Blocking, tripping, pushing, or charging
    b. Screening, fast breaking, rebounding, or weaving
    c. Traveling, double dribble, or kicking the ball

17. In most cases, the penalty for a personal foul is awarding the fouled player either one or two free throws. Personal fouls include:
    a. Striking the ball with the fist, or holding the ball for more than 5 sec when closely guarded

FIGURE 20.5 Continued

>   b. Holding, tripping, pushing, or charging
>   c. Both a and b
>
> 18. Points are scored at a rate of:
>   a. 1 point for field goal, 2 points for free throw
>   b. 2 points for field goal, 1 point for free throw
>   c. 2 points for field goal, 2 points for free throw
>
> 19. A jump ball is called when:
>   a. Two players have one or both hands firmly on the ball and neither can gain possession without undue roughness
>   b. A player holds the ball for more than 5 sec when closely guarded
>   c. Both a and b occur
>
> 20. Technical fouls include:
>   a. Tripping, pushing, hacking, or charging
>   b. Traveling, double dribble, goal tending, or failure to observe the 3-sec rule
>   c. Too many time outs, delay of game, or unsportsmanlike conduct

FIGURE 20.5   Continued

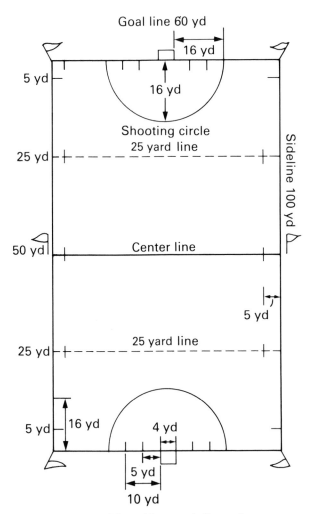

FIGURE 20.6   Field markings and dimensions

FIELD HOCKEY

Field hockey is a popular team sport that has been played predominately by girls in the United States. Many clubs across the country are affiliated with the United States Field Hockey Association, and offer playing experiences for participants age 18 years and older. In other countries, the game is also played by men and is a popular Olympic sport. Many high schools and colleges offer field hockey competition for girls and women.

The regulation game is played with 11 players on each team. The object of the game is to move a ball with a stick into the opponent's goal, which is 4-ft wide and 7-ft high. The game is started with a bully, or face-off, at midfield by the center forward of each team. Besides the goalkeeper, a team usually has 5 forwards, 3 halfbacks, and 2 fullbacks. The field is 60 yd by 100 yd with a 16-yd striking circle (Figure 20.6).

Hockey equipment includes the ball, sticks, shin guards, and the goalkeeper's full-length leg pads and kickers for the shoes. The ball is composed of cork and twine and is covered in leather. Sticks vary in length from 30 to 37 in. Junior high students use sticks that are 30–34 in. long, and high school students use sticks that are 35–37 in. All regulation sticks have a flat surface on one side and a rounded surface on the other. Only the flat side can be used for legal hits.

The game can be modified in several ways for secondary physical education units. The number of players and the field size can be reduced. Goals can be improvised by using boundary cones, high jump standards, or even soccer goals. A whiffle ball or a rubber or plastic ball can be used, and plastic sticks that are flat on both sides are available. A flat plastic puck is recommended for play on the gymnasium floor. Goalies should wear a face mask, chest protector, and shin guards from softball or lacrosse equipment. The game can be enjoyable for both boys and girls in a coeducational unit. Field hockey can be played indoors, outdoors, or on a cement surface.

Sequence of Skills

Grip In is the basic grip (Figure 20.7). The left hand is placed on the top of the stick as though "shaking hands." The right hand is placed 6–8 in. below the left hand. The palms of the hands will face each other in most situations. The right hand can slide up the stick for a drive shot and for a reverse stick. The lower position is used for dribbling and for most passes.

Dribbling

Dribbling is propelling the ball downfield in a controlled manner. It can be done straight down the field or zigzagging to the left and right. In straight dribbling (Figure 20.8), the arms are kept in front of the body. The flat side of the stick faces forward. Short, controlled taps on the ball are used. The ball

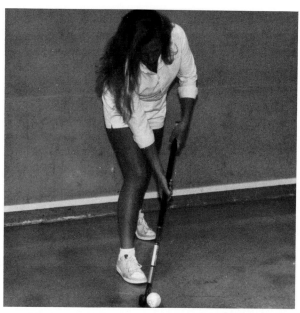

FIGURE 20.8 Straight dribble

should remain in front of the body. The zigzag dribble moves the ball left and right by using a forehand tap to the left and a reverse stick tap to the right. In the reverse stick (Figure 20.9), the stick is turned over, with the toe of the stick pointing down. This type of dribble requires a lot of practice and stick control. The taps to the left and right should be short and controlled.

Passing and Shooting

The drive shot (Figure 20.10) is the most forceful pass for longer distances and goal shots. The hands are together, and the stick comes back and forward in a manner similar to a shortened golf swing. The stick cannot be lifted higher than the shoulder in either the backswing or follow-through. Drive shots can be straight, to the left, or to the right.

The push pass (Figure 20.11) is used for shorter, more accurate passes. The shot is usually executed quickly off the dribble. There is no backswing. The right hand is lower on the stick, and the ball is pushed or swept along the ground.

The scoop is a pass similar to the push pass, but the object is to loft the ball into the air for a shot or to get over an opponent's stick. The top of the stick must be tilted backward so the blade is behind and under the ball to give it loft as the force is applied.

Fielding

Fielding refers to stopping and controlling a moving ball, and must be practiced with balls coming from the right, left, and center. The face of the stick and

FIGURE 20.7 Hand position on the stick

FIGURE 20.11   Push pass

FIGURE 20.9   Reverse stick for zigzag dribble

FIGURE 20.10   Drive shot

the body position need to be adjusted according to the direction in which the ball is traveling. The front fielding position (Figure 20.12) is similar to the straight dribbling position and is used for balls rolling straight toward a person. Balls coming from the left require a regular forehand position with the blade facing to the left. For balls coming from the right, the stick must intercept the ball before it reaches the body. The blade must be turned so that it is facing to the right (Figure 20.13). Fielding requires the ability to absorb the ball's momentum by "giving" with the stick, depending on the speed of the ball.

Tackling and Dodging

Tackling is attempting to take the ball away from an opponent. Tackles can be made straight on or from the left or the right side of an opponent. Timing is important, because the ball must be picked off while it is away from the opponent's stick. The stick is carried low, and the tackler must concentrate on the ball and on the opponent's stick. The speed of the opponent and of the ball must be considered. The tackle should not be a reckless striking of the stick.

Dodging is a skill for evading a tackler and maintaining control of the ball. A dodge can be executed to the left or right side of the tackler, and a scoop shot can also be used to go over an opponent's stick. If a dodge is made to the left, the dodger should move the ball 90 degrees to the left just before the tackle. A dodger moving around to the left is on the stick side, which is the right, of the opponent. This maneuver is a stick-side dodge. A dodge to the right

FIGURE 20.12   Front fielding position

FIGURE 20.13   Fielding from the right

involves moving the ball to the right of the opponent, but the dodger's body must move around the other side of the tackler, that is, the ball goes to the right but the person goes to the left (nonstick-side dodge). This technique is used to avoid an obstruction violation.

Bully or Face-Off

The bully (Figure 20.14) is used only when simultaneous fouls occur. Two players face each other in the middle of the field with their respective sticks facing the direction of the goal where they can score. The bully starts with each player striking the ground on her side of the ball and then touching sticks above the ball. This is repeated three times, and then players attempt to control the ball or to pass it to a teammate.

Goalkeeping

The goalkeeper can kick the ball or block the ball with the body, hands, or stick. Most balls are blocked with the legs or feet, hence the padding on these

areas. Most clears away from the goal are with a kick. The goalie cannot hold the ball or throw the ball away from the goal.

Ideas for Effective Instruction

Drills can be set up for partner work at several stations. Dribbling, passing, shooting, tackling, dodging,

FIGURE 20.14   Bully position

and goalkeeping can be specific stations with varying tasks to be practiced. Use the performance objectives detailed here for the tasks at each station. Set up boundary cones, stopwatches, targets, baskets, and other instructional devices for challenging skill work. Arrange classes so that students spend several minutes working at each of four stations. The station work can then be followed by several small group drills such as 3 on 3, keepaway, or 3-person weave. A modified or regulation game could follow the group work. This variety of learning activities helps to keep students active and motivated.

Remind students continually about the importance of safe stick handling. High-sticking is extremely dangerous and rules must be enforced tightly. A student who commits two high-sticking violations should be placed in a penalty box for 2 min. Body checking, tripping, and hooking with the stick should also be forbidden. A free shot or penalty shot can be used as a penalty for these violations. The teacher must be clear about the rules, regulations, and penalties that are going to be enforced in the game.

Lead-Up Games and Learning Activities

Three-Person Weave

The ball is started by the center person and passed to either the person on the left or right. The person making the pass always runs behind the person who receives the pass. The person receiving the pass then becomes the middle person. This procedure continues downfield.

Partner Passing

Partners stand apart and try to hit as many passes as possible in 30 sec. Each hit is counted. As variations, try the same activity with three people in a triangle, four in a square, or five in a circle.

Circle Keepaway

Students form a circle with one person in the middle. The people in the circle try to keep the ball away from the center person. This can also be played with only three people. The person in the middle is rotated after 1 min.

Circle Dribble

A student dribbles the ball around the circle as fast as possible, concluding the dribble at the next person in the circle. All members of the circle go around quickly. Circles compete against each other or against the clock.

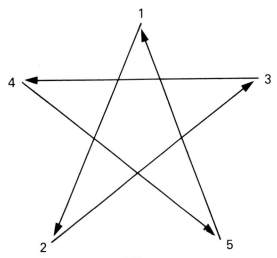

FIGURE 20.15   Star drill

Star Drill

Five classmates make a star formation (Figure 20.15). Number one passes to two, and two to three, and so forth. After passing the ball, the passer runs and takes that person's spot. The passer always follows the pass, and more than one person can be in line. The game can also be played against another team or against the clock.

Dribble and Hit for Distance

Half of the class or group lines up 5 yd behind a drive line. A partner is downfield about 50 yd. On signal, the hitters dribble the 5 yd and hit a drive shot as far as possible. The partner stands over the ball, and a winner is determined. Partners change places after several hits.

No Goalie Field Hockey

The game is played without a goalie. Person-to-person defense can be used. The goal size can also be modified if necessary.

End Zone Hockey

The entire end line of the field is the goal area. Each team designates a certain number of goalies and field players. The goalies must spread out over the entire goal line in order to cover it properly. Goalies and field players change places after a specified number of minutes.

Sideline Hockey

Part of each team lines up on one sideline, while the rest of each team is on the field. The sideline players keep the ball from going out-of-bounds, and they can also pass to the field players. A regulation goal and goalie are used in the game. The sideline and field players switch after 3 min of play. This game can be varied by putting members of each team on both sidelines, thus adding another challenge to the game.

Square Hockey

The game is played on a large square. Each team defends two sides of the square. Some team members are on the square sides as goalies, and others are on the field trying to hit the ball past either of the two end lines. At the start of the game, the teacher can have all students stand on the square and count off. Several numbers can then be called, and those students become the field players.

Half-Circle Hockey

This is similar to square hockey, but each team forms one half of a circle. The half circles connect, and the object is to hit the ball through the opponent's half circle. If the ball comes to rest inside the circle, it belongs to the team nearer the ball. That team can take a shot from the point where the ball stopped.

Modified Coed Field Hockey

This modified game is recommended for coeducational physical education classes. The rules and penalties are as follows:

1. A bully is used to start the game and after each goal.
2. A roll-in is used when the ball goes out-of-bounds.
3. A short corner shot is awarded to the offense when the ball goes past the end line within the striking circle last touching off a defender.
4. A long corner shot is awarded to the offense when the ball goes past the end line outside the striking circle last touching off a defender.
5. A defensive hit is awarded to the defensive team when the ball goes over the end line off an offensive player.
6. The striking circle is the 16-yd half circle around the goal. A free shot is awarded for a foul occurring anywhere outside the striking circle. All players must be 5 yd away.
7. A penalty shot taken from the top of the striking circle is awarded for a defensive foul inside the striking circle.
8. Off sides occurs when an offensive player enters the striking circle before the ball. A defensive hit is awarded at the top of the circle.
9. High-sticking occurs when the stick is raised above the shoulder. The penalty is a free shot or penalty shot and a 2-min time out.
10. Advancing is when a player uses the feet to advance the ball. The penalty is a free shot or a penalty shot.
11. Backing up is when a player uses the feet to stop the ball. The penalty is a free shot or a penalty shot.
12. Hooking, tripping, or dangerous stick use involves using the stick to slow down or trip an opponent. The penalty is a free shot or penalty shot and a 2-min time out.
13. Body checking is vigorous use of the body for blocking and other maneuvers. The penalty is a free shot or penalty shot and a 2-min time out.

Suggested Performance Objectives

These performance objectives can be used to structure the learning activities for station work. They can also be tied to a motivational scheme for earning grades or entry into a playing situation. Teachers might develop a contract from these objectives, which can be modified according to the ability levels of the students in a specific situation. If the objectives are too hard or too easy, they should be rewritten to provide a fair challenge and a successful experience for students.

1. Dribble the ball for 30 yd, 3 consecutive times, using proper technique at all times (straight dribble).
2. Dribble the ball through an obstacle course and back in 30 sec or less (straight dribble).
3. Dribble the ball toward a target and execute a nonstick dodge in 3 of 5 attempts without losing control.
4. Dribble the ball toward a target and execute a stick-side dodge around the target in 3 of 5 attempts without losing control.
5. With a partner, push-pass the ball back and forth (jogging speed) for 30 yd, 2 consecutive times.
6. Push-pass the ball to a target 3 of 5 times from a distance of 10 yd.
7. Shoot 3 of 5 drive shots into the goal from 10 yd (no goalie).
8. Scoop the ball over an obstacle into a basket 3 consecutive times from within a stick-length distance.
9. Dribble the ball from the center of the field toward the goal, and hit 3 drive shots 3 consecutive times without a goalie.
10. Execute proper fielding of the ball from the front, right, and left side, passed by a partner from 10 to 15 yd away (5 times from each side).

11. Dribble the ball for 30 yd, 3 consecutive times, using proper technique at all times (zigzag dribble).
12. Dribble the ball through an obstacle course and back in 30 sec or less (zigzag dribble).
13. Dribble the ball toward a goal and score 2 of 5 drive shots past a goalie from 10 yd.
14. Execute a three-person weave passing drill from a distance of 15–30 yd, 2 consecutive times.
15. Hit 2 of 5 penalty shots past a goalie.
16. Execute a proper tackle from the left, right, and center.
17. Scoop and run with the ball for 25 yd.
18. Dribble 5 yd, then execute a scoop shot. Repeat 5 consecutive times.

Rainy Day Activities

Many of the drills and modified games can be played indoors with a flat plastic-type puck. Teachers can set up station activities for working on performance tasks. Modified games, such as sideline hockey, end zone hockey, and square hockey, can be played indoors with large numbers of students. Strategies, terminology, and penalties can be discussed at indoor sessions.

Suggested Readings

Barnes, M., and Kentwell, R. 1979. *Field Hockey: The Coach and the Player.* 2nd ed. Boston, MA: Allyn and Bacon, Inc.

Fong, D. 1983. *The Coach's Collection of Field Hockey Drills.* West Point, NY: Leisure Press.

Gros, V. 1979. *Inside Field Hockey.* Chicago, IL: Contemporary Books.

Mood, D., Musker, F., and Armbruster, D. 1983. *Sports and Recreational Activities for Men and Women.* 8th ed. St. Louis, MO: C. V. Mosby Co.

National Association for Girls and Women in Sport. 1980. *Field Hockey-Lacrosse Guide.* Reston, VA: AAHPERD,

United States Field Hockey Association. 1979. *The Official Manual of the United States Field Hockey Association.* North Chill, NY.

FLAG FOOTBALL

Football is America's favorite spectator sport. Professional football players are held in high esteem by students. The shape of the football makes throwing and catching more difficult and challenging than similar maneuvers in other sports. Flag and touch football are variations of the game of football, modified so the game can be played without the padding and equipment necessary for tackle football. Flag football is usually the more enjoyable, because it eliminates the arguments about whether someone was touched or not.

Sequence of Skills

Passing

Passing is used to advance the ball downfield to a teammate. The passer looks at the receiver and points the shoulder opposite the throwing arm toward the receiver. The ball is brought up to the throwing shoulder with both hands. The fingers of the throwing hand are placed across the laces of the ball. The weight is transferred to the rear leg in preparation for the throw (Figure 20.16). On throwing, the weight is transferred forward, and a step is taken with the front foot in the direction of the receiver. The throwing arm is extended and the wrist flicked upon release of the ball. The longer the throw

FIGURE 20.16 Preparing to pass

to be made, the higher the angle of release needs to be.

Lateral Pass

Lateral passing is pitching the ball underhand to a teammate. The ball must be tossed sideways or backwards to be a legal lateral that can then be passed again. There is no attempt to make the ball spiral as it does in a pass.

Catching

Since the football is a large and heavy object and can be thrown with great velocity, the catcher must "give" and bring the ball in toward the body (Figures 20.17 and 20.18). In a stationary position, the catcher faces the thrower and plants the feet about shoulder width apart. To catch a ball on the run, the catcher observes the ball by looking over the shoulder. The fingers should be spread and the arms extended to meet the ball. This allows giving with the ball and bringing the ball in toward the body in an attempt to absorb the force of the throw. Students should develop the habit of tucking the ball in close to the body after each catch.

Carrying the Ball

The ball is carried with the arm on the outside and the end of the ball tucked into the notch formed by the elbow and arm. The fingers cradle the forward part of the ball.

Centering

The center moves into position with the feet well spread and the toes pointed straight ahead. The knees are bent in preparation for forward movement. The dominant hand reaches forward slightly and is placed across the laces. The other hand is on the side near the back and guides the ball. The head is between the legs; the center's eyes are on the receiver. The arms are extended, and the ball is propelled by pulling both arms backward and upward. The ball should spiral on its way to the quarterback.

When centering in T formation, only one hand is used. The quarterback places the throwing hand in the crotch of the center and the other hand below with the hands touching at the base of the palms. The ball is given a one-quarter turn as it is centered and placed sideways in the quarterback's hands.

FIGURE 20.17 Catching the ball—thumbs up

FIGURE 20.18 Catching the ball—thumbs down

FIGURE 20.19 Three-point stance

Stance

The two-point stance is used by ends and backs so they can see downfield. The feet are spread shoulder width and the knees are bent slightly. The hands can be placed just above the knees.

The three-point stance (Figure 20.19) is used as a down position in order to move quickly forward or sideways. The feet are spread shoulder width apart with the toes pointing straight ahead. The player leans forward and places the desired hand on the ground while keeping the back parallel to the playing surface. The weight is on the balls of the feet; the head is up. Little weight is placed on the down hand.

The four-point stance is used to move forward quickly. Lateral movement is sacrificed with this stance. It is similar to the three-point stance, but both hands are on the ground and more weight is placed on the hands.

Blocking

The purpose of blocking is to prevent the defensive player from getting the flag of the ball carrier. It is accomplished by keeping the body between the defensive player and the ball carrier. Knocking the defensive player down is not necessary to accomplish a successful block.

Shoulder Block. The shoulder block starts from a three- or four-point stance. The blocker moves forward and makes shoulder contact at chest level of the opponent. The head should be placed between the opponent and the ball carrier in order to move the defensive player away from the ball carrier. The elbows are out and the hands are held near the chest.

Pass Block. The pass block is used when the quarterback is dropping back to throw a pass. The block

can begin from any of the described stances. The blocker moves slightly backward with the rear foot as the opponent charges. The blocker should attempt to stay between the quarterback and the rusher.

Exchanging the Ball

The hand-off is made with the inside hand (nearest the receiver). The ball is held with both hands until the ball carrier is about 6 ft away. It is then shifted to the hand nearer the receiver, with the elbow bent partially away from the body. The receiver comes toward the quarterback with the near arm bent and carried in front of the chest, the palm down. The other arm is carried about waist high, with the palm up. As the ball is exchanged, the receiver clamps down on the ball to secure it.

Punting

The punter starts in standing position with both arms fully extended to receive the ball. The kicking foot is placed slightly forward. After receiving the ball, the kicker takes two steps forward, beginning with the dominant foot. The ball is slightly turned in and held at waist height. The kicking leg is swung forward, and at impact the knee is straightened to provide maximum force. The toes are pointed and the long axis of the ball makes contact on the top of the instep. The ball should be dropped rather than tossed into the air. The drop needs to be mastered before effective punting can occur.

Ideas for Effective Instruction

Since many drills are available for flag football, the authors have devoted this section to delineating the rules and equipment necessary for it. Most of the prerequisites for developing a sound flag football program are listed and discussed.

Uniforms

Rubber-soled shoes should be worn. Metal cleats or spikes are not allowed, nor is any hard surface padding or helmets.

Flags

Flags are available in two colors for team play. All flags should be similar in terms of pulling the flags loose from players. The flag belts have two flags attached, one at each hip. Either flag pulled downs the ball carrier.

Downed Ball

To down a ball carrier, either flag must be withdrawn from the waist by a tackler. The tackler must stop at the point of tackle and hold up the hand with the withdrawn flag. It is illegal for ball carriers to deliberately touch their own flags or to defend them in any manner. Penalty: 15 yards from the point of the foul and loss of a down.

Dead Ball

The ball is ruled dead on a fumble when it hits the ground, or on a wild center when it hits the ground. When a fumble rolls out-of-bounds, the ball is returned to the team that had last full possession of it.

Loss of Flags

If the flag is inadvertently lost, the player is ineligible to handle the ball. The ball then becomes dead if the player is behind the line of scrimmage, or the pass is called incomplete. It is illegal for a player to deliberately withdraw an opponent's flag unless that opponent is in possession of the ball. Such conduct is penalized as unsportsmanlike. Penalty: 15 yards.

Charging and Tackling

The ball carrier may not run through a defensive player, but must attempt to evade the tackler. The tackler must not hold, push, or run through the ball carrier, but must play the flag rather than the person. The officials decide these judgment calls. Penalty: 15 yards and loss of a down offensively, and 15 yards defensively.

Tackling

Tackling is not permitted. The ball is declared dead when defensive play pulls one of the runner's flags. Action against the runner, other than pulling the flag, is unnecessary roughness. Penalty: 15 yards from the point of the foul and loss of a down offensively, and 15 yards from the point of the foul defensively.

Hacking

It is a foul for the ball carrier to hack, push, or straight-arm another player. Penalty: 15 yards from the point of the foul and loss of a down.

Blocking

Line blocking is the same as regulation football. In open-field (out-of-the-line) line blocking, no part of the blocker's body, except the feet, shall be in contact with the ground during the block. Blocking is a type of body checking with the blocker in an upright position and without the use of hands or extended arms. Any rough tactics, such as attempting to run over or batter down an opponent, must be penalized as unnecessary roughness. Unnecessary

Station 1: Passing—Out and In Pattern

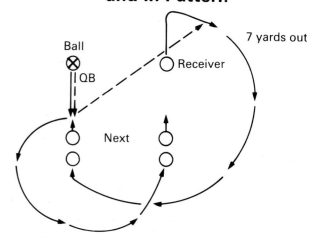

Out pattern: Quarterback takes 5-yd drop, passes ball to receiver at 7 yd.
Rotate in direction of arrows.
Change pattern after all have completed.

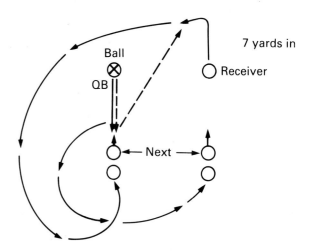

In pattern: Quarterback takes 5-yd drop, passes ball to receiver at 7 yd.
Rotate in direction of arrows.

FIGURE 20.20 Passing

roughness may be declared if the blocker uses knees or elbows in blocking. Penalty: 15 yards and loss of a down offensively, and 15 yards and first down defensively.

Passing

A forward pass may be thrown from any point behind the line of scrimmage. The passer is declared down if a flag is withdrawn by a defensive player, or if a flag falls out on its own before passer's arm is engaged in the throwing motion. It is the responsibility of the officials to make this decision.

Station 2: Punt

Receivers take punt formation after receiving all balls.

Punters take receiving formation after punting all balls.

Ball is hiked to punter.
Ball is punted to receivers.
Rotate in direction of arrows.

FIGURE 20.21 Punting

Station 3: Lateral passing right and left

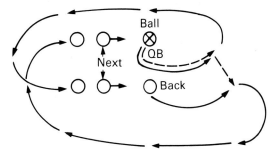

Right lateral: Quarterback rolls to right 5 to 7 yd.
Lateral to halfback at swing position.
Rotate in direction of arrows.

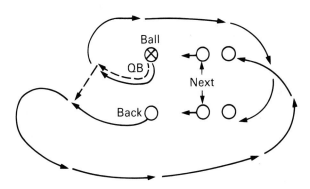

Left lateral: Quarterback rolls to left 5 to 6 yd.
Lateral to halfback in swing position.
Rotate in direction of arrows.

FIGURE 20.22 Lateral passing

Downs

A team has four downs to advance the ball from wherever they take over to score. If the team fails to score in four downs, its opponents gain possession of the ball at the spot where the ball is declared dead on the fourth down. To obtain a first down, the offensive team must complete three forward passes out of four downs. A forward pass is a pass thrown from behind the line of scrimmage past the line of scrimmage.

Miscellaneous Penalties

- Illegal use of flags   15 yards
- Offensive use of hands   15 yards
- Defensive illegal use of hands   15 yards
- Off side   5 yards
- Pushing ball carrier out-of-bounds   15 yards
- Ball carrier pushing the interference   15 yards

- Ineligible person downfield   5 yards
- Illegal procedure   5 yards

Practice Using Station Teaching

Stations can be organized to develop football skills. The following is an example of how this might be done.

- Station 1—Passing (Figure 20.20)
- Station 2—Punting (Figure 20.21)
- Station 3—Lateral passing (Figure 20.22)
- Station 4—Centering (Figure 20.23)

After each group has completed the drill, the instructor gives a signal for rotation to the next station. The first "hutt" will be the signal used at all stations. In Figures 20.20 through 20.23, dashed lines indicate the direction of the ball; straight lines indicate the direction in which the player is to move; a circle with an X in the center marks the position of the

Station 4: Centering Drill
Shotgun formation

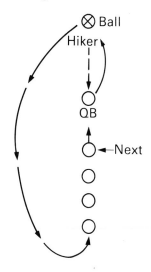

Ball is centered to quarterback.
Each center takes 3 hikes, then rotates.
Rotate in direction of arrows.

FIGURE 20.23   Centering

ball, the quarterback, or the center; and an empty circle represents the position of any other player.

Lead-Up Games and Learning Activities

The following lead-up games can be enjoyable ways to broaden the variety of activities in a football unit. They also avoid one student dominating a skilled position while others simply go through the motions of blocking.

Five Passes

The game can be played on a football field, but the size of the field is not critical and any large area is satisfactory. Players scatter on the field. The object of the game is for one team (identified by pinnies) to make five consecutive passes to five different players without losing control of the ball. This scores one point. The defense may play the ball only and may not make personal contact. No player is allowed to take more than three steps when in possession of the ball, or the ball is given to the other team.

There is no penalty when the ball hits the ground. It remains in play, but this interrupts the five-pass sequence, which starts over. Students should call the number of consecutive passes out loud.

Kick Over

The game is played on a football field with a 10-yd end zone. Teams are scattered at opposite ends of the field. The object is to punt the ball over the other team's goal line. If the ball is caught in the end zone, no score results. A ball kicked into the end zone and not caught scores a goal. If the ball is kicked beyond the end zone on the fly, a score is made regardless of whether the ball is caught.

Play is started by one team with a punt from a point 20–30 ft in front of their own goal line. On a punt, if the ball is not caught, the team must kick from the point of recovery. If the ball is caught, the team also kicks from the point of recovery. When the ball is caught, three long strides are allowed to advance the ball for a kick. It is a good idea to number students and to allow them to kick in rotation so all receive equal practice.

Fourth Down

Six to eight players are on a team and play in an area roughly half the size of a football field. Every play is a fourth down, which means that the play must score or the team loses the ball. No kicking is permitted, and players may pass at any time from any spot in any direction. There can be a series of passes on any play, either from behind or beyond the line of scrimmage.

The teams start in the middle of the field with possession determined by a coin toss. The ball is put into play by centering. The back receiving the ball runs or passes to any teammate. The receiver has the same options. No blocking is permitted. After each touchdown, the ball is brought to the center of the field and the nonscoring team resumes play. The ball is downed when the player's flag is pulled. If a player makes an incomplete pass beyond the line of scrimmage, the ball is brought to the spot from which it was thrown.

Positions are rotated so everyone has a chance to be the quarterback. The rotation occurs after every down. The quarterback rotates to center, which ensures that everyone plays all positions.

Captain Football

The game is played on half of a football field. Five yards beyond each goal is a 6-ft by 6-ft square, which is the box. The teams must be identified with pinnies. The object of the game is to complete a pass to the captain in the box.

To begin, the players line up at opposite ends of the field. One team kicks off from its 10-yd line to the other team. The game then becomes keepaway, with one team trying to secure possession of the ball and the other team trying to retain possession until a successful pass can be made to the captain in the box. To score a touchdown, the captain must catch the ball on the fly and still keep both feet in the box.

A player may run sideways or backwards when in possession of the ball. Players may not run forward but are allowed momentum (two steps) if receiving or intercepting a ball. More than two steps is penalized by loss of possession.

The captain is allowed three attempts to catch a pass, or one successful goal before a new player is rotated into the box. A ball hitting the ground in bounds remains in play. Players may not bat or kick a free ball. Penalty is the awarding of the ball to the other team out-of-bounds.

Aerial Ball

Aerial ball is similar to flag football with the following differences. The ball may be passed at any time. It can be thrown at any time beyond the line of scrimmage: immediately after an interception, during a kickoff, or during a received kick. Players have four downs to score a touchdown. If the ball is thrown from behind the line of scrimmage and an incomplete pass results, the ball is returned to the previous spot on the line of scrimmage. If the pass originates otherwise and is incomplete, the ball is placed at the point from which the pass was thrown.

Because the ball can be passed at any time, no downfield blocking is permitted. A player may screen the ball carrier but cannot make a block. Screening is defined as running between the ball carrier and the defense.

Suggested Performance Objectives

Basic Objectives

1. Throw 10 overhand passes to the chest area of a partner who is standing 10 yd away. Practice correct holding, point of release, and follow-through techniques of passing (1 point).
2. Throw 3 or 4 consecutive passes beyond a target positioned 20 yd away (1 point).
3. Facing the opposite direction from a partner 5 yd away, execute a proper center stance with feet well spread and toes pointed straight ahead, knees bent, and two hands on the ball. Snap the ball back through the legs 10 consecutive times (1 point).
4. With a partner centering the ball, from a distance of 10 yd punt the ball using proper technique to another set of partners 15 yd away, 3 consecutive times (1 point).
5. Same as Task 4, except at a distance of 20 yd (1 point).
6. Punt the ball 3 consecutive times within the boundary lines of the field and beyond a distance of 20 yd (1 point).
7. With a partner, run a "quick" pass pattern and catch the ball 2 of 3 times (5–7-yd pattern) (1 point).
8. With a partner, run a 10–15-yd "down and in" pass pattern and catch the ball 2 of 3 times (1 point).
9. With a partner, run a 10–15-yd "down and out" pass pattern and catch the ball 2 of 3 times (1 point).
10. With a partner, run a 5–7-yd "hook" pattern and catch the ball 2 of 3 times (1 point).

Optional Objectives

1. With a partner centering the ball, from a distance of 10 yd, punt the football using proper technique to another set of partners 15 yd away, 3 consecutive times (2 points).
2. Same as Task 1, but at a distance of 20 yd (2 points).
3. Center-snap 4 of 6 times through a tire positioned 5 yd away (2 points).
4. Throw 3 of 4 consecutive passes beyond a target positioned 20 yd away (2 points).
5. Throw 4 of 6 passes through a tire from a distance of 10 yd (2 points).

Suggested Readings

AAHPERD. 1980. *Rules for Coeducational Activities and Sports*. Reston, VA: AAHPERD.

Brace, D. K. 1965. *Skills Test Manual: Football*. Reston, VA: AAHPERD.

Seaton, D. C., et al. 1983. *Physical Education Handbook*. 7th ed. Englewood Cliffs, NJ: Prentice-Hall, Inc.

Standbury, D., and DeSantis, F. 1961. *Touch Football*. New York: Sterling Publishing Co.

LACROSSE

Lacrosse is played in the United States, Australia, and England, and it is the national sport of Canada. In the United States, lacrosse is most popular in the Middle Atlantic States. The game was originated by American Indians as early as the 16th century. The Indians played each game with over one hundred players and often with as many as a thousand players.

Lacrosse is a wide open game that offers aerobic activity for players. The game can be easily modified to suit all skill and age levels. Examples of modified games are Soft Lacrosse which is played in a gym or on a field with a lacrosse stick, ball, and goals; Plastic Lacrosse is played with modified plastic sticks and does not require as much skill as regulation lacrosse; Box Lacrosse is played in an arena or lacrosse box and requires the highest skill, and Field Lacrosse which is played on a soccer-size field with playing area behind each goal.

Sequence of Skills

Gripping the Stick.   Position the dominant hand at least halfway down the handle of the stick, palm up. The other hand grips the stick at the end with the palm down. The stick should be held close to the body with relaxed hands and wrists (Figure 20.24).

Throwing.   Bring the head of the stick backwards while keeping the eyes focused on the target. Step with the opposite foot in the direction of the throw. Keep the elbows high and throw overhand to improve accuracy. The hands should be kept shoulder width apart (don't push the ball). Break the wrists on follow-through with the head of the stick pointing to the target at the end of the throw.

Catching.   Reach to meet the ball and "give" with the arms when the ball makes contact with the stick. Move the feet and align the body with the path of the oncoming ball. When catching, allow the dominant hand to slide on the handle for better stick control. The following techniques are used for catching balls at various levels:

1. **Above the shoulders.** Extend the crosse in the path of the ball. When the ball is caught, rotate the dominant hand sharply inward to protect it from a defender.
2. **Between the shoulders and knees.** Extend the face of the stick directly toward the ball. When caught, move the head of the crosse upward.
3. **Below the knees.** Rotate the handle outward and upward following the reception.

FIGURE 20.24   Gripping the crosse

4. **Head high.** Put the face of the crosse directly in the path of the ball with the head and shoulders dropping to the left. Rotate the crosse inward with the dominant hand upon reception.
5. **Ball on the weak hand side of the body.** Bring the dominant hand across the body to put the crosse in the path of the ball. Cross the leg on the dominant side in front of the other leg while turning the body. After catch, move the head of the crosse upward.

Scooping.   When fielding ground balls, bend the knees and the back. Keep the butt end of the stick away form the midline of the body. Scoop the ball up with a slight shovel motion. As soon as the ball enters the stick, the player needs to break to the right or left to elude the defender.

Dodging.   There are four basic dodges used by an offensive player who has the ball in an attempt to evade the defender:

1. **Face dodge.** The player with the ball fakes throwing the ball. When the crosse is about even with the head, it is twisted to the nondominant side. The offensive player then drops the shoulders and head slightly to the nondominant side, brings the leg on the dominant side across the other leg, and runs around the defender.
2. **Change-of-pace dodge.** Run quickly in one direction, stop suddenly and reverse directions. Continue this pattern of movement until the opportunity to move past the defender arises.
3. **Toss dodge.** When the offensive player meets the defender, the ball is tossed on the ground or in the air past the defender. The player then moves past the defender and recovers the ball.
4. **Force dodge.** The offensive player approaches the defender with the back side of the body. This causes the defender to retreat. The offensive player fakes to the left and right until an opportunity to run past the defender occurs.

Goaltending.   The main duties of the goalie are to stop the ball, direct the defense, and start the offense by passing the ball out to the side or down the field. The goalie should be positioned as follows: Feet shoulder width apart with the knees bent. Decrease the shooting angle for the offensive player by moving in an arc about 3 ft from the goal mouth with short shuffle steps. When the ball is behind the goal, the goalie should operate in the same arc, favoring the ball side. If regulation equipment is lacking, it is highly recommended that the goalie wear a softball catcher's mask and chest protector during shooting drills and games.

Ideas for Effective Instruction

Equipment

The lacrosse ball is solid rubber and white or orange in color. It is slightly smaller than a baseball, but just as hard. When dropped from a height of 6 ft above a solid wooden floor, it must bounce 43–51 in. The lacrosse stick may be 40–72 in. long with the exception of the goalie's stick which may be any length. For physical education, plastic sticks and balls are recommended (Figure 20.25). The net of the stick is between 6½ and 10 in. The net is made of gut, rawhide, or nylon. Players wear gloves and a helmet with a face mask in regulation lacrosse.

Game Play

Lacrosse is often played in a football stadium. In physical education classes, it can be played on any field, gym, or court with portable goals. The regulation field is 110 yds long with the goals 80 yds apart, leaving 15 yds behind each goal. The field is 60 yds wide, but current rules allow for the width to be reduced to 53⅓ yds, which is the width of a football field (Figure 20.26). A rectangular box, 35 by 40 yds surrounds each goal and is called the goal area. The goal consists of 2 vertical posts joined by a top crossbar. The posts are 6 ft apart and the top crossbar is 6 ft from the ground.

There are 10 players on a team including a goalie, 3 midfielders, 3 attackers, and 3 defenders. The goalie guards the goal and receives support from the defenders. The defenders must remain in their half of the field. The midfielders serve as "rovers" and

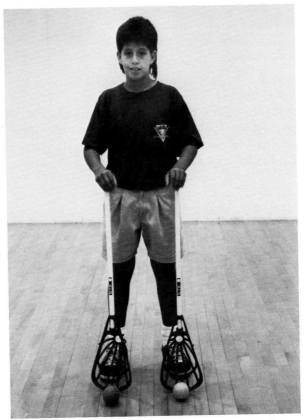

FIGURE 20.25 Examples of plastic sticks and balls

roam the entire field operating as both offensive and defensive players. One of the midfielders handles each faceoff and is called the center. The attackers remain in the offensive half of the field and attempt shots on goal. The attackers, defenders, and

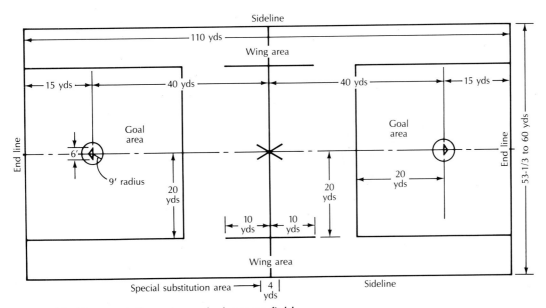

FIGURE 20.26 Markings and dimensions of a lacrosse field

the goalies often play the entire game, but the mid-fielders are often substituted.

Basic Rules

Faceoff.   Play begins with a faceoff (a draw) at the start of each quarter and after a goal is scored (Figure 20.27). The ball is placed between the back side of the opponents' sticks. All players must be in their assigned positions for the faceoff. On signal, players in the wing areas are released, but all other players are confined until a player gains possession of the ball, the ball goes out of bounds, or the ball crosses either of the goal line areas.

Offside Rule.   Each team must have three players located on its attack half and four players on its defensive half of the field. This prevents piling up around the goal.

Out-of-Bounds.   When a player throws or carries the ball out-of-bounds, the opposing team gets possession. However, when a loose ball goes out-of-bounds as a result of a shot taken at the goal, it is awarded to the team whose player is closest to it at the exact time it rolls out-of-bounds.

Checking.   Body checking is allowed in regulation play in an attempt to dislodge the ball. Football blocks can be legally made on the player with the ball or on those who are going for a loose ball 5 yds away. Checking an opponent with the body or stick is a common practice and is used to dislodge the ball.

Penalty Box.   There are two types of fouls: personal and technical. Personal fouls are more serious than technical fouls and result in suspension for 1–3 min based on the severity and intention of the foul. Personal fouls are assigned for illegal personal contact, tripping, and unsportsmanlike conduct. Technical fouls usually result in a 30 sec suspension from the game if the player does not have the ball. If the offending team has the ball, it loses possession of the ball. Technical fouls are assigned for the following infractions:

- *Interference* with the opponent without the ball.
- *Holding* any part of the opponent's body.
- *Pushing*, particularly from the rear.
- *Illegal action with the stick* or playing the game without the stick.
- *Withholding the ball from play* by lying on it or trapping it longer than necessary to gain control.
- *Illegal procedure* occurs when (1) an offensive player steps in the opponent's crease when the ball is in the attacking half of the field or (2) a defending player with the ball runs through the crease.
- *Offside* occurs when a team has less than three players in its attack half or less than four players in the defensive half of the field.

Modified Rules

The regulation rules for lacrosse can be modified for use in a physical education setting where equipment and facilities are limited. The following is an example of various modifications.

1. Reduce the number of players to less than 10 so players have more opportunity to handle the ball. Try assigning players to zones so all students have the opportunity to play the ball. This helps prevent the most dominant players from always "hogging" the ball.
2. No stick or body contact is allowed. Encourage students to play the ball rather than the opponent. If a violation occurs, a penalty shot is awarded at the spot of the infraction.
3. Players must keep both hands on their sticks at all times. A penalty shot is awarded at the spot of the infraction.
4. If a ball goes out of bounds, the team that did not touch it last may run it in or pass it in.
5. To steal the ball from an opponent, only stick on stick tactics may be used (no body contact).
6. To encourage teamwork and passing skills, two passes must be made before each shot on goal.
7. Play should be continuous without any stalling tactics. If problems develop in this area, add a time limit for holding the ball. For example, if the ball is held more than 5 sec, it is turned over to the other team at the point of infraction.
8. The ball is a "free ball" when it is on the ground

FIGURE 20.27   Starting play with a faceoff

or in the air. Stick contact is allowed at these times *without* body contact.

Organization and Skill Work

A number of drills and lead-up games can be used to teach the fundamentals of lacrosse. See the units on basketball, soccer, and hockey for additional activities which can be modified for lacrosse.

Drills

Throwing and Catching.
1. Practice throwing the ball against a wall.
2. With a partner, begin throwing and catching in close proximity. Gradually move apart until clearing passes are made.
3. Play keepaway in groups of three.
4. Use the jack-in-the-box drill. The "jack" is located midway between the two other players, each with a ball. The "jack" receives a pass from one of the end players, who is about 10 yds away. The "jack" passes the ball back to that player, rotates 180 degrees, and receives a pass from the other end player. Change "jack" players frequently.
5. Use buddy passing for learning to pass on the move. Buddies jog around the area and pass back and forth to each other. Increase the challenge by giving each a ball.
6. Use the three-person rush and three-person weave similar to the common basketball drills.

Scooping. Organize the class into groups of three. Two students are positioned on one side with the third student across from them, 30 ft away. The ball is placed in the middle. One of the two students positioned on the same side runs to the ball, scoops it up and carries it a few steps before dropping it. Continuing forward, the student runs behind the player on the opposite side. This player runs forward, scoops up the ball, carries it a few steps, drops it and moves forward behind the remaining student. The pattern continues.

Shooting. A line of 4–5 students face the goal. A "feeder" behind the goal passes the ball to a shooter who cuts toward the goal or moves to a different position. After the shot on goal, the shooter becomes the "feeder." Rotate goalies frequently.

Dodging. Practice all types of dodges with a partner using one ball per two students.

Defense. Three players form a circle with a 20 yd radius. Two offensive players try to keep the ball away form the defensive player while remaining in the circle.

Leadup Games

Three-Second No Steps. Players cannot take any steps with the ball. In addition, the ball may be not be held longer than 3 sec or it is turned over to the other team.

Halfcourt Lacrosse. The offensive team gets five attempts to score. Each shot on goal counts as an offensive attempt. Offense and defense switch roles after the five attempts.

Five Touch. At least 5 members of a team must touch the ball before a goal can be scored.

Suggested Readings

Brackenridge, C. 1978. *Women's Lacrosse*. Woodbury, NY: Barrons.

Hartman, P. E. 1968. *Lacrosse: Fundamentals*. Columbus, OH: Merrill Publishing Co.

Hinkman, J. 1975. *Box Lacrosse: The Fastest Game on Two Feet*. Radnor, PA: University Press.

Liebich, T. 1981. *Coach Lacrosse: Teaching the Fundamentals*. Vancouver, BC: British Columbia Lacrosse Association.

Schrader, R., and Everden, S. 1977. *Team Sports: A Competency Based Approach*. Dubuque, IA: Kendall/Hunt Publishing Co.

Scott, R. 1976. *Lacrosse: Technique and Tradition*. Baltimore, MD: Johns Hopkins University Press.

SOCCER

Soccer, the most popular game in the world, is now rapidly gaining popularity among youth in the United States. Many sport clubs and programs run by organizations such as the YMCA, YWCA, Boys' Clubs, and municipal recreation departments now sponsor soccer teams, and many school districts are now including soccer in their intramural and athletic programs.

Soccer is known throughout the rest of the world as "football." The game is said to have originated in England around the 10th century, but in fact, the Romans played a game similar to soccer. Soccer was brought to the United States about 1870 and was played by women in an organized fashion in 1919.

From a physical education standpoint, one of the advantages of soccer is that it is one of the few sports that depends primarily on foot-eye coordination for success. Many kickers in American football are soccer-style kickers. The long hours of kicking practice have contributed to their success.

The object of the game is to move the ball down the field by foot, body, or head contact to score goals and to prevent the opposing team from scoring. Soccer demands teamwork and the coordination of individual skills into group goals. Position play becomes important as students become more skilled. It is an excellent game for cardiovascular development, because it demands a great deal of running and body control.

Sequence of Skills

The skills of soccer are difficult to master, so instructors should teach the skills through short practice sessions. Many drills and lead-up games can be used to make the practice sessions interesting and novel.

Dribbling

The purpose of dribbling in soccer is similar to basketball, that is, to maintain control of the ball and advance it before passing off to a teammate or shooting on goal. The ball is advanced by pushing it with the inside or outside of the front of the foot (Figure 20.28). The player should keep the ball close during the dribble, rather than kicking it and then running after it. Practice should involve learning to run in different patterns such as weaving, dodging, and twisting or turning with the ball.

Kicking

The purpose of the kick is to pass the ball to a teammate or to take a shot on goal. When passing, the performer plants the nonkicking foot alongside the ball with the foot pointing in the desired direc-

FIGURE 20.29   Instep kick

tion of the kick. The ball is contacted with the inside portion of the instep of the foot (Figure 20.29). The body weight shifts forward after the kick. The pass can also be made with the outside of the foot, although this kick will not move the ball as great a distance or with as much velocity. It is an excellent kick for passing without breaking stride or for passing to the side.

In kicking for a shot on goal, the procedure is similar to the inside-of-the-foot kick. The nonkicking foot is planted alongside the ball with the toes pointing in the direction of the goal. The ball is contacted on the instep, followed by a snap of the lower leg and follow-through.

Trapping

The purpose of trapping is to deflect a moving ball and bring it under control so it may be advanced or passed. Any part of the body may contact the ball except the hands or arms. Effective trapping will result in the ball dropping in front of the body in position to be advanced.

The sole-of-the-foot trap is most commonly used and is often called wedging. The ball is contacted between the foot and the ground just as the ball hits the ground. The ball is swept away under control immediately after the trap.

The shin trap is done by moving to meet the ball just as it hits the ground in front of the lower legs. The ball is trapped between the inside of the lower leg and the ground.

The chest trap (Figure 20.30) is executed by arching the trunk of the body backwards and giving with the ball on contact. The giving occurs with the body

FIGURE 20.28   Dribbling

FIGURE 20.30 Absorbing the force in a chest trap

collapsing, so the ball does not rebound and drops in front of the player.

Heading

Heading can be an effective way of propelling a ball in the air to a teammate or on goal. The player should strike the ball with the head, rather than waiting for the ball to hit the head. The player leans backward as the ball approaches. The head is up, with the eyes following the ball. On contact, the head moves forward and strikes the ball near the hairline on the forehead. The body also swings forward as the follow-through is completed.

Tackling

Tackling is used defensively to take the ball away from an offensive player who is dribbling or attempting to pass. The single-leg tackle is used when approaching an opponent directly, from behind, or from the side. Effective tackling depends, in large part, on being able to anticipate the opponent's next move with the foot. One leg reaches for the ball while the weight is supported on the other. The knees should be bent so good balance is maintained.

Focus should be on a clean tackle rather than on body contact. The object is to reach out and bring the ball to the body, or to kick the ball away and then continue to pursue it.

Goalkeeping

Goalkeeping involves stopping shots by catching or otherwise stopping the ball. Goalkeepers should become adept at catching low, rolling balls, at diving on rolling balls, at catching airborne balls waist high and below, and at catching airborne balls waist high and above. The diving movements are the reason the goalie may choose to wear knee, elbow, and hip pads.

Students should get in the habit of catching low, rolling balls in much the same manner as a baseball outfielder: Get down on one knee, with the body behind the ball to act as a backstop, and catch it with both hands, fingers pointing toward the ground. If diving for a ball is necessary, the goalie must throw the body behind it and cradle it with the hands. The body should always be between the goal and the ball.

The goalie may also punch the ball in order to deflect it if the ball is not catchable. The ball can be deflected off other body parts if it is not punchable.

After a ball is caught by the goalkeeper, it is thrown to a teammate. The ball can also be kicked, but this is less desirable because it is less accurate. Effective throws allow teammates to place the ball in action immediately.

Ideas for Effective Instruction

Soccer is played with two teams of 11 players each. For young players, however, decreasing the size of the teams is more effective. This results in each player's handling the ball more often and feeling an integral part of the soccer team.

Many of the drills, such as dribbling, kicking, and punting, can be learned individually. This means that one ball per player will ensure the maximum amount of practice time. Many types of balls can be used besides a regulation soccer ball. Playground balls (8½ in.) can be used if they are deflated slightly. Many students will play a more aggressive game of soccer if a foam-rubber training ball is used. They become less fearful of being hit by the ball and are willing to kick it with maximum velocity.

Field sizes can be reduced in order to increase the activity level of the game. The regulation game is played on a field with dimensions illustrated in Figure 20.31. Soccer is meant to be played on grass. If a hard surface is used, deflate the ball so that it is not as live and will not bounce so readily.

The drills used for developing soccer skills should help all participants in achieving proper form. For

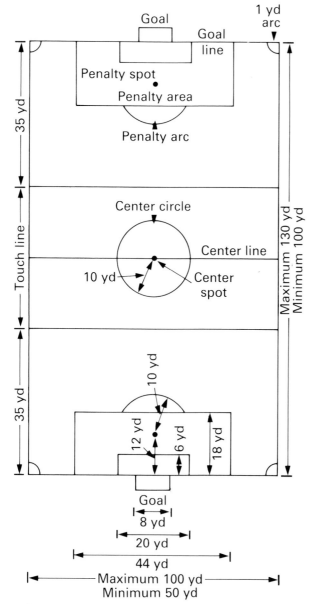

FIGURE 20.31 Regulation soccer field

example, if students are asked to pass and trap together, drills should focus on developing both skills, yet students are sometimes asked to kick with velocity, so the students trapping are fearful of getting hurt. Those students then develop an improper trapping style. An excellent source for many drills and activities to enhance the play of soccer is *Teaching Soccer* by Thomson (1980).

Lead-Up Games and Learning Activities

The following lead-up games are excellent for getting students involved in soccer activities. They emphasize participation and action. The lead-up activities are often more fun for the majority of students than an actual soccer game, because these activities develop specific skills in which students may lack expertise.

Circle Kickball

Players are in circle formation. They kick the ball with the side of the foot back and forth inside the circle. The object is to kick the ball out of the circle beneath shoulder level. A point is scored against each of the players where the ball left the circle. If the lost ball is clearly the fault of a single player, however, then the point is scored against that player only. Players who kick the ball over the shoulders of the circle players have a point scored against them. Players with the fewest points scored against them are the winners. The game works well with a foam training ball because the ball can be kicked at someone from a short distance.

Soccer Croquet

The game is similar to croquet in that the object is for one ball to hit another. One player kicks a ball and tries to hit another ball lying ahead. Kickers alternate until a hit is made, which scores one point for the kicker. The game continues until a player scores a specified number of points.

Soccer Keepaway

Players are spaced evenly around a circle about 10 yd in diameter with one player in the center. The object of the game is to keep the player in the center from touching the ball. The ball is passed back and forth as in soccer. If the center player touches the ball with a foot, the person who kicked the ball goes in the center. If there is an error, the person responsible changes places with the one in the center.

Diagonal Soccer

Two corners are marked off with cones 5 ft from the corners on both sides, outlining triangular dead areas. Each team lines up as illustrated in Figure 20.32 and protects two adjacent sides of the square. The size of the area depends on the size of the class and must be adjusted accordingly. Dead areas on opposite corners mark the opposing team's goal line. To begin competition, three players from each team move into the playing area in their own half of the space. These are the active players. During play, they may roam anywhere in the square. The other players act as line guards.

To score, the active players must kick the ball through the opposing team's line (beneath shoulder height). When a score is made, active players rotate to the sidelines, and new players take their place.

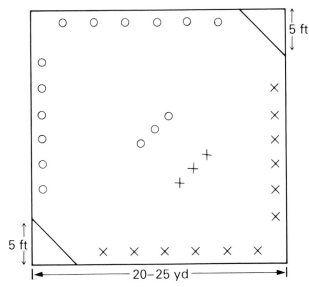

FIGURE 20.32 Diagonal soccer

1. A team allows the ball to go through its line below shoulder height.
2. A team touches the ball illegally.
3. A team kicks the ball over the other team's line above shoulder height.

Sideline Soccer

The teams line up on the sidelines of a large square with the end lines open. Three active players from each team are called from the end of the team line. These players remain active until a point is scored, and then they are rotated to the other end of the line (Figure 20.33).

The object is to kick the ball over the end line, which has no defenders, between cones that define the scoring area. The active players on each team compete against each other, aided by their team-mates on the sidelines.

To start play, a referee drops the ball between two opposing players at the center of the field. To score, the ball must be kicked last by an active player and must go over the end line at or below shoulder height. Regular rules prevail with the restrictions of no pushing, holding, tripping, or other rough play. For out-of-bounds, the team on the side of the field where the ball went out-of-bounds is awarded a free kick near that spot. No score can result from a free kick. Violation of the touch rule also results in a free kick.

Players on the sidelines may block the ball with their bodies, but cannot use their hands. The team against which the point was scored starts the ball for the next point. Only active players may score. A point is scored for the opponents whenever any of the following occurs:

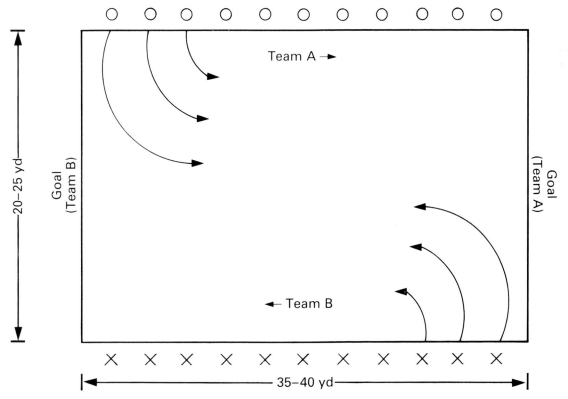

FIGURE 20.33 Sideline soccer

Line Soccer

Two goal lines are drawn 180–210 ft apart. A restraining line is drawn 15 ft in front of and parallel to each goal line. Field width can vary from 90 to 105 ft. Each team stands on one goal line, which it defends. The referee stands in the center of the field, holding a ball (Figure 20.34). At the whistle, three players (or more if the teams are large) run to the center from the right side of each line and become active players. The referee drops the ball to the ground, and the players try to kick it through the other team defending the goal line. The players in the field may advance by kicking only.

A score is made when an active player kicks the ball through the opposing team and over the end line, providing the kick was made from outside the restraining line. Place cones on the field corners to define the goal line. A player rotation system should be set up.

Line players act as goalies and are permitted to catch the ball. After being caught, the ball must be laid down immediately and either rolled or kicked. It cannot be punted or drop-kicked. One point is scored when the ball is kicked through the opponent's goal line below shoulder level. One point is also scored in cases of a personal foul involving pushing, kicking, tripping, or similar acts.

For illegal touching by the active players, a direct

free kick is given from a point 12 yd in front of the penalized team's goal line. All active players on the defending team must be to one side until the ball is kicked. Only goalies may defend. A time limit of 2 min should be set for any group of active players. When no goal is scored during this time, a halt is called at the end of 2 min and players are changed.

An out-of-bounds ball is awarded to the opponents of the team last touching the ball. The regular soccer throw-in from out-of-bounds should be used. If the ball goes over the shoulders of the defenders at the end line, any end-line player may retrieve the ball and put it into play with a throw or kick.

Minisoccer

The playing area (Figure 20.35) can be adjusted, depending on the size and skill of the players. A reasonable playing area is probably 150 by 225 ft. A goal, 24 ft wide, is on each end of the field, marked by jumping standards. A 12-ft semicircle on each end outlines the penalty area. The center of the semicircle is at the center of the goal.

The game follows the general rules of soccer, with one goalie for each side. The corner kick, not played in other lead-up games, needs to be introduced. This kick is used when the ball goes over the end line but not through the goal, and was last touched by the defense. The ball is taken to the nearest corner for a direct free kick, and a goal can

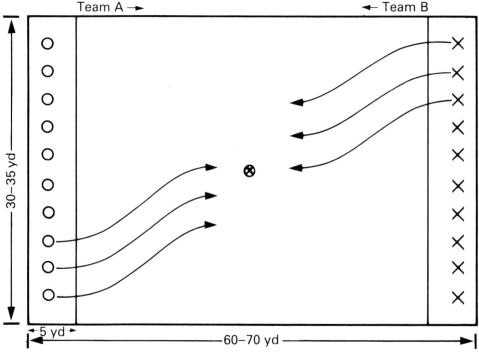

FIGURE 20.34 Line soccer

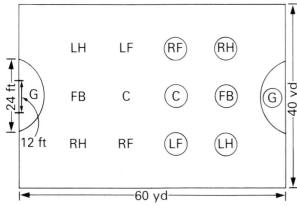

FIGURE 20.35 Minisoccer field

be scored from the kick. If the attacking team last touched the ball, the goalkeeper kick is awarded. The goalie puts the ball down and place-kicks it forward. The players are designated as center forward, outside right halfback, fullback, and goalie. Players should rotate positions at regular intervals. The forwards play in the front half of the field and the guards in the back half, but neither position is restricted to these areas entirely, and all may cross the center line without penalty.

A foul by the defense within its penalty area (semicircle) results in a penalty kick, taken from a point 12 yd distant, directly in front of the goal. Only the goalie is allowed to defend. The ball is in play, with others waiting outside the penalty area. Emphasize position play, and encourage the lines of three to spread out and hold their position.

Suggested Performance Objectives

The following contracts are an example of pass-fail requirements designed for three skill levels: introductory, intermediate, and advanced. The contracts can be used in intermediate or advanced soccer classes, or in a heterogeneously grouped class to challenge students of varying abilities.

Introductory Unit

Kicking

1. Execute a push pass, low drive, and lofted drive. Satisfy the instructor that these are understood and can be executed with the preferred foot.

Passing

(All objectives may be performed with the preferred foot.)
2. Push-pass 3 of 5 passes from 10 yd to partner.
3. Low-drive 3 of 5 passes from 15 yd to partner.
4. Loft-drive 3 of 5 passes from 20 yd to partner.

Dribbling

5. Dribble a distance of 20 yd twice with one or both feet. The ball must not be allowed to stray more than 5 yd.

Shooting

6. Shoot the ball with the preferred foot from 18 yd into an empty goal 8 of 10 times.

Heading

7. Head the ball back to serving partner 8 of 10 times over a distance of 5 yd. The partner must be able to catch the ball.

Control of the Ball

8. Control 3 of 5 passes on the ground using the feet only.
9. Control 3 of 5 passes in the air using the head, chest, or thigh.

Game Situation

10. Show an understanding of pass, run, and control in a minisoccer game situation.

Rules of the Game

11. Score 80% on a rules-of-the-game test. One retake is permissible.

Introductory Unit: Optional Requirements

Goalkeeping

1. Save 6 of 10 shots from 18 yd. The shots must be on target.
2. Punt the ball 25 yd 4 of 5 times.

Juggling

3. Keep the ball in the air with at least 10 consecutive touches. Hands or arms may not be used.

Field Dimensions

4. Diagram a full-size soccer field and give dimensions.

Grading

Thirteen passes are required for a unit pass. The instructor reserves the right to lower the number of required passes for the unit as necessary.

Intermediate Unit

Kicking

1. Satisfy the instructor that the techniques of the push pass, low drive, and lofted drive are understood and can be executed with both feet.

Passing

2. Push Pass: Complete 4 of 5 passes with the preferred foot from 10 yd. The passes must go between two cones placed 5 yd apart. Complete 3 of 5 passes with the nonpreferred foot.

3. Low Drive: Complete 4 of 5 passes with the preferred foot from 10 yd. The passes must go between two cones placed 8 yd apart. Complete 3 of 5 passes with the nonpreferred foot.

4. Lofted Drive: Complete 4 of 5 passes with the preferred foot from 10 yd. The passes must go over an obstacle 6 ft high. Complete 3 of 5 passes with the nonpreferred foot.

Dribbling

5. Dribble through 6 cones over 25 yd, 4 times with no misses. Both feet must be used.

6. Dribble around an advancing goalkeeper and score a goal 3 of 5 times.

Shooting

7. Shoot the ball with the preferred foot from 18 yd into an empty goal 9 of 10 times.

8. Same as task 7, except with the nonpreferred foot, 7 of 10 times.

Heading

9. Head the ball to a serving partner 9 of 10 times over a distance of 10 yd. The partner must be able to catch the ball without its touching the ground.

Control of the Ball

10. Control 4 of 5 passes on the ground. Use the feet only.

11. Control 4 of 5 passes in the air. The head, chest, and thighs must be used.

Corner Kick

12. Propel 3 of 5 corner kicks inside the penalty area. The ball may not touch the ground between the corner and the penalty area.

Throw-In

13. Throw the ball with two hands to a partner 10 yd away 4 of 5 times. Partner must be able to catch the ball.

Juggle

14. Juggle the ball at least 10 consecutive times without allowing it to touch the ground.

Tackling

15. Successfully complete 3 of 5 front block tackles on a partner dribbling a ball at a walking pace.

Goalkeeping

16. Kick goal kicks at least 20 yd in the air 4 of 5 times.

17. Punt the ball 25 yd 4 of 5 times.

18. Save at least 6 of 10 on-target shots from the 18-yd line.

Rules of the Game

19. Score 80% on a rules-of-the-game test. One retest is allowed.

Intermediate Unit: Optional Requirements

Officiating

1. Help officiate at least 2 games.

2. Know the roles of the referee and linesman.

3. Know the correct positioning of officials at corner kicks, goal kicks, and penalties.

Volleying

4. Volley 4 of 5 goals from outside the goal area with the preferred foot.

Swerving or Bending the Ball

5. Bend the ball into the goal from the goal line 3 of 5 times with the preferred foot.

Penalty Kicks

6. Score 7 of 10 penalty kicks against a recognized peer goalkeeper.

Power and Distance Kicking

7. Score 2 of 5 goals into an empty goal from the halfway line.

Grading

Twenty passes are required for a unit completion.

Advanced Unit: Basic Requirements

Passing

1. Push-pass 4 of 5 passes with the preferred foot from a distance of 10 yd between 2 cones, placed 5 yd apart, while running with the ball. Complete 3 of 5 passes with the nonpreferred foot.

2. Low-drive 4 of 5 passes with the preferred foot from a distance of 15 yd between 2 cones, placed 8 yd apart, while running with the ball. Complete 3 of 5 passes with the nonpreferred foot.

Dribbling

3. Dribble through 9 cones over a distance of 40

yd and back to the start in 30 sec or less. Both feet must be used and no cones may be omitted.

4. Dribble around an advancing goalkeeper and score 4 of 5 times. The goalkeeper must be beaten to the left and to the right at least once.

Shooting

5. Score 10 of 10 shots into an empty goal from outside the 18-yd line with the preferred foot, and 9 of 10 shots with the nonpreferred foot.
6. Score 8 of 10 penalty kicks against a recognized peer goalkeeper.
7. Volley 4 of 5 goals from a serving partner, from outside the goal area, with the preferred foot, and 3 of 5 with the nonpreferred foot.
8. Serve or bend the ball from the goal line into the goal 3 of 6 times with the preferred foot. The ball must be placed within 1 ft of the line any distance from the post.

Heading

9. Head the ball back to a serving partner 9 of 10 times over a distance of 10 yd. The partner must be able to catch the ball.
10. Head the ball back and forth with a partner a minimum of 10 times without touching the ground.
11. Head 9 of 10 serves from a partner into an empty goal from a distance of 10 yd.

Control of the Ball

12. Control 9 of 10 passes on the ground with the preferred foot.
13. Control 8 of 10 passes on the ground with the nonpreferred foot.
14. Control 9 of 10 passes from a partner with the head.
15. Control 9 of 10 serves from a partner with the chest.
16. Control 9 of 10 serves from a partner with the preferred thigh, and 8 of 10 with the nonpreferred thigh.

Corner Kick

17. Kick 9 of 10 corner kicks into the penalty area with the preferred foot from the preferred side. The ball may not touch the ground between the corner and the penalty area.
18. Kick 8 of 10 corner kicks into the penalty area from the nonpreferred side (same conditions as task 17).

Throw-In

19. Throw the ball with both hands to a partner 15 yd away, 9 of 10 times. The throw must be placed so partner is able to catch the ball.

20. Throw the ball to a moving partner at least 10 yd away. Partner must be able to catch the ball.

Juggling

21. Juggle the ball at least 20 times without its touching the ground. Head, foot, and thigh must be used. Start with the ball on the ground, and get it into the air using the feet.
22. Juggle the ball with a partner. At least 10 passes must be made. No restrictions are placed on the number of touches by each player.

Tackling

23. Block tackle a partner jogging with the ball 8 of 10 times successfully.
24. Slide tackle a partner jogging with the ball 3 of 5 times successfully.

Goalkeeping

25. Kick 4 of 5 goal kicks at least 20 yd before hitting the ground.
26. Punt the ball at least 30 yd 4 of 5 times.
27. Save 7 of 10 shots on target from outside the 18-yd line.

Game Rules and Strategy

28. A thorough understanding of the rules of the game and principles of strategy must be demonstrated.
29. A score of 80% or higher must be achieved on a test covering the rules of the game. One retake is allowed.

Advanced Unit: Optional Requirements

Officiating

1. At least 3 games must be officiated.

Grading

Twenty-six passes must be obtained to successfully complete the unit.

Rainy Day Activities

Figure 20.36 is an example of a combination word search and fill-in-the-blank.

Suggested Readings

Ingels, N. B., Jr. 1976. *Coaching Youth Soccer*. Monterey, CA: Page-Ficklin Publications.

Thomson, W. 1977. *Soccer Coaching Methods*. Monterey, CA: Page-Ficklin Publications.

Thomson, W. 1980. *Teaching Soccer*. Minneapolis, MN: Burgess Publishing Co.

```
D A G T F E I N T B H M
S H N F F F O K C I K N
R A I O C Z S O C C E R
K L D R I B B L I N G E
C F A W W N E K G Q O N
I B E A L J Y O X T A R
K A H R D T A O U U L O
L C X D L L B W D J I C
A K O A R E F E R E E S
O C N Q T H R O W I N A
G E O D N A L G N E X E
P B T G Y J Z K X V O D
```

1. When the ball has passed over the line, between the two posts and under the crossbar, it is called a _____ .

2. _____ blows the whistle when the ball goes out-of-bounds.

3. Free chance to score a goal _____ .

4. A way to put the ball into play when it goes out-of-bounds _____ .

5. This sport came over from our mother country, which was _____ .

6. When last played by a defenseperson and rolled out-of-bounds, it shall be kicked from the _____ of the field.

7. This is the only player able to pick up the ball _____ .

8. To start the game or after a goal is scored _____ .

9. The last line of defense before the goalie _____ .

10. When you pass the ball using your head, it is called _____ the ball.

11. A fake or swerve with the body is a _____ .

12. After the ball, last touched by the attacking team, passes over the end line, the offense puts the ball in play by using a _____ .

13. _____ is a way of moving the ball.

14. Front offensive linemen are called _____ .

15. The name of this sport is _____ .

FIGURE 20.36 Name that sport

SOFTBALL _____

Softball raises controversy among physical education teachers. Some instructors believe that it is a game in which one only catches "varicose veins" from standing around. On the other hand, since it is a less-active game, softball is often played by adults for many years. When the skill level of the participants is developed, the game can be enjoyable. If skill is lacking, emphasis should be placed on developing skills and on individual practice.

Softball can be taught effectively by using stations. This gives students ample practice in many different skills and avoids the situation in which students play only one position and specialize in skills. Softball can be played coeducationally, and many of the lead-up games make the activity enjoyable and suited to students' ability levels.

Sequence of Skills

Equipment and Facilities

Softball is played on a diamond with the dimensions shown in Figure 20.37. Lines can be applied to the field with chalk or can be burned into the grass with a solvent that kills the grass and leaves a brown line.

Softball requires some specialized equipment. When ordering gloves, about 20% should be left-handed, and enough balls should be ordered so that each student has one. This allows many drills to be undertaken without waiting for the balls to be returned. Available equipment should include a set of bases for each diamond; bats of varying sizes (aluminum are the most durable); fielders' gloves; catcher's glove, protector, and face mask; and batting tees. For less experienced players, the soft softball is most desirable because it helps alleviate the fear that some players have of the ball. When a regulation softball is used, students often learn to dodge the ball, rather than catch it. Some teachers have had success with the large 16-in. ball. It moves slower, cannot be hit as far, and allows the game to be played in a smaller area. The drawback is that the large ball is difficult to throw because of its size.

Catching

Catching involves moving the body into the path of the ball. There are two ways to hold the hands for catching fly balls. For a low ball, the fielder keeps the fingers in and the thumbs turned outward. For a ball above waist level, the thumbs are turned inward and the fingers outward. The arms and hands extend and reach for the ball. As the ball comes into the glove, the arms, hands, and body give to create a soft home for the ball.

When catching grounders, move into the path of the ball, and then move toward the ball, and catch it on a "good" hop. Keep the eyes on the ball and follow it into the glove. The feet are spread, the seat is kept down, and the hands are carried low and in front. The weight is on the balls of the feet or on the toes, and the knees are bent to lower the body. As the ball is caught, the fielder straightens up, takes a step in the direction of the throw, and makes the throw.

Throwing

The ball is generally held with a three- or four-fingered grip. Smaller students usually have to use the four-fingered grip. The fingers should be spaced evenly, and the ball held with the fingertips.

Because throwing is a complex motor pattern, it is difficult to break the skill into component parts. At best, throwing skills can be slowed down about 10% in an effort to teach proper throwing technique. If a mature pattern of throwing has not been developed, students should focus on throwing for velocity rather than accuracy. After proper form has been learned, accuracy becomes a prime objective.

Overhand Throw. The player stands with the opposite side (from the throwing arm) facing the target. The hand with the ball is brought back, over the head, at just above shoulder height. The non-throwing hand is raised in front of the body. The weight is on the rear foot (away from the target) with the front foot advanced toward the target. The arm comes forward with the elbow leading, and the ball is thrown with a downward snap of the wrist (Figure 20.38). The weight of the body is shifted simultaneously with the throw to the front foot. The rear foot rotates forward, and the throwing hand ends facing the ground during the follow-through. The eyes should be kept on the target throughout the throw.

Sidearm Throw. The sidearm throw is similar to the overhand throw, except that the entire motion is kept near a horizontal plane. The sidearm throw, which uses a quick, whiplike motion, is for shorter, quicker throws than the overhand. The sidearm throw should be used only for short infield throws, because the sideways motion causes a spin on the ball, that results in a curved path.

Underhand Throw. The underhand throw is used for short distances, such as throwing to the pitcher covering first base, or the person on second base throwing to the shortstop covering second base. The player faces the target, and the hand is swung back-

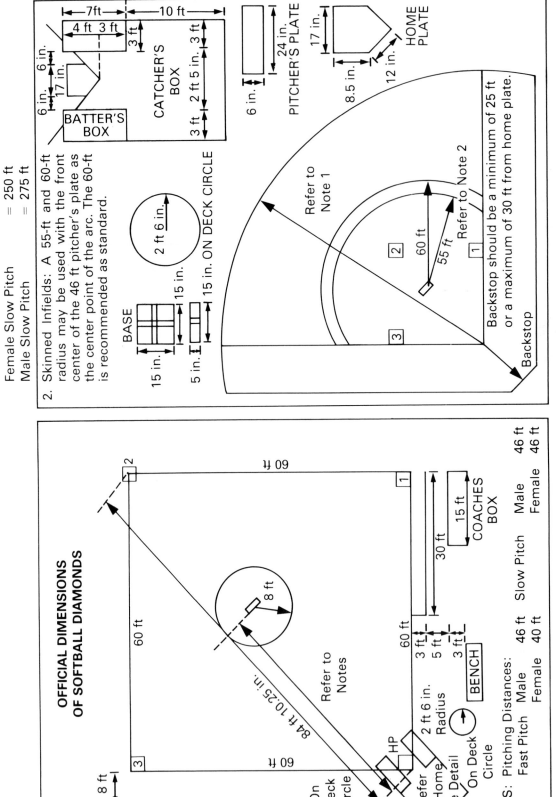

NOTES: 1. Minimum Fence Distances:
       Male & Female Fast Pitch = 225 ft
       Female Slow Pitch   = 250 ft
       Male Slow Pitch   = 275 ft

2. Skinned Infields: A 55-ft and 60-ft radius may be used with the front center of the 46 ft pitcher's plate as the center point of the arc. The 60-ft is recommended as standard.

OFFICIAL DIMENSIONS OF SOFTBALL DIAMONDS

NOTES: Pitching Distances:

	Male	Female
Fast Pitch	46 ft	40 ft
Slow Pitch	46 ft	46 ft

FIGURE 20.37 Softball diamonds

FIGURE 20.38 Overhand throw

FIGURE 20.39 Pitching from the rubber

ward with the palm facing forward. The arm is then moved forward in a pendulum swing with the elbow slightly bent. The weight shifts to the front foot during the toss.

Pitching.   The pitcher must begin with both feet touching the rubber (Figure 20.39). The ball is held in front of the body with the pitcher facing home plate. The pitching hand is brought backward in a pendulum swing, and the wrist is cocked at the back of the swing. The pitcher steps forward on the opposite foot and swings the arm forward. The wrist is snapped, and the ball is released from the fingertips as the arm finishes moving in an upward, lifting fashion. The follow-through should be accompanied by a forward step of the foot on the throwing side, so the player is in a fielding position.

Fielding Position

Infielders should assume the ready position in a semi-crouch, with the legs spread shoulder width apart, knees bent slightly, and hands on or in front of the knees (Figure 20.40). The weight is distributed evenly on both feet so the player can move easily to the left or right. To field a grounder, the fielder moves as quickly as possible into the path of the ball, then moves forward, and plays the ball on a good hop. The glove should be kept near the ground

FIGURE 20.40 Infield catching

and raised only as the ball rises. (A common mistake is to not put the glove down soon enough.) The eyes follow the ball into the glove and the head is kept down. As the ball is caught, the fielder straightens up, takes a step in the direction of the throw, and releases the ball.

To catch a ground ball in the outfield, the player should employ the sure-stop method (Figure 20.41). This involves using the body as a barrier. The fielder drops to one knee in order to block the ball with the body if the catch is missed. This method should be used when runners are on base.

Batting

The bat is gripped with the dominant hand above and adjacent to the nondominant hand. The feet should be positioned comfortably apart, and the front of the body faces the plate. The knees are slightly bent and the weight is distributed equally on both feet. The hands and the bat are held shoulder high and slightly behind the rear foot. The elbows are away from the body, the wrists cocked, and the bat held in an upward position (Figure 20.42). The ball should be followed with the eyes as long as possible. The stride begins by stepping toward the ball with the front foot. The hips are rotated, followed by the trunk and forward shoulder. The arms are extended, wrists snapped, and contact is made with the ball in front of the forward hip. Different grips on the bat can be tried, including the choke and long grip.

FIGURE 20.41 Sure-stop fielding

FIGURE 20.42 Batting position

Batters should avoid using poor techniques such as lifting the front foot high off the ground, stepping back with the rear foot, dropping the elbows, or crouching or bending forward.

Base Running

After a hit, the batter should run hard with the head up and eyes looking down the base path. The runner moves past the bag, tagging it in the process, and turns out into foul territory, unless it is an extra base hit. If it is an extra base hit, the runner swings 5–6 ft to the right of the base line, about two-thirds of the way down the base path, and makes the turn toward second.

Runners on base must stay in contact with it until the pitcher releases the ball. The next base is faced, with one foot forward and the other foot touching the base in a push-off position (Figure 20.43). The knees are flexed, and the upper body leans toward the next base.

Ideas for Effective Instruction

Safety is important, and throwing the bat is a constant problem. The members of the batting team should stand behind the backstop or on the side opposite the batter. Techniques to make the batter think about the bat are: carrying the bat to first base;

FIGURE 20.43 Push-off position

changing ends of the bat before dropping it; or placing the bat in a circle before running. It is usually best not to allow sliding, because sliding can lead to injury if the proper equipment is not available. The catcher should always wear protective gear. In the early stages of practice, soft softballs can be used.

Many of the lead-up games were developed to increase the number of people who get to bat in each inning. One strategy for effective batting practice is to have a member of the batting team pitch so the ball is easy to hit. Players should rotate positions often. Another idea is to have players rotate to a new position each inning. This has the effect of making the players supportive of each other, since the quality of the game depends on all of the participating players.

Station teaching is excellent for developing softball skills. It ensures that participants have the opportunity to practice a wide variety of activities. Players who are particularly skilled in an activity can help others. Teachers should position themselves at a different station each day to ensure that they have instructed all students at all stations over a 1- to 2-wk period.

Figure 20.44 is an example of station teaching. Five stations are developed, so the teacher can make a full rotation in one week. Task cards are placed at each station, so students know exactly what is expected of them.

Station 1. Catching Ground Balls

1. Roll the ball straight to the person.
2. Roll the ball to the left side. Increase the distance.

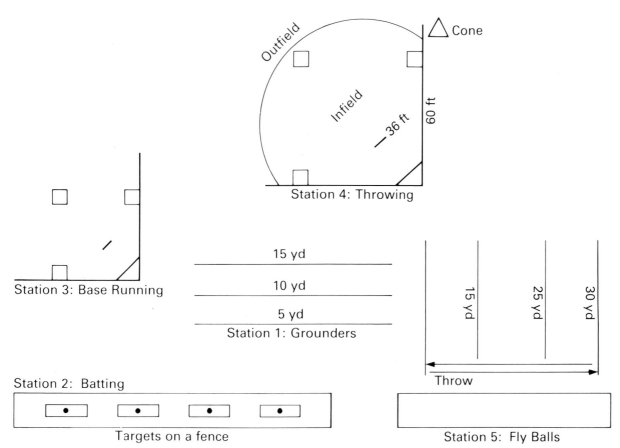

FIGURE 20.44 Station work

3. Roll the ball to the right side. Increase the distance.
4. Roll the ball in an unpredictable direction.
5. Bat the ball in different directions. Start at 5 yd and increase the distance up to 20 yd from the fielder.

Station 2. Batting

1. Work in groups of three with a batting tee. One person fields, one bats, and the other shags the ball. Hit 10 balls.
2. Same as 1, except pitch the ball to the batter.
3. Try placing the ball. Call the direction where you are going to hit the ball, and then do so.

Station 3. Base Running

1. Run the bases using a circle technique. Have a partner time you.
2. Run the bases using a clover technique. Decide which you prefer and which allows you to run the bases faster.
3. Bunt and run to first. Have your partner time you.
4. Play "In a Pickle" in groups of three.

Station 4. Throwing

1. One person stands at each base plus a catcher behind home plate. Practice throwing to each of the bases from each position. Rotate positions after each person has had 3 throws.
2. Throw the ball from the outfield. Throw the ball through a cutoff person. Make 5 throws and rotate to catcher position.
3. Those not throwing should back up the other positions and act as cutoff persons.

Station 5. Fly Balls

1. Throw fly balls back and forth.
2. Vary the height and direction of the throw so teammates have to move into the flight of the ball.
3. Make teammates move backward and forward to catch the ball.
4. Bat some flies and play the game "Five Hundred".

Lead-Up Games and Learning Activities

Two-Pitch Softball

Two-Pitch is played like regulation softball except that a member of the team at bat pitches. Every member of the team must have an opportunity to pitch. The batter receives only two pitched balls to hit, and the ball hit must be fair or it is an out. The pitcher does not field the ball, and no balls or strikes are called.

In a Pickle

A base runner is "in a pickle" when caught between two bases and in danger of being tagged out. To begin, both fielders are on a base with a runner in the middle. The goal is for the player in the middle to get to a base safely. If done, that person scores a point. In either case, rotation occurs.

Five Hundred

A batter hits balls to a group of fielders. The goal is to score 500 points. When the total is reached, that person becomes the new batter. Fielders earn 100 points for catching a fly ball, 75 points for catching a ball on one bounce, 50 points for catching a ball after two bounces, and 25 points for any other ball. The points must total exactly 500 or the total immediately earned is subtracted from the fielder's score. Points are also subtracted if an error is made.

Home Run

The critical players are a batter, a catcher, a pitcher, and one fielder. All other players are fielders and take positions throughout the area. The batter hits a pitch and on a fair ball must run to first base and back home before the ball can be returned to the catcher. The batter is out whenever any of the following occur: a fly ball is caught; a strike-out occurs; or on a fair ball, the ball beats the batter back to home plate. The number of home runs per batter can be limited, and a rotation plan should be developed. The distance to first base may have to be varied, depending on the strength and skill of the players.

Workup

This is a game of rotating positions each time an out is made. The game is played using regulation softball rules. Three batters are up at bat. Each time there is an out, the players move up one position, and the player making the last out goes to right field. The pitcher moves up to catcher, the person on first base to pitcher, and all others move up one position. If a fly ball is caught, the batter and the person catching the ball exchange places.

Babe Ruth Ball

The outfield is divided into three sections: left, center, and right field. The batter calls the field to which he or she intends to hit. The pitcher throws pitches that the batter can hit easily. The batter remains in position as long as he or she hits to the designated field. Field choices are rotated. The batter gets only one swing, but may let a pitch go by. There is no base running.

Speedy Baseball

Speedy baseball is played like regular softball with the following exceptions.

1. The pitcher is from the team at bat and must not interfere with or touch a batted ball on penalty of the batter being called out.
2. The team coming to bat does not wait for the fielding team to get set. Since it has its own pitcher, the pitcher gets the ball to the batter just as quickly as the batter can grab a bat and get ready. The fielding team has to hustle to get to their places.
3. Only one pitch is allowed per batter. Batters must hit a fair ball or they are out. The pitch is made from about two thirds of the normal pitching distance.
4. No stealing is permitted.
5. No bunting is permitted. The batter must take a full swing.

Suggested Performance Objectives

The following is an example of a contract that might be used in a softball unit.

Contract Specifications

1. Reward schedule will be based on three progressive levels of achievement: Level A = 5 points; Level B = 3 points; and Level C = 1 point.
2. Evaluation is primarily by peers, with occasional evaluations done by the instructor. Each contract requirement must be checked off by placing peer or instructor initials and a date by the requirement number.
3. Rewards are based on total point accumulations:
   * 50 points — Admission to softball picnic
   * 65 points — Entrance to advanced softball unit
   * 80 points — One-week choice of favorite physical education activities

Contract Requirements

Throwing Tasks

1. Standing 45 ft from a partner who is inside a hoop, complete 5 consecutive underhand pitches to that person without causing him or her to move outside of the hoop (C = 1 point).
2. Standing 60 ft from a partner who is inside a hoop, complete 5 overhand throws to that person without forcing him or her to move more than 1 ft outside the hoop (B = 3 points).

3. Be able to demonstrate the proper stance, wind-up, and delivery of the windmill pitch to the instructor (B = 3 points).
4. From a designated area of the outfield, situated 150 ft (boys) or 100 ft (girls) away, throw the softball through the air directly to a 10-ft wide circle chalked in front of home plate. To count, the throw must bounce only once before landing or going through the circle. Student must make 3 of 5 throws to qualify for points (B = 3 points).
5. Display pitching skills by striking out 3 or more batters or by allowing no more than 5 base hits in an actual game (A = 5 points).
6. From an outfield or relay position, throw out a baserunner at any base in an actual game (A = 5 points).

Fielding Tasks

1. Demonstrating correct fielding stance, cleanly field 5 consecutive ground or fly balls hit by partner (C = 1 point).
2. Play a game of Pepper with a group of no more than 6 players, demonstrating good bat control, hand-eye coordination, and fielding skills (B = 3 points).
3. Play a game of 500 with no more than 5 players and demonstrate skills in catching flies and line drives and in fielding ground balls (B = 3 points).
4. In an actual game situation, participate in a successful double play (A = 5 points).
5. Perform a diving or over-the-head catch in an actual game situation (A = 5 points).

Hitting Tasks

1. Watch a film loop of hitting by Ted Williams (C = 1 point).
2. Using a batting tee, hit 5 consecutive softballs, on the fly or on the ground, past the 80-ft semicircle line marked off in chalk (C = 1 point).
3. Execute proper bunting form and ability by dumping 3 of 5 attempts into designated bunting areas along the first or third base lines (B = 3 points).
4. In an actual game, make 2 or more base hits (A = 5 points).
5. Hit a triple or home run in an actual game (A = 5 points).
6. During an actual game, observe an opponent or teammate's swing. Write down the strong and weak points of that particular swing and bring them to the instructor's attention. The instructor will then match observations with your critique (A = 5 points).

Optional Requirements

1. Make a diagram of an official softball diamond on posterboard. Illustrate proper field dimensions (A = 5 points).

2. On a piece of paper, show how batting average and earned run average are compiled (A = 5 points).

3. Watch a college or fast-pitch softball game on TV or at the actual setting. Record the score, place, teams, and date of the contest. List the strengths and weaknesses of each team, and note how weaknesses could be corrected (A = 5 points).

4. Umpire a game for 3 or more innings (A = 5 points).

5. Keep accurate score in an official scorebook for 3 or more innings (A = 5 points).

Suggested Readings

AAHPERD. N.A.G.W.S. 1977. *Softball Guide*. Reston, VA: AAHPERD.

Brace, D. 1966. *Skills Test Manual—Softball for Boys*. Reston, VA: AAHPERD.

Brace, D. 1966. *Skills Test Manual—Softball for Girls*. Reston, VA: AAHPERD.

Dobson, M., and Sisley, B. 1971. *Softball for Girls*. New York: Ronald Press Company.

Ledbetter, V. 1964. *Coaching Baseball*. Dubuque, IA: Wm. C. Brown Group.

TEAM HANDBALL

Team handball is an exciting and challenging game that combines skills from basketball, soccer, water polo, and hockey. It involves running, dribbling, jumping, passing, catching, throwing, and goal tending. The object of the game is to move a small soccer ball down the field by passing and dribbling and then to throw the ball into a goal area that is 3 meters wide and 2 meters high.

The game is relatively simple to learn and can be enjoyed by both sexes. It is inexpensive to add to the curriculum and can be played indoors, outdoors, or on a tennis court. Virtually any space can be adapted or modified for team handball. The play is rapid and involves continuous running, making the sport a good cardiovascular activity. Because the game is relatively new to the United States, many students will be inexperienced. A unit on team handball can provide students with a fresh challenge and increased motivation, and teachers should enjoy introducing a new activity.

Basic Rules

In regulation play, each team has six court players and one goalie. The six court players cover the entire court. A player is allowed three steps before and after dribbling the ball. There is no limit on the number of dribbles. Dribbling is, however, discouraged because passing is more effective. A double dribble is a violation. A player can hold the ball for 3 sec only before passing, dribbling, or shooting. No player except the goalie can kick the ball in any way.

The court is marked (Figure 20.45) with a 6-meter goal area, a 7-meter penalty line, and a 9-meter free throw line. The goal is 2 by 3 meters. The goal area inside the 6-meter line is only for the goalie. Other players are not allowed in this area. The 7-meter line is used for a major penalty shot, and the 9-meter line is used for a minor penalty shot. A regulation court is 20 by 40 meters.

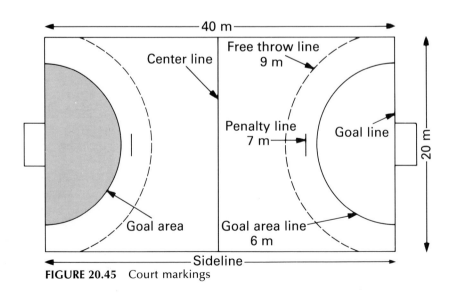

FIGURE 20.45   Court markings

FIGURE 20.46   Two sizes of team handballs

One point is awarded for a goal. Violations and penalties are similar to basketball. A free throw is taken from the point of the violation, and defense must remain 3 meters away while protecting the goal. A penalty throw is awarded from the 7-meter line for a major violation. A major violation occurs when an offensive player who is inside the 9-meter line in a good shooting position is fouled. During a penalty throw, all players must be behind the 9-meter line.*

The official team handball looks like a small soccer ball (Figure 20.46). The men's ball is 23 in. in circumference, and the women's ball is 21 in. A smaller minihandball is available for younger students. Handballs are carried by most sporting goods dealers. Playground balls and small volleyballs can be substituted if necessary. The goals can be improvised by using boundary cones, tape on the wall, rope through a chain-link fence, soccer goals, field hockey goals, or by building some regulation goals. The floor lines can be marked with floor tape or by putting boundary cones along the area where the lines should be. A basketball court can be easily modified for team handball by setting boundary cones along the

---

*The specific rules of team handball are available from the United States Team Handball Federation, 1750 E. Boulder, Colorado Springs, CO 80909.

goal area and by using the free throw lane for the width of the goal (Figure 20.47).

Sequence of Skills

Team handball is a good unit to follow basketball, soccer, or water polo because it uses many of the same skills. The techniques and skill work are similar to those activities.

Passing

Team handball is a passing game, and many different passes can be used for short and medium ranges. The passing fundamentals are similar to those of basketball.

Chest, Bounce, and Overhead Passes.   All two-handed passes, similar to those in basketball.

One-Handed Shoulder or Baseball Pass.   Similar to an overhand throw in baseball. If the student cannot grip the ball, the ball can rest on a flexed hand with the fingers spread (Figure 20.48).

Side-Arm Pass.   Similar to the shoulder pass, except that the ball is released three-quarters to side arm to avoid a defender.

Shovel Pass.   A one- or two-handed underhand pass used for releasing the ball quickly and thus avoiding a defender (Figure 20.49).

Hand-Off Pass.   Similar to a quarterback handing the ball off to a running back. The receiver forms a pocket for the ball (Figure 20.50).

Roller Pass.   The ball is simply rolled along the floor to a teammate when all other passing lanes are blocked.

Hook Pass.   Similar to the hook shot in basketball in which the passer hooks the ball over or around a defender. A jump may be added before the pass (Figure 20.51).

Jump Pass.   Usually made with a shoulder pass. The passer jumps over or around a defender and throws the ball (Figure 20.52).

Behind-the-Back Pass.   Similar to the basketball pass. Can be effective because the smaller ball is easier to control than a basketball.

Dribbling

Dribbling in handball is the same as the basketball skill, but the ball is harder to control because it is small and the ball surface is uneven. Players need to get used to the legal three steps before and after dribbling, as well as the 3-sec holding rule. Dribbling should be practiced some but should in general be discouraged in team handball.

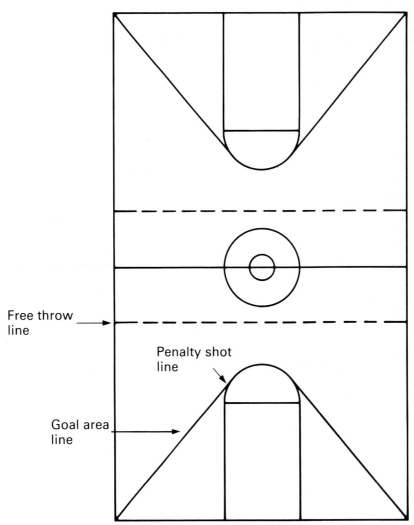

Free throw
line

Penalty shot
line

Goal area
line

FIGURE 20.47 Modified basketball court for team handball

Goal Shooting

All of the aforementioned passes can also be used for shots on goal. The following shots are the most popular:

Jump Shot. Because the offensive player can jump outside the goal area and land in the goal area after a shot, the jump shot is the most popular shot. Shooters run three steps, jump, and shoot, using the one-handed shoulder throw. This is the same as a one-handed shoulder pass, except that it is a shot on goal. The shot can be used with or without a defender.

Dive Shot. The dive shot is a good shot on either wing, because the shooter can dive or fall away from an opponent.

Lob Shot. When a goalie comes out too far to defend, the shooter can lob the ball up and over the goalie's outstretched arms.

Penalty Shot. The penalty shot is the one-on-one free shot with only the goalie defending. The shooter must keep one foot stationary and cannot touch the 7-meter penalty line until the ball is thrown. The ball must be shot in 3 sec. The goalie must be 3 meters or more away from the shooter. The shoulder or side-arm throw is usually most efficient for this shot.

Behind-the-Back. The shooter can fake a shot to the right and then bring the ball behind the back and the defender for a shot. The behind-the-back shot can be executed to either side.

There are a few general principles involved in goal shooting.

1. Attack the high or low corners on each shot.
2. Shoot primarily between the 6- and 9-meter line.
3. Find the open offensive player to take the shot.
4. Do not force a shot that is not open.

FIGURE 20.48   Shoulder pass

FIGURE 20.50   Hand-off pass

FIGURE 20.49   Shovel pass

FIGURE 20.51   Hook pass

FIGURE 20.52 Jump pass

5. Do not shoot too far down on the wings because the angle is too extreme.
6. Use the floor or ground to bounce shots into the goal.
7. Jump shots toward the goal are effective. The ball must be released before the shooter lands in the goal area.
8. Develop a wide variety of goal shots.

Goal Tending

The position of goalie, the most important defender on the team, requires quick hands and feet and fast reaction time. All parts of the body can be used to deflect shots. The goalie also starts the offense after saving shots. The goalie needs to learn how to cut down shooting angles by moving out from the goal, depending on where the ball is located on the court. Goalies should practice saving shots in all four corners of the goal. They need to understand all of the rules governing the goalkeeper.

Defensive Strategy

The defensive strategy is similar to basketball in that person-to-person and zone defense are popular. Beginning players should start with the person-to-per-

son defense and learn how to stay with an offensive player. Zone defenses can be 6–0, 5–1, 4–2, and 3–3, with each person playing an area or zone. The back players in the zone are back against the goal line, while the front players are just inside the 9-meter line. The zone rotates with the ball as passes are made around the court.

Offensive Strategy

The offense starts the game with a throw-on from the center line. A throw-on also initiates play after each goal. All six offensive players line up at the center line, and one teammate throws the ball to another. The defense is in position, using either a zone or person-to-person defense. Offensive strategy is similar to basketball with picks, screens, rolls, and movement to open up shots on goal. With a zone defense, short, quick passes are made in an over-loaded portion of the zone.

Ideas For Effective Instruction

Set up learning stations for passing, shooting, goal tending, dribbling, and defensive work. The performance objectives in this section, for example, are useful for structuring practice time at each station. Students can play with Nerf, or comparable foam rubber balls, playground balls, and volleyballs to get more practice attempts and to help beginning goalies perfect their skills. Group drills from basketball are applicable to team handball defense, offense, passing, and dribbling. Include various instructional devices for targets in passing, timing for dribbling through cones, or narrowing the goal area for shots to the corners. Penalty shots should be practiced daily. Competitive-type drills are enjoyable and motivating for most students.

Modified Games

No Bounce, No Steps, and No Contact

Students are forced to pass the ball rather than dribble. The walking or traveling rule from basketball is in effect, because students are usually comfortable with this rule. The no contact rule gives the offense an advantage. The 3-sec rule should remain in effect to force quick passes and deter holding of the ball.

Three Bounces, Three Steps, and No Contact

This game is closer to the regulation game and provides a gradual adjustment to the team handball rules. A variation would have the 3-bounce and 3-sec rules, but with no steps allowed. Getting students used to the 3-step rule is difficult.

Sideline Team Handball

Sideline handball can be played when space is limited and the class is crowded. Extra team members spread out along each sideline. These sideline players can receive passes from teammates and can help pass the ball down the court. Sideline members can only pass the ball, however, and the 3-sec rule applies to them. One sideline can be one team, and the other sideline the other team. A challenging variation is to have different team members on each sideline. This distribution forces the active players to sharpen their passing skills.

Suggested Performance Objectives

1. Dribble the ball with the right hand (standing position) for 10 consecutive times.
2. Same as Task 1, but with the left hand.
3. Dribble the ball with the right hand (moving forward) from the center line to the goal line without losing the dribble.
4. Same as Task 3, but with the left hand.
5. Pass the ball to a partner standing 10 ft away with a two-handed chest pass to the chest area (between chin and waist) 8 of 10 times.
6. Pass the ball to a partner standing 10 ft away with a two-handed bounce pass to the waist area 8 of 10 times.
7. Pass the ball to a partner standing 10 ft away with a two-handed overhead pass to the chest area 8 of 10 times.
8. Pass the ball to a partner standing 10 ft away with a one-handed overhead pass to the chest area 8 of 10 times.
9. While running from the center line, pass alternately a two-handed chest and bounce pass that can be caught by a partner running at a parallel distance of 12 ft with 3 of 4 passes hitting the partner.
10. While standing 7 meters from the goal, hit 3 of 5 goals.
11. Defend 3 of 5 attempted shots taken by a partner from a distance of 7 meters.
12. Dribble the ball with the right hand (moving forward) from the center line to the goal area without losing the dribble. Jump up and make a goal 3 of 5 times.
13. From 6 meters, hit a target 5 consecutive times with the following passes: roller, hook, jump, shovel, one-handed shoulder, side-arm, and behind-the-back.
14. From 9 meters away, hit 2 of 5 goals.
15. From 9 meters away, defend 4 of 5 goal shots.
16. Dribble through a set of 6 cones in 25 sec.

Suggested Readings

Cavanaugh, M. 1983. Team handball. In N. Dougherty (ed.) *Physical Education and Sport for the Secondary School Student*. Reston, VA: AAHPERD.

Cuesta, J. G. 1981. *Team Handball Techniques*. Colorado Springs, CO: United States Team Handball Federation.

Neil, G. 1976. *Modern Team Handball: Beginner to Expert*. Montreal, Canada: McGill University.

Team Handball—Official Rules of the Game. 1981. Colorado Springs, CO: United States Team Handball Federation.

Team Handball, Racquetball, Orienteering. 1979–1981. National Association for Girls and Women in Sport Guide. Reston, VA: AAHPERD.

VOLLEYBALL

Since volleyball was adopted as an Olympic sport in 1964, it has gained a great deal of visibility through the media. The activity has grown in popularity throughout the world. In the United States, power volleyball has become a vigorous sport that many pursue in school and in recreational leagues. Volleyball is challenging, lends itself to coeducational participation, and can be modified in several ways to suit the abilities of many students.

Most states offer competitive volleyball for girls in the secondary schools. Many boys have had little interest in or experience with organized volleyball. Secondary physical education programs should offer coeducational volleyball classes to encourage both boys and girls. With the increased recreational volleyball offerings in the YMCAs, community centers, and city recreational programs, students will be able to participate in and enjoy this activity for many years.

Sequence of Skills

Volleyball is difficult to play without a basic skills foundation. Help students to master these skills before beginning regulation games. Devising modified games for beginning level students is important, because they will not be able to play a regulation game. (A few students would dominate, and the remaining students would become quickly frustrated.) The type of ball, the height of the net, and the rules of the game can all be adjusted to ensure a successful experience for beginning students.

Serves

Underhand Serve. The underhand serve position (Figure 20.53) starts with the left leg forward and both knees bent slightly. The ball is held in the left hand about waist height. The right arm starts with

FIGURE 20.53 Underhand serve

FIGURE 20.54 Overhand floater serve

a long backswing and then comes forward, the right hand striking the ball just below the midline. The striking hand can be open or slightly closed, and the heel of the hand should contact the ball. The body weight is transferred from the rear foot to the front foot as the ball is contacted. The armswing follow-through should be in a straight line.

Overhand Serve. The overhand floater serve (Figure 20.54) has no spin on the ball. The legs are

staggered, with the left leg forward. The ball is held about shoulder height with the left hand under the ball and the right hand behind it. The ball is tossed 2 or 3 ft up above the right shoulder. The right arm is brought back, behind the ear, and then extended fully to hit the ball. The heel of the hand strikes the ball slightly below the midline. Little follow-through is used, because the ball should float or wobble like a knuckle ball.

Students who lack the strength or ability to get the ball over the net can begin serving closer to the net and the net can be lowered. As students develop skill, they should move back gradually to the regulation distance. Targets can be placed on the floor for work on accuracy as skill improves.

Passing and Setting

This skill involves moving the ball from one teammate to another. Forearm passes are used primarily for receiving a serve or a spike. Overhand set passes are used primarily for setting the ball into position for a spike. All passes require quick footwork while keeping a low center of gravity, which is necessary for getting under the ball.

Forearm Passes. In the forearm bump pass, the ball is hit off the forearms. The feet are about shoulder width apart, and one foot is ahead of the other. The knees are bent and the arms extended forward. The hands can be joined in several ways, as shown in Figure 20.55. The forearms are rolled outward to provide a flat, parallel surface for the ball (Figure 20.56). The elbows must be locked together on contact with the ball. The upward movement of the arms and legs depends on the speed of the ball and on the required distance of the pass. Passers must watch the ball carefully. Forearm passes can be made in different directions and also with one arm if necessary.

FIGURE 20.55 Ways of clasping hands for a forearm pass

FIGURE 20.56   Position for a forearm pass

Overhand or Set Passes.   In overhand passes, the body is set up under the ball, which is directly above the passer's nose. The hands are cupped to form a triangle-shaped window. The knees are bent and the legs are about shoulder width apart and in a stride position (Figure 20.57). The ball is contacted simultaneously with the fingers and thumbs of both hands. The legs, body, and arms uncoil into the ball in one smooth movement. Sets can be made from a front position facing the target and from a back position with the back to the target.

Spiking

Spiking is an offensive maneuver, which involves hitting the ball above the net and downward into the opponent's court. A spiker usually takes three or four steps toward the net. A final step with the right foot followed by a close step with the left foot precedes takeoff. With both feet together, the spiker then jumps vertically straight up. The arms swing forward during the jump. As the arms come forward to about shoulder height, the back begins to arch, and the right arm is cocked behind the head. The left arm starts the forward motion downward, and the right arm uncoils and attacks the ball. The elbow leads the striking arm and shoulder. The striking hand is open and rigid, and the palm of the hand strikes the ball (Figure 20.58).

Blocking

Blocking is a defensive maneuver used to stop the ball from going over the net. Blocking can be done by any of the three players on the front line. Blockers

FIGURE 20.57   Overhand pass and front set position

FIGURE 20.58   Spiking position

can jump and reach over the net, as long as the ball has not been touched by the offensive player. Blockers should leave the floor slightly after the spiker. The takeoff starts with the legs bent at the knees. After the jump, the arms extend fully upward, as high as possible. The fingers are spread as wide as possible. The hands are held rigid and no wider apart than the width of the ball. As the blocker comes down, the arms are drawn back to the body, and the feet and legs absorb the landing.

Ideas for Effective Instruction

Volleyball lends itself to station work on forearm passes, sets, serves, and spiking. The performance objectives listed in the contract at the end of this unit can be posted on task cards at the various stations. A class period could include work on the performance objectives, group skill work, and a modified game. It is important to adjust the height of the net, the rules of the game, and the type of ball used so that inexperienced students can keep the ball in play. Foam rubber balls and beach balls are excellent for beginners.

Many passing, setting, and serving activities can be done with partners. Having one partner toss the ball, and the other partner pass or set, is a good introductory drill. A smooth wall is useful for passing and setting practice, and small groups in a circle can also be effective for passing and setting. For serving practice, several players can line up along both base lines of a court and serve several balls at one time. Servers can practice anywhere along the base line. Beginning servers should always move closer to the net.

Setting and spiking drills can be arranged with a setter in the center forward position and a line of spikers in either the on-hand or off-hand position. The spiker tosses the ball to the setter and awaits a setup for a spike. Several ball chasers on the other side of the net can be useful. Net recovery shots can be practiced on a properly stretched net. One partner tosses the ball into the net, and the other player tries to recover the ball with a forearm pass.

Competitive situations are fun for drill work (e.g., sets in a row, passes with a partner, serves to a target area, or spikes to an area). These competitive challenges can be individual, with partners, or among small groups. The contract included here offers many challenges that can be modified for students of different ability levels.

Lead-Up and Modified Games

Leader Ball

Organize students into several teams. The leader of each team stands about 5 yd away from teammates. The teammates can be in single file or standing side by side facing the leader. The leader uses a forearm pass or set and hits the ball to the first person in line. That person hits the ball back to the leader and goes quickly to the end of the line. The object is

to hit the ball to all teammates quicker than the other teams.

Zigzag Relay

Half of the players on one team stand side by side about 2–3 yd apart, and face the other half of their team. The ball is started at one end and passed or set, back and forth, down the line across a distance of 5 yd. The object is to control the ball and move it down the line quickly. The winning team is the fastest in getting the ball up and down the line to all team members. More than one ball can be added for variety.

Keep It Up

A group must keep the ball up in the air or against a wall for a specified amount of time. The group can be in a circle or arranged single file for the wall drill. Passes, sets, or alternating of the two can be used.

Beach Ball or Nerf Ball Volleyball

Regulation rules are followed, except that the server must move up close to the net. A beach ball or Nerf ball is easier to control than a regular volleyball.

One-Bounce Volleyball

Regular rules are followed, except that the ball can bounce one time on each side. The bounce can occur after the serve, pass, or set. A variation of this game is to allow two or three bounces.

Volley Tennis

The game can be played on a tennis court or on a volleyball court. The net is put on the ground, as in tennis, and the ball is put in play with a serve. It may bounce once or can be passed directly to a teammate. The ball should be hit three times before going over the net. Spiking is common because of the low net.

Sitting or Kneeling Volleyball

Sitting or kneeling volleyball is a good indoor game to play on a mat or in the gym. The net is lowered according to the general size and ability level of the group. An overhead pass starts the game. Court size and number of players can vary.

Serve and Catch

"Serve and catch" is started with a ball on each side of the net. Several balls are served at the same time, and all balls must be caught on the other side. Once the balls are caught, they can be served from the opposing serving area. The object is to catch the ball and quickly serve so that your opponent cannot catch the ball. A scorer from each side is necessary.

Rotation Under the Net

The game, played with two, three, or four people on a team, is started with one team on each side of the net and with two or three other teams waiting in line to enter the game. The teacher begins the game by tossing the ball up on either side of the net. The ball must be hit three times, with the third hit going over the net. No spiking is allowed. The winning team rotates under the net, a new team rotates into their place, and the losing team rotates off the court and becomes the last team in line. The teacher throws the ball up in the air quickly as the teams are rotating. All teams must move quickly to the proper court. The game is fast-moving and involves passing, setting, and court coverage. It is a good game for high school students who have developed passing and setting skills.

Three-Hit Volleyball

Three-hit volleyball is similar to regular volleyball, but the ball must be hit three times on a side with the third hit going over the net.

Minivolleyball

This is a modified game for students age 9–12. The net is 6 ft 10 in., and the court is 15 by 40 ft. Three students are on a team, with two front line players and one back line player. The rules are similar to regulation volleyball.

Blind-Man Volleyball

A cover is put over the net so that it is impossible to see what is happening on the other side. Regulation volleyball rules are followed. Teams must be ready, because they never know when the ball is coming over the net. A scorer is necessary for both sides of the net.

Regulation Volleyball—Serves Modified

Regulation rules are followed, but the server can have two attempts, or the service distance is shortened.

Suggested Performance Objectives

Contracts have been used successfully with volleyball units at both the junior and senior high levels. The following contract employs a point system that is tied to a grading system as the reward for accomplishing the performance objectives. This contract (or any of the performance objectives) can be

modified according to the abilities of the students and the facilities available.

Core Objectives

Forearm Pass

1. Bump 12 consecutive forearm passes against the wall at a height of at least 10 ft (1 point).
2. Bump 12 consecutive forearm passes into the air at a height of at least 10 ft (1 point).
3. Bump 10 consecutive forearm passes over the net with the instructor or a classmate (1 point).

Overhead Set Pass

4. Hit 15 consecutive set passes against the wall at a height of at least 10 ft (1 point).
5. Hit 15 consecutive set passes into the air at a height of at least 10 ft (1 point).
6. Hit 12 consecutive set passes over the net with the instructor or a classmate (1 point).

Serves

7. Hit 3 consecutive underhand serves into the right half of the court (1 point).
8. Hit 3 of 4 underhand serves into the left half of the court (1 point).
9. Hit 3 consecutive overhand serves inbounds (1 point).

Attendance and Participation

10. Be dressed and ready to participate at 8:00 A.M. ($\frac{1}{5}$ of a point for each day = 5 points total).
11. Participate in 15 games (1 point).
12. Score 90% or better on a rules, strategies, and techniques test (2 attempts only, 5 points).

Optional Objectives

1. Standing 2 ft from the backline, bump 3 of 5 forearm passes into an 8-ft circle surrounding the setter's position. The height must be at least 10 ft. The ball will be thrown by the instructor or a classmate (1 point).
2. Bump 3 of 5 forearm passes over the net at a height of at least 12 ft that land inbounds and not more than 8 ft from the backline (1 point).
3. Standing in the setter's position (center forward), hit 3 consecutive overhead sets at least 10 ft high that land in a 5-ft circle where the spiker would be located. The ball will be thrown by the instructor or a classmate (1 point).
4. Hit 3 of 5 overhead passes over the net at least 12 ft high that land inbounds and not more than 8 ft from the backline (1 point).
5. Standing in the setter's position (center forward), hit 3 of 5 back sets at least 10 ft high

that land in a 5-ft circle where the spiker would be located. The ball will be thrown by the instructor or a classmate (1 point).

6. Volley 12 consecutive times over the net with the instructor or a classmate by alternating forearm passes and overhead passes (1 point).

7. Alternate forearm passes and overhead passes in the air at a height of 10 ft or more, 12 consecutive times (1 point).

8. Spike 3 of 4 sets inbounds from an on-hand position—three-step approach, jump, extend arm, hand contact (1 point).

9. Spike 3 of 5 sets inbounds from an off-hand position (1 point).

10. Recover 3 consecutive balls from the net. Recoveries must be playable, that is, 8 ft high in the playing area (1 point).

11. Hit 3 consecutive overhand serves into the right half of the court (1 point).

12. Hit 3 of 4 overhand serves into the left half of the court (1 point).

13. Hit 3 of 5 overhand serves under a rope 15 ft high that land in the back half of the court (1 point).

14. Officiate at least 3 games, using proper calls and signals (1 point).

15. Coach a team for the class tournament—planning strategy, substitution, and scheduling (1 point).

16. Devise and carry out a research project that deals with volleyball. Check with the instructor for ideas (1 point).

Grade Structure

A = 34 points; **B** = 28 points; **C** = 10 points

Suggested Readings

Bertucci, R., ed. 1979. *Championship Volleyball by the Experts*. West Point, NY: Leisure Press.

Scates, A. E. 1976 *Winning Volleyball*. 2nd ed. Boston, MA: Allyn and Bacon, Inc..

Slaymaker, T., and Brown, V. 1983. *Power Volleyball*. 3rd ed. Philadelphia, PA: W. B. Saunders Co.

21 INDIVIDUAL SPORTS

Individual sports are excellent lifetime recreational activities because many of them require little equipment. The focus for instruction in these units should be on the benefits of participation.

AQUATICS

An aquatics instructional program in the secondary schools is an excellent addition to a balanced curriculum. Unfortunately, few school districts have the facilities necessary to implement swimming and related aquatics programs. It is, however, often possible to bus students to swimming pools outside the school. These may be municipal pools, YMCA and YWCA pools, or the facilities of various private organizations.

Swimming classes require teacher expertise in the area. Rotating teaching responsibilities is mandatory so that teachers with experience are used in the swimming instructional program. The swimming program can also have an aquatic games component, which focuses on learning to adjust to the water. The aquatic games can be taught by a less qualified teacher. All aquatics teachers, regardless of assignment, should have the American Red Cross Water Safety Instruction certification.

The pool should be clean and warm. Nothing turns students off faster than having to swim in a pool that is inadequately heated. A pool with a uniform depth of 3 to 4 ft of water is often preferable for teaching nonswimmers, because the students can stand up immediately if they have a problem. This offers beginning swimmers a measure of confidence. For intermediate and advanced swimmers, a standard pool, which can be used for diving as well as swimming, is preferable.

Keep lessons short in terms of time spent in the water. Students tire easily when learning new skills, and they can practice some skills out of the water.

Since swimming is an important lifetime skill, it is most desirable that students leave the class with a positive feeling about the instruction. Introducing students to any new activity is difficult, and most students need extra encouragement and patience as they begin to overcome their fears of the water.

Sequence of Skills

A difficult aspect of teaching swimming to junior and senior high school students is the tremendous range of ability and experience that students bring to the class. Some students may not know how to swim, whereas others may have been swimming competitively since they were three years old. This necessitates homogeneous groupings according to ability. The skills to be taught may therefore range from drown-proofing and survival skills to the American Red Cross Water Safety Instruction certification.

Because aquatics is a highly specialized activity involving specific skills that must be learned, it is difficult to develop meaningful lead-up activities. The authors recommend the text *Teaching Aquatics* (Torney and Clayton, 1981) to teachers who are interested in creating a meaningful instructional program. It includes chapters on developing a successful instructional program, teaching essential aquatic skills, springboard diving skills, and life-saving skills. A chapter is also offered on the evaluation of swimming skills. Of particular aid to the less experienced teacher is a series of performance analysis sheets to help in evaluating various strokes and dives.

Another approach that has been effective in the school setting is to play a wide variety of aquatic games. Many of the games do not require swimming skills, but students often learn to overcome their fear of water through participation. The games are demanding on the cardiovascular system, and help develop strength and balance. An excellent source for aquatic games is the *Physical Education Handbook,* 7th edition (Seaton et al., 1983).

References

Seaton, D. C., et al. 1983. *Physical Education Handbook.* 7th ed. Englewood Cliffs, NJ: Prentice-Hall, Inc.

Torney, J. A., Jr., and Clayton, R. D. 1981. *Teaching Aquatics.* Minneapolis, MN: Burgess Publishing Co.

Suggested Readings

American National Red Cross. 1968. *Swimming and Water Safety.* Washington, DC: American National Red Cross.

American National Red Cross. 1968. *Swimming and Water Safety Courses: Instructors Manual.* Washington, DC: American National Red Cross.

Arnold, C. G., ed. 1979. *Aquatic Safety and Lifesaving Programs.* 2nd ed. New York: National YMCA Program Materials.

Arnold, L., and Freeman, R. W. 1972. *Progressive Swimming and Springboard Diving Program.* New York: National YMCA Program Materials.

Hallett, B., and Clayton, R. D., eds. 1980. *Course Syllabus: Teacher of Swimming.* Reston, VA: AAHPERD.

Lanoue, F. R. 1963. *Drownproofing.* Englewood Cliffs, NJ: Prentice-Hall, Inc.

ARCHERY

Archery has long been recognized as an appealing activity for both sexes of all ages, and for the handicapped. The two most popular forms are target archery and field archery. Target archery involves shooting a specific number of arrows from a given distance at a target with five or ten concentric circles. Scoring is completed by adding up the points for each arrow striking the target. This is the most popular archery activity taught in secondary school programs. Field archery involves 28 stationary targets of assorted sizes and shapes placed at varying distances. Field shooting requires a larger area and considerable safety procedures. It is especially appealing to the hunter and bow fisherman.

Archery seems to be quite popular with certain individuals. Many families enjoy participating together, for archery activities can be enjoyed by all family members.

Sequence of Skills

Bracing the Bow

There are several methods used for stringing or bracing the bow. One method involves using a bowstringer device made of a 5-ft rope with a leather cup on each end. The cups are put on both ends of the bow with the string hanging down toward the

FIGURE 21.1 Bowstringer

ground in front of the body. After placing one string loop in position, place one foot on the center of the bowstringer, and pull the bow straight up with one hand. Use the free hand to slide the free string loop into place. To unstring the bow, reverse the process. Figure 21.1 is an example of another type of bowstringer.

Another stringing technique is called the *step-through method* (Figure 21.2). Start by placing the bottom string loop in position, then put the bottom curve of the bow across the top of the right ankle, and step between the string and the bow with the left foot. Use the left hand to bend the bow against the left thigh until the string loop can be moved into place with the right hand. Be sure to keep the face away from the bow tip.

FIGURE 21.2 Step-through method

Stance

The feet should straddle the shooting line and be shoulder width apart. The toes are in a direct line with the target. The knees should be relaxed, and a comfortable standing posture maintained (Figure 21.3).

Nocking the Arrow

Hold the bow horizontally in the left hand, and place the nock of the arrow on the nocking point of the string. The odd-colored feather should face away from the bow. Use the index finger of the left hand to steady the arrow on the arrow rest.

Extend and Draw

The string is on the first joint of three fingers of the right hand. The index finger is above the arrow, and the next two fingers are below the arrow. Rotate the bow to a vertical position with the left arm parallel to the ground. Extend the left arm and draw the string toward the body with the right hand. Keep the right elbow parallel to the ground. Be sure the fingers of the bow hand are loose and relaxed.

Anchor and Hold

The string should touch the nose, lips, and chin, while the index finger touches under the center of the chin. The anchor point should be the same for every shot.

Aiming

Target archery has two basic methods of aiming—point of aim and bowsights. The beginner should probably use the point-of-aim technique, which in-volves finding a spot somewhere on a vertical line drawn above, through, and below the middle of the target. This point of aim will vary according to the distance from the target. To locate the point, align the eye and the arrow with an object on the vertical line through the center of the target. Shoot several rounds and then adjust the point of aim up or down accordingly. A mechanical bowsight (Figure 21.4) can be mounted on the bow and used by aligning the center of the target through the aperture. The aperture is then adjusted up or down, or left or right, depending on the pattern of the arrows for that shooting distance. The aperture position is then noted for each distance and is used in the future.

Release and Afterhold

As the arrow is released, the back muscles remain tight while the string fingers relax. The relaxed drawing hand moves backward slightly along the neck. The bow arm and head remain steady until the arrow hits the target.

Retrieving Arrows

Arrows in a target should be removed by placing the arrow between the index and middle finger of the left hand. The palm of the hand should be away from the target facing the archer. The right hand should be placed on the arrow close to the target. The arrow is removed by gently twisting and pulling at the same angle at which the arrow entered. If the fletching is inside the target, the arrow should be pulled through the target. Arrows should be carried with the points together and the feathers spread out to prevent damage.

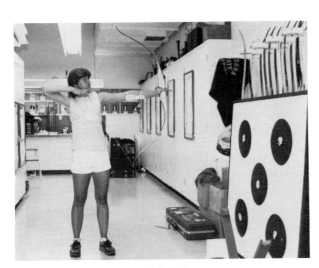

FIGURE 21.3   Stance and full draw

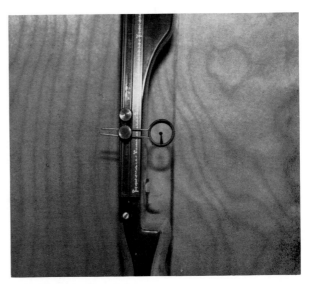

FIGURE 21.4   Bowsight

Ideas for Effective Instruction

Equipment

The composition of bows is primarily wood, fiberglass, or a laminated combination of the two. Both straight and recurved bows are available. The recurved bow has curved ends to provide additional leverage, which increases the velocity of the arrow. Bows also have different weights and lengths. Archers should select a bow based on their strength and skill. Starting with a lighter bow is best, and then progressing to a heavier one as skill and strength are developed. In class situations, teachers should try to have a variety of bows available for different ability levels. Figure 21.5 shows the parts of a bow.

Arrow shafts are made of wood, fiberglass, or aluminum. The term fletching refers to the feathers or plastic material used to stabilize the flight of the arrow. It is important for the beginning archer to get the proper length arrow. A good method for determining proper length is to have someone hold

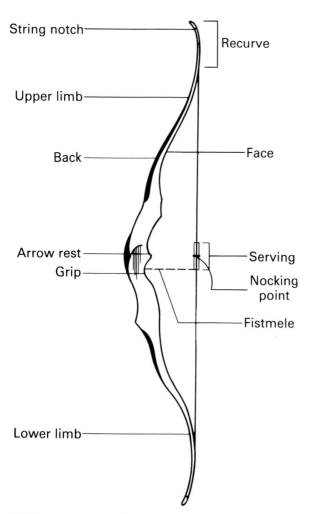

FIGURE 21.5 Parts of a bow

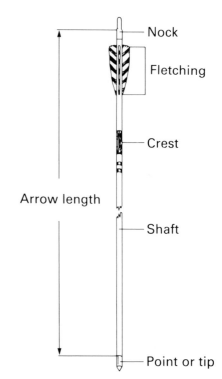

FIGURE 21.6 Parts of an arrow

a yardstick against the sternum and perpendicular to the body, while the individual extends the arms with the palms on either side of the yardstick. The point at which the fingertips touch the yardstick is the correct arrow length. For beginners, it is better to have long arrows. Many different types of points and feathers are available. Figure 21.6 shows the parts of an arrow.

Many types of finger tabs and shooting gloves are also available for protection and to promote smooth release. An arm guard should be used to prevent the bowstring from slapping the bow arm and to keep long clothing sleeves snug to the body. Movable and stationary quivers are used to transport arrows and sometimes to support the bow while retrieving arrows.

General Rules

1. Archers must straddle a shooting line. Arrows should always be pointed down-range.
2. An end of six arrows is usually shot at one time. A round consists of a number of ends shot at several distances.
3. Values for rings in a target are as follows:

Five-Ring Scoring		*Ten-Ring Scoring*	
Gold	= 9	Gold	= 10, 9
Red	= 7	Red	= 8, 7
Blue	= 5	Blue	= 6, 5
Black	= 3	Black	= 4, 3
White	= 1	White	= 2, 1

4. An arrow that bisects two colors scores the higher of the two values.

5. An arrow that bounces off a target or passes through a target is given 7 points if there is a witness.

6. The petticoat, or outside area of the target, counts as a miss.

Organization, Skill Work, and Safety

Beginning students can experience success quickly if the instructor moves the target close to them (10 yd or less). Students can then move away from the target as their skill level increases. A safe environment is important. Make sure that students follow strict rules for shooting procedures. Partner work is useful for checking form, reminding about safety procedures, and giving feedback. A form for a rating scale or checklist for shooting can also be useful and motivating to some students. Several checklists are available from the sources listed at the end of the unit.

Time should be spent with partners and observers to make sure that they are actively involved in the learning process and concentrating on the specific shooting skills. Make sure that all students are mentally involved, even when they are not shooting.

Lead-Up Games and Learning Activities

Relays

Each team has one target and each person has one arrow. The first person in line shoots and then goes to the end of the line. All team members shoot one arrow and then the team score is tallied. The team with the highest score is the winner.

Turkey Shoot

Each team draws a turkey about the size of a target on a piece of paper. The turkey is placed on the target. Each team tries to hit the turkey as many times as possible.

Tic-Tac-Toe or Bingo

Balloons or a target with squares are placed on the regular target—three rows of three for tic-tac-toe, or five rows of five for bingo. The object is to hit three or five in a row vertically, horizontally, or diagonally. The game can be for individuals or for teams.

Target Work-Up

Start with four or five students on a target. Shoot an end of four arrows and tally the score. The highest scorer moves up one target, and the lowest scorer moves down a target. This can be an individual or partner activity.

Tape Shooting

Place two pieces of masking tape across the target, one vertically and one horizontally. The object is to hit either piece of tape. This can also be an individual or team event.

Suggested Performance Objectives

Core Objectives

Objectives 1, 2, and 3 should be completed before the student is allowed to shoot on the range.

1. On a written test covering safety rules, archery terminology, and scoring, the student will score at least 70%. (Two attempts allowed.)

2. The student will demonstrate how to brace and unbrace the bow. Grading is on a pass-fail basis.

3. The student will demonstrate the 9 steps of the shooting technique (i.e., stand, nock, extend, draw, anchor, hold, aim, release, and afterhold). Grading is on a pass-fail basis.

4. At a distance of 10 yd, the student will hit the target at least 5 of 6 times and score a minimum of 28 points.

5. At a distance of 15 yd, the student will hit the target 4 of 6 times and score a minimum of 24 points.

6. At a distance of 20 yd, the student will hit the target 4 of 6 times and score a minimum of 24 points.

7. The student will participate in a minimum of 2 out of 3 novelty archery events.

Optional Activities (Worth Extra Credit)

1. On a written test covering safety rules, archery terminology, and scoring, the student will score 100% (1 attempt only and worth 3 extra points).

2. At a distance of 10 yd, the student will hit the target 6 of 6 times and score at least 40 points (5 extra points).

3. At a distance of 15 yd, the student will hit the target 5 of 6 times and score at least 40 points (5 extra points).

4. At a distance of 20 yd, the student will hit the target 5 of 6 times and score at least 38 points (5 extra points).

5. The student will write a two-page report on the history of archery, complete with bibliography (3 extra points).

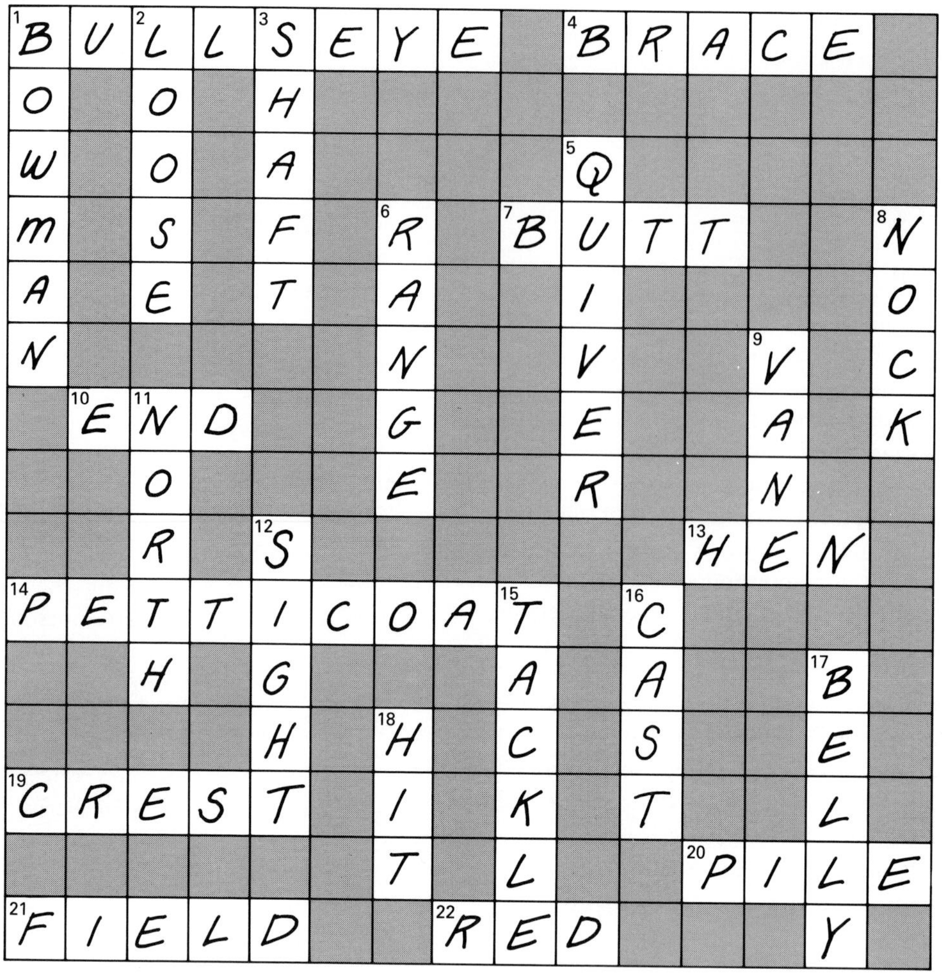

The crossword puzzle grid contains the following filled-in answers:

Across:
- 1. BULLSEYE
- 4. BRACE
- 7. BUTT
- 10. END
- 13. HEN
- 14. PETTICOAT
- 19. CREST
- 20. PILE
- 21. FIELD
- 22. RED

Down:
- 1. BOWMAN
- 2. LOOSE
- 3. SHAFT
- 5. QUIVER
- 6. RANGE
- 8. NOCK
- 9. VANE
- 11. NORTHS (NORTHS / reading NORTH...)
- 12. SIGHT
- 15. TACKLE
- 16. CAST
- 17. BELLY
- 18. HITTILT (HIT)

Across

1. Gold circle in center of target
4. Procedure used in stringing bow
7. Another name for an archery target
10. Six arrows
13. The two feathers not at right angles to the nock
14. Area of target face outside the white ring
19. Colored stripes below the feathers
20. Pointed tip of the arrow
21. Long-range shooting
22. Colored circle on target that counts seven points

Down

1. Individual who participates in archery
2. Act of releasing bowstring during a shot
3. Main part of the arrow
5. Receptacle to hold or carry arrows
6. Shooting area
8. Groove in end of arrow where bowstring is placed
9. The feather of an arrow
11. Best orientation for placing targets outdoors
12. Used to assist the archer in aiming
15. Archery equipment
16. Distance a bow is able to shoot
17. Side of bow nearest the string
18. An arrow that contacts the target for a score

FIGURE 21.7 Archery crossword puzzle

6. The student will participate in all 3 days of novelty archery events (3 extra points).

7. The student will design and put up a bulletin board about archery (5 extra points).

Reinforcement Menu

1. Objectives 1, 2, and 3 must be met before students are allowed to shoot.

2. Post the checklist of objectives on the bulletin board.

3. Post on the bulletin board the high ends and high rounds for each class.

4. Post on the bulletin board the results of the class tournament for each distance.

5. Give ribbons to winners of novelty events.

6. Award extra credit points for exceeding skill requirements.

Rainy Day Activities

Discussion and practice can focus on these skills.

- Eye dominance
- Stance
- Nock
- Extend
- Bow hand position
- String hand and arm position
- Draw
- Anchor
- Tighten-hold
- Aim
- Tighten-release
- Afterhold

Archery tackle can be discussed in detail (i.e., bows, arrows, accessories). Crossword puzzles (Figure 21.7) and word searches are also enjoyable activities for inclement weather.

Suggested Readings

Barrett, J. A. 1973 *Archery*. 2nd ed. Pacific Palisades, CA: Goodyear Publishing Co.

Broer, M. 1971. *Individual Sports for Women*. 5th ed. Philadelphia: W. B. Saunders Co.

Dintiman, G. B., and Barrow, L. M. 1970. *A Comprehensive Manual of Physical Education Activities for Men*. New York: Appleton-Century-Crofts.

McKinney, W. C. 1975. *Archery*. 3rd ed. Dubuque, IA: Wm. C. Brown Group.

National Association for Girls and Women in Sport. 1979–1980. *Archery-Fencing Guide*. Reston, VA: AAHPERD.

Seidel, B. L., et al. 1980. *Sports Skills: A Conceptual Approach to Meaningful Movement*. 2nd ed. Dubuque, IA: Wm. C. Brown Group.

Sysler, B. L., and Fox, E. R. 1978. *Lifetime Sports for the College Student*. 3rd ed. Dubuque, IA: Kendall/Hunt Publishing Co.

BOWLING

The game of bowling today is a form of kingpins, the first bowling game to use finger holes in the ball. The sport has changed from a simple game played outdoors to a complex mechanized game played in large modern facilities.

Bowling has become one of our most widely enjoyed recreational activities. Any family member may participate, because the game is suitable for all ages and both sexes. Bowling can be played in any season, and facilities are usually available at most times of the day. Leagues are popular, and many businesses sponsor employee leagues. Schools have intramural leagues, and many bowling establishments organize leagues for children. These leagues are usually sanctioned by the proper national organization.

The play in bowling consists of rolling balls down a wooden alley with the object of knocking over ten wooden pins positioned at the far end of the alley. The bowler stands any distance behind the foul line and takes three, four, or five steps before releasing the ball down the alley. If the player touches the alley beyond the foul line, a foul is called, and the ball counts as one ball bowled. No score is made on a foul, and the pins knocked down are immediately replaced. In bowling and duckpins, the pins knocked down after the first ball rolled are cleared away before the next ball is rolled. In candlepins, knocked down pins are not cleared away. Each bowler has ten frames in which to knock down as many pins as possible. If a bowler knocks down all of the pins in ten frames of bowling, a perfect score of 300 is attained.

Sequence of Skills

Picking Up the Ball

If in an alley area, face the direction of the returning balls. Place the hands on opposite sides of the ball and lift the ball to a comfortable position in front of the body before placing the fingers and thumb in the holes. Avoid placing the thumb and fingers in the holes to pick up the ball, as this places strain on the bowling hand.

Gripping the Ball

Holding the ball in the left hand (if right-handed), place the two middle fingers in the holes first and then slip the thumb in the thumbhole. Do not squeeze the ball with the fingertips, but maintain contact by slightly pressing the palm side of the fingers and thumb toward the palm area of the ball. The little finger and index finger are relaxed and flat on the ball.

Stance

The stance is the stationary position that the bowler holds before approaching the foul line. The development of a stance, which varies among bowlers, is essential for consistency in bowling. To locate the starting position, stand with the back to the foul line, walk four and one-half steps, stop, turn, and face the pins. The number of steps will vary with the three-, four-, or five-step approach. Standing erect, place the feet parallel to each other, or the left foot may be slightly in front of the right foot. The feet should be about 1.5 in. apart. The weight is on the left foot, and the knees are slightly bent. The head is up, and the shoulders are level.

The ball is held at waist level and slightly to the right. The arm is straight from the shoulder to the wrist. The ball will be pushed out during the first step and will swing down directly below the shoulder. The wrist is kept straight and stiff during the pendulum swing. The elbow moves back alongside the body and should not be braced on the hip. The ball is supported by the nonbowling hand. The shoulders, hips, and feet are square with the pins when the stance is established.

After learning the basic stance, the bowler can develop a personal style. Some leading bowlers hold the ball approximately level with the chin and a few inches from the body. Proficient bowlers usually hold the ball at waist level and a few inches away from the body. The upper torso leans slightly forward. Taller bowlers sometimes use a half crouch and a shorter backswing.

Aiming

The method of aim should be decided after the footwork, timing, and method of rolling the ball have been established. The bowler should then experiment to find the preferable method of aim. Spot bowling is recommended.

1. **Pin bowling**—The bowler looks at the pins and draws an imaginary line between the point of delivery and the point on the pins at which the ball will be aimed. This line will be the route of the ball. The usual point to hit is the 1–3 pocket.
2. **Spot bowling**—The bowler draws an imaginary line from the point of delivery to some spot down the lane, usually at the division boards where the maple meets pine. Most lanes have triangular markings for spot bowlers.

Approach and Delivery

One-Step Delivery

One-step delivery should be learned before the three-, four-, or five-step delivery. The stance for the one-step delivery differs from the general stance discussed previously. The foot opposite the bowling arm is behind. Extend the bowling hand, and after extension, drop the hand slowly to the side and simultaneously lean forward, bending the knees. Keep the arm relaxed and the wrist straight. Swing the arm forward to eye level, back to waist level, and forward again to eye level. The stance for the one-step delivery is assumed. The hands are at waist height as if gripping the ball. Push the arms forward, release the left hand, and complete the pendulum swing.

Repeat the push-away and the pendulum swing, but as the arm swings forward (at the completion of the swing), slide ahead on the foot opposite the bowling arm. Keep the shoulders straight and the body facing straight ahead. Practice the simultaneous movement of arm and foot. No ball is necessary when first learning the approach and delivery. When the timing is learned, then add the ball.

Four-Step Delivery

The four-step delivery is the most popular. The stance is with the opposite foot forward, as presented earlier. Starting with the right foot, take four brisk walking strides forward. Repeat the four-step walk, making the fourth step a slide. At the completion of the slide, the full body weight should be on the sliding foot, knee bent, and shoulders parallel to the foul line. The forward foot should be pointed toward the pins.

To coordinate the delivery, the bowler should assume the stance, start the four-step walk, and push the ball out, down, back, and forward so that the arm movements coordinate with the steps (one, two, three, slide). As the foot slides, the ball comes forward and is released. At the release, the thumb is out, and the fingers and wrist are turning and lifting the ball. The right leg swings forward for balance, and the right arm, which was straight throughout the backswing, bends at the elbow for the follow-through. The body then straightens to get more lift on the ball.

Different types of balls can be thrown, depending on how the ball is released.

1. **Straight ball**—The wrist and forearm are kept straight throughout the entire delivery. The thumb is on top of the ball, at 12 o'clock position, and the index finger is at 2 o'clock.
2. **Hook ball**—The ball is held throughout the ap-

proach, delivery, and release with the thumb at 10 o'clock and the index finger at 12 o'clock. If the ball hooks too much, move the thumb toward the 12 o'clock position.

Ideas for Effective Instruction

Gymnasium Bowling Sets

Gymnasium bowling sets are available through many equipment dealers. They usually contain ten plastic pins, a triangular sheet for pin setup, score sheets, and one hard plastic ball. Sizes of the finger holes will vary, and so may the weight of the ball. The cost is approximately $60.00 per set.

Score Sheets

Score sheets can be drawn and duplicated. Sheets are included in gym sets, or an instructor can check with a local establishment about purchasing or a possible donation.

General Rules and Scoring

1. A game consists of ten frames. Each bowler is allowed two deliveries in each frame, with the exception of the tenth frame in which three are allowed if a spare or strike is scored.
2. The score is an accumulated total of pins knocked down plus bonus points for spares and strikes.
3. If all ten pins are knocked down on the first ball rolled, it is a strike. The scorer counts ten plus the total of the next two balls rolled.
4. If all pins are knocked down with two balls rolled, it is a spare. The scorer counts ten plus the number of pins knocked down on the next ball rolled.
5. If no pins are knocked down when a ball is

rolled, the bowler is charged with an error. This includes gutter balls.
6. If pins left after the first ball constitute a split, a circle is made on the scoresheet around the number of pins knocked down.
7. A foul results if the bowler steps across the foul line.
8. Pin setup and numbering is shown in Figure 21.8.

Symbols for Scoring

Figure 21.9 is a sample score sheet showing all of the standard scoring symbols.

Etiquette

1. Take your turn promptly.
2. The bowler to the right has the right-of-way. Wait until the bowler on the right is finished before assuming stance.
3. Stay on your approach.
4. Step back off the approach after delivery.
5. Use your ball only, and use the same ball throughout.
6. Do not talk to a player who is on the approach.
7. Respect all equipment and the establishment.
8. Competition is encouraged, but be gracious in any case.
9. Return all equipment to its proper place.

Organization and Skill Work

Teach skills in sequence. Once the basic grip and stance have been taught (group situation), stations can be used for skill practice. Contracts with study guides can inform and motivate students.

Depending on the unit structure, students can work at stations on skills to be checked off, or they may be involved in lead-up games, engaged in minitournaments (using gym sets), or practicing skills at a bowling facility. Since bowling skills are perfected through constant practice, the unit should be designed for maximum activity.

If space is available, mock lanes can be made (Figure 21.10). Using mock lanes can enhance the number of students involved in activity while using a smaller space. Students are able to practice the approach, release, and spotting without pins. They can work in pairs, taking turns practicing and rolling the ball back.

Team games with the mock lanes and gymnasium bowling sets can be enjoyable. Hand out score sheets and have students record their scores. Scorers sign their name, and score sheets are checked for correct scoring procedure. Games with mock lanes and gymnasium sets can be used as a lead-up to bowling at a nearby facility.

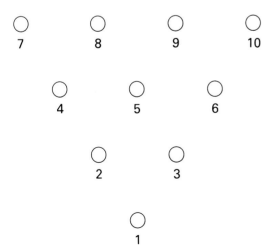

FIGURE 21.8 Pin setup and numbering

Scoring Symbols

Miss	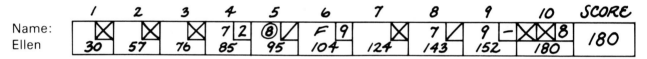	Error, gutter ball

Miss — Error, gutter ball

Foul — Touching or going beyond foul line

Split — Pins left after first roll: Headpin must be down and a ball's width between remaining pins.

Spare — Knocking down all pins in two rolls

Strike — Knocking down all pins in one roll

Double — Two strikes in a row

Turkey — Three strikes in a row

Sample Scoring

FIGURE 21.9 Symbols and sample scoring

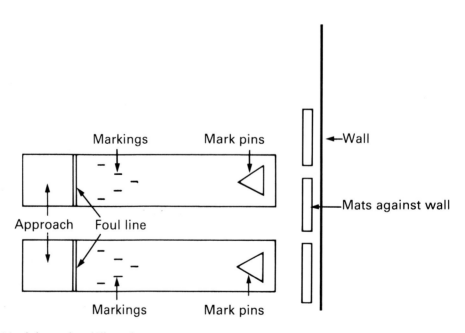

FIGURE 21.10 Mock lanes for skill work

Lead-Up Games and Learning Activities

Red Pin

Use regulation alleys or lanes set up on the gym floor. One pin is painted red (tape may be substituted). The bowler rolls one ball in each frame. The bowler scores only if the red pin is upset. The pinsetter makes no attempt to specifically place the red pin. It will occur in random placement. Because only one ball is rolled, no spares are scored. Strikes are possible and should be scored as in regulation bowling. This activity can be used for team or individual competition.

Scotch Bowling

This activity can be played on regulation lanes or in a gym with marked lanes. Students choose a partner and decide who will roll the first ball. Partners then alternate throughout the game, which is scored like regulation bowling.

Shuffle-Bowl

The game is played on a shuffleboard court using shuffleboard cues, disc, and bowling pins or Indian clubs. The discs are slid at the pins. Play and scoring are carried out as in regulation bowling.

Skittles

Use an open area, wooden discs, and ten small pins or Indian clubs. Slide or pitch the discs at the pins from a specified distance. Use regulation scoring.

Three Pins

Regulation equipment or the gymnasium with marked lanes can be used for play. The bowler attempts to knock down the 1-2-3 combination by hitting the 1-3 pocket (1-2, if left-handed). One ball is allowed for each turn. Players start with 20 points. Three pins down subtracts 3 points, two down subtracts 2 points, and one pin down subtracts 1 point. The first player to reach zero points is the winner.

Soccer Bowling

Any open area, indoors or outdoors, is suitable for play. Soccer balls and wooden pins are used, and the game is scored like regulation bowling.

Basket Bowling

Play in an alley marked on the gym floor. Allow a 15-ft approach. Use two indoor softballs and a metal wastebasket propped up on its side with two bricks or similar objects facing the foul line. Five to ten players and one retriever make up a team. Each player attempts to roll two balls into the wastebasket. Rotate and trade places with the retriever. One point is scored for each basket made, and the high scorer wins. If teams play against one another, use a time limit. Each player is allowed five turns. If the bowler steps over the foul line, one point is subtracted. If the ball is bounced on the alley, one point is subtracted. An official scorekeeper and judge are necessary.

Scoring Work Sheets

Figure 21.11 shows a scoring work sheet, including problems.

Crossword Puzzle

A bowling crossword (Figure 21.12) makes a good rainy day activity or an alternative activity for students not at a station.

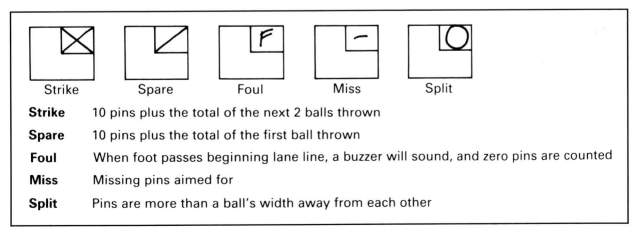

Strike	Spare	Foul	Miss	Split

Strike	10 pins plus the total of the next 2 balls thrown
Spare	10 pins plus the total of the first ball thrown
Foul	When foot passes beginning lane line, a buzzer will sound, and zero pins are counted
Miss	Missing pins aimed for
Split	Pins are more than a ball's width away from each other

FIGURE 21.11 Scoring work sheet

SCORING COMBINATIONS

Strike and Spare

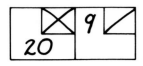

Example: Strike equals 10 plus the next two shots, which totaled 9, and a spare, which also equals 10, for a total of 20.

10 + 9 + 1 = 20

Spare and Strike

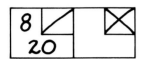

Example: This counts as 10 plus the next ball, which was a strike, so you can count that as 10 + 10 = 20.

Strike and Strike

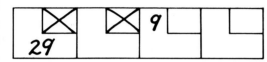

Example: At this point, there is still no score recorded. The scoring would be 10 + 10 plus the next shot. If the first shot in the third frame were 9, then 29 would go in the first frame.

10 + 10 + 9 = 29

Scoring Examples

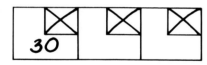

10 + 10 + 10 = 30

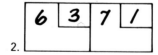

Example Game

Total 196 game

Problems

1.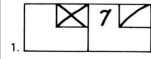

2.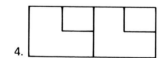

3.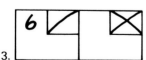

4. (blank frames)

5.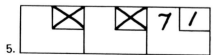

FIGURE 21.11   Continued

FIGURE 21.12 Crossword puzzle

Across

3. A missed spare
5. Bowling using a spot or arrow on the lane
8. Object used to knock down pins
11. Knocking down all pins with first ball of frame
12. The lane
14. Object bowling ball is used to knock down
15. Three strikes in a row made by one bowler in a single game
16. The front pin or no. 1 pin
18. To tighten up under pressure
19. Knocking down all the pins with two balls of a single frame
20. The ball passes and does not hit or knock down any of the pins

Down

1. Number of pins used
2. Two strikes in a row
4. Number of times you could roll the ball in a frame
6. Bowling using pins as an aim
7. A hidden pin, a pin directly behind another pin
9. The troughs on either side of the lane
10. A score box where the points are tallied
12. Act of moving to the foul line to deliver the ball
13. A bonus of the next two balls rolled is awarded for one of these
17. Touching beyond the foul line
19. Two or more pins left standing after the first roll, neither of which is the head pin or side by side

Helpful Hints
Numbers 5 and 8 across and 6 down are two words

FIGURE 21.12   Continued

CONTRACTS, TESTS, AND RATING FORM

Contract

1. Bowl six games at any lane. Keep score and turn in the score sheet to the instructor. On a separate sheet, state the two basic rules for scoring. List and explain the symbols used in scoring (1–10 points).
2. Research and write a paper on the history of bowling using at least four sources. The paper should be typed double-spaced and include a bibliography (1–10 points).
3. Learn the correct way to pick up and hold the ball. Be able to demonstrate the hand positions, footwork, and release. Be able also to demonstrate the hand position that creates a hook, a straight ball, and a backup ball. Performance is evaluated on the basis of an oral explanation to the instructor (1–15 points).
4. Watch at least one tournament, either live or on television, for an hour, or observe an hour of league bowling. Report in writing about how this type of bowling differs from open bowling (1–10 points).
5. Obtain a rule book from the Women's International Bowling Congress (WIBC) and find out what special prizes are awarded in sanctioned leagues. Illustrate and explain the patches and award procedures (1–5 points).
6. Visit a lane and ask the operator for an inspection of an automatic pinsetter in operation. Find out how to operate the ball clearer, how to turn on the teleprompter, and how to reset the pins. Discover where the trouble bell and the foul line indicator are located and how the foul line operates. When ready, take a short quiz from the instructor on this information (1–20 points).
7. Make a poster diagramming a lane. Enlarge and make offset drawings of the approach area and the pin-fall area. Write a short paper telling how one might use this information when bowling (1–10 points).
8. Compile a list of 15 bowling terms and a definition of each (1–15 points).
9. Take a written examination on bowling covering etiquette, scoring, handicaps, averages, techniques, terminology, history, and rules (1–25 points).
10. Demonstrate the proper stance, the four-step delivery, and the position of the hands on each step (1–5 points).

11. Write a paper describing the following: moonlight bowling, headpin tournament, 3-6-9 tournament (1–15 points).
12. Practice spare bowling of a single pin until 4 out of 10 shots are made. (Have the proprietor take all but one pin out of the rack, and shoot at any set that the automatic pin spotter provides.) When ready, test yourself by trying 10 consecutive shots. Record the score as either a miss or a spare. Use any score sheet provided by the alley, and turn it in for credit (1–25 points).

   Grades will be determined as follows: 140–155 points = A; 125–139 points = B; 110–124 points = C; 90–109 = D. No one can fail a contract, because work that is not done properly will be returned. Work must be redone until it is performed correctly.

Test

Figure 21.13 is a bowling quiz that could be administered at the conclusion of the unit.

Rating Form

A rating form (Figure 21.14) is useful for partner work and when facilities are limited. The form enables students who are not participating actively to be cognitively involved. The instructor should spend some time helping students learn to use the form correctly.

Suggested Readings

American Bowling Congress, Film Library, Public Relations Department, 1572 E. Capital Drive, Milwaukee, WI 53211.

Doornink, R. H., ed. 1972. *Physical Education Activity Units of Instruction.* Department of Physical Education for Men, Washington State University.

El Paso Public Schools. 1970. *Physical Education Curriculum Guide.* El Paso, TX.

National Association for Girls and Women in Sport. 1979–1981. *Bowling-Golf.* Reston, VA: AAHPERD.

Sysler, B. L., and Fox, E. R. 1978. *Lifetime Sports for the College Student.* 3rd ed. Dubuque, IA: Kendall/Hunt Publishing Co.

Match the definitions to the terms.

Terms	Definition
_____ 1. Four parts of a delivery	A. Wrist straight and fairly firm
_____ 2. Three-, four-, or five-step	B. Adjustment
_____ 3. Knocking down all pins with two balls	C. Strike
_____ 4. Grip beginning bowlers should use	D. Foul line
_____ 5. Proper wrist position	E. Hook
_____ 6. Knocking down all pins with the first ball	F. Conventional
_____ 7. Ball supported with first joint of the bowling fingers	G. Spare
_____ 8. Line separating the approach and lane	H. Push-away, pendulum backswing, release, and follow-through
_____ 9. Release ball over target, comes up light in pocket, move right with feet	I. Approach
_____ 10. Release ball with fingers at 4 or 5 o'clock	J. Fingertip

FIGURE 21.13 Bowling quiz

Name _____

Bowler

APPROACH
- Push away on first step
- Push-away: out and down—elbow straight
- Backswing: straight—in line with boards
- Backswing: to shoulder level
- Steps: smooth, gliding, even rhythm
- Steps: increase in length and speed
- Slide on left foot

RELEASE
- Shoulders: parallel to foul line
- Shoulders: level
- Upper body: inclined forward
- Left foot: in line with boards
- Weight balanced on left foot
- Thumb in 12 o'clock position
- Ball first strikes alley 1.5 ft in front of left foot
- Follow-through: straight and to shoulder height

AIM
- Approach: straight, in line with boards
- Release: proper dot or dots at foul line
- Crosses proper dart
- Where does ball strike pins? (e.g., 1–3, 1, 3, 1–2)

Place a (√) in proper square if the item is performed correctly.
Place a (−) if it is not correct.

FIGURE 21.14 Bowling rating form

396

GOLF

Each weekend millions of golfers everywhere try to obtain a tee-off time to hit and chase a little white ball around an 18-hole golf course. Golf may appear to be a simple sport, but it is actually a complex activity made up of many different shots or strokes (e.g., woods, long irons, short irons, pitching, chipping, and putting). It is quite challenging and proves to be fascinating to people of all abilities and ages, from 8 to 80. Golf is truly a lifetime sport that can be enjoyed by all people.

Sequence of Skills

The two primary methods of teaching golf are the swing or whole method and the position or part method. Both approaches lead to the same result—square contact with good acceleration. Both teaching methods can be effective, but the whole method seems easier and faster to learn, which makes it better suited to the limited time available for a physical education unit.

The order of skills to be learned in a beginning class follows: grip; stance; alignment; iron shots—half swing, three-quarter swing, and full swing; wood shots—half swing, three-quarter swing, and full swing; putting; chipping; pitching; and the bunker shot.

FIGURE 21.15   Golf stance

Grip

Encourage students to use the overlap grip (80% of all golfers use this grip). Place the left hand on the club in the following manner: First support the club with the right hand and let the left hand hang naturally at the side, then bring the left hand in until it contacts the grip of the club and wrap it around. (Checkpoint: The V formed by the thumb and index finger should point directly to the center of the body, and two knuckles should be visible on the left hand when looking straight down at the grip.) Place the right hand by letting it also hang naturally at the side. Bring it in to meet the club and wrap the fingers around the club so the little finger of the right hand lies over the index finger of the left hand. The thumb of the left hand should fit nicely into the palm of the right hand. (Checkpoint: The V formed by the thumb and index finger of the right hand should point to the center of the body or slightly to the right of center.) A final check on the grip is to extend all fingers and let the club fall to the ground. If the grip is correct, the club will fall straight down between the legs and feet.

Stance

The golf stance should be both comfortable and relaxed. There is a slight bend in the knees and at the waist. The arms and shoulders are relaxed (Figure 21.15). The feet are shoulder width apart for the driver and closer together for the shorter clubs. The ball is positioned within a 6-in. span, starting inside the left heel for the driver and moving toward the center of the stance for the wedge.

Lift the club straight out in front of the body at waist level and swing it back and forth similar to a baseball bat swing. After three or four swings, return to a balanced position in the center. Bend forward from the waist until the club touches the ground. Now relax, and the club will move in slightly closer to the body. It is important that the waist bend lowers the club and not the arms. The relationship between arms and body remains the same until relaxation occurs. (Checkpoint: The preceding check can be applied to every club in the bag. It illustrates how far forward or back the ball must be played and the distance the student should stand from the ball.)

Alignment

A simple procedure for achieving alignment involves the following steps:

1. Stand about 10 ft behind the ball and draw an imaginary line from the flag to the ball.

2. Move to the side of the ball and set the club face square to the target line. Both feet should be together with the ball centered.

3. Grip the club first and then spread the feet apart on a line parallel to the target line. The ball should be on line with the target, and the feet should be on a parallel line just left of the target. The distance between the toes and the ball is approximately 1½ ft.

Half Swing

Each student's swing will vary according to the person's stature, degree of relaxation, understanding of the swing, and natural ability. The half swing is started by bringing the club halfway back to a position parallel to the ground and then letting the club swing forward to the same position in front (Figure 21.16). The swing should be similar to the swing of a pendulum, and the grass should be brushed in both the backswing and forward swing. When the club is parallel to the ground in the backswing, the toe of the club should point straight up, and the grip end of the club should match the line of the feet. At the end of the forward swing, the toe should be straight up again, and the far end of the club should match the line of the feet. After students can do a half swing, introduce the ball. Tell them to concentrate on swinging the club correctly and on the proper alignment procedures.

Three-Quarter Swing

The three-quarter swing is simply an extension of the half swing. The hands reach approximately shoulder height on the backswing and on the forward swing. Many students may be at this point already, because most usually swing longer than they think.

Full Swing

A full swing is characterized by a club shaft that is almost parallel to or parallel to the ground at the top of the backswing (Figure 21.17). The full swing is a further extension of the half and three-quarter swings. At the top of the backswing, the clubhead should point to the ground, and the shaft should point toward the target. The club face will thus be square, and the plane will be correct.

The golf swing actually begins at the top of the backswing. The backswing is simply preparation. Students should visualize the full swing as a circle drawn in the air with the clubhead. The circle starts at the top of the backswing and is completed at the finish of the forward swing. Students should watch the clubhead draw the actual circle two or three times, always keeping the circle out in front. This will help them maintain one plane throughout the swing.

FIGURE 21.16   Half swing forward

FIGURE 21.17   Full swing

At this point, students should have the feel of the full swing, and it is time to experiment with different irons. Try the 5 iron, 9 iron, and finally the 3 iron. Concentration is still on the swing, for the same swing is used with every club. Once patterns of error have developed (i.e., slicing), students can begin to focus on changing a specific aspect of the total swing.

Woods

The same progression should be used to teach wood shots from the half to the full swing. The first wood hit should be the 3 wood from the tee. Next, move to the driver or 1 wood from the tee, and then experiment with the 3 wood off the ground. Students should move halfway down the club's grip to begin swinging. Tee the ball so the top edge of the club comes one quarter to one half of the way up the ball. The stance will be at its widest (shoulder width), and the ball will automatically be positioned forward, inside the left heel.

Putting

Identical to the pendulum of a clock, the putter is an extension of the arms and shoulders, and swings as one unit an equal distance back and forward. The feel is best obtained by having students grip as far down the shaft as they can reach. Square the putter to the target line and stroke straight back and straight through. Have students try the following putting techniques.

1. Use a reverse overlap grip in which the index finger of the left hand lies over the little finger of the right. This allows the whole right hand to be on the club for control.
2. The stance may be wide or narrow, and the ball may be centered in the stance or forward, remaining inside the left heel. If the ball is forward, a slight weight shift to the left must accompany this stance.
3. Place the dominant eye directly over the ball to improve visualization of the target line.
4. Feel the putter accelerating through contact. This may require shortening the backswing slightly.
5. If the ball misses the hole, overshooting the putt is preferable.
6. Keep the putter blade low to the ground to assure good ball contact.

Learn to judge break, or the roll of the green, by standing behind the ball and looking at the line between the ball and the hole, and also at the slant of the entire green. Visualize throwing a pail of water toward the hole, and picture which way the water would run. For most putts (i.e., 4 ft or less) play the ball to the opposite inside edge of the cup. If the putt is longer, gradually move to the edge of the cup, and eventually outside the cup as a point of aim. The point of aim may be a spot on the imaginary line to the hole, or a point even with the hole but to one side. In both cases, the break takes the ball into the hole.

Chip, Pitch, and Bunker Shots

A chip shot is used when the ball is slightly off the green and there is room to hit the ball approximately halfway to the hole. The ball must land on the green and roll close to the hole. If there is not enough room to roll the ball to the hole, then a higher trajectory pitch shot is used. The pitch shot should land at the target. The bunker shot is used for coming out of a sand trap.

A chip shot usually requires a 7 iron and a putting-type stroke. A good technique is to have the students stand off the green and toss the ball underhand so that it rolls to within 4 ft of the hole. Students then place a tee in the green where the ball hit. The tee becomes the target for the chip shot.

The pitch shot should be practiced at different distances with different sized targets (i.e., the greater the distance, the larger the target). Baskets, Hula-Hoops, and parachutes are possibilities at 10, 30, and 50 yd. The 9 iron or wedge is used with a one-quarter, one-half, or three-quarter swing, depending on the distance and the circumstances. Students should learn to make a smooth swing and to let the loft of the club hit the ball. The ball should land at the target and roll slightly forward.

The long jump landing pit can be used for bunker shot practice. Students should use a wedge or 9 iron and concentrate on the following:

1. Open the club face at address.
2. Line up 2 in. behind the ball and focus on that spot, not on the ball.
3. Barely scrape the sand with a one-quarter through full swing, depending on the distance required to land the ball.
4. Always follow through with the club.

Ideas for Effective Instruction

Introduce and stress safety rules on the first day of class. A golf ball or club can cause serious damage, and thus strict adherence to safety rules must be demanded. If the class is large and space is limited, safety officers may be appointed who can help manage ball retrieving, changing from station to station, and other responsibilities assigned by the instructor.

The following are safety suggestions that may help in class organization:

1. Allow ample swing space between students for any group formation.
2. Do not carry clubs while retrieving balls.
3. If space is limited, take students back of the line for individual correction.
4. Do not retrieve balls until instructed.
5. Group the left-handed players together at the far end of the hitting line, facing the right-handed players.
6. Be certain that equipment is in top condition at all times, and tell students to notify the instructor if equipment needs repair.
7. Caution students never to swing toward one another, even without a ball.

Start students with a high iron (7, 8, or 9), so they will experience success quicker. Students need to understand that developing a golf swing takes a lot of practice and is not an easy skill to master. Make sure that students are not overloaded with information and that they receive ample practice time. Depending on the amount of equipment available, teachers may want to assign partner work and to use a swing rating form. This motivates students without clubs to be more involved cognitively and improves their observation skills.

Learning stations can be arranged in the gymnasium or in outdoor fields. An example of an indoor facility, including irons, woods, chipping, pitching, and putting, is shown in Figure 21.18. An outdoor area could be arranged in a similar manner (i.e., around a football or baseball field).

Learning Activities

Modified Courses

Many teachers set up a short golf course in the field space they have available. Broomsticks, traffic cones, and hoops can serve as pins, tees, and holes. A power mower can be used to shape the fairways and greens. If it is impossible to dig holes, students can "hole out" when the ball strikes the target or when they are within a club's length of the target. Whiffle balls, plastic balls, or regular golf balls can be used, depending on what is available. All types of hazards can be set up using tires, hurdles, jump ropes, and cones. Specific course etiquette and rules can be taught with a modified course.

Putting

Miniature putting courses can be set up on smooth grass surfaces, carpeted areas, old carpet pieces, blankets, towels, mats, canvas, and even smooth floors if a whiffle ball is used. Paper cups, pieces of colored paper, shoe boxes, bleach containers, cans, and jars are possibilities for holes.

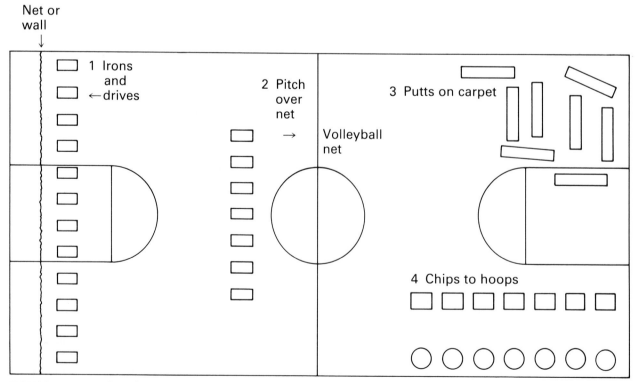

FIGURE 21.18 Indoor facility for golf

GOLF RATING SCALE

1. Grip (4 points—1 each)

   _____ Right-hand V is straight up or slightly right

   _____ Two knuckles of left hand showing

   _____ Grip tension is correct

   _____ Hands completely on grip of club

2. Stance (4 points—$\frac{1}{2}$ each)

   _____ Feet proper width apart

   _____ Standing proper distance from ball

   _____ Weight even over feet (ask)

   _____ Knees bent properly

   _____ Proper bend from waist

   _____ Arms hanging naturally

   _____ No unnecessary tension in arms and hands

   _____ No unnecessary tension in legs

3. Alignment (3 points—1 each)

   _____ Not left of target

   _____ Not right of target

   _____ Proper sequence of address. (Draw imaginary line and pick a spot on the line. Set club square, feet together. Place right foot first on parallel line. Take last look at target.)

4. Swing (10 points—1 each)

   _____ One piece take away

   _____ Head did not move up and down

   _____ Head did not move back and forth

   _____ Left arm extended

   _____ A complete coil is present

   _____ Club toe up to target—backswing—at parallel level

   _____ Club toe up to target—forward swing—at parallel level

   _____ Club accelerates through ball

   _____ Club continues after contact

   _____ Facing target at the finish

Points	Performance
10	Good contact, good trajectory, good direction
9	Good contact, good trajectory, fair direction
8	Good contact, fair trajectory, fair direction
6	Fair contact, fair trajectory, fair direction
4	2 items fair, 1 item barely acceptable
2	1 item fair, 2 items barely acceptable
0	Miss or near miss

FIGURE 21.19 Golf rating scale

Partner Golf

Playing on a regular course or on a putting course, partners alternate hitting or putting toward the pin. If the class size is large, use groups of three or four.

Target Golf

Establish a number of concentric circles and point values around a target. Rope, jump ropes, or lime can be used to mark the circles. The distance and size of the circles can vary according to the club used. This activity can be done with individuals or teams.

Rainy Day Activities

Rainy days are a good time to have a "spell down" with questions on rules, fundamentals, etiquette, and types of matches. Crossword puzzles and word searches are available in the suggested readings. Short putting courses can be set up in the indoor space available.

Skill Tests

Many of the drills and game situations already mentioned can be used for evaluation. Here are a few other possibilities:

1. Parachute—Count the number of 7, 8, or 9 iron shots that land on the parachute in 10 trials.
2. Putting—Play 9 holes on a practice green and keep score. Ideally, each student would score 2 per hole to par the course.
3. Chipping—Count the number of balls that end up inside the 4-ft radius circle.
4. Pitching—Pitch 10 balls at each station (10, 20, and 40 yd), and count the number of balls that land inside the target area.
5. Bunker Shot—Arrange a string in a circle with a 10-ft radius around one hole, and count the number of bunker shots that finish inside the circle after 10 trials.

A rating scale can be used as part of an evaluation scheme or as a part of the learning activities done with partners (Figure 21.19).

Suggested Readings

AAHPERD. 1966. *Ideas for Golf Instruction—A Planning Guide for Schools.* Reston, VA: AAHPERD.

Jones, E. 1952. *Swing the Clubhead.* New York: Arno Press.

Jones, E., and Brown, I. 1937. *Swinging into Golf.* New York: McGraw-Hill Book Co.

Kennington, D. 1981. *The Sourcebook of Golf.* Phoenix, AZ: Oryx Press.

National Association for Girls and Women in Sport. 1979–1981 *Bowling-Golf.* Reston, VA: AAHPERD.

Seidel, B. L., et al. 1980. *Sports Skills: A Conceptual Approach to Meaningful Movement.* 2nd ed. Dubuque, IA: Wm. C. Brown Group.

GYMNASTICS

Gymnastics refers to the performance of a routine on a piece of heavy apparatus or on a large mat. The routines are evaluated by a panel of judges on a ten-point scale. The gymnastics events for men include parallel bars, horizontal bar, long horse vaulting, still rings, pommel horse, and floor exercise. Women's events include the uneven parallel bars, balance beam, side horse vaulting, and floor exercise. In many major gymnastics competitions, the participants must perform a compulsory or set routine and an optional or original routine.

Varying forms of gymnastics were the most common activity in early physical education programs. These different forms of gymnastics were brought to the United States. primarily from Germany and Sweden. Gymnastics became popular through clubs formed in the communities, YMCAs, and the public schools. Private gymnastics clubs and sport schools are still popular, and gymnastics is still taught in some secondary schools and colleges in the United States. Many adults continue to enjoy gymnastics as a lifetime recreational activity. In some geographic areas, competition is available through the private clubs for various age groups.

Instructional units in gymnastics and tumbling are an excellent way to achieve a balanced secondary physical education curriculum. Unfortunately, many school districts do not have the heavy apparatus. In these situations, an extensive unit on tumbling should be incorporated in the program. Gymnastics activities offer students an interesting variety of challenges and should be available for students to explore and experience.

Sequence of Skills

Each gymnastics event is a highly specialized area that incorporates many specific skills and techniques. A sequence of skills should be taught on each piece of apparatus and for floor exercise. In a coeducational class, eight pieces of apparatus and two different floor exercise routines can be offered if the equipment is available. Comprehensive texts with in-depth information on the sequence of skills for each event are listed in the suggested readings. Gymnastics teachers need to have an extensive background in the teaching strategies and safety procedures for all of the individual events. Teachers should analyze carefully the abilities and characteristics of their students, the time allotted to the gymnastics unit, and the pieces of equipment available for instruction. Safety is especially important because of the hazards posed by many of the gymnastics events.

Ideas for Instruction

Each piece of apparatus and the floor exercise can be arranged as a specific learning area for students. After students are introduced to each area and given introductory tasks to perform, they can be distributed evenly throughout the area. This ensures that students will have maximum opportunity to attempt the various skills. Each student can be given a performance card to record the completion of tasks. The tasks can be written as performance objectives or as simple cues. These objectives (Figure 21.20) and the recording forms (Figure 21.21) will help motivate students to use class time in a productive manner.

A gymnastics meet with student judges is an enjoyable culminating activity. Teams can be organized, and students can select their favorite events. Students work with a partner or in groups of three for safety purposes. One person performs and the partner spots. Spotting must be explained carefully to

**BEGINNING GYMNASTICS
PARALLEL BARS—PERFORMANCE OBJECTIVES**

1. Stand at the end of the bars and grasp both bars with hands on top of the bars. Jump up so that your arms are now straight. Walk down the bars, moving one hand at a time (hand-walking).

2. From a standing position at the end of the bars with both hands on top of the bars, jump up until your arms are straight. Now hop down the bars by moving both hands at the same time (hopping travel).

3. Jump to a *cross-arm support* (both arms straight with your body between the bars) and swing your legs forward, straddling the bars with legs on top of the bars. Now lean forward and place your hands in front of your legs. Swing your legs down off the bars and then up in front again. Repeat this sequence to traverse the length of the bar (traveling).

4. Jump to a cross-arm support (both arms straight) and swing your legs forward and backward, showing control and trying to swing your legs high both ways (leg swings).

5. Place your upper arms (by your shoulders) on top of the bars and swing your legs forward and backward. Hold on to the bars with your hands for balance (upper-arm support swings).

6. Jump to a cross-arm support (both arms straight) and bend your arms as far as you can while you lower your body down between the bars. Now straighten your arms and lift yourself back up to where you started. Try this at least three times in a row (still dips).

7. Place the hands in a *reverse grip* on both bars. Lean back and lift your legs and hips up and over your head until your feet almost touch the floor, then return to the position from which you started (skin-the-cat, both bars).

8. From a cross-arm support (both arms straight), lean on one arm, then bring the other hand to the other bar. (You should now be in a front support on one bar.) Finish the turn by leaning to one side and placing your hand on the other bar in a straight-arm cross-arm support. You are now facing the opposite direction from the way you started (half turn).

9. Stand outside the bars facing one bar. Grasp the bar with both hands in a regular grip. Bring your legs up and between your hands until they almost touch the floor under you, then go back to the way you started (skin-the-cat, one bar).

10. Jump up to a cross-arm support (both arms straight). Lift your legs up in front until they are at the same height as the bars and try to hold that position, like an "L," for a few seconds (L-seat).

11. From a cross-arm support (both arms straight), swing both legs backward and over one bar so you have your stomach facing the bar as you go over. Land on the outside of the bars with one arm holding on for balance (front vault dismount).

12. From a cross-arm support (both arms straight), swing both legs forward and lift your body over one bar with your seat facing the bar. Land on the outside of the bar, facing sideways to the bar, with one hand holding on for balance (rear vault dismount).

13. From a standing position between the bars and facing one end, grasp the bars with a reverse grip. Lean back and lift both legs up and over your head like the beginning of a backward roll. Straddle your legs at the top and put them on top of the bars so you end up in a straddle seat (backward roll mount to a straddle seat).

14. Jump to a cross-arm support (both arms straight). Lean forward as if you were starting a forward roll. Stick your elbows out to the sides to stay on top of the bars as you roll. Continue rolling forward as your legs go up and over your head (forward roll).

15. Jump to a cross-arm support (both arms straight). Lean forward and stick both elbows out to the sides so the top part of your arms rests on top of the bars. Extend your legs straight up over your head so you are upside down. Hold your hands on the bars for balance. For safety, come down the same way you went up (shoulder stand).

FIGURE 21.20 Performance objectives for the parallel bars

Name	Core Objectives										Optional Objectives				
	1	2	3	4	5	6	7	8	9	10	1	2	3	4	5
Parallel bars															
Rings															
Floor exercise															
Long horse															
Horizontal bar															
Pommel horse															
Uneven bars															
Balance beam															
Side horse															

FIGURE 21.21   Performance objective monitoring form

students, and the importance of spotting must be continually reinforced.

Suggested Readings

Cooper, P., and Trnka, M. 1982. *Teaching Gymnastic Skills to Men and Women*. Minneapolis, MN: Burgess Publishing Co.

Drury, B., and Schmid, A. B. 1972. *Gymnastics for Women*. Palo Alto, CA: National Press Books.

Mood, D., Musker, F., and Armbruster, D. 1983. *Sports and Recreational Activities for Men and Women*. 8th ed. St. Louis, MO: C. V. Mosby Co.

Zakrajsek, D., and Carnes, L. 1986. *Learning Experiences: An Approach to Teaching Physical Activities*. Champaign, IL: Human Kinetics Publishers.

JOGGING

Joggers and road races are probably the most visible form of the fitness renaissance. Millions take to the road regularly for fitness and sport reasons. Various types of distances for running events have become popular with men and women of all ages. Marathons, triathalons, 15-km, 10-km, 5-km, and 2-mi fun runs are being offered virtually every weekend. People in all areas of the country run in all kinds of weather. Secondary students in physical education programs should have positive experiences with running, because this is a potential lifetime activity that can contribute to fitness and be a form of play. Jogging is an easy, inexpensive activity that can be done individually or with a group.

Sequence of Skills

Jogging is simply slow running. It is different from walking in that both feet leave the ground during the flight or airborne phase. In walking, one foot is always in contact with the ground.

Running Form

Chapter 18 gives in-depth coverage to running form on pages 313–314. Teachers should spend time working on running form, emphasizing one aspect of form with each drill. Students can overlearn the position of the head, hands, arms, knees, feet, and body lean. In distance running, the stride is shorter than in sprinting, and the heel of the foot should strike the ground before the ball of the foot. Breathing should be natural, through both nose and mouth.

Designing a Program

Students need to understand how to design a jogging program to meet their individual objectives. Programs will differ according to those objectives. Some students want to lose weight, others may want to condition themselves for skiing, and others will want to improve their time in 10-km races. Program goals may vary, but students should all understand how the principles of frequency, intensity, and duration apply to a running program. Proper warm-up, cool down, and stretching and strengthening activities must be taught. These are covered in Chapter 18, pages 295–302.

Equipment

Runners must obtain adequate running shoes. Many are available at prices ranging from $20.00 to over $100.00. They should have a well-cushioned, elevated heel and a durable bottom surface. The toes should not rub the front of the shoe, and the tongue and lining should be padded. The sole must be flexible, with two layers for absorbing shock. An arch support should be built into running shoes.

The remaining equipment (shorts, socks, sweat suits, rain suits, jackets, hats, mittens, and so forth) is a matter of personal preference depending on the weather. Comfort is the key, with loose-fitting, non-irritating material. Extremely cold and warm weather can be dangerous. Students should understand how to prevent problems by dressing properly and avoiding certain weather conditions.

Ideas for Effective Instruction

Beginners should understand that jogging is an individual activity that can be noncompetitive. If students choose to be competitive runners, that is fine and is a personal choice. Teachers should reinforce this attitude by reducing the emphasis on running races in a jogging unit. The unit emphasis can be on personal improvement and accomplishing individual goals.

Jog-Walk-Jog

Beginners can be given a distance to cover by alternating jogging and walking. They progress by gradually reducing the walking and increasing the jogging. Various students can be assigned different distances, depending on their abilities. This technique can be used for jogging on a track. Students can jog the straightaways and walk the curves for 1 mi.

Timed Runs

Students can be given a set time of a certain number of minutes. They then try to jog continuously for the designated time. (Teachers blow a whistle every minute or half minute.)

Other Running Activities

Refer to Chapter 18 for descriptions of activities such as form running, file running, walk-sprint-jog, pace work, random running, and Fartlek. All can be modified for a jogging unit.

Group Runs

Divide students into small groups of similar ability. The group can run together for a certain time or

distance. They should be encouraged to use the "talk test" during the run. This refers to the ability to comfortably carry on a conversation during a run as an indicator of proper jogging intensity.

Training Heart Rate

After students have learned about training heart rates (see Chapter 18, page 294), they can check their heart rates at rest before running, after running so many minutes, and again immediately after a run. This will help them to understand the concepts of training heart rate, recovery heart rate, and jogging at sufficient intensity.

Orienteering Runs

A jogging unit can include several orienteering meets emphasizing running from point to point on the school grounds. Draw a map with 10 checkpoints that must be found by the students. Each checkpoint has a secret clue, such as a letter, word, color, or team name. Students can work alone or with a partner. (See Chapter 23 for more orienteering ideas.)

Cross-Country Runs

Map out a cross-country course around the school grounds and in neighboring areas, and hold a meet with a chute for finishers and numbers distributed for the finishing positions. Arrange teams and establish categories for beginners, intermediates, and advanced runners. Set time limits, and allow students to run time trials to determine their category or team. Students can choose to be on a team or to run for individual improvement.

Exercise Trails

Set up an exercise trail around the school grounds with several stations for stretching and strengthening various muscle groups. Use a boundary cone with a sign to mark each station, and give students a rough map showing where each station is located. After completing a station activity, students should jog to the next station. The stations can be set up so the students get a total body workout. After a certain period of time, the trail can be modified.

Running with Equipment

Some students with special interests may want to run with a piece of equipment (e.g., dribbling a soccer ball or a basketball). Others may want to carry a football or roll a Hula-Hoop. Let students be creative, as long as they are engaged in a safe activity. Running with equipment adds variety to activities and is a good motivational device.

McKemy Jogging Club

1	2	3	4	5	6	7	8	9	10	11	12	13	14	15
16	17	18	19	20	21	22	23	24	25	26	27	28	29	30
31	32	33	34	35	36	37	38	39	40	41	42	43	44	45
46	47	48	49	50	51	52	53	54	55	56	57	58	59	60
61	62	63	64	65	66	67	68	69	70	71	72	73	74	75
76	77	78	79	80	81	82	83	84	85	86	87	88	89	90
91	92	93	94	95	96	97	98	99	100	101	102	103	104	105
106	107	108	109	110	111	112	113	114	115	116	117	118	119	120
121	122	123	124	125	126	127	128	129	130	131	132	133	134	135
136	137	138	139	140	141	142	143	144	145	146	147	148	149	150
151	152	153	154	155	156	157	158	159	160	161	162	163	164	165
166	167	168	169	170	171	172	173	174	175	176	177	178	179	180
181	182	183	184	185	186	187	188	189	190	191	192	193	194	195
196	197	198	199	200	201	202	203	204	205	206	207	208	209	210
211	212	213	214	215	216	217	218	219	220	221	222	223	224	225
226	227	228	229	230	231	232	233	234	235	236	237	238	239	240
241	242	243	244	245	246	247	248	249	250	251	252	253	254	255
256	257	258	259	260	261	262	263	264	265	266	267	268	269	270
271	272	273	274	275	276	277	278	279	280	281	282	283	284	285
286	287	288	289	290	291	292	293	294	295	296	297	298	299	300
301	302	303	304	305	306	307	308	309	310	311	312	313	314	315
316	317	318	319	320	321	322	323	324	325	326	327	328	329	330

500-Mile Jogging Club

NAME: _____ DATE: _____

When finished with the month, please bring this card to the Intramural Office in the PE West Gym to record your miles.

	Mon	Tues	Wed	Thurs	Fri	Sat	Sun	Total

Only distances of ½ mi or more will be recorded.

Previous Total _____
Monthly Total _____
Total to Date _____

** Mileage will be kept on record for one year. **

FIGURE 21.22   Mileage charts

Running Evaluation	Always	Some	Never	Comment
Head still				
Eyes ahead				
Hands relaxed				
Elbows at 90 degrees				
Arms moving straight forward and back				
Hand comes back to front pocket				
Arms gently brush sides				
Feet straight ahead				
Knee drive straight ahead				
Knee action not too high				
Feet, knee, and hip in line				
Body lean slight—5 degrees from feet				
Foot strike on heel				
Stride short for distance				

FIGURE 21.23 Running rating form

Mileage Cards and Maps

Many people enjoy keeping a record of the distances covered. Goals can be established for a given time period. Students can jog across the state by coloring in a route or moving a pin to a given point as they accumulate miles. Mileage cards or charts (Figure 21.22) can be kept individually, or they can be posted in the locker room or on a bulletin board. Individual or group competitions can be set up based on number of miles accumulated.

Rating Forms

A rating form (Figure 21.23) can be developed for both student and teacher use. Students should learn how to use the form and check each other. Both the runner and the rater must understand the form.

Rainy Day Activities

Many of these activities (e.g., rating forms, pace work, timed runs) can be modified for running in the gymnasium. If the gym is also not available, there are many interesting running topics that teachers can discuss with students. These include training methods, safety, injuries, equipment, health benefits, exercise and calories, marathons, Cooper's program, and the female runner. The suggested readings are filled with discussion topics.

Suggested Readings

Fixx, J. 1977. *The Complete Book of Running*. New York: Random House.
Henderson, J. 1977. *Jog, Run, Race*. Mountain View, CA: World Publications.
Runner's World Magazine. Box 366, Mountain View, CA 94042.

RESISTANCE TRAINING

Various forms of resistance training have become extremely popular activities for general conditioning. Adults and students of all ages are lifting weights and working on resistance machines in schools, health clubs, YMCAs, and in their homes. Current research has made women aware of the misconceptions about and benefits of resistance training. Coaches and athletes involved in different sports are using extensive resistance training programs to improve performance. Resistance training is now well entrenched in the activity habits of society.

A properly developed resistance training program can produce positive changes in the body composition and in a person's performance. People engaged in resistance training look better, feel better, and perform daily activities better. All of these results have contributed to the popularity of the sport.

Many different types of resistance training equipment are available. Machines such as the Universal Gym, Nautilus equipment, the Orthotron, and the Cybex II are used commonly for training programs. Each machine offers a number of different advantages. Free weights, including different types of dumbbells and barbells, are still quite popular and are available in most weight rooms. Physical education programs need to analyze carefully such factors as cost, space, objectives, and usage before purchasing resistance training equipment.

Sequence of Skills

Principles, Terminology, and Safety

Beginning resistance trainers need to understand the basic principles of training relative to their specific objectives. Students must understand the definitions of strength, endurance, flexibility, warm-up, cool down, sets, repetitions, frequency, rest intervals, and the various types of lifts for specific muscle groups. The type and number of lifts are determined by a student's objectives. Proper form must be understood in order to gain maximum benefits and to complete the activities safely. Spotting techniques are a necessity for certain lifts, especially with heavy weights. Safety in the weight lifting area must be stressed constantly. Chapter 18 gives general information on these aspects of resistance training (see pp. 306–307). Additional specific information is available in the suggested readings listed at the end of this unit.

Spotting

Spotters are people who stand by a lifter to provide help when necessary. Spotters are concerned about preventing a weight from falling or slipping if the lifter cannot control the weight. All students should understand the spotting procedures for a specific lift. They can check the equipment for proper alignment, tightened collars, and so forth, and they can be aware of the position of other students in the area. Specific attention should be paid to each lift, especially with heavier weights.

Breathing

Lifters should try to be consistent and natural in their breathing. Most experts agree that breathing should follow a pattern of exhaling during exertion and inhaling as the weight is returned to the starting position. With heavy weights, many lifters take a deep breath before the lift and hold the breath until the final exertion. The final exhalation helps complete the lift. Care is necessary, because holding the breath too long can make a person light-headed and may even cause one to faint.

Grips

The three major grips are the overhand (Figure 21.24), underhand (Figure 21.25), and alternating

FIGURE 21.24   Overhand grip

FIGURE 21.25   Underhand grip

FIGURE 21.26   Alternating grip

(Figure 21.26). These grips are used with different types of lifts (i.e., the overhand with the palms down is used for the bench press, the underhand with the palms up is used for curls, and the alternating with one palm up and the other down is used with the dead lift).

Body Position

With free weights, it is especially important to get the feet, arms, and body aligned properly for lifting and removing weights from power racks or squat stands. Carelessness in alignment can result in an unbalanced position, which can, in turn, result in dropping the weights or in poor lifting technique. Each lift requires a different position, depending on whether the bar is being lifted from the floor or from a rack. Spotters must understand the type of lift to be executed and their specific responsibility. For example, with a back squat, the following steps should be followed:

1. Check the collars to see that they are tightened.
2. Grip the bar and space the hands wider than the shoulders.
3. Align the middle of the back under the midpoint of the bar.
4. Use a pad or towel to cushion the bar against the back.
5. Bend the knees and align the body vertically under the bar.
6. Keep the head up and lift the weight straight up.
7. Move out from the rack and assume a comfortable foot position about shoulder width apart.
8. Perform the lift with a spotter on either side of the bar.

Upper Body Lifts

Bench Press. Use an overhand grip with hands slightly wider than the shoulders. Bring the bar down to the chest and press up over the shoulders (Figure 21.27). Exhale on the press upward.

Curl. Use an underhand grip with the arms about shoulder width. Curl the bar up the shoulders and extend downward slowly to a straight arm position (Figure 21.28). A reverse curl can be used with an overhand grip.

Bent or Upright Rowing. Both lifts use an overhand grip about shoulder width. The bent position starts with the barbell on the floor and the body bent at the hips (Figure 21.29). The knees are bent slightly. The bar is pulled to the chest while the back is stable. The upright position (Figure 21.30) starts with the bar across the thighs. The bar is pulled up to the chin area and returned slowly.

FIGURE 21.27   Bench press

Military Press.   An overhand grip slightly wider than the shoulders is used in a standing or sitting position. The bar is pressed upward from the chest and returned (Figure 21.31). A variation brings the bar down behind the head and then back up.

Bench Pullover.   Lying on a a bench, the bar is gripped overhand and is pulled straight up and over the face from the floor (Figure 21.32).

FIGURE 21.28   Curl

FIGURE 21.29 Bent rowing

FIGURE 21.31 Military press

FIGURE 21.30 Upright rowing

FIGURE 21.32 Bench pullover

Shoulder Shrugs. With a straight barbell across the thighs or with two dumbbells at the sides of the body (Figure 21.33), the shoulders are raised or shrugged as high as possible and then returned to the starting position.

Triceps Extension. A barbell, two dumbbells, or a machine can be used. With the barbell, the weight bar is started overhead with an overhand grip, and is then lowered slowly behind the head and extended back to the starting position (Figure 21.34). With a machine, the bar is brought down in front of the body.

Lateral Raises. Lateral raises are done using an overhand grip with dumbbells. A standing (Figure 21.35) or bent position can be used. The weights start at the sides or on the floor and are raised laterally with straight arms.

FIGURE 21.33 Shoulder shrugs

FIGURE 21.34 Triceps extension

FIGURE 21.36 Back squat

FIGURE 21.35 Standing lateral raise

FIGURE 21.37 Dead lift

Lower Body Lifts

Front and Back Squat. Use an overhand grip with the bar across the front of the shoulders or across the upper back muscles. The knees are bent to a position in which the thighs are parallel to the floor (Figure 21.36).

Dead Lift. Starting in a squat position with the weight on the floor, the feet are about shoulder width apart, and an alternating grip is used (Figure 21.37). The arms are kept straight and the back flat as the weight is lifted and the body comes to an erect position with the bar across the thighs.

Power Clean. The power clean is a complex lift that starts in the same position as the dead lift, but with an overhand grip (Figure 21.38A). The lift includes a start, an acceleration, and a catch phase. The bar is pulled up, past the waist (Figure 21.38B), and ends up above the chest. The lifter must control both the weight and the body as the weight moves through the starting position to the catch position.

Leg Curls and Extension. Equipment calls for a machine attached to a bench. The extension (Figure 21.39) starts in a sitting position with the feet under a lower, padded section. The arms grip the sides of the bench, and the upper body is leaning slightly back. The legs are extended until they are parallel to the floor. The leg curl (Figure 21.40) uses the upper padded section of the machine. The lifter is

FIGURE 21.38a   Power clean—ready position

FIGURE 21.38b   Power clean—intermediate position

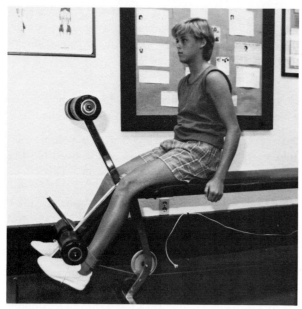

FIGURE 21.39   Leg extension

on the stomach, and the heels are hooked behind the pad. The heels are then pulled up toward the buttocks and lowered.

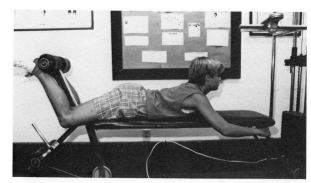

FIGURE 21.40   Leg curl

FIGURE 21.41   Heel raises

Heel Raises.   Begin on the balls of the feet and the toes over a stable board or step. The lifter holds a weight in each hand at the sides (Figure 21.41). The heels are then raised and lowered.

Learning Activities

Circuit Training

An effective strategy for organizing the activities in the weight room is to set up a circuit with a number of stations (Figure 21.42). The students can be divided into groups and rotated after a certain number of minutes. Students perform a specific number of sets and repetitions at each station.

Each student should keep a daily log of the sets and repetitions and of the weights that were lifted. These records are important in organizing a progression and should help to motivate the students. Figures 21.43 and 21.44 are examples of daily lifting records for an upper body and lower body circuit. Depending on the equipment and facilities available,

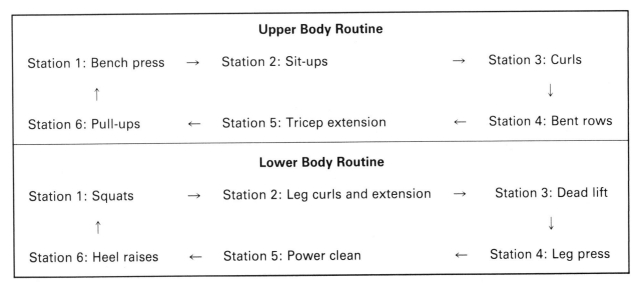

FIGURE 21.42 Weight training circuit

Date							Date					
Sets	1	2	3	4	5	6	1	2	3	4	5	6
Bench												
Curls												
Tricep												
Dips												
Lateral pull												
Rows												
Pull-ups												

FIGURE 21.43 Daily lifting record — upper body

Date							Date					
Sets	1	2	3	4	5	6	1	2	3	4	5	6
Power clean												
Dead lift												
Leg press												
Leg curls												
Squat												
Sit-ups												

FIGURE 21.44 Daily lifting record — lower body

CLUB REQUIREMENTS

Requirements—To become a member, you must lift a combined total of 5.2 times your weight. The three required lifts are bench press, dead lift, and squat.

Weight Class		Required Total	Weight Class		Required Total
100–109	=	520	160–169	=	832
110–119	=	572	170–179	=	884
120–129	=	624	180–189	=	936
130–139	=	676	190–199	=	988
140–149	=	728	200–209	=	1040
150–159	=	780	210–219	=	1092
			220 and up	=	1144

Each participant is allowed three tries for each lift. Weight may be added to the previous lift, but may not be subtracted from the previous lift.

Name _____ Date _____ Class 10, 11, 12

Body weight _____ Required total lift _____

	1st	2nd	3rd	Best of three lifts
Bench press	_____	_____	_____	_____
Dead lift	_____	_____	_____	_____
Squat	_____	_____	_____	_____
			Total	_____

Coach's signature _____

FIGURE 21.45 Motivational club criteria for weight lifters

a good approach is to develop a circuit for both lower body exercises and upper body exercises. Students can alternate days performing upper and lower body workouts. Aerobic conditioning activities can also be alternated with the resistance training. Many teachers like to add variety to the circuit routines by changing stations regularly.

Partner Resistance Activities

Chapter 18 describes a number of partner resistance activities that can be used to supplement and add variety to a resistance training unit. These can also be added to a circuit, or can be scheduled as an entire day's lesson. They are useful in situations in which equipment is limited. For example, while students are waiting their turn to use a weight machine, they can perform several resistance activities. Isometric exercises can also be used in these situations.

Muscle-of-the-Day

Another good learning activity is to present students with information about one muscle at the end of each lesson. The name of the muscle and its functions are written on a card and placed on the wall of the weight room. A quick review of the muscles covered plus the addition of a new muscle takes place each day. This is a good concluding activity after each day's workout. Specific information on the muscular system is available in Chapter 16.

Motivational Devices

Resistance training offers tangible evidence of improvement in the various lifts. This improvement can be tied to many different motivational devices: T-shirts, certificates, and becoming a member of a club are popular examples of awards for lifting certain amounts of weight. These types of devices can be quite simple, yet are effective and meaningful for many students. Figure 21.45 is a good example of motivational club criteria used at Westwood High School in Mesa, Arizona. The club is available to students in the weight training classes.

Suggested Readings

Schwarzenegger, A., and Hall, D. 1977. *Arnold: The Education of a Body Builder.* New York: Simon and Schuster.

Seaton, D., et al. 1983. *Physical Education Handbook.* 7th ed. Englewood Cliffs, NJ: Prentice-Hall, Inc.

Stone, W., and Kroll, W. 1980. *Sports Conditioning and Weight Training.* Boston, MA: Allyn and Bacon, Inc.

Ward, B. 1983. Weight training (Chapter 23). In N. Dougherty (ed.) *Physical Education and Sport for the Secondary School Student.* Reston, VA: AAHPERD.

ROPE JUMPING

Rope jumping can be a demanding activity enjoyed by all ages and ability levels. The American Heart Association has endorsed rope jumping for years because of its positive effects on cardiovascular endurance. It is an inexpensive activity that can be done in a limited amount of space, indoors or outside. Through rope jumping, students develop rhythm, timing, and coordination, as well as fitness. The numerous jumping activities can challenge all ability levels. The rope can be turned many ways at varying speeds and the jumper can use a variety of foot patterns. Individual, partner, and small group activities are available.

Rope jumping is a useful carry-over activity that can be enjoyed throughout one's life. Developing creative rope jumping routines and skills can be a challenge to students. Because of the rhythmic aspect of jumping rope, teachers should add popular music to enhance everyone's motivational level.

Sequence of Skills

Several types of ropes are available that are useful for teaching the skill to secondary students. Sash cord and hard weave synthetic ropes can be used, but the best jump ropes are made of plastic links with a plastic handle that turns. The rope should be heavy enough to maintain a rhythmic rotation. The length of the rope will vary according to the height of the student. Proper length can be determined by standing in the middle of the rope and pulling the ends up to the armpits or slightly higher (Figure 21.46). If the ends of the rope reach beyond that area, students can wrap the extra rope around the hands, or get a longer rope if the one tested is too

FIGURE 21.46   Correct jump rope length

short. Most secondary students will need a 8-, 9-, or 10-ft jump rope.

Body Position and Rhythm

Jumping rope requires proper body position and alignment. The head should be up with the eyes looking ahead. Good balance is a must with the feet, ankles, and legs close together. The body is erect during the jump. The knees flex and extend slightly with each jump. The elbows are kept close to the body at approximately a 90-degree angle. The basic jump should be straight up and down and about 1 in. high. The rope should be turned primarily with the wrists and forearms. Effective jumpers land on the balls of their feet and stay in one spot.

The speed at which the rope turns is referred to as the rhythm. Slow-time (half-time) rhythm involves turning the rope 60–90 revolutions per min. The student jumps, rebounds, and then jumps again as the rope comes through. A rebound is a slight bend at the knee in order to carry or keep the rhythm. The student does not actually leave the ground during a rebound. Slow time is the easiest rhythm for beginners. Fast-time rhythm involves turning the rope 120–180 turns per min. There is no rebound because the rope and the feet must move faster. In double-time rhythm, the rope is turned at the same speed as slow time, but instead of using a rebound, the performer executes a different type of step while the rope is coming around. Double-time rhythm is the most difficult to learn, because the feet and the turning of the rope must be coordinated. The feet must move quickly while the rope turns slowly.

Individual Steps

The following are foot patterns that can be used with all three rhythm patterns—slow time, fast time, and double time. Students should try the patterns in slow time before moving on to fast and double time.

Two-Foot Basic Step.   The student jumps over the rope with both feet together. In slow time, there is a rebound in between each turn of the rope.

Alternate-Foot Step (Jog Step).   The student alternates feet with every jump. The unweighted leg is bent slightly at the knee (Figure 21.47). A variation can have students jump a consecutive number of times on one foot before switching feet. For example, a student might jump five times on the right foot and then five on the left foot. With a fast-time rhythm, this step looks like jogging.

Side Swings—Left or Right.   The student moves the rope to either side of the body and jumps off both feet in time with the rope (Figure 21.48). The student does not actually jump over the rope. This is a good technique to use to work on timing and cardiovascular fitness because it is demanding.

Swing Step Forward or Sideways.   Same as the jog step, except the unweighted leg swings forward or sideways rather than backward. The student can alternate the forward swing with the side swing on each foot.

Rocker Step.   The student starts with one leg in front of the other. As the rope comes around, the weight is shifted from the front leg to the back leg and alternates each time the rope goes around. The student rocks back and forth, from front foot to back foot.

Legs Spread Forward and Backward (Scissors). The student starts with one leg forward and one leg back, similar to the starting position for the rocker step. As the rope turns, the front leg is shifted back and the back leg is shifted forward. The position of the legs shifts each time the rope is turned.

Legs Crossed Sideways (Jumping Jack).   The student starts with the legs straddled sideways. As the rope is turned, the legs are crossed with the right leg in front. Another straddle position is next, and then the legs are crossed again with the left leg in front. This sequence is repeated. The jump can also be executed with the feet coming together, instead of crossing each time, similar to the foot pattern of a jumping jack exercise.

Toe-Touches Forward or Backward.   The student starts with one foot forward. The toe of the forward foot is pointed down and touches the ground. As the rope turns, the feet trade places, and the opposite toe touches the ground. For the backward toe-touch, the foot starts in a backward position with the toe touching. The feet then alternate positions with each jump.

Shuffle Step.   The student starts with the weight on the left foot and the toe of the right foot touching

FIGURE 21.47   Alternate foot step

FIGURE 21.48   Side Swings

the heel of the left foot. As the rope turns, the student steps to the right and the feet trade places. The left toe is now touching the right heel. The step is then repeated in the opposite direction.

Ski Jump. The student keeps both feet together and jumps to the left and right sideways over a line. This motion is similar to that of a skier. The jump can be performed with the rope going forward or backward.

Heel-Toe Jump. The student jumps off the right foot and extends the left leg forward, touching the heel to the ground. On the next jump the left foot is brought back beside the right foot with the toe touching the ground. The pattern is then repeated with the right foot touching the heel, then toe.

Heel Click. The student starts by completing several sideways swing steps in preparation for this pattern. As the leg swings out to the side, the opposite foot is brought up and the heels are touched together. The heel click can be completed on either side.

Crossing Arms. Crossing the arms can be added to all of the basic foot patterns. In crossing the arms, the hands actually trade places. The hands must be brought all the way across the body and kept low. The upper body crouches forward slightly from the waist. Crossing can also be used for backward jumping. Students can learn to cross and uncross after a certain number of jumps.

Double Turns. A double turn occurs when the rope passes under the feet twice during the same jump. The student must jump higher and rotate the rope faster. The jump should be about 6 in. high, and a slight forward crouch is necessary to speed up the turn. Students should try consecutive double turns forward or backward. Various foot patterns can also be tried with double turns.

Sideways Jumping. The rope is turned sideways with one hand over the head and the other hand extended down between the legs in front of the body. As the rope is turned, the student jumps the rope one leg at a time. The weight is shifted back and forth between the legs as the rope turns around the body. Students can turn the rope either left or right, and either hand can be held overhead. Students should try the technique several ways.

Shifting from Forward to Backward Jumping. There are several ways to change jumping direction. The first way is to begin jumping forward. As the rope starts downward, the student executes a left or right side swing. A half turn should be made in the same direction as the rope. As the rope is coming out of the side swing, the student must bring it up in a backwards motion. This motion can be completed to either side, as long as the turn is toward the rope side.

Another way to execute the shift is to make a half turn while the rope is above the head with the arms extended upward. The rope will hesitate slightly and then should be brought down in the opposite direction.

A final shifting strategy is from a cross-arm position. As the rope is going overhead, the student uncrosses the arms and makes a half turn. This starts the rope turning in the opposite direction. The key is to uncross the arms and turn simultaneously.

Partner Activities

A wide variety of challenging combinations can be performed with partners using one rope. The partners can start jumping together, or one person can run into position after the other partner has started jumping. Partner activities can be fun with students the same size. They are more challenging when performed with students of varying sizes.

1. One person turns the rope forward or backward:
   a. Partner faces the turner for a specific number of jumps.
   b. Partners are back to back for a specific number of jumps.
   c. Partner turns in place — quarter turn, half turn, and so on.
   d. Partner dribbles a basketball while jumping.
   e. Partners match foot patterns (e.g., jog step, swing step).
   f. Partners complete double turns.

2. Two students turn the rope forward or backward:
   a. Partners stand side by side, facing the same direction.
   b. Partners face opposite directions.
   c. Repeat activities 2a and 2b with elbows locked.
   d. Repeat a, b, and c while hopping on one foot.
   e. Partners are back to back turning one rope with the right or left hand.
   f. Repeat variation e while turning in a circle — both directions.

3. Three students jump together with one turning the rope, one in front, and the other in back. This can be done forward and backward.

4. Two students, each with a rope, face each other. One student turns the rope forward, and the other turns backward, so the ropes are going in the same direction. Partners jump over both ropes on one jump. Students should then change their rope direction.

5. One student turns the rope. The partner comes in from the side, takes one handle of the rope, and begins turning. The partner's entrance must be timed so the rhythm of the rope remains constant. The partner then leaves and enters from the other side. This stunt can be performed with a forward or backward turn.

6. Partners face each other, turning one rope with the right hand. One partner turns to the left and exits from jumping while continuing to turn the rope for the other partner. After several turns, the partner who was out returns to the starting position. A variation can be tried with the partner turning to the right one-quarter turn.

Ideas for Effective Instruction

Rope jumping is a good example of an activity that can be improved with practice. Remind students constantly that these skills will be perfected only with regular practice. Such reminders help keep students from getting discouraged quickly.

Students should first try new jumping techniques without the rope to get the basic idea. They can then try the stunt with a slow-time rhythm with a rebound in between each movement. As they improve, fast time and double time can be tried. Some students may need to practice turning the rope in one hand to the side of the body to develop the necessary rhythm. Students should practice timing their jump with the rope turning at the side. An instructor might do some partner jumping with a student who is having trouble with timing. Another effective instructional strategy is to use a movie, videotape, or loop film to give students a visual model of the skill. Several are listed in the suggested readings section of this chapter.

Students need plenty of room for practicing. Care should be taken, because the ropes can be dangerous to a person's face and eyes. Horseplay with the jump ropes cannot be tolerated.

Ropes can be color coded for various sizes. Students can help distribute and collect the ropes so they do not get tangled. Student helpers can hold their arms out to the sides, and the other students can place the ropes over their arms. Music with different tempos provides a challenge and motivates many students.

Learning Activities

In addition to the foot patterns, rhythms, turning patterns, and partner activities that have been mentioned, there are other effective learning activities that can be done individually, in small groups, or with the entire class.

Follow-the-Leader

Students can work with a partner, a small group, or the entire class—moving forward, backward, diagonally, or sideways—following a designated leader. Various foot patterns can also be used while moving.

Leader in the Circle

The students follow the leader who is in the center of a circle. This activity can be done with large or small circles. The leader calls the name of the next leader after a designated time period or after a certain number of foot patterns have been executed.

Relays

Many different jump rope relays can be played with boundary cones and various types of jumps. For example:

1. Jog-step down around the cone and back (forward turns).
2. Same as variation 1, but with backward turns.
3. Jog-step backward using forward turns.
4. Same as variation 3, but with backward turns.
5. Hop to the cone on one foot and hop back on the other.
6. Ski-jump down, and forward swing-step back.
7. Jog-step through a series of 6 cones, do 10 sit-ups, and jog-step back.
8. Use a two-foot basic step going down, do 5 rocker steps, 5 scissor steps, and come back with a two-foot basic step.
9. Partners (side by side with one rope, elbows locked, both facing forward) go down forward and come back backwards.
10. Partners (side by side with one rope, one person facing forward, the other facing backward) go down and back with a forward turn.

Routines

Various routines can be developed individually with guidelines for foot patterns, change of direction, crossing over, changing levels, rope speed, and routine length. Small groups can also make up routines, choose music, and perform together, and partner routines can be developed with two people using one rope. An example of the guidelines for a small group routine follows:

1. Two min or less—5 members per group
2. Two changes of direction (e.g., forward, backward, diagonal)
3. Two changes of floor pattern (e.g., circle, square, back to back)
4. Two changes of levels (e.g., high, low)

Jump Rope Skills	Number of Successful Completions		
*Individual Skills	5	10	15
1. Two-foot			
2. One-foot hop			
3. Alternate foot			
4. Side swings			
5. Swing step forward			
6. Swing step sideways			
7. Rocker			
8. Scissors			
9. Legs crossed			
10. Toe touch forward			
11. Toe touch backward			
12. Shuffle			
13. Ski			
14. Heel-toe			
15. Heel click			
16. Crossing arms			
17. Double turns			
18. Sideways			
19. Forward to backward			
20. Backward to forward			
*Four variations of these skills can be completed using a forward or backward turn of the rope and slow-time or fast-time rhythm.			

FIGURE 21.49 Jump rope rating scale

5. Five changes of foot patterns (e.g., rocker, basic two-step)
6. One change of rope direction
7. One double turn

Rating Scales

Develop rating scales for each of the various skills to be learned with the jump rope. The scale can be developed for varying degrees of proficiency. Show students how to use the scale as a learning activity and as part of the grading scheme. The scale in Figure 21.49 focuses on individual skills; another scale could be developed for partner skills.

Contracts

Performance objectives can be written for each of the various jump rope skills. Objectives can be set up as a learning contract that is tied to a grading scheme or to a reward system involving certain enjoyable activities. Completion of a specified number of objectives would equal an A, B, and so forth. The performance objectives should serve as learning activities that motivate students. Students can check each other as they accomplish the objectives.

Rainy Day Activities

All jump rope activities are good for rainy days because they can be performed indoors in a limited space. Hallways and gymnasium foyers are possible areas for jump rope activities. Students can work on individual skills if a limited space is available. A rotation schedule may have to be arranged so that some students are practicing while partners are observing and using a rating scale or checking off performance objectives on a contract. Students can also devote time to learning the appropriate terminology for foot patterns and rhythms.

Suggested Readings and Films

Cassidy, J. 1983. *Pumping Plastic: The Jump Rope Fitness Plan*. Stanford, CA: Klutz Press.

Cowgill, S., and Cowgill, N. (Instructional videotape on rope jumping), 1005 E. Phoenix Rd., Grand Island, NE 68801.

Mitchell, C. 1978. *Perfect Exercise: The Hop, Skip, and Jump Way to Health*. New York: Pocket Books.

Moyer, M. (Color film, *Rope Skipping—Basic Steps*), 900 Federal Ave., Seattle, WA 98102.

Skolnik, P. L. 1974. *Jump Rope*. New York: Workman Publishing Co.

TRACK AND FIELD

Track and field events consist of running, jumping, weight throwing, and vaulting. Running events include sprinting short distances, running middle and longer distances, and hurdling over barriers. Relay races with four team members are run over various distances. The jumping events include the high jump, long jump, and triple jump. The throwing events are the shot put, discus, javelin, and hammer throw. The vaulting event is the pole vault.

In the United States, instruction in track and field activities as part of the physical education program began in the late 1890s. Both men and women have been interested in pursuing these events for various reasons. The tremendous variety of skills necessary for running, jumping, throwing, and vaulting provides people with an exciting challenge.

Track and field should continue to be an important part of the secondary school physical education program. Students with different body types are able to find success in some track and field activity. All students should have the opportunity to explore and experience the wide variety of challenges of this unit.

Secondary schools have changed to metric distances for the running events. These distances vary some from state to state and from men's events to women's events. The men's running events usually include the following: 100, 200, 400, 800, 1600, and 3,200 meter; 400-, and 1,600-meter relay; 110-meter high hurdles, and 400-meter intermediate hurdles.

The field events for men usually include the high jump, long jump, triple jump, pole vault, shot put, discus, javelin, and hammer (only in certain states). Women's running events are similar to the men's, but the women run only one hurdle race, which is 100 meters. The 1,600-meter relay race is sometimes replaced with a medley relay consisting of 100, 100, 200, and 400 meters. In the field events, the women do not pole vault, triple jump, or throw the hammer. It is interesting to note that women are finally being allowed officially to run longer distances (e.g., 1,600 and 3,200 meters). The 1984 Olympic Games in Los Angeles marked the first Olympic marathon for women.

Sequence of Skills

Since track and field is a highly specialized area that includes many specific skills and techniques for each of the running, jumping, vaulting, and throwing events, it is difficult to cover adequately all of these activities in a limited space. Several good texts are available with in-depth information about specific events and the skills involved. Much of what should be taught will depend on the abilities of the students, the length of time allotted to the unit, and the equipment available for instruction. Teachers developing units for track and field should refer to the suggested readings.

Ideas for Instruction

Each event in track and field can serve as a learning station for students. After students are introduced to the events, they can rotate from station to station and work on each activity. Keep a clipboard at each station with records of each day's best performances in an activity. The day-to-day records can be used for motivation and as evidence of individual improvement. A class track meet is an enjoyable culminating activity. Teams can be organized and a regulation dual meet conducted.

Suggested Readings

Bowerman, W. 1972. *Coaching Track and Field*. Boston, MA: Houghton Mifflin Co.

Doherty, J. 1976. *Track and Field Omnibook*. 3rd ed. Los Altos, CA: Track and Field News Press.

Powell, J. 1971. *Track and Field Fundamentals for Teacher and Coach*. 3rd ed. Champaign, IL: Stipes Publishing Co.

22 DUAL SPORTS

Dual sport activities usually require two to four players. They are often played by adults during leisure time. These activities are excellent for participation throughout life.

BADMINTON

Badminton is popular in schools from the junior and senior high through college levels. Competition at the college level is popular nationally and internationally. The activity is considered a lifetime sport and can be enjoyed by all in a recreational setting.

The game is played with a shuttlecock and racquet on a court with a net set at a height of 5 ft. The court is marked for both doubles and singles competition. A toss of a coin or a spin of the racquet determines service or court choice. The game begins with a serve from the right-hand service court to an opponent standing in the opposite right-hand service court.

Sequence of Skills

Grips

Forehand. With the racquet lying across the palm and fingers of the racquet hand, the index finger should be separated from the rest of the fingers. Wrap the thumb around the other side of the handle. The grip resembles a handshake and is called the "pistol grip." This grip is used for serving and forehand shots.

Backhand. Move the thumb to a straightened position and to the right of the handle. Rotate the rest of the hand one-fourth of a turn to the right (if right-handed). Regardless of the grip used, the player should make contact with the shuttlecock as early and as high as possible. This gives the player a better angle for return and for more controlled shots, and forces an opponent to move quickly.

Serves

Ready Position and Preparatory Action. Stand with the nonracquet foot forward and the weight mainly on the racquet foot. The feet should be approximately 12–15 in. apart. The nonracquet shoulder is toward the receiver, with the racquet held waist-high and behind the body. Keep the wrist cocked.

The shuttlecock must be contacted below the waist at the instant of the serve. Either a forehand or backhand shot may be used, but the forehand is most common. Until the serve is delivered, the server and receiver must be in their legal service courts. Part of both players' feet must remain in contact with the ground.

Singles Service. Review the ready position. Extend the nonracquet arm and drop the shuttle-cock before starting to move the racquet forward. As weight is shifted to the front foot, rotate the shoulders and hips. As contact is made below the waist, the wrist and forearm rotate. The racquet arm should follow through high and be extended over the left shoulder at completion of service. Most serves will be long and high. A short serve is, however, effective if your opponent is playing too deep.

Doubles Service. The stance is similar to the singles serve. Contact the shuttlecock closer to waist height and slightly more toward the server's racquet-hand side. Guide the shuttlecock instead of hitting it. The wrist does not uncock. Just prior to contacting the shuttlecock, shift the weight from the racquet foot to the nonracquet foot. Little follow-through or rotation occurs. The shuttlecock should peak in height just before the net and be descending as it clears the net.

Forehand Shots

Clear. Get in ready position with the feet and shoulders parallel to the net. Hold the racquet slightly to the backhand side, and bend the knees slightly. Contact the shuttlecock as high as possible and in front of the body. The racquet face should be tilted upward, and the shuttlecock should clear the opponent's racquet and land close to the backline.

Drop. When contact with the shuttlecock is made, the racquet face should be flat and pointing ahead or slightly downward. The shuttlecock is gently guided over the net. Remember to follow through. The shuttlecock should just drop over the net into the opponent's forecourt.

Smash. Extend the arm when the shuttlecock is hit in front of the body. Rotation of the wrist and forearm is performed quickly. The downward angle of the racquet face is more important than the racquet speed. The shot should only be attempted from the front three-fourths of the court.

Backhand Shots

Ready Position. From the forehand position, turn so that the racquet shoulder faces the net. The weight should be on the nonracquet foot, the racquet shoulder up, and the forearm slightly down and across the chest. While shifting the weight to the racquet foot, the body rotates toward the net. As the wrist leads, the racquet extends upward. The racquet arm and elbow should be fully extended at contact. The thumb should not point upward.

Clear. Hitting hard and upward, contact the shuttlecock as high as possible and hit it over the opponent's racquet. Contact should be made in front of the body with the racquet face flat to the target.

Drop. As the shuttlecock is guided over the net, the racquet should be flat and pointed ahead or slightly downward. The shuttlecock should land close to the net.

Underhand Shots

Ready Position. Place the racquet foot forward, and the racquet face parallel to the ground. Cock the wrist and make contact as close to net height as possible.

Forehand Net Clear. The forehand net clear is a high, deep shot similar to the singles deep serve. Turn the shoulder slightly toward the net, and cock the wrist. An inward rotation of the wrist and a lifting of the forearm occur just before contact. Proceed to follow through with the elbow slightly bent.

Backhand Net Clear. The racquet foot is forward, and the racquet shoulder turned to the net. Contact

the shuttlecock as close to net height as possible. As the player moves toward the net, the wrist should be cocked. An outward rotation is used for the backhand. The shot is high and deep into the opponent's court.

Forehand Net Drop. Review the forehand net clear. The net drop is guided over the net with a lifting motion. The shuttlecock should drop quickly.

Backhand Net Drop. This is the same motion as the forehand net drop, except that the backhand grip is used. The shuttlecock should be contacted close to net height.

Ready Position for Receiving

The feet should be parallel and positioned slightly wider apart than the shoulders. Bend the knees slightly with the weight forward. Hold the racquet with the head up and to the backhand side of the body.

Doubles Strategy

Up and Back. One player plays close shots while the partner plays deep shots.

Side by Side. Each partner plays half of the court and is responsible for close or deep shots in his or her half of the court.

Combination. Both side-by-side and up-and-back formations are used. Regardless of the strategy, partners should always call for the shot ("Mine!") to avoid accidental injuries.

Ideas for Effective Instruction

Racquets and Shuttlecocks

The racquet frame can be made of metal or wood (Figure 22.1). It is usually 26 in. long and weighs between 3.75 and 5.5 oz. Nylon is commonly the choice of material for stringing the racquet. The metal frame racquets are desirable because they do not warp or require a press for storage.

The weight of the shuttlecock is between 73 and 85 grains, with 14–16 feathers. If authentic feathers are used, the shuttlecocks should be stored in a damp place. If nylon feathers are used, the shuttlecocks will be more durable and reasonably priced, which is desirable in the school setting.

Net

The top of the net is 5 ft from the floor at its midpoint. It is 5 ft 1 in. at the posts. The net is 30 in. in depth and 20 ft long.

FIGURE 22.1   Badminton racquets and shuttlecocks

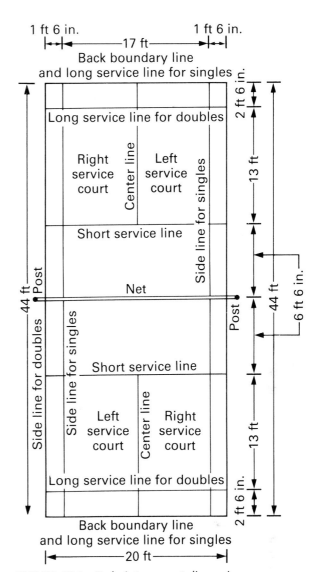

FIGURE 22.2   Badminton court dimensions

Court

Figure 22.2 shows the dimensions of a badminton court.

Games and Match

Eleven points make a game in women's singles. All doubles and men's singles games are 15 points. A match constitutes two games out of three. As soon as a side wins two games, the match is over. The winner of the previous game serves the next game. Players change courts after the first and second games. In the third game, players change after 8 points in a 15-point game and after 6 points in an 11-point game.

Scoring

Only the serving side scores and continues to do so until an error is committed.

Setting

If the score becomes tied, the game may be extended by the player or side first reaching the tied score. In a 15-point game, the set may occur at 13–13 (setting to 5 points) or 14–14 (setting to 3 points). In an 11-point game, the score may be set at 10–10 (setting to 2 points) or 9–9 (setting to 3 points). A set game continues, but the score called is now 0–0, or "Love all." The first player or side to reach set score wins. If a side chooses not to set, the regular game is completed.

Singles Play

The first serve is taken from the right service court and received cross court (diagonally) in the opponent's right service court. All serves on 0 or an even score are served and received in the right-hand court. All serves on an odd score are served and received in the left service court.

Doubles Play

In the first inning, the first service is one hand only. In all other innings, the serving team gets to use two hands. At the beginning of each inning, the player in the right court serves first. Partners rotate only after winning a point.

Even and odd scores are served from the same court as in singles play. If a player serves out of turn or from the incorrect service court and wins the rally, a let will be called. The let must be claimed by the receiving team before the next serve.

If a player standing in the incorrect court takes the serve and wins the rally, it will be a let, provided the let is claimed before the next serve. If either of the above cases occurs and the side at fault loses the rally, the mistake stands, and the players' positions are not corrected for the rest of the game.

Faults

A fault committed by the serving side (in-side) results in a side out, while a fault committed by the receiving side (out-side) results in a point for the server. A fault occurs in any of the following situations.

1. During the serve, the shuttlecock is contacted above the server's waist, or the racquet head is held above the hand.
2. During the serve, the shuttlecock does not fall within the boundaries of the diagonal service court.
3. During the serve, some part of both feet of the server and receiver do not remain in contact

with the court, inside the boundary lines, until the shuttlecock leaves the racquet of the server. Feet on the boundary lines are considered out-of-bounds.

Organization and Skill Work

An effective way to add variety and skill work to classes is to create a series of stations. The stations can be arranged to use the space available in the gymnasium, and can focus on badminton skills, conditioning activities, or a combination of both (Figure 22.3).

Partner activities are helpful with accompanying rating scales or checklists like the one following.

- **Partner Activities:** Low doubles serve
- **Equipment:** One badminton racquet and five shuttlecocks per couple
- **Procedure:** One person is the server, and the other is the helper with a trained eye. The server follows the steps below, and the helper checks off the skills as they are completed.

1. Standing behind the 6 ft 6 in. line from the wall, drop the bird and hit it underhand against the wall. Repeat at least 5 times. The trained eye must be

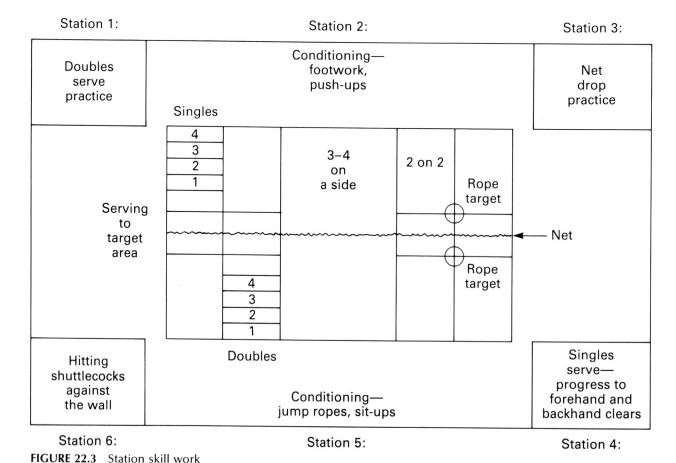

FIGURE 22.3 Station skill work

looking for and giving feedback on the following criteria:

a. Keep both feet on the ground until after the shuttlecock is contacted.

b. Hold the shuttlecock at chest height.

c. Contact the shuttlecock below the waist level.

d. Keep the racquet head below the wrist at point of contact.

e. Keep the wrist firm, cocked throughout the stroke.

f. Shuttlecock is guided, not hit.

2. From the same position behind the line, direct 3 of 5 serves above the 5 ft 1 in. line on the wall and below the 18 in. line above it. Switch positions, and if you were serving, become the helper. Help your partner and remember that you are the trained eye who sees what your partner is doing. Partners repeat the first two steps.

3. Move to the court and take about 5 practice serves. Keep the serve under the 18 in. line. Now do 5 serves and have your partner record your score. This score is to help you determine your accuracy. Switch positions again and repeat step 3.

4. Now try step 3 using your backhand.

Tournament play works well for badminton. Ladder, pyramid, or round robin tournaments can add a competitive flavor to the class.

The use of marking tape on floor and walls, jump ropes on the court, fleece balls, and task cards can give the teacher more stations for a circuit. This enables the student to progress at a personalized skill level. Minigames or lead-up games played on the courts allow for skill work, competition, and enjoyment. Regulation games and tournament play can gradually replace the lead-up games. Students should also be trained as scorekeepers and line or service judges.

Lead-Up Games and Learning Activities

Doubles Drop

After the short serve and underhand drop are taught, a "doubles drop game" can be played between the net and the short service line.

Overhead Clear

After the long serve and the overhead clear are taught, an overhead clear "rally" could be attempted. Try to keep the shuttlecock in play at least 5 times in a row; then try 10 times in a row, 15 times, and so forth.

Designated Shots

After the underhand clear is taught, work on a "designated shots rally." Start with a short serve, return with an underhand drop, return with an underhand clear, and return with an overhead clear. Keep clearing with overhead and underhand clears.

Server versus Receiver

After the "flick" serve and "push" return are taught, play a server versus receiver game. The receiver must try to return as many as possible of the server's 20 serves in a row, 10 from the right and 10 from the left. The server gets a point each time the receiver misses the return. The receiver gets a point if the server misses the serve. Reverse server and receiver roles.

Clear-Smash

After the smash is taught, play a long serve and overhead clear game. Start with a long serve, return with an overhead clear, and keep clearing until someone makes a short clear shot, then smash the short clear. Server is awarded one point if the smash is not returned, or loses one point if the smash is returned. Repeat the rally and try to make points by well-placed smashes.

Drive Rally

After the drive shot is taught, organize a drive rally with four players. Drive crosscourt and down the alley. If the drive shot is too high, smash return it.

Advanced Combination Drill

Start the rally with a long serve and return with an overhead drop, return with an underhand drop, return with an underhand clear to the opponent's backhand side, return with a backhand overhead clear, and return with an overhead clear unless the return shot is short. If the shot is short, use a smash.

Volleyball Badminton

Four players are on each team. Assigned positions rotate as in volleyball.

Three Per Team

Alternate servers, and the "up" player plays the net shots.

Name the Shot

After five days of the badminton unit, challenge students to name the shots (Figure 22.4).

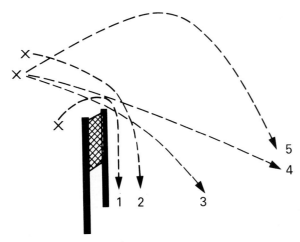

1. Net drop
2. Drop
3. Smash
4. Drive
5. Clear

FIGURE 22.4   Name the shot

Word Scramble

Students who complete station skill work early can be asked to unscramble the puzzle in Figure 22.5.

Suggested Performance Objectives

Core Objectives

All directions given are for right-handed players.

Short or Low Serves

1. Standing 6 ft 6 in. from the wall, serve the shuttlecock 10 times in a row between the 5 ft and 6 ft marks on the wall (1 point).

2. Standing behind the short service line on the right side of the court, serve the shuttlecock crosscourt over the net 10 times and get 7 out of 10 in the court (1 point).

3. Repeat step 2 from the left side of the service court (1 point).

4. Standing behind the short service line, next to the center line in the right court, serve the shuttlecock crosscourt over the net, between the net and a rope 1 ft above it. Repeat 5 times in a row from the right, then 5 times from the left (1 point).

5. Standing behind the short service line, next to the center line in the right-hand court, serve 10 short serves in a row to the receiver's backhand side on the court (1 point).

6. Repeat step 5, standing in the left-hand court (1 point).

Long Serves

1. Standing to the right of and next to the center line, 12 ft from the net, serve 10 long serves in a row to the opposite court (1 point).

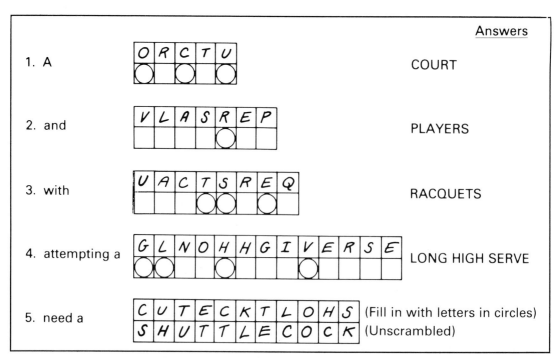

FIGURE 22.5   Word scramble

2. Repeat step 1 from the left service court (1 point).

3. Repeat step 1, but the serves must land in the backhand area marked on the court. Serve 5 long serves in a row to this area (1 point).

Underhand Clears: Forehand and Backhand

1. Standing between the net and the short service line, drop the shuttlecock and underhand clear on the forehand side, 10 clears in a row to the back 4 ft of the court marked for doubles (1 point).

2. Repeat step 1 on the backhand side (1 point).

3. Standing 6 ft behind the short service line, underhand clear on the forehand side 5 clears in a row to the back 4 ft of the doubles court (1 point).

4. Repeat step 3 on the backhand side (1 point).

Drops

1. Standing just behind the short service line on the right court, underhand drop on the forehand side a tossed shuttlecock from your partner. Return 10 drops in a row from the forehand side (1 point).

2. Repeat step 1 on the backhand side (1 point).

3. Repeat steps 1 and 2 from the left court (2 points).

4. Standing anywhere just behind the short service line, a partner tosses the shuttlecock barely over the net, alternating between your forehand and backhand on the toss. Underhand drop 10 in a row back between the net and a rope stretched 1 ft above the net (1 point).

Overhead Clears: Forehand

1. Standing within 12 ft of the net, a partner underhand clears the shuttlecock. Return 10 shuttlecocks in a row with an overhead forehand clear into the doubles court, at least 10 ft from the net (1 point).

2. Repeat step 1, returning 10 in a row to the back 4 ft of the doubles court (1 point).

3. Repeat step 1, returning 10 in a row alternating from right court to left court, at least 10 ft from the net (1 point).

Attendance and Participation

1. Arrive on time for class, dressed and ready to participate (1/3 of a point per day, up to 6 points maximum).

2. Participation in 15 games: 13 doubles and 2 singles (1 point).

Optional Objectives

1. Standing next to the center line on the right court and just behind the short service line, "flick" serve the shuttle 5 times in a row to the back 3 ft of the doubles service court (1 point). Repeat on the left (1 point).

2. Standing in the right receiving court for doubles, "push" return 5 short serves in a row either to the server's backhand side or down the side alley next to server. Repeat on the left (1 point).

3. Standing 6 ft from the short service line next to the center line on the right court, return 5 long serves in a row to the backhand side of the server with an overhead clear (1 point).

4. Repeat step 3, standing in the left court (1 point).

5. A server sets up short, high shots 6–8 in. from the net. Standing 6 ft from the short service line, smash 5 in a row within 15 ft of the net (1 point).

6. Repeat step 5, smashing 5 in a row down the left side of the court (1 point).

7. Repeat step 5, smashing 5 in a row down the right side of the court (1 point).

8. Standing within 10 ft of the short service line, return 10 of your opponent's smashes back over the net as smashes (1 point).

9. Standing within the last 5 ft of the back court, overhead drop opponent's clears to you. Drop 5 shuttlecocks to the right court side between the net and the short service line (1 point).

10. Repeat step 9 on the left court between the net and the short service line (1 point).

11. Stand on the center line, 6 ft from the short service line. Partner sets up low, flat serves down the forehand alley. Hit 5 forehand drives in a row down that alley (1 point).

12. Repeat step 11, hitting 5 backhand drives down the backhand-side alley (1 point).

13. Standing within 12 ft of the net, from a high clear set up by a partner, backhand 5 overhead clears in a row to the back 6 ft of the doubles court (1 point).

14. Standing 15 ft or farther from the net, backhand 5 overhead clears in a row to the back 4 ft of the doubles court (1 point).

Skill Tests

Badminton courts can be marked in many different ways to provide students with a challenge in perfect-

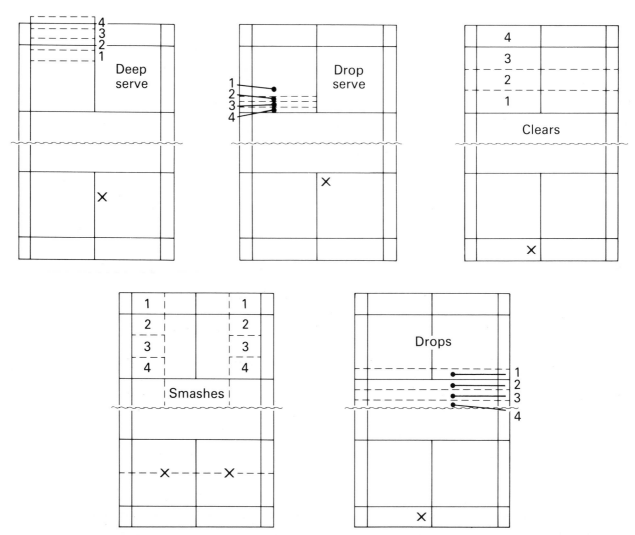

FIGURE 22.6 Skills test

ing their skills (Figure 22.6). Using white shoe polish or masking tape, number portions of the target area in an ascending manner, from the easiest to the most difficult shots. Courts can be marked for deep serves, low serves, clears, drops, and drives. The teacher determines the number of attempts that each student is allowed.

Suggested Readings

Bloss, M. V. 1975. *Badminton*. 3rd ed. Dubuque, IA: Wm. C. Brown Group.

El Paso Public Schools. 1970. *Physical Education Curriculum Guide*. El Paso, TX.

National Association for Girls and Women in Sport. 1982. *Tennis-Badminton-Squash Guide*. Reston, VA: AAHPERD.

Pelton, B. C. 1971. *Badminton*. Englewood Cliffs, NJ: Prentice-Hall.

Poole, J. 1973. *Badminton*. 2nd ed. Pacific Palisades, CA: Goodyear Publishing Co.

Sysler, B. L., and Fox, E. R. 1978. *Lifetime Sports for the College Student*. 3rd ed. Dubuque, IA: Kendall/ Hunt Publishing Co.

FRISBEE

Frisbee is a new, exciting lifetime physical activity that can offer success and a challenge at all ability levels. It can be played on almost any size field or gymnasium area and can be used with individuals, small groups, or teams. The International Frisbee Disc Association, which numbers over 100,000 members, has statistics showing that more Frisbee discs are sold yearly in the United States than footballs and basketballs combined. An annual World Championship held in the Rose Bowl draws large crowds to watch competitors focus on distance, accuracy, free style, and other games.

A number of factors make Frisbee disc sports an attractive new activity for physical education. A Frisbee costs only $4.00 to $8.00, depending on the type and quality of the disc. Frisbee provides excellent skills practice in throwing, catching, and eye-hand coordination, as well as offering many interesting individual challenges and team activities. The low injury risks and the attraction to students are positive factors. The sport can be effective in a coeducational environment, and offers flexibility in terms of participants' ages and abilities and in terms of program space and time. Both team and individual skills can be learned with the Frisbee and used for a lifetime of enjoyment.

Sequence of Skills

Throws

Backhand Throw.   The thumb is on the top of the disc and the remaining fingers are under the rim. The index finger can also be placed on the outside lip of the disc. Coil the wrist and arm across the chest. Step forward and release the disc (keeping it level) with a snap of the wrist (Figure 22.7).

Backhand (Across the Chest) Curves.   Use the same technique as the straight backhand but release the disc at an angle, with the lower side being the desired direction. Throw curves both left and right by tilting the disc.

Underhand Throw.   Use a backhand grip or put the index finger on the lip of the disc. Step with the opposite foot, bring the disc underhand past the body, and release level about waist height with a wrist snap (Figure 22.8).

Thumber Throw.   Hook the thumb under the disc and put the four fingers on top. Bring the disc down from the ear in a sidearm motion and release when the disc is even with the body. Avoid a follow-through with the disc.

Sidearm Throw.   Put the index and middle finger under the disc and the thumb on top. The two fingers can be together on the lip, or one can be on the lip and one in the middle of the disc (Figure 22.9). Release the disc in a motion similar to the thumber.

Overhand Wrist Flip.   Grip the disc with the fingers on top and the thumb under the lip. Cock the wrist backward and start the throw behind the back at shoulder level (Figure 22.10). Flip the wrist forward to a point in line with the body.

FIGURE 22.7   Backhand throw

FIGURE 22.8   Underhand throw

FIGURE 22.9   Sidearm throw

FIGURE 22.10   Overhand wrist flip

Catches

Sandwich Catch. Catch the disc with one hand on top and the other on the bottom with the disc in the middle. Alternate hands from top to bottom on different occasions.

C-Catch. Make a *C* with the thumb and fingers. Watch the disc into the *C* and close the fingers on the disc. Throws below the waist should have the thumb up, and those above the waist should have thumb down.

Additional Skills

1. **Skip-throw off the ground.** Tip the forward edge down and skip the disc to a partner.
2. **Tipping.** Use the finger, knee, head, toe, heel, or elbow. Watch the disc make contact with the various body parts and tip the disc in the air.
3. **Catches.** Catch with the finger, behind the back and head, between the legs, and one-handed.
4. **Air brushing.** Strike the disc on its side to give it rotation.

Ideas for Effective Instruction

Frisbee discs are available from over 30 different companies. Avoid the cheapest discs because they will not fly without turning over. Whamo Company in San Gabriel, California, is the oldest and largest manufacturer of flying discs. They have an excellent

World Class Series ranging from 97 to 165 g. These discs are reasonably priced for secondary schools. Many companies use discs for advertising, and it is often possible to acquire promotional discs at a discount.

Instruction can begin by having partners, positioned about 5 yd apart, work on the basic backhand and sandwich catch. As students improve, have them move farther apart and use the backhand curves with the C-catch and the one-handed catch. Be sure to keep beginning students spread out and away from buildings, fences, and other obstacles, since the disc is difficult to control. Next, the underhand throw, thumber, and sidearm can be introduced with several fancy catches.

After students have the basic idea, create four stations that focus on accuracy, distance, accuracy and distance combined, and loft time. Many station variations can be designed to challenge students. Check the following section on activities for specific ideas. Frisbee golf is a particularly good activity for beginners with few developed skills.

Lead-Up Games and Learning Activities
Throw for Distance

Set up five or six cones at varying distances and let students experiment with different throws for distance.

Throw for Distance and Accuracy

Mark a line with varying distances and have students throw as far as possible on the line. Subtract from the total throw distance, the distance of the Frisbee landing point away from the line. Students should develop both distance and accuracy.

Throw for Accuracy

Make a large circular target, about 9 or 10 ft in diameter, on the ground with rope or jump ropes. Set cones at 10-, 15-, 20-, and 25-yd distances. Let students have five attempts at each distance, and record the number of accurate throws. Another variation is to hang a Hula-Hoop from a tree or goal post and have students throw through the hoop. Award one point for hitting the hoop and two points for going through the hoop.

Time Aloft

Record the time from disc release until it hits the ground.

Throw and Catch with Self

The object of this activity is to throw the disc as far forward as possible and then to run and catch the Frisbee. A starting line is designated at which the disc must be released, and distance is measured from that line. The disc must be caught.

Follow-the-Leader

One player makes a specific throw and the second player must try to make the same throw. The first player must match the catch of the second player.

Twenty-One

Players stand 10 yd apart and throw the disc back and forth. The throws must be accurate and catchable. One point is awarded for a two-handed catch and 2 points for a one-handed catch. A player must get 21 points and win by 2 points.

Frisbee Tennis

The same game as regular tennis, but the player must catch the Frisbee and throw from that spot. The serve starts to the right of the center mark and must go to the opposite back court, not into the service box.

Ultimate

Ultimate is a team game with seven or more on a side. The object is to move the Frisbee down the field by passing and to score by passing across the goal line to a teammate. The person with the disc can only pivot and pass to a teammate. If the Frisbee is grounded not caught, intercepted, or goes out-of-bounds, the defending team gains possession.

Guts

Five to seven players on a team stand behind a line 15 yd from the opponents' line. The goal line is 10 yd wide. The object is to throw so hard that the opponents cannot make a one-handed catch. The Frisbee can be tipped by several people as long as a one-handed catch is used. The receiving team gets a point if the throw is too high, too wide, or too low. The height is determined by having the team stretch their arms straight up, usually 7 to 8 ft high. The first team to score 21 points wins. Use extra caution with beginners and younger students. Move the goals back a bit and match ability levels.

Frisbee Soccer

The game is played like soccer, but the disc is thrown to teammates and at the goal. If the disc is dropped, the defenders play offense. Rules can be modified to include two goalies and limitations on the number of steps possible.

Frisbee Softball

The game is similar to regular softball. The pitcher throws the disc to the batter, who must catch the disc and throw it into play past the pitcher. If the batter drops the pitch, it is a strike. No bunting or stealing is allowed. The other rules of softball apply.

Frisbee Golf

Frisbee or disc golf is a favorite game of many students. Boundary cones with numbers can be used for tees, and holes can be boxes, Hula-Hoops, trees, tires, garbage cans, or any other available equipment on the school grounds. Put the course together on a map for students (Figure 22.11) and start them at different holes to decrease the time spent waiting to tee off. Regulation golf rules apply. The students can jog between throws for increased activity.

Disc Golf—Rules and Regulations

- **General Guideline.** Disc golf is played like regular golf. One stroke is counted for each time the disc is thrown and when a penalty is incurred. The object is to acquire the lowest score.
- **T-Throws.** T-throws must be completed within or behind the designated tee area.
- **Lie.** The lie is the spot on or directly underneath the spot where the previous throw landed.

Frisbee Golf Course

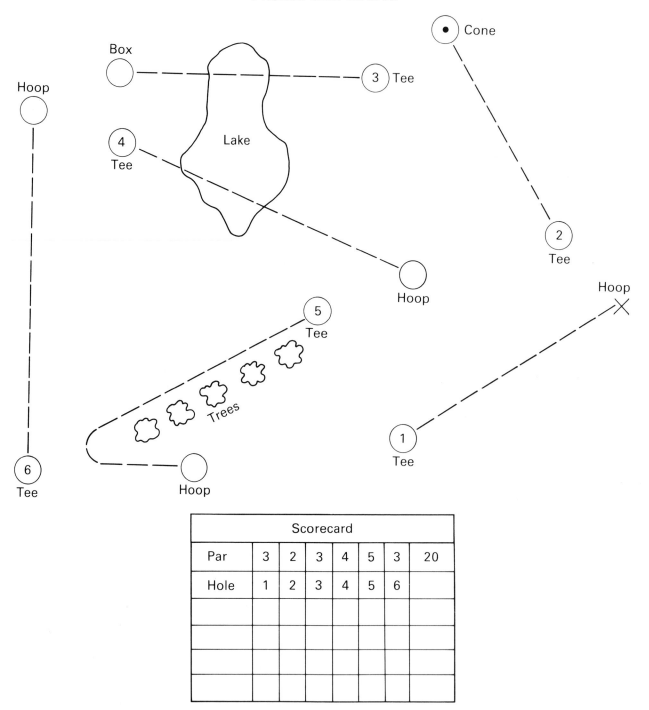

FIGURE 22.11   Frisbee golf course and scorecard

Scorecard							
Par	3	2	3	4	5	3	20
Hole	1	2	3	4	5	6	

- **Throwing Order.** The player whose disc is the farthest from the hole throws first. The player with the least number of throws on the previous hole tees off first.
- **Fairway Throws.** Fairway throws must be made with the foot closest to the hole on the lie. A run-up is allowed.
- **Dog Leg.** A dog leg is one or more designated trees or poles in the fairway that must be passed on the outside when approaching the hole. There is a 2-stroke penalty for missing a dog leg.
- **Putt Throw.** A putt throw is any throw within 10 ft of the hole. A player may not move past

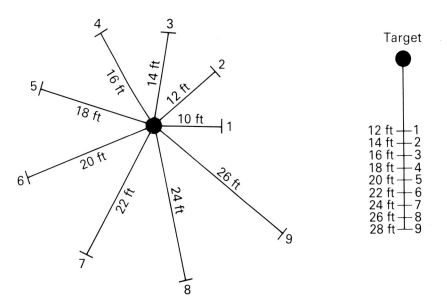

FIGURE 22.12 Around nine game

the point of the lie in making the putt throw. Falling or jumping putts are not allowed.

- **Unplayable Lies.** Any disc that comes to rest 6 or more ft above the ground is unplayable. The next throw must be played from a new lie directly underneath the unplayable lie (1 stroke penalty).
- **Out-of-Bounds.** A throw that lands out-of-bounds must be played from the point where the disc went out (1 stroke penalty).
- **Course Courtesy.** Do not throw until the players ahead are out of range.
- **Completion of Hole.** A disc that comes to rest in the hole (box or hoop) or strikes the designated hole (tree or pole) constitutes successful completion of that hole.

Around Nine

A target is set up with nine different throwing positions around it, each 2 ft farther away (Figure 22.12). The throwing positions can be clockwise or counterclockwise around the target. They can also be in a straight line from the target. Points are awarded based on the throwing position number (i.e., number 7 means 7 points for hitting the target). The game can be played indoors or out.

One-Step

This game is a variation of Guts. Opponents stand 20–30 yd apart. The object is to throw the disc accurately to the opponent so she or he can catch it while taking only one step. If the throw is off target, the thrower receives a point. If the throw is

accurate and the receiver drops the disc, the receiver is awarded 1 point. The first player with 5 points loses the match.

Suggested Performance Objectives

1. Throw 10 consecutive backhands through a Hula-Hoop from 10 yd.
2. Same as Objective 1, using underhand throws.
3. Same as Objective 1, using sidearm throws.
4. Same as Objective 1, using thumber throws.
5. Same as Objective 1, using overhand wrist flips.
6. Throw a Frisbee 30 yd or more using two different throws.
7. Curve the disc around a tree and land it in a designated target area 3 of 5 attempts.
8. Same as Objective 7, but use the opposite curve.
9. Catch 10 consecutive sandwich catches.
10. Catch 10 consecutive thumbs-down catches above the waist.
11. Same as Objective 10, with thumbs up below the waist.
12. Catch 3 of 5 behind the head, behind the back, or between the legs.
13. Make 5 consecutive one-handed catches, both left and right.
14. Throw 5 consecutive skips into a target area.
15. Score 30 or less on a round of Frisbee golf.

These are just a few of the possibilities for challenging students with Frisbee performance objectives. The objectives could be combined with a grading scheme or used with learning stations for skill development. Activities need to be field-tested in

Introduction
What is Frisbee?
Types
Activities
Backhand throw
Sandwich catch
Backhand curves
C-catch
Underhand throw
	Review
	Backhands—
	curves
	Underhands
	Catches
	Teach
	Frisbee golf
	Activity
	Play 6 holes of golf
		Review
		Throws—catches
		Teach
		Thumber
		Sidearm
		Overhand flip
		Activities
		Four stations:
		    Distance
		    Accuracy
		    Curves
		    Partner work
			Review
			Throws—catches
			Teach
			Fancy catches
			Activities
			Follow-the-Leader
			Twenty-One
			One Step
				Review
				Fancy catches
				Teach
				Throw to self
				Activities
				Frisbee softball
				Frisbee soccer

Review
All throws
Teach
Skipping
Tipping
Brushing
Activities
Four stations:
    Distance with
    accuracy
    Self-catch
    Accuracy
    Partner work
	Review
	All catches
	Teach
	Free style
	Activity
	Ultimate
		Review
		Skipping, tipping,
		brushing, free
		style
		Activities
		Four stations: skill
		work
		Frisbee tennis
		Frisbee golf
			Activity
			9 holes of Frisbee
			golf
				Activities
				Four stations:
				    Skill work
				    Evaluation
				Around Nine
				Follow-the-Leader
				Twenty-One
				One Step

Review Skills for station work **Activities** Four stations Frisbee softball	**Activities** Ultimate Frisbee soccer	**Activities** Station work Evaluation Guts Around Nine Follow-the-Leader Twenty-One One Step	**Activities** 9 holes of Frisbee golf	**Activities** Station work Evaluation Ultimate Frisbee softball Guts

FIGURE 22.13   Frisbee block plan

order to establish fair distances and criterion levels for various age students and ability groups.

Figure 22.13 is a 3-wk Frisbee unit for junior high school students.

Rainy Day Activities

1. Review and teach rules and strategies for the various Frisbee games.
2. Set up a short putting (Frisbee golf) course in the gym, hallway, or locker room.
3. Review grips, throws, releases, and so forth.
4. Discuss Frisbee literature, and have students read and report on specific information.
5. Discuss the various types and sizes of discs and the purpose of each type.
6. Set up an indoor tossing accuracy test and let students work at improving their accuracy.
7. Develop a crossword puzzle or Frisbee word searches.
8. Assign a group of students to develop a crossword puzzle or a word search.
9. Devise and give a test on terminology.
10. Discuss with students the skills and activities of Frisbee and how Frisbee can fit into their lifestyles.
11. Have students develop rules and regulations for a new game that will be played when the weather clears.
12. Invite a local Frisbee club or expert to class to give a demonstration and instruction on Frisbee techniques and skills.

Suggested Readings

Danna, M., and Poynter, D. 1978. *Frisbee Players' Handbook*. Santa Barbara, CA: Parachuting Publications.
Frisbee World Magazine. The International Frisbee Association, P.O. Box 970, San Gabriel, CA 91776.
International Frisbee Disc Association. 1978. *The Discourse.* San Gabriel, CA.
Tips, C. 1979. *Frisbee by the Masters.* Millbrae, CA: Celestial Arts.
Tips, C., and Roddick, D. 1979. *Frisbee Disc Sports and Games.* Millbrae, CA: Celestial Arts.

RACQUETBALL

The game of racquetball is a direct descendant from the game of paddleball, which was first played in the 1920s. In the 1940s, a racquet with strings was introduced and became known as "paddle rackets." This sport grew in popularity, and in 1969 the International Racquetball Association was established, and "racquetball" was born. Within the last ten years, the game has grown tremendously in popularity. This growth has brought about a comparable increase in the number of facilities, changes in racquet style, and a livelier ball. A Neilson Company survey found that racquetball was the fastest growing participation sport from 1976 to 1979.

Racquetball can be played on a one-, three-, or four-walled court. The most popular is the enclosed four-wall court with a ceiling, but the other types of courts are more common at the junior and senior high school levels. The game can be played with two people (singles), three people (cutthroat), or four people (doubles). The object is to win each rally by serving or returning the ball so the opponent is unable to keep the ball in play. A rally is over when a side makes an error or is unable to return the ball to the front wall before it touches the floor twice. Note that one can score only when one is serving.

Sequence of Skills

Grip, Eastern Style

Forehand.   Form a *V* on the top bevel of the handle with the thumb and index finger (Figure 22.14). Rest the thumb on the knuckle of the middle finger on the left side bevel of the handle. The palm of the hand should be approximately level with the bottom of the racquet. The index finger should be in a pistol grip position.

Backhand.   Rotate one-quarter turn to the left (counterclockwise) (Figure 22.15). The *V* is now on the upper part of the left bevel.

FIGURE 22.14   Forehand grip

FIGURE 22.15   Backhand grip

Ready Position

The feet should be shoulder width apart and the knees slightly flexed. The back is bent slightly forward, and the head is up. The weight is on the balls of the feet. The racquet should be in front of the body at about chest height. Stand in the middle of the court, approximately 4 ft behind the short line.

Forehand

From the ready position, pivot until facing the right sidewall with the left shoulder forward (Figure 22.16). Bring the wrist back beside the right ear, and point the racquet toward the ceiling. The weight is on the back foot. Start the forward swing with the racquet, and shift the weight from the back to the front foot. Rotate the shoulders and hips toward the front wall. Contact with the ball should be in line with the instep of the front foot. Keep the eyes on the ball and follow through across the body.

FIGURE 22.16   Forehand

FIGURE 22.17   Backhand

Backhand

Follow the same technique as the forehand, but contact the ball when it is about 6 in. from the lead foot (Figure 22.17).

Backwall Shot

Proper setup position is the key to any backwall shot. Watch the ball carefully and set up with the weight on the rear foot and the racquet by the ear. Step forward and stroke into the ball at the proper position, as stated in the previous discussion.

Serve

Drive.   Hit the serve low and hard to the back corner where the back and sidewalls join. This usually goes to the receiver's backhand.

Crosscourt Z.   Serve so that the ball strikes the front wall 3–4 ft from the sidewall and then rebounds to the sidewall and bounces deep in the opposite corner. The speed and height of the serve can be varied to create different angles for the opponent.

Lob.   The lob is a change-of-pace serve that hits high on the front wall and stays close to the sidewall. It should land deep in the back court and drop straight down.

Ceiling Shot

The ceiling shot is a defensive shot to move the opponent back and to open up the front center court. The shot can be hit with a forehand, backhand, or overhead stroke, depending on the position of the ball. If the ball is above the head, an overhead shot can be used. A forehand or backhand can otherwise be used. The overhead shot is similar to a tennis serve. The elbow leads the movement, and the arm stretches overhead to contact the ball with an extended arm. The object is to place the shot close to the front wall on the ceiling. It is usually hit to the opponent's backhand side, tightly against the sidewall.

Passing Shot

The passing shot is an offensive shot that is hit low and hard to either side of the opponent, just out of reach. The object is to keep the ball close to the sidewall and low enough so the ball does not come off the back wall to any degree. The shot is a wise choice when the opponent is out of center position to either side of the court.

Kill Shot

The kill is an offensive shot hit low on the front wall. It is impossible to return if hit accurately. It can be hit straight into the front wall or can be hit off the sidewall into the front wall.

Ideas for Effective Instruction

Racquets are made of wood, fiberglass, aluminum, and various other combinations such as graphite and fiberglass. They have different weights, shapes, strings, and grip sizes. Wood racquets are cheaper but heavier; fiberglass racquets are lighter but less durable. Aluminum is lightweight and durable, but is quite expensive. Grips are usually leather or rubber. Leather seems to provide a better grip, but is not as durable as the rubber. Grip size is the circumference of the handle in inches (i.e., $4\frac{1}{8}$, $4\frac{5}{8}$).

Racquetballs are quite lively and will break after some usage, so having extras is a good idea. Eye guards are available as a safety measure, and some players may want to wear a glove to provide a better grip.

It is usually best to have two students working in one court with one student on each side of the court. If more students must be placed on each court, then designate partners and have one hitting and one chasing balls or throwing setups. Have two hitters and two nonhitters per court. The nonhitter can perform a variety of functions such as analyzing strokes, checking safety, or using a rating scale. Keep the hitters close to the sidewalls to give everyone more room.

Skill work can be accomplished easily by practicing performance objectives in a contract. It is best to start with a bounce-and-hit method and progress to a setup throw off the wall. Either of these methods can be done alone or with a partner. Some students need to practice bouncing the ball and throwing the ball off the wall. Take time to show students how to perform these skills.

Stress the importance of safety on the court because of the confined area and the dangerous implements. Players should be encouraged to wear eye guards, and should be reminded never to turn around and expose the face to a person hitting from behind them. All players must tie the wrist strings snugly around the wrist to avoid losing control of the racquet and injuring others. Finally, players should be reminded that the rules of racquetball stress safety. Whenever there is any chance of endangering the opponent either by hitting with the racquet or by bodily contact, let the ball go and play the point over.

Lead-Up Games and Learning Activities

Ceiling Games

This is a change-of-pace game that requires students to use the ceiling shot. After the serve, a certain number of shots must hit the ceiling before or after hitting the front wall. If the ball does not hit the ceiling, it is a point or side out. A useful variation is to change the required number of ceiling shots that a person must hit each time. For example, start with one and then increase the required number. Or, require all ceiling shots after the serve.

Five Points and Out

This modified game allows five serves or less each time the serve changes hands. After five points are scored, the opponents change positions (server to receiver). The opponents change positions normally if a side out is forced before the five points are scored. This modification keeps opponents from dominating the scoring through an exceptionally strong serve.

Eight Ball Rally

After the serve, each person must hit the ball four times before a point can be scored. This forces a longer rally and encourages work on different shots.

Backhand Rally

After the serve, a player must hit a certain number of backhand shots before a point is scored or a side out is forced. Start with one required backhand and then increase the number gradually.

Accuracy Drills

A challenging activity is to mark off the courts with targets on the floor and walls. Jump ropes, boundary cones, boxes, and masking tape are useful for constructing targets. Challenge the entire class to make five lob serves, five forehands, five backhands, five Z serves, and five drive serves to the target areas. Kill shots off the back wall and sidewalls can be practiced to marked areas on the front wall. Announce the winner in each category. Vary the size of the targets and the designated skills each day.

Cutthroat and Doubles

Cutthroat is played with three people. The server plays the other two players. Doubles is two players versus two.

Rotation

Rotation involves students playing a 5-min game. A whistle is then blown and students rotate to the court on the left if they are ahead and stay where they are if behind. The object of the game is to move up to the last court. Rotation is also enjoyable when playing doubles. Teammates move ahead a court if they are leading when the whistle blows.

Suggested Performance Objectives

These performance objectives can be used for skill work, as a motivational device, and as part of an evaluation scheme. Students can evaluate each other or evaluation can be a combination of peer and teacher observation. A checklist can be used daily or weekly, and students can be required to complete a certain number of checklists before entering the class tournament.

Beginning Skills

Forehand Drive

1. Standing 3 ft behind the short line and 3 ft from the sidewall, bounce the ball off the sidewall and execute a proper forehand drive, hitting the front wall below the 8-ft line, 4 consecutive times.
2. Standing 3 ft behind the receiving line and 3 ft from the sidewall, bounce the ball off the sidewall and execute a proper forehand drive, hitting the front wall below the 8-ft line, 4 consecutive times.
3. Standing 3 ft behind the service line and in the middle of the court, feed the ball to the front wall and then execute a proper forehand drive below the 8-ft line, 3 of 4 times.
4. Standing 3 ft behind the short line and in the middle of the court, feed the ball to the front wall and then execute a proper forehand drive below the 8-ft line, 3 of 4 times.

Backhand Drive

5. Repeat task 1 using proper backhand drive.
6. Repeat task 2 using proper backhand drive.
7. Repeat task 3 using proper backhand drive.
8. Repeat task 4 using proper backhand drive.

Backwall Shot

9. Standing approximately 10 ft from the back wall, bounce the ball off the floor and then off the back wall and execute a forehand backwall shot, hitting the front wall below the 8-ft line, 3 of 4 times.
10. Repeat task 9 using the backhand backwall shot (1 point).
11. Standing approximately in the middle of the court, feed the ball to the front wall so it bounces off the floor and the back wall, and execute a forehand backwall shot, hitting the front wall below the 8-ft line, 3 of 4 times.
12. Repeat task 11 using the backhand drive.

Serves

13. Hit 3 of 5 drive serves to the left court that land within 3 ft of the sidewall in the back court and are otherwise legal.
14. Hit 3 of 5 crosscourt serves to the left court that land within 3 ft of the sidewall and are otherwise legal.
15. Hit 3 of 5 lob serves to the left court that land within 3 ft of the sidewall, do not bounce out from the back more than 3 ft, and are otherwise legal.
16. Repeat task 13 to the right court.
17. Repeat task 14 to the right court.
18. Repeat task 15 to the right court.

Ceiling Shot

19. Standing in back court, bounce the ball high enough to execute a proper overhand forehand ceiling shot so the ball hits ceiling, front wall, floor, and hits low off the back wall 3 of 4 times.
20. Repeat task 19 using regular forehand stroke.

Pinch Shot

21. Standing at midcourt, bounce the ball and execute a proper forehand pinch shot so the ball hits the sidewall, front wall, bounces at least 2 times, and hits the other sidewall 3 of 4 times.
22. Repeat task 21 using backhand stroke.

Intermediate and Advanced Skills

23. Repeat task 1 hitting front wall below the 3-ft line.
24. Repeat task 2 hitting front wall below the 3-ft line.
25. Repeat task 3 hitting front wall below the 3-ft line.
26. Repeat task 4 hitting front wall below the 3-ft line.
27. Repeat task 1 using proper backhand drive and hitting front wall below the 3-ft line.
28. Repeat task 2 using proper backhand drive and hitting front wall below the 3-ft line.
29. Repeat task 3 using proper backhand drive and hitting front wall below the 3-ft line.
30. Repeat task 4 using proper backhand drive and hitting front wall below the 3-ft line.
31. Repeat task 9 hitting front wall below the 3-ft line.
32. Repeat task 9 using the backhand backwall shot and hitting front wall below the 3-ft line.
33. Repeat task 11 hitting front wall below the 3-ft line.
34. Repeat task 11 using the backhand drive and hitting front wall below the 3-ft line.

Introduction What is racquetball? Grips—ready position Forehand stroke Backhand stroke Contract procedures Practice bounce and hit Rule of the day	**Review** Grip, forehand, backhand Equipment **Teach** Serves—drive, Z, lob **Activities** Serves—practice Bounce and hit Rule of the day	**Review** Serves, rules **Teach** Backwall shots Hinders **Activities** Backwall practice Serve practice Rule of the day	**Review** Forehand, backhand **Teach** Court position Kill shots **Activities** Performance objectives or short game Rule of the day	**Review** Backwall shots **Teach** Ceiling shots Passing shots **Activities** Ceiling games One, two, or three shots
Review Problem rules Serve strategy Court coverage **Activities** Accuracy drills Drive serve Lob serve Backhand Backhand games One or two shots	**Teach** Cutthroat Doubles **Activities** Performance objectives Eight ball rally Rotation work up	**Review** Problem areas **Activities** Performance objectives Five and out Ceiling games	**Review** Rules **Activities** Performance objectives Regular game Cutthroat or doubles	**Review** Kill shots **Activity** Rotation work up
Activities Performance objectives Backhand games Regular game Tournament	**Review** Rules, strategy Shots, serves **Activities** Performance objectives Tournament games	Written exam **Activities** Performance objectives Tournament games	**Activities** Performance objectives Tournament games Cutthroat or doubles	Final performance objectives work Review course objectives Final games Return exam

FIGURE 22.18 Racquetball block plan

35. Repeat task 19 using backhand stroke.
36. Repeat task 20 using backhand stroke.
37. Repeat task 21 with feed off the front wall.
38. Repeat task 22 with feed off the front wall.
39. Repeat task 1 hitting the front wall below the 1-ft line (kill shot), 3 of 4 times.
40. Repeat task 3 hitting the front wall below the 1-ft line, 3 of 4 times.
41. Repeat task 14 using the backhand in the right court, 3 of 4 times.
42. Repeat task 15 using the backhand in the right court, 3 of 4 times.

Block Plan

Figure 22.18 is a sample block plan for racquetball.

Rainy Day Activities

1. Review rules and strategies for serving, court position, passing shots, singles play, cutthroat, and doubles play.
2. Have students critique several racquetball articles or a chapter from an activity book.
3. Develop a crossword puzzle or word searches on racquetball.
4. Assign a group of students to develop a crossword puzzle or word search.
5. Work on serving against a wall indoors. Speed and distances can be modified according to the available space.
6. Have on hand a variety of racquets, balls, gloves, and eye guards, and discuss the advantages of each.

7. Show loop films on racquetball.
8. Devise and administer a test on terms and strategy.
9. Discuss caloric expenditure playing racquetball.
10. Point out the health-related benefits of playing racquetball.

Suggested Readings

Brumfield, C., and Bairstow, J. 1978. *Off the Wall.* New York: The Dial Press.

Keeley, S. 1976. *The Complete Book of Racquetball.* Northfield, IL: DBI Books.

Leve, C. 1973. *Inside Racquetball.* Chicago, IL: Henry Regnery Co.

Reznik, J. W., Matthews, D. O., and Peterson, J. 1972. *Racquetball for Men and Women.* Champaign, IL: Stipes Publishing Company.

Pangrazi, R. P. 1987. *Racquetball, Sport for Life Series.* Glenview, IL: Scott, Foresman and Company.

Shay, A., and Leve, C. 1976. *Winning Racquetball.* Chicago, IL: Henry Regnery Co.

Stafford, R. 1975. *Racquetball: The Sport for Everyone.* Memphis, TN: S. C. Toof.

Strandemo, S., and Bruns, B. 1977. *The Racquetball Book.* New York: Pocket Books.

RHYTHMS

The urge to express oneself rhythmically has been characteristic of the human race throughout time. Dances have been done as religious rituals, as national and cultural customs, and as declaration of war. Current dances are borrowed from many cultures and groups both ancient and modern. Since the United States is a melting pot of cultures, we have a broad and diverse range of folk dances representing many peoples.

Every generation dances. It is important that students learn the dances of the past as they develop new dances unique to their group. A wide variety of social skills can be learned through social dancing. Often, if people are not taught dance skills during the school-aged years, they are hesitant to participate in later years. The rhythmic program should thus be viewed as an integral part of the physical education program. If dance skills are not taught as part of the program, they probably will not be taught at all.

Sequence of Skills

The program should consist of four major parts: square dance, folk and round dances, social dance steps, and country swing and western dance. Such a large number of skills and dances can be taught that it is impossible to list all of the activities here.

Instead, the authors make reference to a text that offers supplementary and comprehensive coverage. Another concern is that different geographic areas have favorite dances and rhythmic activities peculiar to each. The authors could not offer activities that would be comprehensive enough in the rhythms area to suit all readers.

Square Dance

The text *Dance a While* by Harris, Pittman, and Waller (1988) is an excellent source for square dancing. The basic movements of square dance are detailed in progression from Level 1A, beginner basics, to Level 5, intermediate basics. Fifty skills are listed and explained in clear and concise terms. A classified index of square dances is also provided, along with the basic skills that are developed in each dance and the level of difficulty. Each dance description contains the necessary performance instructions and recommended records.

Country Swing and Western Dance

Country swing and western dance is popular with junior and senior high school students. The number of dance moves is limited only by the imagination of the dancers. An excellent source for a step-by-step approach to the moves can be found in a text titled *The Complete Book of Country Swing and Western Dance* by Livingston (1981). The text is illustrated in a step-by-step fashion with photographs, and is easy to follow. The shuffle step is also included.

Folk and Round Dance

There are many folk and round dances of varying difficulty. When the dances are presented, the background and history of the dance should be shared with students. The *Dance a While* text (1988) offers a rich repertoire of dances. A classified index detailing the basic steps, formations, and degree of difficulty is most useful. Directions for the dances are given, along with recommended records.

Social Dance Steps

Social dance steps should be developed in the rhythms unit. Steps most commonly taught are the waltz, fox-trot, swing, tango, rumba, samba, cha-cha, and bossa nova. Each can be presented with the basic steps taught first, followed by one or two variations. With junior high school youngsters, the dance steps can be learned individually and then with a partner. Emphasis should be placed on creating an enjoyable atmosphere since peer pressure to succeed is great. Instructors can develop a positive class attitude by demonstrating proper dance etiquette and by showing their enjoyment of the activity. The *Dance a While* text (1988) is recommended as a valuable source.

References

Harris, J. A., Pittman, A. M., and Waller, M. S. 1988. *Dance a While*. New York: Macmillan Publishing Co.

Livingston, P. 1981. *The Complete Book of Country Swing and Western Dance*. Garden City, NY: Doubleday & Co.

Suggested Readings

Ellfeldt, L. 1967. *Folk Dance*. Brown Physical Education Activity Series. Dubuque, IA: Wm. C. Brown Group.

Hall, J. T. 1969. *Folk Dance*. Goodyear Physical Education Series. Pacific Palisades, CA: Goodyear Publishing Co. 1969.

Heaton, A. 1971. *Techniques of Teaching Ballroom Rhythms*. Dubuque, IA: Kendall/Hunt Publishing Co.

Jensen, C. R., and Jensen, M. B. 1973. *Square Dancing*. Provo, UT: Brigham Young University Press.

Kraus, R. G., and Sadlo, L. 1964. *Beginning Social Dance*. Belmont, CA: Wadsworth Publishing Co.

Lidster, M. D., and Tamburini, D. H. 1965. *Folk Dance Progressions*. Belmont, CA: Wadsworth Publishing Co.

Spiesman, M. C. 1970. *Folk Dancing*. Philadelphia: W. B. Saunders Co.

TENNIS

Developing from a crude handball game played in 14th century France, the game of tennis became one of the most popular sports of the 1980s. Part of its popularity stems from the fact that it is truly a game for a lifetime. Children as young as 6 years old can learn to play. In fact, most of today's superstars began playing at very early ages. Chris Evert-Lloyd, one of the top female players of this era, still plays with a two-handed backhand, a skill she acquired when she did not have sufficient strength to hit one-handed as a child.

Tennis can also be played well by older age groups. The United States Tennis Association (USTA), which is the governing body for tennis in the United States, conducts national championships and has established national rankings for age groups beginning with the 12-year-old-and-under group, through the 70-year-old-and-over group. Another reason for the popularity of tennis is that men and women can compete on the same court at the same time (mixed doubles). Few other serious sports offer this possibility. The popularity of tennis is noticeable as one sees thousands of tennis courts across the country, usually with people waiting in line to play. The huge audiences at such classic tournaments as Wimbledon and the U.S. Open also attest to the game's popularity.

Although some tennis is played on grass courts (e.g., Wimbledon), and some is played on clay courts, most American tennis is played on hard surfaces such as asphalt or cement. The court is separated by a net, which is 3 ft high at the center and 3.5 ft high at the net posts.

In singles, one player is on each side of the net. In doubles, two players are on each side of the net. Each player has a racquet. The ball is put into play with a serve. After the return of the serve, players may hit the ball before it bounces, or may allow the ball to bounce once before hitting it. The object of the game is to legally hit the ball over the net into the opponent's court. Most coaches of the sport will say that to win, all you have to do is to hit the ball over the net one more time than the opponent does.

Sequence of Skills

Tennis skills fall into five basic categories. Some skills may not fit exactly into any one category, but for organizational purposes, these five will suffice: volley, ground strokes, lob, overhead, and serve.

Volley

The volley (Figure 22.19) should be the first stroke learned because it is the simplest stroke. The eye-hand coordination involved is similar to that involved in catching a thrown ball, a skill most students have mastered by high school. The volley requires no backswing, and the ball does not bounce, so timing is simplified.

Ground Strokes

The forehand (Figure 22.20) and backhand (Figure 22.21) ground strokes are considered to be the foundation of a solid game. The forehand is the easier of the two for most people and should be learned first. The backhand is more difficult but not too difficult to learn with proper instruction.

Lob

After learning the ground strokes, the lob is relatively easy. It is basically a ground stroke, hit at a different angle. Backswing and body position are identical to those of the ground stroke.

Overhead

The overhead and serve are different from the other strokes and require learning new patterns. The overhead, or smash, should be taught first, as this stroke resembles a simplified service motion (Figure

FIGURE 22.19 Volley

FIGURE 22.21 Backhand

FIGURE 22.20 Forehand

FIGURE 22.22 Overhead

22.22). When the skill of hitting an overhead has been mastered, students will find it easier to learn to hit a serve.

Serve

The serve (Figure 22.23) is a complicated stroke, and some tennis coaches prefer to introduce it as soon as possible to give students the maximum amount of time to master it. If the serve is the last skill taught, however, students are by then more familiar with the equipment, have a better feel for the game, and may be more successful with this skill.

FIGURE 22.23   Serve

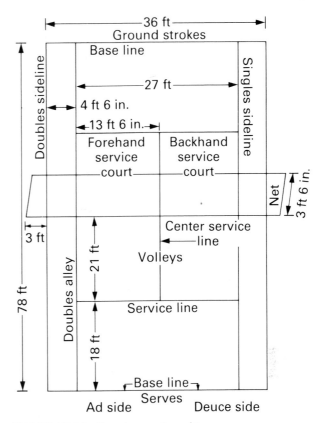

FIGURE 22.24   Tennis court markings

Ideas for Effective Instruction

The Court

The game of tennis is played on a court as diagrammed in (Figure 22.24). A working knowledge of the court areas is vital to the student, not only for its importance in playing the game, but also in following the instructions in the contract included here.

Singles Sideline.   The singles sideline delineates the playing court for singles. A ball landing on the sideline is in play.

Doubles Sideline.   The doubles sideline delineates the playing court for doubles. A ball landing on the doubles sideline is in play in doubles.

Doubles Alley.   The doubles alley is the area of the court in play in doubles after the serve. It includes the doubles sideline.

Base Line.   The base line delineates the length of the court for both singles and doubles. When hitting a serve, the player must stand behind the base line and may not touch it or step over it onto the court until the ball has left the racquet. A ball landing on the base line is in play.

Service Line.   The service line delineates the length of the service court. A serve must land between the net and the service line or on the service line to be in play.

Center Service Line.   The center service line divides the service court into deuce and ad sides. A serve hitting the center service line is in play.

Ad Court.   The ad court is the service court to the receiver's left. Any time an odd number of points has been played, the serve is made to this court (i.e., 15–0, 30–40, ad in, or ad out).

Deuce Court.   The deuce court is the service court to the receiver's right. Any time an even number of points has been played, the serve is made to this court (i.e., 0–0, 15–15, 40–15, deuce).

The Match

Most people play tennis to try to win the match. To win a match, a player must win a predetermined number of sets (usually two out of three). To win a set, a player must win six games with at least a two-game margin. If a set ties at six games each, a tie breaker is played to determine the winner of the set. To win a game, a player must be the first to win four points. Each of these terms is explained in the following discussion.

Points and Games

A player wins a point if the opponent fails to legally return the ball, or if the opponent, while serving, fails to legally put the ball into play. The opponent will be awarded a point in any of these situations: The ball is allowed to bounce more than once before it is returned, the ball is returned so that it does not cross the net or land within the playing court, the ball is hit twice while it is being returned, the player is touched by the ball while it is in play, or the net is touched while the ball is in play.

Two methods are currently used for scoring games. The conventional scoring progression is love–15–30–40–game. Both players start love (zero) and a player must win 4 points to win the game. The one exception is that a player must win by a 2-point margin. If the server leads 40–30 and the receiver wins the next point, the score is deuce. The next player who wins two consecutive points wins the game. At deuce, if the server wins the following point, the score is advantage in. However, if the receiver wins the point, the score is advantage out. When a player with the advantage wins the next point, that player also wins the game.

Another scoring system, called no-ad, or VASS, simplifies this process, speeds the game along, and is better suited for physical education classes in which time limits are a factor. In this system, points are counted 0–1–2–3–game. A 2-point lead is not required because the first player to win a fourth point wins the game. Using this system, there is no ad or deuce.

Sets

The first player (or doubles team) to win 6 games wins the set if they have a 2-game lead. A set might therefore last only 6 games (6–0), or might go to 10 or more games (6–4). If a set is tied at 5 games all, the winner of the next game would go up 6–5, and would not have the necessary 2-game margin to win the set. Should the leader win the next game, that player would also win the set, 7–5. If a set ties at 6 games each, however, a tie breaker is used. The winner of the tie breaker is the winner of the set, and the score is recorded at 7–6.

Tie Breaker

The USTA has established that the 12-point tie breaker be used at 6-all. This occurs in the following manner:

1. The player who served the first game of the set serves the first point.
2. The receiver of point 1 serves points 2 and 3, and the serve changes after every 2 points from that time.
3. Players change sides of the net at every 6 points (6–0, 3–3, 6–6).

4. The tie breaker is won by the first player to reach 7 points with at least a 2-point margin. If the first player to reach 7 does not have a 2-point margin, play continues until one player establishes a 2-point lead.

Match

In women's tennis and in almost all of men's tennis, the winner of a match is determined by the first player or team to win 2 sets. Some men's tennis is played to the best 3 of 5 sets, and thus if Smith defeated Jones (6–4, 3–6, 7–6, (9–7)), Smith won the first set 6–4, lost the second set 6–3, and won the third set in a tie breaker, the score of which was 9–7.

General Rules

The match usually begins with players spinning a racquet to determine who will serve the first game. The winner of the toss can choose to serve or to receive, and can also choose which side of the net to begin from, or can elect to have the opponent decide. After the initial choices are made, the opponent makes all other choices.

One player serves for a whole game. The first serve is hit from the right side of the court into the diagonal service area. The server has two chances to put the ball into play. If the serve is a fault, the second ball is served. If this serve is also a fault, the server loses the point. Any serve that touches the net but still lands in the proper service court is a "let," and the serve is hit again. After the first point of the game, the following serve takes place from the left side of the court. The serve alternates back and forth on each successive point throughout the game.

An exception to this rule applies to no-ad scoring. At 3–3 in no-ad, the receiver chooses the side into which the serve will be made. The serve is not automatically made to the deuce side, as might be expected, but the receiver may choose to receive from either side. The opponent then serves the next game in the same manner. The serve alternates after each successive game for the entire match. In doubles, each team may choose which player serves first for that team, and this alternates each time it is that team's serve.

At the conclusion of every odd-numbered game, players change sides of the net. After the first, third, and fifth game, and so forth, there is a court change.

Tennis is governed by a strict set of rules, which cover every imaginable situation. A thorough knowledge of these rules is important for the tennis instructor. A copy of the rules of tennis can be ordered from the USTA (see Suggested Readings).

Etiquette

Rules of etiquette are a vital part of tennis. Except for large tournaments and professional matches, referees and ball retrievers are seldom present at tennis matches. Rules of etiquette must be followed for the game of tennis to be enjoyable to all.

Most rules of etiquette can be summed up in the motto: "Do unto others as you would have them do unto you." For instance, if a ball was not seen clearly as being out or in, play it over. When the point is over, try to return the balls to the opponent, not merely in the general direction.

Never enter a court (or walk behind one) while a rally is in progress. If one must walk through a court, wait until there is a court change.

A rule of tennis states that any interference during play shall cause a "let," and the point will be replayed. If the opponent claims that there was a distraction during play, do not hesitate to play the point over.

Minimize verbal outbursts on the court. Not only is it distracting to the opponent, but it may be bothering players on other courts. Never throw racquets or slam balls around in anger. This is dangerous and unsportsmanlike.

Organization and Skill Work

Most tennis classes are organized along traditional lines, that is, groups of students show the instructor the proper grips, stances, backswings, and so forth, at the same time. Another method of organizing the class is to allow students to progress at their own rate. This can be accomplished through the use of a contract with performance objectives. Each student knows exactly what is expected and moves from one task to the next when able.

Prepare a contract for each student in the class. As the students come to class, give them a contract, access to balls and racquets, and encourage them to get started.

When the entire class has arrived, call them together for an organizational meeting. These meetings might include a "tennis tip" for the day, some comment about the contract, or some skill analysis. The meeting should be short so that most of the class time can be devoted to practicing and mastering skills.

Roll-keeping is simplified through this process. The contracts that have not been passed out belong to those who are absent. A record of attendance can be a part of each person's contract.

If stations are used, each court can be designated for a particular skill (i.e., one court for volleys, one for ground strokes, and one for serving). Provide plenty of balls (beginners will fare as well with older balls as with newer ones) and racquets. Post the suggested skill tasks on the net or fence, and let the students progress at personalized rates. The instructor should be available for questions and feedback. Do not hesitate to intervene when a student is having difficulty.

Skill Work

The strength of the contract system is that it allows the teacher to help specific students with particular problems. Once the class has started, the teacher is free to roam the courts and to help students who are having problems.

Key points to remember in teaching basic skills include the following:

Volley

1. Watch the ball hit the racquet.
2. Footwork — Step across to hit the volley (a volley to the right should have a final step with the left foot).
3. Minimize backswing — Swing no farther back than the shoulder.
4. Punch the ball and follow through.
5. Never drop the racquet head below the wrist. Bend the knees instead.
6. Squeeze the racquet grip when making contact with the ball.

Ground Strokes

1. Change grips for the backhand and forehand.
2. Early backswing — Get the racquet back as soon as possible.
3. Set up with the side of the body to the net.
4. Contact the ball even with the front foot; do not wait until the ball gets into the body.
5. Contact the ball with the racquet perpendicular to the ground.
6. Follow through.
7. Keep the knees bent throughout.

Lobs

1. Set up exactly like ground strokes.
2. Open the racquet face (approximately 45 degrees).
3. Lift up through the swing and finish with a high follow-through.

Overheads

1. Racquet is in "backscratcher" position; get it there as soon as possible.
2. Side of body is turned toward the net.
3. Contact the ball in front of the body. Do not let it float overhead.

Serves

1. First and foremost, control the toss.
2. Use continental or backhand grip. (This will cause a slice serve, which is the most consistent.)
3. "Throw" the racquet at the ball; use plenty of wrist and elbow.
4. Follow through; the back foot (from the stance) should end up on the court.

Safety

Tennis is a safe sport. Most injuries that occur are self-inflicted, such as ankle sprains, muscle sprains, or blisters. A few precautions can help prevent unnecessary injuries. For example,

1. Warm up properly before beginning play.
2. Never leave loose balls lying around the court.
3. Never hit balls (especially serves) when the player opposite is not ready.
4. Communicate. Both players on a doubles team going for an overhead can cost the team a point and cause an injury.
5. Wear appropriate footwear.

Lead-Up Games, Modified Games, and Rainy Day Activities

Practice is often enhanced, especially for advanced players when stroke practice is conducted under gamelike conditions. Many students find it enjoyable to compete. The following drills can be done competitively.

Twenty-One

In the game of Twenty-One, both players must remain behind the base line. The ball is put into play when either player drops the ball and hits a ground stroke. From that point on, the game uses the same rules as tennis, except that neither player may volley.

Advanced players can include the rule that any ball landing in front of the service line is out, or the ball may be approached from behind and volleyed. The first player to accrue 21 points wins.

Approach Game

To practice approaching the net, players use half of the court, from doubles sideline to center service line. After starting with a ground stroke, the first player moves halfway to the service line. After returning the first ball, player two moves halfway to the service line. After their next shots, players move to the service line and then continue to close in as

far as possible, hitting volleys and half volleys. The game may be played to any total, usually 10 or 15.

Lob-Smash

Begin with one player at the net and the other at the base line. Base-line players hit a lob, which is returned with an overhead. They play out the point and begin again. After 10 points, players change positions. The winner is the player with the most points after these 20 points have been played. Lob-smash can also be played with doubles.

Short Game

Players begin at the service lines and hit soft ground strokes. The ball may not land behind the service line. Regular tennis scoring can be used or a point total can be set.

Return Drill

The return drill can be used to improve a player's return. One player practices returns while three to five players alternate serves. The receiver returns from the court (either ad or deuce) for the entire time. Servers get two serves, just like the real game, and play the point. Only the server gets a point when a rally is won. When a server gets a designated number of points (usually 4 or 5), the receiver and server exchange places, and all servers' scores return to 0. Each receiver thus gets at least 12–15 returns before rotating off. The next time this same player becomes the receiver, returns are made from the opposite court. A variation is to have all servers serve and volley.

Half-Court Volleys

Divide the court into halves (as in the Approach game). One player begins at the net, the other at the base line. The volleyer puts the ball into play, and the player at the base line must hit a passing shot (ground stroke). The ball must be kept in the half-court. Play to 10 points, switch places, and continue for 10 more points.

As a variation, after the initial shot, the groundstroker may hit lobs and may take the net if the opportunity arises.

Backboard Practice

If wall space is available in the gymnasium, ground strokes or volleys can be hit against the gym wall.

Service Practice

The gymnasium is an excellent place for beginners to practice the toss. Any line on the gym floor can be substituted for the base line. Soft foam-rubber tennis balls are excellent for practice of the entire service motion in the gym.

Volleys

Without a net, players can practice volleys indoors. Have them stand 10–20 ft apart and hit soft volleys to each other.

Suggested Performance Objectives

Students should work with a partner. When an objective has been mastered to specification, have a partner (or instructor, where indicated) initial the task. Each task is worth 1 point, unless stated otherwise. The tasks are designed to be progressively more difficult. A student should therefore not proceed to a new task until all preliminary tasks have been completed. The court markings in Figure 22.24 will aid in the comprehension of many of the tasks. Students should refer to the diagram as needed until the markings are learned.

Volley

1. Without a racquet, assume a ready position (feet shoulder width apart, knees bent, weight forward, hands in front of the body). Have a partner toss tennis balls to the dominant side. Stepping with the opposite foot, reach forward and catch 5 consecutive balls thrown from a distance of 15 ft.
2. From the ready position, gripping the racquet at its head, and using proper footwork (instructor will demonstrate), hit 5 consecutive forehand volleys to your partner who feeds the balls from a distance of 15 ft. (Balls may not bounce.)
3. Same as task 2, but grip racquet just above the grip (5 consecutive).
4. Demonstrate to instructor the continental grip. This is the grip with which volleys are hit.
5. Same as task 2, but use the continental grip, and grip the racquet on the grip (5 consecutive).
6. Same as task 2, but use the backhand side of racquet (5 consecutive).
7. Same as task 2, but grip racquet just above the grip and use backhand (5 consecutive).
8. Same as task 5, but use backhand (5 consecutive).
9. Stand halfway between the net and the service line. Partner or instructor will stand across the net at the base line and drop and hit balls at you. Volley 8 of 10 forehands across the net into the singles court.
10. Same as task 9, but use backhand (8 of 10).
11. Standing as in task 9, partner will randomly hit

to your forehand and backhand side. Volley 8 of 10 balls into the singles court.
12. Same as task 11, but balls must land in the singles court behind the service line (8 of 10).
13. From a distance of at least 6 ft from a wall, hit 15 consecutive volleys above a 3-ft mark. The ball may not touch the ground.

Ground Strokes

1. Demonstrate to the instructor the eastern forehand and backhand grips.
2. Without a ball, practice 20 consecutive alternate forehand and backhand ground strokes, alternating the grip each time.
3. Standing behind the base line, drop and hit 10 consecutive forehands across the net into the singles court.
4. Same as task 3, but use backhand (10 consecutive).
5. Stand behind the base line. Partner stands 20 ft away and bounces balls to your forehand. Hit 5 of 7 forehands across the net into the singles court.
6. Same as task 5, but use backhand (5 of 7).
7. Standing behind the base line with a partner across the net, have partner hit or toss balls to your forehand. Hit 8 of 10 forehands across the net into the singles court.
8. Same as task 7, but use backhand (8 of 10).
9. Same as tasks 7 and 8, but have partner toss randomly to your forehand and backhand (8 of 10).
10. Standing behind a line 27 ft from the backboard, hit 10 consecutive ground strokes that strike the backboard on or above the white line, which is 3 ft above the ground.
11. Same as task 10, but hit 20 consecutive ground strokes.
12. With a partner (or instructor) at opposite base line, rally 20 consecutive ground strokes (ball may bounce more than once on each side of the net).

Lobs

1. From the base line, drop and hit 5 consecutive forehand lobs into the opposite singles court behind the service line. Balls must be hit high enough so that your partner, from volley position, cannot touch them with the racquet.
2. Same as task 1, but hit backhand lobs (5 consecutive).
3. With partner tossing or hitting balls from the other side of the net, hit 5 consecutive forehand lobs into the opposite singles court behind the service line.

4. Same as task 3, but hit backhand lobs (5 consecutive).

Serves

1. Demonstrate to the teacher the proper service stance and grip.
2. Using an overhead throwing motion, throw 5 consecutive balls into the service court from the base line on both deuce and ad sides (10 total).
3. Demonstrate proper toss technique to the instructor.
4. Lay the racquet on the ground with the face 6 in. in front of your front foot. Using the nonracquet hand, toss balls approximately 2 ft higher than your head, 3 of 5 must hit the racquet face or frame.
5. Make your normal toss into the air, and using the racquet hand, without a racquet, come through the service motion and hit 5 consecutive balls with the palm of your hand.
6. With a racquet in the "back-scratcher" position, hit 5 of 7 serves into the proper service court.
7. Demonstrate to the instructor an acceptable full backswing for the service.
8. Same as task 6, but use the full backswing to hit 5 of 7 serves into the forehand service court.
9. Place 4 empty tennis ball cans in the outside corner of the forehand service box. Serve until you have knocked over 1 can.
10. Same as task 9, but place cans in the inside corner.
11. Same as task 9, but place cans in the backhand court.
12. Same as task 9, but place cans in the inside corner of the backhand court.

Overheads

1. Using the service grip and standing in service area (at the net), have a partner hit short lobs. Allow the ball to bounce. Hit 3 of 5 forehand overheads into singles court.
2. Same as task 1, but hit the ball before it bounces (3 of 5).
3. Same as task 1, but stand behind the base line (3 of 5).
4. Same as task 1, but hit 6 consecutive balls.
5. Same as task 2, but hit 6 consecutive balls.
6. Same as task 3, but hit 6 consecutive balls.

Suggested Readings: Rules

The following publications contain material pertaining to rules and regulations. All may be purchased from the Publications Department, United States Tennis Association Education and Research Center, 729 Alexander Road, Princeton, NJ 08540.

The Rules of Tennis.
Rules of Tennis and Cases and Decisions.
A Friend at Court (Rules, cases, decisions, officials, and officiating).
The Code (Unwritten rules players should follow in unofficiated matches).

Additional References

Braden, V., and Bruns, B. 1977. *Vic Braden's Tennis for the Future.* Boston: Little, Brown & Co.

Brown, J. 1976. *Tennis: Teaching, Coaching, and Directing Programs.* Englewood Cliffs, NJ: Prentice-Hall, Inc.

Claxton, D. 1980. Tennis Contracts. Unpublished Material, Grand Canyon College, Physical Education Department, Phoenix, AZ.

Gould, K. 1971. *Tennis, Anyone?* Palo Alto, CA: National Press Books.

Murphy, B., and Murphy, C. 1962. *Tennis Handbook.* New York: The Ronald Press Co.

23

OUTDOOR ADVENTURE ACTIVITIES

Many physical education programs have added popular adventure activities to the curriculum over the past ten years. Rock climbing, caving, canoeing, orienteering, and backpacking are just a few examples. Many students are interested in these activities, which are challenging and provide a sense of risk and adventure. Activities that can be added to the curriculum in order to provide a degree of risk and adventure are ropes course activities, orienteering, and group initiative games.

ROPES COURSE ACTIVITIES

Ropes course activities involve obstacles that use ropes, cables, logs, trees, ladders, tires, swings, cargo nets, rings, and other equipment to present students with a challenge that usually has a degree of controlled risk. These obstacles require students to climb, swing, crawl, and balance themselves. Beneath many of the obstacles are water, mud, people, cargo nets, and trees. All of the activities are completed with student spotters or a safety belay line of some type under the direct supervision of the teacher. The activities can be linked together in sequence or they can be utilized as separate challenges. Certain activities require strength and endurance, while others require balance and coordination. The ropes course activities can function as lead-up activities for rock climbing, caving, rappelling, or other adventure activities.

Teachers need to be certain that students begin with activities containing little risk. Student safety is always the most important factor. Generally, the beginning ropes course activities are situated close to the ground with many spotters available, thereby assuring students that little danger is involved. As they gain knowledge, experience, physical skill, and confidence, students can move to higher and more challenging obstacles. Teachers need to be aware of varying ability levels of students and not require all students to attempt the same activities unless they

are ready for the obstacle. Some students will display fear of these types of activities and should be encouraged rather than pushed.

Ropes course activities, just like any other adventure activity, can be risky and have the potential for physical injury if safety factors are overlooked. The authors recommend that teachers seek the advice of experienced ropes course builders before constructing any of these activities (see Suggested Readings at the end of this section). Ropes course activities can be built into the existing environment or posts and logs can be placed in the ground. The following are examples of ropes course activities that could be utilized in a program.

Commando Crawl

In this activity, the student crawls across the top of a 2-in. manila hawser rope by placing the chest on the rope and passing the rope under the body. One foot is hooked over the top of the rope and the other leg hangs down for balance. The student slowly pulls his or her way across the rope by using the arms and the top leg. The student should be spotted on both sides of the rope in case of a fall. If a fall does occur, the spotters should catch the student and slowly lower him or her to the ground. The rope should be secured to two trees 4 to 5 ft high above the ground. A bowline knot can be used on one side of the rope and the opposite side should be

FIGURE 23.1 Commando crawl

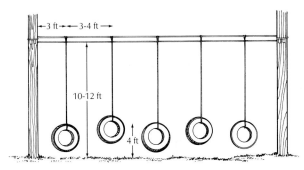

FIGURE 23.2 Tire swing

FIGURE 23.3 Kitten crawl

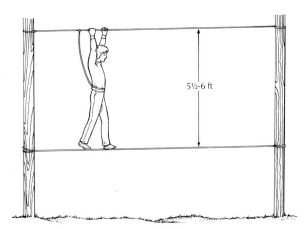

FIGURE 23.4 Two-rope bridge

wrapped around the tree and tied off with two half hitches. Wooden blocks may be secured to the trees below the rope to prevent the rope from slipping.

Tire Swing

Students swing across a set of tires that are secured to a top rope or cable. The tires are set at varying heights above the ground anywhere from 3 to 4 ft high. The tires should be 3–4 ft apart. The top cable should be 10–12 ft above the ground. Spotters should be placed on both sides of the student as they proceed in order to prevent a fall.

Kitten Crawl

Students crawl along two parallel inclined ropes that are secured at 5 ft high at one end and at 2 ft high at the other end. Students should be on all fours and can slowly crawl up or down the rope. Spotters should be aware that the participants can fall through the middle of the two ropes as well as over the sides. Wooden blocks can be used to prevent the rope from slipping down on the secured ends. The height of the ropes can be varied according to ability levels of the participants.

Two Rope Bridge

Two parallel ropes about 5–6 ft apart are secured to trees or posts. The students stand sideways on

the bottom rope and hold on to the top rope with their hands. They slowly slide their way across the rope. The height of the bottom rope should be less than 5–6 ft for beginners. If the height of the bottom rope is higher than 6 ft, then a belay or safety system should be used. A 15-ft swami belt or waist loop of 1-in. tubular nylon flat rope can be wrapped around the student's waist and attached with a carabineer to a belay line. The top of the belay line can be attached with a carabineer to the top rope of the bridge. Spotters can be used for lower bridges and they should follow the participant across the rope and be ready for a fall.

Three Rope Bridge

The three rope Burma bridge has been used in many areas for crossing various ravines, rivers, and mountain passes. It consists of two parallel ropes about waist high for handholds and a bottom rope to walk on. A number a V-shaped ropes should be placed about 2 ft apart along the bridge to support all three ropes (see Figure 23.5). A rope or cable across the top of the bridge should be constructed for attaching a safety line. A swami belt can be attached to the

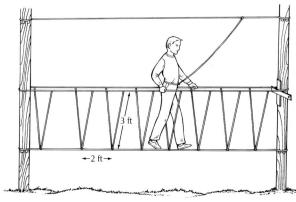

FIGURE 23.5 Three-rope bridge

FIGURE 23.6 Tension traverse

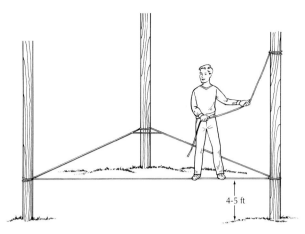

FIGURE 23.7 Triangle tension traverse

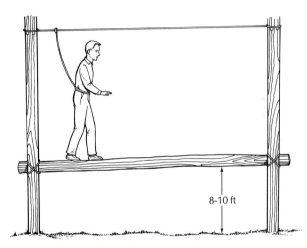

FIGURE 23.8 Balance beam

student and then clipped to the top line with carabineers and a piece of nylon webbing. The height of the bridge can vary; it can be low or high depending on the local area. It is exciting to place the bridge over a natural obstacle if possible. It is important to use wooden blocks to prevent the ropes from slipping in order to assure that the ropes are kept tight.

Tension Traverse

The student balances and moves across a rope suspended between two trees. A top support rope is attached to one tree and the student applies tension on this rope for balance while sliding across the rope. The student should slide sideways across the rope. One hand should hold the support rope at the waist and the other hand should hold the rope above the head (see Figure 23.6). The bottom rope is 2–3 ft above the ground and should always be taut. Again, wooden blocks should be used to prevent the rope from slipping down. Spotters should be used for safety and the students should be instructed to let go of the support rope and jump off if they are going to fall. If they hold on to the top rope while falling, they will swing into the tree or post.

Triangle Tension Traverse

This activity is similar to the tension traverse and adds two more sides to the activity. The bottom rope is placed in a triangle and the student starts at one intersection of the triangle. The student balances and moves around the triangle with a top support rope similar to the straight tension traverse. Spotters should be used for safety as the students move around the triangle. The height of the bottom rope should be 4–5 ft and it should be taut and blocked to prevent slipping.

Balance Beam

The balance beam is a log attached between two trees or posts anywhere from 5 to 10 ft high. It is

a good obstacle that can be used as a bridge between two other rope activities. The students simply walk across the beam. If several beams are used in a course, they can be constructed at varying heights. If the beam is higher than 5 ft, a top safety belay line should be used. If the beam is lower than 5 ft, then student spotters are necessary for safety.

Inclined Log

The inclined log is simply a balance beam that is placed at an angle. It is effective for beginners to walk on an obstacle that moves from the ground to a higher level. Students can walk up the log, bear crawl on all fours, or hug the log as they move up, depending on their comfort level. A moving belay should be set up slightly off center from the log so that students will not fall into the log. As students move up the height of the log, the belay person or spotters should move with them (see Figure 23.9). The log should be notched to enhance the footing and nailed and lashed to the trees or posts for support.

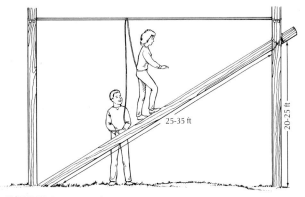

FIGURE 23.9   Inclined log

FIGURE 23.10   Swinging log

Swinging Log

Students walk along a moving log that is suspended from trees by ropes. The log should never be more than 1 ft above the ground because falls will be frequent in this activity. All rocks, stumps, and objects should be cleared away from the area. The log should be notched where the ropes are attached to hold them in place. The upper attachment of the ropes should be blocked in order to prevent any slipping. Rubber tires can be nailed to the trees to prevent damage from the moving log. Participants need to move carefully to avoid falling on the log itself. Spotters can be used to help the students keep their balance.

Cargo Net Jump

Students move up an inclined log to a jumping platform and then jump into a cargo net in the tucked position. The cargo net should be 1-in. manila rope with a small mesh. A rope ladder could be used to exit the net. The net can be secured 15–20 ft above the ground or less and the jumping platform should be about 5 ft higher than the net. The corners of the net should be secured and blocked to avoid

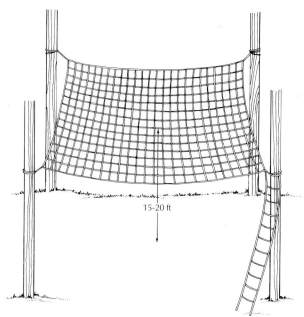

FIGURE 23.11   Cargo net jump

slipping. These secured corners should be inspected regularly before each use. The instructor needs to be careful with students on a jumping platform. Students should be instructed to jump into the center of the net, and only one student should be allowed in the net at a time.

Giant's Ladder

The students balance, jump, and swing up a giant ladder that is made of logs. The ladder encourages

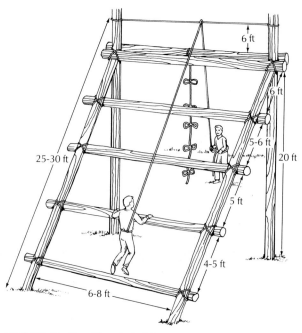

FIGURE 23.12   Giant's ladder

development of balance, strength, agility, and endurance. Students stand and balance on the first rung and then jump to the next rung and land on the chest or abdominal area. The feet swing free below the rung; students then pull upward onto the rung and get ready to move up to the next rung. The rungs get farther apart as the student moves higher on the ladder. The second rung is 4–5 ft from the first and the third rung is 5–6 ft up the ladder (see Figure 23.12). Students must be belayed throughout the climb. A top cable should be used to attach the belay rope. The instructor should keep a tight belay on students so they do not swing into any of the logs.

GROUP INITIATIVE ACTIVITIES ——

Group initiative activities are physical and mental challenges that require the cooperation and joint efforts of a group of students. They require the group to think, plan, and execute a strategy for solving the challenge. Teamwork and cooperation are necessary. These activities force students to work together. Some of the activities involve risk, excitement, and adventure; thus, proper safety and supervision strategies must be implemented. These activities can be completed indoors or outdoors. They can be conducted in conjunction with ropes course activities or as totally separate activities. Many of them require a few special props in order to be effective.

Electric Fence

The object is to get a group of students over the "electric fence" without touching the fence. A piece of rope is stretched between two trees. The rope should be 5 ft off the ground. The students should be given a 4 by 4 beam that is about 8 ft long to help them. Students are not allowed to use the support trees, nor are they allowed to reach under the rope. They can reach over the top of the rope. There are many solutions. A good procedure is to have the group hold the beam on their shoulders and get a few stronger people over first. Then they can hold the beam on the opposite side for the others.

Boardwalk

This involves the use of four 2 by 4 boards that are 10–12 ft long. Two sets of two boards are connected by ropes and eye bolts. About 10 students stand on two of the boards and then hold the other boards at about waist level (see Figure 23.14). Working together, the students alternate lifting the boards and move forward as a group. All must keep their feet on the boards. It can be a race or just a challenge to work together.

FIGURE 23.13 Electric fence

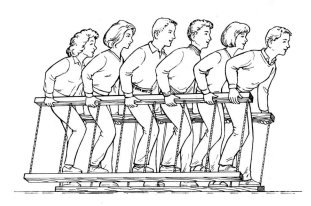

FIGURE 23.14 Boardwalk

Platforms

A group of 6–8 students stands on the first of three platforms. The platforms are 14 ft apart in a straight line. The students are given a 12-ft board and a 4-ft board. The challenge is to move the group from platform to platform without touching the ground with either the boards or any person in the group. The best solution is to extend the smaller board out from the platform about 2 ft and get the entire group to stand on this board. Then, a smaller person can walk out on the board and place the 12-ft board to the next platform and walk across. After 3 or 4 people have reached the second platform, the boards need to be switched so the smaller one is now on the second platform. This process continues until all students are on the third platform.

FIGURE 23.15 Platforms

Nitro Crossing

The object is to get each member of a group to swing across an area with a bucket of "nitro" (water) without spilling it. The swing rope must be attached to some type of tree limb or cross board that provides a good swinging area. Two trip boards need to be placed about 1 ft off the ground on either side of the swing area (see Figure 23.16). The trip boards can be on top of cones or blocks of wood. Half of the group starts on one side and half starts on the other side. They try to swing their group members to the opposite side without spilling the nitro.

The Beam and the Wall

The object of this activity is to move a group of students over a log beam about 8 ft above the ground or a solid wooden wall that is 12–14 ft above the ground. The group cannot use the support trees or posts. They must work together to support each member up and over the obstacle. The wall can be built with a walkway on the back side for the students to stand. Once students get to the top, they can reach down and help others up.

Faith Fall and Trust Dive

The individual falls backward into the arms of a group of students. The individual stands on a balance beam or similar elevated object. The group lines up shoulder to shoulder in two opposite and facing lines. The arms are extended and alternated with the arms of the person directly across wrists. Do not allow students to lock wrists because the partners may bump heads. The individual falls when the catching line is ready.

FIGURE 23.16 Nitro crossing

FIGURE 23.17 The beam

FIGURE 23.20   Trust dive

Human Circle Pass

The group forms a tight circle about 6 ft in diameter, with the arms up in a catching position. One person is put in the middle and closes his or her eyes. When ready, the person falls backward, forward, or sideways into the hands of the group members. They support and pass the individual around the circle. Everyone takes a turn being in the center of the circle.

Human Line Pass

Students sit in a line on the ground with legs straight out, feet touching the person in front of them. The first person in line stands and sits back into the hands of the sitting people who pass the person backward over their heads. The process continues until all people have been passed. Spotters can be placed on each side of the line to ensure safety.

Lightbulb Change

The group is in the dark and cannot proceed until the lightbulb is changed. The goal is to form a pyramid high enough to reach the ceiling (13–15 ft) to change the bulb. A piece of tape can be used to show the highest spot reached by the group. A wall with no windows or protruding objects should be used. Spotters can also be used to may sure than no one falls backward.

High Water

This is similar to the lightbulb change, but the groups compete against one another to see which can make

FIGURE 23.18   The wall

FIGURE 23.19   Faith fall

FIGURE 23.21 Lightbulb or high water

the highest mark on the wall with a piece of chalk or tape.

Sasquatch Race

Two groups are formed and are instructed to make a moving object with a specified number of feet and hands on the ground. Everybody must be part of the group and joined to the others. After the sasquatch is built, the two groups race to a finish line.

Platform Stand

A platform with 20- to 24-in. sides can be used as the base of support. The object is to get as many people as possible standing on the platform simultaneously. The pose must be held for 8 sec.

Stream Crossing

Students must move from one side of the area to the other without touching the floor. They are given small carpet squares on which to move across the "stream." Fewer than the necessary number of squares are handed out, however, so students have

FIGURE 23.22 Platform stand

to pass the squares back and forth in order to get their team across. The first team to move all members across the stream is declared the winner.

Height Alignment

Each member of the group keeps his or her eyes closed and is instructed to align him- or herself in a single file line from shortest person to tallest person. The students cannot talk and can use only their hands to figure out the arrangement.

ORIENTEERING

Orienteering is a challenging outdoor adventure activity that combines cross-country running and the ability to read a map and use a compass. It has been called the thinking sport because rapid decisions need to be made in determining which route to follow so that a minimum of time and energy is used. Ideally, the orienteering competition should take place in a wilderness area that is not familiar to the participants. Orienteering events can be set up for beginners, novices, and experts, thus enabling people of all ages and abilities to take part and find success in these activities. The need for both physical and mental skills can result in an enjoyable experience for all students and members of a family.

Orienteering activities can be easily modified and adapted to secondary physical education programs. Many activities can be completed in a classroom or gymnasium or on the school grounds.* Teachers can

*Special thanks to John W. Horstman, Meadow Lake School, Robbinsdale Area Schools, Robbinsdale, Minnesota, for many of the orienteering activities.

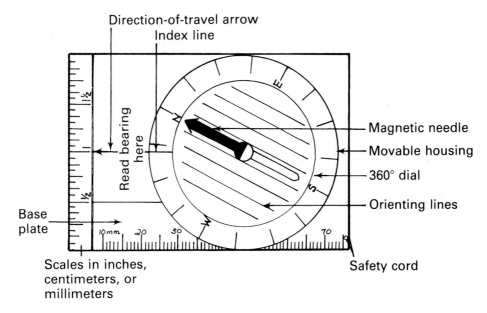

FIGURE 23.23   Parts of a compass

use compasses and homemade maps of the school grounds to develop a challenging unit. A nearby park or a vacant lot can add great variety to orienteering courses.

Sequence of Skills

The basic skills involved in orienteering include reading a topography map, using a compass, and pacing various distances. Since many students have had little experience with these skills, it is important to introduce new information and terminology slowly. Students can perform many of the activities with a partner, so there will be two heads working together on a problem. Teachers can include a variety of maps, a compass, and new pacing activities each day to keep the students challenged. Many activity types and "hands on" experiences should be incorporated in the unit. Competitive events can be added after students begin to understand the basic map and compass skills. The block plan at the end of this unit will provide some ideas for the sequencing of learning activities.

Learning Activities

Compass Activities

Parts of the Compass. Make the students aware of the basic parts of the compass and how the instrument works (Figure 23.23).

Compass Bearings and Directions. Have the students complete the directions and degrees in Figure 23.24.

Following a Bearing. Discuss how to hold the compass properly. Give students a bearing to find and follow. Have them stand in one line facing the instructor. Call out a bearing and have them rotate their bodies in place until they are facing the bearing direction.

Landmarks. The teacher calls out various visible landmarks, and students shoot a bearing from where they are standing to the landmark.

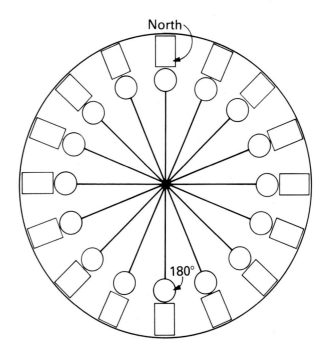

FIGURE 23.24   Compass bearings and directions

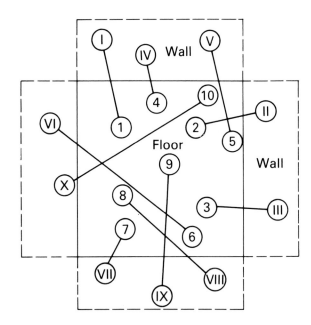

Scorecard	
Number	Bearing
1–I	_____
2–II	_____
3–III	_____
4–IV	_____
5–V	_____
6–VI	_____
7–VII	_____
8–VIII	_____
9–IX	_____
10–X	_____

FIGURE 23.25 Numbers and numerals

Forming a Triangle. Place a penny or other small object on the ground. Set any bearing less than 90 degrees. Walk ten paces on that bearing. Add 120 degrees and walk another ten paces. Repeat the procedure again and end up where you started. This drill can be repeated with another bearing and a different number of paces.

Forming a Square. This is basically the same as "Forming a Triangle" except that 90-degree bearings are added each time, and four sides are formed. The distance must be the same each time.

Numbers and Numerals. Tape the numbers 1–10 on the floor in scattered positions around the gymnasium (Figure 23.25). Next, tape the Roman numerals I–X in scattered positions on the gymnasium walls. The students begin by standing on any of the numbers on the floor and shooting a bearing to the corresponding numeral on the wall. This drill can be made competitive by trying for the fastest time and correct bearing.

Forming a Christmas Tree. On a piece of graph paper, have students place a dot in the southeast quadrant of the paper. From this starting dot, have them draw a line the following distances and on the appropriate bearing (Figure 23.26).

Map Bearings. Students learn to determine the bearing between points on a map. The teacher puts several points on a map and then tells the students to find the bearing and distance between the points. Ten numbered points might be shown, and students can find the bearing and distance from 1 to 2, from

Bearing	Distance (cm)	Bearing	Distance (cm)
1. 269	2.2		
2. 2	2.7	9. 136	6.3
3. 266	4.9	10. 293	1.9
4. 30	6.5	11. 141	5.2
5. 246	2.6	12. 284	2.4
6. 34	5.0	13. 125	5.2
7. 244	2.0	14. 271	5.1
8. 37	4.6	15. 179	2.7

FIGURE 23.26 Forming a Christmas Tree

2 to 3, and so forth. Advanced orienteering can include a discussion of magnetic declination and the addition or subtraction of declination.

Destination Unknown. Divide the class into four teams. Each team follows the given bearings and paces (Figure 23.27). All teams should end up at the same destination.

Schoolyard Compass Game and Competitive Compass Game. These are two challenging compass games that are available from The Silva Company.* The games are inexpensive and can be set up easily in a school situation.

*The Silva Company, 2466 State Road 39 North, LaPorte, Indiana 46350.

Divide students into four groups. Each team should follow the given bearings and paces, which will bring them all to the same destination.

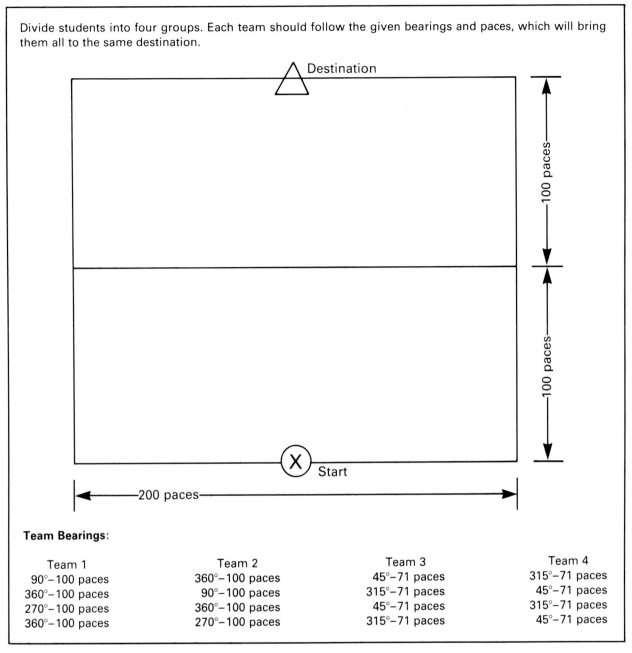

Team Bearings:

Team 1	Team 2	Team 3	Team 4
90°–100 paces	360°–100 paces	45°–71 paces	315°–71 paces
360°–100 paces	90°–100 paces	315°–71 paces	45°–71 paces
270°–100 paces	360°–100 paces	45°–71 paces	315°–71 paces
360°–100 paces	270°–100 paces	315°–71 paces	45°–71 paces

FIGURE 23.27   Destination unknown

Map Activities

Mapping the School. Students draw up rough maps of the school grounds with all of the various buildings, fields, and identification points. These maps can later be used in orienteering competitions.

Map Squares. Cut up several topography maps of the local area into small squares. Students try to locate the cut squares on an uncut map. Have the students identify points of interest, symbols, distances, contour lines, vegetation, roads, water, and so forth.

Map Symbol Relay. Draw a map symbol on one side of an index card and write the name of a different symbol on the back of the card. A duplicate set of cards is necessary for each team in the relay (i.e., four teams means four sets of cards). The game begins with the cards on one side of the gym and the teams on the opposite side. The teacher calls out the first symbol, such as a school. The first member of the team runs to the cards, finds the symbol, and then runs back to the team. The name of the next symbol to be found is on the back of the card with the school symbol. The game continues until all of

Contour Identification Problem. Have the students compare some actual terrain contours with the map representations. Training models are available from Silva, and the teacher can develop a number of contour representations for learning activities. The following are a few examples:

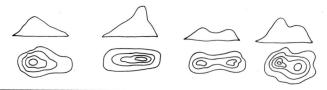

FIGURE 23.28   Contour problems

the cards are played. Students waiting in line can be reviewing symbols. Students who select the wrong symbol must run back and find the correct symbol.

Taking a Trip.   Label 10 to 15 points on several topography maps, and have students calculate the actual distance between a certain number of points. They can figure in map distance and in actual mileage. Next, have the students estimate how many

days would be necessary to complete the trip. They should be able to describe what the terrain is like and where the water stops are located.

Contour Identification.   Have students identify various mountainous and hilly areas from the way those areas look on a contour map. Figure 23.28 is an example of contour problems.

Map Problems.   Map activities, such as Figure 23.29, can be made up for a local situation.

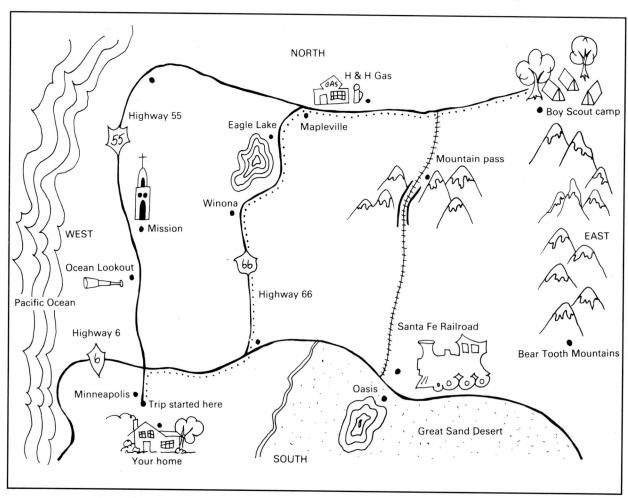

FIGURE 23.29   Map problems

The dotted line on the map shows how you drove from your home to the Boy Scout camp. The questions that follow are about the map. Circle the best answer on this sheet.

1. When you started your trip, in what direction did you go first?

   North   South   East   West

2. If you had walked west of Minneapolis, what would you have come to?

   Great Sand Desert   Ocean Lookout   Pacific Ocean

3. When you got to Highway 66, what town did you pass first?

   Mapleville   Winona   H & H Gas

4. The mission is _____ of the Pacific Ocean.

   North   South   East   West

5. The Santa Fe Railroad runs _____ and _____ .

   North   South   East   West

6. The Scout camp is _____ of H & H Gas.

   North   South   East   West

7. The oasis is _____ of Highway 6

   North   South   East   West

8. From the ocean lookout, what direction is the Bear Tooth mountain range?

   North   South   East   West

9. The first town west of the Scout camp is:

   Winona   H & H Gas   Mapleville

10. In the winter the birds fly _____ .

    North   South   East   West

FIGURE 23.29 Continued

Dot-to-Dot Hike. Students start at the X in the northwest corner (Figure 23.30) and draw in the figure by following the directions. Students can develop their own dot-to-dot hike making other figures.

Direction Walk. Students follow the directions on a piece of graph paper (Figure 23.31).

Pacing Activities

Distance by Pace. Orienteers must be able to judge distance by their pace. One pace equals two steps. A good drill for determining the length of pace is to set up a course that is 100 ft long. Students walk, jog, or run the course, and count the number of times that the right foot hits the ground. The length of the course (100 ft) is then divided by the number of paces in order to determine length of pace. Pace is usually rounded off to the nearest 6 in. Pace will vary with walking, jogging, and running.

Distance by Time. One-mile courses can be set up in a variety of terrain conditions, such as open road, open field, open woods, vegetated areas, dense woods, and mountainous areas. Students cover these areas by walking or jogging and record their times. The ability to cover a given distance at a consistent pace can be used later for competitive meets.

Competitive Orienteering Events

After students have received instruction in the use of the compass, maps, and pacing, competitive events can be introduced. Students should understand that they can compete against the environment, themselves, their peers, and elapsed time. It is not necessary to win the event to be successful.

Cross-Country or Point-to-Point Orienteering

Ten checkpoints are set up over the entire school grounds or park area. Teachers develop a map of

Dot-to-Dot Hike—Follow the directions from the starting point and draw in the figure.

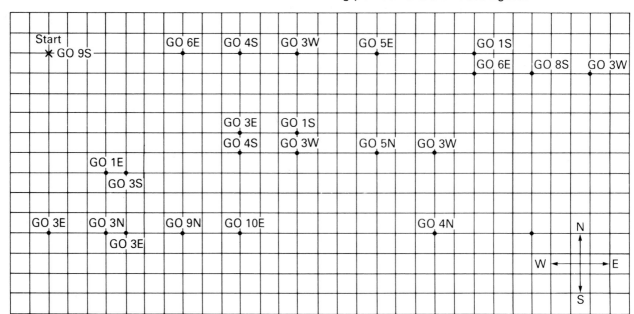

FIGURE 23.30 Dot-to-dot hike

the area to be covered, and duplicate maps are made up for all participants. Each participant uses a map and compass to find the checkpoints as quickly as possible. The compass is not necessary if instruments are not available. Decisions about the best route must be made quickly as participants begin. Several master maps should be set out with the locations of the checkpoints. Participants copy the checkpoints from the master map onto their own map. The time spent in copying down the checkpoints can be included in the overall accumulated time.

Each checkpoint should have a secret letter, word, or name that students must record on some type of card to show that they actually visited the checkpoint. In regulation meets, a coded punch with a number or letter is used at each control site. These punches are available from The Silva Company, but they are not a necessity. Checkpoints can be a boundary cone, an index card, an envelope, or something similar.

Score Orienteering

In score orienteering, each checkpoint has a designated point value. The checkpoints that are hardest to find and farthest away from the starting point are assigned the highest point totals. The object of the event is to accumulate the most points within a set time. Students are given a map of the area on which they copy the locations of the checkpoints from a master map. Students must visit as many sites as possible within the time limit and then return to

the starting point. If they are late, they can be disqualified or assessed a penalty. Students use some type of standard card to record the clue at each checkpoint that they visit.

Descriptive Orienteering

This type of event requires a compass and pacing skills instead of a map. Students attempt to find the checkpoints as quickly as possible by following a bearing (90 degrees), a distance (50 yd), and a descriptive clue (small tree). The descriptive clue can be eliminated with more advanced participants. Students start at a designated master point and return to that point each time before starting toward the next point. In this way, teachers at the master point can monitor student progress throughout the meet. The checkpoints can all have letters, words, or team names. Each student is given a sheet similar to the one shown in Figure 23.32. A more challenging variation is to give students only the bearing and distance to one checkpoint. When they find that checkpoint, they will find the bearing and distance posted for the next checkpoint. Students must find each checkpoint to get directions to the next point. Students can be started at different checkpoints.

Block Plan

Figure 23.33 is a sample block plan that offers a suggested 15-day unit for orienteering. The activities recommended in the block plan are available in this section or in Darst and Armstrong (1980).

Direction Walk—From the starting point marked X, follow the given distances in the appropriate direction. Use a pencil to trace your route. What is it?

1W, 1NW, 1E, 1S, 1W, 4S, 2SW, 1S, 1SW, 2S, 2W, 1NE, 4N, 1SW, 4W, 1NW, 1SW, 1S, 1SW, 2S, 2W, 1NE, 4N, 5NW, 2N, 1E, 2NE, 1E, 2N, 4SE, 8E, 2SE

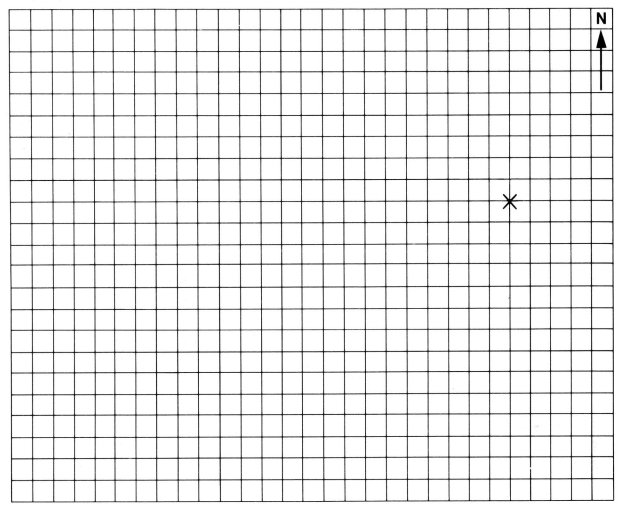

FIGURE 23.31   Direction walk

ORIENTEERING 1

In the Answers column, fill in the key word or letter that you find at each checkpoint.

Checkpoint	Bearing	Description	Distance	Answers
1	90°	Backstop	50 yd	
2	180°	Goal post	100 m	
3	230°	Cottonwood	200 ft	
4	160°	Irrigation	35 yd	
5	341°	Hoop	75 m	
6	45°	Palo verde	400 ft	
7	106°	Trash barrel	150 yd	
8	270°	Power pole	250 ft	
9	78°	Fence post	350 yd	
10	200°	Jumping pit	40 m	

FIGURE 23.32   Descriptive orienteering sheet

1. **Introduction** What is orienteering? Brief history Directions and degrees Dot-to-dot problems Compass rose activity	2. **Review** Directions and degrees **Teach** Maps, symbols, scales, contours **Activities** Map the School Map Squares Contour Identification	3. **Review** Maps, symbols, etc. **Teach** Parts of compass How to hold **Activities** Taking a bearing Dial a bearing Magnetic influence	4. **Review** Compass and bearings **Teach** Landmark bearings Map bearings **Activities** Boy Scout map problem Sea adventure Christmas Tree	5. **Review** Map bearings Map symbols **Teach** Pacing **Activities** Distance by pace Triangle game Square game Map symbol relay
6. **Review** Pacing **Teach** Orienteering Point-to-point Score Descriptive Relay **Activities** Taking a Trip Numbers and Numerals Destination Unknown	7. **Review** Orienteering **Activity** Descriptive meet— Have students return to master table each time for the next bearing, cue, and distance.	8. **Teach** Magnetic declination **Activities** Declination problems Meridian map and compass fun Point-to-point activity Schoolyard compass game	9. **Review** Pacing Bearings Orienteering **Activity** Point-to-point meet	10. **Review** Declination **Activities** Descriptive meet (short) Cues picked up at the next control Competitive compass game, or pacing by time and distance
11. **Review** Materials for written exam **Activities** Score orienteering meet (20 min) Landmark bearings for skill test	12. **Activities** Relay orienteering meet Schoolyard compass game and competitive compass game for skill test	13. Written examination Pacing—distance by time	14. Final score orienteering exam meet (Off-campus if possible)	15. Final point-to-point orienteering meet (Off-campus if possible)

FIGURE 23.33 Orienteering block plan

Suggested Performance Objectives

These objectives could be used in a junior high school unit on orienteering.

1. Identify the compass points.
2. Name the parts of a compass.
3. Find a compass bearing on a map.
4. Follow a compass bearing on the ground.
5. Shoot bearings on key points.
6. Identify map symbols.
7. Identify map distances.
8. Determine pace for 100 yd.
9. Form a triangle using 3 bearings.
10. Form a square using 4 bearings.
11. Complete an orienteering course in a time designated by the teacher.
    Standard no. 1 = 5 points
    Standard no. 2 = 3 points
    Standard no. 3 = 1 point
12. Take a 10-question exam on orienteering.
    Score: 100% = 5 points
    90% = 4 points
    80% = 3 points
    70% = 2 points
    60% = 1 point

Suggested Readings

Darst, P., and Armstrong, G. 1980. *Outdoor Adventure Activities for School and Recreation Programs.* Minneapolis, MN: Burgess Publishing Co.

Disley, J. 1967. *Orienteering.* Harrisburg, PA: Stackpole Books.
Gilchrist, J. 1973. *Teaching Orienteering.* Willowdale, ON: Canadian Orienteering Service.
Kjellstrom, B. 1975. *Be Expert with Map and Compass.* New York: Charles Scribner's Sons.

SUGGESTED READINGS

Darst, P., and Armstrong, G. 1980. *Outdoor Adventure Activities for School and Recreation Programs.* Minneapolis, MN: Burgess Publishing Co.
Fluegelman, A., ed. 1976. *The New Games Book.* Garden City, NY: Doubleday and Co.
Fluegelman, A. 1981. *More New Games.* Englewood Cliffs, NJ: Prentice-Hall Publishing Co.
Orlick, T. 1982. *The Second Cooperative Sports and Games Book.* New York: Pantheon Books/Random House.
Rohnke, K. 1989. *Cowstails and Cobras II: A Guide to Games, Initiatives, Ropes Courses, and Adventure Curriculum.* Dubuque, IA: Kendall/Hunt Publishing Company.
Rohnke, K. 1984. *Silver Bullets: A Guide to Initiative Problems, Adventure Games, and Trust Activities.* Hamilton, MA: Project Adventure.
Simpson, B. 1974. *Initiative Games.* Butler, PA: Encounter Four, Butler County Community College.
Webster, S. 1989. *Ropes Course Safety Manual: An Instructor's Guide to Initiatives and Low and High Elements.* Dubuque, IA: Kendall/Hunt Publishing Company.

INDEX